OPERATIONS MANAGEMENT

Flexible Version

TENTH EDITION

OPERATIONS
MANAGEMENT

Lecture Guide & Activities Manual

TENTH EDITION

JAY
HEIZER

Jesse H. Jones Professor of Business Administration
Texas Lutheran University

BARRY
RENDER

Charles Harwood Professor of Operations Management
Crummer Graduate School of Business
Rollins College

Prentice Hall

Boston Columbus Indianapolis New York San Francisco Upper Saddle River
Amsterdam Cape Town Dubai London Madrid Milan Munich Paris Montreal Toronto
Delhi Mexico City Sao Paulo Sydney Hong Kong Seoul Singapore Taipei Tokyo

Editorial Director: Sally Yagan
Editor in Chief: Eric Svendsen
Senior Acquisitions Editor: Chuck Synovec
Editorial Project Manager: Mary Kate Murray
Editorial Assistant: Jason Calcano
Director of Marketing: Patrice Lumumba Jones
Marketing Manager: Anne Fahlgren
Marketing Assistant: Melinda Jones
Senior Managing Editor: Judy Leale
Project Manager: Mary Kate Murray
Senior Operations Supervisor: Arnold Vila
Operations Specialist: Cathleen Petersen
Manager, Design Development: John Christiana
Interior and Cover Designer: Laura Gardner
Manager, Visual Research: Beth Brenzel

Manager, Rights and Permissions: Zina Arabia
Image Permission Coordinator: Annette Linder
Photo Researcher: Sheila Norman
Manager, Cover Visual Research & Permissions: Karen Sanatar
Cover Photo: Igor Dutina/iStockphoto.com
Permissions Project Manager: Shannon Barbe
Media Project Manager, Editorial: Allison Longley
Media Project Manager, Production: Lisa Rinaldi
Supplements Editor: Mary Kate Murray
Full-Service Project Management: PreMediaGlobal
Composition: PreMediaGlobal
Printer/Binder: Courier/Kendalville
Cover Printer: Lehigh-Phoenix Color/Hagerstown
Text Font: 10/12 Times

Credits and acknowledgments borrowed from other sources and reproduced, with permission, in this textbook appear on appropriate page within text (or on page P1).

Microsoft® and Windows® are registered trademarks of the Microsoft Corporation in the U.S.A. and other countries. Screen shots and icons reprinted with permission from the Microsoft Corporation. This book is not sponsored or endorsed by or affiliated with the Microsoft Corporation.

10 9 8 7 6 5 4 3 2 1

Prentice Hall
is an imprint of

www.pearsonhighered.com

ISBN 10:   0-13-216584-8
ISBN 13: 978-0-13-216584-6

Brief Table of Contents

PART ONE

Introduction to Operations Management 1-1

1. Operations and Productivity 1-1
2. Operations Strategy in a Global Environment 2-1
3. Project Management 3-1
4. Forecasting 4-1

PART TWO

Designing Operations 5-1

5. Design of Goods and Services 5-1
6. Managing Quality 6-1
   Supplement 6: Statistical Process Control S6-1
7. Process Strategy and Sustainability 7-1
   Supplement 7: Capacity and Constraint Management S7-1
8. Location Strategies 8-1
9. Layout Strategies 9-1
10. Human Resources, Job Design, and Work Measurement 10-1

PART THREE

Managing Operations 11-1

11. Supply-Chain Management 11-1
    Supplement 11: Outsourcing as a Supply-Chain Strategy S11-1

12. Inventory Management 12-1
13. Aggregate Planning 13-1
14. Material Requirements Planning (MRP) and ERP 14-1
15. Short-Term Scheduling 15-1
16. JIT and Lean Operations 16-1
17. Maintenance and Reliability 17-1

PART FOUR

Quantitative Modules A-1

A. Decision-Making Tools A-1
B. Linear Programming B-1
C. Transportation Models C-1
D. Waiting-Line Models D-1
E. Learning Curves E-1
F. Simulation F-1

Online Tutorials

1. Statistical Tools for Managers T1-1
2. Acceptance Sampling T2-1
3. The Simplex Method of Linear Programming T3-1
4. The MODI and VAM Methods of Solving Transportation Problems T4-1
5. Vehicle Routing and Scheduling T5-1

Letter to the Student

Operations Management can be one of the most exciting courses in your college program. We hope that you, as a student of operations management, will find *Operations Management, Flexible Version, Tenth Edition* an ideal way to learn the subject. We have created this innovative learning system to help you in your study of the field. This unique combination of *text* and *Lecture Guide & Activities Manual* with extensive Web site support costs significantly less than a traditional textbook. Moreover, the *Lecture Guide & Activities Manual* (the part you should bring to each class) is smaller and lighter than the standard text—easing weight in your backpack! The idea is for the text to be a reference and the *Lecture Guide & Activities Manual* to bridge the gap between the text and the lecture.

The first page of each chapter in the *Lecture Guide & Activities Manual* begins with a chapter outline, a brief introduction, and a series of questions that address the major ideas and concepts of the chapter. If you answer these questions before attending class, you will have an important head start.

Each chapter contains headings for the major topics and critical teaching points, figures, charts, and tables relevant to that topic—but most importantly, each chapter has lots of extra space for you to take notes. We think you can take better notes and get more from the lecture when you can focus on note taking rather than redrawing outlines, figures, charts, and tables. Practice Problems are also included, as is room for the solutions and necessary notes. The *Lecture Guide & Activities Manual* also contains all the homework problems in case your instructor wants to assign any of this material in class. At the end of each chapter, supplement, and module, there is a two-page Rapid Review. This detailed, yet concise, summary of the main points and equations in the chapter will help you prepare for homework, exams, and lectures by capturing the essence of the material.

myomlab, a new resource to aid your learning, ties together all elements in this book into an innovative learning tool, a homework tool, and an assessment center. By using myomlab, you will have access to problems from the *Lecture Guide & Activities Manual* to work online at any time. If you need help with a problem, you can click directly to the relevant text page, watch us solve a similar problem, walk through other sample problems, or seek other useful forms of help. Take a moment to read through the inside front cover of the *text* or visit **www.myomlab.com** for more information.

The full support and resources of the extensive Web site (**www.pearsonhighered.com/heizer**) are also available to make the learning process complete. For instance, the Web site includes PowerPoint presentations, self-study quizzes, virtual company tours, and learning objectives for each chapter. Quizzes are automatically graded and can be forwarded to the instructor if you so desire.

We hope that this new approach to learning helps you enjoy your operations management journey.

Jay Heizer, Ph.D.
Texas Lutheran University
Email: jheizer@tlu.edu

Barry Render, Ph.D.
Rollins College
Email: brender@rollins.edu

1 Operations and Productivity

Chapter Outline

What Is Operations Management?

Organizing to Produce Goods and Services

Why Study OM?

What Operations Managers Do

The Heritage of Operations Management

Operations in the Service Sector

Exciting New Trends in Operations
   Management

The Productivity Challenge

Ethics and Social Responsibility

Ethical Dilemma
Discussion Questions
Problems
Case Studies: National Air Express;
   Frito-Lay: Operations Management in
   Manufacturing; Hard Rock Cafe:
   Operations Management in Services
Rapid Review

Production is the creation of goods and services. Operations Management is the set of activities that creates value by using labor, capital, and management to transform inputs (raw materials) into desired outputs (goods and services). The operations manager's job is to ensure that this transformation takes place efficiently. This text identifies 10 decisions that are critical to effective and efficient operations management.

BEFORE COMING TO CLASS, READ CHAPTER 1 IN YOUR TEXT AND ANSWER THESE QUESTIONS.

1. Define operations management. _____

_____

_____

2. What are the distinctions between goods and services? _____

_____

_____

3. What is the difference between production and productivity? _____

_____

_____

4. Explain single-factor productivity. _____

_____

_____

5. Explain how to perform a multifactor productivity analysis. _____

_____

_____

6. What are the critical variables in productivity? _____

_____

_____

WHAT IS OPERATIONS MANAGEMENT? (See Flexible Version p. 4)

Production

ORGANIZING TO PRODUCE GOODS AND SERVICES

(See Flexible Version pp. 4–5)

Three Functions All Organizations Perform

1. _____

2. _____

3. _____

WHY STUDY OM? (See Flexible Version pp. 6–7)

WHAT OPERATIONS MANAGERS DO (See Flexible Version pp. 7–8)

Ten Decision Areas of OM (See Flexible Version p. 7)

1. Design of Goods and Services (Chapter 5)

2. Managing Quality (Chapter 6 and Supplement 6)

3. Process and Capacity Design (Chapter 7 and Supplement 7)

4. Location (Chapter 8)

5. Layout Design (Chapter 9)

6. Human Resources and Job Design (Chapter 10)

7. Supply Chain Management (Chapter 11 and Supplement 11)

8. Inventory, MRP, and JIT (Chapters 12, 14, and 16)

9. Scheduling (Chapters 13 and 15)

10. Maintenance (Chapter 17)

THE HERITAGE OF OPERATIONS MANAGEMENT

(See Flexible Version pp. 8–10)

Whitney
Taylor
Ford/Sorensen
Gilbreth
Shewhart
Deming

OPERATIONS IN THE SERVICE SECTOR (See Flexible Version pp. 10–12)

Attributes of Goods (tangible product)	Attributes of Services (intangible product)
Product can be resold.	Reselling a service is unusual.
Product can be inventoried.	Many services cannot be inventoried.
Product is often consistent.	Product may be unique.
Some aspects of quality are measurable.	Many aspects of quality are difficult to measure.
Selling is distinct from production.	Selling is often a part of the service.
Low customer interaction.	High customer interaction.
Product is transportable.	Provider, not product, is often transportable.
Site of facility is important for cost.	Site of facility is important for customer contact.
Often easy to automate.	Often knowledge based and difficult to automate.
Revenue is generated primarily from the tangible product.	Revenue is generated primarily from the intangible services.

◀ **TABLE 1.3**
Differences between Goods and Services

EXCITING NEW TRENDS IN OPERATIONS MANAGEMENT

(See Flexible Version pp. 12–13)

1. **Ethics**

2. **Global focus**

3. **Rapid product development**

4. **Environmentally sensitive and sustainable production; recycling**

5. **Mass customization**

6. **Empowerment, lean production**

7. **Partnering with suppliers, collaboration, outsourcing**

8. **JIT shipments**

THE PRODUCTIVITY CHALLENGE (See Flexible Version pp. 13–19)

$$\text{Productivity} = \frac{\text{Units produced}}{\text{Input used}} \qquad (1\text{-}1)$$

PRACTICE PROBLEM 1.1 ■ Productivity

Mance Fraily, the production manager at Ralts Mills, can currently expect his operation to produce 1,000 square yards of fabric for each ton of raw cotton. Each ton of raw cotton requires 5 labor-hours to process. He believes that he can buy a better quality raw cotton, which will enable him to produce 1,200 square yards per ton of raw cotton with the same labor-hours.

What will be the impact on productivity (measured in square yards per labor-hour) if he purchases the higher quality raw cotton?

PRACTICE PROBLEM 1.2 ■ Productivity

C. A. Ratchet, the local auto mechanic, finds that it usually takes him 2 hours to diagnose and fix a typical problem. What is his daily productivity (assume an 8-hour day)?

Mr. Ratchet believes he can purchase a small computer troubleshooting device that will allow him to find and fix a problem in the incredible (at least to his customers!) time of 1 hour. He will, however, have to spend an extra hour each morning adjusting the computerized diagnostic device. What will be the impact on productivity if he purchases the device?

Multifactor Productivity (See Flexible Version p. 15)

$$\text{Productivity} = \frac{\text{Output}}{\text{Labor} + \text{Material} + \text{Energy} + \text{Capital} + \text{Miscellaneous}} \quad (1\text{-}2)$$

PRACTICE PROBLEM 1.3 ■ Multifactor Productivity

Joanna French is currently working a total of 12 hours per day to produce 240 dolls. She thinks that by changing the paint used for the facial features and fingernails that she can increase her rate to 360 dolls per day. Total material cost for each doll is approximately $3.50; she has to invest $20 in the necessary supplies (expendables) per day; energy costs are assumed to be only $4 per day; and she thinks she should be making $10 per hour for her time. Viewing this from a total (multifactor) productivity perspective, what is her productivity at present and with the new paint?

PRACTICE PROBLEM 1.4 ■ Multifactor Productivity

How would total (multifactor) productivity change if using the new paint raised Ms. French's material costs by $0.50 per doll?

PRACTICE PROBLEM 1.5 ■ Multifactor Productivity

If she uses the new paint, by what amount could Ms. French's material cost increase without reducing total (multifactor) productivity?

Additional Practice Problem Space

Productivity Variables (See Flexible Version pp. 16–18)

1. Labor

2. Capital

3. Management

ETHICS AND SOCIAL RESPONSIBILITY (See Flexible Version p. 19)

Ethical Dilemma

Major corporations with overseas subcontractors (such as IKEA in Bangladesh, Unilever in India, and Nike in China) have been criticized, often with substantial negative publicity, when children as young as 10 have been found working in the subcontractor's facilities. The standard response is to perform an audit and then enhance controls so it does not happen again. In one such case, a 10-year-old was terminated. Shortly thereafter, the family, without the 10-year-old's contribution to the family income, lost its modest home, and the 10-year-old was left to scrounge in the local dump for scraps of metal. Was the decision to hire the 10-year-old ethical? Was the decision to terminate the 10-year-old ethical?

Discussion Questions

1. Why should one study operations management?
2. Identify four people who have contributed to the theory and techniques of operations management.
3. Briefly describe the contributions of the four individuals identified in the preceding question.
4. Figure 1.1 outlines the operations, finance/accounting, and marketing functions of three organizations. Prepare a chart similar to Figure 1.1 outlining the same functions for one of the following:
   a) a newspaper
   b) a drugstore
   c) a college library
   d) a summer camp
   e) a small costume-jewelry factory

5. Answer Question 4 for some other organization, perhaps an organization where you have worked.
6. What are the three basic functions of a firm?
7. Name the 10 decision areas of operations management.
8. Name four areas that are significant to improving labor productivity.
9. The U.S., and indeed much of the world, has been described as a "knowledge society." How does this affect productivity measurement and the comparison of productivity between the U.S. and other countries?
10. What are the measurement problems that occur when one attempts to measure productivity?
11. Mass customization and rapid product development were identified as current trends in modern manufacturing operations. What is the relationship, if any, between these trends? Can you cite any examples?
12. What are the five reasons productivity is difficult to improve in the service sector?
13. Describe some of the actions taken by Taco Bell to increase productivity that have resulted in Taco Bell's ability to serve "twice the volume with half the labor."

Problems*

• **1.1** John Lucy makes wooden boxes in which to ship motorcycles. John and his three employees invest a total of 40 hours per day making the 120 boxes.
a) What is their productivity?
b) John and his employees have discussed redesigning the process to improve efficiency. If they can increase the rate to 125 per day, what will be their new productivity?
c) What will be their unit *increase* in productivity per hour?
d) What will be their percentage change in productivity? **Px**

• **1.2** Riverside Metal Works produces cast bronze valves on a 10-person assembly line. On a recent day, 160 valves were produced during an 8-hour shift.
a) Calculate the labor productivity of the line.
b) The manager at Riverside changed the layout and was able to increase production to 180 units per 8-hour shift. What is the new labor productivity per labor-hour?
c) What is the percentage of productivity increase? **Px**

• **1.3** This year, Benson, Inc., will produce 57,600 hot water heaters at its plant in Yulee, Florida, in order to meet expected global demand. To accomplish this, each laborer at the Yulee plant will work 160 hours per month. If the labor productivity at the plant is 0.15 hot water heaters per labor-hour, how many laborers are employed at the plant?

• **1.4** As a library or Internet assignment, find the U.S. productivity rate (increase) last year for the (a) national economy, (b) manufacturing sector, and (c) service sector.

• **1.5** Lori produces "Final Exam Care Packages" for resale by her sorority. She is currently working a total of 5 hours per day to produce 100 care packages
a) What is Lori's productivity?
b) Lori thinks that by redesigning the package, she can increase her total productivity to 133 care packages per day. What will be her new productivity?
c) What will be the percentage increase in productivity if Lori makes the change? **Px**

•• **1.6** Eric Johnson makes billiard balls in his New England plant. With recent increases in his costs, he has a newfound interest in efficiency. Eric is interested in determining the productivity of his organization. He would like to know if his organization is maintaining

*Note: **Px** means the problem may be solved with POM for Windows and/or Excel OM.

the manufacturing average of 3% increase in productivity. He has the following data representing a month from last year and an equivalent month this year:

	Last Year	Now
Units produced	1,000	1,000
Labor (hours)	300	275
Resin (pounds)	50	45
Capital invested ($)	10,000	11,000
Energy (BTU)	3,000	2,850

Show the productivity percentage change for each category and then determine the improvement for labor-hours, the typical standard for comparison. **Px**

•• **1.7** Eric Johnson (using data from Problem 1.6) determines his costs to be as follows:
• *Labor:* $10 per hour
• *Resin:* $5 per pound
• *Capital expense:* 1% per month of investment
• *Energy:* $.50 per BTU.

Show the percent change in productivity for one month last year versus one month this year, on a multifactor basis with dollars as the common denominator. **Px**

• **1.8** Kleen Karpet cleaned 65 rugs in October, consuming the following resources:

Labor:	520 hours at $13 per hour
Solvent:	100 gallons at $5 per gallon
Machine rental:	20 days at $50 per day

a) What is the labor productivity per dollar?
b) What is the multifactor productivity? **Px**

•• **1.9** David Upton is president of Upton Manufacturing, a producer of Go-Kart tires. Upton makes 1,000 tires per day with the following resources:

Labor:	400 hours per day @ $12.50 per hour
Raw material:	20,000 pounds per day @ $1 per pound
Energy:	$5,000 per day
Capital costs:	$10,000 per day

a) What is the labor productivity per labor-hour for these tires at Upton Manufacturing?

b) What is the multifactor productivity for these tires at Upton Manufacturing?

c) What is the percent change in multifactor productivity if Upton can reduce the energy bill by $1,000 per day without cutting production or changing any other inputs? **Px**

•• **1.10** Sawyer's, a local bakery, is worried about increased costs—particularly energy. Last year's records can provide a fairly good estimate of the parameters for this year. Judy Sawyer, the owner, does not believe things have changed much, but she did invest an additional $3,000 for modifications to the bakery's ovens to make them more energy efficient. The modifications were supposed to make the ovens at least 15% more efficient. Sawyer has asked you to check the energy savings of the new ovens and also to look over other measures of the bakery's productivity to see if the modifications were beneficial. You have the following data to work with:

	Last Year	Now
Production (dozen)	1,500	1,500
Labor (hours)	350	325
Capital investment ($)	15,000	18,000
Energy (BTU)	3,000	2,750

Px

•• **1.11** Cunningham Performance Auto, Inc., modifies 375 autos per year. The manager, Peter Cunningham, is interested in obtaining a measure of overall performance. He has asked you to provide him with a multifactor measure of last year's performance as a benchmark for future comparison. You have assembled the following data. Resource inputs were: labor, 10,000 hours; 500 suspension and engine modification kits; and energy, 100,000 kilowatt-hours. Average labor cost last year was $20 per hour, kits cost $1,000 each, and energy costs were $3 per kilowatt-hour. What do you tell Mr. Cunningham? **Px**

•• **1.12** Lake Charles Seafood makes 500 wooden packing boxes for fresh seafood per day, working in two 10-hour shifts. Due to increased demand, plant managers have decided to operate three 8-hour shifts instead. The plant is now able to produce 650 boxes per day.

a) Calculate the company's productivity before the change in work rules and after the change.

b) What is the percentage increase in productivity?

c) If production is increased to 700 boxes per day, what is the new productivity? **Px**

•• **1.13** Charles Lackey operates a bakery in Idaho Falls, Idaho. Because of its excellent product and excellent location, demand has increased by 25% in the last year. On far too many occasions, customers have not been able to purchase the bread of their choice. Because of the size of the store, no new ovens can be added. At a staff meeting, one employee suggested ways to load the ovens differently so that more loaves of bread can be baked at one time. This new process will require that the ovens be loaded by hand, requiring additional manpower. This is the only thing to be changed. If the bakery makes 1,500 loaves per month with a labor productivity of 2.344 loaves per labor-hour, how many workers will Lackey need to add? (*Hint:* Each worker works 160 hours per month.)

•• **1.14** Refer to Problem 1.13. The pay will be $8 per hour for employees. Charles Lackey can also improve the yield by purchasing a new blender. The new blender will mean an increase in his investment. This added investment has a cost of $100 per month, but he will achieve the same output (an increase to 1,875) as the change in labor-hours. Which is the better decision?

a) Show the productivity change, in loaves per dollar, with an increase in labor cost (from 640 to 800 hours).

b) Show the new productivity, in loaves per dollar, with only an increase in investment ($100 per month more).

c) Show the percent productivity change for labor and investment.

•• **1.15** Refer to Problems 1.13 and 1.14. If Charles Lackey's utility costs remain constant at $500 per month, labor at $8 per hour, and cost of ingredients at $0.35 per loaf, but Charles does not purchase the blender suggested in Problem 1.14, what will the productivity of the bakery be? What will be the percent increase or decrease?

•• **1.16** In December, General Motors produced 6,600 customized vans at its plant in Detroit. The labor productivity at this plant is known to have been 0.10 vans per labor-hour during that month. 300 laborers were employed at the plant that month.

a) How many hours did the average laborer work that month?

b) If productivity can be increased to 0.11 vans per hour, how many hours would the average laborer work that month?

•• **1.17** Natalie Attired runs a small job shop where garments are made. The job shop employs eight workers. Each worker is paid $10 per hour. During the first week of March, each worker worked 45 hours. Together, they produced a batch of 132 garments. Of these garments, 52 were "seconds" (meaning that they were flawed). The seconds were sold for $90 each at a factory outlet store. The remaining 80 garments were sold to retail outlets at a price of $198 per garment. What was the labor productivity, in dollars per labor-hour, at this job shop during the first week of March?

▶ **Refer to** myomlab for these additional homework problems: 1.18–1.19

Case Studies

▶ National Air Express

National Air is a competitive air-express firm with offices around the country. Frank Smith, the Chattanooga, Tennessee, station manager, is preparing his quarterly budget report, which will be presented at the Southeast regional meeting next week. He is very concerned about adding capital expense to the operation when business has not increased appreciably. This has been the worst first quarter he can remember: snowstorms, earthquakes, and bitter cold. He has asked Martha Lewis, field services supervisor, to help him review the available data and offer possible solutions.

Service Methods

National Air offers door-to-door overnight air-express delivery within the U.S. Smith and Lewis manage a fleet of 24 trucks to handle freight in the Chattanooga area. Routes are assigned by area, usually delineated by zip code boundaries, major streets, or key geographical features, such as the Tennessee River. Pickups are generally handled between 3:00 P.M. and 6:00 P.M., Monday through Friday. Driver routes are a combination of regularly scheduled daily stops and pickups that the customer calls in as needed. These call-in pickups are dispatched by radio to the driver. Most call-in customers want as late a pickup as possible, just before closing (usually at 5:00 P.M.).

When the driver arrives at each pickup location, he or she provides supplies as necessary (an envelope or box if requested) and must receive a completed air waybill for each package. Because the industry is extremely competitive, a professional, courteous driver is essential to retaining customers. Therefore, Smith has always been concerned that drivers not rush a customer to complete his or her package and paperwork.

Budget Considerations

Smith and Lewis have found that they have been unable to meet their customers' requests for a scheduled pickup on many occasions in the past quarter. Although, on average, drivers are not handling any more business, they are unable on some days to arrive at each location on time. Smith does not think he can justify increasing costs by $1,200 per week for additional trucks and drivers while productivity (measured in shipments per truck/day) has remained flat. The company has established itself as the low-cost operator in the industry but has at the same time committed itself to offering quality service and value for its customers.

Discussion Questions

1. Is the productivity measure of shipments per day per truck still useful? Are there alternatives that might be effective?
2. What, if anything, can be done to reduce the daily variability in pickup call-ins? Can the driver be expected to be at several locations at once at 5:00 P.M.?
3. How should package pickup performance be measured? Are standards useful in an environment that is affected by the weather, traffic, and other random variables? Are other companies having similar problems?

Source: Adapted from a case by Phil Pugliese under the supervision of Professor Marilyn M. Helms, University of Tennessee at Chattanooga. Reprinted by permission.

▶ Frito-Lay: Operations Management in Manufacturing

Video Case

Frito-Lay, the massive Dallas-based subsidiary of PepsiCo, has 38 plants and 48,000 employees in North America. Seven of Frito-Lay's 41 brands exceed $1 billion in sales: Fritos, Lay's, Cheetos, Ruffles, Tostitos, Doritos, and Walker's Potato Chips. Operations is the focus of the firm—from designing products for new markets, to meeting changing consumer preferences, to adjusting to rising commodity costs, to subtle issues involving flavors and preservatives—OM is under constant cost, time, quality, and market pressure. Here is a look at how the 10 decisions of OM are applied at this food processor.

In the food industry, product development kitchens experiment with new products, submit them to focus groups, and perform test marketing. Once the product specifications have been set, processes capable of meeting those specifications and the necessary quality standards are created. At Frito-Lay, quality begins at the farm, with onsite inspection of the potatoes used in Ruffles and the corn used in Fritos. Quality continues throughout the manufacturing process, with visual inspections and with statistical process control of product variables such as oil, moisture, seasoning, salt, thickness, and weight. Additional quality evaluations are conducted throughout shipment, receipt, production, packaging, and delivery.

The production process at Frito-Lay is designed for large volumes and small variety, using expensive special-purpose equipment, and with swift movement of material through the facility. Product-focused facilities, such as Frito-Lay's, typically have high capital costs, tight schedules, and rapid processing. Frito-Lay's facilities are located regionally to aid in the rapid delivery of products because freshness is a critical issue. Sanitary issues and necessarily fast processing of products put a premium on an efficient layout. Production lines are designed for balanced throughput and high utilization. Cross-trained workers, who handle a variety of production lines, have promotion paths identified for their particular skill set. The company rewards employees with medical, retirement, and education plans. Its turnover is very low.

The supply chain is integral to success in the food industry; vendors must be chosen with great care. Moreover, the finished food product is highly dependent on perishable raw materials. Consequently, the supply chain brings raw material (potatoes, corn, etc.) to the plant securely and rapidly to meet tight production schedules. For instance, from the time that potatoes are picked in St. Augustine, Florida, until they are unloaded at the Orlando plant, processed, packaged, and shipped from the plant is under 12 hours. The requirement for fresh product requires on-time, just-in-time deliveries combined with both low raw material and finished goods inventories. The continuous-flow nature of the specialized equipment in the production process permits little work-in-process inventory. The plants usually run 24/7. This means that there are four shifts of employees each week.

Tight scheduling to ensure the proper mix of fresh finished goods on automated equipment requires reliable systems and effective maintenance. Frito-Lay's workforce is trained to recognize problems early, and professional maintenance personnel are available on every shift. Downtime is very costly and can lead to late deliveries, making maintenance a high priority.

Source: Professors Beverly Amer (Northern Arizona University), Barry Render (Rollins College), and Jay Heizer (Texas Lutheran University).

Discussion Questions*

1. From your knowledge of production processes and from the case and the video, identify how each of the 10 decisions of OM is applied at Frito-Lay.
2. How would you determine the productivity of the production process at Frito-Lay?
3. How are the 10 decisions of OM different when applied by the operations manager of a production process such as Frito-Lay versus a service organization such as Hard Rock Cafe (see the Hard Rock Cafe video case below)?

*You may wish to view the video that accompanies this case before addressing these questions.

▶ Hard Rock Cafe: Operations Management in Services

Video Case

In its 39 years of existence, Hard Rock has grown from a modest London pub to a global power managing 129 cafes, 12 hotels/casinos, live music venues, and a huge annual Rockfest concert. This puts Hard Rock firmly in the service industry—a sector that employs over 75% of the people in the U.S. Hard Rock moved its world headquarters to Orlando, Florida, in 1988 and has expanded to more than 40 locations throughout the U.S., serving over 100,000 meals each day. Hard Rock chefs are modifying the menu from classic American—burgers and chicken wings—to include higher-end items such as stuffed veal chops and lobster tails. Just as taste in music changes over time, so does Hard Rock Cafe, with new menus, layouts, memorabilia, services, and strategies.

At Orlando's Universal Studios, a traditional tourist destination, Hard Rock Cafe serves over 3,500 meals each day. The cafe employs about 400 people. Most are employed in the restaurant, but some work in the retail shop. Retail is now a standard and increasingly prominent feature in Hard Rock Cafes (since close to 48% of revenue comes from this source). Cafe employees include kitchen and wait staff, hostesses, and bartenders. Hard Rock employees are not only competent in their job skills but are also passionate about music and have engaging personalities. Cafe staff is scheduled down to 15-minute intervals to meet seasonal and daily demand changes in the tourist environment of Orlando. Surveys are done on a regular basis to evaluate quality of food and service at the cafe. Scores are rated on a 1 to 7 scale, and if the score is not a 7, the food or service is a failure.

Hard Rock is adding a new emphasis on live music and is redesigning its restaurants to accommodate the changing tastes. Since Eric Clapton hung his guitar on the wall to mark his favorite bar stool, Hard Rock has become the world's leading collector and exhibitor of rock 'n' roll memorabilia, with changing exhibits at its cafes throughout the world. The collection includes 1,000s of pieces, valued at $40 million. In keeping with the times, Hard Rock also maintains a Web site, **www.hardrock.com**, which receives over 100,000 hits per week, and a weekly cable television program on VH-1. Hard Rock's brand recognition, at 92%, is one of the highest in the world.

Discussion Questions*

1. From your knowledge of restaurants, from the video, from the *Global Company Profile* that opens this chapter, and from the case itself, identify how each of the 10 decisions of operations management is applied at Hard Rock Cafe.
2. How would you determine the productivity of the kitchen staff and wait staff at Hard Rock?
3. How are the 10 decisions of OM different when applied to the operations manager of a service operation such as Hard Rock versus an automobile company such as Ford Motor Company?

*You may wish to view the video that accompanies this case before addressing these questions.

Main Heading	Review Material	PEARSON myomlab
WHAT IS OPERATIONS MANAGEMENT? (p. 4)	▪ **Production**—The creation of goods and services. ▪ **Operations management (OM)**—Activities that relate to the creation of goods and services through the transformation of inputs to outputs.	**VIDEOS 1.1 and 1.2** OM at Hard Rock OM at Frito-Lay
ORGANIZING TO PRODUCE GOODS AND SERVICES (pp. 4–5)	All organizations perform three functions to create goods and services: 1. *Marketing*, which generates demand 2. *Production/operations,* which creates the product 3. *Finance/accounting,* which tracks how well the organization is doing, pays the bills, and collects the money	
WHY STUDY OM? (pp. 6–7)	We study OM for four reasons: 1. To learn how people organize themselves for productive enterprise 2. To learn how goods and services are produced 3. To understand what operations managers do 4. Because OM is a costly part of an organization	
WHAT OPERATIONS MANAGERS DO (pp. 7–8)	▪ **Management process**—The application of planning, organizing, staffing, leading, and controlling to achieve objectives. Ten major OM decisions are required of operations managers: 1. Design of goods and services 2. Managing quality 3. Process and capacity design 4. Location strategy 5. Layout strategy 6. Human resources, job design, and work measurement 7. Supply-chain management 8. Inventory, material requirements planning, and JIT (just-in-time) 9. Intermediate and short-term scheduling 10. Maintenance About 40% of *all* jobs are in OM. Operations managers possess job titles such as plant manager, quality manager, process improvement consultant, and operations analyst.	
THE HERITAGE OF OPERATIONS MANAGEMENT (pp. 8–10)	Significant events in modern OM can be classified into five eras: 1. Early concepts (1776–1880)—Labor specialization (Smith, Babbage), standardized parts (Whitney) 2. Scientific management (1880–1910)—Gantt charts (Gantt), motion and time studies (Gilbreth), process analysis (Taylor), queuing theory (Erlang) 3. Mass production (1910–1980)—Assembly line (Ford/Sorensen), statistical sampling (Shewhart), economic order quantity (Harris), linear programming (Dantzig), PERT/CPM (DuPont), material requirements planning 4. Lean production (1980–1995)—Just-in-time, computer-aided design, electronic data interchange, total quality management, Baldrige Award, empowerment, kanbans 5. Mass customization (1995–present)—Globalization, Internet/e-commerce, enterprise resource planning, international quality standards, finite scheduling, supply-chain management, mass customization, build-to-order, sustainability	
OPERATIONS IN THE SERVICE SECTOR (pp. 10–12)	▪ **Services**—Economic activities that typically produce an intangible product (such as education, entertainment, lodging, government, financial, and health services). Almost all services and almost all goods are a mixture of a service and a tangible product. ▪ **Service sector**—The segment of the economy that includes trade, financial, lodging, education, legal, medical, and other professional occupations. Services now constitute the largest economic sector in postindustrial societies. The huge productivity increases in agriculture and manufacturing have allowed more of our economic resources to be devoted to services. Many service jobs pay very well.	
EXCITING NEW TRENDS IN OPERATIONS MANAGEMENT (pp. 12–13)	Some of the current challenges for operations managers include: • High ethical and social responsibility; increased legal and professional standards • Global focus; international collaboration • Rapid product development; design collaboration • Environmentally sensitive production; green manufacturing; sustainability • Mass customization • Empowered employees; enriched jobs • Supply-chain partnering; joint ventures; alliances • Just-in-time performance; lean; continuous improvement	

Main Heading	Review Material	
THE PRODUCTIVITY CHALLENGE (pp. 13–19)	■ **Productivity**—The ratio of outputs (goods and services) divided by one or more inputs (such as labor, capital, or management). High production means producing many units, while high productivity means producing units efficiently. Only through increases in productivity can the standard of living of a country improve. U.S. productivity has averaged 2.5% per year for over a century. $$\text{Productivity} = \frac{\text{Units produced}}{\text{Input used}} \qquad (1\text{-}1)$$ ■ **Single-factor productivity**—Indicates the ratio of one resource (input) to the goods and services produced (outputs). ■ **Multifactor productivity (total factor productivity)**—Indicates the ratio of many or all resources (inputs) to the goods and services produced (outputs). Multifactor Productivity $$= \frac{\text{Output}}{\text{Labor} + \text{Material} + \text{Energy} + \text{Capital} + \text{Miscellaneous}} \qquad (1\text{-}2)$$ Measurement problems with productivity include: (1) the quality may change, (2) external elements may interfere, and (3) precise units of measure may be lacking. ■ **Productivity variables**—The three factors critical to productivity improvement are labor (10%), capital (38%), and management (52%). ■ **Knowledge society**—A society in which much of the labor force has migrated from manual work to work based on knowledge.	**myomlab** Problems: 1.1–1.17 Virtual Office Hours for Solved Problems: 1.1, 1.2
ETHICS AND SOCIAL RESPONSIBILITY (p. 19)	Among the many ethical challenges facing operations managers are (1) efficiently developing and producing safe, quality products; (2) maintaining a clean environment; (3) providing a safe workplace; and (4) honoring stakeholder commitments.	

Self Test

■ **Before taking the self-test,** refer to the learning objectives listed at the beginning of the chapter and the key terms listed at the end of the chapter.

LO1. Productivity increases when:
 a) inputs increase while outputs remain the same.
 b) inputs decrease while outputs remain the same.
 c) outputs decrease while inputs remain the same.
 d) inputs and outputs increase proportionately.
 e) inputs increase at the same rate as outputs.

LO2. Services often:
 a) are tangible.
 b) are standardized.
 c) are knowledge based.
 d) are low in customer interaction.
 e) have consistent product definition.

LO3. Productivity:
 a) can use many factors as the numerator.
 b) is the same thing as production.
 c) increases at about 0.5% per year.
 d) is dependent upon labor, management, and capital.
 e) is the same thing as effectiveness.

LO4. Single-factor productivity:
 a) remains constant.

 b) is never constant.
 c) usually uses labor as a factor.
 d) seldom uses labor as a factor.
 e) uses management as a factor.

LO5. Multi-factor productivity:
 a) remains constant.
 b) is never constant.
 c) usually uses substitutes as common variables for the factors of production.
 d) seldom uses labor as a factor.
 e) always uses management as a factor.

LO6. Productivity increases each year in the United States are a result of three factors:
 a) labor, capital, management
 b) engineering, labor, capital
 c) engineering, capital, quality control
 d) engineering, labor, data processing
 e) engineering, capital, data processing

Answers: LO1. b; **LO2.** c; **LO3.** d; **LO4.** c; **LO5.** c; **LO6.** a.

2 Operations Strategy in a Global Environment

Chapter Outline

A Global View of Operations

Developing Missions and Strategies

Achieving Competitive Advantage Through Operations

Ten Strategic OM Decisions

Issues in Operations Strategy

Strategy Development and Implementation

Global Operations Strategy Options

Ethical Dilemma
Discussion Questions
Problems
Case Studies: Minit-Lube; Strategy at Regal Marine; Hard Rock Cafe's Global Strategy
Rapid Review

Today's operations manager must have a global view of operations strategy. The rapid growth of world trade means that many organizations are compelled to extend their firms into an unforgiving global environment. Missions and strategies must obtain a competitive advantage that provides an economic purpose for customers.

The idea is to create customer value in an efficient and sustainable way. Managers create value via some combination of three strategies. The three strategies are *differentiation*, *low cost*, and *response*.

BEFORE COMING TO CLASS, READ CHAPTER 2 IN YOUR TEXT AND ANSWER THESE QUESTIONS.

1. What are missions and strategies? _____

_____

2. Identify three strategic approaches to competitive advantage. _____

_____

_____

3. What are the 10 critical decisions of operations management?_____

_____

_____

_____

4. Define key success factors and core competencies. _____

_____

_____

5. What are four global approaches to operations? _____

_____

_____

A GLOBAL VIEW OF OPERATIONS (See Flexible Version pp. 26–29)

1. Cost Reduction

2. Supply Chain Improvement

3. Better Goods/Services

4. Understand Markets

5. Learning

6. Global Talent

Cultural and Ethical Issues (See Flexible Version p. 29)

DEVELOPING MISSIONS AND STRATEGIES (See Flexible Version pp. 30–31)

Mission (See Flexible Version p. 30)

Strategy (See Flexible Version pp. 30–31)

ACHIEVING COMPETITIVE ADVANTAGE THROUGH OPERATIONS (See Flexible Version pp. 31–34)

Competing on Differentiation (See Flexible Version pp. 31–32)

Competing on Cost (See Flexible Version p. 32)

Competing on Response (See Flexible Version pp. 32–34)

TEN STRATEGIC OM DECISIONS (See Flexible Version pp. 35–36)

1. Design of Goods and Services

2. Managing Quality

3. Process and Capacity Design

4. Location

5. Layout Design

6. Human Resources and Job Design

7. Supply Chain Management

8. Inventory, MRP, and JIT

9. Scheduling

10. Maintenance

ISSUES IN OPERATIONS STRATEGY (See Flexible Version pp. 36–39)

STRATEGY DEVELOPMENT AND IMPLEMENTATION

(See Flexible Version pp. 39–41)

SWOT Analysis (See Flexible Version p. 39)

Strengths

Weaknesses

Opportunities

Threats

Key Success Factors (KSF) (See Flexible Version pp. 39–41)

PRACTICE PROBLEM 2.1 ■ OM Strategy

Identify how changes in the external environment may affect the OM strategy for a company. For example, what impact are the following factors likely to have on OM strategy?

a. The occurrence of a major storm or hurricane.

b. Terrorist attacks of September 11, 2001.

c. The much discussed decrease in the quality of American primary and secondary school systems.

d. Trade legislation such as WTO and NAFTA and changes in tariffs and quotas.

e. The rapid rate at which the cost of health insurance is increasing.

f. The Internet.

PRACTICE PROBLEM 2.2 ■ OM Strategy

Identify how changes in the internal environment affect the OM strategy for a company. For example, what impact are the following factors likely to have on OM strategy?

a. The increased use of local and wide area networks (LANs and WANs).

b. An increased emphasis on service.

c. The increased role of women in the workplace.

d. The seemingly increasing rate at which both internal and external environments change.

GLOBAL OPERATIONS STRATEGY OPTIONS (See Flexible Version pp. 42–44)

International Strategy (See Flexible Version p. 42)

Multi-Domestic Strategy (See Flexible Version p. 43)

Global Strategy (See Flexible Version p. 43)

Transnational Strategy (See Flexible Version pp. 43–44)

Ethical Dilemma

As a manufacturer of athletic shoes whose image, indeed performance, is widely regarded as socially responsible, you find your costs increasing. Traditionally, your athletic shoes have been made in Indonesia and South Korea. Although the ease of doing business in those countries has been improving, wage rates have also been increasing. The labor-cost differential between your present suppliers and a contractor who will get the shoes made in China now exceeds $1 per pair. Your sales next year are projected to be 10 million pairs, and your analysis suggests that this cost differential is not offset by any other tangible costs; you face only the political risk and potential damage to your commitment to social responsibility. Thus, this $1 per pair savings should flow directly to your bottom line. There is no doubt that the Chinese government engages in censorship, remains repressive, and is a long way from a democracy. Moreover, you will have little or no control over working conditions, sexual harassment, and pollution. What do you do and on what basis do you make your decision?

Discussion Questions

1. Based on the descriptions and analyses in this chapter, would Boeing be better described as a global firm or a transnational firm? Discuss.
2. List six reasons to internationalize operations.
3. Coca-Cola is called a global product. Does this mean that Coca-Cola is formulated in the same way throughout the world? Discuss.
4. Define *mission*.
5. Define *strategy*.
6. Describe how an organization's *mission* and *strategy* have different purposes.
7. Identify the mission and strategy of your automobile repair garage. What are the manifestations of the 10 OM decisions at the garage? That is, how is each of the 10 decisions accomplished?
8. As a library or Internet assignment, identify the mission of a firm and the strategy that supports that mission.
9. How does an OM strategy change during a product's life cycle?
10. There are three primary ways to achieve competitive advantage. Provide an example, not included in the text, of each. Support your choices.
11. Given the discussion of Southwest Airlines in the text, define an *operations* strategy for that firm.
12. How must an operations strategy integrate with marketing and accounting?

Problems

• **2.1** The text provides three primary ways—strategic approaches (differentiation, cost, and response)—for achieving competitive advantage. Provide an example of each not given in the text. Support your choices. (*Hint:* Note the examples provided in the text.)

•• **2.2** Within the food service industry (restaurants that serve meals to customers, but not just fast food), find examples of firms that have sustained competitive advantage by competing on the basis of (1) cost leadership, (2) response, and (3) differentiation. Cite one example in each category; provide a sentence or two in support of each choice. Do not use fast-food chains for all categories. (*Hint:* A "99¢ menu" is very easily copied and is not a good source of sustained advantage.)

•• **2.3** Browse through *The Wall Street Journal* or the financial section of a daily paper, or read business news online. Seek articles that constrain manufacturing innovation and productivity—workers aren't allowed to do this, workers are not or cannot be trained to do that, this technology is not allowed, this material cannot be handled by workers, and so forth. Be prepared to share your articles in class discussion.

•• **2.4** Match the product with the proper parent company and country in the table below:

Product	Parent Company	Country
Arrow Shirts	a. Volkswagen	1. France
Braun Household Appliances	b. Bidermann International	2. Great Britain
Lotus Autos	c. Bridgestone	3. Germany
Firestone Tires	d. Campbell Soup	4. Japan
Godiva Chocolate	e. Credit Lyonnais	5. U.S.
Häagen-Dazs Ice Cream (USA)	f. Tata	6. Switzerland
Jaguar Autos	g. Procter & Gamble	7. Malaysia
MGM Movies	h. Michelin	8. India
Lamborghini Autos	i. Nestlé	
Goodrich Tires	j. Proton	
Alpo Pet Foods		

••• **2.5** Identify how changes within an organization affect the OM strategy for a company. For instance, discuss what impact the following internal factors might have on OM strategy:
a) Maturing of a product.
b) Technology innovation in the manufacturing process.
c) Changes in laptop computer design that builds in wireless technology.

••• **2.6** Identify how changes in the external environment affect the OM strategy for a company. For instance, discuss what impact the following external factors might have on OM strategy:
a) Major increases in oil prices.
b) Water- and air-quality legislation.
c) Fewer young prospective employees entering the labor market.

d) Inflation versus stable prices.
e) Legislation moving health insurance from a pretax benefit to taxable income.

•• **2.7** Develop a ranking for corruption in the following countries: Mexico, Turkey, Denmark, the U.S., Taiwan, Brazil, and another country of your choice. (*Hint:* See sources such as *Transparency International*, *Asia Pacific Management News*, and *The Economist*.)

•• **2.8** Develop a ranking for competitiveness and/or business environment for Britain, Singapore, the U.S., Hong Kong, and Italy. (*Hint:* See the *Global Competitive Report*, *World Economic Forum*, Geneva, and *The Economist*.)

Case Studies

▶ Minit-Lube

A substantial market exists for automobile tune-ups, oil changes, and lubrication service for more than 200 million cars on U.S. roads. Some of this demand is filled by full-service auto dealerships, some by Sears and Firestone, and some by other tire/service dealers. However, Minit-Lube, Mobil-Lube, Jiffy-Lube and others have also developed strategies to accommodate this opportunity.

Minit-Lube stations perform oil changes, lubrication, and interior cleaning in a spotless environment. The buildings are clean, painted white, and often surrounded by neatly trimmed landscaping. To facilitate fast service, cars can be driven through three abreast. At Minit-Lube, the customer is greeted by service representatives who are graduates of Minit-Lube U. The Minit-Lube school is not unlike McDonald's Hamburger University near Chicago or Holiday Inn's training school in Memphis. The greeter takes the order, which typically includes fluid checks (oil, water, brake fluid, transmission fluid, differential grease) and the necessary lubrication, as well as filter changes for air and oil. Service personnel in neat uniforms then move into action. The standard three-person team has

one person checking fluid levels under the hood, another assigned interior vacuuming and window cleaning, and the third in the garage pit, removing the oil filter, draining the oil, checking the differential and transmission, and lubricating as necessary. Precise task assignments and good training are designed to move the car into and out of the bay in 10 minutes. The idea is to charge no more, and hopefully less, than gas stations, automotive repair chains, and auto dealers, while providing better service.

Discussion Questions

1. What constitutes the mission of Minit-Lube?
2. How does the Minit-Lube operations strategy provide competitive advantage? (*Hint:* Evaluate how Minit-Lube's traditional competitors perform the 10 decisions of operations management vs. how Minit-Lube performs them.)
3. Is it likely that Minit-Lube has increased productivity over its more traditional competitors? Why? How would we measure productivity in this industry?

► Strategy at Regal Marine

Video Case

Regal Marine, one of the U.S.'s 10 largest power-boat manufacturers, achieves its mission—providing luxury performance boats to customers worldwide—using the strategy of differentiation. It differentiates its products through constant innovation, unique features, and high quality. Increasing sales at the Orlando, Florida, family-owned firm suggest that the strategy is working.

As a quality boat manufacturer, Regal Marine starts with continuous innovation, as reflected in computer-aided design (CAD), high-quality molds, and close tolerances that are controlled through both defect charts and rigorous visual inspection. In-house quality is not enough, however. Because a product is only as good as the parts put into it, Regal has established close ties with a large number of its suppliers to ensure both flexibility and perfect parts. With the help of these suppliers, Regal can profitably produce a product line of 22 boats, ranging from the $14,000 19-foot boat to the $500,000 44-foot Commodore yacht.

"We build boats," says VP Tim Kuck, "but we're really in the 'fun' business. Our competition includes not only 300 other boat, canoe, and yacht manufacturers in our $17 billion industry, but home theaters, the Internet, and all kinds of alternative family entertainment." Fortunately Regal has been paying down debt and increasing market share.

Regal has also joined with scores of other independent boat makers in the American Boat Builders Association. Through economies of scale in procurement, Regal is able to navigate against billion-dollar competitor Brunswick (makers of the Sea Ray and Bayliner brands). The *Global Company Profile* featuring Regal Marine (which opens Chapter 5) provides further background on Regal and its strategy.

Discussion Questions*

1. State Regal Marine's mission in your own words.
2. Identify the strengths, weaknesses, opportunities, and threats that are relevant to the strategy of Regal Marine.
3. How would you define Regal's strategy?
4. How would each of the 10 operations management decisions apply to operations decision making at Regal Marine?

*You may wish to view the video that accompanies the case before addressing these questions.

► Hard Rock Cafe's Global Strategy

Video Case

Hard Rock brings the concept of the "experience economy" to its cafe operation. The strategy incorporates a unique "experience" into its operations. This innovation is somewhat akin to mass customization in manufacturing. At Hard Rock, the experience concept is to provide not only a custom meal from the menu but a dining event that includes a unique visual and sound experience not duplicated anywhere else in the world. This strategy is succeeding. Other theme restaurants have come and gone while Hard Rock continues to grow. As Professor C. Markides of the London Business School says, "The trick is not to play the game better than the competition, but to develop and play an altogether different game."* At Hard Rock, the different game is the experience game.

From the opening of its first cafe in London in 1971, during the British rock music explosion, Hard Rock has been serving food and rock music with equal enthusiasm. Hard Rock Cafe has 40 U.S. locations, about a dozen in Europe, and the remainder scattered throughout the world, from Bangkok and Beijing to Beirut. New construction, leases, and investment in remodeling are long term; so a global strategy means special consideration of political risk, currency risk, and social norms in a context of a brand fit. Although Hard Rock is one of the most recognized brands in the world, this does not mean its cafe is a natural everywhere. Special consideration must be given to the supply chain for the restaurant and its accompanying retail store. About 48% of a typical cafe's sales are from merchandise.

The Hard Rock Cafe business model is well defined, but because of various risk factors and differences in business practices and employment law, Hard Rock elects to franchise about half of its cafes. Social norms and preferences often suggest some tweaking of menus for local taste. For instance, Hard Rock focuses less on hamburgers and beef and more on fish and lobster in its British cafes.

Because 70% of Hard Rock's guests are tourists, recent years have found it expanding to "destination" cities. While this has been a winning strategy for decades, allowing the firm to grow from 1 London cafe to 157 facilities in 57 countries, it has made Hard Rock susceptible to economic fluctuations that hit the tourist business hardest. So Hard Rock is signing a long-term lease for a new location in Nottingham, England, to join recently opened cafes in Manchester and Birmingham—cities that are not standard tourist destinations. At the same time, menus are being upgraded. Hopefully, repeat business from locals in these cities will smooth demand and make Hard Rock less dependent on tourists.

Discussion Questions†

1. Identify the strategy changes that have taken place at Hard Rock Cafe since its founding in 1971.
2. As Hard Rock Cafe has changed its strategy, how has its responses to some of the 10 decisions of OM changed?
3. Where does Hard Rock fit in the four international operations strategies outlined in Figure 2.9? Explain your answer.

*Constantinos Markides, "Strategic Innovation," *MIT Sloan Management Review* 38, no. 3 (spring 1997): 9.

†You may wish to view the video that accompanies this case before addressing these questions.

PEARSON
myomlab

Main Heading	Review Material	
A GLOBAL VIEW OF OPERATIONS (pp. 26–29)	Domestic business operations decide to change to some form of international operations for six main reasons: 1. Reduce costs (labor, taxes, tariffs, etc.) 2. Improve supply chain 3. Provide better goods and services 4. Understand markets 5. Learn to improve operations 6. Attract and retain global talent ■ **Maquiladoras**—Mexican factories located along the U.S.–Mexico border that receive preferential tariff treatment. ■ **World Trade Organization (WTO)**—An international organization that promotes world trade by lowering barriers to the free flow of goods across borders. ■ **NAFTA**—A free trade agreement between Canada, Mexico, and the United States. ■ **European Union (EU)**—A European trade group that has 27 member states. Other trade agreements include APEC (the Pacific Rim countries), SEATO (Australia, New Zealand, Japan, Hong Kong, South Korea, New Guinea, and Chile), MERCOSUR (Argentina, Brazil, Paraguay, and Uruguay), and CAFTA (Central America, the Dominican Republic, and the United States). The World Trade Organization helps to make uniform the protection of both governments and industries from foreign firms that engage in unethical conduct.	
DEVELOPING MISSIONS AND STRATEGIES (pp. 30–31)	An effective operations management effort must have a *mission* so it knows where it is going and a *strategy* so it knows how to get there. ■ **Mission**—The purpose or rationale for an organization's existence. ■ **Strategy**—How an organization expects to achieve its missions and goals. The three strategic approaches to competitive advantage are: 1. Differentiation 2. Cost leadership 3. Response	**VIDEO 2.1** Operations Strategy at Regal Marine
ACHIEVING COMPETITIVE ADVANTAGE THROUGH OPERATIONS (pp. 31–34)	■ **Competitive advantage**—The creation of a unique advantage over competitors. ■ **Differentiation**—Distinguishing the offerings of an organization in a way that the customer perceives as adding value. ■ **Experience differentiation**—Engaging the customer with a product through imaginative use of the five senses, so the customer "experiences" the product. ■ **Low-cost leadership**—Achieving maximum value, as perceived by the customer. ■ **Response**—A set of values related to rapid, flexible, and reliable performance. Differentiation can be attained, for example, through innovative design, by providing a broad product line, by offering excellent after-sale service, or through adding a sensory experience to the product or service offering. Cost leadership can be attained, for example, via low overhead, effective capacity use, or efficient inventory management. Response can be attained, for example, by offering a flexible product line, reliable scheduling, or speedy delivery.	**VIDEO 2.2** Hard Rock's Global Strategy
TEN STRATEGIC OM DECISIONS (pp. 35–36)	■ **Operations decisions**—The strategic decisions of OM are goods and service design, quality, process and capacity design, location selection, layout design, human resources and job design, supply-chain management, inventory, scheduling, and maintenance.	
ISSUES IN OPERATIONS STRATEGY (pp. 36–39)	■ **Resources view**—A view in which managers evaluate the resources at their disposal and manage or alter them to achieve competitive advantage. ■ **Value-chain analysis**—A way to identify the elements in the product/service chain that uniquely add value. ■ **Five-forces analysis**—A way to analyze the five forces in the competitive environment. The potential competing forces in Porter's five-forces model are (1) immediate rivals, (2) potential entrants, (3) customers, (4) suppliers, and (5) substitute products. Different issues are emphasized during different stages of the product life cycle: • **Introduction**—Company strategy: Best period to increase market share, R&D engineering is critical. OM strategy: Product design and development critical, frequent product and process design changes, short production runs, high production costs, limited models, attention to quality. • **Growth**—Company strategy: Practical to change price or quality image, strengthen niche. OM strategy: Forecasting critical, product and process reliability, competitive	

Main Heading	Review Material	myomlab
	product improvements and options, increase capacity, shift toward product focus, enhance distribution. • **Maturity**—Company strategy: Poor time to change image or price or quality, competitive costs become critical, defend market position. OM strategy: Standardization, less rapid product changes (more minor changes), optimum capacity, increasing stability of process, long production runs, product improvement and cost cutting. • **Decline**—Company strategy: Cost control critical. OM strategy: Little product differentiation, cost minimization, overcapacity in the industry, prune line to eliminate items not returning good margin, reduce capacity.	
STRATEGY DEVELOPMENT AND IMPLEMENTATION (pp. 39–41)	▪ **SWOT analysis**—A method of determining internal strengths and weaknesses and external opportunities and threats. The strategy development process first involves performing environmental analysis, followed by determining the corporate mission, and finally forming a strategy. ▪ **Key success factors (KSFs)**—Activities or factors that are key to achieving competitive advantage. ▪ **Core competencies**—A set of skills, talents, and activities that a firm does particularly well. A core competence may be a subset of, or a combination of, KSFs. ▪ **Activity map**—A graphical link of competitive advantage, KSFs, and supporting activities. An operations manager's job is to implement an OM strategy, provide competitive advantage, and increase productivity.	Virtual Office Hours for Solved Problem: 2.1
GLOBAL OPERATIONS STRATEGY OPTIONS (pp. 42–44)	▪ **International business**—A firm that engages in cross-border transactions. ▪ **Multinational corporation (MNC)**—A firm that has extensive involvement in international business, owning or controlling facilities in more than one country. ▪ **International strategy**—A strategy in which global markets are penetrated using exports and licenses. ▪ **Multidomestic strategy**—A strategy in which operating decisions are decentralized to each country to enhance local responsiveness. ▪ **Global strategy**—A strategy in which operating decisions are centralized and headquarters coordinates the standardization and learning between facilities. ▪ **Transnational strategy**—A strategy that combines the benefits of global-scale efficiencies with the benefits of local responsiveness. These firms transgress national boundaries. The four operations strategies for approaching global opportunities can be classified according to local responsiveness and cost reduction: 1. **International**—Little local responsiveness and little cost advantage 2. **Multidomestic**—Significant local responsiveness but little cost advantage 3. **Global**—Little local responsiveness but significant cost advantage 4. **Transnational**—Significant local responsiveness and significant cost advantage	

Self Test

▪ **Before taking the self-test,** refer to the learning objectives listed at the beginning of the chapter and the key terms listed at the end of the chapter.

LO1. A mission statement is beneficial to an organization because it:
a) is a statement of the organization's purpose.
b) provides a basis for the organization's culture.
c) identifies important constituencies.
d) details specific income goals.
e) ensures profitability.

LO2. The three strategic approaches to competitive advantage are _____, _____, and _____.

LO3. The 10 decisions of OM:
a) are functional areas of the firm.
b) apply to both service and manufacturing organizations.
c) are the goals that are to be achieved.
d) form an action plan to achieve a mission.
e) are key success factors.

LO4. The relatively few activities that make a difference between a firm having and not having a competitive advantage are known as:
a) activity maps.
b) SWOT.
c) key success factors.
d) global profile.
e) response strategy.

LO5. A company that is organized across international boundaries, with decentralized authority and substantial autonomy at each business via subsidiaries, franchises, or joint ventures, has:
a) a global strategy.
b) a transnational strategy.
c) an international strategy.
d) a multidomestic strategy.
e) a regional strategy.

Answers: **LO1.** a; **LO2.** differentiation, cost leadership, response; **LO3.** b; **LO4.** c; **LO5.** c.

3 Project Management

Chapter Outline

The Importance of Project Management

Project Planning

Project Scheduling

Project Controlling

Project Management Techniques:
    PERT and CPM

Determining the Project Schedule

Variability in Activity Times

Cost-Time Trade-Offs and Project Crashing

A Critique of PERT and CPM

Using Microsoft Project to Manage
    Projects

Ethical Dilemma

Discussion Questions

Problems

*Case Studies: Southwestern University:
    (A); Project Management at Arnold
    Palmer Hospital; Managing Hard Rock's
    Rockfest*

Active Model Exercise

Classroom Activities

Rapid Review

Many projects that organizations undertake are large and complex. And almost every manager worries about how to manage such projects effectively. It is a difficult problem and the stakes are high. Expensive cost overruns and unnecessary delays can occur due to poor project planning.

The first step in planning and scheduling a project is to develop the work breakdown structure. The time, cost, resource requirements, predecessors, and person(s) responsible are identified for each activity. When this has been done, a schedule for the project can be developed using such techniques as the *Program Evaluation and Review Technique* (PERT) and the *Critical Path Method* (CPM).

BEFORE COMING TO CLASS, READ CHAPTER 3 IN YOUR TEXT AND ANSWER THESE QUESTIONS.

1. What is a work breakdown structure? _____
   _____

2. Explain the difference between AOA and AON networks. _____
   _____

3. Explain forward and backward passes. _____
   _____
   _____

4. What is the critical path and why is it important? _____
   _____
   _____

5. Explain how to calculate the variance of activity times. _____
   _____

6. What would you do to "crash" a project? _____
   _____

7. Explain how to use Microsoft Project software. _____
   _____

THE IMPORTANCE OF PROJECT MANAGEMENT

(See Flexible Version p. 50)

Three Phases in the Management of Projects

1. Planning
2. Scheduling
3. Controlling

PROJECT PLANNING   (See Flexible Version pp. 50–53)

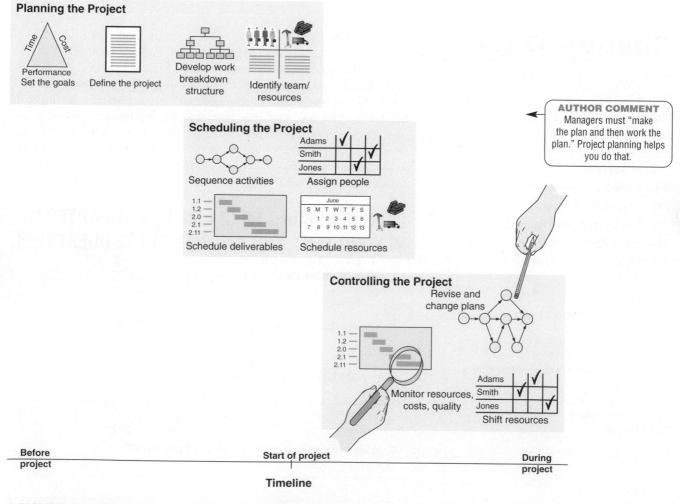

Planning the Project

Time   Cost   Performance
Set the goals

Define the project

Develop work breakdown structure

Identify team/ resources

Scheduling the Project

Sequence activities

Adams	✓		
Smith			✓
Jones		✓	

Assign people

1.1
1.2
2.0
2.1
2.11

Schedule deliverables

June
S M T W T F S
   1 2 3 4 5 6
7 8 9 10 11 12 13

Schedule resources

AUTHOR COMMENT
Managers must "make the plan and then work the plan." Project planning helps you do that.

Controlling the Project

Revise and change plans

1.1
1.2
2.0
2.1
2.11

Monitor resources, costs, quality

Adams	✓	✓	
Smith	✓		
Jones			✓

Shift resources

Before project   Start of project   During project

Timeline

▲ **FIGURE 3.1**   **Project Planning, Scheduling, and Controlling**

Work Breakdown Structure (WBS)   (See Flexible Version pp. 52–53)

Level

1. Project
2.   Major Tasks
3.   Subtasks
4.   Activities ("work package")

PROJECT SCHEDULING (See Flexible Version pp. 53–54)

● **Gantt Charts** (See Flexible Version p. 53)

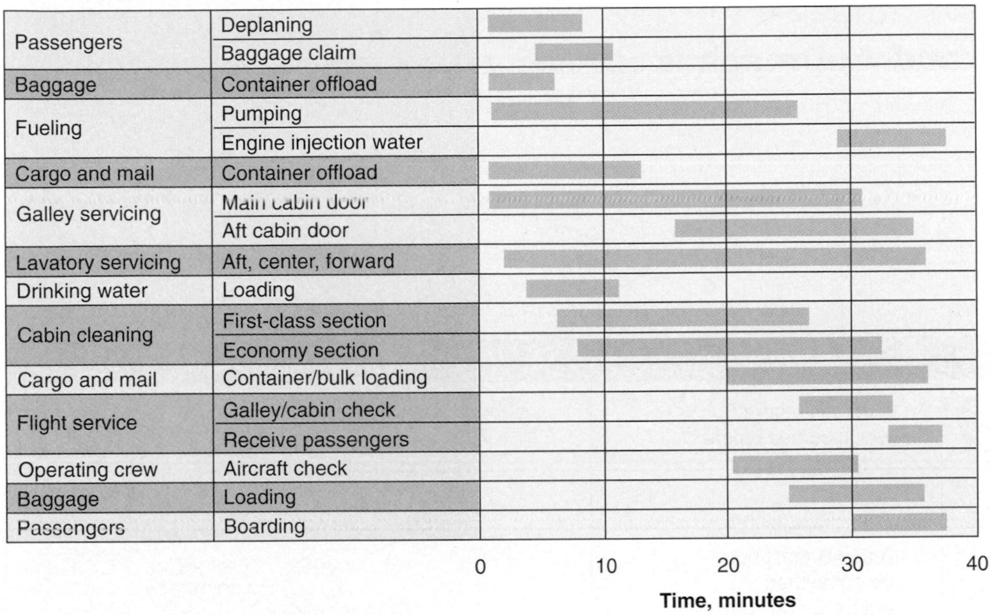

Passengers	Deplaning					
	Baggage claim					
Baggage	Container offload					
Fueling	Pumping					
	Engine injection water					
Cargo and mail	Container offload					
Galley servicing	Main cabin door					
	Aft cabin door					
Lavatory servicing	Aft, center, forward					
Drinking water	Loading					
Cabin cleaning	First-class section					
	Economy section					
Cargo and mail	Container/bulk loading					
Flight service	Galley/cabin check					
	Receive passengers					
Operating crew	Aircraft check					
Baggage	Loading					
Passengers	Boarding					

0   10   20   30   40

Time, minutes

◀ **FIGURE 3.4**

Gantt Chart of Service Activities for a Delta Jet during a 40-Minute Layover

Delta hopes to save $50 million a year with this turnaround time, which is a reduction from its traditional 60-minute routine.

PROJECT CONTROLLING (See Flexible Version p. 54)

●

PROJECT MANAGEMENT TECHNIQUES: PERT AND CPM

(See Flexible Version pp. 55–60)

Six Basic Steps in PERT and CPM

1. Define the project and prepare the WBS.
2. Develop the relationship among the activities.
3. Draw the network.
4. Assign time/cost estimates to activities.
5. Compute the critical path.
6. Use the network to plan, schedule, monitor, and control.

●

PERT and CPM Can Answer Several Questions
(See Flexible Version p. 55)

Network Diagrams and Approaches (See Flexible Version pp. 55–56)

Activity-on-Node (AON)

Activity-on-Arrow (AOA)

Dummy Activity

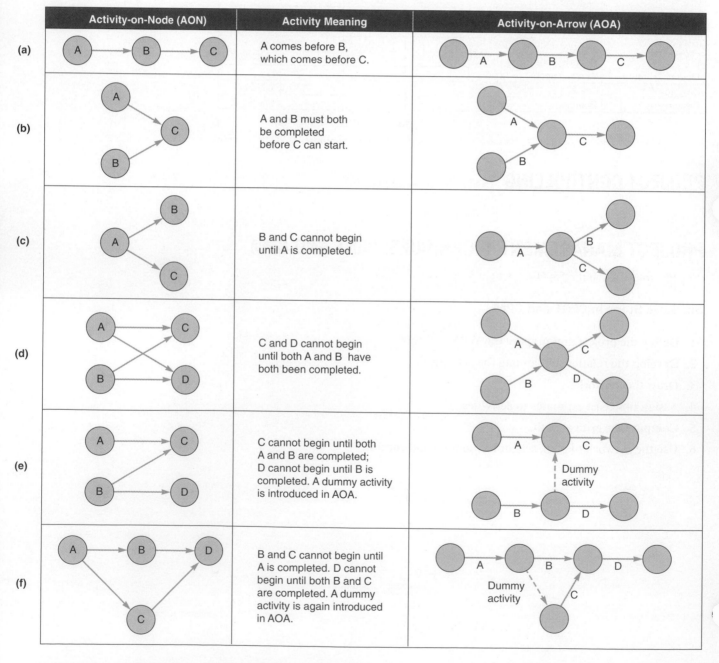

▲ FIGURE 3.5 A Comparison of AON and AOA Network Conventions

PRACTICE PROBLEM 3.1 ■ Drawing an AON Network

The following represent activities in a major construction project. Draw the network to represent this project.

Activity	Immediate Predecessor
A	—
B	—
C	A
D	B
E	B
F	C, E
G	D
H	F, G

DETERMINING THE PROJECT SCHEDULE (See Flexible Version pp. 60–65)

Critical Path Analysis (See Flexible Version pp. 60–61)

Earliest Start (ES)

Earliest Finish (EF)

Latest Start (LS)

Latest Finish (LF)

Forward Pass (See Flexible Version pp. 61–63)

Backward Pass (See Flexible Version pp. 63–64)

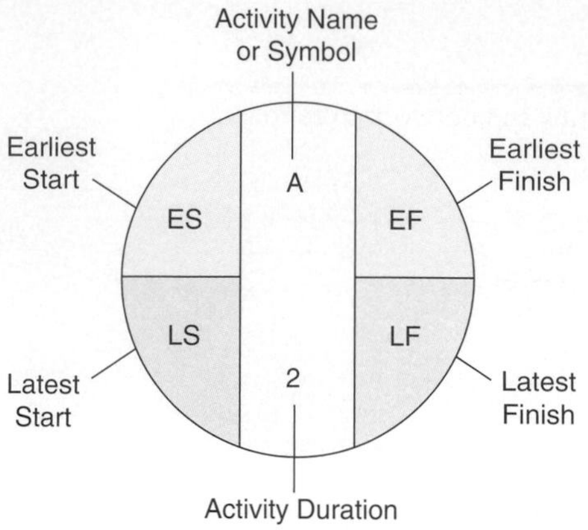

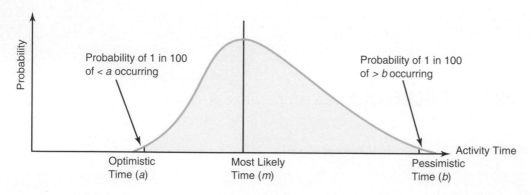

◀ **FIGURE 3.10**
Notation Used in Nodes for Forward and Backward Pass

Slack Time (See Flexible Version pp. 64–65)

$$\text{Slack} = \text{LS} - \text{ES} \quad \text{or} \quad \text{Slack} = \text{LF} - \text{EF} \tag{3-5}$$

VARIABILITY IN ACTIVITY TIMES (See Flexible Version pp. 65–71)

Three Time Estimates in PERT (See Flexible Version pp. 66–67)

Optimistic Time *(a)*
Pessimistic Time *(b)*
Most Likely Time *(m)*

◀ **FIGURE 3.12**
Beta Probability Distribution with Three Time Estimates

Expected time
$$t = (a + 4m + b)/6 \tag{3-6}$$

Variance of activity completion time $= [(b - a)/6]^2 \tag{3-7}$

PRACTICE PROBLEM 3.2 ■ Critical Path

Given the following time chart and network diagram, find the critical path.

Activity	a	m	b	t	Variance
A	2	3	4	3	1/9
B	1	2	3	2	1/9
C	4	5	12	6	16/9
D	1	3	5	3	4/9
E	1	2	3	2	1/9

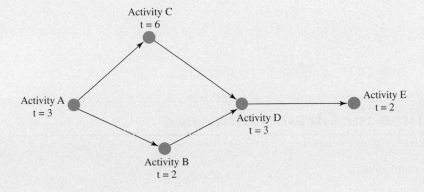

Additional Practice Problem Space

Probability of Project Completion (See Flexible Version pp. 68–71)

Project variance $(\sigma_p^2) = \Sigma$ (variances on critical path)

Project standard deviation $(\sigma_p) = \sqrt{\text{Project variance}}$ (3-8)

PRACTICE PROBLEM 3.3 ■ Variance

What is the variance in completion time for the critical path found in Practice Problem 3.2?

Project Completion Time for Given Confidence Levels (See Flexible Version p. 69)

$Z = (\text{due date} - \text{expected date of completion})/\sigma_p$ (3-9)

PRACTICE PROBLEM 3.4 ■ Probabilities of Project Completion

A project has an expected completion time of 40 weeks and a standard deviation of 5 weeks. It is assumed that the project completion time is normally distributed.

a. What is the probability of finishing the project in 50 weeks or less?

b. What is the probability of finishing the project in 38 weeks or less?

c. The due date for the project is set so that there is a 90% chance that the project will be finished by this date. What is the date?

Additional Practice Problem Space

COST–TIME TRADE-OFFS AND PROJECT CRASHING

(See Flexible Version pp. 71–73)

Normal (or Standard) Time

Normal Cost

Crash Time

Crash Cost

$$\text{Crash cost per period} = \frac{(\text{Crash cost} - \text{Normal cost})}{(\text{Normal time} - \text{Crash time})} \qquad (3\text{-}11)$$

Four Steps in Crashing a Project

1. _____

2. _____

3. _____

4. _____

PRACTICE PROBLEM 3.5 ■ Crashing

Development of a new deluxe version of a particular software product is being considered. The activities necessary for the completion of this project are listed in the following table along with their costs and completion times in weeks.

Activity	Normal Time	Crash Time	Normal Cost	Crash Cost	Immediate Predecessor
A	4	3	2,000	2,600	—
B	2	1	2,200	2,800	A
C	3	3	500	500	A
D	8	4	2,300	2,600	A
E	6	3	900	1,200	B, D
F	3	2	3,000	4,200	C, E
G	4	2	1,400	2,000	F

a. What is the project expected completion date?

b. What is the total cost required for completing this project in normal time?

c. If you wish to reduce the time required to complete this project by 1 week, which activity should be crashed, and how much will this increase the total cost?

Additional Practice Problem Space

A CRITIQUE OF PERT AND CPM   (See Flexible Version pp. 73–74)

Advantages   (See Flexible Version p. 73)

Disadvantages   (See Flexible Version p. 74)

USING MICROSOFT PROJECT TO MANAGE PROJECTS

(See Flexible Version pp. 74–77)

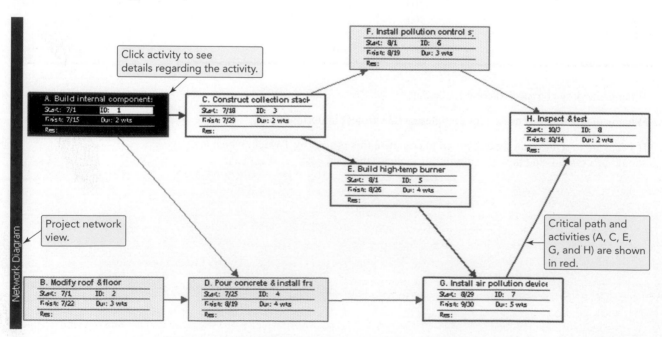

▲ PROGRAM 3.2   Project Network in Microsoft Project for Milwaukee Paper Manufacturing

Ethical Dilemma

Two examples of massively mismanaged projects are TAURUS and the "Big Dig." The first, formally called the London Stock Exchange Automation Project, cost $575 million before it was finally abandoned. Although most IT projects have a reputation for cost overruns, delays, and underperformance, TAURUS set a new standard.

But even TAURUS paled next to the biggest, most expensive public works project in U.S. history—Boston's 15-year-long Central Artery/Tunnel Project. Called the Big Dig, this was perhaps the poorest and most felonious case of project mismanagement in decades. From a starting $2 billion budget to a final price tag of $15 billion, the Big Dig cost more than the Panama Canal, Hoover Dam, or Interstate 95, the 1,919-mile highway between Maine and Florida.

Read about one of these two projects (or another of your choice) and explain why it faced such problems. How and why do project managers allow such massive endeavors to fall into such a state? What do you think are the causes?

Discussion Questions

1. Give an example of a situation in which project management is needed.
2. Explain the purpose of project organization.
3. What are the three phases involved in the management of a large project?
4. What are some of the questions that can be answered with PERT and CPM?
5. Define *work breakdown structure*. How is it used?
6. What is the use of Gantt charts in project management?
7. What is the difference between an activity-on-arrow (AOA) network and an activity-on-node (AON) network? Which is primarily used in this chapter?
8. What is the significance of the critical path?
9. What would a project manager have to do to crash an activity?
10. Describe how expected activity times and variances can be computed in a PERT network.
11. Define *early start*, *early finish*, *late finish*, and *late start* times.
12. Students are sometimes confused by the concept of critical path, and want to believe that it is the *shortest* path through a network. Convincingly explain why this is not so.
13. What are dummy activities? Why are they used in activity-on-arrow (AOA) project networks?
14. What are the three time estimates used with PERT?
15. Would a project manager ever consider crashing a noncritical activity in a project network? Explain convincingly.
16. How is the variance of the total project computed in PERT?
17. Describe the meaning of slack, and discuss how it can be determined.
18. How can we determine the probability that a project will be completed by a certain date? What assumptions are made in this computation?
19. Name some of the widely used project management software programs.

Problems*

•   **3.1** The work breakdown structure for building a house (levels 1 and 2) is shown below:

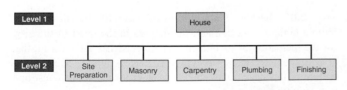

a) Add two level-3 activities to each of the level-2 activities to provide more detail to the WBS.
b) Select one of your level-3 activities and add two level-4 activities below it.

••   **3.2** Robert Mefford has decided to run for a seat as Congressman from the House of Representative district 34 in California. He views his 8-month campaign for office as a major project and wishes to create a work breakdown structure (WBS) to help control the detailed scheduling. So far, he has developed the pieces of the WBS shown in the next column.

Help Mr. Mefford by providing details where the blank lines appear. Are there any other major (level-2) activities to create? If so, add an ID no. 1.6 and insert them.

Level	Level ID No.	Activity
1	1.0	Develop political campaign
2	1.1	Fund-raising plan
3	1.11	_____
3	1.12	_____
3	1.13	_____
2	1.2	Develop a position on major issues
3	1.21	_____
3	1.22	_____
3	1.23	_____
2	1.3	Staffing for campaign
3	1.31	_____
3	1.32	_____
3	1.33	_____
3	1.34	_____
2	1.4	Paperwork compliance for candidacy
3	1.41	_____
3	1.42	_____
2	1.5	Ethical plan/issues
3	1.51	_____

•   **3.3** Draw the activity-on-node (AON) project network associated with the following activities for Dave Carhart's consulting company project. How long should it take Dave and his team to complete this project? What are the critical path activities?

*Note: **PX** means the problem may be solved with POM for Windows and/or Excel OM.

Activity	Immediate Predecessor(s)	Time (days)
A	—	3
B	A	4
C	A	6
D	B	6
E	B	4
F	C	4
G	D	6
H	E, F	8

• **3.4** Given the activities whose sequence is described by the following table, draw the appropriate activity-on-arrow (AOA) network diagram.

a) Which activities are on the critical path?
b) What is the length of the critical path?

Activity	Immediate Predecessor(s)	Time (days)
A	—	5
B	A	2
C	A	4
D	B	5
E	B	5
F	C	5
G	E, F	2
H	D	3
I	G, H	5

• **3.5** Using AOA, diagram the network described below for Sarah McComb's construction project. Calculate its critical path. How long is the minimum duration of this network?

Activity	Nodes	Time (weeks)	Activity	Nodes	Time (weeks)
J	1–2	10	N	3–4	2
K	1–3	8	O	4–5	7
L	2–4	6	P	3–5	5
M	2–3	3			

•• **3.6** Shirley Hopkins is developing a program in leadership training for middle-level managers. Shirley has listed a number of activities that must be completed before a training program of this nature could be conducted. The activities, immediate predecessors, and times appear in the accompanying table:

Activity	Immediate Predecessor(s)	Time (days)
A	—	2
B	—	5
C	—	1
D	B	10
E	A, D	3
F	C	6
G	E, F	8

a) Develop an AON network for this problem.
b) What is the critical path?
c) What is the total project completion time?
d) What is the slack time for each individual activity?

•• **3.7** Task time estimates for a production line setup project at Robert Klassen's Ontario factory are as follows:

Activity	Time (in hours)	Immediate Predecessors
A	6.0	—
B	7.2	—
C	5.0	A
D	6.0	B, C
E	4.5	B, C
F	7.7	D
G	4.0	E, F

a) Draw the project network using AON.
b) Identify the critical path.
c) What is the expected project length?
d) Draw a Gantt chart for the project.

•• **3.8** The City Commission of Nashville has decided to build a botanical garden and picnic area in the heart of the city for the recreation of its citizens. The precedence table for all the activities required to construct this area successfully is given on the bottom of this page. Draw the Gantt chart for the whole construction activity.

▼ TABLE 3.8

Code	Activity	Description	Time (in hours)	Immediate Predecessor(s)
A	Planning	Find location; determine resource requirements	20	None
B	Purchasing	Requisition of lumber and sand	60	Planning
C	Excavation	Dig and grade	100	Planning
D	Sawing	Saw lumber into appropriate sizes	30	Purchasing
E	Placement	Position lumber in correct locations	20	Sawing, excavation
F	Assembly	Nail lumber together	10	Placement
G	Infill	Put sand in and under the equipment	20	Assembly
H	Outfill	Put dirt around the equipment	10	Assembly
I	Decoration	Put grass all over the garden, landscape, paint	30	Infill, outfill

•• **3.9** Refer to the table in Problem 3.8.
a) Draw the AON network for the construction activity.
b) Draw the AOA network for the construction activity.

• **3.10** The activities needed to build an experimental chemical contaminant tracking machine at Charlie Cook Corp. are listed in the following table. Construct an AON network for these activities.

Activity	Immediate Predecessor(s)	Activity	Immediate Predecessor(s)
A	—	E	B
B	—	F	B
C	A	G	C, E
D	A	H	D, F

• **3.11** Charlie Cook (see Problem 3.10) was able to determine the activity times for constructing his chemical contaminant tracking machine. Cook would like to determine ES, EF, LS, LF, and slack for each activity. The total project completion time and the critical path should also be determined. Here are the activity times:

Activity	Time (weeks)	Activity	Time (weeks)
A	6	E	4
B	7	F	6
C	3	G	10
D	2	H	7

• **3.12** The activities described by the following table are given for the Duplaga Corporation:

Activity	Immediate Predecessor(s)	Time
A	—	9
B	A	7
C	A	3
D	B	6
E	B	9
F	C	4
G	E, F	6
H	D	5
I	G, H	3

a) Draw the appropriate AON PERT diagram for Ed Duplaga's management team.
b) Find the critical path.
c) What is the project completion time? **Px**

• **3.13** A small renovation of a Hard Rock Cafe gift shop has six activities (in hours). For the following estimates of *a*, *m*, and *b*, calculate the expected time and the standard deviation for each activity:

Activity	a	m	b
A	11	15	19
B	27	31	41
C	18	18	18
D	8	13	19
E	17	18	20
F	16	19	22

Px

•• **3.14** McGee Carpet and Trim installs carpet in commercial offices. Andrea McGee has been very concerned with the amount of time it took to complete several recent jobs. Some of her workers are very unreliable. A list of activities and their optimistic completion time, the most likely completion time, and the pessimistic completion time (all in days) for a new contract are given in the following table:

Activity	Time (days)			Immediate Predecessor(s)
	a	m	b	
A	3	6	8	—
B	2	4	4	—
C	1	2	3	—
D	6	7	8	C
E	2	4	6	B, D
F	6	10	14	A, E
G	1	2	4	A, E
H	3	6	9	F
I	10	11	12	G
J	14	16	20	C
K	2	8	10	H, I

a) Determine the expected completion time and variance for each activity.
b) Determine the total project completion time and the critical path for the project.
c) Determine ES, EF, LS, LF, and slack for each activity.
d) What is the probability that McGee Carpet and Trim will finish the project in 40 days or less? **Px**

•• **3.15** The following is a table of activities associated with a project at Bill Figg Enterprises, their durations, and what activities each must precede:

Activity	Duration (weeks)	Precedes
A (start)	1	B, C
B	1	E
C	4	F
E	2	F
F (end)	2	—

a) Draw an AON diagram of the project, including activity durations.
b) Define the critical path, listing all critical activities in chronological order.
c) What is the project duration (in weeks)?
d) What is the slack (in weeks) associated with any and all noncritical paths through the project?

•• **3.16** Assume that the activities in Problem 3.15 have the following costs to shorten: A, $300/week; B, $100/week; C, $200/week; E, $100/week; and F, $400/week. Assume also that you can crash an activity down to 0 weeks in duration and that every week you can shorten the project is worth $250 to you. What activities would you crash? What is the total crashing cost?

••• **3.17** Bill Fennema, president of Fennema Construction, has developed the tasks, durations, and predecessor relationships in the following table for building new motels. Draw the AON network and answer the questions that follow.

		Time Estimates (in weeks)		
Activity	Immediate Predecessor(s)	Optimistic	Most Likely	Pessimistic
A	—	4	8	10
B	A	2	8	24
C	A	8	12	16
D	A	4	6	10
E	B	1	2	3
F	E, C	6	8	20
G	E, C	2	3	4
H	F	2	2	2
I	F	6	6	6
J	D, G, H	4	6	12
K	I, J	2	2	3

a) What is the expected (estimated) time for activity C?

b) What is the variance for activity C?

c) Based on the calculation of estimated times, what is the critical path?

d) What is the estimated time of the critical path?

e) What is the activity variance along the critical path?

f) What is the probability of completion of the project before week 36? **Px**

••• **3.18** What is the minimum cost of crashing the following project that James Walters manages at Ball State University by 4 days?

Activity	Normal Time (days)	Crash Time (days)	Normal Cost	Crash Cost	Immediate Predecessor(s)
A	6	5	$ 900	$1,000	—
B	8	6	300	400	—
C	4	3	500	600	—
D	5	3	900	1,200	A
E	8	5	1,000	1,600	C

Px

•• **3.19** Three activities are candidates for crashing on a project network for a large computer installation (all are, of course, critical). Activity details are in the following table:

Activity	Predecessor	Normal Time	Normal Cost	Crash Time	Crash Cost
A	—	7 days	$6,000	6 days	$6,600
B	A	4 days	1,200	2 days	3,000
C	B	11 days	4,000	9 days	6,000

a) What action would you take to reduce the critical path by 1 day?

b) Assuming no other paths become critical, what action would you take to reduce the critical path one additional day?

c) What is the total cost of the 2-day reduction? **Px**

••• **3.20** Development of a new deluxe version of a particular software product is being considered by Ravi Behara's software house. The activities necessary for the completion of this project are listed in the following table:

Activity	Normal Time (weeks)	Crash Time (weeks)	Normal Cost	Crash Cost	Immediate Predecessor(s)
A	4	3	$2,000	$2,600	—
B	2	1	2,200	2,800	—
C	3	3	500	500	—
D	8	4	2,300	2,600	A
E	6	3	900	1,200	B
F	3	2	3,000	4,200	C
G	4	2	1,400	2,000	D, E

a) What is the project completion date?

b) What is the total cost required for completing this project on normal time?

c) If you wish to reduce the time required to complete this project by 1 week, which activity should be crashed, and how much will this increase the total cost?

d) What is the maximum time that can be crashed? How much would costs increase? **Px**

••• **3.21** The estimated times and immediate predecessors for the activities in a project at Caesar Douglas's retinal scanning company are given in the following table. Assume that the activity times are independent.

Activity	Immediate Predecessor	Time (weeks)		
		a	m	b
A	—	9	10	11
B	—	4	10	16
C	A	9	10	11
D	B	5	8	11

a) Calculate the expected time and variance for each activity.

b) What is the expected completion time of the critical path? What is the expected completion time of the other path in the network?

c) What is the variance of the critical path? What is the variance of the other path in the network?

d) If the time to complete path A–C is normally distributed, what is the probability that this path will be finished in 22 weeks or less?

e) If the time to complete path B–D is normally distributed, what is the probability that this path will be finished in 22 weeks or less?

f) Explain why the probability that the *critical path* will be finished in 22 weeks or less is not necessarily the probability that the *project* will be finished in 22 weeks or less. **Px**

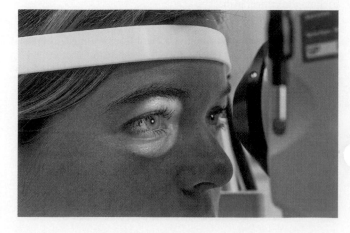

• • •   **3.22** Jack Kanet Manufacturing produces custom-built pollution control devices for medium-size steel mills. The most recent project undertaken by Jack requires 14 different activities.

a) Jack's managers would like to determine the total project completion time (in days) and those activities that lie along the critical path. The appropriate data are shown in the following table.

b) What is the probability of being done in 53 days?

c) What date results in a 99% probability of completion?

Activity	Immediate Predecessor(s)	Optimistic Time	Most Likely Time	Pessimistic Time
A	—	4	6	7
B	—	1	2	3
C	A	6	6	6
D	A	5	8	11
E	B, C	1	9	18
F	D	2	3	6
G	D	1	7	8
H	E, F	4	4	6
I	G, H	1	6	8
J	I	2	5	7
K	I	8	9	11
L	J	2	4	6
M	K	1	2	3
N	L, M	6	8	10

Px

• • •   **3.23** Dream Team Productions, a firm hired to coordinate the release of the movie *Paycheck* (starring Uma Thurman and Ben Affleck), identified 16 activities to be completed before the release of the film.

a) How many weeks in advance of the film release should Dream Team have started its marketing campaign? What is the critical path? The tasks (in time units of weeks) are as follows:

Activity	Immediate Predecessors	Optimistic Time	Most Likely Time	Pessimistic Time
A	—	1	2	4
B	—	3	3.5	4
C	—	10	12	13
D	—	4	5	7
E	—	2	4	5
F	A	6	7	8
G	B	2	4	5.5
H	C	5	7.7	9
I	C	9.9	10	12
J	C	2	4	5
K	D	2	4	6
L	E	2	4	6
M	F, G, H	5	6	6.5
N	J, K, L	1	1.1	2
O	I, M	5	7	8
P	N	5	7	9

b) If activities I and J were not necessary, what impact would this have on the critical path and the number of weeks needed to complete the marketing campaign? **Px**

• •   **3.24** Using PERT, Harold Benson was able to determine that the expected project completion time for the construction of a pleasure yacht is 21 months, and the project variance is 4.

a) What is the probability that the project will be completed in 17 months?

b) What is the probability that the project will be completed in 20 months?

c) What is the probability that the project will be completed in 23 months?

d) What is the probability that the project will be completed in 25 months?

e) What is the due date that yields a 95% chance of completion? **Px**

• • •   **3.25** Bolling Electronics manufactures DVD players for commercial use. W. Blaker Bolling, president of Bolling Electronics, is contemplating producing DVD players for home use. The activities necessary to build an experimental model and related data are given in the following table:

Activity	Normal Time (weeks)	Crash Time (weeks)	Normal Cost ($)	Crash Cost ($)	Immediate Predecessor(s)
A	3	2	1,000	1,600	—
B	2	1	2,000	2,700	—
C	1	1	300	300	—
D	7	3	1,300	1,600	A
E	6	3	850	1,000	B
F	2	1	4,000	5,000	C
G	4	2	1,500	2,000	D, E

a) What is the project completion date?

b) Crash this project to 10 weeks at the least cost.

c) Crash this project to 7 weeks (which is the maximum it can be crashed) at the least cost. **Px**

• • •   **3.26** The Maser is a new custom-designed sports car. An analysis of the task of building the Maser reveals the following list of relevant activities, their immediate predecessors, and their duration:*

Job Letter	Description	Immediate Predecessor(s)	Normal Time (days)
A	Start	—	0
B	Design	A	8
C	Order special accessories	B	0.1
D	Build frame	B	1
E	Build doors	B	1
F	Attach axles, wheels, gas tank	D	1
G	Build body shell	B	2
H	Build transmission and drivetrain	B	3
I	Fit doors to body shell	G, E	1
J	Build engine	B	4
K	Bench-test engine	J	2
L	Assemble chassis	F, H, K	1
M	Road-test chassis	L	0.5
N	Paint body	I	2

Job Letter	Description	Immediate Predecessor(s)	Normal Time (days)
O	Install wiring	N	1
P	Install interior	N	1.5
Q	Accept delivery of special accessories	C	5
R	Mount body and accessories on chassis	M, O, P, Q	1
S	Road test car	R	0.5
T	Attach exterior trim	S	1
U	Finish	T	0

a) Draw a network diagram for the project.
b) Mark the critical path and state its length.
c) If the Maser had to be completed 2 days earlier, would it help to:
   i) Buy preassembled transmissions and drivetrains?
   ii) Install robots to halve engine-building time?
   iii) Speed delivery of special accessories by 3 days?
d) How might resources be borrowed from activities on the noncritical path to speed activities on the critical path? **P℟**

*Source: James A. D. Stoner and Charles Wankel, *Management*, 3rd ed. (Upper Saddle River, NJ: Prentice Hall): 195.

▶ **Refer to myomlab ⟳ for these additional homework problems: 3.27–3.33**

Case Studies

▶ Southwestern University: (A)*

Southwestern University (SWU), a large state college in Stephenville, Texas, 30 miles southwest of the Dallas/Fort Worth metroplex, enrolls close to 20,000 students. In a typical town–gown relationship, the school is a dominant force in the small city, with more students during fall and spring than permanent residents.

A longtime football powerhouse, SWU is a member of the Big Eleven conference and is usually in the top 20 in college football rankings. To bolster its chances of reaching the elusive and long-desired number-one ranking, in 2003, SWU hired the legendary Bo Pitterno as its head coach.

One of Pitterno's demands on joining SWU had been a new stadium. With attendance increasing, SWU administrators began to face the issue head-on. After 6 months of study, much political arm wrestling, and some serious financial analysis, Dr. Joel Wisner, president of Southwestern University, had reached a decision to expand the capacity at its on-campus stadium.

Adding thousands of seats, including dozens of luxury skyboxes, would not please everyone. The influential Pitterno had argued the need for a first-class stadium, one with built-in dormitory rooms for his players and a palatial office appropriate for the coach

of a future NCAA champion team. But the decision was made, and *everyone*, including the coach, would learn to live with it.

The job now was to get construction going immediately after the 2009 season ended. This would allow exactly 270 days until the 2010 season opening game. The contractor, Hill Construction (Bob Hill being an alumnus, of course), signed his contract. Bob Hill looked at the tasks his engineers had outlined and looked President Wisner in the eye. "I guarantee the team will be able to take the field on schedule next year," he said with a sense of confidence. "I sure hope so," replied Wisner. "The contract penalty of $10,000 per day for running late is nothing compared to what Coach Pitterno will do to you if our opening game with Penn State is delayed or canceled." Hill, sweating slightly, did not need to respond. In football-crazy Texas, Hill Construction would be *mud* if the 270-day target was missed.

Back in his office, Hill again reviewed the data (see Table 3.6) and noted that optimistic time estimates can be used as crash times. He then gathered his foremen. "Folks, if we're not 75% sure we'll finish this stadium in less than 270 days, I want this project crashed! Give me the cost figures for a target date of 250 days—also for 240 days. I want to be *early*, not just on time!"

*This integrated study runs throughout the text. Other issues facing Southwestern's football expansion include (B) forecasting game attendance (Chapter 4); (C) quality of facilities (Chapter 6); (D) break-even analysis for food services (Supplement 7 Web site); (E) location of the new stadium (Chapter 8 Web site); (F) inventory planning of football programs (Chapter 12 Web site); and (G) scheduling of campus security officers/staff for game days (Chapter 13).

▼ **TABLE 3.6**   Southwestern University Project

Activity	Description	Predecessor(s)	Time Estimates (days) Optimistic	Time Estimates (days) Most Likely	Time Estimates (days) Pessimistic	Crash Cost/Day
A	Bonding, insurance, tax structuring	—	20	30	40	$1,500
B	Foundation, concrete footings for boxes	A	20	65	80	3,500
C	Upgrading skybox stadium seating	A	50	60	100	4,000
D	Upgrading walkways, stairwells, elevators	C	30	50	100	1,900
E	Interior wiring, lathes	B	25	30	35	9,500
F	Inspection approvals	E	0.1	0.1	0.1	0
G	Plumbing	D, F	25	30	35	2,500
H	Painting	G	10	20	30	2,000
I	Hardware/AC/metal workings	H	20	25	60	2,000
J	Tile/carpet/windows	H	8	10	12	6,000
K	Inspection	J	0.1	0.1	0.1	0
L	Final detail work/cleanup	I, K	20	25	60	4,500

Discussion Questions

1. Develop a network drawing for Hill Construction and determine the critical path. How long is the project expected to take?
2. What is the probability of finishing in 270 days?
3. If it is necessary to crash to 250 or 240 days, how would Hill do so, and at what costs? As noted in the case, assume that optimistic time estimates can be used as crash times.

▶ Project Management at Arnold Palmer Hospital

Video Case

The equivalent of a new kindergarten class is born every day at Orlando's Arnold Palmer Hospital. With more than 12,300 births in 2005 in a hospital that was designed in 1989 for a capacity of 6,500 births a year, the newborn intensive care unit was stretched to the limit. Moreover, with continuing strong population growth in central Florida, the hospital was often full. It was clear that new facilities were needed. After much analysis, forecasting, and discussion, the management team decided to build a new 273-bed building across the street from the existing hospital. But the facility had to be built in accordance with the hospital's Guiding Principles and its uniqueness as a health center dedicated to the specialized needs of women and infants. Those Guiding Principles are: *Family-centered focus, a healing environment where privacy and dignity are respected, sanctuary of caring that includes warm, serene surroundings with natural lighting, sincere and dedicated staff providing the highest quality care, and patient-centered flow and function.*

The vice president of business development, Karl Hodges, wanted a hospital that was designed from the inside out by the people who understood the Guiding Principles, who knew most about the current system, and who were going to use the new system, namely, the doctors and nurses. Hodges and his staff spent 13 months discussing expansion needs with this group, as well as with patients and the community before developing a proposal for the new facility on December 17, 2001. An administrative team created 35 user groups, which held over 1,000 planning meetings (lasting from 45 minutes to a whole day). They even created a "Supreme Court" to deal with conflicting views on the multifaceted issues facing the new hospital.

Funding and regulatory issues added substantial complexity to this major expansion, and Hodges was very concerned that the project stay on time and within budget. Tom Hyatt, director of facility development, was given the task of onsite manager of the $100 million project, in addition to overseeing ongoing renovations, expansions, and other projects. The activities in the multiyear project for the new building at Arnold Palmer are shown in Table 3.7.

▼ **TABLE 3.7**   Expansion Planning and Arnold Palmer Hospital Construction Activities and Times[a]

Activity	Scheduled Time	Precedence Activity(ies)
1. Proposal and review	1 month	—
2. Establish master schedule	2 weeks	1
3. Architect selection process	5 weeks	1
4. Survey whole campus and its needs	1 month	1
5. Conceptual architect's plans	6 weeks	3
6. Cost estimating	2 months	2, 4, 5
7. Deliver plans to board for consideration/decision	1 month	6

(Continued)

▼ TABLE 3.7   Continued

Activity	Scheduled Time	Precedence Activity(ies)
8. Surveys/regulatory review	6 weeks	6
9. Construction manager selection	9 weeks	6
10. State review of need for more hospital beds ("Certificate of Need")	3.5 months	7, 8
11. Design drawings	4 months	10
12. Construction documents	5 months	9, 11
13. Site preparation/demolish existing building	9 weeks	11
14. Construction start/building pad	2 months	12, 13
15. Relocate utilities	6 weeks	12
16. Deep foundations	2 months	14
17. Building structure in place	9 months	16
18. Exterior skin/roofing	4 months	17
19. Interior buildout	12 months	17
20. Building inspections	5 weeks	15, 19
21. Occupancy	1 month	20

ªThis list of activities is abbreviated for purposes of this case study. For simplification, assume each week = .25 months (i.e., 2 weeks = .5 month, 6 weeks = 1.5 months, etc.).

Discussion Questions*

1. Develop the network for planning and construction of the new hospital at Arnold Palmer.
2. What is the critical path and how long is the project expected to take?
3. Why is the construction of this 11-story building any more complex than construction of an equivalent office building?

4. What percent of the whole project duration was spent in planning that occurred prior to the proposal and reviews? Prior to the actual building construction? Why?

*You may wish to view the video accompanying this case before addressing these questions.

► Managing Hard Rock's Rockfest

Video Case

At the Hard Rock Cafe, like many organizations, project management is a key planning tool. With Hard Rock's constant growth in hotels and cafes, remodeling of existing cafes, scheduling for Hard Rock Live concert and event venues, and planning the annual Rockfest, managers rely on project management techniques and software to maintain schedule and budget performance.

"Without Microsoft Project," says Hard Rock Vice President Chris Tomasso, "there is no way to keep so many people on the same page." Tomasso is in charge of the Rockfest event, which is attended by well over 100,000 enthusiastic fans. The challenge is pulling it off within a tight 9-month planning horizon. As the event approaches, Tomasso devotes greater energy to its activities. For the first 3 months, Tomasso updates his Microsoft Project charts monthly. Then at the 6-month mark, he updates his progress weekly. At the 9-month mark, he checks and corrects his schedule twice a week.

Early in the project management process, Tomasso identifies 10 major tasks (called level-2 activities in a work breakdown struc-

ture, or WBS):[†] talent booking, ticketing, marketing/PR, online promotion, television, show production, travel, sponsorships, operations, and merchandising. Using a WBS, each of these is further divided into a series of subtasks. Table 3.8 identifies 26 of the major activities and subactivities, their immediate predecessors, and time estimates. Tomasso enters all these into the Microsoft Project software.[‡] Tomasso alters the Microsoft Project document and the time line as the project progresses. "It's okay to change it as long as you keep on track," he states.

The day of the rock concert itself is not the end of the project planning. "It's nothing but surprises. A band not being able to get to the venue because of traffic jams is a surprise, but an 'anticipated' surprise. We had a helicopter on stand-by ready to fly the band in," says Tomasso.

On completion of Rockfest in July, Tomasso and his team have a 3-month reprieve before starting the project planning process again.

► TABLE 3.8

Some of the Major Activities and Subactivities in the Rockfest Plan

Activity	Description	Predecessor(s)	Time (weeks)
A	Finalize site and building contracts	—	7
B	Select local promoter	A	3
C	Hire production manager	A	3
D	Design promotional Web site	B	5
E	Set TV deal	D	6
F	Hire director	E	4

(Continued)

G	Plan for TV camera placement	F	2	◀ **TABLE 3.8** **Continued**
H	Target headline entertainers	B	4	
I	Target support entertainers	H	4	
J	Travel accommodations for talent	I	10	
K	Set venue capacity	C	2	
L	Ticketmaster contract	D, K	3	
M	On-site ticketing	L	8	
N	Sound and staging	C	6	
O	Passes and stage credentials	G, R	7	
P	Travel accommodations for staff	B	20	
Q	Hire sponsor coordinator	B	4	
R	Finalize sponsors	Q	4	
S	Define/place signage for sponsors	R, X	3	
T	Hire operations manager	A	4	
U	Develop site plan	T	6	
V	Hire security director	T	7	
W	Set police/fire security plan	V	4	
X	Power, plumbing, AC, toilet services	U	8	
Y	Secure merchandise deals	B	6	
Z	Online merchandise sales	Y	6	

Discussion Questions[§]

1. Identify the critical path and its activities for Rockfest. How long does the project take?
2. Which activities have a slack time of 8 weeks or more?
3. Identify five major challenges a project manager faces in events such as this one.
4. Why is a work breakdown structure useful in a project such as this? Take the 26 activities and break them into what you think should be level-2, level-3, and level-4 tasks.

[†]The level-1 activity is the Rockfest concert itself.

[‡]There are actually 127 activities used by Tomasso; the list is abbreviated for this case study.

[§]You may wish to view the video accompanying this case before addressing these questions.

Active Model Exercise

ACTIVE MODEL 3.1 is a simulation that evaluates changes in Example 6 in your text. It is illustrated at **www.myomlab.com** or **www.pearsonhighered.com/heizer**.

Classroom Activities

▶ A Project Management Decision-Making Game: Rock'n Bands

Rock'n Bands[1]

Your company, Planners 'R Us, specializes in effectively managing projects. Previous experience has involved conference management systems, commercial construction, and software development projects.

A new, intriguing project offers another opportunity to apply your project management expertise. The university you just graduated from wishes to put together a music festival, *Rock'n Bands*. This will feature a number of top music groups, and should attract interest from students, local residents, and music fans throughout the region.

Your company has met with university officials to develop a list of activities required to make *Rock'n Bands* a reality. The list on the next page includes twelve activities as well as their durations and immediate predecessors. The project plan is also described visually on the next page with a network diagram. The subscripts on each activity denote the number of weeks of work that activity is expected to require. Arrows denote the order of activities. For instance, activity E cannot be started until activity A is completed, and activity H cannot be started until both C and D are completed. The start and end nodes are dummy nodes and do not

[1]The events, activity durations, and overall scenario represented in this game are purely fictional. No relationship to an upcoming music concert, real or implied, is suggested.

need to be worked on. Note that at the beginning of the project, activities A, C, and D are available to start working on, as they have no predecessor activities. *Be sure to understand the diagram before reading further.*

Your job is to allocate workers to tasks each week during the project. Planners 'R Us has agreed to complete the project in 10 weeks (finishing 2 weeks before the Festival), and wants to minimize the costs associated with the project. All tasks A–K must be completed in 10 weeks. You have four (4) workers, although you do not need to use all of them every week—there are other tasks they can do in your company.

For bookkeeping purposes, your company will charge $200 per week for each worker that you use. If you happen to need an additional worker, there is one (1) available, but that person would then not get their other work done; thus, you will be charged $300 per week for the additional worker. In addition, if the project is

"late," there will be complications during the last 2 weeks before the Festival, costing Planners 'R Us $2000 per week due to a serious loss of goodwill and plenty of negative publicity.

The final cost to consider involves expediting tasks. You can assign an extra worker to a task in any given week in order to finish it in less time. For instance, if a task requires 2 weeks but you assign 2 workers, it will be completed in 1 week. However, putting two workers on a task is not quite as efficient as having one worker complete it from start to finish. Doing this requires additional coordination (by you) and may require some overtime by the workers. These costs total an additional $100 per week. The most workers that can be assigned to any task in a week are two (since having three or more requires so much additional coordination that no reduction in time is achieved). To summarize, the most workers on any given task is two (2) per week, and the total number of workers you may employ for any week is at most five (5).

Activity	Description	Duration (weeks)	Immediate Predecessors
A	Contract negotiation with selected music groups	3	–
B	Find a construction firm and build the stage	5	C
C	Contract negotiation with roadies	2	–
D	Screen and hire security personnel	3	–
E	Ticket distribution arrangements	1	A
F	Organize advertising brochures and souvenir program printing	4	D
G	Logistical arrangements for music group transportation	1	E
H	Sound equipment arrangements	3	C, D
I	Processing of travel visas (for international groups)	5	F, H
J	Hire parking staff and make parking arrangements	4	E, B, H
K	Distribute media passes and arrange for MTV recording	5	G
L	Arrange for concession sales and restroom facilities	2	F

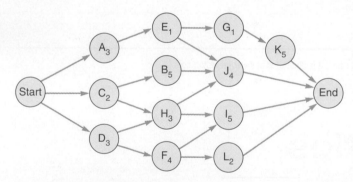

Being an experienced manager, you are aware that all projects involve various uncertainties (e.g., delays, additional requirements, or even improved efficiency) that can occur at any time. Since you do not want to lose your reputation for ontime delivery in Planners 'R Us, you are determined to plan the project well and be as efficient as possible from the first week on.

For now, you want to develop a plan for the whole project, but the only decision that needs to be implemented is how to allocate workers for the first week. Report this decision to the instructor (the reporting sheet on the next page may help with this). After all teams have reported their decisions for first week allocations, the instructor will let you know of any changes that may occur regarding the project. Then, you will make decisions for the second week.

Designed by: Ken Klassen, Brock University
Keith Willoughby, Bucknell University

Note: This game has been developed for educational purposes. It may be used, disseminated, and modified for educational purposes, but it may not be sold. In all uses of the game, the original developers must be acknowledged (as has been done above).

© 2003, Ken Klassen & Keith Willoughby

▶ Project Crashing Using MSProject: Hard Rock Concert Case

Each year, Hard Rock organizes a huge concert called the "Rock Fest." Some 100,000 rock and roll fans attend the Rock Fest. Planning for the concert begins many months before the actual concert date. This year, the concert will take place on the Saturday of Labor Day

weekend, September 3rd. Planning for the concert begins on January 28th. As a recent operations management graduate, you have been hired to help schedule this year's concert. Hard Rock follows a normal workweek and observes all traditional holidays. Specifically these holidays include: Good Friday (March 25th), Memorial Day (May 30th), July 4th, and Labor Day (September 5th). All planning activities must be complete by September 3rd.

Below is a table detailing the specific activities associated with staging Rock Fest. Included in the table are precedence activities, the normal amount of time and normal amount of cost associated with each task, and the number of days an activity can be shortened to and its total cost to crash to that time.

For this case, you are to do the following:

1. Using Microsoft Project, enter the activities, durations, and predecessors under "Normal" conditions. Print this entry screen. This is your "**Before**" entry screen.
2. Once these activities are entered, print the Network Diagram. This will be your "**Before**" Network Diagram.

3. Identify the Critical path in your initial diagram.
4. Print the Slack Table for your initial diagram.
5. Now, shorten this project so that the concert can take place as planned (September 3rd). Identify the tasks you will shorten to achieve this goal and adjust the durations of these activities so that the "finish time" indicates the concert can take place as scheduled. This is your "**After**" or "**Crashed**" entry screen.
6. Print a new Network Diagram showing the new critical path. This will be your "**After**" Network Diagram.
7. Print a new Slack Table.
8. What is the Total Cost of putting on this concert and how much extra did you have to spend to get the concert on schedule?

Prepared by: Gary LaPoint, School of Management, Syracuse University

Activity	Description	Predecessors	Normal Time in Days	Normal Time Cost	Task Can Be Shortened to:	Total Cost of Shortened Time
A	Finalize sites and facility contracts		28	$10,000		
B	Select Concert Promoter	A	14	$7,500		
C	Hire production Manager	B	21	$5,000		
D	Design promotional Web site	B	25	$15,000		
E	Finalize TV rights	B	60	$8,000	50	$10,000
F	Hire Director	B	28	$7,500		
G	Plan for TV camera placement	F	13	$7,250		
H	Target headline entertainers	B	45	$12,500	41	$16,000
I	Target support entertainers	H	43	$11,000		
J	Travel accommodations for talent	I	4	$6,000	3	$6,600
K	Set venue capacity	C	3	$2,000		
L	Sign TicketMaster contract	B, D, K	17	$6,000		
M	Onsite ticketing	L	6	$1,500	5	$2,000
N	Lease sound and staging equipment	C	8	$5,500		
O	Passes and stage credentials	G, R, P	4	$2,500	2	$3,000
P	Travel accommodations for staff	U, W	4	$4,000		
Q	Hire Sponsor Coordinator	B	21	$5,900		
R	Finalize sponsors	Q	35	$9,000	32	$10,500
S	Define and place signage for sponsors	Q, E, X	8	$3,000		
T	Sign concession contracts	B, K	32	$8,000		
U	Hire Operations Manager	B	48	$5,500	43	$8,500
V	Develop site plan	U	31	$9,000	28	$10,200
W	Hire Security Director	B	20	$4,200		
X	Hire Support Staff	U, W	17	$3,600		
Y	Develop police/fire security plan	W	55	$10,000	50	$15,000
Z	Develop traffic plan	W, M, J, T	20	$9,500	18	$10,350

(Continued)

Activity	Description	Predecessors	Normal Time in Days	Normal Time Cost	Task Can Be Shortened to:	Total Cost of Shortened Time
AA	Determine reqmts for power, facilities	V	30	$6,200	26	$7,200
BB	Secure merchandise deals	B	25	$6,100		
CC	Secure online merchandise sales	BB	20	$4,700		
DD	Install power/plumbing/ AC/toilet svcs	AA	6	$9,500		
EE	Construct stage	C, N, V, AA, DD	2	$7,000		
FF	Test sound/lighting	O, DD, EE	2	$3,000	1	$4,500
GG	Ready for concert	Y, Z, CC, S, FF	1			

Chapter 3 *Rapid* Review

3

Main Heading	Review Material	myomlab
THE IMPORTANCE OF PROJECT MANAGEMENT (p. 50)	The management of projects involves three phases: 1. **Planning**—This phase includes goal setting, defining the project, and team organization. 2. **Scheduling**—This phase relates people, money, and supplies to specific activities and relates activities to each other. 3. **Controlling**—Here the firm monitors resources, costs, quality, and budgets. It also revises or changes plans and shifts resources to meet time and cost demands.	**VIDEO 3.1** Project Management at Hard Rock's Rockfest
PROJECT PLANNING (pp. 50–53)	Projects can be defined as a series of related tasks directed toward a major output. ■ **Project organization**—An organization formed to ensure that programs (projects) receive the proper management and attention. ■ **Work breakdown structure (WBS)**—Defines a project by dividing it into more and more detailed components.	Problem 3.1
PROJECT SCHEDULING (pp. 53–54)	■ **Gantt charts**—Planning charts used to schedule resources and allocate time. Project scheduling serves several purposes: 1. It shows the relationship of each activity to others and to the whole project. 2. It identifies the precedence relationships among activities. 3. It encourages the setting of realistic time and cost estimates for each activity. 4. It helps make better use of people, money, and material resources by identifying critical bottlenecks in the project.	Problem 3.8
PROJECT CONTROLLING (p. 54)	Computerized programs produce a broad variety of PERT/CPM reports, including (1) detailed cost breakdowns for each task, (2) total program labor curves, (3) cost distribution tables, (4) functional cost and hour summaries, (5) raw material and expenditure forecasts, (6) variance reports, (7) time analysis reports, and (8) work status reports.	**VIDEO 3.2** Project Management at Arnold Palmer Hospital
PROJECT MANAGEMENT TECHNIQUES: PERT AND CPM (pp. 55–60)	■ **Program evaluation and review technique (PERT)**—A project management technique that employs three time estimates for each activity. ■ **Critical path method (CPM)**—A project management technique that uses only one estimate per activity. ■ **Critical path**—The computed *longest* time path(s) through a network. PERT and CPM both follow six basic steps. The activities on the critical path will delay the entire project if they are not completed on time. ■ **Activity-on-node (AON)**—A network diagram in which nodes designate activities. ■ **Activity-on-arrow (AOA)**—A network diagram in which arrows designate activities. In an AOA network, the nodes represent the starting and finishing times of an activity and are also called *events*. ■ **Dummy activity**—An activity having no time that is inserted into a network to maintain the logic of the network. A dummy ending activity can be added to the end of an AON diagram for a project that has multiple ending activities.	Problems: 3.3–3.7, 3.9, 3.10, 3.12, 3.15 Virtual Office Hours for Solved Problems: 3.1, 3.2
DETERMINING THE PROJECT SCHEDULE (pp. 60–65)	■ **Critical path analysis**—A process that helps determine a project schedule. To find the critical path, we calculate two distinct starting and ending times for each activity: • *Earliest start (ES)* = Earliest time at which an activity can start, assuming that all predecessors have been completed • *Earliest finish (EF)* = Earliest time at which an activity can be finished • *Latest start (LS)* = Latest time at which an activity can start, without delaying the completion time of the entire project • *Latest finish (LF)* = Latest time by which an activity has to finish so as to not delay the completion time of the entire project ■ **Forward pass**—A process that identifies all the early start and early finish times. $$ES = \text{Maximum } EF \text{ of all immediate predecessors} \quad (3\text{-}1)$$ $$EF = ES + \text{Activity time} \quad (3\text{-}2)$$ ■ **Backward pass**—A process that identifies all the late start and late finish times. $$LF = \text{Minimum } LS \text{ of all immediate following activities} \quad (3\text{-}3)$$ $$LS = LF - \text{Activity time} \quad (3\text{-}4)$$ ■ **Slack time**—Free time for an activity. $$\text{Slack} = LS - ES \quad \text{or} \quad \text{Slack} = LF - EF \quad (3\text{-}5)$$	Problems: 3.11, 3.14, 3.15, 3.17, 3.20, 3.22, 3.23, 3.26

Main Heading	Review Material	PEARSON myomlab
	The activities with zero slack are called *critical activities* and are said to be on the critical path. The critical path is a continuous path through the project network that starts at the first activity in the project, terminates at the last activity in the project, and includes only critical activities.	Virtual Office Hours for Solved Problem: 3.3 **ACTIVE MODEL 3.1**
VARIABILITY IN ACTIVITY TIMES (pp. 65–71)	■ **Optimistic time** (*a*)—The "best" activity completion time that could be obtained in a PERT network. ■ **Pessimistic time** (*b*)—The "worst" activity time that could be expected in a PERT network. ■ **Most likely time** (*m*)—The most probable time to complete an activity in a PERT network. When using PERT, we often assume that activity time estimates follow the beta distribution. $$\text{Expected activity time } t = (a + 4m + b)/6 \qquad (3\text{-}6)$$ $$\text{Variance of Activity Completion Time} = [(b - a)/6]^2 \qquad (3\text{-}7)$$ $$\sigma_p^2 = \text{Project variance} = \Sigma(\text{variances of activities on critical path}) \qquad (3\text{-}8)$$ $$Z = (\text{Due date} - \text{expected date of completion})/\sigma_p \qquad (3\text{-}9)$$ $$\text{Due date} = \text{Expected completion time} + (Z \times \sigma_p) \qquad (3\text{-}10)$$	Problems: 3.13, 3.14. 3.21, 3.24 Virtual Office Hours for Solved Problems: 3.4, 3.5, 3.6
COST–TIME TRADE-OFFS AND PROJECT CRASHING (pp. 71–73)	■ **Crashing**—Shortening activity time in a network to reduce time on the critical path so total completion time is reduced. $$\text{Crash cost per period} = \frac{(\text{Crash cost} - \text{Normal cost})}{(\text{Normal time} - \text{Crash time})} \qquad (3\text{-}11)$$	Problems: 3.16, 3.18, 3.19, 3.25 Virtual Office Hours for Solved Problem: 3.7
A CRITIQUE OF PERT AND CPM (pp. 73–74)	As with every technique for problem solving, PERT and CPM have a number of advantages as well as several limitations.	
USING MICROSOFT PROJECT TO MANAGE PROJECTS (pp. 74–77)	Microsoft Project, the most popular example of specialized project management software, is extremely useful in drawing project networks, identifying the project schedule, and managing project costs and other resources.	

Self Test

■ **Before taking the self-test,** refer to the learning objectives listed at the beginning of the chapter and the key terms listed at the end of the chapter.

LO1. Which of the following statements regarding Gantt charts is true?
   a) Gantt charts give a timeline and precedence relationships for each activity of a project.
   b) Gantt charts use the four standard spines: Methods, Materials, Manpower, and Machinery.
   c) Gantt charts are visual devices that show the duration of activities in a project.
   d) Gantt charts are expensive.
   e) All of the above are true.

LO2. Which of the following is true about AOA and AON networks?
   a) In AOA, arrows represent activities.
   b) In AON, nodes represent activities.
   c) Activities consume time and resources.
   d) Nodes are also called *events* in AOA.
   e) All of the above.

LO3. Slack time equals:
   a) ES + *t*.
   b) LS – ES.
   c) zero.
   d) EF – ES.

LO4. The critical path of a network is the:
   a) shortest-time path through the network.
   b) path with the fewest activities.
   c) path with the most activities.
   d) longest-time path through the network.

LO5. PERT analysis computes the variance of the total project completion time as:
   a) the sum of the variances of all activities in the project.
   b) the sum of the variances of all activities on the critical path.
   c) the sum of the variances of all activities not on the critical path.
   d) the variance of the final activity of the project.

LO6. The crash cost per period:
   a) is the difference in costs divided by the difference in times (crash and normal).
   b) is considered to be linear in the range between normal and crash.
   c) needs to be determined so that the smallest cost values on the critical path can be considered for time reduction first.
   d) all of the above.

Answers: LO1. c; **LO2.** e; **LO3.** b; **LO4.** d; **LO5.** b; **LO6.** d.

4 Forecasting

Chapter Outline

What is Forecasting?

The Strategic Importance of Forecasting

Seven Steps in the Forecasting System

Forecasting Approaches

Time-Series Forecasting

Associative Forecasting Methods:
    Regression and Correlation Analysis

Monitoring and Controlling Forecasts

Forecasting in the Service Sector

Ethical Dilemma
Discussion Questions
Problems
Case Studies: Southwestern University:
    (B); Digital Cell Phone, Inc. ;
    Forecasting at Hard Rock Cafe
Active Model Exercises
Rapid Review

Forecasts are an essential part of efficient service and manufacturing operations. Demand forecasts drive a firm's production, capacity, and scheduling decisions and affect the financial, marketing, and personnel planning functions.

Both qualitative and quantitative techniques are used to forecast demand. Qualitative approaches employ judgment, experience, intuition, and a host of other factors that are difficult to quantify. Quantitative forecasting uses historical data and causal, or associative, relations to project future demands.

BEFORE COMING TO CLASS, READ CHAPTER 4 IN YOUR TEXT AND ANSWER THESE QUESTIONS.

1. What are the three forecasting time horizons? _____

    _____

2. What are the four qualitative forecasting models and when are they used? _____

    _____

3. What is the difference between the naïve, moving average, exponential smoothing, and trend methods? _____

    _____

4. What are three measures of forecast accuracy? _____

    _____

5. Explain how to develop seasonal indexes. _____

    _____

    _____

6. How do you conduct a regression and correlation analysis? _____

    _____

    _____

7. What is a tracking signal? _____

    _____

WHAT IS FORECASTING? (See Flexible Version pp. 86–87)

Forecasting Time Horizons (See Flexible Version pp. 86–87)

1. Short-Range
2. Medium-Range
3. Long-Range

Types of Forecasts (See Flexible Version p. 87)

1. Economic Forecasts
2. Technological Forecasts
3. Demand Forecasts

THE STRATEGIC IMPORTANCE OF FORECASTING

(See Flexible Version pp. 87–88)

SEVEN STEPS IN THE FORECASTING SYSTEM (See Flexible Version p. 88)

1. Determine the Use of the Forecast
2. Select the Items to Be Forecasted
3. Determine the Time Horizon of the Forecast
4. Select the Forecasting Model(s)
5. Gather the Data Needed
6. Make the Forecast
7. Validate and Implement the Results

FORECASTING APPROACHES (See Flexible Version pp. 89–90)

Qualitative Methods (See Flexible Version p. 89)

1. Jury of Executive Opinion

2. Delphi

3. Sales Force Composite

4. Consumer Market Survey

Quantitative Methods (See Flexible Version pp. 89–90)

1. Time-Series Models

2. Associative (Regression) Model

TIME-SERIES FORECASTING (See Flexible Version pp. 90–108)

Decomposition (See Flexible Version p. 90)

1. **Trend**

2. **Seasonality**

3. **Cycles**

4. **Random Variations**

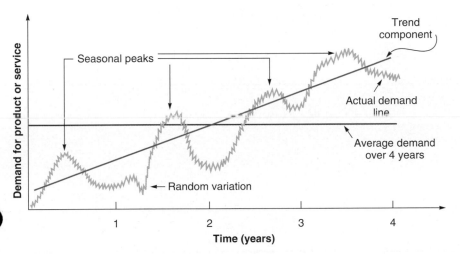

> **AUTHOR COMMENT**
> Forecasting is easy when demand is stable. But with trend, seasonality, and cycles considered, the job is a lot more interesting.

▲ **FIGURE 4.1**   **Demand Charted over 4 Years with a Growth Trend and Seasonality Indicated**

Naive Approach (See Flexible Version pp. 90–91)

Moving Averages (See Flexible Version pp. 91–94)

$$\text{Moving average} = \frac{\Sigma \text{ Demand in previous } n \text{ periods}}{n} \qquad (4\text{-}1)$$

PRACTICE PROBLEM 4.1 ■ Moving Averages

Auto sales at Carmen's Chevrolet are as follows. Develop a 3-week moving average.

Week	Auto Sales
1	8
2	10
3	9
4	11
5	10
6	13
7	—

Additional Practice Problem Space

Weighted Moving Averages (See Flexible Version pp. 92–93)

$$\text{Weighted moving average} = \frac{\Sigma \, (\text{Weight for period } n)(\text{Demand in period } n)}{\Sigma \, \text{Weights}} \qquad (4\text{-}2)$$

PRACTICE PROBLEM 4.2 ■ Practice Problem 4.1 with Weights

Carmen's decides to forecast auto sales by weighting the 3 weeks as follows:

Weights Applied	Period
3	Last week
2	Two weeks ago
1	Three weeks ago
6	Total

Additional Practice Problem Space

Exponential Smoothing (See Flexible Version pp. 94–95)

New forecast = Last period's forecast
+ α (Last period's actual demand − Last period's forecast)   (4-3)

where α = smoothing constant between 0 and 1

PRACTICE PROBLEM 4.3 ■ Exponential Smoothing

A firm uses simple exponential smoothing with $\alpha = 0.1$ to forecast demand. The forecast for the week of January 1 was 500 units, whereas the actual demand turned out to be 450 units. Calculate the demand forecast for the week of January 8.

Additional Practice Problem Space

Measuring Forecast Error (See Flexible Version pp. 95–98)

1. **Mean Absolute Deviation (MAD)**

$$\text{MAD} = \frac{\Sigma |\text{Actual} - \text{Forecast}|}{n} \tag{4-5}$$

2. **Mean Squared Error (MSE)**

$$\text{MSE} = \frac{\Sigma (\text{Forecast errors})^2}{n} \tag{4-6}$$

3. **Mean Absolute Percent Error (MAPE)**

$$\text{MAPE} = \frac{\sum\limits_{i=1}^{n} 100 |\text{Actual}_i - \text{Forecast}_i| / \text{Actual}_i}{n} \tag{4-7}$$

PRACTICE PROBLEM 4.4 ■ Using MAD to Evaluate Two Exponential Smoothing Models

Exponential smoothing is used to forecast automobile battery sales. Two values of α are examined: $\alpha = 0.8$ and $\alpha = 0.5$. Evaluate the accuracy of each smoothing constant. Which is preferable? (Assume the forecast for January was 22 batteries.) Actual sales are as follows:

Month	Actual Battery Sales	Forecast
January	20	22
February	21	
March	15	
April	14	
May	13	
June	16	

Additional Practice Problem Space

Exponential Smoothing with Trend Adjustment

(See Flexible Version pp. 98–101)

$$\text{Forecast including trend } (FIT_t) = \text{Exponentially smoothed forecast } (F_t)$$
$$+ \text{ Exponentially smoothed trend } (T_t) \qquad \text{(4-8)}$$

α = smoothing constant for average

β = smoothing constant for trend

Practice Problem Space

Trend Projections (See Flexible Version pp. 101–103)

Least Squares Method

$$\hat{y} = a + bx \qquad \text{(4-11)}$$

Where: y is:

a is:

b is:

x is:

$$b = \frac{\Sigma xy - n\bar{x}\,\bar{y}}{\Sigma x^2 - n\bar{x}^2} \qquad \text{(4-12)}$$

$$a = \bar{y} - b\bar{x} \qquad \text{(4-13)}$$

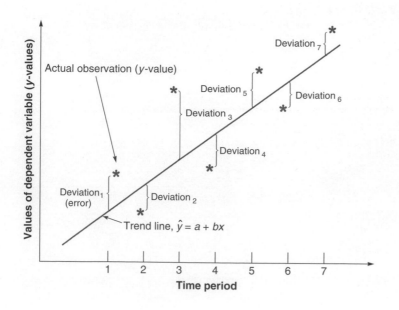

◀ **FIGURE 4.4**
The Least Squares Method for Finding the Best-Fitting Straight Line, Where the Asterisks Are the Locations of the Seven Actual Observations or Data Points

PRACTICE PROBLEM 4.5 ■ Trend Projection

Use the sales data given below to determine (a) the least squares trend line and (b) the predicted value for 2011 sales.

Year	Sales (units)
2004	100
2005	110
2006	122
2007	130
2008	139
2009	152
2010	164

To minimize computations, transform the value of x (time) to simpler numbers. In this case, designate year 2004 as year 1, 2005 as year 2, and so on.

Additional Practice Problem Space

Seasonal Variations in Data (See Flexible Version pp. 103–108)

PRACTICE PROBLEM 4.6 ■ Quarterly Seasons

Over the past year, Meredith and Smunt Manufacturing had annual sales of 10,000 portable water pumps. The average quarterly sales for the past 5 years have averaged: spring 4,000; summer 3,000; fall 2,000; and winter 1,000. Compute the quarterly index.

PRACTICE PROBLEM 4.7 ■ Forecasting with Seasonal Data

Using the data in Practice Problem 4.6, Meredith and Smunt Manufacturing expects sales of pumps to grow by 10% next year. Compute next year's sales and the sales for each quarter.

Additional Practice Problem Space

ASSOCIATIVE FORECASTING METHODS: REGRESSION AND CORRELATION ANALYSIS (See Flexible Version pp. 108–113)

Associative Model

Dependent Variable (y)

Independent Variable (x)

$$\hat{y} = a + bx$$

Practice Problem Space

Standard Error of the Estimate (See Flexible Version pp. 110–111)

Correlation Coefficients (*r*) (See Flexible Version pp. 111–113)

$$r = \frac{n\Sigma xy - \Sigma x \Sigma y}{\sqrt{[n\Sigma x^2 - (\Sigma x)^2][n\Sigma y^2 - (\Sigma y)^2]}}$$ (4-16)

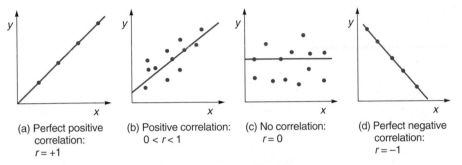

(a) Perfect positive correlation: $r = +1$

(b) Positive correlation: $0 < r < 1$

(c) No correlation: $r = 0$

(d) Perfect negative correlation: $r = -1$

▲ **FIGURE 4.10**   **Four Values of the Correlation Coefficient**

Coefficient of Determination (*r²*) (See Flexible Version pp. 112–113)

Multiple-Regression Analysis (See Flexible Version p. 113)

$$\hat{y} = a + b_1x_1 + b_2x_2 + \cdots + b_nx_n$$ (4-17)

MONITORING AND CONTROLLING FORECASTS

(See Flexible Version pp. 113–116)

Tracking Signal

$$\text{Tracking signal} = \frac{\text{Cumulative error}}{\text{MAD}}$$

$$= \frac{\Sigma(\text{Actual demand in period } i - \text{Forecast demand in period } i)}{\text{MAD}}$$ (4-18)

$$\text{where MAD} = \frac{\Sigma|\text{Actual} - \text{Forecast}|}{n}$$

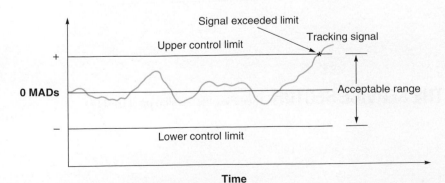

◄ **FIGURE 4.11**
A Plot of Tracking Signals

PRACTICE PROBLEM 4.8 ■ Tracking Signals and MAD

Given the following forecast demand and actual demand for 10-foot fishing boats, compute the tracking signal and MAD.

Year	Forecast Demand	Actual Demand
1	78	71
2	75	80
3	83	101
4	84	84
5	88	60
6	85	73

Additional Practice Problem Space

FORECASTING IN THE SERVICE SECTOR (See Flexible Version pp. 116–117)

Ethical Dilemma

In 2009, the board of regents responsible for all public higher education funding in a large Midwestern state hired a consultant to develop a series of enrollment forecasting models, one for each college. These models used historical data and exponential smoothing to forecast the following year's enrollments. Based on the model, which included a smoothing constant (α) for each school, each college's budget was set by the board. The head of the board personally selected each smoothing constant based on what she called her "gut reactions and political acumen."

What do you think the advantages and disadvantages of this system are? Answer from the perspective of (a) the board of regents and (b) the president of each college. How can this model be abused and what can be done to remove any biases? How can a *regression model* be used to produce results that favor one forecast over another?

Discussion Questions

1. What is a qualitative forecasting model, and when is its use appropriate?
2. Identify and briefly describe the two general forecasting approaches.
3. Identify the three forecasting time horizons. State an approximate duration for each.
4. Briefly describe the steps that are used to develop a forecasting system.
5. A skeptical manager asks what medium-range forecasts can be used for. Give the manager three possible uses/purposes.
6. Explain why such forecasting devices as moving averages, weighted moving averages, and exponential smoothing are not well suited for data series that have trends.
7. What is the basic difference between a weighted moving average and exponential smoothing?
8. What three methods are used to determine the accuracy of any given forecasting method? How would you determine whether time-series regression or exponential smoothing is better in a specific application?
9. Research and briefly describe the Delphi technique. How would it be used by an employer you have worked for?
10. What is the primary difference between a time-series model and an associative model?

11. Define time series.
12. What effect does the value of the smoothing constant have on the weight given to the recent values?
13. Explain the value of seasonal indices in forecasting. How are seasonal patterns different from cyclical patterns?
14. Which forecasting technique can place the most emphasis on recent values? How does it do this?
15. In your own words, explain adaptive forecasting.
16. What is the purpose of a tracking signal?
17. Explain, in your own words, the meaning of the correlation coefficient. Discuss the meaning of a negative value of the correlation coefficient.
18. What is the difference between a dependent and an independent variable?
19. Give examples of industries that are affected by seasonality. Why would these businesses want to filter out seasonality?
20. Give examples of industries in which demand forecasting is dependent on the demand for other products.
21. What happens to the ability to forecast for periods farther into the future?

Problems*

•   **4.1** The following gives the number of pints of type A blood used at Woodlawn Hospital in the past 6 weeks:

Week of	Pints Used
August 31	360
September 7	389
September 14	410
September 21	381
September 28	368
October 5	374

a) Forecast the demand for the week of October 12 using a 3-week moving average.

b) Use a 3-week weighted moving average, with weights of .1, .3, and .6, using .6 for the most recent week. Forecast demand for the week of October 12.
c) Compute the forecast for the week of October 12 using exponential smoothing with a forecast for August 31 of 360 and $\alpha = .2$. **PX**

••   **4.2**

Year	1	2	3	4	5	6	7	8	9	10	11
Demand	7	9	5	9	13	8	12	13	9	11	7

Note: **PX** means the problem may be solved with POM for Windows and/or Excel OM.

a) Plot the data from the previous page on a graph. Do you observe any trend, cycles, or random variations?

b) Starting in year 4 and going to year 12, forecast demand using a 3-year moving average. Plot your forecast on the same graph as the original data.

c) Starting in year 4 and going to year 12, forecast demand using a 3-year moving average with weights of .1, .3, and .6, using .6 for the most recent year. Plot this forecast on the same graph.

d) As you compare forecasts with the original data, which seems to give the better results? **Px**

• **4.3** Refer to Problem 4.2. Develop a forecast for years 2 through 12 using exponential smoothing with $\alpha = .4$ and a forecast for year 1 of 6. Plot your new forecast on a graph with the actual data and the naive forecast. Based on a visual inspection, which forecast is better? **Px**

• **4.4** A check-processing center uses exponential smoothing to forecast the number of incoming checks each month. The number of checks received in June was 40 million, while the forecast was 42 million. A smoothing constant of .2 is used.

a) What is the forecast for July?

b) If the center received 45 million checks in July, what would be the forecast for August?

c) Why might this be an inappropriate forecasting method for this situation? **Px**

•• **4.5** The Carbondale Hospital is considering the purchase of a new ambulance. The decision will rest partly on the anticipated mileage to be driven next year. The miles driven during the past 5 years are as follows:

Year	Mileage
1	3,000
2	4,000
3	3,400
4	3,800
5	3,700

a) Forecast the mileage for next year using a 2-year moving average.

b) Find the MAD based on the 2-year moving average forecast in part (a). (*Hint:* You will have only 3 years of matched data.)

c) Use a weighted 2-year moving average with weights of .4 and .6 to forecast next year's mileage. (The weight of .6 is for the most recent year.) What MAD results from using this approach to forecasting? (*Hint:* You will have only 3 years of matched data.)

d) Compute the forecast for year 6 using exponential smoothing, an initial forecast for year 1 of 3,000 miles, and $\alpha = .5$. **Px**

•• **4.6** The monthly sales for Telco Batteries, Inc., were as follows:

Month	Sales
January	20
February	21
March	15
April	14
May	13
June	16
July	17
August	18
September	20
October	20
November	21
December	23

a) Plot the monthly sales data.

b) Forecast January sales using each of the following:
   i. Naive method.
   ii. A 3-month moving average.
   iii. A 6-month weighted average using .1, .1, .1, .2, .2, and .3, with the heaviest weights applied to the most recent months.
   iv. Exponential smoothing using an $\alpha = .3$ and a September forecast of 18.
   v. A trend projection.

c) With the data given, which method would allow you to forecast next March's sales? **Px**

•• **4.7** The actual demand for the patients at Omaha Emergency Medical Clinic for the first six weeks of this year follows:

Week	Actual No. of Patients
1	65
2	62
3	70
4	48
5	63
6	52

Clinic administrator Marc Schniederjans wants you to forecast patient demand at the clinic for week 7 by using this data. You decide to use a weighted moving average method to find this forecast. Your method uses four actual demand levels, with weights of 0.333 on the present period, 0.25 one period ago, 0.25 two periods ago, and 0.167 three periods ago.

a) What is the value of your forecast?

b) If instead the weights were 20, 15, 15, and 10, respectively, how would the forecast change? Explain why.

c) What if the weights were 0.40, 0.30, 0.20, and 0.10, respectively? Now what is the forecast for week 7? **Px**

• **4.8** Daily high temperatures in St. Louis for the last week were as follows: 93, 94, 93, 95, 96, 88, 90 (yesterday).

a) Forecast the high temperature today, using a 3-day moving average.

b) Forecast the high temperature today, using a 2-day moving average.

c) Calculate the mean absolute deviation based on a 2-day moving average.

d) Compute the mean squared error for the 2-day moving average.

e) Calculate the mean absolute percent error for the 2-day moving average. **Px**

••• **4.9** Dell uses the CR5 chip in some of its laptop computers. The prices for the chip during the past 12 months were as follows:

Month	Price per Chip	Month	Price per Chip
January	$1.80	July	$1.80
February	1.67	August	1.83
March	1.70	September	1.70
April	1.85	October	1.65
May	1.90	November	1.70
June	1.87	December	1.75

a) Use a 2-month moving average on all the data and plot the averages and the prices.

b) Use a 3-month moving average and add the 3-month plot to the graph created in part (a).

c) Which is better (using the mean absolute deviation): the 2-month average or the 3-month average?

d) Compute the forecasts for each month using exponential smoothing, with an initial forecast for January of $1.80. Use $\alpha = .1$, then $\alpha = .3$, and finally $\alpha = .5$. Using MAD, which α is the best? **Px**

•• **4.10** Data collected on the yearly registrations for a Six Sigma seminar at the Quality College are shown in the following table:

Year	1	2	3	4	5	6	7	8	9	10	11
Registrations (000)	4	6	4	5	10	8	7	9	12	14	15

a) Develop a 3-year moving average to forecast registrations from year 4 to year 12.

b) Estimate demand again for years 4 to 12 with a 3-year weighted moving average in which registrations in the most recent year are given a weight of 2, and registrations in the other 2 years are each given a weight of 1.

c) Graph the original data and the two forecasts. Which of the two forecasting methods seems better? **Px**

• **4.11** a) Use exponential smoothing with a smoothing constant of 0.3 to forecast the registrations at the seminar given in Problem 4.10. To begin the procedure, assume that the forecast for year 1 was 5,000 people signing up.

b) What is the MAD? **Px**

•• **4.12** Consider the following actual and forecast demand levels for Big Mac hamburgers at a local McDonald's restaurant:

Day	Actual Demand	Forecast Demand
Monday	88	88
Tuesday	72	88
Wednesday	68	84
Thursday	48	80
Friday		

The forecast for Monday was derived by observing Monday's demand level and setting Monday's forecast level equal to this demand level. Subsequent forecasts were derived by using exponential smoothing with a smoothing constant of 0.25. Using this exponential smoothing method, what is the forecast for Big Mac demand for Friday? **Px**

••• **4.13** As you can see in the following table, demand for heart transplant surgery at Washington General Hospital has increased steadily in the past few years:

Year	1	2	3	4	5	6
Heart Transplants	45	50	52	56	58	?

The director of medical services predicted 6 years ago that demand in year 1 would be 41 surgeries.

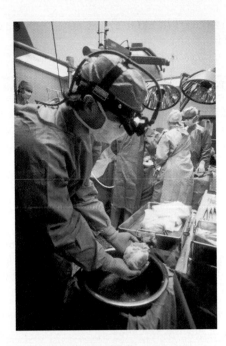

a) Use exponential smoothing, first with a smoothing constant of .6 and then with one of .9, to develop forecasts for years 2 through 6.

b) Use a 3-year moving average to forecast demand in years 4, 5, and 6.

c) Use the trend-projection method to forecast demand in years 1 through 6.

d) With MAD as the criterion, which of the four forecasting methods is best? **Px**

•• **4.14** Following are two weekly forecasts made by two different methods for the number of gallons of gasoline, in thousands, demanded at a local gasoline station. Also shown are actual demand levels, in thousands of gallons:

	Forecasts		
Week	Method 1	Method 2	Actual Demand
1	0.90	0.80	0.70
2	1.05	1.20	1.00
3	0.95	0.90	1.00
4	1.20	1.11	1.00

What are the MAD and MSE for each method? **Px**

• **4.15** Refer to Solved Problem 4.1 on page 119 of the Flexible Version. Use a 3-year moving average to forecast the sales of Volkswagen Beetles in Nevada through 2010. What is the MAD? **Px**

• **4.16** Refer to Solved Problem 4.1 on page 119 of the Flexible Version. Using the trend projection method, develop a forecast for the sales of Volkswagen Beetles in Nevada through 2010. What is the MAD? **Px**

• **4.17** Refer to Solved Problem 4.1 on page 119 of the Flexible Version. Using smoothing constants of .6 and .9, develop forecasts for the sales of VW Beetles. What effect did the smoothing constant have on the forecast? Use MAD to determine which of the three smoothing constants (.3, .6, or .9) gives the most accurate forecast. **Px**

•••• **4.18** Consider the following actual (A_t) and forecast (F_t) demand levels for a product:

Time Period, t	Actual Demand, A_t	Forecast Demand, F_t
1	50	50
2	42	50
3	56	48
4	46	50
5		

The first forecast, F_1, was derived by observing A_1 and setting F_1 equal to A_1. Subsequent forecasts were derived by exponential smoothing. Using the exponential smoothing method, find the forecast for time period 5. (*Hint:* You need to first find the smoothing constant, α.)

••• **4.19** Income at the law firm Smith and Wesson for the period February to July was as follows:

Month	February	March	April	May	June	July
Income (in $ thousand)	70.0	68.5	64.8	71.7	71.3	72.8

Use trend-adjusted exponential smoothing to forecast the law firm's August income. Assume that the initial forecast for February is $65,000 and the initial trend adjustment is 0. The smoothing constants selected are $\alpha = .1$ and $\beta = .2$. **Px**

••• **4.20** Resolve Problem 4.19 with $\alpha = .1$ and $\beta = .8$. Using MSE, determine which smoothing constants provide a better forecast. **Px**

• **4.21** Refer to the trend-adjusted exponential smoothing illustration in Example 7 on pages 99–100 of the Flexible Version. Using $\alpha = .2$ and $\beta = .4$, we forecast sales for 9 months, showing the detailed calculations for months 2 and 3. In Solved Problem 4.2 on page 119 of the Flexible Version, we continued the process for month 4.

In this problem, show your calculations for months 5 and 6 for F_t, T_t, and FIT_t. **Px**

• **4.22** Refer to Problem 4.21. Complete the trend-adjusted exponential-smoothing forecast computations for periods 7, 8, and 9. Confirm that your numbers for F_t, T_t, and FIT_t match those in Table 4.1 (p. 100 of your Flexible Version). **Px**

•• **4.23** Sales of vegetable dehydrators at Bud Banis's discount department store in St. Louis over the past year are shown in the next column. Management prepared a forecast using a combination of exponential smoothing and its collective judgment for the 4 months (March, April, May, and June of 2010).
a) Compute MAD and MAPE for management's technique.
b) Do management's results outperform (i.e., have smaller MAD and MAPE than) a naive forecast?
c) Which forecast do you recommend, based on lower forecast error? **Px**

Month	2009–2010 Unit Sales	Management's Forecast
July	100	
August	93	
September	96	
October	110	
November	124	
December	119	
January	92	
February	83	
March	101	120
April	96	114
May	89	110
June	108	108

•• **4.24** Howard Weiss, owner of a musical instrument distributorship, thinks that demand for bass drums may be related to the number of television appearances by the popular group Stone Temple Pilots during the previous month. Weiss has collected the data shown in the following table:

Demand for Bass Drums	3	6	7	5	10	7
Stone Temple Pilots' TV Appearances	3	4	7	6	8	5

a) Graph these data to see whether a linear equation might describe the relationship between the group's television shows and bass drum sales.
b) Use the least-squares regression method to derive a forecasting equation.
c) What is your estimate for bass drum sales if the Stone Temple Pilots performed on TV nine times last month?
d) What are the correlation coefficient (r) and the coefficient of determination (r^2) for this model, and what do they mean? **Px**

• **4.25** The following gives the number of accidents that occurred on Florida State Highway 101 during the past 4 months:

Month	Number of Accidents
January	30
February	40
March	60
April	90

Forecast the number of accidents that will occur in May, using least-squares regression to derive a trend equation. **Px**

• **4.26** In the past, Arup Mukherjee's tire dealership in Pensacola sold an average of 1,000 radials each year. In the past 2 years, 200 and 250, respectively, were sold in fall, 350 and 300 in winter, 150 and 165 in spring, and 300 and 285 in summer. With a major expansion planned, Mukherjee projects sales next year to increase to 1,200 radials. What will be the demand during each season?

•• **4.27** Mark Cotteleer owns a company that manufactures sail-boats. Actual demand for Mark's sailboats during each season in 2006 through 2009 was as follows:

	Year			
Season	2006	2007	2008	2009
Winter	1,400	1,200	1,000	900
Spring	1,500	1,400	1,600	1,500
Summer	1,000	2,100	2,000	1,900
Fall	600	750	650	500

Mark has forecasted that annual demand for his sailboats in 2011 will equal 5,600 sailboats. Based on this data and the multiplicative seasonal model, what will the demand level be for Mark's sailboats in the spring of 2011?

•• **4.28** Attendance at Los Angeles's newest Disney-like attraction, Vacation World, has been as follows:

Quarter	Guests (in thousands)	Quarter	Guests (in thousands)
Winter '07	73	Summer '08	124
Spring '07	104	Fall '08	52
Summer '07	168	Winter '09	89
Fall '07	74	Spring '09	146
Winter '08	65	Summer '09	205
Spring '08	82	Fall '09	98

Compute seasonal indices using all of the data. **Px**

• **4.29** Central States Electric Company estimates its demand trend line (in millions of kilowatt hours) to be:

$$D = 77 + 0.43Q$$

where Q refers to the sequential quarter number and $Q = 1$ for winter 1986. In addition, the multiplicative seasonal factors are as follows:

Quarter	Factor (index)
Winter	.8
Spring	1.1
Summer	1.4
Fall	.7

Forecast energy use for the four quarters of 2011, beginning with winter.

• **4.30** Brian Buckley has developed the following forecasting model:

$$\hat{y}\ 36 + 4.3x$$

where $\hat{y}$ = demand for Aztec air conditioners and
             x = the outside temperature (°F)

a) Forecast demand for the Aztec when the temperature is 70°F.
b) What is demand when the temperature is 80°F?
c) What is demand when the temperature is 90°F? **Px**

•• **4.31** Coffee Palace's manager, Joe Felan, suspects that demand for mocha latte coffees depends on the price being charged. Based on

historical observations, Joe has gathered the following data, which show the numbers of these coffees sold over six different price values:

Price	Number Sold
$2.70	760
$3.50	510
$2.00	980
$4.20	250
$3.10	320
$4.05	480

Using these data, how many mocha latte coffees would be forecast to be sold according to simple linear regression if the price per cup were $2.80? **Px**

• **4.32** The following data relate the sales figures of the bar in Marty and Polly Starr's small bed-and-breakfast inn in Marathon, Florida, to the number of guests registered that week:

Week	Guests	Bar Sales
1	16	$330
2	12	270
3	18	380
4	14	300

a) Perform a linear regression that relates bar sales to guests (not to time).
b) If the forecast is for 20 guests next week, what are the sales expected to be? **Px**

• **4.33** The number of transistors (in millions) made at a plant in Japan during the past 5 years follows:

Year	Transistors
1	140
2	160
3	190
4	200
5	210

a) Forecast the number of transistors to be made next year, using linear regression.
b) Compute the mean squared error (MSE) when using linear regression.
c) Compute the mean absolute percent error (MAPE). **Px**

• **4.34** The number of auto accidents in a certain region is related to the regional number of registered automobiles in thousands (X_1), alcoholic beverage sales in $10,000s ($X_2$), and rainfall in inches (X_3). Furthermore, the regression formula has been calculated as:

$$Y = a + b_1X_1 + b_2X_2 + b_3X_3$$

where

Y = number of automobile accidents
$a = 7.5$
$b_1 = 3.5$
$b_2 = 4.5$
$b_3 = 2.5$

Calculate the expected number of automobile accidents under conditions a, b, and c:

	X_1	X_2	X_3
(a)	2	3	0
(b)	3	5	1
(c)	4	7	2

Px

•• **4.35** John Howard, a Mobile, Alabama, real estate developer, has devised a regression model to help determine residential housing prices in South Alabama. The model was developed using recent sales in a particular neighborhood. The price (Y) of the house is based on the size (square footage $= X$) of the house. The model is:

$$Y = 13,473 + 37.65X$$

The coefficient of correlation for the model is 0.63.
a) Use the model to predict the selling price of a house that is 1,860 square feet.
b) An 1,860-square-foot house recently sold for $95,000. Explain why this is not what the model predicted.
c) If you were going to use multiple regression to develop such a model, what other quantitative variables might you include?
d) What is the value of the coefficient of determination in this problem? **Px**

• **4.36** Accountants at the firm Michael Vest, CPAs, believed that several traveling executives were submitting unusually high travel vouchers when they returned from business trips. First, they took a sample of 200 vouchers submitted from the past year. Then they developed the following multiple-regression equation relating expected travel cost to number of days on the road (x_1) and distance traveled (x_2) in miles:

$$\hat{y} = \$90.00 + \$48.50x_1 + \$.40x_2$$

The coefficient of correlation computed was .68.
a) If Wanda Fennell returns from a 300-mile trip that took her out of town for 5 days, what is the expected amount she should claim as expenses?
b) Fennell submitted a reimbursement request for $685. What should the accountant do?
c) Should any other variables be included? Which ones? Why? **Px**

•• **4.37** Sales of music stands at Johnny Ho's music store in Columbus, Ohio, over the past 10 weeks are shown in the table below.
a) Forecast demand for each week, including week 10, using exponential smoothing with $\alpha = .5$ (initial forecast $= 20$).

Week	Demand	Week	Demand
1	20	6	29
2	21	7	36
3	28	8	22
4	37	9	25
5	25	10	28

b) Compute the MAD.
c) Compute the tracking signal. **Px**

•• **4.38** City government has collected the following data on annual sales tax collections and new car registrations:

Annual Sales Tax Collections (in millions)	1.0	1.4	1.9	2.0	1.8	2.1	2.3
New Car Registrations (in thousands)	10	12	15	16	14	17	20

Determine the following:
a) The least-squares regression equation.
b) Using the results of part (a), find the estimated sales tax collections if new car registrations total 22,000.
c) The coefficients of correlation and determination. **Px**

•• **4.39** Dr. Susan Sweeney, a Providence, Rhode Island, psychologist, specializes in treating patients who are agoraphobic (i.e., afraid to leave their homes). The following table indicates how many patients Dr. Sweeney has seen each year for the past 10 years. It also indicates what the robbery rate was in Providence during the same year:

Year	1	2	3	4	5	6	7	8	9	10
Number of Patients	36	33	40	41	40	55	60	54	58	61
Robbery Rate per 1,000 Population	58.3	61.1	73.4	75.7	81.1	89.0	101.1	94.8	103.3	116.2

Using trend analysis, predict the number of patients Dr. Sweeney will see in years 11 and 12 as a function of time. How well does the model fit the data? **Px**

•• **4.40** Using the data in Problem 4.39, apply linear regression to study the relationship between the robbery rate and Dr. Sweeney's patient load. If the robbery rate increases to 131.2 in year 11, how many phobic patients will Dr. Sweeney treat? If the robbery rate drops to 90.6, what is the patient projection? **Px**

••• **4.41** Bus and subway ridership for the summer months in London, England, is believed to be tied heavily to the number of tourists visiting the city. During the past 12 years, the following data have been obtained:

Year (summer months)	Number of Tourists (in millions)	Ridership (in millions)
1	7	1.5
2	2	1.0
3	6	1.3
4	4	1.5
5	14	2.5
6	15	2.7
7	16	2.4
8	12	2.0
9	14	2.7
10	20	4.4
11	15	3.4
12	7	1.7

a) Plot these data and decide if a linear model is reasonable.
b) Develop a regression relationship.
c) What is expected ridership if 10 million tourists visit London in a year?
d) Explain the predicted ridership if there are no tourists at all.
e) What is the standard error of the estimate?
f) What is the model's correlation coefficient and coefficient of determination? **Px**

... 4.42 Des Moines Power and Light has been collecting data on demand for electric power in its western subregion for only the past 2 years. Those data are shown in the table at the top of the next page.

To plan for expansion and to arrange to borrow power from neighboring utilities during peak periods, the utility needs to be able to forecast demand for each month next year. However, the standard forecasting models discussed in this chapter will not fit the data observed for the 2 years.

Demand in Megawatts		
Month	Last Year	This Year
January	5	17
February	6	14
March	10	20
April	13	23
May	18	30
June	15	38
July	23	44
August	26	41
September	21	33
October	15	23
November	12	26
December	14	17

a) What are the weaknesses of the standard forecasting techniques as applied to this set of data?
b) Because known models are not appropriate here, propose your own approach to forecasting. Although there is no perfect solution to tackling data such as these (in other words, there are no 100% right or wrong answers), justify your model.
c) Forecast demand for each month next year using the model you propose.

... 4.43 Emergency calls to the 911 system of Gainesville, Florida, for the past 24 weeks are shown in the following table:

Week	1	2	3	4	5	6	7	8	9	10	11	12
Calls	50	35	25	40	45	35	20	30	35	20	15	40
Week	13	14	15	16	17	18	19	20	21	22	23	24
Calls	55	35	25	55	55	40	35	60	75	50	40	65

a) Compute the exponentially smoothed forecast of calls for each week. Assume an initial forecast of 50 calls in the first week, and use $\alpha = .2$. What is the forecast for week 25?
b) Reforecast each period using $\alpha = .6$.
c) Actual calls during week 25 were 85. Which smoothing constant provides a superior forecast? Explain and justify the measure of error you used. **Px**

... 4.44 Using the 911 call data in Problem 4.43, forecast calls for weeks 2 through 25 with a trend-adjusted exponential smoothing model. Assume an initial forecast for 50 calls for week 1 and an initial trend of zero. Use smoothing constants of $\alpha = .3$. and $\beta = .2$. Is this model better than that of Problem 4.43? What adjustment might be useful for further improvement? (Again, assume that actual calls in week 25 were 85.) **Px**

... 4.45 The following are monthly actual and forecast demand levels for May through December for units of a product manufactured by the N. Tamimi Pharmaceutical Company:

Month	Actual Demand	Forecast Demand
May	100	100
June	80	104
July	110	99
August	115	101
September	105	104
October	110	104
November	125	105
December	120	109

What is the value of the tracking signal as of the end of December? **Px**

.. 4.46 Thirteen students entered the business program at Hillcrest College 2 years ago. The following table indicates what each student scored on the high school SAT math exam and their grade-point averages (GPAs) after students were in the Hillcrest program for 2 years.

Student	A	B	C	D	E	F	G
SAT Score	421	377	585	690	608	390	415
GPA	2.90	2.93	3.00	3.45	3.66	2.88	2.15
Student	H	I	J	K	L	M	
SAT Score	481	729	501	613	709	366	
GPA	2.53	3.22	1.99	2.75	3.90	1.60	

a) Is there a meaningful relationship between SAT math scores and grades?
b) If a student scores a 350, what do you think his or her GPA will be?
c) What about a student who scores 800?

... 4.47 City Cycles has just started selling the new Z-10 mountain bike, with monthly sales as shown in the table. First, co-owner Amit wants to forecast by exponential smoothing by initially setting February's forecast equal to January's sales with $\alpha = .1$. Co-owner Barbara wants to use a three-period moving average.

	Sales	Amit	Barbara	Amit's Error	Barbara's Error
January	400	—			
February	380	400			
March	410				
April	375				
May					

a) Is there a strong linear trend in sales over time?

b) Fill in the table with what Amit and Barbara each forecast for May and the earlier months, as relevant.

c) Assume that May's actual sales figure turns out to be 405. Complete the table's columns and then calculate the mean absolute deviation for both Amit's and Barbara's methods.

d) Based on these calculations, which method seems more accurate? **Px**

•• **4.48** Sundar Balakrishnan, the general manager of Precision Engineering Corporation (PEC), thinks that his firm's engineering services contracted to highway construction firms are directly related to the volume of highway construction business contracted with companies in his geographic area. He wonders if this is really so, and if it is, can this information help him plan his operations better by forecasting the quantity of his engineering services required by construction firms in each quarter of the year? The following table presents the sales of his services and total amounts of contracts for highway construction over the past 8 quarters:

Quarter	1	2	3	4	5	6	7	8
Sales of PEC Services (in $ thousands)	8	10	15	9	12	13	12	16
Contracts Released (in $ thousands)	153	172	197	178	185	199	205	226

a) Using this data, develop a regression equation for predicting the level of demand of Precision's services.

b) Determine the coefficient of correlation and the standard error of the estimate. **Px**

•••• **4.49** Salinas Savings and Loan is proud of its long tradition in Topeka, Kansas. Begun by Teresita Salinas 20 years after World War II, the S&L has bucked the trend of financial and liquidity problems that has repeatedly plagued the industry. Deposits have increased slowly but surely over the years, despite recessions in 1983, 1988, 1991, 2001, and 2008. Ms. Salinas believes it is necessary to have a long-range strategic plan for her firm, including a 1-year forecast and preferably even a 5-year forecast of deposits. She examines the past deposit data and also peruses Kansas's gross state product (GSP) over the same 44 years. (GSP is analogous to gross national product [GNP] but on the state level.) The resulting data are in the following table:

Year	Deposits[a]	GSP[b]	Year	Deposits[a]	GSP[b]
1966	.25	.4	1988	6.2	2.5
1967	.24	.4	1989	4.1	2.8
1968	.24	.5	1990	4.5	2.9
1969	.26	.7	1991	6.1	3.4
1970	.25	.9	1992	7.7	3.8
1971	.30	1.0	1993	10.1	4.1
1972	.31	1.4	1994	15.2	4.0
1973	.32	1.7	1995	18.1	4.0
1974	.24	1.3	1996	24.1	3.9
1975	.26	1.2	1997	25.6	3.8
1976	.25	1.1	1998	30.3	3.8
1977	.33	.9	1999	36.0	3.7
1978	.50	1.2	2000	31.1	4.1
1979	.95	1.2	2001	31.7	4.1
1980	1.70	1.2	2002	38.5	4.0
1981	2.3	1.6	2003	47.9	4.5
1982	2.8	1.5	2004	49.1	4.6
1983	2.8	1.6	2005	55.8	4.5
1984	2.7	1.7	2006	70.1	4.6
1985	3.9	1.9	2007	70.9	4.6
1986	4.9	1.9	2008	79.1	4.7
1987	5.3	2.3	2009	94.0	5.0

[a]In $ millions.
[b]In $ billions.

a) Using exponential smoothing, with $\alpha = .6$. then trend analysis, and finally linear regression, discuss which forecasting model fits best for Salinas's strategic plan. Justify the selection of one model over another.

b) Carefully examine the data. Can you make a case for excluding a portion of the information? Why? Would that change your choice of model? **Px**

▶ Refer to myomlab 🌐 for these additional homework problems: 4.50–4.62

Case Studies

▶ Southwestern University: (B)*

Southwestern University (SWU), a large state college in Stephenville, Texas, enrolls close to 20,000 students. The school is a dominant force in the small city, with more students during fall and spring than permanent residents.

Always a football powerhouse, SWU is usually in the top 20 in college football rankings. Since the legendary Bo Pitterno was hired as its head coach in 2003 (in hopes of reaching the elusive number 1 ranking), attendance at the five Saturday home games each year increased. Prior to Pitterno's arrival, attendance generally averaged 25,000 to 29,000 per game. Season ticket sales bumped up by 10,000 just with the announcement of the new coach's arrival. Stephenville and SWU were ready to move to the big time!

The immediate issue facing SWU, however, was not NCAA ranking. It was capacity. The existing SWU stadium, built in 1953, has seating for 54,000 fans. The following table indicates attendance at each game for the past 6 years.

One of Pitterno's demands upon joining SWU had been a stadium expansion, or possibly even a new stadium. With attendance increasing, SWU administrators began to face the issue head-on. Pitterno had wanted dormitories solely for his athletes in the stadium as an additional feature of any expansion.

SWU's president, Dr. Joel Wisner, decided it was time for his vice president of development to forecast when the existing stadium would "max out." The expansion was, in his mind, a given. But

Wisner needed to know how long he could wait. He also sought a revenue projection, assuming an average ticket price of $50 in 2010 and a 5% increase each year in future prices.

Discussion Questions

1. Develop a forecasting model, justifying its selection over other techniques, and project attendance through 2011.
2. What revenues are to be expected in 2010 and 2011?
3. Discuss the school's options.

*This integrated case study runs throughout the text. Other issues facing Southwestern's football stadium include (A) managing the stadium project (Chapter 3); (C) quality of facilities (Chapter 6); (D) break-even analysis of food services (Supplement 7 Web site); (E) locating the new stadium (Chapter 8 Web site); (F) inventory planning of football programs (Chapter 12 Web site); and (G) scheduling of campus security officers/staff for game days (Chapter 13).

Southwestern University Football Game Attendance, 2004–2009

Game	2004 Attendees	Opponent	2005 Attendees	Opponent	2006 Attendees	Opponent
1	34,200	Baylor	36,100	Oklahoma	35,900	TCU
2[a]	39,800	Texas	40,200	Nebraska	46,500	Texas Tech
3	38,200	LSU	39,100	UCLA	43,100	Alaska
4[b]	26,900	Arkansas	25,300	Nevada	27,900	Arizona
5	35,100	USC	36,200	Ohio State	39,200	Rice

Game	2007 Attendees	Opponent	2008 Attendees	Opponent	2009 Attendees	Opponent
1	41,900	Arkansas	42,500	Indiana	46,900	LSU
2[a]	46,100	Missouri	48,200	North Texas	50,100	Texas
3	43,900	Florida	44,200	Texas A&M	45,900	Prairie View A&M
4[b]	30,100	Miami	33,900	Southern	36,300	Montana
5	40,500	Duke	47,800	Oklahoma	49,900	Arizona State

[a]Homecoming games.

[b]During the 4th week of each season, Stephenville hosted a hugely popular southwestern crafts festival. This event brought tens of thousands of tourists to the town, especially on weekends, and had an obvious negative impact on game attendance.

▶ Digital Cell Phone, Inc.

Paul Jordan has just been hired as a management analyst at Digital Cell Phone, Inc. Digital Cell manufactures a broad line of phones for the consumer market. Paul's boss, John Smithers, chief operations officer, has asked Paul to stop by his office this morning. After a brief exchange of pleasantries over a cup of coffee, he says he has a special assignment for Paul: "We've always just made an educated guess about how many phones we need to make each month. Usually we just look at how many we sold last month and plan to produce about the same number. This sometimes works fine. But most months we either have too many phones in inventory or we are out of stock. Neither situation is good."

Handing Paul the table shown here, Smithers continues, "Here are our actual orders entered for the past 36 months. There are 144 phones per case. I was hoping that since you graduated recently from the University of Alaska, you might have studied some techniques that would help us plan better. It's been awhile since I was in

Orders Received, by Month

Month	Cases 2007	Cases 2008	Cases 2009
January	480	575	608
February	436	527	597
March	482	540	612
April	448	502	603
May	458	508	628
June	489	573	605
July	498	508	627
August	430	498	578
September	444	485	585
October	496	526	581
November	487	552	632
December	525	587	656

college—I think I forgot most of the details I learned then. I'd like you to analyze these data and give me an idea of what our business will look like over the next 6 to 12 months. Do you think you can handle this?"

"Of course," Paul replies, sounding more confident than he really is. "How much time do I have?"

"I need your report on the Monday before Thanksgiving—that would be November 20th. I plan to take it home with me and read it during the holiday. Since I'm sure you will not be around during the holiday, be sure that you explain things carefully so that I can understand your recommendation without having to ask you any more questions. Since you are new to the company, you should know that

Source: Professor Victor E. Sower, Sam Houston State University.

I like to see all the details and complete justification for recommendations from my staff."

With that, Paul was dismissed. Arriving back at his office, he began his analysis.

Discussion Question

1. Prepare Paul Jordan's report to John Smithers using regression analysis. Provide a summary of the cell phone industry outlook as part of Paul's response.
2. Adding seasonality into your model, how does the analysis change?

▶ Forecasting at Hard Rock Cafe

Video Case

With the growth of Hard Rock Cafe—from one pub in London in 1971 to more than 129 restaurants in more than 40 countries today—came a corporatewide demand for better forecasting. Hard Rock uses long-range forecasting in setting a capacity plan and intermediate-term forecasting for locking in contracts for leather goods (used in jackets) and for such food items as beef, chicken, and pork. Its short-term sales forecasts are conducted each month, by cafe, and then aggregated for a headquarters view.

The heart of the sales forecasting system is the point-of-sale (POS) system, which, in effect, captures transaction data on nearly every person who walks through a cafe's door. The sale of each entrée represents one customer; the entrée sales data are transmitted daily to the Orlando corporate headquarters' database. There, the financial team, headed by Todd Lindsey, begins the forecast process. Lindsey forecasts monthly guest counts, retail sales, banquet sales, and concert sales (if applicable) at each cafe. The general managers of individual cafes tap into the same database to prepare a daily forecast for their sites. A cafe manager pulls up prior years' sales for that day, adding information from the local Chamber of Commerce or Tourist Board on upcoming events such as a major convention, sporting event, or concert in the city where the cafe is located. The daily forecast is further broken into hourly sales, which drives employee scheduling. An hourly forecast of $5,500 in sales translates into 19 workstations, which are further broken down into a specific number of wait staff, hosts, bartenders, and kitchen staff. Computerized scheduling software plugs in people based on their availability. Variances between forecast and actual sales are then examined to see why errors occurred.

Hard Rock doesn't limit its use of forecasting tools to sales. To evaluate managers and set bonuses, a 3-year weighted moving average is applied to cafe sales. If cafe general managers exceed their targets, a bonus is computed. Todd Lindsey, at corporate headquarters, applies weights of 40% to the most recent year's sales, 40% to the year before, and 20% to sales 2 years ago in reaching his moving average.

An even more sophisticated application of statistics is found in Hard Rock's menu planning. Using multiple regression, managers

can compute the impact on demand of other menu items if the price of one item is changed. For example, if the price of a cheeseburger increases from $7.99 to $8.99, Hard Rock can predict the effect this will have on sales of chicken sandwiches, pork sandwiches, and salads. Managers do the same analysis on menu placement, with the center section driving higher sales volumes. When an item such as a hamburger is moved off the center to one of the side flaps, the corresponding effect on related items, say french fries, is determined.

Hard Rock's Moscow Cafe[a]

Month	1	2	3	4	5	6	7	8	9	10
Guest count (in thousands)	21	24	27	32	29	37	43	43	54	66
Advertising (in $ thousand)	14	17	25	25	35	35	45	50	60	60

[a]These figures are used for purposes of this case study.

Discussion Questions*

1. Describe three different forecasting applications at Hard Rock. Name three other areas in which you think Hard Rock could use forecasting models.
2. What is the role of the POS system in forecasting at Hard Rock?
3. Justify the use of the weighting system used for evaluating managers for annual bonuses.
4. Name several variables besides those mentioned in the case that could be used as good predictors of daily sales in each cafe.
5. At Hard Rock's Moscow restaurant, the manager is trying to evaluate how a new advertising campaign affects guest counts. Using data for the past 10 months (see the table above) develop a least squares regression relationship and then forecast the expected guest count when advertising is $65,000.

*You may wish to view the video that accompanies this case before answering these questions.

Active Model Exercises

ACTIVE MODELS 4.1 4.2 4.3 4.4 These four Active Model exercises are simulations that allow you to evaluate changes in Examples 1, 4, 7, and 8, respectively, in your text. They are illustrated at **www.myomlab.com** or **www.pearsonhighered.com/heizer**.

Chapter 4 *Rapid* Review

Main Heading	Review Material	
WHAT IS FORECASTING? (pp. 86–87)	■ **Forecasting**—The art and science of predicting future events. ■ **Economic forecasts**—Planning indicators that are valuable in helping organizations prepare medium- to long-range forecasts. ■ **Technological forecasts**—Long-term forecasts concerned with the rates of technological progress. ■ **Demand forecasts**—Projections of a company's sales for each time period in the planning horizon.	
THE STRATEGIC IMPORTANCE OF FORECASTING (pp. 87–88)	*The forecast is the only estimate of demand until actual demand becomes known.* Forecasts of demand drive decisions in many areas, including: *Human resources, Capacity, Supply-chain management.*	**VIDEO 4.1** Forecasting at Hard Rock Cafe
SEVEN STEPS IN THE FORECASTING SYSTEM (p. 88)	Forecasting follows seven basic steps: 1. Determine the use of the forecast; 2. Select the items to be forecasted; 3. Determine the time horizon of the forecast; 4. Select the forecasting model(s); 5. Gather the data needed to make the forecast; 6. Make the forecast; 7. Validate and implement the results.	
FORECASTING APPROACHES (pp. 89–90)	■ **Quantitative forecasts**—Forecasts that employ mathematical modeling to forecast demand. ■ **Qualitative forecast**—Forecasts that incorporate such factors as the decision maker's intuition, emotions, personal experiences, and value system. ■ **Jury of executive opinion**—Takes the opinion of a small group of high-level managers and results in a group estimate of demand. ■ **Delphi method**—Uses an interactive group process that allows experts to make forecasts. ■ **Sales force composite**—Based on salespersons' estimates of expected sales. ■ **Consumer market survey**—Solicits input from customers or potential customers regarding future purchasing plans. ■ **Time series**—Uses a series of past data points to make a forecast.	
TIME-SERIES FORECASTING (pp. 90–108)	■ **Naïve approach**—Assumes that demand in the next period is equal to demand in the most recent period. ■ **Moving averages**—Uses an average of the *n* most recent periods of data to forecast the next period. $$\text{Moving average} = \frac{\sum \text{Demand in previous } n \text{ periods}}{n} \quad (4\text{-}1)$$ $$\text{Weighted moving average} = \frac{\sum(\text{Weight for period } n)(\text{Demand in period } n)}{\sum \text{Weights}} \quad (4\text{-}2)$$ ■ **Exponential smoothing**—A weighted-moving-average forecasting technique in which data points are weighted by an exponential function. ■ **Smoothing constant**—The weighting factor, α, used in an exponential smoothing forecast, a number between 0 and 1. Exponential smoothing formula: $\quad F_t = F_{t-1} + \alpha(A_{t-1} - F_{t-1}) \quad (4\text{-}4)$ ■ **Mean absolute deviation (MAD)**—A measure of the overall forecast error for a model. $$\text{MAD} = \frac{\sum|\text{Actual} - \text{Forecast}|}{n} \quad (4\text{-}5)$$ ■ **Mean squared error (MSE)**—The average of the squared differences between the forecast and observed values. $$\text{MSE} = \frac{\sum(\text{Forecast errors})^2}{n} \quad (4\text{-}6)$$ ■ **Mean absolute percent error (MAPE)**—The average of the absolute differences between the forecast and actual values, expressed as a percentage of actual values. $$\text{MAPE} = \frac{\sum_{i=1}^{n} 100|\text{Actual}_t - \text{Forecast}_t|/\text{Actual}_t}{n} \quad (4\text{-}7)$$	Problems: 4.1, 4.2, 4.3, 4.4, 4.5, 4.6, 4.7, 4.8, 4.9, 4.10, 4.11–4.23, 4.25–4.29, 4.33, 4.37, 4.39, 4.43, 4.44, 4.47, 4.49 Virtual Office Hours for Solved Problems: 4.1–4.4 **ACTIVE MODELS: 4.1–4.4**

Main Heading	Review Material	myomlab

Exponential Smoothing with Trend Adjustment

Forecast including trend (FIT_t) = Exponentially smoothed forecast (F_t)
  + Exponentially smoothed trend (T_t)   (4-8)

- **Trend projection**—A time-series forecasting method that fits a trend line to a series of historical data points and then projects the line into the future for forecasts.

Trend Projection and Regression Analysis

$$\hat{y} = a + bx, \text{ where } b = \frac{\Sigma xy - n\bar{x}\bar{y}}{\Sigma x^2 - n\bar{x}^2}, \text{ and } a = \bar{y} - b\bar{x} \qquad (4\text{-}11),(4\text{-}12),(4\text{-}13)$$

- **Seasonal variations**—Regular upward or downward movements in a time series that tie to recurring events.
- **Cycles**—Patterns in the data that occur every several years.

ASSOCIATIVE FORECASTING METHODS: REGRESSION AND CORRELATION ANALYSIS (pp. 108–113)	■ **Linear-regression analysis**—A straight-line mathematical model to describe the functional relationships between independent and dependent variables. ■ **Standard error of the estimate**—A measure of variability around the regression line. ■ **Coefficient of correlation**—A measure of the strength of the relationship between two variables. ■ **Coefficient of determination**—A measure of the amount of variation in the dependent variable about its mean that is explained by the regression equation. ■ **Multiple regression**—An associative forecasting method with > 1 independent variable. Multiple regression forecast: $\hat{y} = a + b_1 x_1 + b_2 x_2$ (4-17)	Problems: 4.24, 4.30–4.32, 4.34–4.36, 4.38, 4.40, 4.41, 4.46, 4.48
MONITORING AND CONTROLLING FORECASTS (pp. 113–116)	■ **Tracking signal**—A measurement of how well the forecast is predicting actual values. $$\text{Tracking signal} = \frac{\sum (\text{Actual demand in period } i - \text{ Forecast demand in period } i)}{\text{MAD}}$$ (4-18) ■ **Bias**—A forecast that is consistently higher or lower than actual values of a time series. ■ **Adaptive smoothing**—An approach to exponential smoothing forecasting in which the smoothing constant is automatically changed to keep errors to a minimum. ■ **Focus forecasting**—Forecasting that tries a variety of computer models and selects the best one for a particular application.	Problems: 4.37, 4.45
FORECASTING IN THE SERVICE SECTOR (pp. 116–117)	Service-sector forecasting may require good short-term demand records, even per 15-minute intervals. Demand during holidays or specific weather events may also need to be tracked.	

Self Test

- **Before taking the self-test,** refer to the learning objectives listed at the beginning of the chapter and the key terms listed at the end of the chapter.

LO1. Forecasting time horizons include:
- a) long range.
- b) medium range.
- c) short range.
- d) all of the above.

LO2. Qualitative methods of forecasting include:
- a) sales force composite.
- b) jury of executive opinion.
- c) consumer market survey.
- d) exponential smoothing.
- e) all except (d).

LO3. The difference between a *moving-average* model and an *exponential smoothing* model is that _____.

LO4. Three popular measures of forecast accuracy are:
- a) total error, average error, and mean error.
- b) average error, median error, and maximum error.
- c) median error, minimum error, and maximum absolute error.
- d) mean absolute deviation, mean squared error, and mean absolute percent error.

LO5. Average demand for iPods in the Rome, Italy, Apple store is 800 units per month. The May monthly index is 1.25. What is the seasonally adjusted sales forecast for May?
- a) 640 units   b) 798.75 units   c) 800 units   d) 1,000 units
- e) cannot be calculated with the information given

LO6. The main difference between simple and multiple regression is _____.

LO7. The tracking signal is the:
- a) standard error of the estimate.
- b) cumulative error.
- c) mean absolute deviation (MAD).
- d) ratio of the cumulative error to MAD.
- e) mean absolute percent error (MAPE).

Answers: LO1. d; **LO2.** e; **LO3.** exponential smoothing is a weighted moving-average model in which all prior values are weighted with a set of exponentially declining weights; **LO4.** d; **LO5.** d ; **LO6.** simple regression has only one independent variable ; **LO7.** d.

5

Design of Goods and Services

Chapter Outline

Goods and Services Selection

Generating New Products

Product Development

Issues for Product Design

Ethics, Environmentally-Friendly Designs, and Sustainability

Time-Based Competition

Defining a Product

Documents for Production

Service Design

Application of Decision Trees to Product Design

Transition to Production

Ethical Dilemma
Discussion Questions
Problems
Case Studies: De Mar's Product Strategy; Product Design at Regal Marine
Active Model Exercise
Rapid Review

Selection and design of goods and services are fundamental to an organization's strategy and have major implications throughout the operations function. The objective of product decisions is to develop and implement a product strategy that meets the demands of the marketplace with a competitive advantage. The product strategy often determines the focus of the competitive advantage—a focus that may be via differentiation, low cost, rapid response, or a combination of these.

BEFORE COMING TO CLASS, READ CHAPTER 5 IN YOUR TEXT AND ANSWER THESE QUESTIONS.

1. Identify the four stages of a product's life cycle. _____
_____

2. What is the product development system? _____
_____

3. What is a house of quality? _____
_____

4. What is time-based competition? _____
_____

5. Identify how firms define products and services. _____
_____

6. What documents are used to facilitate production of products? _____
_____
_____

7. How do customers participate in the design and production of services?
_____

8. How can a decision tree be applied to product design? _____
_____

GOODS AND SERVICES SELECTION   (See Flexible Version pp. 126–129)

Product Life Cycles   (See Flexible Version pp. 127–128)

Product-by-Value Analysis   (See Flexible Version pp. 128–129)

GENERATING NEW PRODUCTS   (See Flexible Version pp. 129–130)

Opportunities, Considerations, and Issues
(See Flexible Version p. 129)

Importance of New Products   (See Flexible Version pp. 129–130)

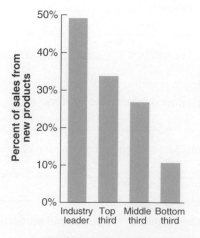

The higher the percentage of sales from the last 5 years, the more likely the firm is to be a leader.

▲ FIGURE 5.2   Innovation and New Products Yield Results for Both Manufacturing and Services

PRODUCT DEVELOPMENT (See Flexible Version pp. 130–135)

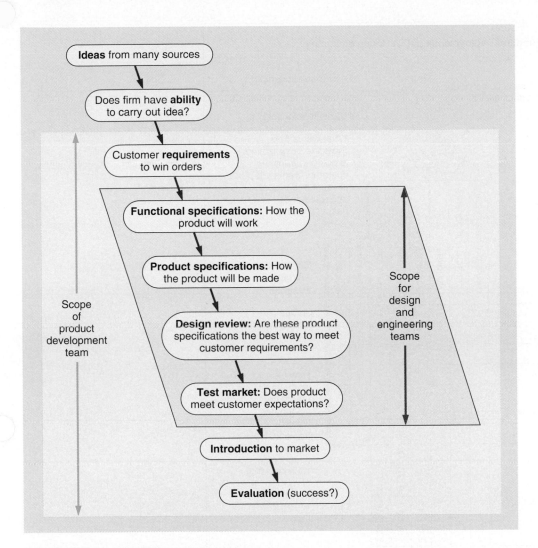

▲ **FIGURE 5.3** **Product Development Stages**

Product concepts are developed from a variety of sources, both external and internal to the firm. Concepts that survive the product idea stage progress through various stages, with nearly constant review, feedback, and evaluation in a highly participative environment to minimize failure.

Quality Function Deployment (See Flexible Version pp. 131–133)

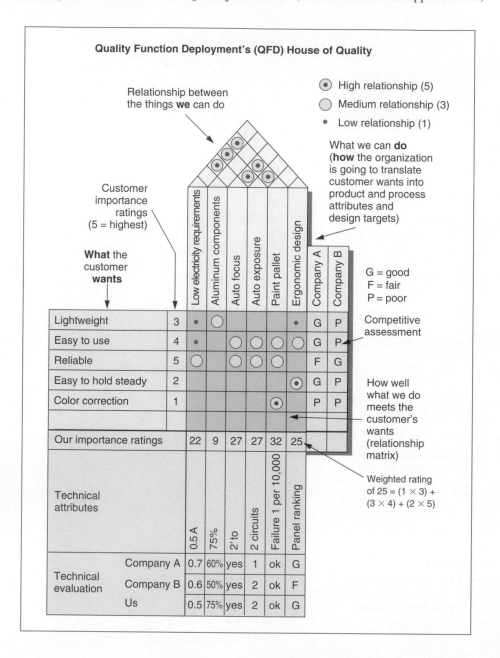

Quality Function Deployment's (QFD) House of Quality

PRACTICE PROBLEM 5.1 ■ QFD

You wish to compete in the super premium ice cream market. The task is to determine the *wants* of the super premium market and the attributes/*hows* to be met by your firm. Use the house of quality concept.

Market research has revealed that customers feel four factors are significant when making a buying decision. A "rich" taste is most important, followed by smooth texture, distinct flavor, and a sweet taste. From a production standpoint, important factors are the sugar content, the amount of butterfat, low air content, and natural flavors.

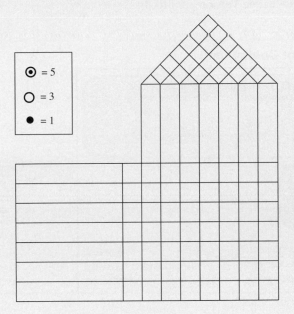

ISSUES FOR PRODUCT DESIGN (See Flexible Version pp. 135–137)

Robust Design (See Flexible Version p. 135)

Modular Design (See Flexible Version p. 135)

Computer-Aided Design (CAD) (See Flexible Version pp. 136–137)

Computer-Aided Manufacturing (CAM)
(See Flexible Version p. 137)

Virtual Reality Technology (See Flexible Version p. 137)

Value Analysis (See Flexible Version p. 137)

ETHICS, ENVIRONMENTALLY-FRIENDLY DESIGNS, AND SUSTAINABILITY (See Flexible Version pp. 138–140)

Goals

Guidelines

Laws and Industry Standards

TIME-BASED COMPETITION (See Flexible Version pp. 140–142)

Product Development Continuum

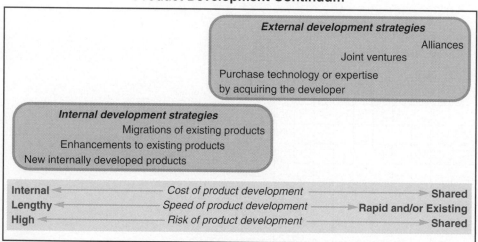

External development strategies

Alliances

Joint ventures

Purchase technology or expertise
by acquiring the developer

Internal development strategies

Migrations of existing products

Enhancements to existing products

New internally developed products

Internal	← Cost of product development →	Shared
Lengthy	← Speed of product development →	Rapid and/or Existing
High	← Risk of product development →	Shared

AUTHOR COMMENT
Managers seek a variety of approaches to obtain speed to market. The president of one U.S. firm says: "If I miss one product cycle, I'm dead."

▲ **FIGURE 5.6** Product Development Continuum

DEFINING A PRODUCT (See Flexible Version pp. 142–144)

Written Specifications (See Flexible Version p. 142)

Engineering Drawings (See Flexible Version p. 142)

Bills-of-Material (See Flexible Version pp. 142–143)

Make-or-Buy Decisions (See Flexible Version p. 143)

Group Technology (See Flexible Version p. 144)

**(a)   Bill of Material
for a Panel Weldment**

NUMBER	DESCRIPTION	QTY
A 60-71	PANEL WELDM'T	1
A 60-7	LOWER ROLLER ASSM.	1
R 60-17	ROLLER	1
R 60-428	PIN	1
P 60-2	LOCKNUT	1
A 60-72	GUIDE ASSM. REAR	1
R 60-57-1	SUPPORT ANGLE	1
A 00-4	ROLLER ASSM.	1
02-50-1150	BOLT	1
A 60-73	GUIDE ASSM. FRONT	1
A 60-74	SUPPORT WELDM'T	1
R 60-99	WEAR PLATE	1
02-50-1150	BOLT	1

**(b)   Hard Rock Cafe's Hickory
BBQ Bacon Cheeseburger**

DESCRIPTION	QTY
Bun	1
Hamburger patty	8 oz.
Cheddar cheese	2 slices
Bacon	2 strips
BBQ onions	1/2 cup
Hickory BBQ sauce	1 oz.
Burger set	
Lettuce	1 leaf
Tomato	1 slice
Red onion	4 rings
Pickle	1 slice
French fries	5 oz.
Seasoned salt	1 tsp.
11-inch plate	1
HRC flag	1

AUTHOR COMMENT
Hard Rock's recipe here serves the same purpose as a bill of material in a factory: It defines the product for production.

▲ **FIGURE 5.9**   Bills of Material Take Different Forms in a Manufacturing Plant (a) and a Restaurant (b), but in Both Cases, the Product Must Be Defined

PRACTICE PROBLEM 5.2 ■ BOM

Prepare a bill-of-material for a ham and cheese sandwich.

DOCUMENTS FOR PRODUCTION (See Flexible Version pp. 144–146)

Assembly Drawing

Assembly Chart

Route Sheet

Work Order

Engineering Change Notices (ECNs)

Configuration Management

Product Life-Cycle Management (PLM)

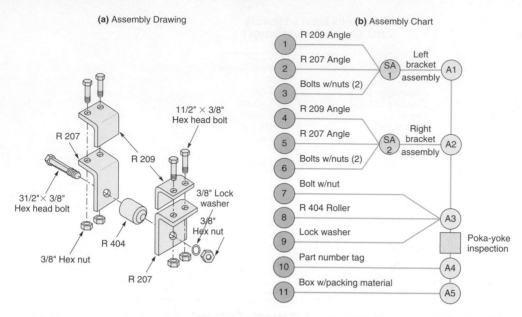

(a) Assembly Drawing

(b) Assembly Chart

▲ **FIGURE 5.11   Assembly Drawing and Assembly Chart**

PRACTICE PROBLEM 5.3 ■ Assembly Chart

Prepare an assembly chart for a ham and cheese sandwich.

SERVICE DESIGN (See Flexible Version pp. 146–148)

APPLICATION OF DECISION TREES TO PRODUCT DESIGN (See Flexible Version pp. 149–150)

PRACTICE PROBLEM 5.4 ■ Decision Tree

Michael's Engineering, Inc., manufactures components for the ever-changing notebook computer business. Michael is considering moving from a small custom design facility to an operation capable of much more rapid design of components. This means that Michael must consider upgrading his CAD equipment. Option 1 is to purchase two new desktop CAD systems at $100,000 each. Option 2 is to purchase an integrated system and the related server at $500,000. Michael's sales manager has estimated that if the market for notebook computers continues to expand, sales over the life of the system will be $1,000,000. He places the odds of this happening at 40%. He thinks the likelihood of the market having already peaked to be 60% and the sales to be only $700,000. What do you suggest Michael do and what is the EMV of this decision?

Additional Practice Problem Space

TRANSITION TO PRODUCTION (See Flexible Version p. 150)

Ethical Dilemma

John Edwards, president of Edwards Toy Company, Inc., in South Carolina, has just reviewed the design of a new pull-toy locomotive for 1- to 3-year-olds. John's design and marketing staff are very enthusiastic about the market for the product and the potential of follow-on circus train cars. The sales manager is looking forward to a very good reception at the annual toy show in Dallas next month. John, too, is delighted, as he is faced with a layoff if orders do not improve.

John's production people have worked out the manufacturing issues and produced a successful pilot run. However, the quality testing staff suggests that under certain conditions, a hook to attach cars to the locomotive and the crank for the bell can be broken off. This is an issue because children can choke on small parts such as these. In the quality test, 1- to 3-year-olds were unable to break off these parts; there were *no* failures. But when the test simulated the force of an adult tossing the locomotive into a toy box or a 5-year-old throwing it on the floor, there were failures. The estimate is that one of the two parts can be broken off 4 times out of 100,000 throws. Neither the design nor the material people know how to

make the toy safer and still perform as designed. The failure rate is low and certainly normal for this type of toy, but not at the Six Sigma level that John's firm strives for. And, of course, someone, someday may sue. A child choking on the broken part is a serious matter. Also, John was recently reminded in a discussion with legal counsel that U.S. case law suggests that new products may not be produced if there is "actual or foreseeable knowledge of a problem" with the product.

The design of successful, ethically produced, new products, as suggested in this chapter, is a complex task. What should John do?

Discussion Questions

1. Why is it necessary to document a product explicitly?
2. What techniques do we use to define a product?
3. In what ways is product strategy linked to product decisions?
4. Once a product is defined, what documents are used to assist production personnel in its manufacture?
5. What is time-based competition?
6. Describe the differences between joint ventures and alliances.
7. Describe four organizational approaches to product development. Which of these is generally thought to be best?
8. Explain what is meant by robust design.
9. What are three specific ways in which computer-aided design (CAD) benefits the design engineer?
10. What information is contained in a bill of material?
11. What information is contained in an engineering drawing?
12. What information is contained in an assembly chart? In a process sheet?
13. Explain what is meant in service design by the "moment of truth."
14. Explain how the house of quality translates customer desires into product/service attributes.
15. What is meant by *sustainability* in the context of operations management?
16. What strategic advantages does computer-aided design provide?

Problems*

•• **5.1** Construct a house of quality matrix for a wristwatch. Be sure to indicate specific customer wants that you think the general public desires. Then complete the matrix to show how an operations manager might identify specific attributes that can be measured and controlled to meet those customer desires.

•• **5.2** Using the house of quality, pick a real product (a good or service) and analyze how an existing organization satisfies customer requirements.

•• **5.3** Prepare a house of quality for a mousetrap.

•• **5.4** Conduct an interview with a prospective purchaser of a new bicycle and translate the customer's *wants* into the specific *hows* of the firm.

•• **5.5** Prepare a bill of material for (a) a pair of eyeglasses and its case or (b) a fast-food sandwich (visit a local sandwich shop like Subway, McDonald's, Blimpie, Quizno's; perhaps a clerk or the manager will provide you with details on the quantity or weight of various ingredients—otherwise, estimate the quantities).

•• **5.6** Draw an assembly chart for a pair of eyeglasses and its case.

•• **5.7** Prepare a script for telephone callers at the university's annual "phone-a-thon" fund raiser.

•• **5.8** Prepare an assembly chart for a table lamp.

••• **5.9** Prepare a product-by-value analysis for the following products, and given the position in its life cycle, identify the issues likely to confront the operations manager, and his or her possible actions. Product Alpha has annual sales of 1,000 units and a contribution of $2,500; it is in the introductory stage. Product Bravo has annual sales of 1,500 units and a contribution of $3,000; it is in the growth stage. Product Charlie has annual sales of 3,500 units and a contribution of $1,750; it is in the decline stage.

•• **5.10** Given the contribution made on each of the three products in the following table and their position in the life cycle, identify a reasonable operations strategy for each:

Product	Product Contribution (% of selling price)	Company Contribution (%: total annual contribution divided by total annual sales)	Position in Life Cycle
Kindle 2	30	40	Growth
Netbook computer	30	50	Introduction
Hand calculator	50	10	Decline

•• **5.11** The product design group of Flores Electric Supplies, Inc., has determined that it needs to design a new series of switches. It must decide on one of three design strategies. The market forecast is for 200,000 units. The better and more sophisticated the design strategy and the more time spent on value engineering,

*Note: **Px** means the problem may be solved with POM for Windows and/or Excel OM.

the less will be the variable cost. The chief of engineering design, Dr. W. L. Berry, has decided that the following costs are a good estimate of the initial and variable costs connected with each of the three strategies:

a) *Low-tech:* A low-technology, low-cost process consisting of hiring several new junior engineers. This option has a fixed cost of $45,000 and variable-cost probabilities of .3 for $.55 each, .4 for $.50, and .3 for $.45.

b) *Subcontract:* A medium-cost approach using a good outside design staff. This approach would have a fixed cost of $65,000 and variable-cost probabilities of .7 of $.45, .2 of $.40, and .1 of $.35.

c) *High-tech:* A high-technology approach using the very best of the inside staff and the latest computer-aided design technology. This approach has a fixed cost of $75,000 and variable-cost probabilities of .9 of $.40 and .1 of $.35.

What is the best decision based on an expected monetary value (EMV) criterion? (*Note:* We want the lowest EMV, as we are dealing with costs in this problem.) **Px**

•• **5.12** Clarkson Products, Inc., of Clarkson, New York, has the option of (a) proceeding immediately with production of a new top-of-the-line stereo TV that has just completed prototype testing or (b) having the value analysis team complete a study. If Ed Lusk, VP for operations, proceeds with the existing prototype (option a), the firm can expect sales to be 100,000 units at $550 each, with a probability of .6 and a .4 probability of 75,000 at $550. If, however, he uses the value analysis team (option b), the firm expects sales of 75,000 units at $750, with a probability of .7 and a .3 probability of 70,000 units at $750. Value analysis, at a cost of $100,000, is only used in option b. Which option has the highest expected monetary value (EMV)? **Px**

•• **5.13** Residents of Mill River have fond memories of ice skating at a local park. An artist has captured the experience in a drawing and is hoping to reproduce it and sell framed copies to current and former residents. He thinks that if the market is good he can sell 400 copies of the elegant version at $125 each. If the market is not good, he will sell only 300 at $90 each. He can make a deluxe version of the same drawing instead. He feels that if the market is good he can sell 500 copies of the deluxe version at $100 each. If the market is not good, he will sell only

400 copies at $70 each. In either case, production costs will be approximately $35,000. He can also choose to do nothing. If he believes there is a 50% probability of a good market, what should he do? Why? **Px**

•• **5.14** Ritz Products's materials manager, Bruce Elwell, must determine whether to make or buy a new semiconductor for the wrist TV that the firm is about to produce. One million units are expected to be produced over the life cycle. If the product is made, start-up and production costs of the *make* decision total $1 million, with a probability of .4 that the product will be satisfactory and a .6 probability that it will not. If the product is not satisfactory, the firm will have to reevaluate the decision. If the decision is reevaluated, the choice will be whether to spend another $1 million to redesign the semiconductor or to purchase. Likelihood of success the second time that the make decision is made is .9. If the second *make* decision also fails, the firm must purchase. Regardless of when the purchase takes place, Elwell's best judgment of cost is that Ritz will pay $.50 for each purchased semiconductor plus $1 million in vendor development cost.

a) Assuming that Ritz must have the semiconductor (stopping or doing without is not a viable option), what is the best decision?
b) What criteria did you use to make this decision?
c) What is the worst that can happen to Ritz as a result of this particular decision? What is the best that can happen? **Px**

•• **5.15** Page Engineering designs and constructs air conditioning and heating systems for hospitals and clinics. Currently, the company's staff is overloaded with design work. There is a major design project due in 8 weeks. The penalty for completing the design late is $14,000 per week, since any delay will cause the facility to open later than anticipated and cost the client significant revenue. If the company uses its inside engineers to complete the design, it will have to pay them overtime for all work. Page has estimated that it will cost $12,000 per week (wages and overhead), including late weeks, to have company engineers complete the design. Page is also considering having an outside engineering firm do the design. A bid of $92,000 has been received for the completed design. Yet another option for completing the design is to conduct a joint design by having a third engineering company complete all electromechanical components of the design at a cost of $56,000. Page would then complete the rest of the design and control systems at an estimated cost of $30,000.

Page has estimated the following probabilities of completing the project within various time frames when using each of the three options. Those estimates are shown in the following table:

| | Probability of Completing the Design | | | |
Option	On Time	1 Week Late	2 Weeks Late	3 Weeks Late
Internal Engineers	.4	.5	.1	—
External Engineers	.2	.4	.3	.1
Joint Design	.1	.3	.4	.2

What is the best decision based on an expected monetary value criterion? (*Note:* You want the lowest EMV because we are dealing with costs in this problem.) **Px**

••• **5.16** Use the data in Solved Problem 5.1 on page 131 of the Flexible Version to examine what happens to the decision if Sarah King can increase yields from 59,000 to 64,000 by applying an expensive phosphorus to the screen at an added manufacturing cost of $250,000. Prepare the modified decision tree. What are the payoffs, and which branch has the greatest EMV?

•••• **5.17** Using the house of quality sequence, as described in Figure 5.4 on page 133 of the Flexible Version, determine how you might deploy resources to achieve the desired quality for a product or service whose production process you understand.

•••• **5.18** McBurger, Inc., wants to redesign its kitchens to improve productivity and quality. Three designs, called designs K1, K2, and K3, are under consideration. No matter which design is used, daily demand for sandwiches at a typical McBurger restaurant is for 500 sandwiches. A sandwich costs $1.30 to produce. Non-defective sandwiches sell, on the average, for $2.50 per sandwich. Defective sandwiches cannot be sold and are scrapped. The goal is to choose a design that maximizes the expected profit at a typical restaurant over a 300-day period. Designs K1, K2, and K3 cost $100,000, $130,000, and $180,000, respectively. Under design K1, there is a .80 chance that 90 out of each 100 sandwiches are non-defective and a .20 chance that 70 out of each 100 sandwiches are non-defective. Under design K2, there is a .85 chance that 90 out of each 100 sandwiches are non-defective and a .15 chance that 75 out of each 100 sandwiches are non-defective. Under design K3, there is a .90 chance that 95 out of each 100 sandwiches are non-defective and a .10 chance that 80 out of each 100 sandwiches are non-defective. What is the expected profit level of the design that achieves the maximum expected 300-day profit level? **Px**

▶ Refer to myomlab 🌐 for these additional homework problems: 5.19–5.25

Case Studies

▶ De Mar's Product Strategy

De Mar, a plumbing, heating, and air-conditioning company located in Fresno, California, has a simple but powerful product strategy: *Solve the customer's problem no matter what, solve the problem when the customer needs it solved, and make sure the customer feels good when you leave.* De Mar offers guaranteed, same-day service for customers requiring it. The company provides 24-hour-a-day,

7-day-a-week service at no extra charge for customers whose air conditioning dies on a hot summer Sunday or whose toilet overflows at 2:30 A.M. As assistant service coordinator Janie Walter puts it: "We will be there to fix your A/C on the fourth of July, and it's not a penny extra. When our competitors won't get out of bed, we'll be there!"

De Mar guarantees the price of a job to the penny before the work begins. Whereas most competitors guarantee their work for 30 days, De Mar guarantees all parts and labor for one year. The company assesses no travel charge because "it's not fair to charge customers for driving out." Owner Larry Harmon says: "We are in an industry that doesn't have the best reputation. If we start making money our main goal, we are in trouble. So I stress customer satisfaction; money is the by-product."

De Mar uses selective hiring, ongoing training and education, performance measures, and compensation that incorporate customer satisfaction, strong teamwork, peer pressure, empowerment, and aggressive promotion to implement its strategy. Says credit manager Anne Semrick: "The person who wants a nine-to-five job needs to go somewhere else."

De Mar is a premium pricer. Yet customers respond because De Mar delivers value—that is, benefits for costs. In 8 years, annual sales increased from about $200,000 to more than $3.3 million.

Discussion Questions

1. What is De Mar's product? Identify the tangible parts of this product and its service components.
2. How should other areas of De Mar (marketing, finance, personnel) support its product strategy?
3. Even though De Mar's product is primarily a service product, how should each of the 10 OM decisions in the text be managed to ensure that the product is successful?

Source: Reprinted with the permission of The Free Press, from *On Great Service: A Framework for Action* by Leonard L. Berry. Copyright © 1995 by Leonard L. Berry.

▶ Product Design at Regal Marine

Video Case

With hundreds of competitors in the boat business, Regal Marine must work to differentiate itself from the flock. As we saw in the *Global Company Profile* that opened this chapter in the text, Regal continuously introduces innovative, high-quality new boats. Its differentiation strategy is reflected in a product line consisting of 22 models.

To maintain this stream of innovation, and with so many boats at varying stages of their life cycles, Regal constantly seeks design input from customers, dealers, and consultants. Design ideas rapidly find themselves in the styling studio, where they are placed onto CAD machines in order to speed the development process. Existing boat designs are always evolving as the company tries to stay stylish and competitive. Moreover, with life cycles as short as 3 years, a steady stream of new products is required. A few years ago, the new product was the three-passenger $11,000 Rush, a small but powerful boat capable of pulling a water-skier. This was followed with a 20-foot inboard–outboard performance boat with so many innovations that it won prize after prize in the industry. Another new boat is a redesigned 44-foot Commodore that sleeps six in luxury staterooms. With all these models and innovations, Regal designers and production personnel are under pressure to respond quickly.

By getting key suppliers on board early and urging them to participate at the design stage, Regal improves both innovations and quality while speeding product development. Regal finds that the sooner it brings suppliers on board, the faster it can bring new boats to the market. After a development stage that constitutes concept and styling, CAD designs yield product specifications. The first stage in actual production is the creation of the "plug," a foam-based carving used to make the molds for fiberglass hulls and decks. Specifications from the CAD system drive the carving process. Once the plug is carved, the permanent molds for each new hull and deck design are formed. Molds take about 4 to 8 weeks to make and are all handmade. Similar molds are made for many of the other features in Regal boats—from galley and stateroom components to lavatories and steps. Finished molds can be joined and used to make thousands of boats.

Discussion Questions*

1. How does the concept of product life cycle apply to Regal Marine products?
2. What strategy does Regal use to stay competitive?
3. What kind of engineering savings is Regal achieving by using CAD technology rather than traditional drafting techniques?
4. What are the likely benefits of the CAD design technology?

*You may wish to view the video that accompanies this case before addressing these questions.

Active Model Exercise

ACTIVE MODEL 5.1 is a simulation exercise that evaluates changes in Example 3 in your text. It is illustrated at **www.myomlab.com** or **www.pearsonhighered.com/heizer**.

Main Heading	Review Material	
GOODS AND SERVICES SELECTION (pp. 126–129)	Although the term *products* may often refer to tangible goods, it also refers to offerings by service organizations. *The objective of the product decision is to develop and implement a product strategy that meets the demands of the marketplace with a competitive advantage.* ■ **Product decision**—The selection, definition, and design of products. The four phases of the product life cycle are introduction, growth, maturity, and decline. ■ **Product-by-value analysis**—A list of products, in descending order of their individual dollar contribution to the firm, as well as the *total annual dollar* contribution of the product.	Problem: 5.9 **VIDEO 5.1** Product Strategy at Regal Marine
GENERATING NEW PRODUCTS (pp. 129–130)	Product selection, definition, and design take place on a continuing basis. Changes in product opportunities, the products themselves, product volume, and product mix may arise due to understanding the customer, economic change, sociological and demographic change, technological change, political/legal change, market practice, professional standards, suppliers, or distributors.	
PRODUCT DEVELOPMENT (pp. 130–135)	■ **Quality function deployment (QFD)**—A process for determining customer requirements (customer "wants") and translating them into attributes (the "hows") that each functional area can understand and act on. ■ **House of quality**—A part of the quality function deployment process that utilizes a planning matrix to relate customer wants to how the firm is going to meet those wants. ■ **Product development teams**—Teams charged with moving from market requirements for a product to achieving product success. ■ **Concurrent engineering**—Use of participating teams in design and engineering activities. ■ **Manufacturability and value engineering**—Activities that help improve a product's design, production, maintainability, and use.	
ISSUES FOR PRODUCT DESIGN (pp. 135–137)	■ **Robust design**—A design that can be produced to requirements even with unfavorable conditions in the production process. ■ **Modular design**—A design in which parts or components of a product are subdivided into modules that are easily interchanged or replaced. ■ **Computer-aided design (CAD)**—Interactive use of a computer to develop and document a product. ■ **Design for manufacture and assembly (DFMA)**—Software that allows designers to look at the effect of design on manufacturing of a product. ■ **3-D object modeling**—An extension of CAD that builds small prototypes. ■ **Standard for the exchange of product data (STEP)**—A standard that provides a format allowing the electronic transmission of three-dimensional data. ■ **Computer-aided manufacturing (CAM)**—The use of information technology to control machinery. ■ **Virtual reality**—A visual form of communication in which images substitute for reality and typically allow the user to respond interactively. ■ **Value analysis**—A review of successful products that takes place during the production process.	
ETHICS, ENVIRONMENTALLY-FRIENDLY DESIGNS, AND SUSTAINABILITY (pp. 138–140)	■ **Sustainability**—A production system that supports conservation and renewal of resources. ■ **Life Cycle Assessment (LCA)**—Part of ISO 14000; assesses the environmental impact of a product from material and energy inputs to disposal and environmental releases. Goals for ethical, environmentally friendly designs are (1) developing safe and environmentally sound products, (2) minimizing waste of resources, (3) reducing environmental liabilities, (4) increasing cost-effectiveness of complying with environmental regulations, and (5) being recognized as a good corporate citizen.	
TIME-BASED COMPETITION (pp. 140–142)	■ **Time-based competition**—Competition based on time; rapidly developing products and moving them to market. *Internal development strategies* include (1) new internally developed products, (2) enhancements to existing products, and (3) migrations of existing products. *External development strategies* include (1) purchase the technology or expertise by acquiring the developer, (2) establish joint ventures, and (3) develop alliances. ■ **Joint ventures**—Firms establishing joint ownership to pursue new products or markets. ■ **Alliances**—Cooperative agreements that allow firms to remain independent but pursue strategies consistent with their individual missions.	

Main Heading	Review Material	
DEFINING A PRODUCT (pp. 142–144)	■ **Engineering drawing**—A drawing that shows the dimensions, tolerances, materials, and finishes of a component. ■ **Bill of material (BOM)**—A list of the components, their description, and the quantity of each required to make one unit of a product. ■ **Make-or-buy decision**—The choice between producing a component or a service and purchasing it from an outside source. ■ **Group technology**—A product and component coding system that specifies the type of processing and the parameters of the processing; it allows similar products to be grouped.	myomlab
DOCUMENTS FOR PRODUCTION (pp. 144–146)	■ **Assembly drawing**—An exploded view of a product. ■ **Assembly chart**—A graphic means of identifying how components flow into subassemblies and final products ■ **Route sheet**—A list of the operations necessary to produce a component with the material specified in the bill of material. ■ **Work order**—An instruction to make a given quantity of a particular item. ■ **Engineering change notice (ECN)**—A correction or modification of an engineering drawing or bill of material. ■ **Configuration management**—A system by which a product's planned and changing components are accurately identified. ■ **Product life cycle management (PLM)**—Software programs that tie together many phases of product design and manufacture.	
SERVICE DESIGN (pp. 146–148)	Techniques to reduce costs and enhance the service offering include (1) delaying customization, (2) modularizing, (3) automating, and (4) designing for the "moment of truth."	
APPLICATION OF DECISION TREES TO PRODUCT DESIGN (pp. 149–150)	To form a decision tree, (1) include all possible alternatives (including "do nothing") and states of nature; (2) enter payoffs at the end of the appropriate branch; and (3) determine the expected value of each course of action by starting at the end of the tree and working toward the beginning, calculating values at each step and "pruning" inferior alternatives.	Problems: 5.10–5.15, 5.18 Virtual Office Hours for Solved Problem: 5.1 **ACTIVE** MODEL 5.1
TRANSITION TO PRODUCTION (p. 150)	One of the arts of modern management is knowing when to move a product from development to production; this move is known as *transition to production*.	

Self Test

■ **Before taking the self-test,** refer to the learning objectives listed at the beginning of the chapter and the key terms listed at the end of the chapter.

LO1. A product's life cycle is divided into four stages, including:
    a) introduction.   **b)** growth.
    c) maturity.   **d)** all of the above.

LO2. Product development systems include:
    a) bills of material.   **b)** routing charts.
    c) functional specifications.   **d)** product-by-values analysis.
    e) configuration management.

LO3. A house of quality is:
    a) a matrix relating customer "wants" to the firm's "hows."
    b) a schematic showing how a product is put together.
    c) a list of the operations necessary to produce a component.
    d) an instruction to make a given quantity of a particular item.
    e) a set of detailed instructions about how to perform a task.

LO4. Time-based competition focuses on:
    a) moving new products to market more quickly.
    b) reducing the life cycle of a product.
    c) linking QFD to PLM.
    d) design database availability.
    e) value engineering.

LO5. Products are defined by:
    a) value analysis.   **b)** value engineering.

LO6. A route sheet:
    a) lists the operations necessary to produce a component.
    b) is an instruction to make a given quantity of a particular item.
    c) is a schematic showing how a product is assembled.
    d) is a document showing the flow of product components.
    e) all of the above.

LO7. Four techniques available when a service is designed are:
    a) recognize political or legal change, technological change, sociological demographic change, and economic change.
    b) understand product introduction, growth, maturity, and decline.
    c) recognize functional specifications, product specifications, design review, and test markets.
    d) ensure that customization is done as late in the process as possible, modularize the product, reduce customer interaction, and focus on the moment of truth.

LO8. Decision trees use:
    a) probabilities.   **b)** payoffs.
    c) logic.   **d)** options.
    e) all of the above.

Answers: LO1. d; **LO2.** c; **LO3.** a; **LO4.** a; **LO5.** e; **LO6.** a; **LO7.** d; **LO8.** e.

6 Managing Quality

Chapter Outline

Quality and Strategy

Defining Quality

International Quality Standards

Total Quality Management (TQM)

Tools of TQM

The Role of Inspection

TQM in Services

Ethical Dilemma
Discussion Questions
Problems
Case Studies: Southwestern University:
   (C); The Culture of Quality at Arnold
   Palmer Hospital; Quality at the
   Ritz-Carlton Hotel Company
Active Model Exercise
Rapid Review

Regardless of the organization's strategy, defining and managing quality is crucial. Quality, or lack of quality, impacts the entire organization from supplier to customer and from product design to maintenance. Successful quality management begins with an organizational environment that fosters quality, followed by an understanding of the principles of quality, and then engaging employees in the necessary activities to implement quality. When these things are done well, the product typically obtains a competitive advantage and wins customers.

BEFORE COMING TO CLASS, READ CHAPTER 6 IN YOUR TEXT AND ANSWER THESE QUESTIONS.

1. Define quality and TQM. _____

_____

2. What are ISO standards and why are they important? _____

_____

_____

3. What is Six Sigma? _____

_____

4. Explain how benchmarking is used. _____

_____

5. What are quality robust products and Taguchi concepts? _____

_____

_____

6. What are seven tools of TQM? _____

_____

_____

QUALITY AND STRATEGY (See Flexible Version p. 156)

DEFINING QUALITY (See Flexible Version pp. 156–159)

Quality is the totality of features and characteristics of a product or service that bears on the ability to satisfy stated or implied needs.

Three Other Perspectives to Defining Quality

1. User based:

2. Manufacturing based:

3. Product based:

Implications of Quality (See Flexible Version p. 157)

Cost of Quality (COQ) (See Flexible Version p. 158)

Ethics and Quality Management (See Flexible Version p. 158)

INTERNATIONAL QUALITY STANDARDS (See Flexible Version pp. 159–160)

The Two Major International Standards for Quality

1. ISO 9000
2. ISO 14000

TOTAL QUALITY MANAGEMENT (TQM) (See Flexible Version pp. 160–166)

The Seven Ingredients of Total Quality Management

1. Continuous improvement
2. Six Sigma
3. Employee empowerment
4. Benchmarking
5. Just-in-time
6. Taguchi concepts
7. TQM tools

Taguchi Concepts (See Flexible Version p. 165)

Quality loss function

$$L = D^2C$$

where
L = loss to society
D^2 = square of the distance from the target value
C = cost of the deviation at the specification limit

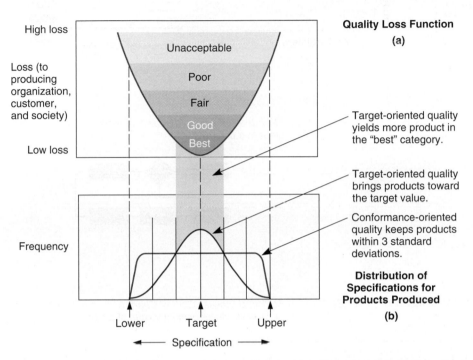

▲ FIGURE 6.5   (a) Quality Loss Function and (b) Distribution of Specifications for Products Produced
Taguchi aims for the target because products produced near the upper and lower acceptable specifications result in higher quality loss function.

The Other Two Taguchi Concepts

1. **Target-oriented quality**
2. **Quality robust products**

TOOLS OF TQM (See Flexible Version pp. 166–170)

Tools for Generating Ideas

(a) *Check Sheet:* An organized method of recording data

Defect	Hour							
	1	2	3	4	5	6	7	8
A	///	/		/	/	/	///	/
B	//	/	/	/			//	///
C	/	//					//	////

(b) *Scatter Diagram:* A graph of the value of one variable vs. another variable

(c) *Cause-and-Effect Diagram:* A tool that identifies process elements (causes) that may effect an outcome

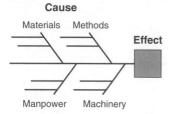

Tools for Organizing the Data

(d) *Pareto Chart:* A graph to identify and plot problems or defects in descending order of frequency

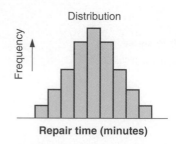

(e) *Flow Chart (Process Diagram):* A chart that describes the steps in a process

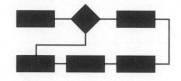

Tools for Identifying Problems

(f) *Histogram:* A distribution showing the frequency of occurrences of a variable

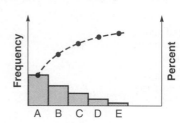

(g) *Statistical Process Control Chart:* A chart with time on the horizontal axis for plotting values of a statistic

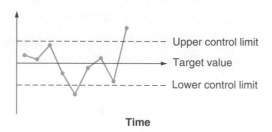

▲ FIGURE 6.6 Seven Tools of TQM

PRACTICE PROBLEM 6.1 ■ Pareto Chart

The accounts receivable department has documented the following defects over a 30-day period:

Category	Frequency
Invoice amount does not agree with the check amount	108
Invoice not on record (not found)	24
No formal invoice issued	18
Check (payment) not received on time	30
Check not signed	8
Invoice number and invoice referenced do not agree	12

Draw the Pareto chart. What conclusions can you draw about defects in the accounts receivable department?

Additional Practice Problem Space

PRACTICE PROBLEM 6.2 ■ Flowchart

Prepare a flowchart for purchasing a Big Mac at the drive-through window at McDonald's.

PRACTICE PROBLEM 6.3 ■ Cause and Effect Diagram (Fish-bone Chart)

Draw a fish-bone chart detailing reasons why a part might not be machined correctly.

PRACTICE PROBLEM 6.4 ■ Process Chart

Develop a process chart for changing an automobile tire.

THE ROLE OF INSPECTION (See Flexible Version pp. 170–172)

When and Where to Inspect

Source Inspection

Poka-Yoke

Attribute Inspection

Variable Inspection

TQM IN SERVICES (See Flexible Version pp. 172–174)

Determinants of Quality

Reliability

Responsiveness

Competence

Access

Courtesy

Communication

Credibility

Security

Understanding/Knowing the Customer

Tangibles

Ethical Dilemma

A lawsuit a few years ago made headlines worldwide when a McDonald's drive-through customer spilled a cup of scalding hot coffee on herself. Claiming the coffee was too hot to be safely consumed in a car, the badly burned 80-year-old woman won $2.9 million in court. (The judge later reduced the award to $640,000.) McDonald's claimed the product was served to the correct specifications and was of proper quality. Further, the cup read "Caution—Contents May Be Hot." McDonald's coffee, at 180°, is substantially hotter (by corporate rule) than typical restaurant coffee, despite hundreds of coffee-scalding complaints in the past 10 years. Similar court cases, incidentally, resulted in smaller verdicts, but again in favor of the plaintiffs. For example, Motor City Bagel Shop was sued for a spilled cup of coffee by a drive-through patron, and Starbucks by a customer who spilled coffee on her own ankle.

Are McDonald's, Motor City, and Starbucks at fault in situations such as these? How do quality and ethics enter into these cases?

Discussion Questions

1. Explain how improving quality can lead to reduced costs.
2. As an Internet exercise, determine the Baldrige Award Criteria. See the Web site **www.quality.nist.gov**.
3. Which 3 of Deming's 14 points do you think are most critical to the success of a TQM program? Why?
4. List the seven concepts that are necessary for an effective TQM program. How are these related to Deming's 14 points?
5. Name three of the important people associated with the quality concepts of this chapter. In each case, write a short sentence about each one summarizing their primary contribution to the field of quality management.
6. What are seven tools of TQM?
7. How does fear in the workplace (and in the classroom) inhibit learning?
8. How can a university control the quality of its output (that is, its graduates)?
9. Philip Crosby said that quality is free. Why?
10. List the three concepts central to Taguchi's approach.
11. What is the purpose of using a Pareto chart for a given problem?

12. What are the four broad categories of "causes" to help initially structure an Ishikawa diagram or cause-and-effect diagram?
13. Of the several points where inspection may be necessary, which apply especially well to manufacturing?
14. What roles do operations managers play in addressing the major aspects of service quality?
15. Explain, in your own words, what is meant by *source inspection*.
16. What are 10 determinants of service quality?
17. Name several products that do not require high quality.
18. What does the formula $\alpha = D^2 C$ mean?
19. In this chapter, we have suggested that building quality into a process and its people is difficult. Inspections are also difficult. To indicate just how difficult inspections are, count the number of *E*s (both capital *E* and lowercase *e*) in the *OM in Action* box "Richey International's Spies" on page 174 in the Flexible Version (include the title but not the footnote). How many did you find? If each student does this individually, you are very likely to find a distribution rather than a single number!

Problems

•   **6.1**   An avant-garde clothing manufacturer runs a series of high-profile, risqué ads on a billboard on Highway 101 and regularly collects protest calls from people who are offended by them. The company has no idea how many people in total see the ad, but it has been collecting statistics on the number of phone calls from irate viewers:

Type	Description	Number of Complaints
R	Offensive racially/ethnically	10
M	Demeaning to men	4
W	Demeaning to women	14
I	Ad is Incomprehensible	6
O	Other	2

a) Depict this data with a Pareto chart. Also depict the cumulative complaint line.
b) What percent of the total complaints can be attributed to the most prevalent complaint?

•   **6.2**   Develop a scatter diagram for two variables of interest (say pages in the newspaper by day of the week; see example in Figure 6.6[b]).

•   **6.3**   Develop a Pareto chart of the following causes of poor grades on an exam:

Reason for Poor Grade	Frequency
Insufficient time to complete	15
Late arrival to exam	7
Difficulty understanding material	25
Insufficient preparation time	2
Studied wrong material	2
Distractions in exam room	9
Calculator batteries died during exam	1
Forgot exam was scheduled	3
Felt ill during exam	4

•   **6.4**   Develop a histogram of the time it took for you or your friends to receive six recent orders at a fast-food restaurant.

••   **6.5**   Theresa Shotwell's restaurant in Tallahassee, Florida, has recorded the following data for eight recent customers:

Customer Number, i	Minutes from Time Food Ordered Until Food Arrived (y_i)	No. of Trips to Kitchen by Waitress (x_i)
1	10.50	4
2	12.75	5
3	9.25	3
4	8.00	2
5	9.75	3
6	11.00	4
7	14.00	6
8	10.75	5

a) Theresa wants you to graph the eight points (x_i, y_i), $i = 1, 2, \ldots 8$. She has been concerned because customers have been waiting too long for their food, and this graph is intended to help her find possible causes of the problem.
b) This is an example of what type of graph?

••   **6.6**   Develop a flowchart (as in Figure 6.6[e] and Example 2 on page 169 in the Flexible Version) showing all the steps involved in planning a party.

••   **6.7**   Consider the types of poor driving habits that might occur at a traffic light. Make a list of the 10 you consider most likely to happen. Add the category of "other" to that list.
a) Compose a check sheet (like that in Figure 6.6[a]) to collect the frequency of occurrence of these habits. Using your check sheet, visit a busy traffic light intersection at four different times of the day, with two of these times being during high-traffic periods (rush hour, lunch hour). For 15 to 20 minutes each visit, observe the frequency with which the habits you listed occurred.
b) Construct a Pareto chart showing the relative frequency of occurrence of each habit.

•• **6.8** Draw a fish-bone chart detailing reasons why an airline customer might be dissatisfied.

•• **6.9** Consider the everyday task of getting to work on time or arriving at your first class on time in the morning. Draw a fish-bone chart showing reasons why you might arrive late in the morning.

•• **6.10** Construct a cause-and-effect diagram to reflect "student dissatisfied with university registration process." Use the "four *M*s" or create your own organizing scheme. Include at least 12 causes.

•• **6.11** Draw a fish-bone chart depicting the reasons that might give rise to an incorrect fee statement at the time you go to pay for your registration at school.

••• **6.12** Mary Beth Marrs, the manager of an apartment complex, feels overwhelmed by the number of complaints she is receiving. Below is the check sheet she has kept for the past 12 weeks. Develop a Pareto chart using this information. What recommendations would you make?

Week	Grounds	Parking/ Drives	Pool	Tenant Issues	Electrical/ Plumbing
1	✓✓✓	✓✓	✓	✓✓✓	
2	✓	✓✓✓	✓✓	✓✓	✓
3	✓✓✓	✓✓✓	✓✓	✓	
4	✓	✓✓✓✓	✓	✓	✓✓
5	✓✓	✓✓✓	✓✓✓✓	✓✓	
6	✓	✓✓✓✓	✓✓		
7		✓✓✓	✓✓	✓✓	
8	✓	✓✓✓✓	✓✓	✓✓✓	✓
9	✓	✓✓	✓		
10	✓	✓✓✓✓	✓✓	✓✓	
11		✓✓✓	✓✓	✓	
12	✓✓	✓✓✓	✓✓✓	✓	

• **6.13** Use Pareto analysis to investigate the following data collected on a printed-circuit-board assembly line:

Defect	Number of Defect Occurrences
Components not adhering	143
Excess adhesive	71
Misplaced transistors	601
Defective board dimension	146
Mounting holes improperly positioned	12
Circuitry problems on final test	90
Wrong component	212

a) Prepare a graph of the data.
b) What conclusions do you reach?

•• **6.14** A list of 16 issues that led to incorrect formulations in Richard Dulski's jam manufacturing unit is provided below:

List of Issues	
1. Incorrect measurement	9. Variability in scale accuracy
2. Antiquated scales	10. Equipment in disrepair
3. Lack of clear instructions	11. Technician calculation off
4. Damaged raw material	12. Jars mislabeled
5. Operator misreads display	13. Temperature controls off
6. Inadequate cleanup	14. Incorrect weights
7. Incorrect maintenance	15. Priority miscommunication
8. Inadequate flow controls	16. Inadequate instructions

Create a fish-bone diagram and categorize each of these issues correctly, using the "four *M*s" method.

•• **6.15** Develop a flowchart for one of the following:
a) Filling up with gasoline at a self-serve station.
b) Determining your account balance and making a withdrawal at an ATM.
c) Getting a cone of yogurt or ice cream from an ice cream store.

•••• **6.16** Boston Electric Generators has been getting many complaints from its major customer, Home Station, about the quality of its shipments of home generators. Daniel Shimshak, the plant manager, is alarmed that a customer is providing him with the only information the company has on shipment quality. He decides to collect information on defective shipments through a form he has asked his drivers to complete on arrival at customers' stores. The forms for the first 279 shipments have been turned in. They show the following over the past 8 weeks:

			Reason for Defective Shipment			
Week	No. of Shipments	No. of Ship- ments with Defects	Incorrect Bill of Lading	Incorrect Truck- load	Damaged Product	Trucks Late
1	23	5	2	2	1	
2	31	8	1	4	1	2
3	28	6	2	3	1	
4	37	11	4	4	1	2
5	35	10	3	4	2	1
6	40	14	5	6	3	
7	41	12	3	5	3	1
8	44	15	4	7	2	2

Even though Daniel increased his capacity by adding more workers to his normal contingent of 30, he knew that for many weeks he exceeded his regular output of 30 shipments per week. A review of his turnover over the past 8 weeks shows the following:

Week	No. of New Hires	No. of Terminations	Total No. of Workers
1	1	0	30
2	2	1	31
3	3	2	32
4	2	0	34
5	2	2	34
6	2	4	32
7	4	1	35
8	3	2	36

a) Develop a scatter diagram using total number of shipments and number of defective shipments. Does there appear to be any relationship?
b) Develop a scatter diagram using the variable "turnover" (number of new hires plus number of terminations) and the number of defective shipments. Does the diagram depict a relationship between the two variables?

c) Develop a Pareto chart for the type of defects that have occurred.

d) Draw a fish-bone chart showing the possible causes of the defective shipments.

• • • **6.17** A recent Gallup poll of 519 adults who flew in the past year (published in *The Economist*, June 16, 2007, p. 6) found the following their number 1 complaints about flying: cramped seats (45), cost (16), dislike or fear of flying (57), security measures (119), poor service (12), connecting flight problems (8), overcrowded planes (42), late planes/waits (57), food (7), lost luggage (7), and other (51).

a) What percentage of those surveyed found nothing they disliked?

b) Draw a Pareto chart summarizing these responses. Include the "no complaints" group.

c) Use the "four *M*s" method to create a fish-bone diagram for the 10 specific categories of dislikes (exclude "other" and "no complaints").

d) If you were managing an airline, what two or three specific issues would you tackle to improve customer service? Why?

▶ **Refer to** myomlab◯ **for these additional homework problems: 6.18–6.21**

Case Studies

▶ Southwestern University: (C)*

The popularity of Southwestern University's football program under its new coach, Bo Pitterno, surged in each of the 5 years since his arrival at the Stephenville, Texas, college. (See Southwestern University: (A) in Chapter 3 and (B) in Chapter 4.) With a football stadium close to maxing out at 54,000 seats and a vocal coach pushing for a new stadium, SWU president Joel Wisner faced some difficult decisions. After a phenomenal upset victory over its archrival, the University of Texas, at the homecoming game in the fall, Dr. Wisner was not as happy as one would think. Instead of ecstatic alumni, students, and faculty, all Wisner heard were complaints. "The lines at the concession stands were too long"; "Parking was harder to find and farther away than in the old days" (that is, before the team won regularly); "Seats weren't comfortable"; "Traffic was backed up halfway to Dallas"; and on and on. "A college president just can't win," muttered Wisner to himself.

At his staff meeting the following Monday, Wisner turned to his VP of administration, Leslie Gardner. "I wish you would take care of these football complaints, Leslie," he said. "See what the *real* problems are and let me know how you've resolved them." Gardner wasn't surprised at the request. "I've already got a handle

on it, Joel," she replied. "We've been randomly surveying 50 fans per game for the past year to see what's on their minds. It's all part of my campuswide TQM effort. Let me tally things up and I'll get back to you in a week."

When she returned to her office, Gardner pulled out the file her assistant had compiled (see Table 6.6). "There's a lot of information here," she thought.

Discussion Questions

1. Using at least two different quality tools, analyze the data and present your conclusions.

2. How could the survey have been more useful?

3. What is the next step?

*This integrated case study runs throughout the text. Other issues facing Southwestern's football stadium include: (A) Managing the renovation project (Chapter 3); (B) Forecasting game attendance (Chapter 4); (D) Break-even analysis of food services (Supplement 7 Web site); (E) Locating the new stadium (Chapter 8 Web site); (F) Inventory planning of football programs (Chapter 12 Web site); and (G) Scheduling of campus security officers/staff for game days (Chapter 13).

▼ **TABLE 6.6** Fan Satisfaction Survey Results (N = 250)

		Overall Grade				
		A	**B**	**C**	**D**	**E**
Game Day	A. Parking	90	105	45	5	5
	B. Traffic	50	85	48	52	15
	C. Seating	45	30	115	35	25
	D. Entertainment	160	35	26	10	19
	E. Printed Program	66	34	98	22	30
Tickets	A. Pricing	105	104	16	15	10
	B. Season Ticket Plans	75	80	54	41	0
Concessions	A. Prices	16	116	58	58	2
	B. Selection of Foods	155	60	24	11	0
	C. Speed of Service	35	45	46	48	76

Respondents

Alumnus	113
Student	83
Faculty/Staff	16
None of the above	38

Open-Ended Comments on Survey Cards:

Parking a mess	More hot dog stands	Put in bigger seats	My company will buy a
Add a skybox	Seats are all metal	Friendly ushers	skybox—build it!
Get better cheerleaders	Need skyboxes	Need better seats	Programs overpriced
Double the parking attendants	Seats stink	Expand parking lots	Want softer seats
Everything is okay	Go SWU!	Hate the bleacher seats	Beat those Longhorns!
Too crowded	Lines are awful	Hot dogs cold	I'll pay for a skybox
Seats too narrow	Seats are uncomfortable	$3 for a coffee? No way!	Seats too small
Great food	I will pay more for better view	Get some skyboxes	Band was terrific
Joe P. for President!	Get a new stadium	Love the new uniforms	Love Pitterno
I smelled drugs being smoked	Student dress code needed	Took an hour to park	Everything is great
Stadium is ancient	I want cushioned seats	Coach is terrific	Build new stadium
Seats are like rocks	Not enough police	More water fountains	Move games to Dallas
Not enough cops for traffic	Students too rowdy	Better seats	No complaints
Game starts too late	Parking terrible	Seats not comfy	Dirty bathroom
Hire more traffic cops	Toilets weren't clean	Bigger parking lot	
Need new band	Not enough handicap spots in lot	I'm too old for bench seats	
Great!	Well done, SWU	Cold coffee served at game	

► **The Culture of Quality at Arnold Palmer Hospital**   **Video Case**

Founded in 1989, Arnold Palmer Hospital is one of the largest hospitals for women and children in the U.S., with 431 beds in two facilities totaling 676,000 square feet. Located in downtown Orlando, Florida, and named after its famed golf benefactor, the hospital, with more than 2,000 employees, serves an 18-county area in central Florida and is the only Level 1 trauma center for children in that region. Arnold Palmer Hospital provides a broad range of medical services including neonatal and pediatric intensive care, pediatric oncology and cardiology, care for high-risk pregnancies, and maternal intensive care.

The Issue of Assessing Quality Health Care

Quality health care is a goal all hospitals profess, but Arnold Palmer Hospital has actually developed comprehensive and scientific means of asking customers to judge the quality of care they receive. Participating in a national benchmark comparison against other hospitals, Arnold Palmer Hospital consistently scores in the top 10% in overall patient satisfaction. Executive Director Kathy Swanson states, "Hospitals in this area will be distinguished largely on the basis of their customer satisfaction. We must have accurate information about how our patients and their families judge the quality of our care, so I follow the questionnaire results daily. The in-depth survey helps me and others on my team to gain quick knowledge from patient feedback." Arnold Palmer Hospital employees are empowered to provide gifts in value up to $200 to patients who find reason to complain about any hospital service such as food, courtesy, responsiveness, or cleanliness.

Swanson doesn't focus just on the customer surveys, which are mailed to patients one week after discharge, but also on a variety of internal measures. These measures usually start at the grassroots level, where the staff sees a problem and develops ways to track performance. The hospital's longstanding philosophy supports the concept that each patient is important and respected as a person. That patient has the right to comprehensive, compassionate family-centered health care provided by a knowledgeable physician-directed team.

Some of the measures Swanson carefully monitors for continuous improvement are morbidity, infection rates, readmission rates, costs per case, and length of stays. The tools she uses daily include Pareto charts, flowcharts, and process charts, in addition to benchmarking against hospitals both nationally and in the southeast region.

The result of all of these efforts has been a quality culture as manifested in Arnold Palmer's high ranking in patient satisfaction and one of the highest survival rates of critically ill babies.

Discussion Questions*

1. Why is it important for Arnold Palmer Hospital to get a patient's assessment of health care quality? Does the patient have the expertise to judge the health care she receives?
2. How would you build a culture of quality in an organization, such as Arnold Palmer Hospital?
3. What techniques does Arnold Palmer Hospital practice in its drive for quality and continuous improvement?
4. Develop a fish-bone diagram illustrating the quality variables for a patient who just gave birth at Arnold Palmer Hospital (or any other hospital).

*You may wish to view the video that accompanies this case before answering these questions.

▶ Quality at the Ritz-Carlton Hotel Company

Video Case

Ritz-Carlton. The name alone evokes images of luxury and quality. As the first hotel company to win the Malcolm Baldrige National Quality Award, the Ritz treats quality as if it is the heartbeat of the company. This means a daily commitment to meeting customer expectations and making sure that each hotel is free of any deficiency.

In the hotel industry, quality can be hard to quantify. Guests do not purchase a product when they stay at the Ritz: They buy an experience. Thus, creating the right combination of elements to make the experience stand out is the challenge and goal of every employee, from maintenance to management.

Before applying for the Baldrige Award, company management undertook a rigorous self-examination of its operations in an attempt to measure and quantify quality. Nineteen processes were studied, including room service delivery, guest reservation and registration, message delivery, and breakfast service. This period of self-study included statistical measurement of process work flows and cycle times for areas ranging from room service delivery times and reservations to valet parking and housekeeping efficiency. The results were used to develop performance benchmarks against which future activity could be measured.

With specific, quantifiable targets in place, Ritz-Carlton managers and employees now focus on continuous improvement. The goal is 100% customer satisfaction: If a guest's experience does not meet expectations, the Ritz-Carlton risks losing that guest to competition.

One way the company has put more meaning behind its quality efforts is to organize its employees into "self-directed" work teams.

Employee teams determine work scheduling, what work needs to be done, and what to do about quality problems in their own areas. In order that they can see the relationship of their specific area to the overall goals, employees are also given the opportunity to take additional training in hotel operations. Ritz-Carlton believes that a more educated and informed employee is in a better position to make decisions in the best interest of the organization.

Discussion Questions*

1. In what ways could the Ritz-Carlton monitor its success in achieving quality?
2. Many companies say that their goal is to provide quality products or services. What actions might you expect from a company that intends quality to be more than a slogan or buzzword?
3. Why might it cost the Ritz-Carlton less to "do things right" the first time?
4. How could control charts, Pareto diagrams, and cause-and-effect diagrams be used to identify quality problems at a hotel?
5. What are some nonfinancial measures of customer satisfaction that might be used by the Ritz-Carlton?

Source: Adapted from C. T. Horngren, S. M. Datar, and G. Foster, *Cost Accounting*, 13th ed. (Upper Saddle River, NJ: Prentice Hall, 2009).

*You may wish to view the video that accompanies this case before addressing these questions.

Active Model Exercise

ACTIVE MODEL 6.1 is a simulation exercise that evaluates changes in Example 1 in your text. It is illustrated at **www.myomlab.com** or **www.pearsonhighered.com/heizer.**

Main Heading	Review Material	
QUALITY AND STRATEGY (p. 156)	Managing quality helps build successful strategies of differentiation, low cost, and *response*. Two ways that quality improves profitability are: <ul><li>*Sales gains* via improved response, price flexibility, increased market share, and/or improved reputation</li><li>*Reduced costs* via increased productivity, lower rework and scrap costs, and/or lower warranty costs</li></ul>	**VIDEO 6.1** The Culture and Quality at Arnold Palmer Hospital
DEFINING QUALITY (pp. 156–159)	An operations manager's objective is to build a total quality management system that identifies and satisfies customer needs. ■ **Quality**—The ability of a product or service to meet customer needs. The American Society for Quality (ASQ) defines quality as "the totality of features and characteristics of a product or service that bears on its ability to satisfy stated or implied needs." The two most well-known quality awards are: <ul><li>*U.S.*: Malcolm Baldrige National Quality Award, named after a former secretary of commerce</li><li>*Japan*: Deming Prize, named after an American, Dr. W. Edwards Deming</li></ul> ■ **Cost of quality (COQ)**—The cost of doing things wrong; that is, the price of non-conformance. The four major categories of costs associated with quality are: *Prevention costs, Appraisal costs, Internal failure,* and *External costs*. Four leaders in the field of quality management are W. Edwards Deming, Joseph M. Juran, Armand Feigenbaum, and Philip B. Crosby.	
INTERNATIONAL QUALITY STANDARDS (pp. 159–160)	■ **ISO 9000**—A set of quality standards developed by the International Organization for Standardization (ISO). ISO 9000 is the only quality standard with international recognition. To do business globally, being listed in the ISO directory is critical. ■ **ISO 14000**—A series of environmental management standards established by the ISO. ISO 14000 contains five core elements: (1) environmental management, (2) auditing, (3) performance evaluation, (4) labeling, and (5) life cycle assessment. As a follow-on to ISO 14000, ISO 24700 reflects the business world's current approach to reuse recovered components from many products.	
TOTAL QUALITY MANAGEMENT (TQM) (pp. 160–166)	■ **Total quality management (TQM)**—Management of an entire organization so that it excels in all aspects of products and services that are important to the customer. Seven concepts for an effective TQM program are (1) continuous improvement, (2) Six Sigma, (3) employee empowerment, (4) benchmarking, (5) just-in-time (JIT), (6) Taguchi concepts, and (7) knowledge of TQM tools. ■ **PDCA**—A continuous improvement model that involves four stages: plan, do, check, and act. The Japanese use the word *kaizen* to describe the ongoing process of unending improvement—the setting and achieving of ever-higher goals. ■ **Six Sigma**—A program to save time, improve quality, and lower costs. In a statistical sense, Six Sigma describes a process, product, or service with an extremely high capability—99.9997% accuracy, or 3.4 defects per million. ■ **Employee empowerment**—Enlarging employee jobs so that the added responsibility and authority is moved to the lowest level possible in the organization. Business literature suggests that some 85% of quality problems have to do with materials and processes, not with employee performance. ■ **Quality circle**—A group of employees meeting regularly with a facilitator to solve work-related problems in their work area. ■ **Benchmarking**—Selecting a demonstrated standard of performance that represents the very best performance for a process or an activity. The philosophy behind just-in-time (JIT) involves continuing improvement and enforced problem solving. JIT systems are designed to produce or deliver goods just as they are needed. ■ **Quality robust**—Products that are consistently built to meet customer needs, in spite of adverse conditions in the production process.	Problems: 6.1, 6.3, 6.5, 6.13, 6.14, 6.16, and 6.17

Main Heading	Review Material	PEARSON myomlab
	■ **Quality loss function (QLF)**—A mathematical function that identifies all costs connected with poor quality and shows how these costs increase as product quality moves from what the customer wants: $L = D^2C$. ■ **Target-oriented quality**—A philosophy of continuous improvement to bring the product exactly on target.	
TOOLS OF TQM (pp. 166–170)	TQM tools that generate ideas include the *check sheet* (organized method of recording data), *scatter diagram* (graph of the value of one variable vs. another variable), and *cause-and-effect diagram*. Tools for organizing the data are the *Pareto chart* and *flowchart*. Tools for identifying problems are the *histogram* (distribution showing the frequency of occurrences of a variable) and *statistical process control chart*. ■ **Cause-and-effect diagram**—A schematic technique used to discover possible locations of quality problems. (Also called an Ishikawa diagram or a fish-bone chart.) The 4 *Ms* (material, machinery/equipment, manpower, and methods) may be broad "causes." ■ **Pareto chart**—A graphic that identifies the few critical items as opposed to many less important ones. ■ **Flowchart**—A block diagram that graphically describes a process or system. ■ **Statistical process control (SPC)**—A process used to monitor standards, make measurements, and take corrective action as a product or service is being produced. ■ **Control chart**—A graphic presentation of process data over time, with predetermined control limits.	**ACTIVE MODEL 6.1**
THE ROLE OF INSPECTION (pp. 170–172)	■ **Inspection**—A means of ensuring that an operation is producing at the quality level expected. ■ **Source inspection**—Controlling or monitoring at the point of production or purchase: at the source. ■ **Poka-yoke**—Literally translated, "foolproof"; it has come to mean a device or technique that ensures the production of a good unit every time. ■ **Attribute inspection**—An inspection that classifies items as being either good or defective. ■ **Variable inspection**—Classifications of inspected items as falling on a continuum scale, such as dimension, size, or strength.	
TQM IN SERVICES (pp. 172–174)	Determinants of service quality: reliability, responsiveness, competence, access, courtesy, communication, credibility, security, understanding/knowing the customer, and tangibles. ■ **Service recovery**—Training and empowering frontline workers to solve a problem immediately.	**VIDEO 6.2** TQM at Ritz-Carlton Hotels

Self Test

■ **Before taking the self-test,** refer to the learning objectives listed at the beginning of the chapter and the key terms listed at the end of the chapter.

LO1. In this chapter, *quality* is defined as:
  a) the degree of excellence at an acceptable price and the control of variability at an acceptable cost.
  b) how well a product fits patterns of consumer preferences.
  c) the totality of features and characteristics of a product or service that bears on its ability to satisfy stated or implied needs.
  d) being impossible to define, but you know what it is.

LO2. ISO 14000 is an international standard that addresses _____.

LO3. If 1 million passengers pass through the Jacksonville Airport with checked baggage each year, a successful Six Sigma program for baggage handling would result in how many passengers with misplaced luggage?
  a) 3.4   b) 6.0
  c) 34   d) 2,700
  e) 6 times the monthly standard deviation of passengers

LO4. The process of identifying other organizations that are best at some facet of your operations and then modeling your organization after them is known as:
  a) continuous improvement.   b) employee empowerment.
  c) benchmarking.   d) copycatting.
  e) patent infringement.

LO5. The Taguchi method includes all except which of the following major concepts?
  a) Employee involvement
  b) Remove the effects of adverse conditions
  c) Quality loss function
  d) Target specifications

LO6. The seven tools of total quality management are _____, _____, _____, _____, _____, _____, and _____.

Answers: LO1. c; **LO2.** environmental management; **LO3.** a; **LO4.** c; **LO5.** a; **LO6.** check sheets, scatter diagrams, cause-and-effect diagrams, Pareto charts, flowcharts, histograms, SPC charts.

Statistical Process Control

Supplement Outline

Statistical Process Control (SPC)

Process Capability

Acceptance Sampling

Discussion Questions

Problems

Case Studies: Bayfield Mud Company;
*   Frito-Lay's Quality-Controlled Potato*
*   Chips; Farm to Fork: Quality at Darden*
*   Restaurants*

Active Model Exercises

Classroom Activity

Rapid Review

Statistical process control (SPC) is a major tool of quality control. We use SPC to measure performance of a process. Control charts for SPC help operations managers distinguish between natural and assignable variations. A process is said to be operating in statistical control when the only source of variation is common (natural) causes. The $\bar{x}$-chart and the R-chart are used for variable sampling, and the p-chart and the c-chart for attribute sampling. The C_{pk} index is a way to express process capability. Operating characteristic (OC) curves facilitate acceptance sampling and provide the manager with tools to evaluate the quality of a production run or shipment.

BEFORE COMING TO CLASS, READ SUPPLEMENT 6 IN YOUR TEXT AND ANSWER THESE QUESTIONS.

1. Explain why control charts are used. _____
   _____

2. What is the central limit theorem? _____
   _____

3. Explain the use of $\bar{x}$- and R-charts. _____
   _____

4. List the 5 steps involved in building control charts. _____
   _____

5. When are p- or c-charts used? _____
   _____

6. Explain what C_p and C_{pk} mean. _____
   _____

7. What is acceptance sampling? _____
   _____

8. Explain how AOQ is used. _____
   _____

STATISTICAL PROCESS CONTROL (SPC) (See Flexible Version pp. 178–191)

Natural Variations

Assignable Variations

Samples

Control Charts

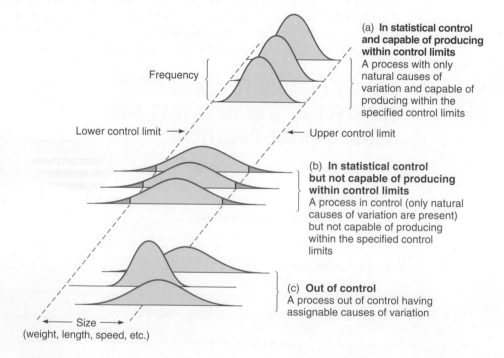

Frequency

Lower control limit →

← Upper control limit

Size →
(weight, length, speed, etc.)

(a) **In statistical control and capable of producing within control limits**
A process with only natural causes of variation and capable of producing within the specified control limits

(b) **In statistical control but not capable of producing within control limits**
A process in control (only natural causes of variation are present) but not capable of producing within the specified control limits

(c) **Out of control**
A process out of control having assignable causes of variation

◀ **FIGURE S6.2**
Process Control: Three Types of Process Outputs

Central Limit Theorem (See Flexible Version pp. 180–181)

$$\bar{\bar{x}} = \mu \qquad \text{Population mean} \qquad\qquad (S6\text{-}1)$$

$$\sigma_{\bar{x}} = \frac{\sigma}{\sqrt{n}} \qquad \text{Standard deviation of the sampling distribution} \qquad (S6\text{-}2)$$

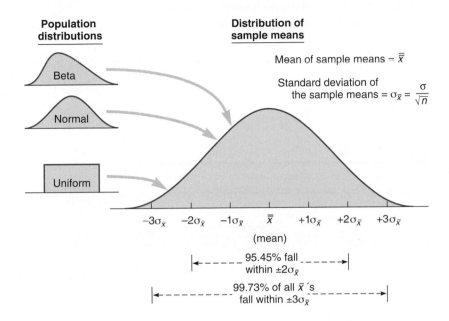

Population distributions

Beta

Normal

Uniform

Distribution of sample means

Mean of sample means = $\bar{\bar{x}}$

Standard deviation of the sample means = $\sigma_{\bar{x}} = \dfrac{\sigma}{\sqrt{n}}$

$-3\sigma_x \quad -2\sigma_{\bar{x}} \quad -1\sigma_{\bar{x}} \quad \bar{\bar{x}} \quad +1\sigma_{\bar{x}} \quad +2\sigma_{\bar{x}} \quad +3\sigma_{\bar{x}}$

(mean)

95.45% fall within $\pm 2\sigma_{\bar{x}}$

99.73% of all $\bar{x}$'s fall within $\pm 3\sigma_{\bar{x}}$

◀ **FIGURE S6.3**
The Relationship between Population and Sampling Distributions
Even though the population distributions will differ (e.g., normal, beta, uniform), each with its own mean (μ) and standard deviation (σ), the distribution of sample means always approaches a normal distribution.

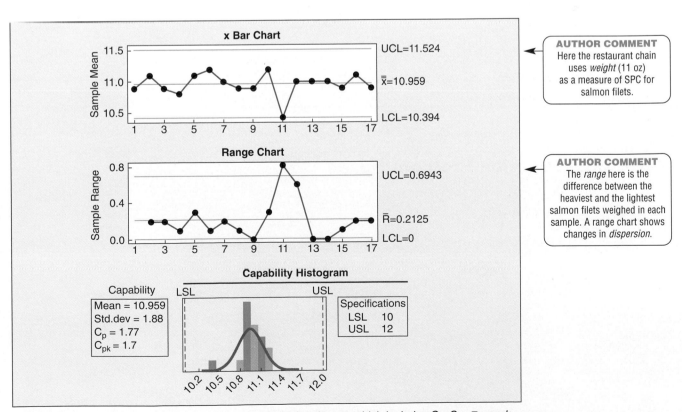

x Bar Chart

Sample Mean

11.5

11.0

10.5

1 3 5 7 9 11 13 15 17

UCL=11.524

$\bar{\bar{x}}$=10.959

LCL=10.394

AUTHOR COMMENT
Here the restaurant chain uses *weight* (11 oz) as a measure of SPC for salmon filets.

Range Chart

Sample Range

0.8

0.4

0.0

1 3 5 7 9 11 13 15 17

UCL=0.6943

$\bar{R}$=0.2125

LCL=0

AUTHOR COMMENT
The *range* here is the difference between the heaviest and the lightest salmon filets weighed in each sample. A range chart shows changes in *dispersion*.

Capability Histogram

Capability

Mean = 10.959
Std.dev = 1.88
C_p = 1.77
C_{pk} = 1.7

LSL   USL

Specifications
LSL   10
USL   12

10.2 10.5 10.8 11.1 11.4 11.7 12.0

Salmon filets are monitored by Darden Restaurant's SPC software, which includes C_p, C_{pk}, $\bar{x}$-, and R-charts and a process capability histogram. The video case study "Farm to Fork," at the end of this supplement, asks you to interpret these figures.

Creating $\bar{x}$ Charts (See Flexible Version p. 181)

If we know the standard deviation of the process population, σ

$$\text{Upper control limit (UCL)} = \bar{\bar{x}} + z\sigma_{\bar{x}} \qquad \text{(S6-3)}$$

$$\text{Lower control limit (LCL)} = \bar{\bar{x}} - z\sigma_{\bar{x}} \qquad \text{(S6-4)}$$

where $\bar{\bar{x}}$ = mean of the sample means or a target value set for the process
   z = number of normal standard deviations (2 for 95.45% confidence,
        3 for 99.73%)
   $\sigma_{\bar{x}}$ = standard deviation of the sample means = $\sigma/\sqrt{n}$
   σ = population (process) standard deviation
   n = sample size

PRACTICE PROBLEM S6.1 ■ Setting $\bar{x}$ Control Limits

Twenty-five engine mounts are sampled each day and found to have an average width of 2 inches, with a standard deviation of 0.1 inches. What are the control limits that include 99.73% of the sample means ($Z = 3$)?

Additional Practice Problem Space

Using the range to set control limits

$$UCL_{\bar{x}} - \bar{\bar{x}} + A_2\bar{R} \qquad \text{(S6-5)}$$

and

$$LCL_{\bar{x}} = \bar{\bar{x}} - A_2\bar{R} \qquad \text{(S6-6)}$$

where $\bar{R}$ = average range of the samples
A_2 = value found in Table S6.1
$\bar{\bar{x}}$ = mean of the sample means

Sample Size, n	Mean Factor, A_2	Upper Range, D_4	Lower Range, D_3
2	1.880	3.268	0
3	1.023	2.574	0
4	.729	2.282	0
5	.577	2.115	0
6	.483	2.004	0
7	.419	1.924	0.076
8	.373	1.864	0.136
9	.337	1.816	0.184
10	.308	1.777	0.223
12	.266	1.716	0.284

◀ **TABLE S6.1**
Factors for Computing Control Chart Limits (3 sigma)

PRACTICE PROBLEM S6.2 ■ $\bar{x}$-Chart with Ranges and Use of Table S6.1

Several samples of size $n = 8$ have been taken from today's production of fence posts. The average post was 3 yards in length, and the average sample range was 0.015 yard. Find the 99.73% upper and lower control limits.

Additional Practice Problem Space

Creating *R*-Charts (See Flexible Version p. 185)

$$UCL_R = D_4\overline{R}$$

(S6-7)

$$LCL_R = D_3\overline{R}$$

(S6-8)

where UCL_R = upper control chart limit for the range
            LCL_R = lower control chart limit for the range
       D_4 and D_3 = values from Table S6.1

PRACTICE PROBLEM S6.3 ■ Range Chart

The average range of a process is 10 pounds. The sample size is 10. Use Table S6.1 to develop upper and lower control limits on the *range*.

Additional Practice Problem Space

Steps to Follow When Using Control Charts

1. Collect 20 to 25 samples, often of n = 4 or 5 observations each, from a stable process and compute the mean and range of each.
2. Compute the overall means, set control limits, and compute the UCL and LCL.
3. Graph the sample means and ranges and see if they fall outside the limits. If the process is not currently stable and in control, use the desired mean, μ, instead of $\overline{\overline{x}}$ to calculate limits.
4. Investigate points and patterns out of control.
5. Collect additional samples and revalidate limits if necessary.

Control Charts for Attributes (See Flexible Version pp. 186–190)

Attributes

p-Charts (See Flexible Version pp. 186–187)

$$\text{UCL}_p = \bar{p} + z\sigma_{\hat{p}} \qquad \text{(S6-9)}$$

$$\text{LCL}_p = \bar{p} - z\sigma_{\hat{p}} \qquad \text{(S6-10)}$$

where $\bar{p}$ = mean fraction defective in the sample
z = number of standard deviations ($z = 2$ for 95.45% limits; $z = 3$ for 99.73% limits)
$\sigma_{\hat{p}}$ = standard deviation of the sampling distribution

$\sigma_{\hat{p}}$ is estimated by the formula:

$$\sigma_{\hat{p}} = \sqrt{\frac{\bar{p}(1 - \bar{p})}{n}} \qquad \text{(S6-11)}$$

where n = size of *each* sample.

PRACTICE PROBLEM S6.4 ■ *p*-Chart Limits

Based on samples of 20 IRS auditors, each handling 100 files, we find that the total number of mistakes in handling files is 220. Find the 95.45% upper and lower control limits.

Additional Practice Problem Space

c-Charts   (See Flexible Version p. 189)

$$\text{Control limits} = \bar{c} \pm 3\sqrt{\bar{c}}$$

(S6-12)

PRACTICE PROBLEM S6.5 ■ *c*-Chart Limits

There have been complaints that the sports page of the *Dubuque Register* has lots of typos. The past 6 days have been examined carefully and the number of typos per page is recorded below. Is the process in control using $Z = 2$?

Day	Number of Typos
Monday	2
Tuesday	1
Wednesday	5
Thursday	3
Friday	4
Saturday	0

Additional Practice Problem Space

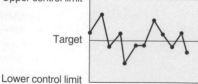

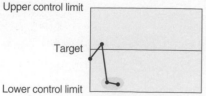

Normal behavior. Process is "in control."

Two points very near lower (or upper) control. Investigate for cause.

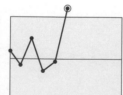

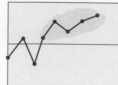

One point out above (or below). Investigate for cause. Process is "out of control."

Run of 5 points above (or below) central line. Investigate for cause.

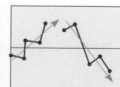

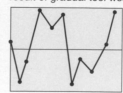

Trends in either direction, 5 points. Investigate for cause of progressive change. This could be the result of gradual tool wear.

Erratic behavior. Investigate.

◀ **FIGURE S6.7**
Patterns to Look for on Control Charts

Source: Adapted from Bertrand L. Hansen, *Quality Control: Theory and Applications* (1991): 65. Reprinted by permission of Prentice Hall, Upper Saddle River, New Jersey.

AUTHOR COMMENT
Workers in companies such as Frito-Lay are trained to follow rules like these.

PROCESS CAPABILITY (See Flexible Version pp. 191–193)

Process Capability Ratio (C_p) (See Flexible Version pp. 191–192)

$$C_p = \frac{\text{Upper specification} - \text{Lower specification}}{6\sigma} \qquad \text{(S6-13)}$$

Process Capability Index (C_pk) (See Flexible Version pp. 192–193)

$$C_{pk} = \text{minimum of} \left[\frac{\text{Upper specification limit} - \bar{X}}{3\sigma}, \frac{\bar{X} - \text{Lower specification limit}}{3\sigma} \right] \qquad \text{(S6-14)}$$

where $\bar{X}$ = process mean
σ = standard deviation of the process population

Practice Problem Space

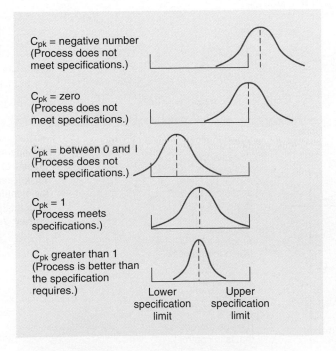

C_{pk} = negative number
(Process does not meet specifications.)

C_{pk} = zero
(Process does not meet specifications.)

C_{pk} = between 0 and 1
(Process does not meet specifications.)

C_{pk} = 1
(Process meets specifications.)

C_{pk} greater than 1
(Process is better than the specification requires.)

Lower specification limit

Upper specification limit

◀ **FIGURE S6.8**
Meanings of C_pk Measures
A C_{pk} index of 1.0 for both the upper and lower control limits indicates that the process variation is within the upper and lower control limits. As the C_{pk} index goes above 1.0, the process becomes increasingly target-oriented with fewer defects. If the C_{pk} is less than 1.0, the process will not produce within the specified tolerance. Because a process may not be centered, or may "drift," a C_{pk} above 1 is desired.

ACCEPTANCE SAMPLING (See Flexible Version pp. 193–196)

Operating Characteristic (OC) Curve

(See Flexible Version pp. 194–195)

Producer's Risk

Consumer's Risk

Acceptable Quality Level (AQL)

Lot Tolerance Percent Defective (LTPD)

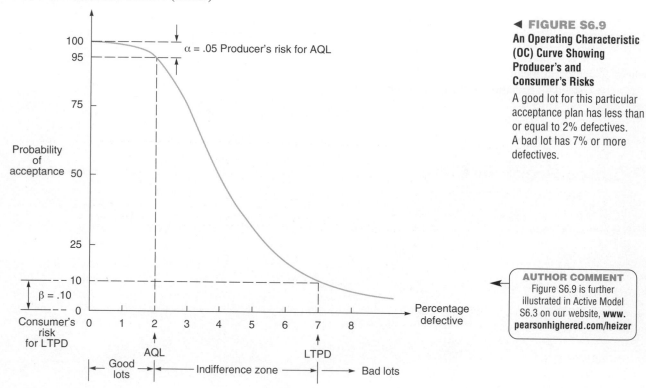

◀ **FIGURE S6.9**
An Operating Characteristic (OC) Curve Showing Producer's and Consumer's Risks

A good lot for this particular acceptance plan has less than or equal to 2% defectives. A bad lot has 7% or more defectives.

AUTHOR COMMENT
Figure S6.9 is further illustrated in Active Model S6.3 on our website, **www. pearsonhighered.com/heizer**

Average Outgoing Quality (AOQ) (See Flexible Version pp. 195–196)

$$AOQ = \frac{(P_d)(P_a)(N - n)}{N}$$

(S6-15)

where P_d = true percent defective of the lot
         P_a = probability of accepting the lot
         N = number of items in the lot
         n = number of items in the sample

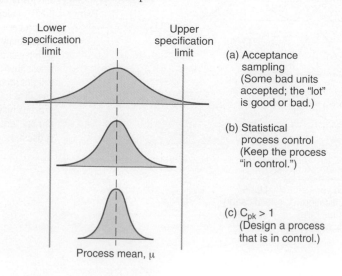

◀ **FIGURE S6.10**
The Application of Statistical Process Techniques Contributes to the Identification and Systematic Reduction of Process Variability

Discussion Questions

1. List Shewhart's two types of variation. What are they also called?
2. Define "in statistical control."
3. Explain briefly what an $\bar{x}$-chart and an R-chart do.
4. What might cause a process to be out of control?
5. List five steps in developing and using $\bar{x}$-charts and R-charts.
6. List some possible causes of assignable variation.
7. Explain how a person using 2-sigma control charts will more easily find samples "out of bounds" than 3-sigma control charts. What are some possible consequences of this fact?
8. When is the desired mean, μ, used in establishing the centerline of a control chart instead of $\bar{x}$?
9. Can a production process be labeled as "out of control" because it is too good? Explain.
10. In a control chart, what would be the effect on the control limits if the sample size varied from one sample to the next?
11. Define C_{pk} and explain what a C_{pk} of 1.0 means. What is C_p?
12. What does a run of 5 points above or below the centerline in a control chart imply?
13. What are the acceptable quality level (AQL) and the lot tolerance percentage defective (LTPD)? How are they used?
14. What is a run test and when is it used?
15. Discuss the managerial issues regarding the use of control charts.
16. What is an OC curve?
17. What is the purpose of acceptance sampling?
18. What two risks are present when acceptance sampling is used?
19. Is a *capable* process a *perfect* process? That is, does a capable process generate only output that meets specifications? Explain.

Problems*

• **S6.1** Boxes of Organic Flakes are produced to contain 14 ounces, with a standard deviation of .1 ounce. Set up the 3-sigma $\bar{x}$-chart for a sample size of 36 boxes. **Px**

• **S6.2** The overall average on a process you are attempting to monitor is 50 units. The process standard deviation is 1.72. Determine the upper and lower control limits for a mean chart, if you choose to use a sample size of 5.
a) Set $z = 3$.
b) Now set $z = 2$. How do the control limits change? **Px**

• **S6.3** Thirty-five samples of size 7 each were taken from a fertilizer-bag-filling machine. The results were: Overall mean = 57.75 lb; Average range = 1.78 lb.
a) Determine the upper and lower control limits of the $\bar{x}$-chart, where $\sigma = 3$.
b) Determine the upper and lower control limits of the R-chart, where $\sigma = 3$. **Px**

• **S6.4** Pioneer Chicken advertises "lite" chicken with 30% fewer calories than standard chicken. When the process for "lite" chicken breast production is in control, the average chicken breast contains 420 calories, and the standard deviation in caloric content of the chicken breast population is 25 calories.

Pioneer wants to design an $\bar{x}$-chart to monitor the caloric content of chicken breasts, where 25 chicken breasts would be chosen at random to form each sample.
a) What are the lower and upper control limits for this chart if these limits are chosen to be *four* standard deviations from the target?
b) What are the limits with three standard deviations from the target? **Px**

• **S6.5** Cordelia Barrera is attempting to monitor a filling process that has an overall average of 705 cc. The average range is 6 cc. If you use a sample size of 10, what are the upper and lower control limits for the mean and range? **Px**

Note: **Px** means the problem may be solved with POM for Windows and/or Excel OM/Excel.

•• **S6.6** Sampling 4 pieces of precision-cut wire (to be used in computer assembly) every hour for the past 24 hours has produced the following results:

Hour	$\bar{x}$	R	Hour	$\bar{x}$	R
1	3.25"	.71"	13	3.11"	.85"
2	3.10	1.18	14	2.83	1.31
3	3.22	1.43	15	3.12	1.06
4	3.39	1.26	16	2.84	.50
5	3.07	1.17	17	2.86	1.43
6	2.86	.32	18	2.74	1.29
7	3.05	.53	19	3.41	1.61
8	2.65	1.13	20	2.89	1.09
9	3.02	.71	21	2.65	1.08
10	2.85	1.33	22	3.28	.46
11	2.83	1.17	23	2.94	1.58
12	2.97	.40	24	2.64	.97

Develop appropriate control charts and determine whether there is any cause for concern in the cutting process. Plot the information and look for patterns. **Px**

•• **S6.7** Auto pistons at Yongpin Zhou's plant in Shanghai are produced in a forging process, and the diameter is a critical factor that must be controlled. From sample sizes of 10 pistons produced each day, the mean and the range of this diameter have been as follows:

Day	Mean (mm)	Range (mm)
1	156.9	4.2
2	153.2	4.6
3	153.6	4.1
4	155.5	5.0
5	156.6	4.5

a. What is the value of $\bar{\bar{x}}$?
b. What is the value of $\bar{R}$?
c. What are the $UCL_{\bar{x}}$ and $LCL_{\bar{x}}$ using 3σ?

d. What are the UCL_R and LCL_R using 3σ?

e. If the true diameter mean should be 155 mm and you want this as your center (nominal) line, what are the new $UCL_{\bar{x}}$ and $LCL_{\bar{x}}$? **Px**

•• **S6.8** Bill Kime's bowling ball factory makes bowling balls of adult size and weight only. The standard deviation in the weight of a bowling ball produced at the factory is known to be 0.12 pounds. Each day for 24 days, the average weight, in pounds, of nine of the bowling balls produced that day has been assessed as follows:

Day	Average (lb)	Day	Average (lb)
1	16.3	13	16.3
2	15.9	14	15.9
3	15.8	15	16.3
4	15.5	16	16.2
5	16.3	17	16.1
6	16.2	18	15.9
7	16.0	19	16.2
8	16.1	20	15.9
9	15.9	21	15.9
10	16.2	22	16.0
11	15.9	23	15.5
12	15.9	24	15.8

a) Establish a control chart for monitoring the average weights of the bowling balls in which the upper and lower control limits are each two standard deviations from the mean. What are the values of the control limits?

b) If three standard deviations are used in the chart, how do these values change? Why? **Px**

•• **S6.9** Whole Grains LLC uses statistical process control to ensure that its health-conscious, low-fat, multigrain sandwich loaves have the proper weight. Based on a previously stable and in-control process, the control limits of the $\bar{x}$- and R-charts are: $UCL_{\bar{x}} = 6.56$. $LCL_{\bar{x}} = 5.84$, $UCL_R = 1.141$, $LCL_R = 0$. Over the past few days, they have taken five random samples of four loaves each and have found the following:

| | Net Weight | | | |
Sample	Loaf #1	Loaf #2	Loaf #3	Loaf #4
1	6.3	6.0	5.9	5.9
2	6.0	6.0	6.3	5.9
3	6.3	4.8	5.6	5.2
4	6.2	6.0	6.2	5.9
5	6.5	6.6	6.5	6.9

Is the process still in control? Explain why or why not. **Px**

••• **S6.10** A process that is considered to be in control measures an ingredient in ounces. Below are the last 10 samples (each of size $n = 5$) taken. The population standard deviation is 1.36.

| | | | | Samples | | | | | |
1	2	3	4	5	6	7	8	9	10
10	9	13	10	12	10	10	13	8	10
9	9	9	10	10	10	11	10	8	12
10	11	10	11	9	8	10	8	12	9
9	11	10	10	11	12	8	10	12	8
12	10	9	10	10	9	9	8	9	12

a) What is the process standard deviation σ? What is $\sigma_{\bar{x}}$?

b) If $z = 3$, what are the control limits for the mean chart?

c) What are the control limits for the range chart?

d) Is the process in control? **Px**

••• **S6.11** Twelve samples, each containing five parts, were taken from a process that produces steel rods. The length of each rod in the samples was determined. The results were tabulated and sample means and ranges were computed. The results were:

Sample	Sample Mean (in.)	Range (in.)
1	10.002	0.011
2	10.002	0.014
3	9.991	0.007
4	10.006	0.022
5	9.997	0.013
6	9.999	0.012
7	10.001	0.008
8	10.005	0.013
9	9.995	0.004
10	10.001	0.011
11	10.001	0.014
12	10.006	0.009

a) Determine the upper and lower control limits and the overall means for $\bar{x}$-charts and R-charts.

b) Draw the charts and plot the values of the sample means and ranges.

c) Do the data indicate a process that is in control?

d) Why or why not? **Px**

•• **S6.12** Eagletrons are all-electric automobiles produced by Mogul Motors, Inc. One of the concerns of Mogul Motors is that the Eagletrons be capable of achieving appropriate maximum speeds. To monitor this, Mogul executives take samples of eight Eagletrons at a time. For each sample, they determine the average maximum speed and the range of the maximum speeds within the sample. They repeat this with 35 samples to obtain 35 sample means and 35 ranges. They find that the average sample mean is 88.50 miles per hour, and the average range is 3.25 miles per hour. Using these results, the executives decide to establish an R chart. They would like this chart to be established so that when it shows that the range of a sample is not within the control limits, there is only approximately a 0.0027 probability that this is due to natural variation. What will be the upper control limit (UCL) and the lower control limit (LCL) in this chart? **Px**

•• **S6.13** The defect rate for data entry of insurance claims has historically been about 1.5%.

a) What are the upper and lower control chart limits if you wish to use a sample size of 100 and 3-sigma limits?

b) What if the sample size used were 50, with 3σ?

c) What if the sample size used were 100, with 2σ?

d) What if the sample size used were 50, with 2σ?

e) What happens to $\sigma_{\hat{p}}$ when the sample size is larger?

f) Explain why the lower control limit cannot be less than 0. **Px**

•• **S6.14** You are attempting to develop a quality monitoring system for some parts purchased from Charles Sox Manufacturing Co. These parts are either good or defective. You have decided to take a sample of 100 units. Develop a table of the appropriate upper and lower control chart limits for various values of the average fraction defective in the samples taken. The values for $\bar{p}$ in this table should range from 0.02 to 0.10 in increments of 0.02. Develop the upper and lower control limits for a 99.73% confidence level.

	n = 100	
$\bar{p}$	UCL	LCL
0.02		
0.04		
0.06		
0.08		
0.10		

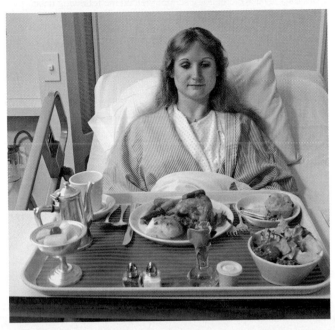

•• **S6.15** The results of inspection of DNA samples taken over the past 10 days are given below. Sample size is 100.

Day	1	2	3	4	5	6	7	8	9	10
Defectives	7	6	9	9	5	6	0	8	9	1

a) Construct a 3-sigma p-chart using this information.
b) If the number of defectives on the next three days are 12, 5, and 13, is the process in control?

• **S6.16** In the past, the defective rate for your product has been 1.5%. What are the upper and lower control chart limits if you wish to use a sample size of 500 and $z = 3$?

• **S6.17** Refer to Problem S6.16. If the defective rate was 3.5% instead of 1.5%, what would be the control limits ($z = 3$)?

•• **S6.18** Five data entry operators work at the data processing department of the Georgia Bank. Each day for 30 days, the number of defective records in a sample of 250 records typed by these operators has been noted, as follows:

Sample No.	No. Defective	Sample No.	No. Defective	Sample No.	No. Defective
1	7	11	18	21	17
2	5	12	5	22	12
3	19	13	16	23	6
4	10	14	4	24	7
5	11	15	11	25	13
6	8	16	8	26	10
7	12	17	12	27	4
8	9	18	4	28	6
9	6	19	6	29	12
10	13	20	16	30	3

a) Establish 3σ upper and lower control limits.
b) Why can the lower control limit not be a negative number?
c) The industry standards for the upper and lower control limits are 0.10 and 0.01, respectively. What does this imply about Georgia Bank's own standards?

•• **S6.19** Detroit Central Hospital is trying to improve its image by providing a positive experience for its patients and their relatives. Part of the "image" program involves providing tasty, inviting patient meals that are also healthful. A questionnaire accompanies each meal served, asking the patient, among other things, whether he or she is satisfied or unsatisfied with the meal. A 100-patient sample of the survey results over the past 7 days yielded the following data:

Day	No. of Unsatisfied Patients	Sample Size
1	24	100
2	22	100
3	8	100
4	15	100
5	10	100
6	26	100
7	17	100

Construct a p-chart that plots the percentage of patients unsatisfied with their meals. Set the control limits to include 99.73% of the random variation in meal satisfaction. Comment on your results.

•• **S6.20** Chicago Supply Company manufactures paper clips and other office products. Although inexpensive, paper clips have provided the firm with a high margin of profitability. Sample size is 200. Results are given for the last 10 samples.

Sample	1	2	3	4	5	6	7	8	9	10
Defectives	5	7	4	4	6	3	5	6	2	8

a) Establish upper and lower control limits for the control chart and graph the data.
b) Is the process in control?
c) If the sample size were 100 instead, how would your limits and conclusions change?

• **S6.21** Peter Ittig's department store, Ittig Brothers, is Amherst's largest independent clothier. The store receives an average of six returns per day. Using $z = 3$, would nine returns in a day warrant action?

•• **S6.22** An ad agency tracks the complaints, by week received, about the billboards in its city:

Week	No. of Complaints
1	4
2	5
3	4
4	11
5	3
6	9

a. What type of control chart would you use to monitor this process and why?
b. What are the 3-sigma control limits for this process? Assume that the historical complaint rate is unknown.
c. Is the process mean in control, according to the control limits? Why or why not?
d. Assume now that the historical complaint rate has been four calls a week. What would the 3-sigma control limits for this process be now? Is the process in control according to the control limits?

•• **S6.23** The school board is trying to evaluate a new math program introduced to second-graders in five elementary schools across the county this year. A sample of the student scores on standardized math tests in each elementary school yielded the following data:

School	No. of Test Errors
A	52
B	27
C	35
D	44
E	55

Construct a c-chart for test errors, and set the control limits to contain 99.73% of the random variation in test scores. What does the chart tell you? Has the new math program been effective? **Px**

•• **S6.24** Telephone inquiries of 100 IRS "customers" are monitored daily at random. Incidents of incorrect information or other nonconformities (such as impoliteness to customers) are recorded. The data for last week follow:

Day	No. of Nonconformities
1	5
2	10
3	23
4	20
5	15

a) Construct a 3-standard deviation c-chart of nonconformities.
b) What does the control chart tell you about the IRS telephone operators? **Px**

••• **S6.25** The accounts receivable department at Rick Wing Manufacturing has been having difficulty getting customers to pay the full amount of their bills. Many customers complain that the bills are not correct and do not reflect the materials that arrived at their receiving docks. The department has decided to implement SPC in its billing process. To set up control charts, 10 samples of 50 bills each were taken over a month's time and the items on the bills checked against the bill of lading sent by the company's shipping department to determine the number of bills that were not correct. The results were:

Sample No.	No. of Incorrect Bills	Sample No.	No. of Incorrect Bills
1	6	6	5
2	5	7	3
3	11	8	4
4	4	9	7
5	0	10	2

a) Determine the value of p-bar, the mean fraction defective. Then determine the control limits for the p-chart using a 99.73% confidence level (3 standard deviations). Is this process in control? If not, which sample(s) were out of control?
b) How might you use the quality tools discussed in Chapter 6 to determine the source of the billing defects and where you might start your improvement efforts to eliminate the causes? **Px**

• **S6.26** The difference between the upper specification and the lower specification for a process is 0.6". The standard deviation is 0.1". What is the process capability ratio, C_p? Interpret this number. **Px**

•• **S6.27** Meena Chavan Corp.'s computer chip production process yields DRAM chips with an average life of 1,800 hours and

$\sigma = 100$ hours. The tolerance upper and lower specification limits are 2,400 hours and 1,600 hours, respectively. Is this process capable of producing DRAM chips to specification? **Px**

•• **S6.28** Blackburn, Inc., an equipment manufacturer in Nashville, has submitted a sample cutoff valve to improve your manufacturing process. Your process engineering department has conducted experiments and found that the valve has a mean (μ) of 8.00 and a standard deviation (σ) of .04. Your desired performance is $\mu = 8.0$ and $\sigma = .045$. What is the C_{pk} of the Blackburn valve? **Px**

•• **S6.29** The specifications for a plastic liner for concrete highway projects calls for a thickness of 3.0 mm $\pm .1$ mm. The standard deviation of the process is estimated to be .02 mm. What are the upper and lower specification limits for this product? The process is known to operate at a mean thickness of 3.0 mm. What is the C_{pk} for this process? About what percentage of all units of this liner will meet specifications? **Px**

•• **S6.30** The manager of a food processing plant desires a quality specification with a mean of 16 ounces, an upper specification limit of 16.5, and a lower specification limit of 15.5. The process has a mean of 16 ounces and a standard deviation of 1 ounce. Determine the C_{pk} of the process. **Px**

•• **S6.31** A process filling small bottles with baby formula has a target of 3 ounces ± 0.150 ounce. Two hundred bottles from the process were sampled. The results showed the average amount of formula placed in the bottles to be 3.042 ounces. The standard deviation of the amounts was 0.034 ounce. Determine the value of C_{pk}. Roughly what proportion of bottles meet the specifications? **Px**

••• **S6.32** As the supervisor in charge of shipping and receiving, you need to determine *the average outgoing quality* in a plant where the known incoming lots from your assembly line have an average defective rate of 3%. Your plan is to sample 80 units of every 1,000 in a lot. The number of defects in the sample is not to exceed 3. Such a plan provides you with a probability of acceptance of each lot of .79 (79%). What is your average outgoing quality? **Px**

••• **S6.33** An acceptance sampling plan has lots of 500 pieces and a sample size of 60. The number of defects in the sample may not exceed 2. This plan, based on an OC curve, has a probability of .57 of accepting lots when the incoming lots have a defective rate of 4%, which is the historical average for this process. What do you tell your customer the average outgoing quality is? **Px**

••• **S6.34** West Battery Corp. has recently been receiving complaints from retailers that its 9-volt batteries are not lasting as long as other name brands. James West, head of the TQM program at West's Austin plant, believes there is no problem because his batteries have had an average life of 50 hours, about 10% longer than competitors' models. To raise the lifetime above this level would require a new level of technology not available to West. Nevertheless, he is concerned enough to set up hourly assembly line checks. Previously, after ensuring that the process was running properly, West took size $n = 5$ samples of 9-volt batteries for each of 25 hours to establish the standards for control chart limits. Those samples are shown in the following table:

West Battery Data—Battery Lifetimes (in hours)

| Hour | Sample | | | | | $\bar{x}$ | R |
	1	2	3	4	5		
1	51	50	49	50	50	50.0	2
2	45	47	70	46	36	48.8	34
3	50	35	48	39	47	43.8	15

Hour	Sample 1	2	3	4	5	$\bar{x}$	R
4	55	70	50	30	51	51.2	40
5	49	38	64	36	47	46.8	28
6	59	62	40	54	64	55.8	24
7	36	33	49	48	56	44.4	23
8	50	67	53	43	40	50.6	27
9	44	52	46	47	44	46.6	8
10	70	45	50	47	41	50.6	29
11	57	54	62	45	36	50.8	26
12	56	54	47	42	62	52.2	20
13	40	70	58	45	44	51.4	30
14	52	58	40	52	46	49.6	18
15	57	42	52	58	59	53.6	17
16	62	49	42	33	55	48.2	29
17	40	39	49	59	48	47.0	20
18	64	50	42	57	50	52.6	22
19	58	53	52	48	50	52.2	10
20	60	50	41	41	50	48.4	19
21	52	47	48	58	40	49.0	18
22	55	40	56	49	45	49.0	16
23	47	48	50	50	48	48.6	3
24	50	50	49	51	51	50.2	2
25	51	50	51	51	62	53.0	12

With these limits established, West now takes 5 more hours of data, which are shown in the following table:

Hour	Sample 1	2	3	4	5
26	48	52	39	57	61
27	45	53	48	46	66
28	63	49	50	45	53
29	57	70	45	52	61
30	45	38	46	54	52

a. Determine means and the upper and lower control limits for $\bar{x}$ and R (using the first 25 hours only).
b. Is the manufacturing process in control?
c. Comment on the lifetimes observed. **Px**

•••• **S6.35** One of Alabama Air's top competitive priorities is on-time arrivals. Quality V.P. Mike Hanna decided to personally monitor Alabama Air's performance. Each week for the past 30 weeks, Hanna checked a random sample of 100 flight arrivals for on-time performance. The table that follows contains the number of flights that did not meet Alabama Air's definition of on time:

Sample (week)	Late Flights	Sample (week)	Late Flights
1	2	16	2
2	4	17	3
3	10	18	7
4	4	19	3
5	1	20	2
6	1	21	3
7	13	22	7
8	9	23	4
9	11	24	3
10	0	25	2
11	3	26	2
12	4	27	0
13	2	28	1
14	2	29	3
15	8	30	4

a. Using a 95% confidence level, plot the overall percentage of late flights ($\bar{p}$) and the upper and lower control limits on a control chart.
b. Assume that the airline industry's upper and lower control limits for flights that are not on time are .1000 and .0400, respectively. Draw them on your control chart.
c. Plot the percentage of late flights in each sample. Do all samples fall within Alabama Airlines's control limits? When one falls outside the control limits, what should be done?
d. What can Mike Hanna report about the quality of service? **Px**

▶ Refer to myomlab ◯ for these additional homework problems: S6.36–S6.52

Case Studies

▶ **Bayfield Mud Company**

In November 2009, John Wells, a customer service representative of Bayfield Mud Company, was summoned to the Houston warehouse of Wet-Land Drilling, Inc., to inspect three boxcars of mudtreating agents that Bayfield had shipped to the Houston firm. (Bayfield's corporate offices and its largest plant are located in Orange, Texas, which is just west of the Louisiana–Texas border.) Wet-Land had filed a complaint that the 50-pound bags of treating agents just received from Bayfield were short-weight by approximately 5%.

The short-weight bags were initially detected by one of Wet-Land's receiving clerks, who noticed that the railroad scale tickets indicated that net weights were significantly less on all three boxcars than those of identical shipments received on October 25, 2009. Bayfield's traffic department was called to determine if lighter-weight pallets were used on the shipments. (This might explain the lighter net weights.) Bayfield indicated, however, that no changes had been made in loading or palletizing procedures. Thus, Wet-Land engineers randomly checked 50 bags and discovered that the average net weight was 47.51 pounds. They noted from past shipments that the process yielded bag net weights averaging exactly 50.0 pounds, with an acceptable standard deviation σ of 1.2 pounds. Consequently, they concluded that the sample indicated a significant short-weight. (The reader may wish to verify this conclusion.)

Bayfield was then contacted, and Wells was sent to investigate the complaint. Upon arrival, Wells verified the complaint and issued a 5% credit to Wet-Land.

Wet-Land management, however, was not completely satisfied with the issuance of credit. The charts followed by their mud engineers on the drilling platforms were based on 50-pound bags of treating agents. Lighter-weight bags might result in poor chemical control during the drilling operation and thus adversely affect drilling efficiency. (Mud-treating agents are used to control the pH and other chemical properties of the core during drilling operation.) This defect could cause severe economic consequences because of the extremely high cost of oil and natural gas well-drilling operations. Consequently, special-use instructions had to accompany the delivery of these shipments to the drilling platforms. Moreover, the short-weight shipments had to be isolated in Wet-Land's warehouse, causing extra handling and poor space utilization. Thus, Wells was informed that Wet-Land might seek a new supplier of mud-treating agents if, in the future, it received bags that deviated significantly from 50 pounds.

The quality control department at Bayfield suspected that the lightweight bags might have resulted from "growing pains" at the Orange plant. Because of the earlier energy crisis, oil and natural gas exploration activity had greatly increased. In turn, this increased activity created increased demand for products produced by related industries, including drilling muds. Consequently, Bayfield had to expand from a one-shift (6:00 A.M. to 2:00 P.M.) to a two-shift (2:00 P.M. to 10:00 P.M.) operation in mid-2007, and finally to a three-shift operation (24 hours per day) in the fall of 2009.

The additional night-shift bagging crew was staffed entirely by new employees. The most experienced foremen were temporarily assigned to supervise the night-shift employees. Most emphasis was placed on increasing the output of bags to meet ever-increasing demand. It was suspected that only occasional reminders were made to double-check the bag weight-feeder. (A double-check is performed by systematically weighing a bag on a scale to determine if the proper weight is being loaded by the weight-feeder. If there is significant deviation from

Time	Average Weight (pounds)	Range		Time	Average Weight (pounds)	Range	
		Smallest	Largest			Smallest	Largest
6:00 A.M.	49.6	48.7	50.7	6:00	46.8	41.0	51.2
7:00	50.2	49.1	51.2	7:00	50.0	46.2	51.7
8:00	50.6	49.6	51.4	8:00	47.4	44.0	48.7
9:00	50.8	50.2	51.8	9:00	47.0	44.2	48.9
10:00	49.9	49.2	52.3	10:00	47.2	46.6	50.2
11:00	50.3	48.6	51.7	11:00	48.6	47.0	50.0
12 Noon	48.6	46.2	50.4	12 Midnight	49.8	48.2	50.4
1:00 P.M.	49.0	46.4	50.0	1:00 A.M.	49.6	48.4	51.7
2:00	49.0	46.0	50.6	2:00	50.0	49.0	52.2
3:00	49.8	48.2	50.8	3:00	50.0	49.2	50.0
4:00	50.3	49.2	52.7	4:00	47.2	46.3	50.5
5:00	51.4	50.0	55.3	5:00	47.0	44.1	49.7
6:00	51.6	49.2	54.7	6:00	48.4	45.0	49.0
7:00	51.8	50.0	55.6	7:00	48.8	44.8	49.7
8:00	51.0	48.6	53.2	8:00	49.6	48.0	51.8
9:00	50.5	49.4	52.4	9:00	50.0	48.1	52.7
10:00	49.2	46.1	50.7	10:00	51.0	48.1	55.2
11:00	49.0	46.3	50.8	11:00	50.4	49.5	54.1
12 Midnight	48.4	45.4	50.2	12 Noon	50.0	48.7	50.9
1:00 A.M.	47.6	44.3	49.7	1:00 P.M.	48.9	47.6	51.2
2:00	47.4	44.1	49.6	2:00	49.8	48.4	51.0
3:00	48.2	45.2	49.0	3:00	49.8	48.8	50.8
4:00	48.0	45.5	49.1	4:00	50.0	49.1	50.6
5:00	48.4	47.1	49.6	5:00	47.8	45.2	51.2
6:00	48.6	47.4	52.0	6:00	46.4	44.0	49.7
7:00	50.0	49.2	52.2	7:00	46.4	44.4	50.0
8:00	49.8	49.0	52.4	8:00	47.2	46.6	48.9
9:00	50.3	49.4	51.7	9:00	48.4	47.2	49.5
10:00	50.2	49.6	51.8	10:00	49.2	48.1	50.7
11:00	50.0	49.0	52.3	11:00	48.4	47.0	50.8
12 Noon	50.0	48.8	52.4	12 Midnight	47.2	46.4	49.2
1:00 P.M.	50.1	49.4	53.6	1:00 A.M.	47.4	46.8	49.0
2:00	49.7	48.6	51.0	2:00	48.8	47.2	51.4
3:00	48.4	47.2	51.7	3:00	49.6	49.0	50.6
4:00	47.2	45.3	50.9	4:00	51.0	50.5	51.5
5:00	46.8	44.1	49.0	5:00	50.5	50.0	51.9

50 pounds, corrective adjustments are made to the weight-release mechanism.)

To verify this expectation, the quality control staff randomly sampled the bag output and prepared the chart on the previous page. Six bags were sampled and weighed each hour.

Discussion Questions

1. What is your analysis of the bag-weight problem?
2. What procedures would you recommend to maintain proper quality control?

Source: Professor Jerry Kinard, Western Carolina University.

▶ Frito-Lay's Quality-Controlled Potato Chips

Video Case

Frito-Lay, the multi-billion-dollar snack food giant, produces billions of pounds of product every year at its dozens of U.S. and Canadian plants. From the farming of potatoes—in Florida, North Carolina, and Michigan—to factory and to retail stores, the ingredients and final product of Lay's chips, for example, are inspected at least 11 times: in the field, before unloading at the plant, after washing and peeling, at the sizing station, at the fryer, after seasoning, when bagged (for weight), at carton filling, in the warehouse, and as they are placed on the store shelf by Frito-Lay personnel. Similar inspections take place for its other famous products, including Cheetos, Fritos, Ruffles, and Tostitos.

In addition to these employee inspections, the firm uses proprietary vision systems to look for defective potato chips. Chips are pulled off the high-speed line and checked twice if the vision system senses them to be too brown.

The company follows the very strict standards of the American Institute of Baking (AIB), standards that are much tougher than those of the U.S. Food and Drug Administration. Two unannounced AIB site visits per year keep Frito-Lay's plants on their toes. Scores, consistently in the "excellent" range, are posted, and every employee knows exactly how the plant is doing.

There are two key metrics in Frito-Lay's continuous improvement quality program: (1) total customer complaints (measured on a complaints per million bag basis) and (2) hourly or daily statistical process control scores (for oil, moisture, seasoning, and salt content, for chip thickness, for fryer temperature, and for weight).

In the Florida plant, Angela McCormack, who holds engineering and MBA degrees, oversees a 15-member quality assurance staff. They watch all aspects of quality, including training employees on the factory floor, monitoring automated processing equipment, and developing and updating statistical process control (SPC) charts. The upper and lower control limits for one check point, salt content in Lay's chips, are 2.22% and 1.98%, respectively. To see exactly how these limits are created using SPC, watch the video that accompanies this case.

Discussion Questions*

1. Angela is now going to evaluate a new salt process delivery system and wants to know if the upper and lower control limits at 3 standard deviations for the new system will meet the upper and lower control specifications previously noted.

The data (in percents) from the initial trial samples are:

Sample 1: 1.98, 2.11, 2.15, 2.06
Sample 2: 1.99, 2.0, 2.08, 1.99
Sample 3: 2.20, 2.10. 2.20, 2.05
Sample 4: 2.18, 2.01, 2.23, 1.98
Sample 5: 2.01, 2.08, 2.14, 2.16

Provide the report to Angela.

2. What are the advantages and disadvantages of Frito-Lay drivers stocking their customers' shelves?
3. Why is quality a critical function at Frito-Lay?

Source: Professors Barry Render, Rollins College; Jay Heizer, Texas Lutheran University; and Beverly Amer, Northern Arizona University.

*You may wish to view the video that accompanies this case before answering these questions.

▶ Farm to Fork: Quality at Darden Restaurants

Video Case

Darden Restaurants, the $5.2 billion owner of such popular brands as Olive Garden, Red Lobster, Seasons 52, and Bahama Breeze, serves more than 300 million meals annually in its 1,700 restaurants across the U.S. and Canada. Before any one of these meals is placed before a guest, the ingredients for each recipe must pass quality control inspections from the source, ranging from measurement and weighing, to tasting, touching, or lab testing. Darden has differentiated itself from its restaurant peers by developing the gold standard in continuous improvement.

To assure both customers and the company that quality expectations are met, Darden uses a rigorous inspection process, employing statistical process control (SPC) as part of its "Farm to Fork" program. More than 50 food scientists, microbiologists, and public health professionals report to Ana Hooper, vice president of quality assurance.

As part of Darden's Point Source program, Hooper's team, based in Southeast Asia (in China, Thailand, and Singapore) and Latin America (in Equador, Honduras, and Chile), approves and inspects—and works with Darden buyers to purchase—more than 50 million pounds of seafood each year for restaurant use. Darden used to build quality in at the end by inspecting shipments as they reached U.S. distribution centers. Now, thanks to coaching and partnering with vendors abroad, Darden needs but a few domestic inspection labs to verify compliance to its exacting standards. Food vendors in source countries know that when supplying Darden, they are subject to regular audits that are stricter than U.S. Food and Drug Administration (FDA) standards.

Two Quality Success Stories

Quality specialists' jobs include raising the bar and improving quality and safety at all plants in their geographic area. The Thai quality representative, for example, worked closely with several of Darden's largest shrimp vendors to convert them to a production-line-integrated quality assurance program. The vendors were able to improve the quality of shrimp supplied and reduce the percentage of defects by 19%.

Likewise, when the Darden quality teams visited fields of growers/shippers in Mexico recently, it identified challenges such as low employee hygiene standards, field food safety problems, lack of portable toilets, child labor, and poor working conditions. Darden addressed these concerns and hired third party independent food safety verification firms to ensure continued compliance to standards.

SPC Charts

SPC charts, such as the one shown on page 184 in the Flexible Version, are particularly important. These charts document pre-cooked food weights; meat, seafood and poultry temperatures; blemishes on produce; and bacteria counts on shrimp—just to name a few. Quality assurance is part of a much bigger process that is key to Darden's success—its supply chain (see Chapter 11 and Supplement 11 for discussion and case studies on this topic). That's because quality comes from the source and flows through distribution to the restaurant and guests.

Discussion Questions*

1. How does Darden build quality into the supply chain?
2. Select two potential problems—one in the Darden supply chain and one in a restaurant—that can be analyzed with a fish-bone chart. Draw a complete chart to deal with each problem.
3. Darden applies SPC in many product attributes. Identify where these are probably used.
4. The SPC chart on page 184 in the Flexible Version (and also on page S6-3 of this *Lecture Guide & Activities Manual*) illustrates Darden's use of control charts to monitor the weight of salmon filets. Given these data, what conclusion do you, as a Darden quality control inspector, draw? What report do you issue to your supervisor? How do you respond to the salmon vendor?

*You might want to view the video that accompanies this case before answering these questions.

Active Model Exercises

ACTIVE MODELS S6.1 S6.2 S6.3 These three Active Model exercises are simulations that allow you to evaluate changes in Examples S4 and S6 and in Figure S6.9, respectively, in your text. They are illustrated at **www.myomlab.com** or **www. pearsonhighered.com/heizer**.

Classroom Activity

▶ Dice Game for Statistical Process Control

1. Take 10 samples of sample size 4. (Roll the dice 40 times.)
2. Calculate the $\bar{x}$ and the Range for each sample.
3. Calculate the $\bar{\bar{x}}$ and the $\bar{R}$.
4. Calculate the UCL and the LCL for the $\bar{x}$ and the R chart.
5. Plot the values for each sample.
6. Is the process in control?
7. Given the upper and lower tolerances desired by the customer, is the process in control?
8. Using the C_{pk} index, is the process capable of operating within those tolerances?

Prepared by: Gary LaPoint, School of Management,
Syracuse University

Record of Observations

Sample Number	1	2	3	4	$\bar{x}$	R
1						
2						
3						
4						
5						
6						
7						
8						
9						
10						
				Average		

UCL$_R$ =

LCL$_R$ =

UCL$_{\bar{x}}$ =

LCL$_{\bar{x}}$ =

C_{pk} =

R-Chart

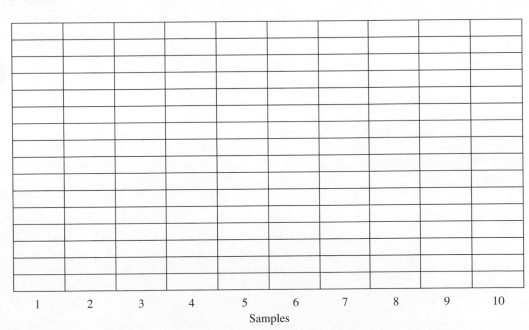

Samples

$\bar{x}$ Chart

Samples

Supplement 6 *Rapid* Review

Main Heading	Review Material	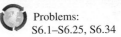

STATISTICAL PROCESS CONTROL (SPC)
(pp. 178–191)

■ **Statistical process control (SPC)**—A process used to monitor standards by taking measurements and corrective action as a product or service is being produced.

■ **Control chart**—A graphical presentation of process data over time.

A process is said to be operating *in statistical control* when the only source of variation is common (natural) causes. The process must first be brought into statistical control by detecting and eliminating special (assignable) causes of variation.

The objective of a process control system is to provide a statistical signal when assignable causes of variation are present.

■ **Natural variations**—The variability that affects every production process to some degree and is to be expected; also known as common cause.

When natural variations form a *normal distribution,* they are characterized by two parameters:
- Mean, μ (the measure of central tendency—in this case, the average value)
- Standard deviation, σ (the measure of dispersion)

As long as the distribution (output measurements) remains within specified limits, the process is said to be "in control," and natural variations are tolerated.

■ **Assignable variation**—Variation in a production process that can be traced to specific causes.

Control charts for the mean, $\bar{x}$, and the range, R, are used to monitor *variables* (outputs with continuous dimensions), such as weight, speed, length, or strength.

■ **$\bar{x}$-chart**—A quality control chart for variables that indicates when changes occur in the central tendency of a production process.

■ **R-chart**—A control chart that tracks the range within a sample; it indicates that a gain or loss in uniformity has occurred in dispersion of a production process.

■ **Central Limit Theorem**—The theoretical foundation for $\bar{x}$-charts, which states that regardless of the distribution of the population of all parts or services, the $\bar{x}$ distribution will tend to follow a normal curve as the number of samples increases:

$$\bar{\bar{x}} = \mu \tag{S6-1}$$

$$\sigma_{\bar{x}} = \frac{\sigma}{\sqrt{n}} \tag{S6-2}$$

The $\bar{x}$-chart limits, if we know the true standard deviation σ of the process population, are:

$$\text{Upper control limit (UCL)} = \bar{\bar{x}} + z\sigma_{\bar{x}} \tag{S6-3}$$

$$\text{Lower control limit (LCL)} = \bar{\bar{x}} + z\sigma_{\bar{x}} \tag{S6-4}$$

where z = the confidence level selected (e.g., $z = 3$ is 99.73% confidence).

The *range*, R, of a sample is defined as the difference between the largest and smallest items. If we do not know the true standard deviation, σ, of the population, the $\bar{x}$-chart limits are:

$$\text{UCL}_{\bar{x}} = \bar{\bar{x}} + A_2\bar{R} \tag{S6-5}$$

$$\text{LCL}_{\bar{x}} = \bar{\bar{x}} - A_2\bar{R} \tag{S6-6}$$

In addition to being concerned with the process average, operations managers are interested in the process dispersion, or range. The R-chart control limits for the range of a process are:

$$\text{UCL}_R = D_4\bar{R} \tag{S6-7}$$

$$\text{LCL}_R = D_3\bar{R} \tag{S6-8}$$

Attributes are typically classified as *defective* or *nondefective.* The two attribute charts are (1) *p*-charts (which measure the *percent* defective in a sample, and (2) *c*-charts (which *count* the number of defects in a sample).

■ **p-chart**—A quality control chart that is used to control attributes:

$$\text{UCL}_p = \bar{p} + z\sigma_{\hat{p}} \tag{S6-9}$$

$$\text{LCL}_p = \bar{p} + z\sigma_{\hat{p}} \tag{S6-10}$$

$$\sigma_{\hat{p}} = \sqrt{\frac{\bar{p}(1 - \bar{p})}{n}} \tag{S6-11}$$

Problems:
S6.1–S6.25, S6.34

VIDEO S6.1
Farm to Fork: Quality at Darden Restaurants

VIDEO S6.2
Frito-Lay's Quality-Controlled Potato Chips

Virtual Office Hours for Solved Problems:
S6.1–S6.3

ACTIVE MODEL S6.1

Main Heading	Review Material	PEARSON myomlab
	■ *c*-chart—A quality control chart used to control the number of defects per unit of output. The Poisson distribution is the basis for *c*-charts, whose 99.73% limits are computed as: $$\text{Control limits} = \bar{c} \pm 3\sqrt{c} \qquad (S6\text{-}12)$$ ■ **Run test**—A test used to examine the points in a control chart to determine whether nonrandom variation is present.	
PROCESS CAPABILITY (pp. 191–193)	■ **Process capability**—The ability to meet design specifications. ■ **C_p**—A ratio for determining whether a process meets design specifications. $$C_p = \frac{(\text{Upper specification} - \text{Lower specification})}{6\sigma} \qquad (S6\text{-}13)$$ ■ **C_{pk}**—A proportion of variation (3σ) between the center of the process and the nearest specification limit: $$C_{pk} = \text{Minimum of}\left[\frac{\text{Upper spec limit} - \bar{X}}{3\sigma}, \frac{\bar{X} - \text{Lower spec limit}}{3\sigma}\right] \quad (S6\text{-}14)$$	Problems: S6.26–S6.31 Virtual Office Hours for Solved Problem: S6.4 **ACTIVE** MODEL **S6.2**
ACCEPTANCE SAMPLING (pp. 193–196)	■ **Acceptance sampling**—A method of measuring random samples of lots or batches of products against predetermined standards. ■ **Operating characteristic (OC) curve**—A graph that describes how well an acceptance plan discriminates between good and bad lots. ■ **Producer's risk**—The mistake of having a producer's good lot rejected through sampling. ■ **Consumer's risk**—The mistake of a customer's acceptance of a bad lot overlooked through sampling. ■ **Acceptable quality level (AQL)**—The quality level of a lot considered good. ■ **Lot tolerance percent defective (LTPD)**—The quality level of a lot considered bad. ■ **Type I error**—Statistically, the probability of rejecting a good lot. ■ **Type II error**—Statistically, the probability of accepting a bad lot. ■ **Average outgoing quality (AOQ)**—The percent defective in an average lot of goods inspected through acceptance sampling: $$AOQ = \frac{(P_d)(P_a)(N - n)}{N} \qquad (S6\text{-}15)$$	Problems: S6.32, S6.33 **ACTIVE** MODEL **S6.3**

Self Test

■ **Before taking the self-test,** refer to the learning objectives listed at the beginning of the supplement and the key terms listed at the end of the supplement.

LO1. If the mean of a particular sample is within control limits and the range of that sample is not within control limits:
  a) the process is in control, with only assignable causes of variation.
  b) the process is not producing within the established control limits.
  c) the process is producing within the established control limits, with only natural causes of variation.
  d) the process has both natural and assignable causes of variation.

LO2. The Central Limit Theorem:
  a) is the theoretical foundation of the *c*-chart.
  b) states that the average of assignable variations is zero.
  c) allows managers to use the normal distribution as the basis for building some control charts.
  d) states that the average range can be used as a proxy for the standard deviation.
  e) controls the steepness of an operating characteristic curve.

LO3. The type of chart used to control the central tendency of variables with continuous dimensions is:
  a) $\bar{x}$-chart.   b) *R*-chart.   c) *p*-chart.
  d) *c*-chart.   e) none of the above.

LO4. If parts in a sample are measured and the mean of the sample measurement is outside the tolerance limits:
  a) the process is out of control, and the cause should be established.

  b) the process is in control but not capable of producing within the established control limits.
  c) the process is within the established control limits, with only natural causes of variation.
  d) all of the above are true.

LO5. Control charts for attributes are:
  a) *p*-charts.   b) *c*-charts.   c) *R*-charts.
  d) $\bar{x}$-charts.   e) both a and b.

LO6. The ability of a process to meet design specifications is called:
  a) Taguchi.   b) process capability.
  c) capability index.   d) acceptance sampling.
  e) average outgoing quality.

LO7. The _____ risk is the probability that a lot will be rejected despite the quality level exceeding or meeting the _____.

LO8. In most acceptance sampling plans, when a lot is rejected, the entire lot is inspected, and all defective items are replaced. When using this technique, the AOQ:
  a) worsens (AOQ becomes a larger fraction).
  b) improves (AOQ becomes a smaller fraction).
  c) is not affected, but the AQL is improved.
  d) is not affected.
  e) falls to zero.

Answers: LO1. b; **LO2.** c; **LO3.** a; **LO4.** a; **LO5.** e; **LO6.** b; **LO7.** producer's risk, AQL; **LO8.** b.

7

Process Strategy and Sustainability

Chapter Outline

Four Process Strategies

Process Analysis and Design

Special Considerations for Service
    Process Design

Selection of Equipment and Technology

Production Technology

Technology in Services

Process Redesign

Sustainability

Ethical Dilemma
Discussion Questions
Problems
Case Studies: Rochester Manufacturing's
    Process Decision; Environmental
    Sustainability at Walmart; Green
    Manufacturing and Sustainability at
    Frito-Lay; Process Analysis at Arnold
    Palmer Hospital; Process Strategy at
    Wheeled Coach
Active Model Exercise
Rapid Review

A process strategy is an organization's approach to transforming resources into goods and services. The objective of a process strategy is to find a way to produce goods and services that meet customer requirements and product specifications within cost and other managerial constraints. This is typically done in one of four ways: (1) process focus, (2) repetitive focus, (3) product focus, or (4) mass customization. In this chapter we examine these four processes and the issues connected with their design.

BEFORE COMING TO CLASS, READ CHAPTER 7 IN YOUR TEXT AND ANSWER THESE QUESTIONS.

1. Describe the differences between the four process strategies. _____
   _____
   _____

2. How are crossover points computed? _____
   _____
   _____

3. List and explain the tools of process analysis. _____
   _____
   _____

4. How do customers interact in process design? _____
   _____
   _____

5. Identify recent advances in production technology. _____
   _____
   _____

6. List and explain the four R's of sustainability. _____
   _____
   _____

FOUR PROCESS STRATEGIES   (See Flexible Version pp. 204–211)

Process Focus   (See Flexible Version pp. 204–205)

Repetitive Focus   (See Flexible Version pp. 205–206)

Product Focus   (See Flexible Version p. 206)

Mass Customization Focus   (See Flexible Version pp. 206–208)

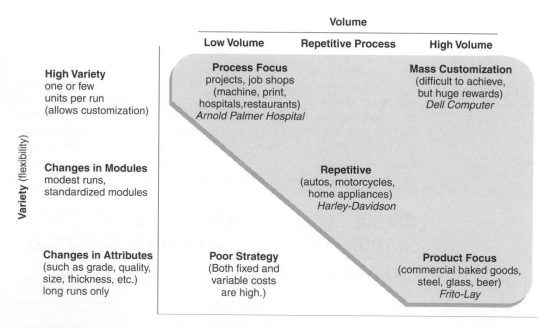

▲ FIGURE 7.1   Process Selected Must Fit with Volume and Variety

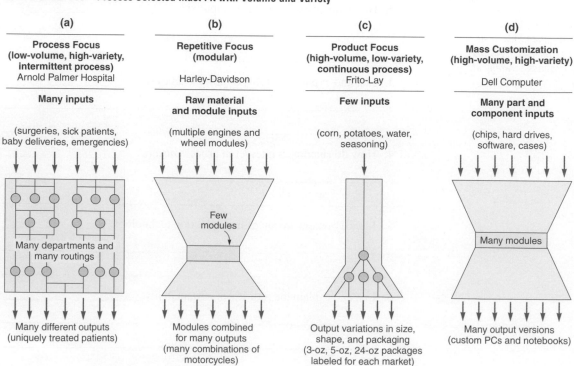

▲ FIGURE 7.2   Process Options

Crossover Charts (See Flexible Version pp. 209–210)

PRACTICE PROBLEM 7.1 ■ Crossover Chart Calculations

Taggert Custom Machine Shop has a contract for 130,000 units of a new product. James Taggert, the owner, has calculated the cost for three process alternatives. Which process should he choose for this new contract?

	General Purpose Equipment (GPE)	Flexible Manufacturing (FMS)	Dedicated Automation (DA)
Fixed Costs	$150,000	$350,000	$950,000
Variable Costs	$10	$8	$6

PRACTICE PROBLEM 7.2 ■ Crossover Chart Graph

Solve Practice Problem 7.1 graphically.

PRACTICE PROBLEM 7.3 ■ Crossover Points

Using either your analytical solution found in Practice Problem 7.1 or the graphical solution found in Practice Problem 7.2, identify the volume ranges where each process should be used.

PRACTICE PROBLEM 7.4 ■ Crossover Analysis

If Taggert Custom Machine is able to convince the customer to renew the contract for another 1 or 2 years, what implications does this have for James Taggert's decision?

Additional Practice Problem Space

PROCESS ANALYSIS AND DESIGN (See Flexible Version pp. 211–214)

Flowchart (See Flexible Version p. 211)

Time-Function Mapping (See Flexible Version pp. 211–212)

Value-Stream Mapping (See Flexible Version pp. 212–213)

Process Charts (See Flexible Version pp. 213–214)

Service Blueprinting (See Flexible Version p. 214)

SPECIAL CONSIDERATIONS FOR SERVICE PROCESS DESIGN

(See Flexible Version pp. 214–217)

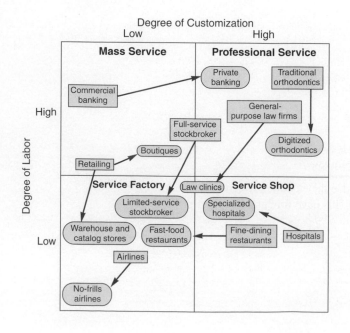

◀ **FIGURE 7.9**
Services Moving toward Specialization and Focus within the Service Process Matrix

Source: Adapted from work by Roger Schmenner, "Service Business and Productivity," *Decision Sciences* 35, no. 3 (Summer 2004): 333–347.

AUTHOR COMMENT
Notice how services find a competitive opportunity by moving from the rectangles to the ovals.

SELECTION OF EQUIPMENT AND TECHNOLOGY

(See Flexible Version pp. 217–218)

PRODUCTION TECHNOLOGY (See Flexible Version pp. 218–220)

1. **Machine Technology**

2. **Automatic Identification System (AIS) and RFID**

3. **Process Control**

4. **Vision Systems**

5. **Robots**

6. **Automated Storage and Retrieval System (ASRS)**

7. **Automated Guided Vehicle (AGV)**

8. **Flexible Manufacturing System (FMS)**

9. **Computer Integrated Manufacturing (CIM)**

TECHNOLOGY IN SERVICES (See Flexible Version pp. 221–222)

Service Industry	Example
Financial Services	Debit cards, electronic funds transfer, automatic teller machines, Internet stock trading, online banking via cell phone.
Education	Online newspapers, online journals, interactive assignments via Web CT, Blackboard, and smart phones.
Utilities and government	Automated one-man garbage trucks, optical mail scanners, flood-warning systems, meters allowing homeowners to control energy usage and costs.
Restaurants and foods	Wireless orders from waiters to the kitchen, robot butchering, transponders on cars that track sales at drive-throughs.
Communications	Interactive TV, ebooks via kindle 2.
Hotels	Electronic check-in/checkout, electronic key/lock systems, mobile Web booking.
Wholesale/retail trade	Point-of-sale (POS) terminals, e-commerce, electronic communication between store and supplier, bar-coded data, RFID.
Transportation	Automatic toll booths, satellite-directed navigation systems, Wi-Fi in automobiles.
Health care	Online patient-monitoring systems, online medical information systems, robotic surgery.
Airlines	Ticketless travel, scheduling, Internet purchases, boarding passes downloaded as two-dimensional bar codes on smart phones.

◀ **TABLE 7.4**
Examples of Technology's Impact on Services

PROCESS REDESIGN (See Flexible Version p. 223)

SUSTAINABILITY (See Flexible Version pp. 223–225)

Resources (See Flexible Version p. 223)

Recycle (See Flexible Version pp. 223–224)

Regulations (See Flexible Version p. 224)

Reputation (See Flexible Version pp. 224–225)

Ethical Dilemma

For the sake of efficiency and lower costs, Premium Standard Farms of Princeton, Missouri, has turned pig production into a standardized product-focused process. Slaughterhouses have done this for a hundred years—but after the animal was dead. Doing it while the animal is alive is a relatively recent innovation. Here is how it works.

Impregnated female sows wait for 40 days in metal stalls so small that they cannot turn around. After an ultrasound test, they wait 67 days in a similar stall until they give birth. Two weeks after delivering 10 or 11 piglets, the sows are moved back to breeding rooms for another cycle. After 3 years, the sow is slaughtered. Animal-welfare advocates say such confinement drives pigs crazy. Premium Standard replies that its hogs are in fact comfortable, arguing that only 1% die before Premium Standard wants them to and that their system helps reduce the cost of pork products.

Discuss the productivity and ethical implications of this industry and these two divergent opinions.

Discussion Questions

1. What is process strategy?
2. What type of process is used for making each of the following products?
   a) beer
   b) wedding invitations
   c) automobiles
   d) paper
   e) Big Macs
   f) custom homes
   g) motorcycles
3. What is service blueprinting?
4. What is process redesign?
5. What are the techniques for improving service productivity?
6. Name the four quadrants of the service process matrix. Discuss how the matrix is used to classify services into categories.
7. What is CIM?
8. What do we mean by a process-control system and what are the typical elements in such systems?
9. Identify *manufacturing* firms that compete on each of the four processes shown in Figure 7.1.
10. Identify the competitive advantage of each of the four firms identified in Discussion Question 9.

11. Identify *service* firms that compete on each of the four processes shown in Figure 7.1.
12. Identify the competitive advantage of each of the four firms identified in Discussion Question 11.
13. What are numerically controlled machines?
14. Describe briefly what an automatic identification system (AIS) is and how service organizations could use AIS to increase productivity and at the same time increase the variety of services offered.
15. Name some of the advances being made in technology that enhance production and productivity.
16. Explain what a flexible manufacturing system (FMS) is.
17. In what ways do CAD and FMS connect?
18. What are the four *R*'s of sustainability?

Problems*

• **7.1** Prepare a flowchart for one of the following:
a) the registration process at a school
b) the process at the local car wash
c) a shoe shine
d) some other process with the approval of the instructor

• **7.2** Prepare a process chart for one of the activities in Problem 7.1.

• **7.3** Prepare a time-function map for one of the activities in Problem 7.1.

• **7.4** Prepare a service blueprint for one of the activities in Problem 7.1.

• **7.5** Meile Machine Shop, Inc., has a 1-year contract for the production of 200,000 gear housings for a new off-road vehicle. Owner Larry Meile hopes the contract will be extended and the volume increased next year. Meile has developed costs for three alternatives. They are general-purpose equipment (GPE), flexible manufacturing system (FMS), and expensive, but efficient, dedicated machine (DM). The cost data follow:

	General-Purpose Equipment (GPE)	Flexible Manufacturing System (FMS)	Dedicated Machine (DM)
Annual contracted units	200,000	200,000	200,000
Annual fixed cost	$100,000	$200,000	$500,000
Per unit variable cost	$ 15.00	$ 14.00	$ 13.00

Which process is best for this contract? **Px**

• **7.6** Using the data in Problem 7.5, determine the economical volume for each process. **Px**

• **7.7** Using the data in Problem 7.5, determine the best process for each of the following volumes: (1) 75,000, (2) 275,000, and (3) 375,000.

• **7.8** Refer to Problem 7.5. If a contract for the second and third years is pending, what are the implications for process selection?

•• **7.9** Stan Fawcett's company is considering producing a gear assembly that it now purchases from Salt Lake Supply, Inc. Salt Lake Supply charges $4 per unit with a minimum order of 3,000 units. Stan estimates that it will cost $15,000 to set up the process and then $1.82 per unit for labor and materials.
a) Draw a graph illustrating the crossover (or indifference) point.
b) Determine the number of units where either choice has the same cost. **Px**

Note: **Px** means the problem may be solved with POM for Windows and/or Excel OM.

•• **7.10** Ski Boards, Inc., wants to enter the market quickly with a new finish on its ski boards. It has three choices: (a) refurbish the old equipment at a cost of $800, (b) make major modifications at the cost of $1,100, or (c) purchase new equipment at a net cost of $1,800. If the firm chooses to refurbish the equipment, materials and labor will be $1.10 per board. If it chooses to make modifications, materials and labor will be $0.70 per board. If it buys new equipment, variable costs are estimated to be $.40 per board.

a) Graph the three total cost lines on the same chart.
b) Which alternative should Ski Boards, Inc., choose if it thinks it can sell more than 3,000 boards?
c) Which alternative should the firm use if it thinks the market for boards will be between 1,000 and 2,000? **Px**

•• **7.11** Susan Meyer, owner/manager of Meyer's Motor Court in Key West, is considering outsourcing the daily room cleanup for her motel to Duffy's Maid Service. Susan rents an average of 50 rooms for each of 365 nights (365 × 50 equals the total rooms rented for the year). Susan's cost to clean a room is $12.50. The Duffy's Maid Service quote is $18.50 per room plus a fixed cost of $25,000 for sundry items such as uniforms with the motel's name. Susan's annual fixed cost for space, equipment, and supplies is $61,000. Which is the preferred process for Susan, and why? **Px**

•• **7.12** Keith Whittingham, as manager of Designs by Whittingham, is upgrading his CAD software. The high-performance

(HP) software rents for $3,000 per month per workstation. The standard-performance (SP) software rents for $2,000 per month per workstation. The productivity figures that he has available suggest that the HP software is faster for his kind of design. Therefore, with the HP software he will need five engineers and with the SP software he will need six. This translates into a variable cost of $200 per drawing for the HP system and $240 per drawing for the SP system. At his projected volume of 80 drawings per month, which system should he rent? **Px**

•• **7.13** Using Figure 7.6 in the discussion of value-stream mapping as a starting point, analyze an opportunity for improvement in a process with which you are familiar and develop an improved process.

•• **7.14** Creative Cabinets, Inc., needs to choose a production method for its new office shelf, the Maxistand. To help accomplish this, the firm has gathered the following production cost data:

Process Type	Annualized Fixed Cost of Plant & Equip.	Variable Costs (per unit) ($)		
		Labor	Material	Energy
Mass Customization	$1,260,000	30	18	12
Intermittent	$1,000,000	24	26	20
Repetitive	$1,625,000	28	15	12
Continuous	$1,960,000	25	15	10

Creative Cabinets projects an annual demand of 24,000 units for the Maxistand. The Maxistand will sell for $120 per unit.
a) Which process type will maximize the annual profit from producing the Maxistand?
b) What is the value of this annual profit? **Px**

Case Studies

▶ Rochester Manufacturing's Process Decision

Rochester Manufacturing Corporation (RMC) is considering moving some of its production from traditional numerically controlled machines to a flexible manufacturing system (FMS). Its computer numerical control machines have been operating in a high-variety, low-volume manner. Machine utilization, as near as it can determine, is hovering around 10%. The machine tool salespeople and a consulting firm want to put the machines together in an FMS. They believe that a $3 million expenditure on machinery and the transfer machines will handle about 30% of RMC's work. There will, of course, be transition and startup costs in addition to this.

The firm has not yet entered all its parts into a comprehensive group technology system, but believes that the 30% is a good estimate of products suitable for the FMS. This 30% should fit very nicely into a "family." A reduction, because of higher utilization, should take place in the number of pieces of machinery. The firm should be able to go from 15 to about 4 machines and personnel should go from 15 to perhaps as low as 3. Similarly, floor space reduction will go from 20,000 square feet to about 6,000. Throughput of orders should also

improve with processing of this family of parts in 1 to 2 days rather than 7 to 10. Inventory reduction is estimated to yield a one-time $750,000 savings, and annual labor savings should be in the neighborhood of $300,000.

Although the projections all look very positive, an analysis of the project's return on investment showed it to be between 10% and 15% per year. The company has traditionally had an expectation that projects should yield well over 15% and have payback periods of substantially less than 5 years.

Discussion Questions

1. As a production manager for RMC, what do you recommend? Why?
2. Prepare a case by a conservative plant manager for maintaining the status quo until the returns are more obvious.
3. Prepare the case for an optimistic sales manager that you should move ahead with the FMS now.

▶ Environmental Sustainability at Walmart

Walmart views "environmental sustainability as one of the most important opportunities for both the future of our business, and the future of our world."* Its environmental vision is clear: ". . . to be supplied 100 percent by renewable energy; to create zero waste; and to sell products that sustain our natural resources and the environment." Its specific goals in the three areas are as follows:

- *Renewable energy:* existing stores are to be 20% more efficient in 7 years, new stores are to be 30% more efficient in 4 years, and the trucking fleet is to be 25% more efficient in 3 years and twice as efficient in 10 years.
- *Zero waste:* 25% reduction in solid waste in 3 years and improved brand packaging through right-sized packaging that uses reusable material.
- *Sustain resources and the environment:* 20% of its 61,000 suppliers will abide by the program within 3 years.

The three above goals make up what Walmart refers to as its Sustainable Value Network. Renewable energy includes global

logistics, Greenhouse Gas (GHG) emissions, and sustainable buildings, in addition to alternative fuels. Waste refers to packaging, operations, and procurement.

Walmart has also launched various experiments and innovations, including the following:

- Building high-efficiency stores using recycled building material and lighting that conserves energy. These new facilities are 25% more energy efficient than the firm's 2005 baseline.
- Purchasing solar-powered equipment at a rate that could put it in the top 10 largest-ever solar-power purchasers in the U.S. Solar power is to be used at 22 locations in Hawaii and California.
- Reducing packaging. For example, changes to packaging for patio sets resulted in 400 fewer shipping containers. And the company used 230 fewer shipping containers to distribute toys.

- Selling reusable bags to reduce the use of disposable plastic bags; encouraging schools to collect plastic bags, for which the schools are paid.
- Adopting a series of aerodynamic innovations for its trucking fleet. It even developed a power unit to warm or cool drivers at night without turning on the truck's engine.

With these policies and initiatives, Walmart hopes to blunt criticism and as a major worldwide employer lead the way in environmental sustainability. As one critic admitted begrudgingly, "Walmart has more green clout than anyone."

Source: Professor Asbjorn Osland, San Jose State University.

Discussion Questions

1. How is Walmart doing in terms of environmental sustainability?
2. Based on library and Internet research, report on other Walmart sustainability efforts.
3. Compare the firm's sustainability plan to those of Home Depot, Target, or other big-box retailers.
4. How much of Walmart's sustainability effort is (a) resource focused, (b) recycle focused, (c) regulation focused, and (d) reputation focused?

*http://walmartstores.com/sustainability

▶ Green Manufacturing and Sustainability at Frito-Lay

Video Case

Frito-Lay, the multi-billion-dollar snack food giant, requires vast amounts of water, electricity, natural gas, and fuel to produce its 41 well-known brands. In keeping with growing environmental concerns, Frito-Lay has initiated ambitious plans to produce environmentally friendly snacks. But even environmentally friendly snacks require resources. Recognizing the environmental impact, the firm is an aggressive "green manufacturer," with major initiatives in resource reduction and sustainability.

For instance, the company's energy management program includes a variety of elements designed to engage employees in reducing energy consumption. These elements include scorecards and customized action plans that empower employees and recognize their achievements.

At Frito-Lay's factory in Casa Grande, Arizona, more than 500,000 pounds of potatoes arrive every day to be washed, sliced, fried, seasoned, and portioned into bags of Lay's and Ruffles chips. The process consumes enormous amounts of energy and creates vast amounts of wastewater, starch, and potato peelings. Frito-Lay plans to take the plant off the power grid and run it almost entirely on renewable fuels and recycled water. The managers at the Casa Grande plant have also installed skylights in conference rooms, offices, and a finished goods warehouse to reduce the need for artificial light. More fuel-efficient ovens recapture heat from exhaust stacks. Vacuum hoses that pull moisture from potato slices to recapture the water and to reduce the amount of heat needed to cook the potato chips are also being used.

Frito-Lay has also built over 50 acres of solar concentrators behind its Modesto, California, plant to generate solar power. The solar power is being converted into heat and used to cook Sun Chips. A biomass boiler, which will burn agricultural waste, is also planned to provide additional renewable fuel.

Frito-Lay is installing high-tech filters that recycle most of the water used to rinse and wash potatoes. It also recycles corn by-products to make Doritos and other snacks; starch is reclaimed and sold, primarily as animal feed, and leftover sludge is burned to create methane gas to run the plant boiler.

There are benefits besides the potential energy savings. Like many other large corporations, Frito-Lay is striving to establish its green credentials as consumers become more focused on environmental issues. There are marketing opportunities, too. The company, for example, advertises that its popular Sun Chips snacks are made using solar energy.

At Frito-Lay's Florida plant, only 3½% of the waste goes to landfills, but that is still 1.5 million pounds annually. The goal is zero waste to landfills. The snack food maker earned its spot in the National Environmental Performance Track program by maintaining a sustained environmental compliance record and making new commitments to reduce, reuse, and recycle at this facility.

Substantial resource reductions have been made in the production process, with an energy reduction of 21% across Frito-Lay's 34 U.S. plants. But the continuing battle for resource reduction continues. The company is also moving toward biodegradable packaging and pursuing initiatives in areas such as office paper, packaging material, seasoning bags, and cans and bottles. While these multiyear initiatives are expensive, they have the backing at the highest levels of Frito-Lay as well as corporate executives at PepsiCo, the parent company.

Discussion Questions*

1. Using resources, regulation, and reputation as a basis, what are the sources of pressure on firms such as Frito-Lay to reduce their environmental footprint?
2. Identify the specific techniques that Frito-Lay is using to become a "green manufacturer."
3. Select another company and compare its green policies to those of Frito-Lay.

*You may wish to view the video that accompanies this case before addressing these questions.

Source: Professors Beverly Amer, Northern Arizona University; Barry Render, Rollins College; and Jay Heizer, Texas Lutheran University.

▶ Process Analysis at Arnold Palmer Hospital

Video Case

The Arnold Palmer Hospital (APH) in Orlando, Florida, is one of the busiest and most respected hospitals for the medical treatment of children and women in the U.S. Since its opening on golfing legend Arnold Palmer's birthday September 10, 1989, more than 1.6 million children and women have passed through its doors. It is the fourth busiest labor and delivery hospital in the U.S. and one of the largest neonatal intensive care units in the Southeast. APH ranks in the top 10% of hospitals nationwide in patient satisfaction.

"Part of the reason for APH's success," says Executive Director Kathy Swanson, "is our continuous improvement process. Our goal is 100% patient satisfaction. But getting there means constantly examining and reexamining everything we do, from patient flow, to cleanliness, to layout space, to a work-friendly environment, to speed of medication delivery from the pharmacy to a patient. Continuous improvement is a huge and never-ending task."

One of the tools the hospital uses consistently is the process flow-chart (like those in Figure 7.1 to 7.3 in this chapter and Figure 6.6e in Chapter 6 in the Flexible Version). Staffer Diane Bowles, who carries the title "clinical practice improvement consultant," charts scores of processes. Bowles's flowcharts help study ways to improve the turn-around of a vacated room (especially important in a hospital that has pushed capacity for years), speed up the admission process, and deliver warm meals warm.

Lately, APH has been examining the flow of maternity patients (and their paperwork) from the moment they enter the hospital until they are discharged, hopefully with their healthy baby a day or two later. The flow of maternity patients follows these steps:

1. Enter APH's Labor & Delivery (L&D) check-in desk entrance.
2. If the baby is born en route or if birth is imminent, the mother and baby are taken directly to Labor & Delivery on the second floor and registered and admitted directly at the bedside. If there are no complications, the mother and baby go to step 6.
3. If the baby is *not* yet born, the front desk asks if the mother is pre-registered. (Most do pre-register at the 28- to 30-week pregnancy mark). If she is not, she goes to the registration office on the first floor.
4. The pregnant woman is then taken to L&D Triage on the 8th floor for assessment. If she is in active labor, she is taken to an L&D room on the 2nd floor until the baby is born. If she is not ready, she goes to step 5.
5. Pregnant women not ready to deliver (i.e., no contractions or false alarm) are either sent home to return on a later date and reenter

the system at that time, or if contractions are not yet close enough, they are sent to walk around the hospital grounds (to encourage progress) and then return to L&D Triage at a prescribed time.
6. When the baby is born, if there are no complications, after 2 hours the mother and baby are transferred to a "mother–baby care unit" room on floors 3, 4, or 5 for an average of 40–44 hours.
7. If there *are* complications with the mother, she goes to an operating room and/or intensive care unit. From there, she goes back to a mother–baby care room upon stabilization—or is discharged at another time if not stabilized. Complications for the baby may result in a stay in the neonatal intensive care unit (NICU) before transfer to the baby nursery near the mother's room. If the baby is not stable enough for discharge with the mother, the baby is discharged later.
8. Mother and/or baby, when ready, are discharged and taken by wheelchair to the discharge exit for pickup to travel home.

Discussion Questions*

1. As Diane's new assistant, you need to flowchart this process. Explain how the process might be improved once you have completed the chart.
2. If a mother is scheduled for a Caesarean-section birth (i.e., the baby is removed from the womb surgically), how would this flowchart change?
3. If *all* mothers were electronically (or manually) pre-registered, how would the flowchart change? Redraw the chart to show your changes.
4. Describe in detail a process that the hospital could analyze, besides the ones mentioned in this case.

*You may wish to view the video that accompanies this case before addressing these questions.

▶ Process Strategy at Wheeled Coach

Video Case

Wheeled Coach, based in Winter Park, Florida, is the world's largest manufacturer of ambulances. Working four 10-hour days each week, 350 employees make only custom-made ambulances: Virtually every vehicle is unique. Wheeled Coach accommodates the marketplace by providing a wide variety of options and an engineering staff accustomed to innovation and custom design. Continuing growth, which now requires that more than 20 ambulances roll off the assembly line each week, makes process design a continuing challenge. Wheeled Coach's response has been to build a focused factory: Wheeled Coach builds nothing but ambulances. Within the focused factory, Wheeled Coach established work cells for every major module feeding an assembly line, including aluminum bodies, electrical wiring harnesses, interior cabinets, windows, painting, and upholstery.

Labor standards drive the schedule so that every work cell feeds the assembly line on schedule, just-in-time for installations. The chassis, usually that of a Ford truck, moves to a station at which the aluminum body is mounted. Then the vehicle is moved to painting. Following a custom paint job, it moves to the assembly line, where it will spend 7 days. During each of these 7 workdays, each work cell delivers its respective module to the appropriate position on the assembly line. During the first day,

electrical wiring is installed; on the second day, the unit moves forward to the station at which cabinetry is delivered and installed, then to a window and lighting station, on to upholstery, to fit and finish, to further customizing, and finally to inspection and road testing. The *Global Company Profile* featuring Wheeled Coach, which opens Chapter 14 in the text, provides further details about this process.

Discussion Questions*

1. Why do you think major auto manufacturers do not build ambulances?
2. What is an alternative process strategy to the assembly line that Wheeled Coach currently uses?
3. Why is it more efficient for the work cells to prepare "modules" and deliver them to the assembly line than it would be to produce the component (e.g., interior upholstery) on the line?
4. How does Wheeled Coach manage the tasks to be performed at each work station?

*You may wish to view the video that accompanies this case before addressing these questions.

Active Model Exercise

ACTIVE MODEL 7.1 is a simulation exercise that evaluates changes in Example 4 in your text. It is illustrated at **www.myomlab.com** or **www.pearsonhighered.com/heizer**.

Main Heading	Review Material	PEARSON myomlab
FOUR PROCESS STRATEGIES (pp. 204–211)	■ **Process strategy**—An organization's approach to transforming resources into goods and services.	Problems: 7.5–7.14
	The objective of a process strategy is to build a production process that meets customer requirements and product specifications within cost and other managerial constraints.	
	Virtually every good or service is made by using some variation of one of four process strategies.	
	■ **Process focus**—A facility organized around processes to facilitate low-volume, high-variety production.	
	The vast majority of global production is devoted to making low-volume, high variety products in process focused facilities, also known as job shops or *intermittent process* facilities.	**VIDEO 7.1** Process Strategy at Wheeled Coach Ambulance
	Process focused facilities have high variable costs with extremely low utilization (5% to 25%) of facilities.	
	■ **Repetitive process**—A product-oriented production process that uses modules.	
	■ **Modules**—Parts or components of a product previously prepared, often in a continuous process.	**ACTIVE** MODEL 7.1
	The repetitive process is the classic assembly line. It allows the firm to use modules and combine the economic advantages of the product-focused model with the customization advantages of the process-focus model.	
	■ **Product focus**—A facility organized around products; a product-oriented, high-volume, low-variety process.	
	Product-focused facilities are also called *continuous processes,* because they have very long, continuous production runs.	
	The specialized nature of a product-focused facility requires high fixed cost; however, low variable costs reward high facility utilization.	
	■ **Mass customization**—Rapid, low-cost production that caters to constantly changing unique customer desires.	
	■ **Build-to-order (BTO)**—Produce to customer order rather than to a forecast.	
	Major challenges of a build-to-order system include: *Product design, Process design, Inventory management, Tight schedules* and *Responsive partners.*	
	■ **Postponement**—The delay of any modifications or customization to a product as long as possible in the production process.	Virtual Office Hours for Solved Problem: 7.1
	■ **Crossover chart**—A chart of costs at the possible volumes for more than one process.	
PROCESS ANALYSIS AND DESIGN (pp. 211–214)	Five tools of process analysis are (1) flowcharts, (2) time-function mapping, (3) value-stream mapping, (4) process charts, and (5) service blueprinting.	Problems: 7.2, 7.3
	■ **Flowchart**—A drawing used to analyze movement of people or materials.	
	■ **Time-function mapping** (or **process mapping**)—A flowchart with time added on the horizontal axis.	
	■ **Value-stream mapping (VSM)**—A tool that helps managers understand how to add value in the flow of material and information through the entire production process.	
	■ **Process charts**—Charts that use symbols to analyze the movement of people or material.	
	Process charts allow managers to focus on value-added activities and to compute the percentage of value-added time (= operation time/total time).	
	■ **Service blueprinting**—A process analysis technique that lends itself to a focus on the customer and the provider's interaction with the customer.	
SPECIAL CONSIDERATIONS FOR SERVICE PROCESS DESIGN (pp. 214–217)	Services can be classified into one of four quadrants, based on relative degrees of labor and customization:	**VIDEO 7.2** Process Analysis at Arnold Palmer Hospital
	1. *Service factory* 2. *Service shop* 3. *Mass service* 4. *Professional service* Techniques for improving service productivity include:	
	■ *Separation*—Structuring service so customers must go where the service is offered	
	■ *Self-service*—Customers examining, comparing, and evaluating at their own pace	
	■ *Postponement*—Customizing at delivery	
	■ *Focus*—Restricting the offerings	
	■ *Modules*—Modular selection of service; modular production	
	■ *Automation*—Separating services that may lend themselves to a type of automation	

Main Heading	Review Material	myomlab
	▪ *Scheduling*—Precise personnel scheduling ▪ *Training*—Clarifying the service options; explaining how to avoid problems	
SELECTION OF EQUIPMENT AND TECHNOLOGY (pp. 217–218)	Picking the best equipment involves understanding the specific industry and available processes and technology. The choice requires considering cost, quality, capacity, and flexibility. ▪ **Flexibility**—The ability to respond with little penalty in time, cost, or customer value.	
PRODUCTION TECHNOLOGY (pp. 218–220)	▪ **Computer numerical control (CNC)**—Machinery with its own computer and memory. ▪ **Automatic identification system (AIS)**—A system for transforming data into electronic form (e.g., bar codes). ▪ **Radio frequency identification (RFID)**—A wireless system in which integrated circuits with antennas send radio waves. ▪ **Process control**—The use of information technology to control a physical process. ▪ **Vision systems**—Systems that use video cameras and computer technology in inspection roles. ▪ **Robot**—A flexible machine with the ability to hold, move, or grab items. ▪ **Automated storage and retrieval systems (ASRS)**—Computer-controlled warehouses that provide for the automatic placement of parts into and from designated places within a warehouse. ▪ **Automated guided vehicle (AGV)**—Electronically guided and controlled cart used to move materials. ▪ **Flexible manufacturing system (FMS)**—Automated work cell controlled by electronic signals from a common centralized computer facility. ▪ **Computer-integrated manufacturing (CIM)**—A manufacturing system in which CAD, FMS, inventory control, warehousing, and shipping are integrated.	
TECHNOLOGY IN SERVICES (pp. 221–222)	Many rapid technological developments have occurred in the service sector. These range from POS terminals and RFID to online newspapers and ebooks.	
PROCESS REDESIGN (p. 223)	▪ Process redesign—The fundamental rethinking of business processes to bring about dramatic improvements in performance. Process redesign often focuses on activities that cross functional lines.	
SUSTAINABILITY (pp. 223–225)	There are four *Rs* to consider when addressing sustainability: (1) the *resources* used by the production process, (2) the *recycling* of production materials and product components, (3) the *regulations* that apply, and (4) the firm's *reputation*.	**VIDEO 7.3** Frito-Lay's Green Manufacturing and Sustainability

Self Test

▪ **Before taking the self-test,** refer to the learning objectives listed at the beginning of the chapter and the key terms listed at the end of the chapter.

LO1. Low-volume, high-variety processes are also known as:
a) continuous processes.
b) process focused.
c) repetitive processes.
d) product focused.

LO2. A crossover chart for process selection focuses on:
a) labor costs.
b) material cost.
c) both labor and material costs.
d) fixed and variable costs.
e) fixed costs.

LO3. Tools for process analysis include all of the following except:
a) flowchart.
b) vision systems.
c) service blueprinting.
d) time-function mapping.
e) value-stream mapping.

LO4. Customer feedback in process design is lower as:
a) the degree of customization is increased.
b) the degree of labor is increased.

c) the degree of customization is lowered.
d) both a and b.
e) both b and c.

LO5. Computer-integrated manufacturing (CIM) includes manufacturing systems that have:
a) computer-aided design, direct numerical control machines, and material handling equipment controlled by automation.
b) transaction processing, a management information system, and decision support systems.
c) automated guided vehicles, robots, and process control.
d) robots, automated guided vehicles, and transfer equipment.

LO6. The four *R's* of sustainability are:
_____, _____, _____, _____.

Answers: LO1. b; LO2. d; LO3. b; LO4. c; LO5. a; LO6: resources, recycling, regulations, reputation.

Capacity and Constraint Management

Supplement Outline

Capacity

Bottleneck Analysis and the Theory of Contraints

Break-Even Analysis

Reducing Risk with Incremented Changes

Applying Expected Monetary Value (EMV) to Capacity Decisions

Applying Investment Analysis to Strategy-Driven Investments

Discussion Questions

Problems

Case Study: Capacity Planning at Arnold Palmer Hospital

Active Model Exercises

Classroom Activity

Rapid Review

Effective utilization of facilities is an important component of process efficiency and hence the operations manager's job. And effective utilization of facilities depends on both capacity being appropriate to demand (a long-run operations decision) and good short- and intermediate-range operations planning that aid in overcoming bottlenecks.

Capacity is the "throughput," or number of units a facility can hold, receive, store, or produce in a period of time. Operations managers must deal with the capacity design, effectiveness, utilization, and efficiency. Break-even analysis helps define the minimum necessary capacity and the Theory of Contraints helps us improve throughput. Expected monetary value helps us make good decisions and net present value determines the discounted value of future cash flows.

BEFORE COMING TO CLASS, READ SUPPLEMENT 7 IN YOUR TEXT AND ANSWER THESE QUESTIONS.

1. Define capacity. _____

_____

2. What is design capacity, effective capacity, and utilization? _____

_____

_____

3. What are the principles of bottleneck management? _____

_____

4. What is meant by "break-even point"? _____

_____

5. How can expected monetary value be applied to capacity decisions?

_____

6. What is the purpose of net present value analysis? _____

_____

CAPACITY (SeeFlexible Version pp. 228–234)

Options for Adjusting Capacity

Time Horizon	Modify capacity	Use capacity
Long-range planning	Add facilities. Add long lead time equipment. ★	
Intermediate-range planning (aggregate planning)	Subcontract. Add equipment. Add shifts.	Add personnel. Build or use inventory.
Short-range planning (scheduling)	★	Schedule jobs. Schedule personnel. Allocate machinery.

★Difficult to adjust capacity as limited options exist

Design Capacity

Effective Capacity

Utilization

Efficiency

Utilization = Actual output/Design capacity   (S7-1)

Efficiency = Actual output/Effective capacity   (S7-2)

Actual (or expected) output = (Effective capacity)(Efficiency)   (S7-3)

PRACTICE PROBLEM S7.1 ■ Utilization, Efficiency, and Output

The design capacity for engine repair in our company is 80 trucks per day. The effective capacity is 40 engines per day, and the actual output is 36 engines per day. Calculate the utilization and efficiency of the operation. If the efficiency for next month is expected to be 82%, what is the expected output?

Additional Practice Problem Space

Capacity and Strategy (See Flexible Version p. 230)

Capacity Considerations (See Flexible Version p. 231)

Managing Demand (See Flexible Version pp. 231–233)

Demand and Capacity Management in the Service Sector (See Flexible Version pp. 233–234)

BOTTLENECK ANALYSIS AND THE THEORY OF CONSTRAINTS

(See Flexible Version pp. 234–238)

Process Time for Stations, Systems, and Cycles

(See Flexible Version pp. 235–237)

Theory of Constraints (See Flexible Version p. 237)

5 Steps:

1.

2.

3.

4.

5.

Bottleneck Management (See Flexible Version pp. 237–238)

PRACTICE PROBLEM S7.2 ■ Capacity Analysis

Stephen Minners's employee team produces chess sets using the production process shown below.

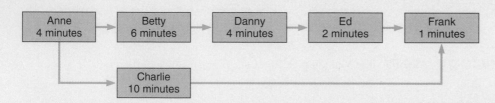

a) What is the process cycle time?
b) What is the capacity of the process?
c) Stephen is considering installing a second machine to speed up Charlie's process (the longest process). Charlie can monitor both machines at the same time. What is the new process cycle time, and what is the new capacity?
d) If the second machine for Charlie is not added, but Betty and Danny are cross-trained so they can both do the work at each other's workstations, what is the new process cycle time? And what is the new capacity?

BREAK-EVEN ANALYSIS (See Flexible Version pp. 238–242)

$$\text{Break-even in units} = \frac{\text{Total fixed cost}}{\text{Price} - \text{Variable cost}} \qquad \text{(S7-4)}$$

$$\text{Break-even in dollars} = \frac{\text{Total fixed cost}}{1 - \dfrac{\text{Variable cost}}{\text{Selling price}}} \qquad \text{(S7-5)}$$

PRACTICE PROBLEM S7.3 ■ Break-Even

Given: F = fixed cost = \$1,000
V = variable cost = \$2/unit
P = selling price = \$4/unit

Find the break-even point in dollars and in units.

PRACTICE PROBLEM S7.4 ■ Break-Even Chart

Develop a break-even chart for Practice Problem S7.3.

PRACTICE PROBLEM S7.5 ■ Break-Even

Jack's Grocery is manufacturing a "store brand" item that has a variable cost of $0.75 per unit and a selling price of $1.25 per unit. Fixed costs are $12,000. Current volume is 50,000 units. The grocery can substantially improve the product quality by adding a new piece of equipment at an additional fixed cost of $5,000. Variable cost would increase to $1, but volume should increase to 70,000 units due to the higher quality product. Should the company buy the new equipment?

PRACTICE PROBLEM S7.6 ■ Break-Even Points

What are the break-even points (dollars and units) for the two processes considered in Practice Problem S7.5?

PRACTICE PROBLEM S7.7 ■ Break-Even Chart

Develop a break-even chart for Practice Problem S7.5.

REDUCING RISK WITH INCREMENTAL CHANGES

(See Flexible Version pp. 242–243)

(a) Leading Strategy
Management leads capacity in periodic increments. Management could also add enough capacity in one period to handle expected demand for multiple periods.

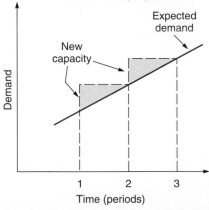

(b) Lag Strategy
Here management lags (chases) demand.

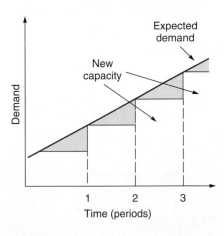

(c) Straddle Strategy
Here management uses average capacity increments to straddle demand.

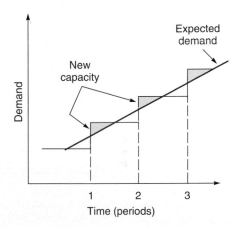

▲ FIGURE S7.6   **Approaches to Capacity Expansion**

Practice Problem Space

APPLYING EXPECTED MONETARY VALUE (EMV) TO CAPACITY DECISIONS (See Flexible Version pp. 243–244)

Practice Problem Space

APPLYING INVESTMENT ANALYSIS TO STRATEGY-DRIVEN INVESTMENTS (See Flexible Version pp. 244–247)

Net Present Value (See Flexible Version pp. 244–247)

$$F = P(1 + i)^N \qquad \text{(S7-7)}$$

$$P = \frac{F}{(1 + i)^N} \qquad \text{(S7-8)}$$

$$P = \frac{F}{(1 + i)^N} = FX \qquad \text{(S7-9)}$$

where F = future value (such as \$110.25 or \$105)
  P = present value (such as \$100.00)
  i = interest rate (such as .05)
  N = number of years (such as 1 year or 2 years)

◀ **TABLE S7.1**
Present Value of $1

Year	5%	6%	7%	8%	9%	10%	12%	14%
1	.952	.943	.935	.926	.917	.909	.893	.877
2	.907	.890	.873	.857	.842	.826	.797	.769
3	.864	.840	.816	.794	.772	.751	.712	.675
4	.823	.792	.763	.735	.708	.683	.636	.592
5	.784	.747	.713	.681	.650	.621	.567	.519
6	.746	.705	.666	.630	.596	.564	.507	.456
7	.711	.665	.623	.583	.547	.513	.452	.400
8	.677	.627	.582	.540	.502	.467	.404	.351
9	.645	.592	.544	.500	.460	.424	.361	.308
10	.614	.558	.508	.463	.422	.386	.322	.270
15	.481	.417	.362	.315	.275	.239	.183	.140
20	.377	.312	.258	.215	.178	.149	.104	.073

◀ **TABLE S7.2**
Present Value of an
Annuity of $1

Year	5%	6%	7%	8%	9%	10%	12%	14%
1	.952	.943	.935	.926	.917	.909	.893	.877
2	1.859	1.833	1.808	1.783	1.759	1.736	1.690	1.647
3	2.723	2.673	2.624	2.577	2.531	2.487	2.402	2.322
4	3.546	3.465	3.387	3.312	3.240	3.170	3.037	2.914
5	4.329	4.212	4.100	3.993	3.890	3.791	3.605	3.433
6	5.076	4.917	4.766	4.623	4.486	4.355	4.111	3.889
7	5.786	5.582	5.389	5.206	5.033	4.868	4.564	4.288
8	6.463	6.210	5.971	5.747	5.535	5.335	4.968	4.639
9	7.108	6.802	6.515	6.247	5.985	5.759	5.328	4.946
10	7.722	7.360	7.024	6.710	6.418	6.145	5.650	5.216
15	10.380	9.712	9.108	8.559	8.060	7.606	6.811	6.142
20	12.462	11.470	10.594	9.818	9.128	8.514	7.469	6.623

PRACTICE PROBLEM S7.8 ■ Present Value

Good news! You are going to receive $6,000 in each of the next 5 years for sale of used machinery. In the meantime, a bank is willing to lend you the present value of the money at a discount of 10% per year. How much cash do you receive now?

Discussion Questions

1. Distinguish between design capacity and effective capacity.
2. What is effective capacity?
3. What is efficiency?
4. How is actual, or expected, output computed?
5. Explain why doubling the capacity of a bottleneck may not double the system capacity.
6. Distinguish between process time of a system and process cycle time.
7. What is the theory of constraints?
8. What are the assumptions of break-even analysis?
9. What keeps plotted revenue data from falling on a straight line in a break-even analysis?
10. Under what conditions would a firm want its capacity to lag demand? to lead demand?
11. Explain how net present value is an appropriate tool for comparing investments.
12. Describe the five-step process that serves as the basis of the theory of constraints.
13. What are the techniques available to operations managers to deal with a bottleneck operation? Which of these does not decrease process cycle time?

Problems*

• **S7.1** If a plant was designed to produce 7,000 hammers per day but is limited to making 6,000 hammers per day because of the time needed to change equipment between styles of hammers, what is the utilization?

• **S7.2** For the past month, the plant in Problem S7.1, which has an effective capacity of 6,500, has made only 4,500 hammers per day because of material delay, employee absences, and other problems. What is its efficiency?

• **S7.3** If a plant has an effective capacity of 6,500 and an efficiency of 88%, what is the actual (planned) output?

• **S7.4** A plant has an effective capacity of 900 units per day and produces 800 units per day with its product mix; what is its efficiency?

• **S7.5** Material delays have routinely limited production of household sinks to 400 units per day. If the plant efficiency is 80%, what is the effective capacity?

• **S7.6** The effective capacity and efficiency for the next quarter at MMU Mfg. in Waco, Texas, for each of three departments are shown:

Department	Effective Capacity	Recent Efficiency
Design	93,600	.95
Fabrication	156,000	1.03
Finishing	62,400	1.05

Compute the expected production for next quarter for each department.

•• **S7.7** Southeastern Oklahoma State University's business program has the facilities and faculty to handle an enrollment of 2,000 new students per semester. However, in an effort to limit class sizes to a "reasonable" level (under 200, generally), Southeastern's dean, Tom Choi, placed a ceiling on enrollment of 1,500 new students. Although there was ample demand for business courses last semester, conflicting schedules allowed only 1,450 new students to take business courses. What are the utilization and efficiency of this system?

•• **S7.8** Under ideal conditions, a service bay at a Fast Lube can serve 6 cars per hour. The effective capacity and efficiency of a Fast Lube service bay are known to be 5.5 and 0.880, respectively. What is the minimum number of service bays Fast Lube needs to achieve an anticipated production of 200 cars per 8-hour day?

• **S7.9** A production line at V. J. Sugumaran's machine shop has three stations. The first station can process a unit in 10 minutes. The second station has two identical machines, each of which can process a unit in 12 minutes (each unit only needs to be processed on one of the two machines). The third station can process a unit in 8 minutes. Which station is the bottleneck station?

•• **S7.10** A work cell at Chris Ellis Commercial Laundry has a workstation with two machines, and each unit produced at the station needs to be processed by both of the machines. (The same unit cannot be worked on by both machines simultaneously.) Each machine has a production capacity of 4 units per hour. What is the process time of the work cell in minutes per unit?

•• **S7.11** The three-station work cell illustrated in Figure S7.7 has a product that must go through one of the two machines at station 1 (they are parallel) before proceeding to station 2.

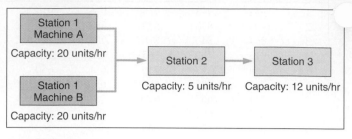

▲ **FIGURE S7.7**

a) What is the process time of the system?
b) What is the bottleneck time of this work cell?
c) What is the process cycle time?
d) If the firm operates 10 hours per day, 5 days per week, what is the weekly capacity of this work cell?

•• **S7.12** The three-station work cell at Pullman Mfg., Inc. is illustrated in Figure S7.8. It has two machines at station 1 in parallel (i.e., the product needs to go through only one of the two machines before proceeding to station 2).
a) What is the process cycle time of this work cell?
b) What is the system process time of this work cell?
c) If the firm operates 8 hours per day, 6 days per week, what is the weekly capacity of this work cell?

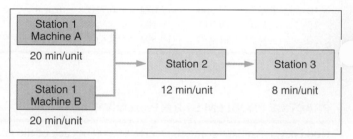

▲ **FIGURE S7.8**

•• **S7.13** The Pullman Mfg., Inc. three-station work cell illustrated in Figure S7.8 has two machines at station 1 in parallel. (The product needs to go through only one of the two machines before proceeding to station 2.) The manager, Ms. Hartley, has asked you to evaluate the system if she adds a parallel machine at station 2.
a) What is the process cycle time of the new work cell?
b) What is the system process time of the new work cell?
c) If the firm operates 8 hours per day, 6 days per week, what is the weekly capacity of this work cell?
d) How did the addition of the second machine at workstation 2 affect the performance of the work cell from Problem S7.12?

• **S7.14** Klassen Toy Company, Inc., assembles two parts (parts 1 and 2): Part 1 is first processed at workstation A for 15 minutes per unit and then processed at workstation B for 10 minutes per unit. Part 2 is simultaneously processed at workstation C for 20 minutes per unit. Work stations B and C feed the parts to an assembler at workstation D, where the two parts are assembled. The time at workstation D is 15 minutes.
a) What is the bottleneck of this process?
b) What is the hourly capacity of the process?

•• **S7.15** A production process at Kenneth Day Manufacturing is shown in Figure S7.9. The drilling operation occurs separately from, and simultaneously with, the sawing and sanding operations.

Sawing 6 units/hr → Sanding 6 units/hr → Welding 2 units/hr → Assembly 0.7 units/hr, Assembly 0.7 units/hr, Assembly 0.7 units/hr; Drilling 2.4 units/hr → Welding

▲ **FIGURE S7.9**

A product needs to go through only one of the three assembly operations (the operations are in parallel).
a) Which operation is the bottleneck?
b) What is the process time of the overall system?
c) What is the process cycle time of the overall system?
d) If the firm operates 8 hours per day, 20 days per month, what is the monthly capacity of the manufacturing process?

• **S7.16** Smithson Cutting is opening a new line of scissors for supermarket distribution. It estimates its fixed cost to be $500.00 and its variable cost to be $0.50 per unit. Selling price is expected to average $0.75 per unit.
a) What is Smithson's break-even point in units?
b) What is the break-even point in dollars? **Px**

• **S7.17** Markland Manufacturing intends to increase capacity by overcoming a bottleneck operation by adding new equipment. Two vendors have presented proposals. The fixed costs for proposal A are $50,000, and for proposal B, $70,000. The variable cost for A is $12.00, and for B, $10.00. The revenue generated by each unit is $20.00.
a) What is the break-even point in units for proposal A?
b) What is the break-even point in units for proposal B? **Px**

• **S7.18** Using the data in Problem S7.17:
a) What is the break-even point in dollars for proposal A if you add $10,000 installation to the fixed cost?
b) What is the break-even point in dollars for proposal B if you add $10,000 installation to the fixed cost? **Px**

• **S7.19** Given the data in Problem S7.17, at what volume (units) of output would the two alternatives yield the same profit? **Px**

•• **S7.20** Janelle Heinke, the owner of Ha'Peppas!, is considering a new oven in which to bake the firm's signature dish, vegetarian pizza. Oven type A can handle 20 pizzas an hour. The fixed costs associated with oven A are $20,000 and the variable costs are $2.00 per pizza. Oven B is larger and can handle 40 pizzas an hour. The fixed costs associated with oven B are $30,000 and the variable costs are $1.25 per pizza. The pizzas sell for $14 each.
a) What is the break-even point for each oven?
b) If the owner expects to sell 9,000 pizzas, which oven should she purchase?
c) If the owner expects to sell 12,000 pizzas, which oven should she purchase?
d) At what volume should Janelle switch ovens? **Px**

• **S7.21** Given the following data, calculate: a) BEP_x; b) $BEP_\$$; and c) the profit at 100,000 units:

$$P = \$8/\text{unit} \quad V = \$4/\text{unit} \quad F = \$50,000 \ \textbf{Px}$$

•• **S7.22** You are considering opening a copy service in the student union. You estimate your fixed cost at $15,000 and the variable cost of each copy sold at $.01. You expect the selling price to average $.05.
a) What is the break-even point in dollars?
b) What is the break-even point in units? **Px**

•• **S7.23** An electronics firm is currently manufacturing an item that has a variable cost of $.50 per unit and a selling price of $1.00 per unit. Fixed costs are $14,000. Current volume is 30,000 units. The firm can substantially improve the product quality by adding a new piece of equipment at an additional fixed cost of $6,000. Variable cost would increase to $.60, but volume should jump to 50,000 units due to a higher-quality product. Should the company buy the new equipment? **Px**

•• **S7.24** The electronics firm in Problem S7.23 is now considering the new equipment and increasing the selling price to $1.10 per unit. With the higher-quality product, the new volume is expected to be 45,000 units. Under these circumstances, should the company purchase the new equipment and increase the selling price? **Px**

•••• **S7.25** Zan Azlett and Angela Zesiger have joined forces to start A&Z Lettuce Products, a processor of packaged shredded lettuce for institutional use. Zan has years of food processing experience, and Angela has extensive commercial food preparation experience. The process will consist of opening crates of lettuce and then sorting, washing, slicing, preserving, and finally packaging the prepared lettuce. Together, with help from vendors, they feel they can adequately estimate demand, fixed costs, revenues, and variable cost per 5-pound bag of lettuce. They think a largely manual process will have monthly fixed costs of $37,500 and variable costs of $1.75 per bag. A more mechanized process will have fixed costs of $75,000 per month with variable costs of $1.25 per 5-pound bag. They expect to sell the shredded lettuce for $2.50 per 5-pound bag.

a. What is the break-even quantity for the manual process?
b. What is the revenue at the break-even quantity for the manual process?
c. What is the break-even quantity for the mechanized process?
d. What is the revenue at the break-even quantity for the mechanized process?
e. What is the monthly profit or loss of the *manual* process if they expect to sell 60,000 bags of lettuce per month?
f. What is the monthly profit or loss of the *mechanized* process if they expect to sell 60,000 bags of lettuce per month?
g. At what quantity would Zan and Angela be indifferent to the process selected?
h. Over what range of demand would the *manual* process be preferred over the mechanized process? Over what range of demand would the *mechanized* process be preferred over the manual process? **Px**

•••• **S7.26** As a prospective owner of a club known as the Red Rose, you are interested in determining the volume of sales dollars necessary for the coming year to reach the break-even point. You have decided to break down the sales for the club into four categories, the first category being beer. Your estimate of the beer sales is that 30,000 drinks will be served. The selling price for each unit will average $1.50; the cost is $.75. The second major category is meals, which you expect to be 10,000 units with an average price of $10.00 and a cost of $5.00. The third major category is desserts and wine, of which you also expect to sell 10,000 units, but with an average price of $2.50 per unit sold and a cost of $1.00 per unit. The final category is lunches and inexpensive sandwiches, which you expect to total 20,000 units at an average price of $6.25 with a food cost of $3.25. Your fixed cost (that is, rent, utilities, and so on) is $1,800 per month plus $2,000 per month for entertainment.
a. What is your break-even point in dollars per month?
b. What is the expected number of meals each day if you are open 30 days a month?

••• **S7.27** As manager of the St. Cloud Theatre Company, you have decided that concession sales will support themselves. The following table provides the information you have been able to put together thus far:

Item	Selling Price	Variable Cost	% of Revenue
Soft drink	$1.00	$ .65	25
Wine	1.75	.95	25
Coffee	1.00	.30	30
Candy	1.00	.30	20

Last year's manager, Jim Freeland, has advised you to be sure to add 10% of variable cost as a waste allowance for all categories.

You estimate labor cost to be $250.00 (5 booths with 2 people each). Even if nothing is sold, your labor cost will be $250.00, so you decide to consider this a fixed cost. Booth rental, which is a contractual cost at $50.00 for *each* booth per night, is also a fixed cost.
a. What is the break-even volume per evening performance?
b. How much wine would you expect to sell at the break-even point?

•• **S7.28** James Lawson's Bed and Breakfast, in a small historic Mississippi town, must decide how to subdivide (remodel) the large old home that will become its inn. There are three alternatives: Option A would modernize all baths and combine rooms, leaving the inn with four suites, each suitable for two to four adults. Option B would modernize only the second floor; the results would be six suites, four for two to four adults, two for two adults only. Option C (the status quo option) leaves all walls intact. In this case, there are eight rooms available, but only two are suitable for four adults, and four rooms will not have private baths. Below are the details of profit and demand patterns that will accompany each option:

Alternatives	Annual Profit under Various Demand Patterns			
	High	p	Average	p
A (modernize all)	$90,000	.5	$25,000	.5
B (modernize 2nd)	$80,000	.4	$70,000	.6
C (status quo)	$60,000	.3	$55,000	.7

Which option has the highest expected monetary value? **Px**

•••• **S7.29** As operations manager of Holz Furniture, you must make a decision about adding a line of rustic furniture. In discussing the possibilities with your sales manager, Steve Gilbert, you decide that there will definitely be a market and that your firm should enter that market. However, because rustic furniture has a different finish than your standard offering, you decide you need another process line. There is no doubt in your mind about the decision, and you are sure that you should have a second process. But you do question how large to make it. A large process line is going to cost $400,000; a small process line will cost $300,000. The question, therefore, is the demand for rustic furniture. After extensive discussion with Mr. Gilbert and Tim Ireland of Ireland Market Research, Inc., you determine that the best estimate you can make is that there is a two-out-of-three chance of profit from sales as large as $600,000 and a one-out-of-three chance as low as $300,000.

With a large process line, you could handle the high figure of $600,000. However, with a small process line you could not and would be forced to expand (at a cost of $150,000), after which time your profit from sales would be $500,000 rather than the $600,000 because of the lost time in expanding the process. If you do not expand the small process, your profit from sales would be held to $400,000. If you build a small process and the demand is low, you can handle all of the demand.

Should you open a large or small process line? **Px**

•• **S7.30** What is the net present value of an investment that costs $75,000 and has a salvage value of $45,000? The annual profit from the investment is $15,000 each year for 5 years. The cost of capital at this risk level is 12%. **Px**

• **S7.31** The initial cost of an investment is $65,000 and the cost of capital is 10%. The return is $16,000 per year for 8 years. What is the net present value? **Px**

•• **S7.32** What is the present value of $5,600 when the interest rate is 8% and the return of $5,600 will not be received for 15 years? **Px**

•• **S7.33** Tim Smunt has been asked to evaluate two machines. After some investigation, he determines that they have the costs shown in the following table. He is told to assume that:
a) the life of each machine is 3 years, and
b) the company thinks it knows how to make 12% on investments no more risky than this one.

	Machine A	Machine B
Original cost	$10,000	$20,000
Labor per year	2,000	4,000
Maintenance per year	4,000	1,000
Salvage value	2,000	7,000

Determine, via the present value method, which machine Tim should recommend. **Px**

•••• **S7.34** Your boss has told you to evaluate two ovens for Tink-the-Tinkers, a gourmet sandwich shop. After some questioning of vendors and receipt of specifications, you are assured that the ovens have the attributes and costs shown in the following table. The following two assumptions are appropriate:

1. The life of each machine is 5 years.
2. The company thinks it knows how to make 14% on investments no more risky than this one.

	Three Small Ovens at $1,250 Each	Two Large Ovens at $2,500 Each
Original cost	$3,750	$5,000
Labor per year in excess of larger models	$ 750 (total)	
Cleaning/ maintenance	$ 750 ($250 each)	$ 400 ($200 each)
Salvage value	$ 750 ($250 each)	$1,000 ($500 each)

a. Determine via the present value method which machine to tell your boss to purchase.
b. What assumption are you making about the ovens?
c. What assumptions are you making in your methodology? **Px**

•••• **S7.35** Bold's Gym, a health club chain, is considering expanding into a new location: the initial investment would be $1 million in equipment, renovation, and a 6-year lease, and its annual upkeep and expenses would be $75,000. Its planning horizon is 6 years out, and at the end, it can sell the equipment for $50,000. Club capacity is 500 members who would pay an annual fee of $600. Bold's expects to have no problems filling membership slots. Assume that the interest rate is 10%. (See Table S7.1)

a. What is the present value profit/loss of the deal?
b. The club is considering offering a special deal to the members in the first year. For $3,000 upfront they get a full 6-year membership (i.e., 1 year free). Would it make financial sense to offer this deal? **Px**

▶ **Refer to** myomlab 🔊 **for these additional homework problems**: S7.36–S7.45

Case Study

▶ Capacity Planning at Arnold Palmer Hospital

Video Case

Since opening day, the Arnold Palmer Hospital has experienced an explosive growth in demand for its services. One of only six hospitals in the U.S. to specialize in health care for women and children, Arnold Palmer Hospital has cared for over 1,500,000 patients who came to the Orlando facility from all 50 states and more than 100 countries. With patient satisfaction scores in the top 10% of U.S. hospitals surveyed (over 95% of patients would recommend the hospital to others), one of Arnold Palmer Hospital's main focuses is delivery of babies. Originally built with 281 beds and a capacity for 6,500 births per year, the hospital steadily approached and then passed 10,000 births. Looking at Table S7.3, Executive Director Kathy Swanson knew an expansion was necessary.

With continuing population growth in its market area serving 18 central Florida counties, Arnold Palmer Hospital was delivering the equivalent of a kindergarten class of babies every day and still not meeting demand. Supported with substantial additional demographic analysis, the hospital was ready to move ahead with a capacity expansion plan and a new 11-story hospital building across the street from the existing facility.

Thirty-five planning teams were established to study such issues as (1) specific forecasts, (2) services that would transfer to the new facility, (3) services that would remain in the existing facility, (4) staffing needs, (5) capital equipment, (6) pro forma accounting data, and (7) regulatory requirements. Ultimately, Arnold Palmer Hospital was ready to move ahead with a budget of $100 million and a commitment to an additional 150 beds. But given the growth of the central Florida region, Swanson decided to expand the hospital in stages: the top two floors would be empty interiors ("shell") to be completed at a later date, and the fourth-floor operating room could be doubled in size when needed. "With the new facility in place, we are now able to handle up to 16,000 births per year," says Swanson.

▼ **TABLE S7.3**
Births at Arnold Palmer Hospital

Year	Births
1995	6,144
1996	6,230
1997	6,432
1998	6,950
1999	7,377
2000	8,655
2001	9,536
2002	9,825
2003	10,253
2004	10,555
2005	12,316
2006	13,070
2007	14,028
2008	14,634

Discussion Questions*

1. Given the capacity planning discussion in the text (see Figure S7.6) what approach is being taken by Arnold Palmer Hospital toward matching capacity to demand?
2. What kind of major changes could take place in Arnold Palmer Hospital's demand forecast that would leave the hospital with an underutilized facility (namely, what are the risks connected with this capacity decision)?
3. Use regression analysis to forecast the point at which Swanson needs to "build out" the top two floors of the new building, namely, when demand will exceed 16,000 births.

*You may wish to view the video accompanying this case before addressing these questions.

Active Model Exercises

ACTIVE MODEL S7.1 based on Example S1 in the text, allows you to stimulate changes in design capacity, utilization, and efficiency based on changes in actual output and effective capacity. It is illustrated at **www.myomlab.com** or **www. pearsonhighered.com/heizer**.

ACTIVE MODEL S7.2 based on Example S5 in the text, allows you to examine how changes in fixed cost, variable cost, and revenue affect break-even points in volume and dollars. It is illustrated at **www.myomlab.com** or **www.pearsonhighered.com/heizer**.

Classroom Activity

▶ The Dice Game

This dice game (based on *The Goal* [Goldratt and Cox, Third Revised Edition, North River Press 2004], Chapter 14) uses groups of five people and demonstrates the detrimental effects of statistical fluctuations on dependent events such as throughput of a production line. Play the game using a die, a random number table, or the RANDBETWEEN function in Excel.

The game places five players in a row. The first player is the supply chain with an unlimited supply of raw material (say pennies or matchsticks). During each round, the first player rolls one die. The number shown is the number of products moved into the raw materials area of player 2. Then player 2 rolls the die and moves the minimum of (a) the roll and (b) the number of products in the raw material area to player 3. This process continues down the line for each player. Player 5's throughput (the minimum of the raw materials available or the die roll) represents the system throughput for that round. Leave the extra units in the raw material areas and play the game for several rounds, say 10 or more.

Observe that the average number from the die (1, 2, 3, 4, 5, and 6) is not 3, but 3.5, and compare that with the actual number of units produced. What can be done to improve throughput? How might you change the game to improve throughput?

Main Heading	Review Material	

CAPACITY
(pp. 228–234)

- **Capacity**—The "throughput," or number of units a facility can hold, receive, store, or produce in a period of time.

Capacity decisions often determine capital requirements and therefore a large portion of fixed cost. Capacity also determines whether demand will be satisfied or whether facilities will be idle.

Determining facility size, with an objective of achieving high levels of utilization and a high return on investment, is critical.

Capacity planning can be viewed in three time horizons:

1. *Long-range* (> 1 year)—Adding facilities and long lead-time equipment
2. *Intermediate-range* (3–18 months)—"Aggregate planning" tasks, including adding equipment, personnel, and shifts; subcontracting; and building or using inventory
3. *Short-range* (< 3 months)—Scheduling jobs and people, and allocating machinery

- **Design capacity**—The theoretical maximum output of a system in a given period, under ideal conditions.

Most organizations operate their facilities at a rate less than the design capacity.

- **Effective capacity**—The capacity a firm can expect to achieve, given its product mix, methods of scheduling, maintenance, and standards of quality.
- **Utilization**—Actual output as a percent of design capacity.
- **Efficiency**—Actual output as a percent of effective capacity.

$$\text{Utilization} = \text{Actual output/Design capacity} \qquad \text{(S7-1)}$$

$$\text{Efficiency} = \text{Actual output/Effective capacity} \qquad \text{(S7-2)}$$

$$\text{Actual (or Expected) output} = \text{(Effective capacity)(Efficiency)} \qquad \text{(S7-3)}$$

Expected output is sometimes referred to as *rated capacity*.

When demand exceeds capacity, a firm may be able to curtail demand simply by raising prices, increasing lead times (which may be inevitable), and discouraging marginally profitable business.

When capacity exceeds demand, a firm may want to stimulate demand through price reductions or aggressive marketing, or it may accommodate the market via product changes.

In the service sector, scheduling customers is *demand management,* and scheduling the workforce is *capacity management.*

When demand and capacity are fairly well matched, demand management in services can often be handled with appointments, reservations, or a first-come, first-served rule. Otherwise, discounts based on time of day may be used (e.g., "early bird" specials, matinee pricing).

When managing demand in services is not feasible, managing capacity through changes in full-time, temporary, or part-time staff may be an option.

Problems:
S7.1–S7.8

Virtual Office Hours for
Solved Problems: S7.1

ACTIVE MODEL **S7.1**

**BOTTLENECK
ANALYSIS AND
THE THEORY OF
CONSTRAINTS**
(pp. 234–238)

- **Capacity analysis**—Determining throughput capacity of workstations or an entire production system.
- **Bottleneck**—The limiting factor or constraint in a system.
- **Process time of a station**—The time to produce a given number of units at that single workstation.
- **Process time of a system**—The time of the longest (slowest) process, the bottleneck.
- **Process cycle time**—The time it takes for a product to go through the production process with no waiting: the longest path through the system.

A system's process time determines its capacity (e.g., one car per minute), while its process cycle time determines potential ability to build product (e.g., 30 hours).

If *n* parallel (redundant) operations are added, the process time of the combined operations will equal $1/n$ times the process time of the original.

With simultaneous processing, an order or product is essentially *split* into different paths to be rejoined later on. The longest path through the system is deemed the process cycle time.

- **Theory of constraints (TOC)**—A body of knowledge that deals with anything limiting an organization's ability to achieve its goals.

Problems:
S7.9–S7.15

Main Heading	Review Material	PEARSON myomlab
BREAK-EVEN ANALYSIS (pp. 238–242)	■ **Break-even analysis**—A means of finding the point, in dollars and units, at which costs equal revenues. *Fixed costs* are costs that exist even if no units are produced. Variable costs are those that vary with the volume of units produced. In the break-even model, costs and revenue are assumed to increase linearly. $$\text{Break-even in units} = \frac{\text{Total Fixed cost}}{\text{Price} - \text{Variable cost}} \quad \text{(S7-4)}$$ $$\text{Break-even in dollars} = \frac{\text{Total Fixed cost}}{1 - \dfrac{\text{Variable cost}}{\text{Selling price}}} \quad \text{(S7-5)}$$ $$\text{Multiproduct Break-even point in dollars} = BEP_\$ = \frac{F}{\sum\left[\left(1 - \dfrac{V_i}{P_i}\right) \times (W_i)\right]} \quad \text{(S7-6)}$$	Problems: S7.16–S7.27 Virtual Office Hours for Solved Problem: S7.3 **ACTIVE MODEL S7.2**
REDUCING RISK WITH INCREMENTAL CHANGES (pp. 242–243)	Demand growth is usually in small units, while capacity additions are likely to be both instantaneous and in large units. To reduce risk, incremental changes that hedge demand forecasts may be a good option. Three approaches to capacity expansion are (1) *leading* strategy, (2) *lag* strategy, and (3) *straddle* strategy. Both lag strategy and straddle strategy delay capital expenditure.	**VIDEO S7.1** Capacity Planning at Arnold Palmer Hospital
APPLYING EXPECTED MONETARY VALUE (EMV) TO CAPACITY DECISIONS (pp. 243–244)	Determining expected monetary value requires specifying alternatives and various states of nature (e.g., demand or market favorability). By assigning probability values to the various states of nature, we can make decisions that maximize the expected value of the alternatives.	Problems: S7.28–S7.29
APPLYING INVESTMENT ANALYSIS TO STRATEGY-DRIVEN INVESTMENTS (pp. 244–247)	■ **Net present value**—A means of determining the discounted value of a series of future cash receipts. $$F = P(1 + i)^N \quad \text{(S7-7)}$$ $$P = \frac{F}{(1 + i)^N} \quad \text{(S7-8)}$$ $$P = \frac{F}{(1 + i)^N} = FX \quad \text{(S7-9)}$$ When making several investments, those with higher net present values are preferable to investments with lower net present values.	Problems: S7.30–S7.35 Virtual Office Hours for Solved Problem: S7.4

Self Test

■ **Before taking the self-test,** refer to the learning objectives listed at the beginning of the supplement and the key terms listed at the end of the supplement.

LO1. Capacity decisions should be made on the basis of:
a) building sustained competitive advantage.
b) good financial returns.
c) a coordinated plan.
d) integration into the company's strategy.
e) all of the above.

LO2. Effective capacity is:
a) the capacity a firm expects to achieve, given the current operating constraints.
b) the percent of design capacity actually achieved.
c) the percent of capacity actually achieved.
d) actual output.
e) efficiency.

LO3. System capacity is based on:
a) process time of the bottleneck.
b) throughput time.
c) process time of the fastest station.
d) throughput time plus waiting time.
e) none of the above.

LO4. The break-even point is:
a) adding processes to meet the point of changing product demands.
b) improving processes to increase throughput.
c) the point in dollars or units at which cost equals revenue.
d) adding or removing capacity to meet demand.
e) the total cost of a process alternative.

LO5. Expected monetary value is most appropriate:
a) when the payoffs are equal.
b) when the probability of each decision alternative is known.
c) when probabilities are the same.
d) when both revenue and cost are known.
e) when probabilities of each state of nature are known.

LO6. Net present value (NPV):
a) is greater if cash receipts occur later rather than earlier.
b) is greater if cash receipts occur earlier rather than later.
c) is revenue minus fixed cost.
d) is preferred over break-even analysis.
e) is greater if $100 monthly payments are received in a lump sum ($1,200) at the end of the year.

Answers: LO1. e; **LO2.** a; **LO3.** a; **LO4.** c; **LO5.** b; **LO6.** b.

8 Location Strategies

Chapter Outline

The Strategic Importance of Location

Factors That Affect Location Decisions

Methods of Evaluating Location
    Alternatives

Service Location Strategy

Ethical Dilemma
Discussion Questions
Problems
Case Studies: Southern Recreational
    Vehicle Company; Locating the Next
    Red Lobster Restaurant; Where to
    Place the Hard Rock Cafe
Active Model Exercise
Rapid Review

Location may determine up to 10% of the total *cost* for an industrial firm. For the service, retail, or professional firm, location tends to be more critical in determining *revenue* than cost. In general, however, the objective of a location strategy is to maximize the benefit of location to the firm.

This chapter covers the factors that a firm should consider in the location decision and the techniques appropriate for that decision. For industrial firms, these issues include tangible costs such as transportation, energy, labor, raw material, and taxes, as well as intangible costs such as quality of education, government, labor, and quality of life. For service firms, issues such as competition, drawing area, purchasing power, parking, security, and rent are important.

BEFORE COMING TO CLASS, READ CHAPTER 8 IN YOUR TEXT AND ANSWER THESE QUESTIONS.

1. What are the seven major factors that affect location decisions? _____

_____

_____

2. How do you compute labor productivity? _____

_____

_____

3. How can the factor-rating method be used in location decisions? _____

_____

_____

4. What is locational break-even analysis? _____

_____

_____

5. What is the center of gravity method and when is it used? _____

_____

_____

6. Identify the differences between service and industrial sector location analysis. _____

_____

_____

THE STRATEGIC IMPORTANCE OF LOCATION

(See Flexible Version pp. 254–255)

FACTORS THAT AFFECT LOCATION DECISIONS

(See Flexible Version pp. 255–258)

Country Decision

Key Success Factors

1. Political risks, government rules, attitudes, incentives
2. Cultural and economic issues
3. Location of markets
4. Labor talent, attitudes, productivity, costs
5. Availability of supplies, communications, energy
6. Exchange rates and currency risk

Region/Community Decision

1. Corporate desires
2. Attractiveness of region (culture, taxes, climate, etc.)
3. Labor availability, costs, attitudes toward unions
4. Cost and availability of utilities
5. Environmental regulations of state and town
6. Government incentives and fiscal policies
7. Proximity to raw materials and customers
8. Land/construction costs

Site Decision

1. Site size and cost
2. Air, rail, highway, and waterway systems
3. Zoning restrictions
4. Proximity of services/supplies needed
5. Environmental impact issues

▲ **FIGURE 8.1** **Some Considerations and Factors That Affect Location Decisions**

Labor Productivity (See Flexible Version p. 256)

$$\frac{\text{Labor cost per day}}{\text{Productivity (that is, units per day)}} = \text{Labor cost per unit}$$

Exchange Rates and Currency Risk (See Flexible Version p. 256)

Costs (See Flexible Version pp. 257–258)

Political Risk, Value, and Culture (See Flexible Version p. 258)

Proximity to Markets (See Flexible Version p. 258)

Proximity to Suppliers (See Flexible Version p. 258)

Proximity to Competitors (Clustering)

(See Flexible Version p. 258)

METHODS OF EVALUATING LOCATION ALTERNATIVES

(See Flexible Version pp. 259–264)

Major Location Evaluation Methods

(See Flexible Version pp. 259–264)

1. **Factor Rating Method**

2. **Locational Break-Even Analysis**

3. **Center of Gravity**

4. **Transportation Model**

The Factor-Rating Method (See Flexible Version pp. 259–260)

Steps in the Factor Rating Method

1. _____

2. _____

3. _____

4. _____

5. _____

6. _____

PRACTICE PROBLEM 8.1 ■ Factor Rating Method

A major drug store chain wishes to build a new warehouse to serve the whole Midwest. At the moment, it is looking at three possible locations. The factors, weights, and ratings being considered are as follows:

Factor	Weights	Ratings Peoria	Ratings Des Moines	Ratings Chicago
Nearness to markets	20	4	7	5
Labor cost	5	8	8	4
Taxes	15	8	9	7
Nearness to suppliers	10	10	6	10

What city should it choose?

Additional Practice Problem Space

Locational Break-Even Analysis

(See Flexible Version pp. 260–261)

- Method of Cost-Volume Analysis Used for Industrial Locations

Steps

1. _____

2. _____

3. _____

PRACTICE PROBLEM 8.2 ■ Break-Even Analysis

Balfour's is considering building a plant in one of three possible locations. They have estimated the following parameters for each location:

Location	Fixed Cost	Variable Cost
Waco, Texas	$300,000	$5.75
Tijuana, Mexico	$800,000	$2.75
Fayetteville, Arkansas	$100,000	$8.00

For what unit sales volume should they choose each location?

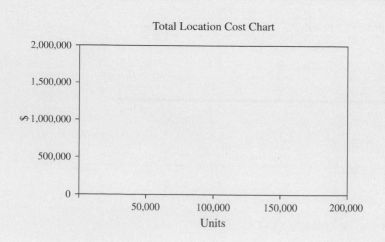

Total Location Cost Chart

Additional Practice Problem Space

Center-of-Gravity Method (See Flexible Version pp. 262–263)

- **Finds Location of Single Distribution Center Serving Several Destinations**
- **Used Primarily for Services**
- **Considers Location, Volume, and Shipping Distance**

$$x\text{-coordinate of the center of gravity} = \frac{\sum_i d_{ix}Q_i}{\sum_i Q_i} \qquad (8\text{-}1)$$

$$y\text{-coordinate of the center of gravity} = \frac{\sum_i d_{iy}Q_i}{\sum_i Q_i} \qquad (8\text{-}2)$$

where d_{ix} = x-coordinate of location i

d_{iy} = y-coordinate of location i

Q_i = Quantity of goods moved to or from location i

PRACTICE PROBLEM 8.3 ■ Center of Gravity Method

Our main distribution center in Phoenix, AZ, is due to be replaced with a much larger, more modern facility that can handle the tremendous needs that have developed with the city's growth. Fresh produce travels to the seven store locations several times a day, making site selection critical for efficient distribution. Using the data in the following table, determine the map coordinates for the proposed new distribution center.

Store Locations	Map Coordinates (x, y)	Truck Round Trips per Day
Mesa	(10,5)	3
Glendale	(3,8)	3
Camelback	(4,7)	2
Scottsdale	(15,10)	6
Apache Junction	(13,3)	5
Sun City	(1,12)	3
Pima	(5,5)	10

(*continued*)

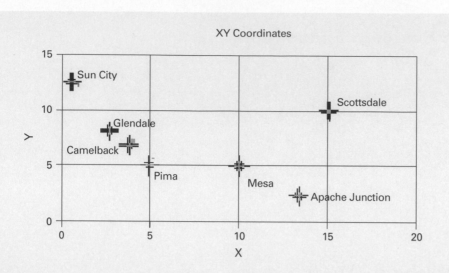

Additional Practice Problem Space

Transportation Model (See Flexible Version pp. 263–264)

- **Finds Amount to Be Shipped from Several Sources to Several Destinations**
- **Used Primarily for Industrial Locations**
- **Type of Linear Programming Model**

SERVICE LOCATION STRATEGY (See Flexible Version pp. 264–268)

Eight major determinants of volume and revenue for the service firm:

1. _____

2. _____

3. _____

4. _____

5. _____

6. _____

7. _____

8. _____

◀ **TABLE 8.6**
Location Strategies—Service vs. Goods-Producing Organizations

Service/Retail/Professional Location	Goods-Producing Location
Revenue Focus	**Cost Focus**
Volume/revenue	**Tangible costs**
Drawing area; purchasing power	Transportation cost of raw material
Competition; advertising/pricing	Shipment cost of finished goods
	Energy and utility cost; labor; raw material; taxes; and so on
Physical quality	
Parking/access; security/lighting; appearance/image	**Intangible and future costs**
	Attitude toward union
Cost determinants	Quality of life
Rent	Education expenditures by state
Management caliber	Quality of state and local government
Operation policies (hours, wage rates)	
Techniques	**Techniques**
Regression models to determine importance of various factors	Transportation method
Factor-rating method	Factor-rating method
Traffic counts	Locational break-even analysis
Demographic analysis of drawing area	Crossover charts
Purchasing power analysis of area	
Center-of-gravity method	
Geographic information systems	
Assumptions	**Assumptions**
Location is a major determinant of revenue	Location is a major determinant of cost
High customer-contact issues are critical	Most major costs can be identified explicitly for each site
Costs are relatively constant for a given area; therefore, the revenue function is critical	Low customer contact allows focus on the identifiable costs
	Intangible costs can be evaluated

Ethical Dilemma

In this chapter, we have discussed a number of location decisions. Consider another: United Air Lines announced its competition to select a town for a new billion-dollar aircraft-repair base. The bidding for the prize of 7,500 jobs paying at least $25 per hour was fast and furious, with Orlando offering $154 million in incentives and Denver more than twice that amount. Kentucky's governor angrily rescinded Louisville's offer of $300 million, likening the bidding to "squeezing every drop of blood out of a turnip."

When United finally selected from among the 93 cities bidding on the base, the winner was Indianapolis and its $320 million offer of taxpayers' money.

But in 2003, with United near bankruptcy, and having fulfilled its legal obligation, the company walked away from the massive center. This left the city and state governments out all that money, with no new tenant in sight. The city now even owns the tools, neatly arranged in each of the 12 elaborately equipped hangar bays. United outsourced its maintenance to mechanics at a Southern firm (which pays one-third of what United gave out in salary and benefits in Indianapolis).

What are the ethical, legal, and economic implications of such location bidding wars? Who pays for such giveaways? Are local citizens allowed to vote on offers made by their cities, counties, or states? Should there be limits on these incentives?

Discussion Questions

1. How is FedEx's location a competitive advantage? Discuss.
2. Why do so many U.S. firms build facilities in other countries?
3. Why do so many foreign companies build facilities in the U.S.?
4. What is clustering?
5. How does factor weighting incorporate personal preference in location choices?
6. What are the advantages and disadvantages of a qualitative (as opposed to a quantitative) approach to location decision making?
7. Provide two examples of clustering in the service sector.
8. What are the major factors that firms consider when choosing a country in which to locate?
9. What factors affect region/community location decisions?
10. Although most organizations may make the location decision infrequently, there are some organizations that make the decision quite regularly and often. Provide one or two examples. How might their approach to the location decision differ from the norm?
11. List factors, other than globalization, that affect the location decision.
12. Explain the assumptions behind the center-of-gravity method. How can the model be used in a service facility location?
13. What are the three steps to locational break-even analysis?
14. "Manufacturers locate near their resources, retailers locate near their customers." Discuss this statement, with reference to the proximity-to-markets arguments covered in the text. Can you think of a counterexample in each case? Support your choices.
15. Why shouldn't low wage rates alone be sufficient to select a location?
16. List the techniques used by service organizations to select locations.
17. Contrast the location of a food distributor and a supermarket. (The distributor sends truckloads of food, meat, produce, etc., to the supermarket.) Show the relevant considerations (factors) they share; show those where they differ.
18. Elmer's Fudge Factory is planning to open 10 retail outlets in Oregon over the next 2 years. Identify (and weight) those factors relevant to the decision. Provide this list of factors and weights.

Problems*

•   **8.1** In Cambodia, 6 laborers, each making the equivalent of $3 per day, can produce 40 units per day. In China, 10 laborers, each making the equivalent of $2 per day, can produce 45 units. In Billings, Montana, two laborers, each making $60 per day, can make 100 units. Based on labor costs only, which location would be most economical to produce the item?

•   **8.2** Refer to Problem 8.1. Shipping cost from Cambodia to Denver, Colorado, the final destination, is $1.50 per unit. Shipping cost from China to Denver is $1 per unit, while the shipping cost from Billings to Denver is $.25 per unit. Considering both labor and transportation costs, which is the most favorable production location?

•• **8.3** You have been asked to analyze the bids for 200 polished disks used in solar panels. These bids have been submitted by three suppliers: Thailand Polishing, India Shine, and Sacramento Glow. Thailand Polishing has submitted a bid of 2,000 baht. India Shine has submitted a bid of 2,000 rupee. Sacramento Glow has submitted a bid of $200. You check with your local bank and find that $1 = 10 baht and $1 = 8 rupee. Which company should you choose?

*Note: **PX** means the problem may be solved with POM for Windows and/or Excel OM.

•   **8.4** Refer to Problem 8.3. If the final destination is New Delhi, India, and there is a 30% import tax, which firm should you choose?

•• **8.5** Subway, with more than 20,000 outlets in the U.S., is planning for a new restaurant in Buffalo, New York. Three locations are being considered. The following table gives the factors for each site.

Factor	Weight	Maitland	Baptist Church	Northside Mall
Space	.30	60	70	80
Costs	.25	40	80	30
Traffic density	.20	50	80	60
Neighborhood income	.15	50	70	40
Zoning laws	.10	80	20	90

a) At which site should Subway open the new restaurant?
b) If the weights for Space and Traffic density are reversed, how would this affect the decision? **PX**

• **8.6** Gayla Delong owns the Oklahoma Warriors, a minor league baseball team in northwest Oklahoma. She wishes to move the Warriors east, to either Atlanta or Charlotte. The table below gives the factors that Gayla thinks are important, their weights, and the scores for Atlanta and Charlotte.

Factor	Weight	Atlanta	Charlotte
Incentive	.4	80	60
Player satisfaction	.3	20	50
Sports interest	.2	40	90
Size of city	.1	70	30

a) Which site should she select?
b) Charlotte just raised its incentive package, and the new score is 75. Why doesn't this impact your decision in part (a)? **Px**

•• **8.7** Insurance Company of Latin America (ILA) is considering opening an office in the U.S. The two cities under consideration are Philadelphia and New York. The factor ratings (higher scores are better) for the two cities are given in the following table. In which city should ILA locate?

Factor	Weight	Philadelphia	New York
Customer convenience	.25	70	80
Bank accessibility	.20	40	90
Computer support	.20	85	75
Rental costs	.15	90	55
Labor costs	.10	80	50
Taxes	.10	90	50 **Px**

•• **8.8** Marilyn Helm Retailers is attempting to decide on a location for a new retail outlet. At the moment, the firm has three alternatives—stay where it is but enlarge the facility; locate along the main street in nearby Newbury; or locate in a new shopping mall in Hyde Park. The company has selected the four factors listed in the following table as the basis for evaluation and has assigned weights as shown:

Factor	Factor Description	Weight
1	Average community income	.30
2	Community growth potential	.15
3	Availability of public transportation	.20
4	Labor availability, attitude, and cost	.35

Helm has rated each location for each factor, on a 100-point basis. These ratings are given below:

	Location		
Factor	Present Location	Newbury	Hyde Park
1	40	60	50
2	20	20	80
3	30	60	50
4	80	50	50

a) What should Helm do?
b) A new subway station is scheduled to open across the street from the present location in about a month, so its third factor score should be raised to 40. How does this change your answer? **Px**

•• **8.9** A location analysis for Temponi Controls, a small manufacturer of parts for high-technology cable systems, has been narrowed down to four locations. Temponi will need to train assemblers, testers, and robotics maintainers in local training centers. Cecilia Temponi, the president, has asked each potential site to offer training programs, tax breaks, and other industrial incentives. The critical factors, their weights, and the ratings for each location are shown in the following table. High scores represent favorable values.

		Location			
Factor	Weight	Akron, OH	Biloxi, MS	Carthage, TX	Denver, CO
Labor availability	.15	90	80	90	80
Technical school quality	.10	95	75	65	85
Operating cost	.30	80	85	95	85
Land and construction cost	.15	60	80	90	70
Industrial incentives	.20	90	75	85	60
Labor cost	.10	75	80	85	75

a) Compute the composite (weighted average) rating for each location.
b) Which site would you choose?
c) Would you reach the same conclusion if the weights for operating cost and labor cost were reversed? Recompute as necessary and explain. **Px**

••• **8.10** Consolidated Refineries, headquartered in Houston, must decide among three sites for the construction of a new oil-processing center. The firm has selected the six factors listed below as a basis for evaluation and has assigned rating weights from 1 to 5 on each factor:

Factor	Factor Name	Rating Weight
1	Proximity to port facilities	5
2	Power-source availability and cost	3
3	Workforce attitude and cost	4
4	Distance from Houston	2
5	Community desirability	2
6	Equipment suppliers in area	3

Management has rated each location for each factor on a 1- to 100-point basis.

Factor	Location A	Location B	Location C
1	100	80	80
2	80	70	100
3	30	60	70
4	10	80	60
5	90	60	80
6	50	60	90

a) Which site will be recommended based on *total* weighted scores?

b) If location B's score for Proximity to port facilities was reset at 90, how would the result change?

c) What score would location B need on Proximity to port facilities to change its ranking? **Px**

•• **8.11** A company is planning on expanding and building a new plant in one of three Southeast Asian countries. Chris Ellis, the manager charged with making the decision, has determined that five key success factors can be used to evaluate the prospective countries. Ellis used a rating system of 1 (least desirable country) to 5 (most desirable) to evaluate each factor.

Key Success Factors	Weight	Candidate Country Ratings		
		Taiwan	Thailand	Singapore
Technology	0.2	4	5	1
Level of education	0.1	4	1	5
Political and legal aspects	0.4	1	3	3
Social and cultural aspects	0.1	4	2	3
Economic factors	0.2	3	3	2

a) Which country should be selected for the new plant?

b) Political unrest in Thailand results in a lower score, 2, for Political and legal aspects. Does your conclusion change?

c) What if Thailand's score drops even further, to a 1, for Political and legal aspects? **Px**

• **8.12** Thomas Green College is contemplating opening a European campus where students from the main campus could go to take courses for 1 of the 4 college years. At the moment, it is considering five countries: Holland, Great Britain, Italy, Belgium, and Greece. The college wishes to consider eight factors in its decision. All the factors have equal weight. The following table illustrates its assessment of each factor for each country (5 is best).

Factor	Factor Description	Holland	Great Britain	Italy	Belgium	Greece
1	Stability of government	5	5	3	5	4
2	Degree to which the population can converse in English	4	5	3	4	3
3	Stability of the monetary system	5	4	3	4	3
4	Communications infrastructure	4	5	3	4	3
5	Transportation infrastructure	5	5	3	5	3

(*continued*)

Factor	Factor Description	Holland	Great Britain	Italy	Belgium	Greece
6	Availability of historic/cultural sites	3	4	5	3	5
7	Import restrictions	4	4	3	4	4
8	Availability of suitable quarters	4	4	3	4	3

a) In which country should Thomas Green College choose to set up its European campus?

b) How would the decision change if the "degree to which the population can converse in English" was not an issue? **Px**

•• **8.13** Daniel Tracy, owner of Martin Manufacturing, must expand by building a new factory. The search for a location for this factory has been narrowed to four sites: A, B, C, or D. The following table shows the results thus far obtained by Tracy by using the factor-rating method to analyze the problem. The scale used for each factor scoring is 1 through 5.

Factor	Weight	Site Scores			
		A	B	C	D
Quality of labor	10	5	4	4	5
Construction cost	8	2	3	4	1
Transportation costs	8	3	4	3	2
Proximity to markets	7	5	3	4	4
Taxes	6	2	3	3	4
Weather	6	2	5	5	4
Energy costs	5	5	4	3	3

a) Which site should Tracy choose?

b) If site D's score for Energy costs increases from a 3 to a 5, do results change?

c) If site A's Weather score is adjusted to a 4, what is the impact? What should Tracy do at this point? **Px**

••• **8.14** An American consulting firm is planning to expand globally by opening a new office in one of four countries: Germany,

Key Success Factors	Weight	Candidate Country Ratings			
		Germany	Italy	Spain	Greece
Level of education					
Number of consultants	.05	5	5	5	2
National literacy rate	.05	4	2	1	1
Political aspects					
Stability of government	0.2	5	5	5	2
Product liability laws	0.2	5	2	3	5
Environmental regulations	0.2	1	4	1	3
Social and cultural Aspects					
Similarity in language	0.1	4	2	1	1
Acceptability of consultants	0.1	1	4	4	3
Economic factors					
Incentives	0.1	2	3	1	5

Italy, Spain, or Greece (see table on prior page). The chief partner entrusted with the decision, L. Wayne Shell, has identified eight key success factors that he views as essential for the success of any consultancy. He used a rating system of 1 (least desirable country) to 5 (most desirable) to evaluate each factor.
a) Which country should be selected for the new office?
b) If Spain's score were lowered in the Stability of government factor, to a 4, how would its overall score change? On this factor, at what score for Spain *would* the rankings change? **Px**

•• **8.15** A British hospital chain wishes to make its first entry into the U.S. market by building a medical facility in the Midwest, a region with which its director, Doug Moodie, is comfortable because he got his medical degree at Northwestern University. After a preliminary analysis, four cities are chosen for further consideration. They are rated and weighted according to the factors shown below:

		City			
Factor	Weight	Chicago	Milwaukee	Madison	Detroit
Costs	2.0	8	5	6	7
Need for a facility	1.5	4	9	8	4
Staff availability	1.0	7	6	4	7
Local incentives	0.5	8	6	5	9

a) Which city should Moodie select?
b) Assume a minimum score of 5 is now required for all factors. Which city should be chosen? **Px**

•• **8.16** The fixed and variable costs for three potential manufacturing plant sites for a rattan chair weaver are shown:

Site	Fixed Cost per Year	Variable Cost per Unit
1	$ 500	$11
2	1,000	7
3	1,700	4

a) Over what range of production is each location optimal?
b) For a production of 200 units, which site is best? **Px**

• **8.17** Peter Billington Stereo, Inc., supplies car radios to auto manufacturers and is going to open a new plant. The company is undecided between Detroit and Dallas as the site. The fixed costs in Dallas are lower due to cheaper land costs, but the variable costs in Dallas are higher because shipping distances would increase. Given the following costs:

	Dallas	Detroit
Fixed costs	$600,000	$800,000
Variable costs	$28/radio	$22/radio

a) Perform an analysis of the volume over which each location is preferable.
b) How does your answer change if Dallas's fixed costs increase by 10%? **Px**

••• **8.18** Audi Motors is considering three sites—A, B, and C—at which to locate a factory to build its new-model automobile, the Audi SUV XL500. The goal is to locate at a minimum-cost site, where cost is measured by the annual fixed plus variable costs of production. Audi Motors has gathered the following data:

Site	Annualized Fixed Cost	Variable Cost per Auto Produced
A	$10,000,000	$2,500
B	$20,000,000	$2,000
C	$25,000,000	$1,000

The firm knows it will produce between 0 and 60,000 SUV XL500s at the new plant each year, but, thus far, that is the extent of its knowledge about production plans.
a) For what values of volume, V, of production, if any, is site C a recommended site?
b) What volume indicates site A is optimal?
c) Over what range of volume is site B optimal? Why? **Px**

•• **8.19** Hugh Leach Corp., a producer of machine tools, wants to move to a larger site. Two alternative locations have been identified: Bonham and McKinney. Bonham would have fixed costs of $800,000 per year and variable costs of $14,000 per standard unit produced. McKinney would have annual fixed costs of $920,000 and variable costs of $13,000 per standard unit. The finished items sell for $29,000 each.
a) At what volume of output would the two locations have the same profit?
b) For what range of output would Bonham be superior (have higher profits)?
c) For what range would McKinney be superior?
d) What is the relevance of break-even points for these cities? **Px**

•• **8.20** The following table gives the map coordinates and the shipping loads for a set of cities that we wish to connect through a central hub.

City	Map Coordinate (x, y)	Shipping Load
A	(5, 10)	5
B	(6, 8)	10
C	(4, 9)	15
D	(9, 5)	5
E	(7, 9)	15
F	(3, 2)	10
G	(2, 6)	5

a) Near which map coordinates should the hub be located?
b) If the shipments from city A triple, how does this change the coordinates? **Px**

•• **8.21** A chain of home health care firms in Louisiana needs to locate a central office from which to conduct internal audits and other periodic reviews of its facilities. These facilities are scattered throughout the state, as detailed in the following table. Each site, except for Houma, will be visited three times each year by a team of workers, who will drive from the central office to the site. Houma will be visited five times a year. Which coordinates represent a good central location for this office? What other factors might influence the office location decision? Where would you place this office? Explain.

City	Map Coordinates	
	X	Y
Covington	9.2	3.5
Donaldsonville	7.3	2.5
Houma	7.8	1.4
Monroe	5.0	8.4
Natchitoches	2.8	6.5
New Iberia	5.5	2.4
Opelousas	5.0	3.6
Ruston	3.8	8.5

Px

•• **8.22** A small rural county has experienced unprecedented growth over the past 6 years, and as a result, the local school district built the new 500-student North Park Elementary School. The district has three older and smaller elementary schools: Washington,

Jefferson, and Lincoln. Now the growth pressure is being felt at the secondary level. The school district would like to build a centrally located middle school to accommodate students and reduce busing costs. The older middle school is adjacent to the high school and will become part of the high school campus.

a) What are the coordinates of the central location?

b) What other factors should be considered before building a school? **Px**

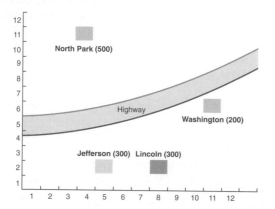

•• 8.23 Todd's Video, a major video rental and TV sales chain headquartered in New Orleans, is about to open its first outlet in Mobile, Alabama, and wants to select a site that will place the new outlet in the center of Mobile's population base. Todd examines the seven census tracts in Mobile, plots the coordinates of the center of each from a map, and looks up the population base in each to use as a weighting. The information gathered appears in the following table.

Census Tract	Population in Census Tract	X, Y Map Coordinates
101	2,000	(25, 45)
102	5,000	(25, 25)
103	10,000	(55, 45)
104	7,000	(50, 20)
105	10,000	(80, 50)
106	20,000	(70, 20)
107	14,000	(90, 25)

a) At what center-of-gravity coordinates should the new store be located?

b) Census tracts 103 and 105 are each projected to grow by 20% in the next year. How will this influence the new store's coordinates? **Px**

•••• 8.24 Eagle Electronics must expand by building a second facility. The search has been narrowed down to locating the new facility in one of four cities: Atlanta (A), Baltimore (B), Chicago (C), or Dallas (D). The factors, scores, and weights follow:

i	Factor	Weight (W_i)	A	B	C	D
1	Labor quality	20	5	4	4	5
2	Quality of life	16	2	3	4	1
3	Transportation	16	3	4	3	2
4	Proximity to markets	14	5	3	4	4
5	Proximity to suppliers	12	2	3	3	4
6	Taxes	12	2	5	5	4
7	Energy supplies	10	5	4	3	3

Scores by Site columns: A B C D

a) Using the factor-rating method, what is the recommended site for Eagle Electronics's new facility?

b) For what range of values for the weight (currently $w_7 = 10$) does the site given as the answer to part (a) remain a recommended site?

•••• 8.25 The EU has made changes in airline regulation that dramatically affect major European carriers such as British International Air (BIA), KLM, Air France, Alitalia, and Swiss International Air.

Data for Problem 8.25		Location								
	Importance Weight	Italy			France			Germany		
Factor		Milan	Rome	Genoa	Paris	Lyon	Nice	Munich	Bonn	Berlin
Financial incentives	85	8	8	8	7	7	7	7	7	7
Skilled labor pool	80	4	6	5	9	9	7	10	8	9
Existing facility	70	5	3	2	9	6	5	9	9	2
Wage rates	70	9	8	9	4	6	6	4	5	5
Competition for jobs	70	7	3	8	2	8	7	4	8	9
Ease of air traffic access	65	5	4	6	2	8	8	4	8	9
Real estate cost	40	6	4	7	4	6	6	3	4	5
Communication links	25	6	7	6	9	9	9	10	9	8
Attractiveness to relocating executives	15	4	8	3	9	6	6	2	3	3
Political considerations	10	6	6	6	8	8	8	8	8	8
Expansion possibilities	10	10	2	8	1	5	4	4	5	6
Union strength	10	1	1	1	5	5	5	6	6	6

With ambitious expansion plans, BIA has decided it needs a second service hub on the continent, to complement its large Heathrow (London) repair facility. The location selection is critical, and with the potential for 4,000 new skilled blue-collar jobs on the line, virtually every city in western Europe is actively bidding for BIA's business.

After initial investigations by Holmes Miller, head of the Operations Department, BIA has narrowed the list to 9 cities. Each is then rated on 12 factors, as shown in the table on the previous page.

a) Help Miller rank the top three cities that BIA should consider as its new site for servicing aircraft.

b) After further investigation, Miller decides that an existing set of hangar facilities for repairs is not nearly as important as earlier thought. If he lowers the weight of that factor to 30, does the ranking change?

c) After Miller makes the change in part (b), Germany announces it has reconsidered its offer of financial incentives, with an additional 200-million-euro package to entice BIA. Accordingly, BIA has raised Germany's rating to 10 on that factor. Is there any change in top rankings in part (b)? **Px**

▶ **Refer to** myomlab ⊙ **for these additional homework problems: 8.26–8.34**

Case Studies

▶ Southern Recreational Vehicle Company

In October 2010, top management of Southern Recreational Vehicle Company of St. Louis, Missouri, announced its plans to relocate its manufacturing and assembly operations to a new plant in Ridgecrest, Mississippi. The firm, a major producer of pickup campers and camper trailers, had experienced 5 consecutive years of declining profits as a result of spiraling production costs. The costs of labor and raw materials had increased alarmingly, utility costs had gone up sharply, and taxes and transportation expenses had steadily climbed upward. In spite of increased sales, the company suffered its first net loss since operations were begun in 1982.

When management initially considered relocation, it closely scrutinized several geographic areas. Of primary importance to the relocation decision were the availability of adequate transportation facilities, state and municipal tax structures, an adequate labor supply, positive community attitudes, reasonable site costs, and financial inducements. Although several communities offered essentially the same incentives, the management of Southern Recreational Vehicle Company was favorably impressed by the efforts of the Mississippi Power and Light Company to attract "clean, labor-intensive" industry and the enthusiasm exhibited by state and local officials, who actively sought to bolster the state's economy by enticing manufacturing firms to locate within its boundaries.

Two weeks prior to the announcement, management of Southern Recreational Vehicle Company finalized its relocation plans. An existing building in Ridgecrest's industrial park was selected (the physical facility had previously housed a mobile home manufacturer that had gone bankrupt due to inadequate financing and poor management); initial recruiting was begun through the state employment office; and efforts to lease or sell the St. Louis property were initiated. Among the inducements offered Southern Recreational Vehicle Company to locate in Ridgecrest were:

1. Exemption from county and municipal taxes for 5 years
2. Free water and sewage services
3. Construction of a second loading dock—free of cost—at the industrial site
4. An agreement to issue $500,000 in industrial bonds for future expansion
5. Public-financed training of workers in a local industrial trade school

In addition to these inducements, other factors weighed heavily in the decision to locate in the small Mississippi town. Labor costs would be significantly less than those incurred in St. Louis; organized labor was not expected to be as powerful (Mississippi is a right-to-work state); and utility costs and taxes would be moderate. All in all, management of Southern Recreational Vehicle Company felt that its decision was sound.

On October 15, the following announcement was attached to each employee's paycheck:

To: Employees of Southern Recreational Vehicle Company

From: Gerald O'Brian, President

The Management of Southern Recreational Vehicle Company regretfully announces its plans to cease all manufacturing operations in St. Louis on December 31. Because of increased operating costs and the unreasonable demands forced upon the company by the union, it has become impossible to operate profitably. I sincerely appreciate the fine service that each of you has rendered to the company during the past years. If I can be of assistance in helping you find suitable employment with another firm, please let me know. Thank you again for your cooperation and past service.

Discussion Questions

1. Evaluate the inducements offered Southern Recreational Vehicle Company by community leaders in Ridgecrest, Mississippi.
2. What problems would a company experience in relocating its executives from a heavily populated industrialized area to a small rural town?
3. Evaluate the reasons cited by O'Brian for relocation. Are they justifiable?
4. What legal and ethical responsibilities does a firm have to its employees when a decision to cease operations is made?

Source: Reprinted by permission of Professor Jerry Kinard, Western Carolina University.

► Locating the Next Red Lobster Restaurant

From its first Red Lobster in 1968, Darden Restaurants has grown the chain to 690 locations, with over $2.6 billion in U.S. sales annually. The casual dining market may be crowded, with competitors such as Chili's, Ruby Tuesday, Applebee's, TGI Friday's, and Outback, but Darden's continuing success means the chain thinks there is still plenty of room to grow. Robert Reiner, director of market development, is charged with identifying the sites that will maximize new store sales without cannibalizing sales at the existing Red Lobster locations.

Characteristics for identifying a good site have not changed in 40 years; they still include real estate prices, customer age, competition, ethnicity, income, family size, population density, nearby hotels, and buying behavior, to name just a few. What *has* changed is the powerful software that allows Reiner to analyze a new site in 5 minutes, as opposed to the 8 hours he spent just a few years ago.

Darden has partnered with MapInfo Corp., whose geographic information system (GIS) contains a powerful module for analyzing a trade area (see the discussion of GIS in the chapter). With the U.S. geo-coded down to the individual block, MapInfo allows Reiner to create a psychographic profile of existing and potential Red Lobster trade areas. "We can now target areas with greatest sales potential," says Reiner.

The U.S. is segmented into 72 "clusters" of customer profiles by MapInfo. If, for example, cluster #7, Equestrian Heights (see MapInfo description below), represents 1.7% of a household base within a Red Lobster trade area, but this segment also accounts for 2.4% of sales, Reiner computes that this segment is effectively spending 1.39 times more than average (Index = 2.4/1.7) and adjusts his analysis of a new site to reflect this added weight.

Cluster	PSYTE 2003	Snapshot Description
7	Equestrian Heights	They may not have a stallion in the barn, but they likely pass a corral on the way home. These families with teens live in older, larger homes adjacent to, or between, suburbs but not usually tract housing. Most are married with teenagers, but 40% are empty nesters. They use their graduate and professional school education— 56% are dual earners. Over 90% are white, non-Hispanic. Their mean family income is $99,000, and they live within commuting distance of central cities. They have white-collar jobs during the week but require a riding lawn mower to keep the place up on weekends.

When Reiner maps the U.S., a state, or a region for a new site, he wants one that is at least 3 miles from the nearest Red Lobster and won't negatively impact its sales by more than 8%; MapInfo pinpoints the best spot. The software also recognizes the nearness of non-Darden competition and assigns a probability of success (as measured by reaching sales potential).

The specific spot selected depends on Darden's seven real estate brokers, whose list of considerations include proximity to a vibrant retail area, proximity to a freeway, road visibility, nearby hotels, and a corner location at a primary intersection.

"Picking a new Red Lobster location is one of the most critical functions we can do at Darden," says Reiner. "And the software we use serves as an independent voice in assessing the quality of an existing or proposed location."

Discussion Questions*

1. Visit the Web site for MapInfo (**www.mapinfo.com**). Describe the psychological profiling (PSYTE) clustering system. Select an industry, other than restaurants, and explain how the software can be used for that industry.
2. What are the major differences in site location for a restaurant vs. a retail store vs. a manufacturing plant?
3. Red Lobster also defines its trade areas based on market size and population density. Here are its seven density classes:

Density Class	Description	Households per Sq. Mile
1	Super Urban	8,000+
2	Urban	4,000–7,999
3	Light Urban	2,000–3,999
4	First Tier Suburban	1,000–1,999
5	Second Tier Suburban	600–999
6	Exurban/Small	100–599
7	Rural	0–99

Note: Density classes are based on the households and land area within 3 miles of the geography (i.e., census tract) using population-weighted centroids.

Ninety-two percent of the Red Lobster restaurants fall into three of these classes. Which three classes do you think the chain has the most restaurants in? Why?

*You may wish to view the video that accompanies this case before answering the questions.

► Where to Place the Hard Rock Cafe

Some people would say that Oliver Munday, Hard Rock's vice president for cafe development, has the best job in the world. Travel the world to pick a country for Hard Rock's next cafe, select a city, and find the ideal site. It's true that selecting a site involves lots of incognito walking around, visiting nice restaurants, and drinking in bars. But that is not where Mr. Munday's work begins, nor where it ends. At the front end, selecting the country and city first involves a

great deal of research. At the back end, Munday not only picks the final site and negotiates the deal but then works with architects and planners and stays with the project through the opening and first year's sales.

Munday is currently looking heavily into global expansion in Europe, Latin America, and Asia. "We've got to look at political risk, currency, and social norms—how does our brand fit into the country," he says. Once the country is selected, Munday focuses on the region and city. His research checklist is extensive, as shown in the list.

Hard Rock's Standard Market Report (for offshore sites)

A. Demographics (local, city, region, SMSA), with trend analysis
   1. Population of area
   2. Economic indicators
B. Visitor market, with trend analysis
   1. Tourists/business visitors
   2. Hotels
   3. Convention center
   4. Entertainment
   5. Sports
   6. Retail
C. Transportation
   1. Airport ←
   2. Rail
   3. Road
   4. Sea/river
D. Restaurants and nightclubs (a selection in key target market areas)
E. Political risk
F. Real estate market
G. Hard Rock Cafe comparable market analysis

subcategories include:
(a) age of airport,
(b) no. of passengers,
(c) airlines,
(d) direct flights,
(e) hubs

Site location now tends to focus on the tremendous resurgence of "city centers," where nightlife tends to concentrate. That's what Munday selected in Moscow and Bogota, although in both locations he chose to find a local partner and franchise the operation. In these two political environments, "Hard Rock wouldn't dream of operating by ourselves," says Munday. The location decision also is at least a 10- to 15-year commitment by Hard Rock, which employs tools such as break-even analysis to help decide whether to purchase land and build, or to remodel an existing facility.

Currently, Munday is considering four European cities for Hard Rock's next expansion. Although he could not provide the names, for competitive reasons, the following is known:

Factor	European City under Consideration				Importance of This Factor at This Time
	A	**B**	**C**	**D**	
A. Demographics	70	70	60	90	20
B. Visitor market	80	60	90	75	20
C. Transportation	100	50	75	90	20
D. Restaurants/ nightclubs	80	90	65	65	10
E. Low political risk	90	60	50	70	10
F. Real estate market	65	75	85	70	10
G. Comparable market analysis	70	60	65	80	10

Discussion Questions*

1. From Munday's Standard Market Report checklist, select any other four categories, such as population (A1), hotels (B2), or restaurants/nightclubs (D), and provide three subcategories that should be evaluated. (See item C1 [airport] for a guide.)
2. Which is the highest rated of the four European cities under consideration, using the table above?
3. Why does Hard Rock put such serious effort into its location analysis?
4. Under what conditions do you think Hard Rock prefers to franchise a cafe?

*You may wish to view the video case before answering the questions.

Active Model Exercise

ACTIVE MODEL 8.1 allows you to simulate important elements in the center-of-gravity model illustrated in Example 3 in the text. It is illustrated at **www.myomlab.com** or **www.pearsonhighered.com/heizer**.

Chapter 8 *Rapid* Review

Main Heading	Review Material	myomlab

THE STRATEGIC IMPORTANCE OF LOCATION
(pp. 254–255)

Location has a major impact on the overall risk and profit of the company. Transportation costs alone can total as much as 25% of the product's selling price. When all costs are considered, location may alter total operating expenses as much as 50%. Companies make location decisions relatively infrequently, usually because demand has outgrown the current plant's capacity or because of changes in labor productivity, exchange rates, costs, or local attitudes. Companies may also relocate their manufacturing or service facilities because of shifts in demographics and customer demand. Location options include (1) expanding an existing facility instead of moving, (2) maintaining current sites while adding another facility elsewhere, and (3) closing the existing facility and moving to another location.

For industrial location decisions, the location strategy is usually minimizing costs. For retail and professional service organizations, the strategy focuses on maximizing revenue. Warehouse location strategy may be driven by a combination of cost and speed of delivery.

The objective of location strategy is to maximize the benefit of location to the firm.

When innovation is the focus, overall competitiveness and innovation are affected by (1) the presence of high-quality and specialized inputs such as scientific and technical talent, (2) an environment that encourages investment and intense local rivalry, (3) pressure and insight gained from a sophisticated local market, and (4) local presence of related and supporting industries.

VIDEO 8.1
Hard Rock's Location Selection

FACTORS THAT AFFECT LOCATION DECISIONS
(pp. 255–258)

Globalization has taken place because of the development of (1) market economics; (2) better international communications; (3) more rapid, reliable travel and shipping; (4) ease of capital flow between countries; and (5) large differences in labor costs.

Labor cost per unit is sometimes called the *labor content* of the product:

Labor cost per unit = Labor cost per day ÷ Production (that is, units per day)

Sometimes firms can take advantage of a particularly favorable exchange rate by relocating or exporting to (or importing from) a foreign country.

- **Tangible costs**—Readily identifiable costs that can be measured with some precision.

- **Intangible costs**—A category of location costs that cannot be easily quantified, such as quality of life and government.

Many service organizations find that proximity to market is *the* primary location factor. Firms locate near their raw materials and suppliers because of (1) perishability, (2) transportation costs, or (3) bulk.

- **Clustering**—Location of competing companies near each other, often because of a critical mass of information, talent, venture capital, or natural resources.

Problems: 8.1–8.4

METHODS OF EVALUATING LOCATION ALTERNATIVES
(pp. 259–264)

- **Factor-rating method**—A location method that instills objectivity into the process of identifying hard-to-evaluate costs.

The six steps of the factor-rating method are:

1. Develop a list of relevant factors called *key success factors*.
2. Assign a weight to each factor to reflect its relative importance in the company's objectives.
3. Develop a scale for each factor (for example, 1 to 10 or 1 to 100 points).
4. Have management score each location for each factor, using the scale in step 3.
5. Multiply the score by the weight for each factor and total the score for each location.
6. Make a recommendation based on the maximum point score, considering the results of other quantitative approaches as well.

- **Locational break-even analysis**—A cost–volume analysis used to make an economic comparison of location alternatives.

The three steps to locational break-even analysis are:

1. Determine the fixed and variable cost for each location.
2. Plot the costs for each location, with costs on the vertical axis of the graph and annual volume on the horizontal axis.
3. Select the location that has the lowest total cost for the expected production volume.

 Problems: 8.5–8.25

Virtual Office Hours for Solved Problems: 8.1, 8.2

ACTIVE MODEL 8.1

Main Heading	Review Material	PEARSON myomlab

■ **Center-of-gravity method**—A mathematical technique used for finding the best location for a single distribution point that services several stores or areas.

The center-of-gravity method chooses the ideal location that minimizes the *weighted* distance between itself and the locations it serves, where the distance is weighted by the number of containers shipped Q_i:

$$x\text{-coordinate of the center of gravity} = \sum_i d_{ix}Q_i \div \sum_i Q_i \qquad (8\text{-}1)$$

$$y\text{-coordinate of the center of gravity} = \sum_i d_{iy}Q_i \div \sum_i Q_i \qquad (8\text{-}2)$$

■ **Transportation model**—A technique for solving a class of linear programming problems.

The transportation model determines the best pattern of shipments from several points of supply to several points of demand in order to minimize total production and transportation costs.

SERVICE LOCATION STRATEGY
(pp. 264–268)

The eight major determinants of volume and revenue for the service firm are:

1. Purchasing power of the customer-drawing area
2. Service and image compatibility with demographics of the customer-drawing area
3. Competition in the area
4. Quality of the competition
5. Uniqueness of the firm's and competitors' locations
6. Physical qualities of facilities and neighboring businesses
7. Operating policies of the firm
8. Quality of management

■ **Geographic information system (GIS)**—A system that stores and displays information that can be linked to a geographic location.

Some of the geographic databases available in many GISs include (1) census data by block, tract, city, county, congressional district, metropolitan area, state, and zip code; (2) maps of every street, highway, bridge, and tunnel in the United States; (3) utilities such as electrical, water, and gas lines; (4) all rivers, mountains, lakes, and forests; and (5) all major airports, colleges, and hospitals.

VIDEO 8.2
Locating the Next Red Lobster Restaurant

Self Test

■ **Before taking the self-test**, refer to the learning objectives listed at the beginning of the chapter and the key terms listed at the end of the chapter.

LO1. The factors involved in location decisions include:
   a) foreign exchange.
   b) attitudes.
   c) labor productivity.
   d) all of the above.

LO2. If Fender Guitar pays $30 per day to a worker in its Ensenada, Mexico, plant, and the employee completes four instruments per 8-hour day, the labor cost/unit is:
   a) $30.00.
   b) $3.75.
   c) $7.50.
   d) $4.00.
   e) $8.00.

LO3. Evaluating location alternatives by comparing their composite (weighted-average) scores involves:
   a) factor-rating analysis.
   b) cost–volume analysis.
   c) transportation model analysis.
   d) linear regression analysis.
   e) crossover analysis.

LO4. On the crossover chart where the costs of two or more location alternatives have been plotted, the quantity at which two cost curves cross is the quantity at which:

   a) fixed costs are equal for two alternative locations.
   b) Variable costs are equal for two alternative locations.
   c) total costs are equal for all alternative locations.
   d) fixed costs equal variable costs for one location.
   e) total costs are equal for two alternative locations.

LO5. A regional bookstore chain is about to build a distribution center that is centrally located for its eight retail outlets. It will most likely employ which of the following tools of analysis?
   a) Assembly-line balancing
   b) Load–distance analysis
   c) Center-of-gravity model
   d) Linear programming
   e) All of the above

LO6. What is the major difference in focus between location decisions in the service sector and in the manufacturing sector?
   a) There is no difference in focus.
   b) The focus in manufacturing is revenue maximization, while the focus in service is cost minimization.
   c) The focus in service is revenue maximization, while the focus in manufacturing is cost minimization.
   d) The focus in manufacturing is on raw materials, while the focus in service is on labor.

Answers: LO1. d; LO2. c; LO3. a; LO4. e; LO5. c; LO6. c.

9 Layout Strategies

Chapter Outline

The Strategic Importance of Layout Decisions

Types of Layout

Office Layout

Retail Layout

Warehousing and Storage Layouts

Fixed-Position Layout

Process-Oriented Layout

Work Cells

Repetitive and Product-Oriented Layout

Ethical Dilemma
Discussion Questions
Problems
Case Studies: State Automobile License Renewals; Laying Out Arnold Palmer Hospital's New Facility; Facility Layout at Wheeled Coach
Active Model Exercise
Rapid Review

Layouts make a substantial difference in operating efficiency. The seven classic layout situations are (1) office, (2) retail, (3) warehouse, (4) fixed position, (5) process oriented, (6) work cells, and (7) product oriented. A variety of techniques have been developed in attempts to solve these layout problems. Industrial firms focus on reducing material movement and assembly-line balancing. Retail firms focus on product exposure. Storage layouts focus on the optimum trade-off between storage costs and material handling costs.

Often the variables in the layout problem are so wide ranging and numerous as to preclude finding an optimal solution. For this reason, layout decisions, although having received substantial research effort, remain something of an art.

BEFORE COMING TO CLASS, READ CHAPTER 9 IN YOUR TEXT AND ANSWER THESE QUESTIONS.

1. Discuss important issues in office layout. _____

_____

2. What are the objectives of retail layout? _____

_____

3. What are ASRS, cross-docking, and random stocking? _____

_____

4. When are fixed-position layouts needed? _____

_____

5. What is the operations manager trying to achieve with process-oriented layout, and when is it used? _____

_____

6. What is a work cell, and why do firms use it? _____

_____

7. What is a product-oriented layout, and when is it used? _____

_____

8. How are assembly lines balanced? _____

_____

THE STRATEGIC IMPORTANCE OF LAYOUT DECISIONS

(See Flexible Version p. 276)

TYPES OF LAYOUT (See Flexible Version pp. 276–278)

1. Office
2. Retail
3. Warehouse
4. Fixed Position
5. Process Oriented
6. Work Cells
7. Product Oriented (Repetitive)

OFFICE LAYOUT (See Flexible Version pp. 278–279)

RETAIL LAYOUT (See Flexible Version pp. 279–281)

WAREHOUSING AND STORAGE LAYOUTS (See Flexible Version pp. 281–282)

Cross-Docking
Random Stocking
Customizing

FIXED-POSITION LAYOUT (See Flexible Version pp. 282–283)

PROCESS-ORIENTED LAYOUT (See Flexible Version pp. 283–287)

$$\text{Minimize cost} = \sum_{i=1}^{n} \sum_{j=1}^{n} X_{ij} C_{ij} \qquad (9\text{-}1)$$

where
n = total number of work centers or departments
i, j = individual departments
X_{ij} = number of loads moved from department i to department j
C_{ij} = cost to move a load between department i and department j

PRACTICE PROBLEM 9.1 ■ Process-Oriented Layout

As in most kitchens, the baking ovens in Lori's Kitchen in New Orleans are located in one area near the cooking burners. The refrigerators are located next to each other, as are the dishwashing facilities. A work area of tabletops is set aside for cutting, mixing, dough rolling, and assembling of final servings, although different table areas may be reserved for each of these functions.

Given the following interdepartmental activity matrix, develop an appropriate layout for Lori's Kitchen.

	Interdepartmental Activity Matrix			
	Cooking Burners (A)	**Refrigerators (B)**	**Dishwashing (C)**	**Work Area (D)**
Cooking Burners (A)	—	7	193	12
Refrigerator (B)		—	4	82
Dishwashing (C)			—	222
Work Area (D)				—

The present layout is

A	B	C	D

with a distance of 10 feet between adjacent areas.
Computing the load × distance measure:

Load × Distance		
A to B	7×10	70
A to C	193×20	3,860
A to D	12×30	360
B to C	4×10	40
B to D	82×20	1,640
C to D	222×10	2,220
Total		8,190

Develop a preferred layout. What is the sum of the loads × distance of your new layout?

Additional Practice Problem Space

WORK CELLS (See Flexible Version pp. 288–291)

Note in both (a) and (b) that U-shaped work cells can reduce material and employee movement. The U shape may also reduce space requirements, enhance communication, cut the number of workers, and make inspection easier.

(a)

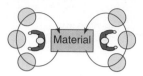

Current layout—workers in small closed areas.

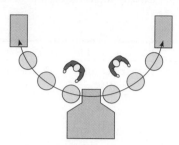

Improved layout—cross-trained workers can assist each other. May be able to add a third worker as added output is needed.

(b)

Current layout—straight lines make it hard to balance tasks because work may not be divided evenly.

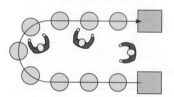

Improved layout—in U shape, workers have better access. Four cross-trained workers were reduced to three.

▲ **FIGURE 9.10** **Improving Layouts by Moving to the Work Cell Concept**

Requirements of Work Cells (See Flexible Version pp. 288–289)

1. _____

2. _____

3. _____

4. _____

Staffing and Balancing (See Flexible Version pp. 289–291)

$$\text{Takt time} = \text{Total work time available/Units required} \tag{9-2}$$

$$\text{Workers required} = \text{Total operation time required/Takt time} \tag{9-3}$$

Practice Problem Space

Focused Work Center (See Flexible Version p. 291)

Focused Factory (See Flexible Version p. 291)

REPETITIVE AND PRODUCT-ORIENTED LAYOUT

(See Flexible Version pp. 292–297)

Fabrication Line

Assembly Line

Assembly-Line Balancing (See Flexible Version pp. 293–297)

1. Cycle time $= \dfrac{\text{Production time available per day}}{\text{Units required per day}}$ (9-4)

2. Minimum number of workstations $= \dfrac{\sum\limits_{i=1}^{n}\text{Time for task } i}{\text{Cycle time}}$ (9-5)

3. Balance the Line Using a Technique in Table 9.4.

◀ **TABLE 9.4**
Layout Heuristics That May Be Used to Assign Tasks to Work Stations in Assembly-Line Balancing

1. *Longest task (operation) time*
2. *Most following tasks*
3. *Ranked positional weight*
4. *Shortest task (operations) time*
5. *Least number of following tasks*

PRACTICE PROBLEM 9.2 ■ Line Balancing

A firm must produce 40 units per day during an 8-hour workday. Tasks, times, and predecessor activities are as follows:

Task	Time (minutes)	Predecessor(s)
A	2	—
B	2	A
C	8	—
D	6	C
E	3	B
F	10	D, E
G	4	F
H	3	G
Total	38 minutes	

Determine the cycle time and the appropriate number of workstations to produce the 40 units per day.

Efficiency

$$\text{Efficiency} = \frac{\sum \text{task times}}{(\text{actual number of workstations}) \times (\text{assigned cycle time})} \quad (9\text{-}6)$$

PRACTICE PROBLEM 9.3 ■ Efficiency

Task Element	Time (minutes)	Element Predecessor
A	1	—
B	1	A
C	2	B
D	1	B
E	3	C, D
F	1	A
G	1	F
H	2	G
I	1	E, H

Given a cycle time of 4 minutes, develop an appropriate layout.

What is the efficiency of your layout?

Additional Practice Problem Space

Ethical Dilemma

Although buried by mass customization and a proliferation of new products of numerous sizes and variations, grocery chains continue to seek to maximize payoff from their layout. Their layout includes a marketable commodity—shelf space—and they charge for it. This charge is known as a *slotting fee.** Recent estimates are that food manufacturers now spend some 13% of sales on trade promotions, which is paid to grocers to get them to promote and discount the manufacturer's products. A portion of these fees is for slotting, but slotting fees drive up the manufacturer's cost. They also put the small company with a new product at a disadvantage, because small companies with limited resources are squeezed out of the market place. Slotting fees may also mean that customers may no longer be able to find the special local brand. How ethical are slotting fees?

*For an interesting discussion of slotting fees, see J. G. Kaikati and A. M. Kaikati, "Slotting and Promotional Allowances," *Supply Chain Management* 11, no. 2 (2006): 140–147; or J. L. Stanton and K. C. Herbst, "Slotting Allowances," *International Journal of Retail & Distribution Management* 34, no. 2/3 (2006): 187–197.

Discussion Questions

1. What are the seven layout strategies presented in this chapter?
2. What are the three factors that complicate a fixed-position layout?
3. What are the advantages and disadvantages of process layout?
4. How would an analyst obtain data and determine the number of trips in:
   a) a hospital?
   b) a machine shop?
   c) an auto-repair shop?
5. What are the advantages and disadvantages of product layout?
6. What are the four assumptions (or preconditions) of establishing layout for high-volume, low-variety products?
7. What are the three forms of work cells discussed in the textbook?
8. What are the advantages and disadvantages of work cells?
9. What are the requirements for a focused work center or focused factory to be appropriate?
10. What are the two major trends influencing office layout?
11. What layout variables would you consider particularly important in an office layout where computer programs are written?
12. What layout innovations have you noticed recently in retail establishments?
13. What are the variables that a manager can manipulate in a retail layout?
14. Visit a local supermarket and sketch its layout. What are your observations regarding departments and their locations?
15. What is random stocking?
16. What information is necessary for random stocking to work?
17. Explain the concept of cross-docking.
18. What is a heuristic? Name several that can be used in assembly-line balancing.

Problems*

•• **9.1** Michael Plumb's job shop has four work areas, A, B, C, and D. Distances in feet between centers of the work areas are:

	A	B	C	D
A	—	4	9	7
B	—	—	6	8
C	—	—	—	10
D	—	—	—	—

Workpieces moved, in 100s of workpieces per week, between pairs of work areas, are:

	A	B	C	D
A	—	8	7	4
B	—	—	3	2
C	—	—	—	6
D	—	—	—	—

Note: **Px** means the problem may be solved with POM for Windows and/or Excel OM.

It costs Michael $1 to move 1 work piece 1 foot. What is the weekly total material handling cost of the layout? **Px**

•• **9.2** A Missouri job shop has four departments—machining (M), dipping in a chemical bath (D), finishing (F), and plating (P)—assigned to four work areas. The operations manager, Mary Marrs, has gathered the following data for this job shop as it is currently laid out (Plan A).

100s of Workpieces Moved Between Work Areas Each Year

Plan A

	M	D	F	P
M	—	6	18	2
D	—	—	4	2
F	—	—	—	18
P	—	—	—	—

Distances Between Work Areas (departments) in Feet

	M	D	F	P
M	—	20	12	8
D		—	6	10
F			—	4
P				—

It costs $0.50 to move 1 workpiece 1 foot in the job shop. Marrs's goal is to find a layout that has the lowest material handling cost.

a) Determine cost of the current layout, Plan A, from the data above.

b) One alternative is to switch those departments with the high loads, namely, finishing (F) and plating (P), which alters the distance between them and machining (M) and dipping (D), as follows:

Distances Between Work Areas (departments) in Feet

Plan B

	M	D	F	P
M	—	20	8	12
D		—	10	6
F			—	4
P				—

What is the cost of *this* layout?

c) Marrs now wants you to evaluate Plan C, which also switches milling (M) and drilling (D), below.

Distance Between Work Areas (departments) in Feet

Plan C

	M	D	F	P
M	—	20	10	6
D		—	8	12
F			—	4
P				—

What is the cost of *this* layout?

d) Which layout is best from a cost perspective? **Px**

• **9.3** Three departments—milling (M), drilling (D), and sawing (S)—are assigned to three work areas in Samuel Smith's machine shop in Baltimore. The number of work pieces moved per day and the distances between the centers of the work areas, in feet, are shown below.

Pieces Moved Between Work Areas Each Day

	M	D	S
M	—	23	32
D		—	20
S			—

Distances Between Centers of Work Areas (departments) in Feet

	M	D	S
M	—	10	5
D		—	8
S			—

It costs $2 to move 1 workpiece 1 foot. What is the cost? **Px**

•• **9.4** Roy Creasey Enterprises, a machine shop, is planning to move to a new, larger location. The new building will be 60 feet long by 40 feet wide. Creasey envisions the building as having six distinct production areas, roughly equal in size. He feels strongly about safety and intends to have marked pathways throughout the building to facilitate the movement of people and materials. See the following building schematic.

Building Schematic (with work areas 1–6)

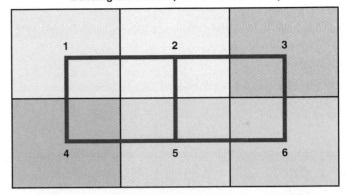

His foreman has completed a month-long study of the number of loads of material that have moved from one process to another in the current building. This information is contained in the following flow matrix.

Flow Matrix between Production Processes

From \ To	Materials	Welding	Drills	Lathes	Grinders	Benders
Materials	0	100	50	0	0	50
Welding	25	0	0	50	0	0
Drills	25	0	0	0	50	0
Lathes	0	25	0	0	20	0
Grinders	50	0	100	0	0	0
Benders	10	0	20	0	0	0

Finally, Creasey has developed the following matrix to indicate distances between the work areas shown in the building schematic.

Distance between Work Areas						
	1	2	3	4	5	6
1		20	40	20	40	60
2			20	40	20	40
3				60	40	20
4					20	40
5						20
6						

What is the appropriate layout of the new building? **Px**

•• **9.5** Registration at Southern University has always been a time of emotion, commotion, and lines. Students must move among four stations to complete the trying semiannual process. Last semester's registration, held in the fieldhouse, is described in Figure 9.20.

You can see, for example, that 450 students moved from the paper-work station (A) to advising (B), and 550 went directly from A to picking up their class cards (C). Graduate students, who for the most part had preregistered, proceeded directly from A to the station where registration is verified and payment collected (D). The layout used last semester is also shown in Figure 9.20. The registrar is preparing to set up this semester's stations and is anticipating similar numbers.

Interstation Activity Mix

	Pick up paperwork and forms (A)	Advising station (B)	Pick up class cards (C)	Verification of status and payment (D)
Paperwork/forms (A)	—	450	550	50
Advising (B)	350	—	200	0
Class cards (C)	0	0	—	750
Verification/payment (D)	0	0	0	—

Existing Layout

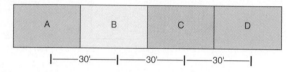

▲ **FIGURE 9.20   Registration Flow of Students**

a) What is the "load × distance," or "movement cost," of the layout shown?
b) Provide an improved layout and compute its movement cost. **Px**

••• **9.6** You have just been hired as the director of operations for Reid Chocolates, a purveyor of exceptionally fine candies. Reid Chocolates has two kitchen layouts under consideration for its recipe making and testing department. The strategy is to provide the best kitchen layout possible so that food scientists can devote their time and energy to product improvement, not wasted effort in the kitchen. You have been asked to evaluate these two kitchen layouts and to prepare a recommendation for your boss, Mr. Reid, so that he can proceed to place the contract for building the kitchens. (See Figure 9.21[a], and Figure 9.21[b].) **Px**

Number of trips between work centers:

From: \ To:	Refrigerator 1	Counter 2	Sink 3	Storage 4	Stove 5
Refrig. 1	0	8	13	0	0
Counter 2	5	0	3	3	8
Sink 3	3	12	0	4	0
Storage 4	3	0	0	0	5
Stove 5	0	8	4	10	0

▲ **FIGURE 9.21(a)   Layout Options**

Kitchen layout #1

Walking distance in feet

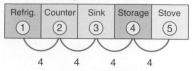

Kitchen layout #2

Walking distance in feet

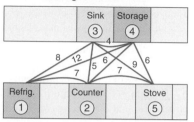

▲ **FIGURE 9.21(b)**

•• **9.7** Reid Chocolates (see Problem 9.6) is considering a third layout, as shown below. Evaluate its effectiveness in trip-distance feet. **Px**

Kitchen layout #3

Walking distance in feet

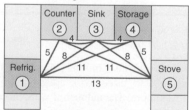

•• **9.8** Reid Chocolates (see Problems 9.6 and 9.7) has yet two more layouts to consider.
a) Layout 4 is shown below. What is the total trip distance?
b) Layout 5, which also follows, has what total trip distance? **Px**

Kitchen layout #4

Walking distance in feet

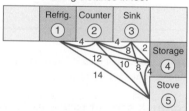

Kitchen layout #5

Walking distance in feet

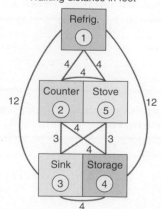

•• 9.9 Six processes are to be laid out in six areas along a long corridor at Linda Babat Accounting Services. The distance between adjacent work centers is 40 feet. The number of trips between work centers is given in the following table:

From	Trips between Processes					
			To			
	A	B	C	D	E	F
A		18	25	73	12	54
B			96	23	31	45
C				41	22	20
D					19	57
E						48
F						

a) Assign the processes to the work areas in a way that minimizes the total flow, using a method that places processes with highest flow adjacent to each other.
b) What assignment minimizes the total traffic flow? **Px**

•• 9.10 After an extensive product analysis using group technology, Bob Buerlein has identified a product he believes should be pulled out of his process facility and handled in a work cell. Bob has identified the following operations as necessary for the work cell. The customer expects delivery of 250 units per day, and the work day is 420 minutes.
a) What is the takt time?
b) How many employees should be cross-trained for the cell?
c) Which operations may warrant special consideration?

Operation	Standard time (min)
Shear	1.1
Bend	1.1
Weld	1.7
Clean	3.1
Paint	1.0

•• 9.11 Stanford Rosenberg Electronics wants to establish an assembly line for producing a new product, the Personal Little Assistant (PLA). The tasks, task times, and immediate predecessors for the tasks are as follows:

Task	Time (sec)	Immediate Predecessors
A	12	—
B	15	A
C	8	A
D	5	B, C
E	20	D

Rosenberg's goal is to produce 180 PLAs per hour.
a) What is the cycle time?
b) What is the theoretical minimum for the number of workstations that Rosenberg can achieve in this assembly line?
c) Can the theoretical minimum actually be reached when workstations are assigned? **Px**

••• 9.12 South Carolina Furniture, Inc., produces all types of office furniture. The "Executive Secretary" is a chair that has been designed using ergonomics to provide comfort during long work

hours. The chair sells for $130. There are 480 minutes available during the day, and the average daily demand has been 50 chairs. There are eight tasks:

Task	Performance Time (min)	Task Must Follow Task Listed Below
A	4	—
B	7	—
C	6	A, B
D	5	C
E	6	D
F	7	E
G	8	E
H	6	F, G

a) Draw a precedence diagram of this operation.
b) What is the cycle time for this operation?
c) What is the *theoretical* minimum number of workstations?
d) Assign tasks to workstations.
e) What is the idle time per cycle?
f) How much total idle time is present each day?
g) What is the overall efficiency of the assembly line? **Px**

•• 9.13 Rita Gibson Appliances wants to establish an assembly line to manufacture its new product, the Mini-Me Microwave Oven. The goal is to produce five Mini-Me Microwave Ovens per hour. The tasks, task times, and immediate predecessors for producing one Mini-Me Microwave Oven are as follows:

Task	Time (min)	Immediate Predecessors
A	10	—
B	12	A
C	8	A, B
D	6	B, C
E	6	C
F	6	D, E

a) What is the *theoretical* minimum for the smallest number of workstations that Gibson can achieve in this assembly line?
b) Graph the assembly line and assign workers to workstations. Can you assign them with the theoretical minimum?
c) What is the efficiency of *your* assignment? **Px**

•• 9.14 The Temple Toy Company has decided to manufacture a new toy tractor, the production of which is broken into six steps. The demand for the tractor is 4,800 units per 40-hour workweek:

Task	Performance Time (sec)	Predecessors
A	20	None
B	30	A
C	15	A
D	15	A
E	10	B, C
F	30	D, E

a) Draw a precedence diagram of this operation.
b) Given the demand, what is the cycle time for this operation?
c) What is the *theoretical* minimum number of workstations?

d) Assign tasks to workstations.

e) How much total idle time is present each cycle?

f) What is the overall efficiency of the assembly line with five stations; and with six stations? **Px**

•• **9.15** The following table details the tasks required for Dallas-based T. Liscio Industries to manufacture a fully portable industrial vacuum cleaner. The times in the table are in minutes. Demand forecasts indicate a need to operate with a cycle time of 10 minutes.

Activity	Activity Description	Immediate Predecessors	Time
A	Attach wheels to tub	—	5
B	Attach motor to lid	—	1.5
C	Attach battery pack	B	3
D	Attach safety cutoff	C	4
E	Attach filters	B	3
F	Attach lid to tub	A, E	2
G	Assemble attachments	—	3
H	Function test	D, F, G	3.5
I	Final inspection	H	2
J	Packing	I	2

a) Draw the appropriate precedence diagram for this production line.

b) Assign tasks to workstations and determine how much idle time is present each cycle?

c) Discuss how this balance could be improved to 100%.

d) What is the *theoretical* minimum number of workstations? **Px**

•• **9.16** Tailwind, Inc., produces high-quality but expensive training shoes for runners. The Tailwind shoe, which sells for $210, contains both gas- and liquid-filled compartments to provide more stability and better protection against knee, foot, and back injuries. Manufacturing the shoes requires 10 separate tasks. There are 400 minutes available for manufacturing the shoes in the plant each day. Daily demand is 60. The information for the tasks is as follows:

Task	Performance Time (min)	Task Must Follow Task Listed Below
A	1	—
B	3	A
C	2	B
D	4	B
E	1	C, D
F	3	A
G	2	F
H	5	G
I	1	E, H
J	3	I

a) Draw the precedence diagram.

b) Assign tasks to the minimum feasible number of workstations according to the "ranked positioned weight" decision rule.

c) What is the efficiency of the process?

d) What is the idle time per cycle? **Px**

•• **9.17** The Mach 10 is a one-person sailboat manufactured by Creative Leisure. The final assembly plant is in Cupertino, California. The assembly area is available for production of the Mach 10 for 200 minutes per day. (The rest of the time it is busy making other products.) The daily demand is 60 boats. Given the following information:

a) Draw the precedence diagram and assign tasks using five workstations.

b) What is the efficiency of the assembly line, using your answer to (a)?

c) What is the *theoretical* minimum number of workstations?

d) What is the idle time per boat produced? **Px**

Task	Performance Time (min)	Task Must Follow Task Listed Below
A	1	—
B	1	A
C	2	A
D	1	C
E	3	C
F	1	C
G	1	D, E, F
H	2	B
I	1	G, H

•• **9.18** Because of the expected high demand for Mach 10, Creative Leisure has decided to increase manufacturing time available to produce the Mach 10 (see Problem 9.17).

a) If demand remained the same but 300 minutes were available each day on the assembly line, how many workstations would be needed?

b) What would be the efficiency of the new system?

c) What would be the impact on the system if 400 minutes were available? **Px**

••• **9.19** Dr. Lori Baker, operations manager at Nesa Electronics, prides herself on excellent assembly-line balancing. She has been told that the firm needs to complete 96 instruments per 24-hour day. The assembly-line activities are:

Task	Time (min)	Predecessors
A	3	—
B	6	—
C	7	A
D	5	A, B
E	2	B
F	4	C
G	5	F
H	7	D, E
I	1	H
J	6	E
K	$\dfrac{4}{50}$	G, I, J

a) Draw the precedence diagram.

b) If the daily (24-hour) production rate is 96 units, what is the highest allowable cycle time?

c) If the cycle time after allowances is given as 10 minutes, what is the daily (24-hour) production rate?

d) With a 10-minute cycle time, what is the theoretical minimum number of stations with which the line can be balanced?

e) With a 10-minute cycle time and six workstations, what is the efficiency?

f) What is the total idle time per cycle with a 10-minute cycle time and six workstations?

g) What is the best work station assignment you can make without exceeding a 10-minute cycle time and what is its efficiency? **Px**

••   9.20 Suppose production requirements in Solved Problem 9.2 (see pp. 301–302 in the Flexible Version) increase and require a reduction in cycle time from 8 minutes to 7 minutes. Balance the line once again, using the new cycle time. Note that it is not possible to combine task times so as to group tasks into the minimum number of workstations. This condition occurs in actual balancing problems fairly often. **Px**

••   9.21 The preinduction physical examination given by the U.S. Army involves the following seven activities:

Activity	Average Time (min)
Medical history	10
Blood tests	8
Eye examination	5
Measurements (e.g., weight, height, blood pressure)	7
Medical examination	16
Psychological interview	12
Exit medical evaluation	10

These activities can be performed in any order, with two exceptions: Medical history must be taken first, and Exit medical evaluation is last. At present, there are three paramedics and two physicians on duty during each shift. Only physicians can perform exit evaluations and conduct psychological interviews. Other activities can be carried out by either physicians or paramedics.

a) Develop a layout and balance the line.
b) How many people can be processed per hour?
c) Which activity accounts for the current bottleneck?
d) What is the total idle time per cycle?
e) If one more physician and one more paramedic can be placed on duty, how would you redraw the layout? What is the new throughput?

•••   9.22 Frank Pianki's company wants to establish an assembly line to manufacture its new product, the iScan phone. Frank's goal is to produce 60 iScans per hour. Tasks, task times, and immediate predecessors are as follows:

Task	Time (sec)	Immediate Predecessors	Task	Time (sec)	Immediate Predecessors
A	40	—	F	25	C
B	30	A	G	15	C
C	50	A	H	20	D, E
D	40	B	I	18	F, G
E	6	B	J	30	H, I

a) What is the theoretical minimum for the number of workstations that Frank can achieve in this assembly line?
b) Use the *most following tasks* heuristic to balance an assembly line for the iScan phone.
c) How many workstations are in your answer to (b)?
d) What is the efficiency of your answer to (b)? **Px**

••••   9.23 As the Cottrell Bicycle Co. of St. Louis completes plans for its new assembly line, it identifies 25 different tasks in the production process. VP of Operations Jonathan Cottrell now faces the job of balancing the line. He lists precedences and provides time estimates for each step based on work-sampling techniques. His goal is to produce 1,000 bicycles per standard 40-hour workweek.

Task	Time (sec)	Precedence Tasks	Task	Time (sec)	Precedence Tasks
K3	60	—	E3	109	F3
K4	24	K3	D6	53	F4
K9	27	K3	D7	72	F9, E2, E3
J1	66	K3	D8	78	E3, D6
J2	22	K3	D9	37	D6
J3	3	—	C1	78	F7
G4	79	K4, K9	B3	72	D7, D8, D9, C1
G5	29	K9, J1	B5	108	C1
F3	32	J2	B7	18	B3
F4	92	J2	A1	52	B5
F7	21	J3	A2	72	B5
F9	126	G4	A3	114	B7, A1, A2
E2	18	G5, F3			

a) Balance this operation, using various heuristics. Which is best and why?
b) What happens if the firm can change to a 41-hour workweek? **Px**

▶ **Refer to** myomlab **for these additional homework problems: 9.24–9.27**

Case Studies

▶ **State Automobile License Renewals**

Henry Coupe, the manager of a metropolitan branch office of the state department of motor vehicles, attempted to analyze the driver's license–renewal operations. He had to perform several steps. After examining the license-renewal process, he identified those steps and associated times required to perform each step, as shown in the following table:

State Automobile License–Renewal Process Times

Step	Average Time to Perform (seconds)
1. Review renewal application for correctness	15
2. Process and record payment	30
3. Check file for violations and restrictions	60
4. Conduct eye test	40
5. Photograph applicant	20
6. Issue temporary license	30

Coupe found that each step was assigned to a different person. Each application was a separate process in the sequence shown. He determined that his office should be prepared to accommodate a maximum demand of processing 120 renewal applicants per hour.

He observed that work was unevenly divided among clerks and that the clerk responsible for checking violations tended to shortcut her task to keep up with the others. Long lines built up during the maximum-demand periods.

Coupe also found that Steps 1 to 4 were handled by general clerks who were each paid $12 per hour. Step 5 was performed by a photographer paid $16 per hour. (Branch offices were charged $10 per hour for each camera to perform photography.) Step 6, issuing temporary licenses, was required by state policy to be handled by uniformed motor vehicle officers. Officers were paid $18 per hour but could be assigned to any job except photography.

A review of the jobs indicated that Step 1, reviewing applications for correctness, had to be performed before any other step could be taken. Similarly, Step 6, issuing temporary licenses, could not be performed until all the other steps were completed.

Henry Coupe was under severe pressure to increase productivity and reduce costs, but he was also told by the regional director that he must accommodate the demand for renewals. Otherwise, "heads would roll."

Discussion Questions

1. What is the maximum number of applications per hour that can be handled by the present configuration of the process?
2. How many applications can be processed per hour if a second clerk is added to check for violations?
3. If the second clerk could be added *anywhere* you choose (and not necessarily to check for violations, as in question 2), what is the maximum number of applications the process can handle? What is the new configuration?
4. How would you suggest modifying the process to accommodate 120 applications per hour? What is the cost per application of this new configuration?

Source: Modified from a case by W. Earl Sasser, Paul R. Olson, and D. Daryl Wyckoff, *Management of Services Operations: Text, Cases, and Readings* (Boston: Allyn & Bacon).

▶ Laying Out Arnold Palmer Hospital's New Facility

Video Case

When Orlando's Arnold Palmer Hospital began plans to create a new 273-bed, 11-story hospital across the street from its existing facility, which was bursting at the seams in terms of capacity, a massive planning process began. The $100 million building, opened in 2006, was long overdue, according to Executive Director Kathy Swanson: "We started Arnold Palmer Hospital in 1989, with a mission to provide quality services for children and women in a comforting, family-friendly environment. Since then we have served well over 1.5 million women and children and now deliver more than 12,000 babies a year. By 2001, we simply ran out of room, and it was time for us to grow."

The new hospital's unique, circular pod design provides a maximally efficient layout in all areas of the hospital, creating a patient-centered environment. *Servicescape* design features include a serene environment created through the use of warm colors, private rooms with pull-down Murphy beds for family members, 14-foot ceilings, and natural lighting with oversized windows in patient rooms. But these radical new features did not come easily. "This pod concept with a central nursing area and pie-shaped rooms resulted from over 1,000 planning meetings of 35 user groups, extensive motion and time studies, and computer simulations of the daily movements of nurses," says Swanson.

In a traditional linear hospital layout, called the *racetrack* design, patient rooms line long hallways, and a nurse might walk 2.7 miles per day serving patient needs at Arnold Palmer. "Some nurses spent 30% of their time simply walking. With the nursing shortage and the high cost of health care professionals, efficiency is a major concern," added Swanson. With the nursing station in the center of 10- or 12-bed circular pods, no patient room is more than 14 feet from a station. The time savings are in the 20% range.

Swanson pointed to Figures 9.22 and 9.23 as examples of the old and new walking and trip distances.*

"We have also totally redesigned our neonatal rooms," says Swanson. "In the old system, there were 16 neonatal beds in a large and often noisy rectangular room. The new building features semiprivate rooms for these tiny babies. The rooms are much improved, with added privacy and a quiet, simulated night atmosphere, in addition to pull-down beds for parents to use. Our research shows that babies improve and develop much more quickly with this layout design. Layout and environment indeed impact patient care!"

Discussion Questions**

1. Identify the many variables that a hospital needs to consider in layout design.
2. What are the advantages of the circular pod design over the traditional linear hallway layout found in most hospitals?
3. Figure 9.22 illustrates a sample linear hallway layout. During a period of random observation, nurse Thomas Smith's day includes 6 trips from the nursing station to each of the 12 patient rooms (back and forth), 20 trips to the medical supply room, 5 trips to the break room, and 12 trips to the linen supply room. What is his total distance traveled in miles?

*Layout and walking distances, including some of the numbers in Figures 9.22 and 9.23, have been simplified for purposes of this case.

**You may wish to view the video that accompanies this case before addressing these questions.

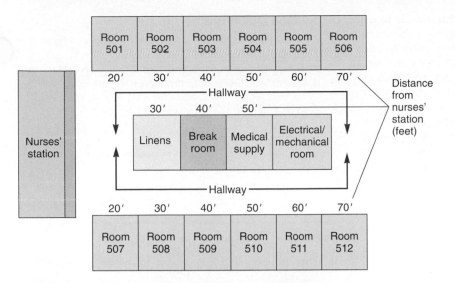

◄ **FIGURE 9.22**
Traditional Hospital Layout
Patient rooms are on two linear hallways with exterior windows. Supply rooms are on interior corridors. This layout is called a "racetrack" design.

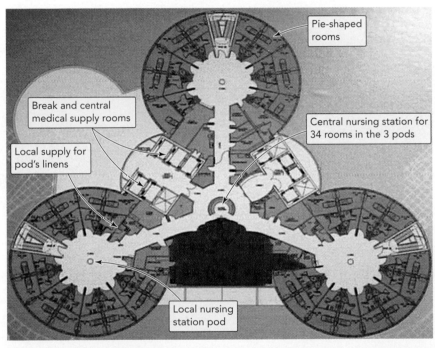

◄ **FIGURE 9.23**
New Pod Design for Hospital Layout
Note that each room is 14 feet from the pod's *local* nursing station. The *break rooms* and the *central medical station* are each about 60 feet from the local nursing pod. Pod *linen supply* rooms are also 14 feet from the local nursing station.

4. Figure 9.23 illustrates an architect's drawing of Arnold Palmer Hospital's new circular pod system. If nurse Susan Jones's day includes 7 trips from the nursing pod to each of the 12 rooms (back and forth), 20 trips to central medical supply, 6 trips to the break room, and 12 trips to the pod linen supply, how many miles does she walk during her shift? What are the differences in the travel times between the two nurses for this random day?

5. The concept of *servicescapes* is discussed in this chapter. Describe why this is so important at Arnold Palmer Hospital and give examples of its use in layout design.

► **Facility Layout at Wheeled Coach**

Video Case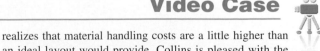

When President Bob Collins began his career at Wheeled Coach, the world's largest manufacturer of ambulances, there were only a handful of employees. Now the firm's Florida plant has a workforce of 350. The physical plant has also expanded, with offices, R&D, final assembly, and wiring, cabinetry, and upholstery work cells in one large building. Growth has forced the painting work cell into a separate building, aluminum fabrication and body installation into another, inspection and shipping into a fourth, and warehousing into yet another.

Like many other growing companies, Wheeled Coach was not able to design its facility from scratch. And although management realizes that material handling costs are a little higher than an ideal layout would provide, Collins is pleased with the way the facility has evolved and employees have adapted.

The aluminum cutting work cell lies adjacent to body fabrication, which, in turn, is located next to the body-installation work cell. And while the vehicle must be driven across a street to one building for painting and then to another for final assembly, at least the ambulance is on wheels. Collins is also satisfied with the flexibility shown in the design of the work cells. Cell construction is flexible and can accommodate changes in product mix and volume. In addition, work cells are typically small and movable, with many work benches and staging racks borne on wheels so that they can be easily rearranged and products transported to the assembly line.

Assembly-line balancing is one key problem facing Wheeled Coach and every other repetitive manufacturer. Produced on a schedule calling for four 10-hour work days per week, once an ambulance is on one of the six final assembly lines, it *must* move forward each day to the next workstation. Balancing just enough workers and tasks at each of the seven workstations is a never-ending challenge. Too many workers end up running into each other; too few can't finish an ambulance in 7 days. Constant shifting of design and mix and improved analysis has led to frequent changes.

Discussion Questions*

1. What analytical techniques are available to help a company like Wheeled Coach deal with layout problems?
2. What suggestions would you make to Bob Collins about his layout?
3. How would you measure the "efficiency" of this layout?

*You may wish to view the video that accompanies this case before addressing these questions.

Active Model Exercise

ACTIVE MODEL 9.1, based on Example 1 in the text, allows you to simulate changing parameters in a process layout analysis. It is illustrated at **www.myomlab.com** or **www.pearsonhighered.com/heizer**.

Main Heading	Review Material	
THE STRATEGIC IMPORTANCE OF LAYOUT DECISIONS (p. 276)	Layout has numerous strategic implications because it establishes an organization's competitive priorities in regard to capacity, processes, flexibility, and cost, as well as quality of work life, customer contact, and image. *The objective of layout strategy is to develop an effective and efficient layout that will meet the firm's competitive requirements.*	
TYPES OF LAYOUT (pp. 276–278)	Types of layout and examples of their typical objectives include: 1. *Office layout:* Locate workers requiring frequent contact close to one another. 2. *Retail layout:* Expose customers to high-margin items. 3. *Warehouse layout:* Balance low-cost storage with low-cost material handling. 4. *Fixed-position layout:* Move material to the limited storage areas around the site. 5. *Process-oriented layout:* Manage varied material flow for each product. 6. *Work-cell layout:* Identify a product family, build teams, and cross-train team members. 7. *Product-oriented layout:* Equalize the task time at each workstation.	
OFFICE LAYOUT (pp. 278–279)	▪ **Office layout**—The grouping of workers, their equipment, and spaces/offices to provide for comfort, safety, and movement of information. A *relationship chart* displays a "closeness value" between each pair of people and/or departments that need to be placed in the office layout.	
RETAIL LAYOUT (pp. 279–281)	▪ **Retail layout**—An approach that addresses flow, allocates space, and responds to customer behavior. Retail layouts are based on the idea that sales and profitability vary directly with customer exposure to products. The main *objective of retail layout is to maximize profitability per square foot of floor space* (or, in some stores, per linear foot of shelf space). ▪ **Slotting fees**—Fees manufacturers pay to get shelf space for their products. ▪ **Servicescape**—The physical surroundings in which a service takes place and how they affect customers and employees.	
WAREHOUSING AND STORAGE LAYOUT (pp. 281–282)	▪ **Warehouse layout**—A design that attempts to minimize total cost by addressing trade-offs between space and material handling. The variety of items stored and the number of items "picked" has direct bearing on the optimal layout. Modern warehouse management is often an automated procedure using *automated storage and retrieval systems* (ASRSs). ▪ **Cross-docking**—Avoiding the placement of materials or supplies in storage by processing them as they are received for shipment. Cross-docking requires both tight scheduling and accurate inbound product identification. ▪ **Random stocking**—Used in warehousing to locate stock wherever there is an open location. ▪ **Customizing**—Using warehousing to add value to a product through component modification, repair, labeling, and packaging.	
FIXED-POSITION LAYOUT (pp. 282–283)	▪ **Fixed-position layout**—A system that addresses the layout requirements of stationary projects. Fixed-position layouts involve three complications: (1) There is limited space at virtually all sites, (2) different materials are needed at different stages of a project, and (3) the volume of materials needed is dynamic.	
PROCESS-ORIENTED LAYOUT (pp. 283–287)	▪ **Process-oriented layout**—A layout that deals with low-volume, high-variety production in which like machines and equipment are grouped together. ▪ **Job lots**—Groups or batches of parts processed together. $$\text{Material handling cost minimization} = \sum_{i=1}^{n}\sum_{j=1}^{n} X_{ij}\,C_{ij} \qquad (9\text{-}1)$$	Problems: 9.1–9.9 Virtual Office Hours for Solved Problem: 9.1 **VIDEO 9.1** Arnold Palmer Hospital **ACTIVE** MODEL 9.1

Main Heading	Review Material	myomlab
WORK CELLS (pp. 288–291)	■ **Work cell**—An arrangement of machines and personnel that focuses on making a single product or family of related products. ■ **Takt time**—Pace of production to meet customer demands. $$\text{Takt time} = \text{Total work time available/Units required} \qquad (9\text{-}2)$$ $$\text{Workers required} = \text{Total operation time required/Takt time} \qquad (9\text{-}3)$$ ■ **Focused work center**—A permanent or semi-permanent product-oriented arrangement of machines and personnel. ■ **Focused factory**—A facility designed to produce similar products or components.	Problem: 9.10
REPETITIVE AND PRODUCT-ORIENTED LAYOUT (pp. 292–297)	■ **Fabrication line**—A machine-paced, product-oriented facility for building components. ■ **Assembly line**—An approach that puts fabricated parts together at a series of workstations; a repetitive process. ■ **Assembly-line balancing**—Obtaining output at each workstation on a production line in order to minimize delay. $$\text{Cycle time} = \text{Production time available per day} \div \text{Units required per day} \qquad (9\text{-}4)$$ $$\text{Minimum number of workstations} = \sum_{i=1}^{n} \text{Time for task } i \div \text{Cycle time} \qquad (9\text{-}5)$$ ■ **Heuristic**—Problem solving using procedures and rules rather than mathematical optimization. Line balancing heuristics include *longest task (operation) time, most following tasks, ranked positional weight, shortest task (operation) time, and least number of following tasks.* $$\text{Efficiency} = \frac{\sum \text{Task times}}{(\text{Actual number of workstations}) \times (\text{Largest assigned cycle time})} \qquad (9\text{-}6)$$	Problems: 9.11–9.22 **VIDEO 9.2** Facility Layout at Wheeled Coach Ambulances Virtual Office Hours for Solved Problem: 9.2

Self Test

■ **Before taking the self-test,** refer to the learning objectives listed at the beginning of the chapter and the key terms listed at the end of the chapter.

LO1. Which of the statements below best describes *office layout*?
 a) Groups workers, their equipment, and spaces/offices to provide for movement of information.
 b) Addresses the layout requirements of large, bulky projects such as ships and buildings.
 c) Seeks the best personnel and machine utilization in repetitive or continuous production.
 d) Allocates shelf space and responds to customer behavior.
 e) Deals with low-volume, high-variety production.

LO2. Which of the following does *not* support the retail layout objective of maximizing customer exposure to products?
 a) Locate high-draw items around the periphery of the store.
 b) Use prominent locations for high-impulse and high-margin items.
 c) Maximize exposure to expensive items.
 d) Use end-aisle locations.
 e) Convey the store's mission with the careful positioning of the lead-off department.

LO3. The major problem addressed by the warehouse layout strategy is:
 a) minimizing difficulties caused by material flow varying with each product.
 b) requiring frequent contact close to one another.
 c) addressing trade-offs between space and material handling.
 d) balancing product flow from one workstation to the next.
 e) none of the above.

LO4. A fixed-position layout:
 a) groups workers to provide for movement of information.
 b) addresses the layout requirements of large, bulky projects such as ships and buildings.
 c) seeks the best machine utilization in continuous production.

 d) allocates shelf space based on customer behavior.
 e) deals with low-volume, high-variety production.

LO5. A process-oriented layout:
 a) groups workers to provide for movement of information.
 b) addresses the layout requirements of large, bulky projects such as ships and buildings.
 c) seeks the best machine utilization in continuous production.
 d) allocates shelf space based on customer behavior.
 e) deals with low-volume, high-variety production.

LO6. For a focused work center or focused factory to be appropriate, the following three factors are required:
 a) _____
 b) _____
 c) _____

LO7. Before considering a product-oriented layout, it is important to be certain that:
 a) _____
 b) _____
 c) _____
 d) _____

LO8. An assembly line is to be designed for a product whose completion requires 21 minutes of work. The factory works 400 minutes per day. Can a production line with five workstations make 100 units per day?
 a) Yes, with exactly 100 minutes to spare.
 b) No, but four workstations would be sufficient.
 c) No, it will fall short even with a perfectly balanced line.
 d) Yes, but the line's efficiency is very low.
 e) Cannot be determined from the information given.

Answers: LO1. a; **LO2.** c; **LO3.** c; **LO4.** b; **LO5.** e; **LO6.** family of products, stable forecast (demand), volume; **LO7.** adequate volume, stable demand, standardized product, adequate/quality supplies; **LO8.** c.

10 Human Resources, Job Design, and Work Measurement

Chapter Outline

Human Resource Strategy for
    Competitive Advantage

Labor Planning

Job Design

Ergonomics and the Work Environment

Methods Analysis

The Visual Workplace

Labor Standards

Ethics

Ethical Dilemma
Discussion Questions
Problems
Case Studies: Jackson Manufacturing
    Company; Hard Rock's Human
    Resource Strategy
Active Model Exercise
Rapid Review

"We hired workers and human beings came instead." Max Firsh's words ring very true to the operations manager because organizations do not function without human beings and do not function well without competent, motivated human beings. The objective of a human resource strategy is to design jobs and manage labor so that people are effectively and efficiently utilized.

This chapter discusses how operations managers can achieve an effective human resource strategy by effective labor planning, job design, a visual workplace, and labor standards to provide a competitive advantage. Labor standards may be established via historical data, time studies, predetermined time standards, and work sampling.

BEFORE COMING TO CLASS, READ CHAPTER 10 IN YOUR TEXT AND ANSWER THESE QUESTIONS.

1. What are the three labor planning staffing policies? _____,
   _____

2. What are the major issues in job design? _____
   _____

3. What are the major ergonomic and work environment issues? _____
   _____

4. What are the four tools of methods analysis? _____
   _____

5. What are the four ways to set labor standards? _____
   _____

6. What is the difference between a normal and a standard time in a time
   study? _____
   _____

7. How do you find the proper sample size for a time study? _____
   _____

HUMAN RESOURCE STRATEGY FOR COMPETITIVE ADVANTAGE (See Flexible Version pp. 306–307)

Constraints on Human Resource Strategy
(See Flexible Version p. 306)

LABOR PLANNING (See Flexible Version pp. 307–308)

JOB DESIGN (See Flexible Version pp. 308–311)

Labor Specialization (See Flexible Version p. 308)

Job Expansion (See Flexible Version pp. 308–309)

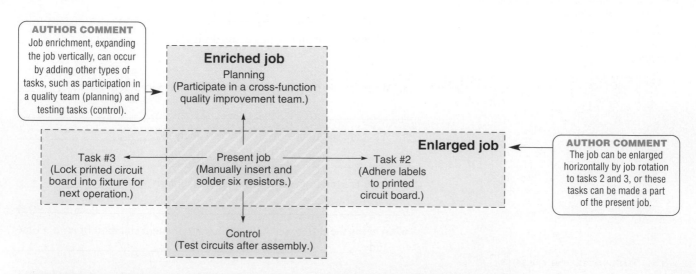

AUTHOR COMMENT
Job enrichment, expanding the job vertically, can occur by adding other types of tasks, such as participation in a quality team (planning) and testing tasks (control).

Enriched job
Planning
(Participate in a cross-function quality improvement team.)

Enlarged job

AUTHOR COMMENT
The job can be enlarged horizontally by job rotation to tasks 2 and 3, or these tasks can be made a part of the present job.

Task #3
(Lock printed circuit board into fixture for next operation.)

Present job
(Manually insert and solder six resistors.)

Task #2
(Adhere labels to printed circuit board.)

Control
(Test circuits after assembly.)

▲ FIGURE 10.2 **An Example of Job Enlargement (*horizontal* job expansion) and Job Enrichment (*vertical* job expansion)**

Psychological Components (See Flexible Version p. 309)

Self-Directed Teams (See Flexible Version p. 310)

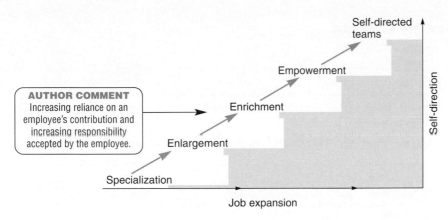

AUTHOR COMMENT
Increasing reliance on an employee's contribution and increasing responsibility accepted by the employee.

Specialization

Enlargement

Enrichment

Empowerment

Self-directed teams

Self-direction

Job expansion

▲ FIGURE 10.3 **Job Design Continuum**

Motivation and Incentive Systems (See Flexible Version p. 311)

ERGONOMICS AND THE WORK ENVIRONMENT

(See Flexible Version pp. 311–314)

Ergonomics/Human Factors

METHODS ANALYSIS (See Flexible Version pp. 314–315)

Flow Diagrams and Process Charts

(See Flexible Version pp. 314–315)

(a)

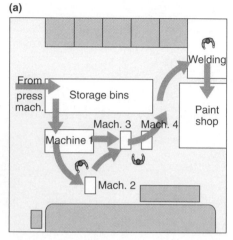

(b)

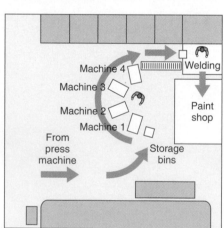

(c)

| Present Method ☐ | | PROCESS CHART | |
| Proposed Method ☒ | | | |

SUBJECT CHARTED *Axle-stand Production* DATE *8/1/10*

CHART BY *JH*

CHART NO. *1*

DEPARTMENT *Work cell for axle stand* SHEET NO. *1* OF *1*

DIST. IN FEET	TIME IN MINS.	CHART SYMBOLS	PROCESS DESCRIPTION
50		○ ➡ ☐ D ▽	*From press machine to storage bins at work cell*
	3	○ ➡ ☐ D ▼	*Storage bins*
5		○ ➡ ☐ D ▽	*Move to machine 1*
	4	● ➡ ☐ D ▽	*Operation at machine 1*
4		● ➡ ☐ D ▽	*Move to machine 2*
	2.5	● ➡ ☐ D ▽	*Operation at machine 2*
4		○ ➡ ☐ D ▽	*Move to machine 3*
	3.5	● ➡ ☐ D ▽	*Operation at machine 3*
4		○ ➡ ☐ D ▽	*Move to machine 4*
	4	● ➡ ☐ D ▽	*Operation at machine 4*
20		○ ➡ ☐ D ▽	*Move to welding*
	Poka-yoke	○ ➡ ■ D ▽	*Poka-yoke inspection at welding*
	4	● ➡ ☐ D ▽	*Weld*
10		○ ➡ ☐ D ▽	*Move to painting*
	4	● ➡ ☐ D ▽	*Paint*
		○ ➡ ☐ D ▽	
97	25		TOTAL

○ = operation; ➡ = transportation; ☐ = inspection; D = delay; ▽ = storage

▲ **FIGURE 10.5** **Flow Diagram of Axle-Stand Production Line at Paddy Hopkirk Factory**

(a) Old method; (b) new method; (c) process chart of axle-stand production using Paddy Hopkirk's new method (shown in b).

PRACTICE PROBLEM 10.1 ■ Process Chart for Sandwich

Develop a *process chart* for making a grilled cheese sandwich. Process charts should be quite detailed, containing all the required elements of the entire process. You should incorporate all the steps necessary for each part of the process of making the sandwich.

Additional Practice Problem Space

Activity and Operations Charts

(See Flexible Version p. 315)

ACTIVITY CHART

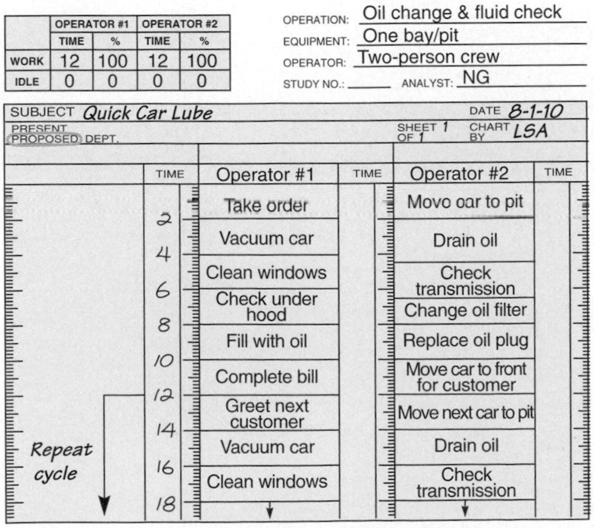

	OPERATOR #1		OPERATOR #2	
	TIME	%	TIME	%
WORK	12	100	12	100
IDLE	0	0	0	0

OPERATION: Oil change & fluid check
EQUIPMENT: One bay/pit
OPERATOR: Two-person crew
STUDY NO.: _____ ANALYST: NG

SUBJECT *Quick Car Lube*   DATE *8-1-10*
PRESENT (PROPOSED) DEPT.   SHEET 1 OF 1   CHART BY *LSA*

	TIME	Operator #1	TIME	Operator #2	TIME
	2	Take order		Move car to pit	
	4	Vacuum car		Drain oil	
	6	Clean windows		Check transmission	
	8	Check under hood		Change oil filter	
	10	Fill with oil		Replace oil plug	
	12	Complete bill		Move car to front for customer	
	14	Greet next customer		Move next car to pit	
Repeat cycle	16	Vacuum car		Drain oil	
	18	Clean windows		Check transmission	

▲ **FIGURE 10.6** Activity Chart for Two-Person Crew Doing an Oil Change in 12 Minutes at Quick Car Lube

OPERATIONS CHART

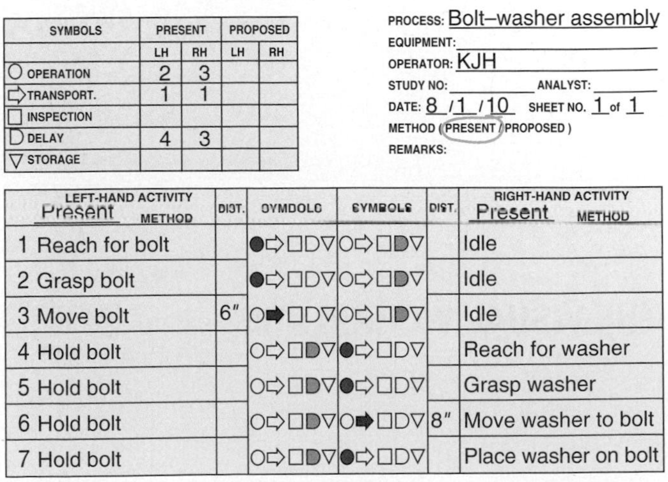

SYMBOLS	PRESENT		PROPOSED	
	LH	RH	LH	RH
○ OPERATION	2	3		
⇨ TRANSPORT.	1	1		
☐ INSPECTION				
D DELAY	4	3		
▽ STORAGE				

PROCESS: Bolt–washer assembly
EQUIPMENT: _____
OPERATOR: KJH
STUDY NO: _____ ANALYST: _____
DATE: 8 /1 /10   SHEET NO. 1 of 1
METHOD (PRESENT / PROPOSED)
REMARKS:

LEFT-HAND ACTIVITY Present METHOD	DIST.	SYMBOLS	SYMBOLS	DIST.	RIGHT-HAND ACTIVITY Present METHOD
1 Reach for bolt		●⇨☐D▽	○⇨☐D▽		Idle
2 Grasp bolt		●⇨☐D▽	○⇨☐D▽		Idle
3 Move bolt	6"	○➡☐D▽	○⇨☐D▽		Idle
4 Hold bolt		○⇨☐D▽	●⇨☐D▽		Reach for washer
5 Hold bolt		○⇨☐D▽	●⇨☐D▽		Grasp washer
6 Hold bolt		○⇨☐D▽	○➡☐D▽	8"	Move washer to bolt
7 Hold bolt		○⇨☐D▽	●⇨☐D▽		Place washer on bolt

▲ **FIGURE 10.7** Operation Chart (left-hand/right-hand chart) for Bolt-Washer Assembly

PRACTICE PROBLEM 10.2 ■ Activity Chart for Laundry

Develop an *activity chart* for doing three loads of laundry. Activity charts should be quite detailed, containing all the required elements of the entire process and the utilization of required resources. For this exercise, assume you will have access to one washing machine and one dryer.

Additional Practice Problem Space

THE VISUAL WORKPLACE (See Flexible Version pp. 315–316)

LABOR STANDARDS   (See Flexible Version pp. 317–328)

1. **Historical**

2. **Time Studies**

3. **Predetermined Time Standards**

4. **Work Sampling**

Historical Experience   (See Flexible Version p. 317)

Time Studies   (See Flexible Version pp. 317–322)

Eight Steps

1.

2.

3.

4.

5.

$$\text{Average observed time} = \frac{(\text{Sum of the times recorded to perform each element})}{\text{Number of observations}} \quad \text{(10-1)}$$

6.

$$\text{Normal time} = (\text{Average observed time}) \times (\text{Performance rating factor}) \quad \text{(10-2)}$$

7.

8.

$$\text{Standard time} = \frac{\text{Total normal time}}{1 - \text{Allowance factor}} \quad \text{(10-3)}$$

PRACTICE PROBLEM 10.3 ■ Normal and Standard Times

Carolyn Barrett, a marketing surveyor, takes an average of 10 minutes to complete a particular questionnaire. Carolyn's performance rating (pace) is 110%, and there is an allowance of 15%.

What is the normal time for completing this questionnaire?

What is the standard time for completing this questionnaire?

PRACTICE PROBLEM 10.4 ■ Additional Practice in Normal and Standard Times

Tom Leonard, of Leonard, Spitz, and Wareham, takes 3 hours and 25 minutes to write an end-of-month report. Tom is rated at 95% (work pace is 95%), and the office has a personal time allowance of 8%. There is no delay time or fatigue time.

What is the normal time for writing an end-of-month report?

What is the standard time for writing an end-of-month report?

PRACTICE PROBLEM 10.5 ■ Using Stopwatch Times

The two steps in preparing chocolate candy bars are molding and packaging. Personal fatigue and delay allowances are set at 15%. The molding machine operator is rated at 110%, and the packer is rated at 80%. Observed times per batch are given as follows:

| Task | Observed Time in Minutes | | | |
	1	2	3	4
Molding	26	30	29	31
Packing	45	50	35	30

Determine the normal and standard times for both tasks.

PRACTICE PROBLEM 10.6 ■ More Practice in Normal and Standard Times

A work-study sample of a manufacturing activity conducted over a 40-hour period shows that a worker with an 85% rating produced 12 parts. The worker's idle time was 10%, and the allowance factor was 12%.

Find the normal and standard times for this activity.

Additional Practice Problem Space

Sampling Error and Sample Size

$$\text{Required sample size} = n = \left(\frac{zs}{h\overline{x}}\right)^2 \tag{10-4}$$

where h = accuracy level desired in percent of the job element, expressed as a decimal
$\qquad (5\% = .05)$
$\quad z$ = number of standard deviations required for desired level of confidence
$\qquad (90\% \text{ confidence} = 1.65; \text{see Table 10.2 or Appendix I for the more common } z \text{ values})$
$\quad s$ = standard deviation of the initial sample
$\quad \overline{x}$ = mean of the initial sample
$\quad n$ = required sample size

▼ **TABLE 10.2** Common *z* Values

Desired Confidence (%)	z Value (standard deviation required for desired level of confidence)
90.0	1.65
95.0	1.96
95.45	2.00
99.0	2.58
99.73	3.00

PRACTICE PROBLEM 10.7 ■ Sample Size

Jim and Bob recently time-studied a janitorial task. From a sample of 75 observations, they computed an average cycle time of 15 minutes with a standard deviation of 2 minutes. Was their sample large enough that one can be 99% confident that the standard time is within 5% of the true value?

Additional Practice Problem Space

Predetermined Time Standards

(See Flexible Version pp. 322–325)

Therbligs

Time Measurement Units (TMUs)

GET and PLACE			DISTANCE RANGE IN IN.	<8	>8 <20	>20 <32
WEIGHT	CONDITIONS OF GET	PLACE ACCURACY	MTM CODE	1	2	3
<2 LB	EASY	APPROXIMATE	AA	20	35	50
		LOOSE	AB	30	45	60
		TIGHT	AC	40	55	70
	DIFFICULT	APPROXIMATE	AD	20	45	60
		LOOSE	AE	30	55	70
		TIGHT	AF	40	65	80
	HANDFUL	APPROXIMATE	AG	40	65	80
>2 LB <18 LB		APPROXIMATE	AH	25	45	55
		LOOSE	AJ	40	65	75
		TIGHT	AK	50	75	85
>18 LB <45 LB		APPROXIMATE	AL	90	106	115
		LOOSE	AM	95	120	130
		TIGHT	AN	120	145	160

◀ **FIGURE 10.9**
Sample MTM Table for GET and PLACE Motion
Time values are in TMUs.

Source: Copyrighted by the MTM Association for Standards and Research. No reprint permission without consent from the MTM Association, 16–01 Broadway, Fair Lawn, NJ 07410. Used with permission of MTM Association for Standards & Research.

PRACTICE PROBLEM 10.8 ■ MTM Calculations

Consider the following task broken down into 5 MTM elements:

	TMUs	Code in MTM Books
Reach to tool box	14.2	R12D
Grasp a tool	3.5	BG1
Separate tool by pressing	10.6	AP2
Turn tool	3.5	T45S
Move and focus eyes	13.4	M12B

What is the total time for the task?

Additional Practice Problem Space

Work Sampling (See Flexible Version pp. 325–328)

Five Steps

1. _____

2. _____

3. _____

4. _____

5. _____

$$n = \frac{z^2 p(1 - p)}{h^2}$$

(10-7)

where n = required sample size

z = standard normal deviate for the desired confidence level

($z = 1$ for 68% confidence, $z = 2$ for 95.45% confidence, and $z = 3$ for 99.73% confidence—these values are obtained from Table 10.2 or the Normal Table in Appendix I)

p = estimated value of sample proportion (of time worker is observed busy or idle)

h = acceptable error level, in percent

Practice Problem Space

ETHICS (See Flexible Version p. 328)

Ethical Dilemma

Birmingham's McWane Inc., with 10 major foundries, is one of the world's largest makers of cast-iron water and sewer pipes. In one of the nation's most dangerous industries, McWane is perhaps the most unsafe, with four times the injury rate of its six competitors combined. Its worker death rate is six times that of its industry's. McWane plants were also found in violation of pollution and emission limits 450 times in a recent 7-year period.

Workers who protest dangerous work conditions claim they are "bull's-eyed"—marked for termination. Supervisors have bullied injured workers and intimidated union leaders. Line workers who fail to make daily quotas get disciplinary actions. Managers have put up safety signs *after* a worker was injured to make it appear the worker ignored posted policies. They alter safety records and doctor machines to cover up hazards. When the government investigated one worker's death in 2000, inspectors found the McWane policy "was not to correct anything until OSHA found it."

McWane plants have also been repeatedly fined for failing to stop production to repair broken pollution controls. Five plants have been designated "high priority" violators by the EPA. Inside the plants, workers have repeatedly complained of blurred vision, severe headaches, and respiratory problems after being exposed, without training or protection, to chemicals used to make pipes. Near one plant in Phillipsburg, New Jersey, school crossing guards have had to wear gas masks—that location alone received 150 violations between 1995 and 2002. McWane's "standard procedure" (according to a former plant manager) is to illegally dump industrial contaminants into local rivers and creeks. Workers wait for night or heavy rainstorms before flushing thousands of gallons from their sump pumps.

Given the following fictional scenarios: What is your position, and what action should you take?

a. On your spouse's recent move to Birmingham, you accepted a job, perhaps somewhat naively, as a company nurse in one of the McWane plants. After 2 weeks on the job you became aware of the work environment noted above.
b. You are a contractor who has traditionally used McWane's products, which meet specifications. McWane is consistently the low bidder. Your customers are happy with the product.
c. You are McWane's banker.
d. You are a supplier to McWane.

Sources: The New York Times (January 9, 2003: E5, (May 26, 2004): A19, and (August 30, 2005): A16; and *The Wall Street Journal* (May 27, 2004): A8

Discussion Questions

1. How would you define a good quality of work life?
2. What are some of the worst jobs you know about? Why are they bad jobs? Why do people want these jobs?
3. If you were redesigning the jobs described in Question 2, what changes would you make? Are your changes realistic? Would they improve productivity (not just *production* but *productivity*)?
4. Can you think of any jobs that push the man–machine interface to the limits of human capabilities?
5. What are the five core characteristics of a good job design?
6. What are the differences among job enrichment, job enlargement, job rotation, job specialization, and employee empowerment?
7. Define ergonomics. Discuss the role of ergonomics in job design.
8. List the techniques available for carrying out methods analysis.
9. Identify four ways in which labor standards are set.
10. What are some of the uses to which labor standards are put?

11. How would you classify the following job elements? Are they personal, fatigue, or delay?
    a) The operator stops to talk to you.
    b) The operator lights up a cigarette.
    c) The operator opens his lunch pail (it is not lunch time), removes an apple, and takes an occasional bite.
12. How do you classify the time for a drill press operator who is idle for a few minutes at the beginning of every job waiting for the setup person to complete the setup? Some of the setup time is used in going for stock, but the operator typically returns with stock before the setup person is finished with the setup.
13. How do you classify the time for a machine operator who, between every job and sometimes in the middle of jobs, turns off the machine and goes for stock?
14. The operator drops a part, which you pick up and hand to him. Does this make any difference in a time study? If so, how?

Problems*

• **10.1** Make a process chart for changing the right rear tire on an automobile.

• **10.2** Draw an activity chart for a machine operator with the following operation. The relevant times are as follows:

Prepare mill for loading (cleaning, oiling, and so on)	.50 min
Load mill	1.75 min
Mill operating (cutting material)	2.25 min
Unload mill	.75 min

••• **10.3** Draw an activity chart (a crew chart similar to Figure 10.6) for a concert (for example, Nickelback, Linkin Park, Lil' Wayne, or Bruce Springsteen) and determine how to put together the concert so the star has reasonable breaks. For instance, at what point is there an instrumental number, a visual effect, a duet, a dance moment, that allows the star to pause and rest physically or at least rest his or her voice? Do other members of the show have moments of pause or rest?

•• **10.4** Make an operations chart of one of the following:
a) Putting a new eraser in (or on) a pencil
b) Putting a paper clip on two pieces of paper
c) Putting paper in a printer

• **10.5** Develop a process chart for installing a new memory board in your personal computer.

• **10.6** Rate a job you have had using Hackman and Oldham's core job characteristics (see p. 309 in the Flexible Version) on a scale from 1 to 10. What is your total score? What about the job could have been changed to make you give it a higher score?

•• **10.7** Using the data in Solved Problem 10.1 on page 329 in the Flexible Version, prepare an activity chart like the one in the Solved Problem, but a second Gas Man also delivers 11 gallons.

•• **10.8** Prepare a process chart for the Jackman in Solved Problem 10.1 on page 329 in the Flexible Version.

•• **10.9** Draw an activity chart for changing the right rear tire on an automobile with:
a) Only one person working
b) Two people working

••• **10.10** Draw an activity chart for washing the dishes in a double-sided sink. Two people participate, one washing, the other rinsing and drying. The rinser dries a batch of dishes from the drip rack as the washer fills the right sink with clean but unrinsed dishes. Then the rinser rinses the clean batch and places them on the drip rack. All dishes are stacked before being placed in the cabinets.

••• **10.11** Your campus club is hosting a car wash. Due to demand, three people are going to be scheduled per wash line. (Three people have to wash each vehicle.) Design an activity chart for washing and drying a typical sedan. You must wash the wheels but ignore the cleaning of the interior, because this part of the operation will be done at a separate vacuum station.

•••• **10.12** Design a process chart for printing a short document on a laser printer at an office. Unknown to you, the printer in the hallway is out of paper. The paper is located in a supply room at the other end of the hall. You wish to make five stapled copies of the document once it is printed. The copier, located next to the printer, has a sorter but no stapler. How could you make the task more efficient with the existing equipment?

• **10.13** If Charlene Brewster has times of 8.4, 8.6, 8.3, 8.5, 8.7, and 8.5 and a performance rating of 110%, what is the normal time for this operation? Is she faster or slower than normal? **Px**

• **10.14** If Charlene, the worker in Problem 10.13, has a performance rating of 90%, what is the normal time for the operation? Is she faster or slower than normal? **Px**

•• **10.15** Refer to Problem 10.13.
a) If the allowance factor is 15%, what is the standard time for this operation?
b) If the allowance factor is 18% and the performance rating is now 90%, what is the standard time for this operation? **Px**

•• **10.16** Maurice Browne recorded the following times assembling a watch. Determine (a) the average time, (b) the normal time, and (c) the standard time taken by him, using a performance rating of 95% and a personal allowance of 8%. **Px**

Assembly Times Recorded

Observation No.	Time (minutes)	Observation No.	Time (minutes)
1	0.11	9	0.12
2	0.10	10	0.09
3	0.11	11	0.12
4	0.10	12	0.11
5	0.14	13	0.10
6	0.10	14	0.12
7	0.10	15	0.14
8	0.09	16	0.09

• **10.17** A Northeast Airlines gate agent, Chip Gilliken, gives out seat assignments to ticketed passengers. He takes an average of 50 seconds per passenger and is rated 110% in performance. How long should a *typical* agent be expected to take to make seat assignments? **Px**

Note: **Px** means the problem may be solved with POM for Windows and/or Excel.

•   **10.18** After being observed many times, Marilyn Jones, a hospital lab analyst, had an average observed time for blood tests of 12 minutes. Marilyn's performance rating is 105%. The hospital has a personal, fatigue, and delay allowance of 16%.
a) Find the normal time for this process.
b) Find the standard time for this blood test. **Px**

•   **10.19** Jell Lee Beans is famous for its boxed candies, which are sold primarily to businesses. One operator had the following observed times for gift wrapping in minutes: 2.2, 2.6, 2.3, 2.5, 2.4. The operator has a performance rating of 105% and an allowance factor of 10%. What is the standard time for gift wrapping? **Px**

•   **10.20** After training, Mary Fernandez, a computer technician, had an average observed time for memory-chip tests of 12 seconds. Mary's performance rating is 100%. The firm has a personal fatigue and delay allowance of 15%.
a) Find the normal time for this process.
b) Find the standard time for this process. **Px**

•• **10.21** Susan Cottenden clocked the observed time for welding a part onto truck doors at 5.3 minutes. The performance rating of the worker timed was estimated at 105%. Find the normal time for this operation.
Note: According to the local union contract, each welder is allowed 3 minutes of personal time per hour and 2 minutes of fatigue time per hour. Further, there should be an average delay allowance of 1 minute per hour. Compute the allowance factor and then find the standard time for the welding activity. **Px**

•• **10.22** A hotel housekeeper, Alison Harvey, was observed five times on each of four task elements, as shown in the following table. On the basis of these observations, find the standard time for the process. Assume a 10% allowance factor.

Element	Performance Rating (%)	Observations (minutes per cycle)				
		1	2	3	4	5
Check minibar	100	1.5	1.6	1.4	1.5	1.5
Make one bed	90	2.3	2.5	2.1	2.2	2.4
Vacuum floor	120	1.7	1.9	1.9	1.4	1.6
Clean bath	100	3.5	3.6	3.6	3.6	3.2

Px

•• **10.23** Virginia College promotes a wide variety of executive-training courses for firms in the Arlington, Virginia, region. Director Marilyn Helms believes that individually typed letters add a personal touch to marketing. To prepare letters for mailing, she conducts a time study of her secretaries. On the basis of the observations shown in the following table, she wishes to develop a time standard for the whole job.

The college uses a total allowance factor of 12%. Helms decides to delete all unusual observations from the time study. What is the standard time?

Element	Observations (minutes)						Performance Rating (%)
	1	2	3	4	5	6	
Typing letter	2.5	3.5	2.8	2.1	2.6	3.3	85
Typing envelope	.8	.8	.6	.8	3.1[a]	.7	100
Stuffing envelope	.4	.5	1.9[a]	.3	.6	.5	95
Sealing, sorting	1.0	2.9[b]	.9	1.0	4.4[b]	.9	125

[a]Disregard—secretary stopped to answer the phone.
[b]Disregard—interruption by supervisor. **Px**

•   **10.24** The results of a time study to perform a quality control test are shown in the following table. On the basis of these observations, determine the normal and standard time for the test, assuming a 23% allowance factor. **Px**

Task Element	Performance Rating (%)	Observations (minutes)				
		1	2	3	4	5
1	97	1.5	1.8	2.0	1.7	1.5
2	105	.6	.4	.7	3.7[a]	.5
3	86	.5	.4	.6	.4	.4
4	90	.6	.8	.7	.6	.7

[a]Disregard—employee is smoking a cigarette (included in personal time).

•• **10.25** Peter Rourke, a loan processor at Wentworth Bank, has been timed performing four work elements, with the results shown in the following table. The allowances for tasks such as this are personal, 7%; fatigue, 10%; and delay, 3%.

Task Element	Performance Rating (%)	Observations (minutes)				
		1	2	3	4	5
1	110	.5	.4	.6	.4	.4
2	95	.6	.8	.7	.6	.7
3	90	.6	.4	.7	.5	.5
4	85	1.5	1.8	2.0	1.7	1.5

a) What is the normal time?
b) What is the standard time? **Px**

•• **10.26** Each year, Lord & Taylor, Ltd., sets up a gift-wrapping station to assist its customers with holiday shopping. Preliminary observations of one worker at the station produced the following sample time (in minutes per package): 3.5, 3.2, 4.1, 3.6, 3.9. Based on this small sample, what number of observations would be necessary to determine the true cycle time with a 95% confidence level and an accuracy of 5%? **Px**

•• **10.27** A time study of a factory worker has revealed an average observed time of 3.20 minutes, with a standard deviation of 1.28 minutes. These figures were based on a sample of 45 observations. Is this sample adequate in size for the firm to be 99% confident that the standard time is within 5% of the true value? If not, what should be the proper number of observations? **Px**

•• **10.28**   Based on a careful work study in the Richard Dulski Corp., the results shown in the following table have been observed:

Element	Observations (minutes) 1	2	3	4	5	Performance Rating (%)
Prepare daily reports	35	40	33	42	39	120
Photocopy results	12	10	36[a]	15	13	110
Label and package reports	3	3	5	5	4	90
Distribute reports	15	18	21	17	45[b]	85

[a]Photocopying machine broken; included as delay in the allowance factor.
[b]Power outage; included as delay in the allowance factor.

a) Compute the normal time for each work element.
b) If the allowance for this type of work is 15%, what is the standard time?
c) How many observations are needed for a 95% confidence level within 5% accuracy? (*Hint:* Calculate the sample size of each element.)

•• **10.29**   The Dubuque Cement Company packs 80-pound bags of concrete mix. Time-study data for the filling activity are shown in the following table. Because of the high physical demands of the job, the company's policy is a 23% allowance for workers.
a) Compute the standard time for the bag-packing task.
b) How many observations are necessary for 99% confidence, within 5% accuracy?

Element	Observations (seconds) 1	2	3	4	5	Performance Rating (%)
Grasp and place bag	8	9	8	11	7	110
Fill bag	36	41	39	35	112[a]	85
Seal bag	15	17	13	20	18	105
Place bag on conveyor	8	6	9	30[b]	35[b]	90

[a]Bag breaks open; included as delay in the allowance factor.
[b]Conveyor jams; included as delay in the allowance factor.

•• **10.30**   Installing mufflers at the Stanley Garage in Golden, Colorado, involves five work elements. Linda Stanley has timed workers performing these tasks seven times, with the results shown in the following table.

Job Element	Observations (minutes) 1	2	3	4	5	6	7	Performance Rating (%)
1. Select correct mufflers	4	5	4	6	4	15[a]	4	110
2. Remove old muffler	6	8	7	6	7	6	7	90
3. Weld/install new muffler	15	14	14	12	15	16	13	105
4. Check/inspect work	3	4	24[a]	5	4	3	18[a]	100
5. Complete paperwork	5	6	8	—	7	6	7	130

[a]Employee has lengthy conversations with boss (not job related).

By agreement with her workers, Stanley allows a 10% fatigue factor, a 10% personal-time factor but no time for delay. To compute standard time for the work operation, Stanley excludes all observations that appear to be unusual or nonrecurring. She does not want an error of more than 5%.
a) What is the standard time for the task?
b) How many observations are needed to assure a 95% confidence level? **Px**

• **10.31**   Bank manager Art Hill wants to determine the percent of time that tellers are working and idle. He decides to use work sampling, and his initial estimate is that the tellers are idle 15% of the time. How many observations should Hill take to be 95.45% confident that the results will not be more than 4% from the true result? **Px**

•• **10.32**   Supervisor Robert Hall wants to determine the percent of time a machine in his area is idle. He decides to use work sampling, and his initial estimate is that the machine is idle 20% of the time. How many observations should Hall take to be 98% confident that the results will be less than 5% from the true results?

••• **10.33**   In the photo on page 318 in the Flexible Version, Tim Nelson's job as an inspector for La-Z-Boy is discussed. Tim is expected to inspect 130 chairs per day.
a) If he works an 8-hour day, how many minutes is he allowed for each inspection (i.e., what is his "standard time")?
b) If he is allowed a 6% fatigue allowance, a 6% delay allowance, and 6% for personal time, what is the normal time that he is assumed to take to perform each inspection?

••• **10.34**   A random work sample of operators taken over a 160-hour work month at Tele-Marketing, Inc., has produced the following results. What is the percent of time spent working?

On phone with customer	858
Idle time	220
Personal time	85

•• **10.35**   A total of 300 observations of Bob Ramos, an assembly-line worker, were made over a 40-hour work week. The sample also showed that Bob was busy working (assembling the parts) during 250 observations.
a) Find the percentage of time Bob was working.
b) If you want a confidence level of 95%, and if 3% is an acceptable error, what size should the sample be?
c) Was the sample size adequate? **Px**

• **10.36**   Sharpening your pencil is an operation that may be divided into eight small elemental motions. In MTM terms, each element may be assigned a certain number of TMUs:

Reach 4 inches for the pencil	6 TMU
Grasp the pencil	2 TMU
Move the pencil 6 inches	10 TMU
Position the pencil	20 TMU
Insert the pencil into the sharpener	4 TMU
Sharpen the pencil	120 TMU
Disengage the pencil	10 TMU
Move the pencil 6 inches	10 TMU

What is the total normal time for sharpening one pencil? Convert your answer into minutes and seconds.

•• 10.37 Supervisor Vic Sower at Huntsville Equipment Company is concerned that material is not arriving as promptly as needed at work cells. A new kanban system has been installed, but there seems to be some delay in getting the material moved to the work cells so that the job can begin promptly. Sower is interested in determining how much delay there is on the part of his highly paid machinists. Ideally, the delay would be close to zero. He has asked his assistant to determine the delay factor among his 10 work cells. The assistant collects the data on a random basis over the next 2 weeks and determines that of the 1,200 observations, 105 were made while the operators were waiting for materials. Use a 95% confidence level and a 3% acceptable error. What report does he give to Sower? **Px**

•••• 10.38 The Winter Garden Hotel has 400 rooms. Every day, the housekeepers clean any room that was occupied the night before. If a guest is checking out of the hotel, the housekeepers give the room a thorough cleaning to get it ready for the next guest. This takes about 30 minutes. If a guest is staying another night, the housekeeper only "refreshes" the room, which takes 15 minutes.

Each day, each housekeeper reports for her 6-hour shift, then prepares her cart. She pushes the cart to her floor and begins work. She usually has to restock the cart once per day; then she pushes it back to the storeroom at the end of the day and puts the things away. Here is a timetable:

1) Arrive at work and stock cart (10 minutes).
2) Push cart to floor (10 minutes).
3) Take morning break (15 minutes).
4) Stop for lunch (30 minutes).
5) Restock cart (20 minutes).
6) Take afternoon break (15 minutes).
7) Push cart back to laundry and store items (20 minutes).

Last night, the hotel was full (all 400 rooms were occupied). People are checking out of 200 rooms. Their rooms will need to be thoroughly cleaned. The other 200 rooms will need to be refreshed.

a) How many minutes per day of actual room cleaning can each housekeeper do?
b) How many minutes of room cleaning will the Winter Garden Hotel need today?
c) How many housekeepers will be needed to clean the hotel today?
d) If *all* the guests checked out this morning, how many housekeepers would be needed to clean the 400 rooms?

▶ Refer to myomlab🔵 for these additional homework problems: 10.39–10.46

Case Studies

▶ Jackson Manufacturing Company

Kathleen McFadden, vice president of operations at Jackson Manufacturing Company, has just received a request for quote (RFQ) from DeKalb Electric Supply for 400 units per week of a motor armature. The components are standard and either easy to work into the existing production schedule or readily available from established suppliers on a JIT basis. But there is some difference in assembly. Ms. McFadden has identified eight tasks that Jackson must perform to assemble the armature. Seven of these tasks are very similar to ones performed by Jackson in the past; therefore, the average time and resulting labor standard of those tasks is known.

The eighth task, an *overload* test, requires performing a task that is very different from any performed previously, however. Kathleen has asked you to conduct a time study on the task to determine the standard time. Then an estimate can be made of the cost to assemble the armature. This information, combined with other cost data, will allow the firm to put together the information needed for the RFQ.

To determine a standard time for the task, an employee from an existing assembly station was trained in the new assembly process. Once proficient, the employee was then asked to perform the task 17 times so a standard could be determined. The actual times observed (in minutes) were as follows:

The worker had a 115% performance rating. The task can be performed in a sitting position at a well-designed ergonomic workstation in an air-conditioned facility. Although the armature itself weighs 10.5 pounds, there is a carrier that holds it so that the operator need only rotate the armature. But the detail work remains high; therefore, the fatigue allowance should be 8%. The company has an established personal allowance of 6%. Delay should be very low. Previous studies of delay in this department average 2%. This standard is to use the same figure.

The workday is 7.5 hours, but operators are paid for 8 hours at an average of $12.50 per hour.

Discussion Questions

In your report to Ms. McFadden, you realize you will want to address several factors:

1. How big should the sample be for a statistically accurate standard (at, say, the 99.73% confidence level and accuracy of 5%)?
2. Is the sample size adequate?
3. How many units should be produced at this workstation per day?
4. What is the cost per unit for this task in direct labor cost?

1	2	3	4	5	6	7	8	9	10	11	12	13	14	15	16	17
2.05	1.92	2.01	1.89	1.77	1.80	1.86	1.83	1.93	1.96	1.95	2.05	1.79	1.82	1.85	1.85	1.99

Source: Professor Hank Maddux, Sam Houston State University.

▶ **Hard Rock's Human Resource Strategy**

Video Case

Everyone—managers and hourly employees alike—who goes to work for Hard Rock Cafe takes Rock 101, an initial 2-day training class. There they receive their wallet-sized "Hard Rock Values" card which they carry at all times. The Hard Rock value system is to bring a fun, healthy, nurturing environment into the Hard Rock Cafe culture.* This initial course and many other courses help employees develop both personally and professionally. The human resource department plays a critical role in any service organization, but at Hard Rock, with its "experience strategy," the human resource department takes on added importance.

Long before Jim Knight, manager of corporate training, begins the class, the human resource strategy of Hard Rock has had an impact. Hard Rock's strategic plan includes building a culture that allows for acceptance of substantial diversity and individuality. From a human resource perspective, this has the benefit of enlarging the pool of applicants as well as contributing to the Hard Rock culture.

Creating a work environment above and beyond a paycheck is a unique challenge. Outstanding pay and benefits are a start, but the key is to provide an environment that works for the employees. This includes benefits that start for part-timers who work at least 19 hours per week (while others in the industry start at 35 hours per week); a unique respect for individuality; continuing training; and a high level of internal promotions—some 60% of the managers are promoted from hourly employee ranks. The company's training is very specific, with job-oriented interactive CDs covering kitchen, retail, and front-of-the-house service. Outside volunteer work is especially encouraged to foster a bond between the workers, their community, and issues of importance to them.

Applicants also are screened on their interest in music and their ability to tell a story. Hard Rock builds on a hiring criterion of bright, positive-attitude, self-motivated individuals with an employee bill of rights and substantial employee empowerment. The result is a unique culture and work environment which, no doubt, contributes to the low turnover of hourly people—one-half the industry average.

The layout, memorabilia, music, and videos are important elements in the Hard Rock "experience," but it falls on the waiters and waitresses to make the experience come alive. They are particularly focused on providing an authentic and memorable dining experience. Like Southwest Airlines, Hard Rock is looking for people with a cause—people who like to serve. By succeeding with its human resource strategy, Hard Rock obtains a competitive advantage.

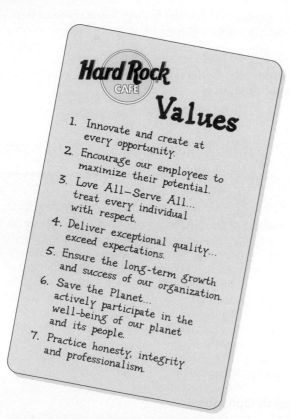

Hard Rock Cafe Values

1. Innovate and create at every opportunity.
2. Encourage our employees to maximize their potential.
3. Love All—Serve All... treat every individual with respect.
4. Deliver exceptional quality... exceed expectations.
5. Ensure the long-term growth and success of our organization.
6. Save the Planet... actively participate in the well-being of our planet and its people.
7. Practice honesty, integrity and professionalism.

Discussion Questions[†]

1. What has Hard Rock done to lower employee turnover to half the industry average?
2. How does Hard Rock's human resource department support the company's overall strategy?
3. How would Hard Rock's value system work for automobile assembly line workers? (*Hint:* Consider Hackman and Oldham's core job characteristics.)
4. How might you adjust a traditional assembly line to address more "core job characteristics"?

[†]Before answering these questions, you may wish to view the video that accompanies this case.

*Hard Rock Cafe's mission, mottos, and operating values are available at **www.hardrock.com/corporate/careers**.

Active Model Exercise

ACTIVE MODEL 10.1, based on Example 5 in the text, simulates the sample size required as a function of the proportion of time spent on a work activity. It is illustrated at **www.myomlab.com** or **www.pearsonhighered.com/heizer**.

Main Heading	Review Material	
HUMAN RESOURCE STRATEGY FOR COMPETITIVE ADVANTAGE (pp. 306–307)	*The objective of a human resource strategy is to manage labor and design jobs so people are effectively and efficiently utilized.* *Quality of work life* refers to a job that is not only reasonably safe with equitable pay but that also achieves an appropriate level of both physical and psychological requirements. *Mutual commitment* means that both management and employees strive to meet common objectives. *Mutual trust* is reflected in reasonable, documented employment policies that are honestly and equitably implemented to the satisfaction of both management and employees.	**VIDEO 10.1** Human Resources at Hard Rock Cafe
LABOR PLANNING (pp. 307–308)	▪ **Labor planning**—A means of determining staffing policies dealing with employment stability, work schedules, and work rules. *Flextime* allows employees, within limits, to determine their own schedules. *Flexible* (or *compressed*) *workweeks* often call for fewer but longer workdays. *Part-time status* is particularly attractive in service industries with fluctuating demand loads.	
JOB DESIGN (pp. 308–311)	▪ **Job design**—Specifies the tasks that constitute a job for an individual or group. ▪ **Labor specialization** (or **job specialization**)—The division of labor into unique ("special") tasks. ▪ **Job enlargement**—The grouping of a variety of tasks about the same skill level; horizontal enlargement. ▪ **Job rotation**—A system in which an employee is moved from one specialized job to another. ▪ **Job enrichment**—A method of giving an employee more responsibility that includes some of the planning and control necessary for job accomplishment; vertical expansion. ▪ **Employee empowerment**—Enlarging employee jobs so that the added responsibility and authority is moved to the lowest level possible. ▪ **Self-directed team**—A group of empowered individuals working together to reach a common goal.	
ERGONOMICS AND THE WORK ENVIRONMENT (pp. 311–314)	▪ **Ergonomics**—The study of the human interface with the environment and machines. The physical environment affects performance, safety, and quality of work life. Illumination, noise and vibration, temperature, humidity, and air quality are controllable by management.	
METHODS ANALYSIS (pp. 314–315)	▪ **Methods analysis**—A system that involves developing work procedures that are safe and produce quality products efficiently. ▪ **Flow diagram**—A drawing used to analyze movement of people or material. ▪ **Process chart**—A graphic representation that depicts a sequence of steps for a process. ▪ **Activity chart**—A way of improving utilization of an operator and a machine or some combination of operators (a crew) and machines. ▪ **Operations chart**—A chart depicting right- and left-hand motions.	Virtual Office Hours for Solved Problems: 10.1
THE VISUAL WORKPLACE (pp. 315–316)	▪ **Visual workplace**—Uses a variety of visual communication techniques to rapidly communicate information to stakeholders.	
LABOR STANDARDS (pp. 317–328)	▪ **Labor standards**—The amount of time required to perform a job or part of a job. Labor standards are set in four ways: (1) historical experience, (2) time studies, (3) predetermined time standards, and (4) work sampling. ▪ **Time study**—Timing a sample of a worker's performance and using it as a basis for setting a standard time. ▪ **Average observed time**—The arithmetic mean of the times for each element measured, adjusted for unusual influence for each element: $$\text{Average observed time} = \frac{\text{Sum of the times recorded to perform each element}}{\text{Number of observations}} \quad (10\text{-}1)$$ ▪ **Normal time**—The average observed time, adjusted for pace: $$\text{Normal time} = (\text{Average observed time}) \times (\text{Performance rating factor}) \quad (10\text{-}2)$$	Virtual Office Hours for Solved Problems: 10.2–10.6 Problems 10.13–10.37

Main Heading	Review Material	

- **Standard time**—An adjustment to the total normal time; the adjustment provides allowances for personal needs, unavoidable work delays, and fatigue:

$$\text{Standard time} = \frac{\text{Total normal time}}{1 - \text{Allowance factor}} \qquad (10\text{-}3)$$

Personal time allowances are often established in the range of 4% to 7% of total time.

$$\text{Required sample size} = n = \left(\frac{zs}{h\overline{x}}\right)^2 \qquad (10\text{-}4)$$

$$n = \left(\frac{zs}{e}\right)^2 \qquad (10\text{-}5)$$

$$s = \sqrt{\frac{\sum (x_i - \overline{x})^2}{n - 1}} = \sqrt{\frac{(\text{Each sample observation} - \overline{x})^2}{\text{Number in sample} - 1}} \qquad (10\text{-}6)$$

- **Predetermined time standards**—A division of manual work into small basic elements that have established and widely accepted times.

The most common predetermined time standard is *methods time measurement* (MTM).

- **Therbligs**—Basic physical elements of motion.
- **Time measurement units (TMUs)**—Units for very basic micromotions in which 1 TMU = 0.0006 min or 100,000 TMUs = 1 hr.
- **Work sampling**—An estimate, via sampling, of the percent of the time that a worker spends on various tasks.

Work sampling sample size for a desired confidence and accuracy:

$$n = \frac{z^2 p(1 - p)}{h^2} \qquad (10\text{-}7)$$

ETHICS
(p. 328)

Management's role is to educate the employee; specify the necessary equipment, work rules, and work environment; and then enforce those requirements.

Self Test

- **Before taking the self-test,** refer to the learning objectives listed at the beginning of the chapter and the key terms listed at the end of the chapter.

LO1. When product demand fluctuates and yet you maintain a constant level of employment, some of your cost savings might include:
- a) reduction in hiring costs.
- b) reduction in layoff costs and unemployment insurance costs.
- c) lack of need to pay a premium wage to get workers to accept unstable employment.
- d) having a trained workforce rather than having to retrain new employees each time you hire for an upswing in demand.
- e) all of the above.

LO2. The difference between *job enrichment* and *job enlargement* is that:
- a) enlarged jobs contain a larger number of similar tasks, while enriched jobs include some of the planning and control necessary for job accomplishment.
- b) enriched jobs contain a larger number of similar tasks, while enlarged jobs include some of the planning and control necessary for job accomplishment.
- c) enriched jobs enable an employee to do a number of boring jobs instead of just one.
- d) all of the above.

LO3. The work environment includes these factors:
- a) Lighting, noise, temperature, and air quality
- b) Illumination, carpeting, and high ceilings
- c) Enough space for meetings and videoconferencing
- d) Noise, humidity, and number of coworkers
- e) Job enlargement and space analysis

LO4. *Methods analysis* focuses on:
- a) the design of the machines used to perform a task.
- b) how a task is accomplished.
- c) the raw materials that are consumed in performing a task.
- d) reducing the number of steps required to perform a task.

LO5. The least preferred method of establishing labor standards is:
- a) time studies.
- b) work sampling.
- c) historical experience.
- d) predetermined time standards.

LO6. The allowance factor in a time study:
- a) adjusts normal time for errors and rework.
- b) adjusts standard time for lunch breaks.
- c) adjusts normal time for personal needs, unavoidable delays, and fatigue.
- d) allows workers to rest every 20 minutes.

LO7. To set the required sample size in a time study, you must know:
- a) the number of employees.
- b) the number of parts produced per day.
- c) the desired accuracy and confidence levels.
- d) management's philosophy toward sampling.

Answers: **LO1.** e; **LO2.** a; **LO3.** a; **LO4.** b; **LO5.** c; **LO6.** c; **LO7.** c.

11 Supply-Chain Management

Chapter Outline

The Supply Chain's Strategic Importance

Ethics and Sustainability

Supply-Chain Economics

Supply-Chain Strategies

Managing the Supply Chain

E-Procurement

Vendor Selection

Logistics Management

Measuring Supply-Chain Performance

Ethical Dilemma
Discussion Questions
Problems
Case Studies: Dell's Value Chain; Darden's
  Global Supply Chains; Arnold Palmer
  Hospital's Supply Chain; Supply-Chain
  Management at Regal Marine
Rapid Review

Most firms spend over 50% of their sales dollar on purchases. Because such a high percentage of an organization's costs are determined by purchasing, relationships with suppliers are critical. Indeed, as firms strive to increase their competitiveness via product customization, higher quality, cost reductions, and speed to market, they place added emphasis on the supply chain. The discipline that manages these relationships is known as *supply-chain management*.

The objective of supply chain management is to build a chain of suppliers that focuses on maximizing value to the ultimate customer.

BEFORE COMING TO CLASS, READ CHAPTER 11 IN YOUR TEXT AND ANSWER THESE QUESTIONS.

1. Why is the supply chain of strategic importance? _____

_____

_____

2. Identify six supply chain strategies. _____

_____

_____

3. Explain issues and opportunities in the supply chain. _____

_____

_____

4. Identify the steps in vendor selection. _____

_____

_____

5. What are the major issues for logistics management? _____

_____

_____

6. How do you compute the percent of assets committed to inventory? ___

_____

7. How do you compute inventory turnover? _____

_____

THE SUPPLY CHAIN'S STRATEGIC IMPORTANCE

(See Flexible Version pp. 336–338)

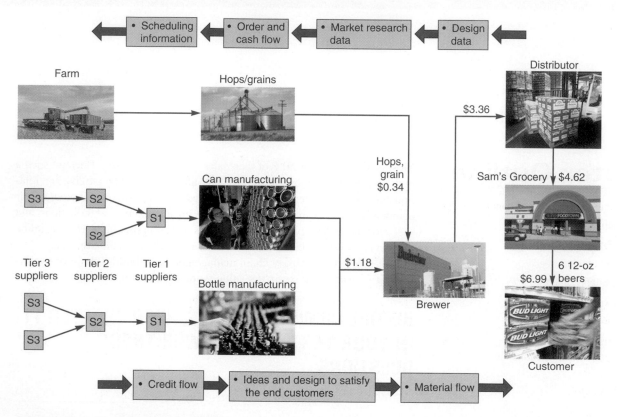

▲ FIGURE 11.1   A Supply Chain for Beer

The supply chain includes all the interactions among suppliers, manufacturers, distributors, and customers. The chain includes transportation, scheduling information, cash and credit transfers, as well as ideas, designs, and material transfers. Even can and bottle manufacturers have their own tiers of suppliers providing components such as glass, lids, labels, packing containers, etc. (Costs are approximate and include substantial taxes.)

Supply-Chain Management   (See Flexible Version pp. 336–337)

Supply-Chain Risk   (See Flexible Version pp. 337–338)

ETHICS AND SUSTAINABILITY   (See Flexible Version pp. 339–340)

SUPPLY-CHAIN ECONOMICS   (See Flexible Version pp. 340–341)

▼ **TABLE 11.4**   Dollars of Additional Sales Needed to Equal $1 Saved through the Supply Chain

Percent Net Profit of Firm	Percent of Sales Spent in the Supply Chain						
	30%	**40%**	**50%**	**60%**	**70%**	**80%**	**90%**
2	$2.78	$3.23	$3.85	$4.76	$6.25	$9.09	$16.67
4	$2.70	$3.13	$3.70	$4.55	$5.88	$8.33	$14.29
6	$2.63	$3.03	$3.57	$4.35	$5.56	$7.69	$12.50
8	$2.56	$2.94	$3.45	$4.17	$5.26	$7.14	$11.11
10	$2.50	$2.86	$3.33	$4.00	$5.00	$6.67	$10.00

PRACTICE PROBLEM 11.1 ■ Supply-Chain Economics

Determine the sales necessary to equal a dollar of savings on purchases for a company that has a net profit of 6% and spends 70% of its revenues on purchases. (Use Table 11.4.)

PRACTICE PROBLEM 11.2 ■ Supply-Chain Economics

Determine the sales necessary to equal a dollar of savings on purchases for a company that has a net profit of 4% and spends 40% of its revenues on purchases. (Use Table 11.4.)

Make or Buy (See Flexible Version p. 341)

Outsourcing (See Flexible Version p. 341)

SUPPLY-CHAIN STRATEGIES (See Flexible Version pp. 341–343)

1. **Many Suppliers**

2. **Few Suppliers**

3. **Vertical Integration**

4. Joint Ventures

5. *Keiretsu* Networks

6. Virtual Companies

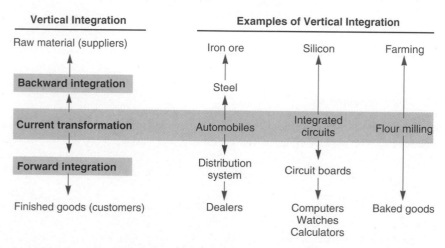

▲ FIGURE 11.2   Vertical Integration Can Be Forward or Backward

MANAGING THE SUPPLY CHAIN (See Flexible Version pp. 343–347)

Agreement on Goals, Trust, and Cultures

Issues in an Integrated Supply Chain
(See Flexible Version pp. 344–345)

Local Optimization, Incentives, Large Lots, Bullwhip Effect

Opportunities in the Integrated Supply Chain
(See Flexible Version pp. 345–347)

Accurate Pull Data

Lotsize Reduction

Single-Stage Control of Replenishment

Vendor Managed Inventory

Collaborative Planning, Forecasting, and Replenishment (CPFR)

Blanket Orders

Standardization

Postponement

Drop Shipping

Pass-Through Facility

Channel Assembly

E-PROCUREMENT (See Flexible Version pp. 347–349)

Electronic Data Interchange (EDI)
(See Flexible Version p. 347)

Online Catalogs (See Flexible Version pp. 347–348)

Auctions (See Flexible Version p. 348)

RFQs (See Flexible Version p. 348)

Real-Time Inventory Tracking (See Flexible Version pp. 348–349)

VENDOR SELECTION (See Flexible Version pp. 349–350)

Vendor Evaluation, Development, and Negotiations
(See Flexible Version pp. 349–350)

LOGISTICS MANAGEMENT (See Flexible Version pp. 350–354)

Distribution Systems: Trucking, Rail, Air, Water, and Pipelines (See Flexible Version p. 351)

Third-Party Logistics (See Flexible Version pp. 351–352)

Shipping Costs (See Flexible Version pp. 352–353)

PRACTICE PROBLEM 11.3 ■ Shipping Costs

Phil Carter, president of Carter Computer Components Corp., has the option of shipping computer transformers from the company's Singapore plant via container ship or airfreight. The typical shipment has a value of $75,000. A container ship takes 24 days and costs $5,000; airfreight takes 1 day and costs $8,000. Holding cost is estimated to be 40% in either case. How should shipments be made?

Additional Practice Problem Space

Security and JIT (See Flexible Version pp. 353–354)

MEASURING SUPPLY-CHAIN PERFORMANCE

(See Flexible Version pp. 354–356)

$$\text{Percentage invested in inventory} = (\text{Total inventory investment}/\text{Total assets}) \times 100 \quad \text{(11-1)}$$

$$\text{Inventory turnover} = \text{Cost of goods sold}/\text{Inventory investment} \quad \text{(11-2)}$$

	Typical Firms	Benchmark Firms
Lead time (weeks)	15	8
Time spent placing an order	42 minutes	15 minutes
Percentage of late deliveries	33%	2%
Percentage of rejected material	1.5%	.0001%
Number of shortages per year	400	4

Source: Adapted from a McKinney & Company report.

◀ **TABLE 11.5**
Metrics for Supply-Chain Performance

Ethical Dilemma

For generations, the policy of Sears Roebuck and Company, the granddaddy of retailers, was not to purchase more than 50% of any of its suppliers' output. The rationale of this policy was that it allowed Sears to move to other suppliers, as the market dictated, without destroying the supplier's ability to stay in business. In contrast, Walmart purchases more and more of a supplier's output. Eventually, Walmart can be expected to sit down with that supplier and explain why the supplier no longer needs a sales force and that the supplier should eliminate the sales force, passing the cost savings on to Walmart.

Sears is losing market share, has been acquired by K-Mart, and is eliminating jobs; Walmart is gaining market share and hiring. What are the ethical issues involved, and which firm has a more ethical position?

Discussion Questions

1. Define *supply-chain management*.
2. What are the objectives of supply-chain management?
3. What is the objective of logistics management?
4. How do we distinguish between the types of risk in the supply chain?
5. What is vertical integration? Give examples of backward and forward integration.
6. What are three basic approaches to negotiations?
7. How does a traditional adversarial relationship with suppliers change when a firm makes a decision to move to a few suppliers?
8. What is the difference between postponement and channel assembly?
9. What is CPFR?
10. What is the value of online auctions in e-commerce?
11. Explain how FedEx uses the Internet to meet requirements for quick and accurate delivery.
12. How does Walmart use drop shipping?
13. What are blanket orders? How do they differ from invoiceless purchasing?
14. What can purchasing do to implement just-in-time deliveries?
15. What is e-procurement?
16. How does Darden Restaurants, described in the *Global Company Profile* in the *Flexible Version*, find competitive advantage in its supply chain?
17. What is SCOR, and what purpose does it serve?

Problems

•• **11.1**   Choose a local establishment that is a member of a relatively large chain. From interviews with workers and information from the Internet, identify the elements of the supply chain. Determine whether the supply chain represents a low-cost, rapid response, or differentiation strategy (refer to Chapter 2). Are the supply-chain characteristics significantly different from one product to another?

•• **11.2**   As purchasing agent for Woolsey Enterprises in Golden, Colorado, you ask your buyer to provide you with a ranking of "excellent," "good," "fair," or "poor" for a variety of characteristics for two potential vendors. You suggest that the "Products" total be weighted 40% and the other three categories' totals be weighted 20% each. The buyer has returned the following ranking:

VENDOR RATING

Company	Excellent (4)	Good (3)	Fair (2)	Poor (1)	Products	Excellent (4)	Good (3)	Fair (2)	Poor (1)
Financial Strength			K	D	Quality	KD			
Manufacturing Range			KD		Price			KD	
Research Facilities	K		D		Packaging			KD	
Geographical Locations		K	D						
Management		K	D		**Sales**				
Labor Relations			K	D	Product Knowledge			D	K
Trade Relations			KD		Sales Calls			K	D
					Sales Service			K	D

Service				
Deliveries on Time		KD		
Handling of Problems		KD		
Technical Assistance		K	D	

DONNA INC. = D
KAY CORP. = K

Which of the two vendors would you select?

•• **11.3**   Using the data in Problem 11.2, assume that both Donna, Inc. and Kay Corp. are able to move all their "poor" ratings to "fair." How would you then rank the two firms?

•• **11.4**   Develop a vendor-rating form that represents your comparison of the education offered by universities in which you considered (or are considering) enrolling. Fill in the necessary data, and identify the "best" choice. Are you attending that "best" choice? If not, why not?

•• **11.5**   Using sources from the Internet, identify some of the problems faced by a company of your choosing as it moves toward, or operates as, a virtual organization. Does its operating as a virtual organization simply exacerbate old problems, or does it create new ones?

• **11.6**   Using Table 11.4, determine the sales necessary to equal a dollar of savings on purchases for a company that has:
a) A net profit of 4% and spends 40% of its revenue on purchases.
b) A net profit of 6% and spends 80% of its revenue on purchases.

• **11.7**   Using Table 11.4, determine the sales necessary to equal a dollar of savings on purchases for a company that has:
a) A net profit of 6% and spends 60% of its revenue on purchases.
b) A net profit of 8% and spends 80% of its revenue on purchases.

•• **11.8**   Your options for shipping $100,000 of machine parts from Baltimore to Kuala Lumpur, Malaysia, are (1) use a ship that will take 30 days at a cost of $3,800, or (2) truck the parts to Los Angeles and then ship at a total cost of $4,800. The second option will take only 20 days. You are paid via a letter of credit the day the parts arrive. Your holding cost is estimated at 30% of the value per year.

a) Which option is more economical?
b) What customer issues are not included in the data presented?

•• **11.9**   If you have a third option for the data in Problem 11.8, and it costs only $4,000 and also takes 20 days, what is your most economical plan?

•• **11.10**   Monczka-Trent Shipping is the logistics vendor for Handfield Manufacturing Co. in Ohio. Handfield has daily shipments of a power-steering pump from its Ohio plant to an auto assembly line in Alabama. The value of the standard shipment is $250,000. Monczka-Trent has two options: (1) its standard 2-day shipment or (2) a subcontractor who will team drive overnight with an effective delivery of 1 day. The extra driver costs $175. Handfield's holding cost is 35% annually for this kind of inventory.

a) Which option is more economical?

b) What production issues are not included in the data presented?

•• **11.11**   Baker Mfg Inc. (see Table 11.8) wishes to compare its inventory turnover to those of industry leaders, who have turnover of about 13 times per year and 8% of their assets invested in inventory.

▼ **TABLE 11.8**   For Problems 11.11 and 11.12

Arrow Distributing Corp.	
Net revenue	$16,500
Cost of sales	$13,500
Inventory	$ 1,000
Total assets	$ 8,600
Baker Mfg. Inc.	
Net revenue	$27,500
Cost of sales	$21,500
Inventory	$ 1,250
Total assets	$16,600

a) What is Baker's inventory turnover?

b) What is Baker's percent of assets committed to inventory?

c) How does Baker's performance compare to the industry leaders?

•• **11.12**   Arrow Distributing Corp. (see Table 11.8) likes to track inventory by using weeks of supply as well as by inventory turnover.

a) What is its weeks of supply?

b) What percent of Arrow's assets are committed to inventory?

c) What is Arrow's inventory turnover?

d) Is Arrow's supply-chain performance, as measured by these inventory metrics, better than that of Baker, in Problem 11.11?

• **11.13**   The grocery industry has an annual inventory turnover of about 14 times. Organic Grocers, Inc., had a cost of goods sold last year of $10.5 million; its average inventory was $1.0 million. What was Organic Grocers's inventory turnover, and how does that performance compare with that of the industry?

•• **11.14**   Mattress Wholesalers, Inc. is constantly trying to reduce inventory in its supply chain. Last year, cost of goods sold was $7.5 million and inventory was $1.5 million. This year, costs of goods sold is $8.6 million and inventory investment is $1.6 million.

a) What were the weeks of supply last year?

b) What are the weeks of supply this year?

c) Is Mattress Wholesalers making progress in its inventory reduction effort?

▶ Refer to myomlab🌐 for this additional homework problem: 11.15

Case Studies

▶ Dell's Value Chain

Dell Computer, with close supplier relationships, encourages suppliers to focus on their individual technological capabilities to sustain leadership in their components. Research and development costs are too high and technological changes are too rapid for any one company to sustain leadership in every component. Suppliers are also pressed to drive down lead times, lot sizes, and inventories. Dell, in turn, keeps its research customer-focused and leverages that research to help itself and suppliers. Dell also constructs special Web pages for suppliers, allowing them to view orders for components they produce as well as current levels of inventory at Dell. This allows suppliers to plan based on actual end customer demand; as a result, it reduces the bullwhip effect. The intent is to work with suppliers to keep the supply chain moving rapidly, products current, and the customer order queue short. Then, with supplier collaboration, Dell can offer the latest options, can build-to-order, and can achieve rapid throughput. The payoff is a competitive advantage, growing market share, and low capital investment.

On the distribution side, Dell uses direct sales, primarily via the Internet, to increase revenues by offering a virtually unlimited variety of desktops, notebooks, and enterprise products. Options displayed over the Internet allow Dell to attract customers that value

choice. Customers select recommended product configurations or customize them. Dell's customers place orders at any time of the day from anywhere in the world. And Dell's price is cheaper; retail stores have additional costs because of their brick-and-mortar model. Dell has also customized Web pages that enable large business customers to track past purchases and place orders consistent with their purchase history and current needs. Assembly begins immediately after receipt of a customer order. Competing firms have previously assembled products filling the distribution channels (including shelves at retailers) before a product reaches the customer. Dell, in contrast, introduces a new product to customers over the Internet as soon as the first of that model is ready. In an industry where products have life cycles measured in months, Dell enjoys a huge early-to-market advantage.

Dell's model also has cash flow advantages. Direct sales allow Dell to eliminate distributor and retailer margins and increase its own margin. Dell collects payment in a matter of days after products are sold. But Dell pays its suppliers according to the more traditional billing schedules. Given its low levels of inventory, Dell is able to operate its business with negative working capital because it manages to receive payment before it pays its suppliers for components. These more traditional supply chains often require 60 or more days for the cash to flow from customer to supplier—a huge demand on working capital.

Dell has designed its order processing, products, and assembly lines so that customized products can be assembled in a matter of hours. This allows Dell to postpone assembly until after a customer order has been placed. In addition, any inventory is often in the form of components that are common across a wide variety of finished products. Postponement, component modularity, and tight scheduling allow low inventory and support mass customization. Dell maximizes the benefit of postponement by focusing on new products for which demand is difficult to forecast. Manufacturers who sell via distributors and retailers find postponement virtually impossible. Therefore, traditional manufacturers are often stuck with product configurations that are not selling while simultaneously being out of the configurations that *are* selling. Dell is better able to match supply and demand.

One of the few negatives for Dell's model is that it results in higher outbound shipping costs than selling through distributors and retailers. Dell sends individual products directly to customers from its factories. But many of these shipments are small (often one or a few products), while manufacturers selling through distributors and retailers ship with some economy of scale, using large shipments via truck to warehouses and retailers, with the end user providing the final portion of delivery. As a result, Dell's outbound transportation costs are higher, but the relative cost is low (typically 2% to 3%), and thus the impact on the overall cost is low.

What Dell has done is build a collaborative supply chain and an innovative ordering and production system. The result is what Dell likes to refer to as its *value chain*—a chain that brings value from supplier to the customer and provides Dell with a competitive advantage.

Discussion Questions

1. How has Dell used its direct sales and build-to-order model to develop an exceptional supply chain?
2. How has Dell exploited the direct sales model to improve operations performance?
3. What are the main disadvantages of Dell's direct sales model?
4. How does Dell compete with a retailer who already has a stock?
5. How does Dell's supply chain deal with the bullwhip effect?

Sources: Adapted from S. Chopra and P. Meindl, *Supply Chain Management*, 3rd ed. (Upper Saddle River, NJ: Prentice Hall, 2007); R. Kapuscinski, et al., "Inventory Decisions in Dell's Supply Chain," *Interfaces* 34, no. 3 (May–June 2004): 191–205; and A. A. Thompson, A. J. Strickland, and J. E. Gamble, "Dell, Inc. in 2006: Can Rivals Beat Its Strategy?" *Crafting and Executing Strategy*, 15th ed. (New York: McGraw-Hill, 2007).

▶ Darden's Global Supply Chains

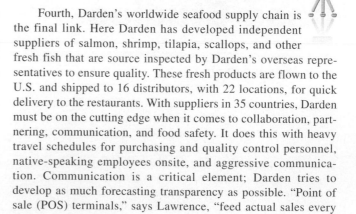

Video Case

Darden Restaurants (subject of the *Global Company Profile* in the *Flexible Version*), owner of popular brands such as Olive Garden and Red Lobster, requires unique supply chains to serve more than 300 million meals annually. Darden's strategy is operations excellence, and Senior VP Jim Lawrence's task is to ensure competitive advantage via Darden's supply chains. For a firm with purchases exceeding $1.5 billion, managing the supply chains is a complex and challenging task.

Darden, like other casual dining restaurants, has unique supply chains that reflect its menu options. Darden's supply chains are rather shallow, often having just one tier of suppliers. But it has four distinct supply chains.

First, "smallware" is a restaurant industry term for items such as linens, dishes, tableware and kitchenware, and silverware. These are purchased, with Darden taking title as they are received at the Darden Direct Distribution (DDD) warehouse in Orlando, Florida. From this single warehouse, smallware items are shipped via common carrier (trucking companies) to Olive Garden, Red Lobster, Bahama Breeze, and Seasons 52 restaurants.

Second, frozen, dry, and canned food products are handled economically by Darden's 11 distribution centers in North America, which are managed by major U.S. food distributors, such as MBM, Maines, and Sygma. This is Darden's second supply line.

Third, the fresh food supply chain (not frozen and not canned), where life is measured in days, includes dairy products, produce, and meat. This supply-chain is B2B, where restaurant managers directly place orders with a preselected group of independent suppliers.

Fourth, Darden's worldwide seafood supply chain is the final link. Here Darden has developed independent suppliers of salmon, shrimp, tilapia, scallops, and other fresh fish that are source inspected by Darden's overseas representatives to ensure quality. These fresh products are flown to the U.S. and shipped to 16 distributors, with 22 locations, for quick delivery to the restaurants. With suppliers in 35 countries, Darden must be on the cutting edge when it comes to collaboration, partnering, communication, and food safety. It does this with heavy travel schedules for purchasing and quality control personnel, native-speaking employees onsite, and aggressive communication. Communication is a critical element; Darden tries to develop as much forecasting transparency as possible. "Point of sale (POS) terminals," says Lawrence, "feed actual sales every night to suppliers."

Discussion Questions*

1. What are the advantages of each of Darden's four supply chains?
2. What are the complications of having four supply chains?
3. Where would you expect ownership/title to change in each of Darden's four supply chains?
4. How do Darden's four supply chains compare with those of other firms, such as Dell or an automobile manufacturer? Why do the differences exist, and how are they addressed?

*You may wish to view the video that accompanies this case before answering these questions.

► Arnold Palmer Hospital's Supply Chain

Video Case

Arnold Palmer Hospital, one of the nation's top hospitals dedicated to serving women and children, is a large business with over 2,000 employees working in a 431-bed facility totaling 676,000 square feet in Orlando, Florida. Like many other hospitals, and other companies, Arnold Palmer Hospital had been a long-time member of a large buying group, one servicing 900 members. But the group did have a few limitations. For example, it might change suppliers for a particular product every year (based on a new lower-cost bidder) or stock only a product that was not familiar to the physicians at Arnold Palmer Hospital. The buying group was also not able to negotiate contracts with local manufacturers to secure the best pricing.

So in 2003, Arnold Palmer Hospital, together with seven other partner hospitals in central Florida, formed its own much smaller, but still powerful (with $200 million in annual purchases) Healthcare Purchasing Alliance (HPA) corporation. The new alliance saved the HPA members $7 million in its first year with two main changes. First, it was structured and staffed to assure that the bulk of the savings associated with its contracting efforts went to its eight members. Second, it struck even better deals with vendors by guaranteeing a *committed* volume and signing not 1-year deals but 3- to 5-year contracts. "Even with a new internal cost of $400,000 to run HPA, the savings and ability to contract for what our member hospitals really want makes the deal a winner," says George DeLong, head of HPA.

Effective supply chain management in manufacturing often focuses on development of new product innovations and efficiency through buyer–vendor collaboration. However, the approach in a service industry has a slightly different emphasis. At Arnold Palmer Hospital, supply-chain opportunities often manifest themselves through the Medical Economic Outcomes Committee. This committee (and its subcommittees) consists of users (including the medical and nursing staff) who evaluate purchase options with a goal of better

medicine while achieving economic targets. For instance, the heart pacemaker negotiation by the cardiology subcommittee allowed for the standardization to two manufacturers, with annual savings of $2 million for just this one product.

Arnold Palmer Hospital is also able to develop custom products that require collaboration down to the third tier of the supply chain. This is the case with custom packs that are used in the operating room. The custom packs are delivered by a distributor, McKesson General Medical, but assembled by a pack company that uses materials the hospital wanted purchased from specific manufacturers. The HPA allows Arnold Palmer Hospital to be creative in this way. With major cost savings, standardization, blanket purchase orders, long-term contracts, and more control of product development, the benefits to the hospital are substantial.

Discussion Questions*

1. How does this supply chain differ from that in a manufacturing firm?
2. What are the constraints on making decisions based on economics alone at Arnold Palmer Hospital?
3. What role do doctors and nurses play in supply-chain decisions in a hospital? How is this participation handled at Arnold Palmer Hospital?
4. Doctor Smith just returned from the Annual Physician's Orthopedic Conference, where she saw a new hip joint replacement demonstrated. She decides she wants to start using the replacement joint at Arnold Palmer Hospital. What process will Dr. Smith have to go through at the hospital to introduce this new product into the supply chain for future surgical use?

*You may wish to view the video that accompanies this case before answering the questions.

► Supply-Chain Management at Regal Marine

Video Case

Like most other manufacturers, Regal Marine finds that it must spend a huge portion of its revenue on purchases. Regal has also found that the better its suppliers understand its end users, the better are both the supplier's product and Regal's final product. As one of the 10 largest U.S. power boat manufacturers, Regal is trying to differentiate its products from the vast number of boats supplied by 300 other companies. Thus, the firm works closely with suppliers to ensure innovation, quality, and timely delivery.

Regal has done a number of things to drive down costs while driving up quality, responsiveness, and innovation. First, working on partnering relationships with suppliers ranging from providers of windshields to providers of instrument panel controls, Regal has brought timely innovation at reasonable cost to its product. Key vendors are so tightly linked with the company that they meet with designers to discuss material changes to be incorporated into new product designs.

Second, the company has joined about 15 other boat manufacturers in a purchasing group, known as American Boat Builders Association, to work with suppliers on reducing the costs of large purchases. Third, Regal is working with a number of local vendors to supply hardware and fasteners directly to the assembly line on a just-in-time basis. In some of these cases, Regal has worked out an

arrangement with the vendor so that title does not transfer until parts are used by Regal. In other cases, title transfers when items are delivered to the property. This practice drives down total inventory and the costs associated with large-lot delivery.

Finally, Regal works with a personnel agency to outsource part of the recruiting and screening process for employees. In all these cases, Regal is demonstrating innovative approaches to supply-chain management that help the firm and, ultimately, the end user. The *Global Company Profile* featuring Regal Marine (which opens Chapter 5 in the *Flexible Version*) provides further background on Regal's operations.

Discussion Questions*

1. What other techniques might Regal use to improve supply-chain management?
2. What kind of response might members of the supply chain expect from Regal in response to their "partnering" in the supply chain?
3. Why is supply-chain management important to Regal?

*You may wish to view the video that accompanies this case before answering the questions.

Chapter 11 *Rapid* Review

Main Heading	Review Material	PEARSON myomlab
THE SUPPLY CHAIN'S STRATEGIC IMPORTANCE (pp. 336–338)	Most firms spend a huge portion of their sales dollars on purchases. ■ **Supply-chain management**—Management of activities related to procuring materials and services, transforming them into intermediate goods and final products, and delivering them through a distribution system. The *objective is to build a chain of suppliers that focuses on maximizing value to the ultimate customer.* Competition is no longer between companies; it is between supply chains.	**VIDEO 11.1** Darden's Global Supply Chain
ETHICS AND SUSTAINABILITY (pp. 339–340)	Ethics includes personal ethics, ethics within the supply chain, and ethical behavior regarding the environment. The Institute for Supply Management has developed a set of Principles and Standards for ethical conduct.	
SUPPLY-CHAIN ECONOMICS (pp. 340–341)	■ **Make-or-buy decision**—A choice between producing a component or service in-house or purchasing it from an outside source. ■ **Outsourcing**—Transferring to external suppliers a firm's activities that have traditionally been internal.	Problems: 11.6, 11.7
SUPPLY-CHAIN STRATEGIES (pp. 341–343)	Six supply-chain strategies for goods and services to be obtained from outside sources are: 1. Negotiating with many suppliers and playing one supplier against another 2. Developing long-term partnering relationships with a few suppliers 3. Vertical integration 4. Joint ventures 5. Developing *keiretsu* networks 6. Developing virtual companies that use suppliers on an as-needed basis ■ **Vertical integration**—Developing the ability to produce goods or services previously purchased or actually buying a supplier or a distributor. ■ *Keiretsu*—A Japanese term that describes suppliers who become part of a company coalition. ■ **Virtual companies**—Companies that rely on a variety of supplier relationships to provide services on demand. Also known as hollow corporations or network companies.	**VIDEO 11.2** Supply-Chain Management at Regal Marine
MANAGING THE SUPPLY CHAIN (pp. 343–347)	Supply-chain integration success begins with mutual agreement on goals, followed by mutual trust, and continues with compatible organizational cultures. Three issues complicate the development of an efficient, integrated supply chain: local optimization, incentives, and large lots. ■ **Bullwhip effect**—Increasing fluctuation in orders or cancellations that often occurs as orders move through the supply chain. ■ **Pull data**—Accurate sales data that initiate transactions to "pull" product through the supply chain. ■ **Single stage control of replenishment**—Fixing responsibility for monitoring and managing inventory for the retailer. ■ **Vendor-managed inventory (VMI)**—A system in which a supplier maintains material for the buyer, often delivering directly to the buyer's using department. ■ **Collaborative planning, forecasting, and replenishment (CPFR)**—A system in which members of a supply chain share information in a joint effort to reduce supply-chain costs. ■ **Blanket order**—A long-term purchase commitment to a supplier for items that are to be delivered against short-term releases to ship. The purchasing department should make special efforts to increase levels of standardization. ■ **Postponement**—Delaying any modifications or customization to a product as long as possible in the production process. Postponement strives to minimize internal variety while maximizing external variety. ■ **Drop shipping**—Shipping directly from the supplier to the end consumer rather than from the seller, saving both time and reshipping costs. ■ **Pass-through facility**—A facility that expedites shipment by holding merchandise and delivering from shipping hubs. ■ **Channel assembly**—A system that postpones final assembly of a product so the distribution channel can assemble it.	**VIDEO 11.3** Arnold Palmer Hospital's Supply Chain

Main Heading	Review Material	PEARSON myomlab
E-PROCUREMENT (pp. 347–349)	▪ **E-procurement**—Purchasing facilitated through the Internet. ▪ **Electronic data interchange (EDI)**—A standardized data-transmittal format for computerized communications between organizations. ▪ **Advanced shipping notice (ASN)**—A shipping notice delivered directly from vendor to purchaser. Online catalogs move companies from a multitude of individual phone calls, faxes, and e-mails to a centralized online system and drive billions of dollars of waste out of the supply chain.	
VENDOR SELECTION (pp. 349–350)	Vendor selection is a three-stage process: (1) vendor evaluation, (2) vendor development, and (3) negotiations. *Vendor evaluation* involves finding potential vendors and determining the likelihood of their becoming good suppliers. *Vendor development* may include everything from training, to engineering and production help, to procedures for information transfer. ▪ **Negotiation strategies**—Approaches taken by supply-chain personnel to develop contractual relationships with suppliers. Three classic types of negotiation strategies are (1) the cost-based price model, (2) the market-based price model, and (3) competitive bidding.	Problems: 11.2, 11.3
LOGISTICS MANAGEMENT (pp. 350–354)	▪ **Logistics management**—An approach that seeks efficiency of operations through the integration of all material acquisition, movement, and storage activities. The total distribution cost in the United States is over 10% of the gross national product (GNP). Five major means of distribution are trucking, railroads, airfreight, waterways, and pipelines. The vast majority of manufactured goods move by truck.	Problems: 11.8–11.10
MEASURING SUPPLY-CHAIN PERFORMANCE (pp. 354–356)	Typical supply-chain benchmark metrics include lead time, time spent placing an order, percent of late deliveries, percent of rejected material, and number of shortages per year: Percent invested in inventory $=$ (Total inventory investment/Total assets) $\times$ 100 (11-1) ▪ **Inventory turnover**—Cost of goods sold divided by average inventory: Inventory turnover $=$ Cost of goods sold $\div$ Inventory investment (11-2) Weeks of supply $=$ Inventory investment $\div$ (Annual cost of goods sold/52 weeks) (11-3) ▪ **Supply Chain Operations Reference (SCOR) Model**—A set of processes, metrics, and best practices developed by the Supply Chain Council. The five parts of the SCOR model are Plan, Source, Make, Deliver, and Return.	Problems: 11.11–11.15 Virtual Office Hours for Solved Problem: 11.1

Self Test

▪ **Before taking the self-test,** refer to the learning objectives listed at the beginning of the chapter and the key terms listed at the end of the chapter.

LO1. The objective of supply-chain management is to _____.

LO2. The term *vertical integration* means to:
  a) develop the ability to produce products that complement or supplement the original product.
  b) produce goods or services previously purchased.
  c) develop the ability to produce the specified good more efficiently.
  d) all of the above.

LO3. The bullwhip effect can be aggravated by:
  a) local optimization.
  b) sales incentives.
  c) quantity discounts.
  d) promotions.
  e) all of the above.

LO4. Vendor selection requires:
  a) vendor evaluation and effective third-party logistics.
  b) vendor development and logistics.

  c) negotiations, vendor evaluation, and vendor development.
  d) an integrated supply chain.
  e) inventory and supply-chain management.

LO5. A major issue in logistics is:
  a) cost of purchases.
  b) vendor evaluation.
  c) product customization.
  d) cost of shipping alternatives.
  e) excellent suppliers.

LO6. Inventory turnover =
  a) Cost of goods sold $\div$ Weeks of supply.
  b) Weeks of supply $\div$ Annual cost of goods sold.
  c) Annual cost of goods sold $\div$ 52 weeks.
  d) Inventory investment $\div$ Cost of goods sold.
  e) Cost of goods sold $\div$ Inventory investment.

Answers: LO1. build a chain of suppliers that focuses on maximizing value to the ultimate customer; **LO2.** b; **LO3.** e; **LO4.** c; **LO5.** d; **LO6.** e.

Outsourcing as a Supply-Chain Strategy

Supplement Outline

What Is Outsourcing?

Strategic Planning and Core Competencies

Risks of Outsourcing

Evaluating Outsourcing Risk with Factor Rating

Advantages and Disadvantages of Outsourcing

Audits and Metrics to Evaluate Performance

Ethical Issues in Outsourcing

Discussion Questions
Problems
Case Studies: Outsourcing to Tata; Outsourcing Offshore at Darden
Rapid Review

Many firms have found added efficiency by procuring non-core goods and services from others. When firms use this strategy they are outsourcing. Outsourcing can be viewed as an extension of the classic make or buy decision, but organizations may extend this technique to outsource entire functions such as accounting, marketing, finance, or even manufacturing.

This supplement introduces factor rating as a technique that can be used to make outsourcing decisions.

BEFORE COMING TO CLASS, READ SUPPLEMENT 11 IN YOUR TEXT AND ANSWER THESE QUESTIONS.

1. How do core competencies relate to outsourcing? _____

_____

_____

2. What are the risks of outsourcing? _____

_____

_____

3. How can factor rating be used to address outsourcing decisions? _____

_____

_____

4. What are the advantages and disadvantages of outsourcing? _____

_____

_____

WHAT IS OUTSOURCING?   (See Flexible Version pp. 360–361)

Outsourcing   (See Flexible Version p. 360)

Offshoring   (See Flexible Version p. 360)

Types of Outsourcing   (See Flexible Version p. 361)

STRATEGIC PLANNING AND CORE COMPETENCIES
(See Flexible Version pp. 361–363)

The Theory of Comparative Advantage
(See Flexible Version pp. 362–363)

RISKS OF OUTSOURCING   (See Flexible Version pp. 363–364)

EVALUATING OUTSOURCING RISK WITH FACTOR RATING
(See Flexible Version pp. 365–366)

Factor Rating of International Risk Factors and Providers   (See Flexible Version pp. 365–366)

Practice Problem Space

ADVANTAGES AND DISADVANTAGES OF OUTSOURCING

(See Flexible Version pp. 367–368)

AUDITS AND METRICS TO EVALUATE PERFORMANCE

(See Flexible Version p. 368)

ETHICAL ISSUES IN OUTSOURCING (See Flexible Version p. 368)

Discussion Questions

1. How would you summarize outsourcing trends?
2. What potential cost saving advantages might firms experience by using outsourcing?
3. What internal issues must managers address when outsourcing?
4. How should a company select an outsourcing provider?
5. What are international risk factors in the outsourcing decision?
6. How can ethics be beneficial in an outsourcing organization?
7. What are some of the possible consequences of poor outsourcing?

Problems*

• **S11.1** Claudia Pragram Technologies, Inc., has narrowed its choice of outsourcing provider to two firms located in different countries. Pragram wants to decide which one of the two countries is the better choice, based on risk-avoidance criteria. She has polled her executives and established four criteria. The resulting ratings for the two countries are presented in the table below, where 1 is a lower risk and 3 is a higher risk.
a) Using the unweighted factor-rating method, which country would you select?
b) If the first two factors (price and nearness) are given a weight of 2, and the last two factors (technology and history) are given a weight of 1, how does your answer change? **Px**

Selection Criterion	England	Canada
Price of service from outsourcer	2	3
Nearness of facilities to client	3	1
Level of technology	1	3
History of successful outsourcing	1	2

• **S11.2** Using the same ratings given in Problem S11.1, assume that the executives have determined four criteria weightings: Price, with a weight of 0.1; Nearness, with 0.6; Technology, with 0.2; and History, with 0.1.
a) Using the weighted factor-rating method, which country would you select?
b) Double each of the weights used in part (a) (to 0.2, 1.2, 0.4, and 0.2, respectively). What effect does this have on your answer? Why? **Px**

*Note: **Px** means the problem may be solved with POM for Windows and/or Excel OM.

• **S11.3** Ranga Ramasesh is the operations manager for a firm that is trying to decide which one of four countries it should research for possible outsourcing providers. The first step is to select a country based on cultural risk factors, which are critical to eventual business success with the provider. Ranga has reviewed outsourcing provider directories and found that the four countries in the table that follows have an ample number of providers from which they can choose. To aid in the country selection step, he has enlisted the aid of a cultural expert, John Wang, who has provided ratings of the various criteria in the table that follows. The resulting ratings are on a 1 to 10 scale, where 1 is a low risk and 10 is a high risk.
a) Using the unweighted factor-rating method, which country should Ranga select based on risk avoidance?
b) If Peru's ratings for "Society value of quality work" and "Individualism attitudes" are each lowered by 50%, how does your answer to part (a) change? **Px**

Culture Selection Criterion	Mexico	Panama	Costa Rica	Peru
Trust	1	2	2	1
Society value of quality work	7	10	9	10
Religious attitudes	3	3	3	5
Individualism attitudes	5	2	4	8
Time orientation attitudes	4	6	7	3
Uncertainty avoidance attitudes	3	2	4	2

•• **S11.4** Using the same ratings given in Problem S11.3(a), assume that John Wang has determined six criteria weightings: Trust, with a weight of 0.4; Quality, with 0.2; Religious, with 0.1; Individualism, with 0.1; Time, with 0.1; and Uncertainty, with 0.1. Using the weighted factor-rating method, which country should Ranga select? **Px**

•• **S11.5** Charles Teplitz's firm wishes to use factor rating to help select an outsourcing provider of logistics services.

a) With weights from 1–5 (5 highest) and ratings 1–100 (100 highest), use the following table to help Teplitz make his decision:

		Rating of Logistics Providers		
Criterion	Weight	Atlanta Shipping	Seattle Delivery	Utah Freight
Quality	5	90	80	75
Delivery	3	70	85	70
Cost	2	70	80	95

b) Teplitz decides to increase the weights for quality, delivery, and cost to 10, 6, and 4, respectively. How does this change your conclusions? Why?

c) If Atlanta Shipping's ratings for each of the factors increase by 10%, what are the new results? **Px**

• **S11.6** Walker Accounting Software is marketed to small accounting firms throughout the U.S. and Canada. Owner George Walker has decided to outsource the company's help desk and is considering three providers: Manila Call Center (Philippines), Delhi Services (India), and Moscow Bell (Russia). The following table summarizes the data Walker has assembled. Which outsourcing firm has the best rating? (Higher weights imply higher importance and higher ratings imply more desirable providers.) **Px**

	Importance	Provider Ratings		
Criterion	Weight	Manila	Delhi	Moscow
Flexibility	0.5	5	1	9
Trustworthiness	0.1	5	5	2
Price	0.2	4	3	6
Delivery	0.2	5	6	6

•••• **S11.7** Price Technologies, a California-based high-tech manufacturer, is considering outsourcing some of its electronics production. Four firms have responded to its request for bids, and CEO Willard Price has started to perform an analysis on the scores his OM team has entered in the table below.

		Ratings of Outsource Providers			
Factor	Weight	A	B	C	D
Labor	w	5	4	3	5
Quality procedures	30	2	3	5	1
Logistics system	5	3	4	3	5
Price	25	5	3	4	4
Trustworthiness	5	3	2	3	5
Technology in place	15	2	5	4	4
Management team	15	5	4	2	1

Weights are on a scale from 1 through 30, and the outsourcing provider scores are on a scale of 1 through 5. The weight for the labor factor is shown as a w because Price's OM team cannot agree on a value for this weight. For what range of values of w, if any, is company C a recommended outsourcing provider, according to the factor-rating method?

Case Studies

▶ Outsourcing to Tata

While some states, such as Tennessee, have been quick to ban or limit international outsourcing of government activities, other state governments have sought to take advantage of low-cost opportunities that international outsourcing can offer.

The state of New Mexico's Labor Department hired Tata Consultancy Services, an Indian outsourcing firm, to redo New Mexico's unemployment compensation computer system. While Tata had completed work for other states, including Pennsylvania and New York, it had never worked on an unemployment compensation system. Also, New Mexico agreed to allow Tata to do all computer software work in India, apparently with insufficient monitoring of progress by New Mexico officials responsible for the outsourcing project.

The new system should have been completed in 6 months, which put the due date in December 2001. Unfortunately, things did not work out well. The initial system was delivered 1 year later. But in late 2004 it was still not working. Also, the outsourcing project went way over the budget of $3.6 million, up to $13 million. The warranty for the system ended in 2003, leaving New Mexico with a situation of either suing Tata to complete the project (it was estimated at 80% complete) or hiring someone to fix it. Tata's position was that it had complied with the outsourcing agreement and was willing to continue fixing the system if it could receive additional compensation to justify additional work.

Discussion Questions

1. Use the process in Table S11.2 on page 362 in the Flexible Version to analyze what New Mexico could have done to achieve a more successful outcome.

2. Is this a case of cultural misunderstanding, or could the same result have occurred if a U.S. firm, such as IBM, had been selected?

3. Conduct your own research to assess the risks of outsourcing any information technology project. (*Computerworld* is one good source.)

► Outsourcing Offshore at Darden

Darden Restaurants, owner of popular brands such as Olive Garden and Red Lobster, serves more than 300 million meals annually in over 1,700 restaurants across the U.S. and Canada. To achieve competitive advantage via its supply chain, Darden must achieve excellence at each step. With purchases from 35 countries, and seafood products with a shelf life as short as 4 days, this is a complex and challenging task.

Those 300 million meals annually mean 40 million pounds of shrimp and huge quantities of tilapia, swordfish, and other fresh purchases. Fresh seafood is typically flown to the U.S. and monitored each step of the way to ensure that 34°F is maintained.

Darden's purchasing agents travel the world to find competitive advantage in the supply chain. Darden personnel from supply chain and development, quality assurance, and environmental relations contribute to developing, evaluating, and checking suppliers. Darden also has seven native-speaking representatives living on other continents to provide continuing support and evaluation of suppliers. All suppliers must abide by Darden's food standards, which typically exceed FDA and other industry standards. Darden expects continuous improvement in durable relationships that increase quality and reduce cost.

Darden's aggressiveness and development of a sophisticated supply chain provides an opportunity for outsourcing. Much food preparation is labor intensive and is often more efficient when handled in bulk. This is particularly true where large volumes may justify capital investment. For instance, Tyson and Iowa Beef prepare meats to Darden's specifications much more economically than can individual restaurants. Similarly, Darden has found that it can outsource both the cutting of salmon to the proper portion size and the cracking/peeling of shrimp more cost-effectively offshore than in U.S. distribution centers or individual restaurants.

Discussion Questions*

1. What are some outsourcing opportunities in a restaurant?
2. What supply-chain issues are unique to a firm sourcing from 35 countries?
3. Examine how other firms or industries develop international supply chains as compared to Darden.
4. Why does Darden outsource harvesting and preparation of much of its seafood?

*You may wish to view the video that accompanies this case study before answering these questions.

Supplement 11 *Rapid* Review

Main Heading	Review Material	
WHAT IS OUTSOURCING? (pp. 360–361)	▪ **Outsourcing**—Procuring from external sources services or products that are normally part of an organization. Some organizations use outsourcing to replace entire purchasing, information systems, marketing, finance, and operations departments. ▪ **Offshoring**—Moving a business process to a foreign country but retaining control of it. Outsourcing is not a new concept; it is simply an extension of the long-standing practice of *subcontracting* production activities. Outsourced manufacturing, also known as contract manufacturing, is becoming standard practice in many industries. Outsourcing implies an agreement (typically a legally binding contract) with an external organization.	**VIDEO S11.1** Outsourcing offshore at Darden
STRATEGIC PLANNING AND CORE COMPETENCIES (pp. 361–363)	▪ **Core competencies**—An organization's unique skills, talents, and capabilities. Core competencies may include specialized knowledge, proprietary technology or information, and unique production methods. *Non-core activities*, which can be a sizable portion of an organization's total business, are good candidates for outsourcing. ▪ **Theory of comparative advantage**—A theory which states that countries benefit from specializing in (and exporting) products and services in which they have relative advantage and importing goods in which they have a relative disadvantage. ▪ **Backsourcing**—The return of business activity to the original firm.	
RISKS OF OUTSOURCING (pp. 363–364)	Perhaps half of all outsourcing agreements fail because of inappropriate planning and analysis. Potential risks of outsourcing include: • In some countries, erratic power grids, difficult local government officials, inexperienced managers, or unmotivated employees • A drop in quality or customer service • Political backlash that results from outsourcing to foreign countries • Changes in employment levels • Changes in facilities and processes needed to receive components in a different state of assembly • Vastly expanded logistics issues, including insurance, customs, and timing The most common reason given for outsourcing failure is that the decision was made without sufficient understanding and analysis.	
EVALUATING OUTSOURCING RISK WITH FACTOR RATING (pp. 365–366)	The factor-rating method is an excellent tool for dealing with both country risk assessment and provider selection problems. Including the home country of the outsourcing firm in a factor-rating analysis helps document the risks that a domestic outsourcing provider poses compared to the risks posed by international providers. Including the home country in the analysis also helps justify final strategy selection to stakeholders who might question it. ▪ **Nearshoring**—Choosing an outsource provider in the home country or in a nearby country. Nearshoring can be a good strategy for businesses and governments seeking both control and cost advantages.	Problems: S11.1–S11.7
ADVANTAGES AND DISADVANTAGES OF OUTSOURCING (pp. 367–368)	Advantages of outsourcing include: • *Cost savings*: The number-one reason driving outsourcing for many firms is the possibility of significant cost savings, particularly for labor. • *Gaining outside expertise*: In addition to gaining access to a broad base of skills that are unavailable in-house, an outsourcing provider may be a source of innovation for improving products, processes, and services. • *Improving operations and service*: An outsourcing provider may have production flexibility. This may allow the client firm to win orders by more quickly introducing new products and services. • *Focusing on core competencies*: An outsourcing provider brings *its* core competencies to the supply chain. This frees up the firm's human, physical, and financial resources to reallocate to the firm's own core competencies.	

Main Heading	Review Material	myomlab
	• *Gaining outside technology*: Firms can outsource to state-of-the-art providers instead of retaining old (legacy) systems. These firms do not have to invest in new technology, thereby cutting risks. • *Other advantages*: The client firm may improve its performance and image by associating with an outstanding supplier. Outsourcing can also be used as a strategy for downsizing, or "reengineering," a firm. Potential disadvantages of outsourcing include: • *Increased transportation costs*: Delivery costs may rise substantially if distance increases from an outsourcing provider to a client firm. • *Loss of control*: This disadvantage can permeate and link to all other problems with outsourcing. When managers lose control of some operations, costs may increase because it's harder to assess and control them. • *Creating future competitors* • *Negative impact on employees*: Employee morale may drop when functions are outsourced, particularly when friends lose their jobs. • *Longer-term impact*: Some disadvantages of outsourcing tend to be longer term than the advantages of outsourcing. In other words, many of the risks firms run by outsourcing may not show up on the bottom line until some time in the future.	
AUDITS AND METRICS TO EVALUATE PERFORMANCE (p. 368)	Outsourcing agreements must specify results and outcomes. Management needs an evaluation process to ensure satisfactory continuing performance. At a minimum, the product or service must be defined in terms of quality, customer satisfaction, delivery, cost, and improvement. When the outsourced product or service plays a major role in strategy and winning orders, the relationship needs to be based on continuing communication, understanding, trust, and performance.	
ETHICAL ISSUES IN OUTSOURCING (p. 368)	Some outsourcing policies linked to ethical principles include: avoid outsourcing in a way that violates religious holidays; don't use outsourcing to move pollution from one country to another; don't use outsourcing to take advantage of cheap labor that leads to employee abuse; don't accept outsourcing that violates basic human rights; don't use outsourcing as a short-term arrangement to reduce costs—view it as a long-term partnership; and don't think an outsourcing agreement will prevent loss of technology, but use the inevitable sharing to build a good relationship with outsourcing firms.	

Self Test

■ **Before taking the self-test,** refer to the learning objectives listed at the beginning of the supplement and the key terms listed at the end of the supplement.

LO1. Core competencies are those strengths in a firm that include:
   a) specialized skills.
   b) unique production methods.
   c) proprietary information/knowledge.
   d) things a company does better than others.
   e) all of the above.

LO2. Outsourcing can be a risky proposition because:
   a) about half of all outsourcing agreements fail.
   b) it saves only about 30% in labor costs.
   c) labor costs are increasing throughout the world.
   d) a non-core competency is outsourced.
   e) shipping costs are increasing.

LO3. Evaluating outsourcing providers by comparing their weighted average scores involves:
   a) factor-rating analysis.
   b) cost-volume analysis.

   c) transportation model analysis.
   d) linear regression analysis.
   e) crossover analysis.

LO4. Advantages of outsourcing include:
   a) focusing on core competencies and cost savings.
   b) gaining outside technology and creating new markets in India for U.S. products.
   c) improving operations by closing plants in Malaysia.
   d) employees wanting to leave the firm.
   e) reduced problems with logistics.

Answers: LO1. e; **LO2.** a; **LO3.** a; **LO4.** a.

12 Inventory Management

Chapter Outline

The Importance of Inventory

Managing Inventory

Inventory Models

Inventory Models for Independent Demand

Probabilistic Models and Safety Stock

Single-Period Model

Fixed-Period (P) Systems

Ethical Dilemma

Discussion Questions

Problems

Case Studies: Zhou Bicycle Company;
*   Sturdivant Sound Systems; Managing*
*   Inventory at Frito-Lay; Inventory Control*
*   at Wheeled Coach*

Active Model Exercises

Classroom Activity

Rapid Review

Inventory represents a major investment for many firms. This investment is often larger than it should be because firms find it easier to have "just-in-case" inventory rather than "just-in-time" inventory. Inventories are of four types:

1. Raw material and purchased components
2. Work-in-process
3. Maintenance, repair, and operating (MRO)
4. Finished goods

This chapter discusses the inventory management topics of ABC analysis, record accuracy, and cycle counting. Three inventory models used to control independent demands are introduced: the EOQ model, the production order quantity model, and the quantity discount model.

BEFORE COMING TO CLASS, READ CHAPTER 12 IN YOUR TEXT AND ANSWER THESE QUESTIONS.

1. What is ABC analysis? _____

_____

2. What is cycle counting? _____

_____

3. What are the basic assumptions of the EOQ model? _____

_____

4. What is the reorder point and how is it computed? _____

_____

5. How does the production order quantity model differ from the EOQ model?

_____

6. What is the quantity discount model? _____

_____

7. What is the meaning of service levels in a probabilistic model? _____

_____

THE IMPORTANCE OF INVENTORY (See Flexible Version pp. 374–375)

Four Types of Inventory (See Flexible Version p. 375)

1. **Raw material**

2. **Work-in-process**

3. **Maintenance, repair, and operating (MRO)**

4. **Finished goods**

MANAGING INVENTORY (See Flexible Version pp. 375–379)

ABC Analysis (See Flexible Version pp. 375–377)

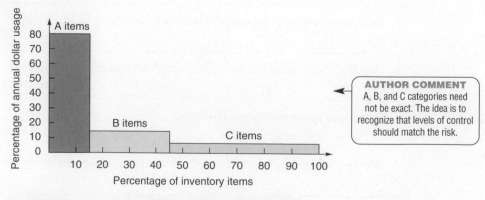

> **AUTHOR COMMENT**
> A, B, and C categories need not be exact. The idea is to recognize that levels of control should match the risk.

▲ **FIGURE 12.2** Graphic Representation of ABC Analysis

PRACTICE PROBLEM 12.1 ■ ABC

Stock Number	ABC Analysis Annual $ Volume	Percent of Annual $ Volume
J24	12,500	46.2
R26	9,000	33.3
L02	3,200	11.8
M12	1,550	5.8
P33	620	2.3
T72	65	0.2
S67	53	0.2
Q47	32	0.1
V20	30	0.1
		100.0

What are the appropriate ABC groups of inventory items?

Additional Practice Problem Space

Inventory Accuracy and Cycle Counting

(See Flexible Version pp. 377–379)

PRACTICE PROBLEM 12.2 ■ Cycle Counting

A firm has 1,000 "A" items (which it counts every week, i.e., 5 days), 4,000 "B" items (counted every 40 days), and 8,000 "C" items (counted every 100 days). How many items should be counted per day?

Service Inventory (See Flexible Version p. 379)

INVENTORY MODELS (See Flexible Version p. 379)

Independent vs. Dependent Demand

(See Flexible Version p. 380)

Holding, Ordering, and Setup Costs (See Flexible Version p. 380)

Category	Cost (and Range) as a Percent of Inventory Value
Housing costs (building rent or depreciation, operating cost, taxes, insurance)	6% (3–10%)
Material handling costs (equipment lease or depreciation, power, operating cost)	3% (1–3.5%)
Labor cost	3% (3–5%)
Investment costs (borrowing costs, taxes, and insurance on inventory)	11% (6–24%)
Pilferage, scrap, and obsolescence	3% (2–5%)
Overall carrying cost	**26%**

◀ TABLE 12.1
Determining Inventory Holding Costs

INVENTORY MODELS FOR INDEPENDENT DEMAND

(See Flexible Version pp. 380–393)

The Basic Economic Order Quantity (EOQ) Model

(See Flexible Version p. 381)

Assumptions

1. _____

2. _____

3. _____

4. _____

5. _____

6. _____

Inventory Usage over Time

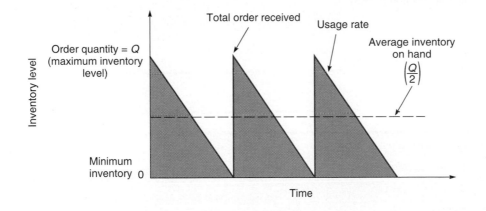

◄ **FIGURE 12.3**
Inventory Usage over Time

> **AUTHOR COMMENT**
> If the maximum we can ever have is Q (say, 500 units) and the minimum is zero, then if inventory is used (or sold) on a fairly steady rate, the average = $(Q + 0)/2 = Q/2$.

Minimizing Costs (See Flexible Version pp. 381–386)

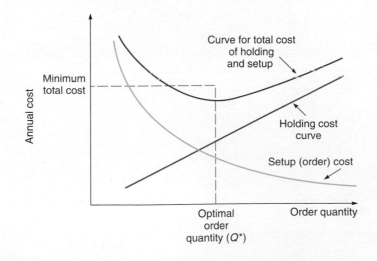

◄ **FIGURE 12.4(c)**
Total Cost as a Function of Order Quantity

> **AUTHOR COMMENT**
> This graph is the heart of EOQ inventory modeling. We want to find the smallest total cost (top curve), which is the sum of the two curves below it.

Definitions for the EOQ model

Q = Number of pieces per order

Q^* = Optimum number of pieces per order (EOQ)

D = Annual demand in units for the inventory item

S = Setup or ordering cost for each order

H = Holding or carrying cost per unit per year

Steps for Solving for Q*

1. _____

2. _____

3. _____

4. _____

EOQ Equation (See Flexible Version p. 383)

$$Q^* = \sqrt{\frac{2DS}{H}}$$

(12-1)

PRACTICE PROBLEM 12.3 ■ EOQ

Assume you have a product with the following parameters:

Annual demand = 360 units

Holding cost per year = $1 per unit

Order cost = $100 per order

What is the EOQ for this product?

$$\text{Expected number of orders} = N = \frac{\text{Demand}}{\text{Order quantity}} = \frac{D}{Q^*}$$

(12-2)

$$\text{Expected time between orders} = T = \frac{\text{Number of working days per year}}{N}$$

(12-3)

PRACTICE PROBLEM 12.4 ■ Number of Orders/Time between Orders

Given the data from Practice Problem 12.3, and assuming a 300-day work year, how many orders should be processed per year? What is the expected time between orders?

Total Costs

Total annual cost = Setup cost + Holding cost $\qquad$ (12-4)

$$TC = \frac{D}{Q}S + \frac{Q}{2}H \qquad (12\text{-}5)$$

PRACTICE PROBLEM 12.5 ■ Total Costs

What is the total cost for the inventory policy used in Practice Problem 12.3?

Additional Practice Problem Space

Robust Model

PRACTICE PROBLEM 12.6 ■ Sensitivity

Based on the material from Practice Problems 12.3 to 12.5, what would the cost be if the demand was actually higher than estimated (e.g., 500 units instead of 360 units), but the EOQ established in Practice Problem 12.3 is used? What will be the actual annual total cost?

Reorder Points (See Flexible Version pp. 386–387)

$$\text{ROP} = (\text{Demand per day})(\text{Lead time for a new order in days}) = d \times L \qquad (12\text{-}6)$$

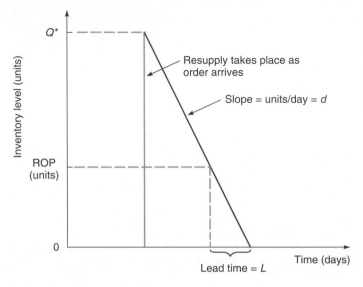

◀ **FIGURE 12.5**
The Reorder Point (ROP) Curve

Q^* is the optimum order quantity, and lead time represents the time between placing and receiving an order.

PRACTICE PROBLEM 12.7 ■ ROP

If demand for an item is 3 units per day, and delivery lead time is 15 days, what should we use for a simple reorder point?

Additional Practice Problem Space

Production Order Quantity Model

(See Flexible Version pp. 387–390)

Q = Number of pieces per order
H = Holding cost per unit per year
p = Daily production rate
d = Daily demand rate, or usage rate
t = Length of the production run in days

$$Q_p^* = \sqrt{\frac{2DS}{H[1 - (d/p)]}}$$

(12-7)

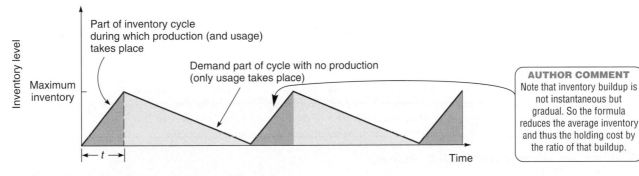

▲ **FIGURE 12.6**   **Change in Inventory Levels over Time for the Production Model**

AUTHOR COMMENT
Note that inventory buildup is not instantaneous but gradual. So the formula reduces the average inventory and thus the holding cost by the ratio of that buildup.

PRACTICE PROBLEM 12.8 ■ Production Order Quantity Model

Assume that our firm produces *Type C* fire extinguishers. We make 30,000 of these fire extinguishers per year. Each extinguisher requires one handle (assume a 300-day work year for daily usage rate purposes). Assume an annual carrying cost of $1.50 per handle, production setup cost of $150, and a daily production rate of 300. What is the optimal production order quantity?

Additional Practice Problem Space

Quantity Discount Models (See Flexible Version pp. 390–393)

Steps:

1. _____

2. _____

3. _____

4. _____

PRACTICE PROBLEM 12.9 ■ Quantity Discount

We use 1,000 electric drills per year in our production process. The ordering cost for these is $100 per order, and the carrying cost is assumed to be 40% of the per-unit cost. In orders of less than 120, drills cost $78 per unit; for orders of 120 or more, the cost drops to $50 per unit.

Should we take advantage of the quantity discount?

Additional Practice Problem Space

PROBABILISTIC MODELS AND SAFETY STOCK

(See Flexible Version pp. 393–398)

Safety Stock (See Flexible Version pp. 393–394)

$$ROP = d \times L + ss \tag{12-11}$$

Annual stockout costs = The sum of the units short $\times$ The probability
$\times$ The stockout cost/unit $\times$ The number of orders per year (12-12)

PRACTICE PROBLEM 12.10 ■ Probabilistic Model

Litely Corp. sells 1,350 of its special decorator light switch per year and places orders for 300 of these switches at a time. Assuming no safety stocks, Litely estimates a 50% chance of no shortages in each cycle and the probability of shortages of 5, 10, and 15 units as 0.2, 0.15, and 0.15, respectively. The carrying cost per unit per year is calculated at $5, and the stockout cost is estimated at $6 ($3 lost profit per switch and another $3 loss of goodwills or future sales). What level of safety stock should Litely use for this product? (Consider safety stocks of 0, 5, 10, and 15 units.)

Additional Practice Problem Space

Service Level (See Flexible Version pp. 394–396)

$$\text{ROP} = \text{Expected demand during lead time} + Z\sigma_{dLT} \tag{12-13}$$

where Z = Number of standard deviations

σ_{dLT} = Standard deviation of demand during lead time

$$Safety\ stock = Z\sigma_{dLT} \tag{12-14}$$

PRACTICE PROBLEM 12.11 ■ Safety Stock

Presume that Litely (see Practice Problem 12.10) carries a modern white kitchen ceiling lamp that is quite popular. The anticipated demand during lead time can be approximated by a normal curve having a mean of 180 units and a standard deviation of 40 units. What safety stock should Litely carry to achieve a 95% service level?

Other Probabilistic Models (See Flexible Version pp. 396–398)

1. Demand is variable and lead time is constant.
2. Lead time is variable and demand is constant.
3. Both demand and lead time are variable.

Demand Is Variable and Lead Time Is Constant.

$$\text{ROP} = (Average\ \text{daily demand} \times \text{Lead time in days}) + Z\sigma_{dLT} \tag{12-15}$$

where σ_{dLT} = Standard deviation of demand during lead time = $\sigma_d\sqrt{\text{Lead time}}$
and σ_d = Standard deviation of demand per day

Lead Time Is Variable and Demand Is Constant.

$$\text{ROP} = (\text{Daily demand} \times Average\ \text{lead time in days}) + Z(\text{Daily demand}) \times \sigma_{LT} \tag{12-16}$$

where σ_{LT} = Standard deviation of lead time in days

Both Demand and Lead Time Are Variable.

$$\text{ROP} = (\text{Average daily demand} \times \text{Average lead time}) + Z\sigma_{dLT} \tag{12-17}$$

where σ_d = Standard deviation of demand per day
σ_{LT} = Standard deviation of lead time in days

and $\sigma_{dLT}\sqrt{(\text{Average lead time} \times \sigma_d^2) + (\text{Average daily demand})^2\sigma_{LT}^2}$

Practice Problem Space

SINGLE-PERIOD MODEL (See Flexible Version pp. 398–399)

$$\text{Service level} = \frac{C_s}{C_s + C_o} \qquad\qquad (12\text{-}18)$$

where C_s = cost of shortage
C_o = cost of overage

FIXED-PERIOD (*P*) SYSTEMS (See Flexible Version pp. 399–400)

Ethical Dilemma

Wayne Hills Hospital in tiny Wayne, Nebraska, faces a problem common to large, urban hospitals as well as to small, remote ones like itself. That problem is deciding how much of each type of whole blood to keep in stock. Because blood is expensive and has a limited shelf life (up to 5 weeks under 1–6°C refrigeration), Wayne Hills naturally wants to keep its stock as low as possible. Unfortunately, past disasters such as a major tornado and a train wreck demonstrated that lives would be lost when not enough blood was available to handle massive needs. The hospital administrator wants to set an 85% service level based on demand over the past decade. Discuss the implications of this decision. What is the hospital's responsibility with regard to stocking lifesaving medicines with short shelf lives? How would you set the inventory level for a commodity such as blood?

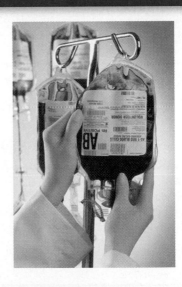

Discussion Questions

1. Describe the four types of inventory.
2. With the advent of low-cost computing, do you see alternatives to the popular ABC classifications?
3. What is the purpose of the ABC classification system?
4. Identify and explain the types of costs that are involved in an inventory system.
5. Explain the major assumptions of the basic EOQ model.
6. What is the relationship of the economic order quantity to demand? to the holding cost? to the setup cost?
7. Explain why it is not necessary to include product cost (price or price times quantity) in the EOQ model, but the quantity discount model requires this information.
8. What are the advantages of cycle counting?
9. What impact does a decrease in setup time have on EOQ?
10. When quantity discounts are offered, why is it not necessary to check discount points that are below the EOQ or points above the EOQ that are not discount points?
11. What is meant by *service level*?
12. Explain the following: All things being equal, the production inventory quantity will be larger than the economic order quantity.
13. Describe the difference between a fixed-quantity (Q) and a fixed-period (P) inventory system.
14. Explain what is meant by the expression "robust model." Specifically, what would you tell a manager who exclaimed, "Uh-oh, we're in trouble! The calculated EOQ is wrong; actual demand is 10% greater than estimated."
15. What is "safety stock?" What does safety stock provide safety against?
16. When demand is not constant, the reorder point is a function of what four parameters?
17. How are inventory levels monitored in retail stores?
18. State a major advantage, and a major disadvantage, of a fixed-period (P) system.

Problems*

•• **12.1** L. Houts Plastics is a large manufacturer of injection-molded plastics in North Carolina. An investigation of the company's manufacturing facility in Charlotte yields the information presented in the table below. How would the plant classify these items according to an ABC classification system? **Px**

L. Houts Plastics Charlotte Inventory Levels

Item Code #	Average Inventory (units)	Value ($/unit)
1289	400	3.75
2347	300	4.00
2349	120	2.50
2363	75	1.50
2394	60	1.75
2395	30	2.00
6782	20	1.15
7844	12	2.05
8210	8	1.80
8310	7	2.00
9111	6	3.00

•• **12.2** Boreki Enterprise has the following 10 items in inventory. Theodore Boreki asks you, a recent OM graduate, to divide these items into ABC classifications.

Item	Annual Demand	Cost/Unit
A2	3,000	$ 50
B8	4,000	12
C7	1,500	45
D1	6,000	10
E9	1,000	20
F3	500	500
G2	300	1,500
H2	600	20
I5	1,750	10
J8	2,500	5

a) Develop an ABC classification system for the 10 items.
b) How can Boreki use this information?
c) Boreki reviews the classification and then places item A2 into the A category. Why might he do so? **Px**

•• **12.3** Jean-Marie Bourjolly's restaurant has the following inventory items that it orders on a weekly basis:

Inventory Item	$ Value/Case	# Ordered/Week
Rib eye steak	135	3
Lobster tail	245	3
Pasta	23	12
Salt	3	2
Napkins	12	2
Tomato sauce	23	11
French fries	43	32
Pepper	3	3
Garlic powder	11	3
Trash can liners	12	3
Table cloths	32	5
Fish filets	143	10
Prime rib roasts	166	6
Oil	28	2

(continued)

Note: **Px** means the problem may be solved with POM for Windows and/or Excel OM.

Inventory Item	$ Value/Case	# Ordered/Week
Lettuce (case)	35	24
Chickens	75	14
Order pads	12	2
Eggs (case)	22	7
Bacon	56	5
Sugar	4	2

a) Which is the most expensive item, using annual dollar volume?
b) Which are C items?
c) What is the annual dollar volume for all 20 items? **Px**

• **12.4** Howard Electronics, a small manufacturer of electronic research equipment, has approximately 7,000 items in its inventory and has hired Joan Blasco-Paul to manage its inventory. Joan has determined that 10% of the items in inventory are A items, 35% are B items, and 55% are C items. She would like to set up a system in which all A items are counted monthly (every 20 working days), all B items are counted quarterly (every 60 working days), and all C items are counted semiannually (every 120 working days). How many items need to be counted each day?

• **12.5** William Beville's computer training school, in Richmond, stocks workbooks with the following characteristics:

$$\text{Demand } D = 19{,}500 \text{ units/year}$$
$$\text{Ordering cost } S = \$25/\text{order}$$
$$\text{Holding cost } H = \$4/\text{unit/year}$$

a) Calculate the EOQ for the workbooks.
b) What are the annual holding costs for the workbooks?
c) What are the annual ordering costs? **Px**

• **12.6** If $D = 8{,}000$ per month, $S = \$45$ per order, and $H = \$2$ per unit per month,
a) What is the economic order quantity?
b) How does your answer change if the holding cost doubles?
c) What if the holding cost drops in half? **Px**

•• **12.7** Henry Crouch's law office has traditionally ordered ink refills 60 units at a time. The firm estimates that carrying cost is 40% of the $10 unit cost and that annual demand is about 240 units per year. The assumptions of the basic EOQ model are thought to apply.
a) For what value of ordering cost would its action be optimal?
b) If the true ordering cost turns out to be much greater than your answer to part a, what is the impact on the firm's ordering policy?

• **12.8** Madeline Thimmes's Dream Store sells water beds and assorted supplies. Her best-selling bed has an annual demand of 400 units. Ordering cost is $40; holding cost is $5 per unit per year.
a) To minimize the total cost, how many units should be ordered each time an order is placed?
b) If the holding cost per unit was $6 instead of $5, what would be the optimal order quantity? **Px**

• **12.9** Southeastern Bell stocks a certain switch connector at its central warehouse for supplying field service offices. The yearly demand for these connectors is 15,000 units. Southeastern estimates its annual holding cost for this item to be $25 per unit. The cost to place and process an order from the supplier is $75. The company

operates 300 days per year, and the lead time to receive an order from the supplier is 2 working days.
a) Find the economic order quantity.
b) Find the annual holding costs.
c) Find the annual ordering costs.
d) What is the reorder point? **P✗**

• **12.10** Lead time for one of your fastest-moving products is 21 days. Demand during this period averages 100 units per day.
a) What would be an appropriate reorder point?
b) How does your answer change if demand during lead time doubles?
c) How does your answer change if demand during lead time drops in half?

• **12.11** Annual demand for the notebook binders at Duncan's Stationery Shop is 10,000 units. Dana Duncan operates her business 300 days per year and finds that deliveries from her supplier generally take 5 working days.
a) Calculate the reorder point for the notebook binders that she stocks.
b) Why is this number important to Duncan?

•• **12.12** Thomas Kratzer is the purchasing manager for the headquarters of a large insurance company chain with a central inventory operation. Thomas's fastest-moving inventory item has a demand of 6,000 units per year. The cost of each unit is $100, and the inventory carrying cost is $10 per unit per year. The average ordering cost is $30 per order. It takes about 5 days for an order to arrive, and the demand for 1 week is 120 units. (This is a corporate operation, and there are 250 working days per year.)
a) What is the EOQ?
b) What is the average inventory if the EOQ is used?
c) What is the optimal number of orders per year?
d) What is the optimal number of days in between any two orders?
e) What is the annual cost of ordering and holding inventory?
f) What is the total annual inventory cost, including the cost of the 6,000 units? **P✗**

•• **12.13** Joe Henry's machine shop uses 2,500 brackets during the course of a year. These brackets are purchased from a supplier 90 miles away. The following information is known about the brackets:

Annual demand:	2,500
Holding cost per bracket per year:	$1.50
Order cost per order:	$18.75
Lead time:	2 days
Working days per year:	250

a) Given the above information, what would be the economic order quantity (EOQ)?
b) Given the EOQ, what would be the average inventory? What would be the annual inventory holding cost?
c) Given the EOQ, how many orders would be made each year? What would be the annual order cost?
d) Given the EOQ, what is the total annual cost of managing the inventory?
e) What is the time between orders?
f) What is the reorder point (ROP)? **P✗**

•• **12.14** Myriah Fitzgibbon, of L.A. Plumbing, uses 1,200 of a certain spare part that costs $25 for each order, with an annual holding cost of $24.

a) Calculate the total cost for order sizes of 25, 40, 50, 60, and 100.
b) Identify the economic order quantity and consider the implications for making an error in calculating economic order quantity. **P✗**

••• **12.15** M. Cotteleer Electronics supplies microcomputer circuitry to a company that incorporates microprocessors into refrigerators and other home appliances. One of the components has an annual demand of 250 units, and this is constant throughout the year. Carrying cost is estimated to be $1 per unit per year, and the ordering cost is $20 per order.
a) To minimize cost, how many units should be ordered each time an order is placed?
b) How many orders per year are needed with the optimal policy?
c) What is the average inventory if costs are minimized?
d) Suppose that the ordering cost is not $20, and Cotteleer has been ordering 150 units each time an order is placed. For this order policy (of $Q = 150$) to be optimal, determine what the ordering cost would have to be. **P✗**

•• **12.16** Race One Motors is an Indonesian car manufacturer. At its largest manufacturing facility, in Jakarta, the company produces subcomponents at a rate of 300 per day, and it uses these subcomponents at a rate of 12,500 per year (of 250 working days). Holding costs are $2 per item per year, and ordering costs are $30 per order.
a) What is the economic production quantity?
b) How many production runs per year will be made?
c) What will be the maximum inventory level?
d) What percentage of time will the facility be producing components?
e) What is the annual cost of ordering and holding inventory? **P✗**

•• **12.17** Radovilsky Manufacturing Company, in Hayward, California, makes flashing lights for toys. The company operates its production facility 300 days per year. It has orders for about 12,000 flashing lights per year and has the capability of producing 100 per day. Setting up the light production costs $50. The cost of each light is $1. The holding cost is $0.10 per light per year.
a) What is the optimal size of the production run?
b) What is the average holding cost per year?
c) What is the average setup cost per year?
d) What is the total cost per year, including the cost of the lights? **P✗**

•• **12.18** Arthur Meiners is the production manager of Wheel-Rite, a small producer of metal parts. Wheel-Rite supplies Cal-Tex, a larger assembly company, with 10,000 wheel bearings each year. This order has been stable for some time. Setup cost for Wheel-Rite is $40, and holding cost is $.60 per wheel bearing per year. Wheel-Rite can produce 500 wheel bearings per day. Cal-Tex is a just-in-time manufacturer and requires that 50 bearings be shipped to it each business day.
a) What is the optimum production quantity?
b) What is the maximum number of wheel bearings that will be in inventory at Wheel-Rite?
c) How many production runs of wheel bearings will Wheel-Rite have in a year?
d) What is the total setup + holding cost for Wheel-Rite? **P✗**

•• **12.19** Cesar Rego Computers, a Mississippi chain of computer hardware and software retail outlets, supplies both educational and commercial customers with memory and storage devices. It currently faces the following ordering decision relating to purchases of high-density disks:

$$D = 36,000 \text{ disks}$$
$$S = \$25$$

$$H = \$0.45$$
$$\text{Purchase price} = \$.85$$
$$\text{Discount price} = \$0.82$$
$$\text{Quantity needed to qualify for the discount} = 6{,}000 \text{ disks}$$

Should the discount be taken? **Px**

•• **12.20** Bell Computers purchases integrated chips at $350 per chip. The holding cost is $35 per unit per year, the ordering cost is $120 per order, and sales are steady, at 400 per month. The company's supplier, Rich Blue Chip Manufacturing, Inc., decides to offer price concessions in order to attract larger orders. The price structure is shown below.

a) What is the optimal order quantity and the minimum cost for Bell Computers to order, purchase, and hold these integrated chips?

Rich Blue Chip's Price Structure

Quantity Purchased	Price/Unit
1–99 units	$350
100–199 units	$325
200 or more units	$300

b) Bell Computers wishes to use a 10% holding cost rather than the fixed $35 holding cost in part a. What is the optimal order quantity, and what is the optimal cost? **Px**

•• **12.21** Wang Distributors has an annual demand for an airport metal detector of 1,400 units. The cost of a typical detector to Wang is $400. Carrying cost is estimated to be 20% of the unit cost, and the ordering cost is $25 per order. If Ping Wang, the owner, orders in quantities of 300 or more, he can get a 5% discount on the cost of the detectors. Should Wang take the quantity discount? **Px**

•• **12.22** The catering manager of LaVista Hotel, Lisa Ferguson, is disturbed by the amount of silverware she is losing every week. Last Friday night, when her crew tried to set up for a banquet for 500 people, they did not have enough knives. She decides she needs to order some more silverware, but wants to take advantage of any quantity discounts her vendor will offer.

For a small order (2,000 or fewer pieces), her vendor quotes a price of $1.80/piece.

If she orders 2,001–5,000 pieces, the price drops to $1.60/piece. 5,001–10,000 pieces brings the price to $1.40/piece, and 10,001 and above reduces the price to $1.25.

Lisa's order costs are $200 per order, her annual holding costs are 5%, and the annual demand is 45,000 pieces. For the best option:
a) What is the optimal order quantity?
b) What is the annual holding cost?
c) What is the annual ordering (setup) cost?
d) What are the annual costs of the silverware itself with an optimal order quantity?
e) What is the total annual cost, including ordering, holding, and purchasing the silverware? **Px**

•• **12.23** Rocky Mountain Tire Center sells 20,000 go-cart tires per year. The ordering cost for each order is $40, and the holding cost is 20% of the purchase price of the tires per year. The purchase price is $20 per tire if fewer than 500 tires are ordered, $18 per tire if 500 or more—but fewer than 1,000—tires are ordered, and $17 per tire if 1,000 or more tires are ordered.
a) How many tires should Rocky Mountain order each time it places an order?
b) What is the total cost of this policy? **Px**

•• **12.24** M. P. VanOyen Manufacturing has gone out on bid for a regulator component. Expected demand is 700 units per month. The item can be purchased from either Allen Manufacturing or Baker Manufacturing. Their price lists are shown in the table. Ordering cost is $50, and annual holding cost per unit is $5.

Allen Mfg.		Baker Mfg.	
Quantity	Unit Price	Quantity	Unit Price
1–499	$16.00	1–399	$16.10
500–999	15.50	400–799	15.60
1,000+	15.00	800+	15.10

a) What is the economic order quantity?
b) Which supplier should be used? Why?
c) What is the optimal order quantity and total annual cost of ordering, purchasing, and holding the component? **Px**

••• **12.25** Chris Sandvig Irrigation, Inc., has summarized the price list from four potential suppliers of an underground control valve. See the table below. Annual usage is 2,400 valves; order cost is $10 per order; and annual inventory holding costs are $3.33 per unit.

Which vendor should be selected and what order quantity is best if Sandvig Irrigation wants to minimize total cost? **Px**

Vendor A		Vendor B	
Quantity	Price	Quantity	Price
1–49	$35.00	1–74	$34.75
50–74	34.75	75–149	34.00
75–149	33.55	150–299	32.80
150–299	32.35	300–499	31.60
300–499	31.15	500+	30.50
500+	30.75		

Vendor C		Vendor D	
Quantity	Price	Quantity	Price
1–99	$34.50	1–199	$34.25
100–199	33.75	200–399	33.00
200–399	32.50	400+	31.00
400+	31.10		

••• **12.26** Emery Pharmaceutical uses an unstable chemical compound that must be kept in an environment where both temperature and humidity can be controlled. Emery uses 800 pounds per month of the chemical, estimates the holding cost to be 50% of the purchase price (because of spoilage), and estimates order costs to be $50 per order. The cost schedules of two suppliers are as follows:

Vendor 1		Vendor 2	
Quantity	Price/lb	Quantity	Price/lb
1–499	$17.00	1–399	$17.10
500–999	16.75	400–799	16.85
1,000+	16.50	800–1,199	16.60
		1,200+	16.25

a) What is the economic order quantity for each supplier?
b) What quantity should be ordered, and which supplier should be used?
c) What is the total cost for the most economic order size?
d) What factor(s) should be considered besides total cost? **Px**

•• **12.27** Barbara Flynn is in charge of maintaining hospital supplies at General Hospital. During the past year, the mean lead time demand for bandage BX-5 was 60 (and was normally distributed).

Furthermore, the standard deviation for BX-5 was 7. Ms. Flynn would like to maintain a 90% service level.
a) What safety stock level do you recommend for BX-5?
b) What is the appropriate reorder point? **Px**

•• 12.28 Based on available information, lead time demand for PC jump drives averages 50 units (normally distributed), with a standard deviation of 5 drives. Management wants a 97% service level.
a) What value of Z should be applied?
b) How many drives should be carried as safety stock?
c) What is the appropriate reorder point? **Px**

••• 12.29 Authentic Thai rattan chairs (shown in the photo) are delivered to Gary Schwartz's chain of retail stores, called The Kathmandu Shop, once a year. The reorder point, without safety stock, is 200 chairs. Carrying cost is $30 per unit per year, and the cost of a stockout is $70 per chair per year. Given the following demand probabilities during the lead time, how much safety stock should be carried?

Demand During Lead Time	Probability
0	0.2
100	0.2
200	0.2
300	0.2
400	0.2 **Px**

•• 12.30 Tobacco is shipped from North Carolina to a cigarette manufacturer in Cambodia once a year. The reorder point, without safety stock, is 200 kilos. The carrying cost is $15 per kilo per year, and the cost of a stockout is $70 per kilo per year. Given the following demand probabilities during the lead time, how much safety stock should be carried?

Demand During Lead Time (kilos)	Probability
0	0.1
100	0.1
200	0.2
300	0.4
400	0.2 **Px**

••• 12.31 Mr. Beautiful, an organization that sells weight training sets, has an ordering cost of $40 for the BB-1 set. (BB-1 stands for Body Beautiful Number 1.) The carrying cost for BB-1 is $5 per set per year. To meet demand, Mr. Beautiful orders large quantities of BB-1 seven times a year. The stockout cost for BB-1 is estimated to be $50 per set. Over the past several years, Mr. Beautiful has observed the following demand during the lead time for BB-1:

Demand During Lead Time	Probability
40	.1
50	.2
60	.2
70	.2
80	.2
90	.1
	1.0

The reorder point for BB-1 is 60 sets. What level of safety stock should be maintained for BB-1? **Px**

•• 12.32 Chicago's Hard Rock Hotel distributes a mean of 1,000 bath towels per day to guests at the pool and in their rooms. This demand is normally distributed with a standard deviation of 100 towels per day, based on occupancy. The laundry firm that has the linen contract requires a 2-day lead time. The hotel expects a 98% service level to satisfy high guest expectations.
a) What is the ROP?
b) What is the safety stock? **Px**

•• 12.33 First Printing has contracts with legal firms in San Francisco to copy their court documents. Daily demand is almost constant at 12,500 pages of documents. The lead time for paper delivery is normally distributed with a mean of 4 days and a standard deviation of 1 day. A 97% service level is expected. Compute First's ROP. **Px**

••• 12.34 Gainesville Cigar stocks Cuban cigars that have variable lead times because of the difficulty in importing the product: Lead time is normally distributed with an average of 6 weeks and a standard deviation of 2 weeks. Demand is also a variable and normally distributed with a mean of 200 cigars per week and a standard deviation of 25 cigars.
a) For a 90% service level, what is the ROP?
b) What is the ROP for a 95% service level?
c) Explain what these two service levels mean. Which is preferable? **Px**

••• 12.35 Kim Clark has asked you to help him determine the best ordering policy for a new product. The demand for the new product has been forecasted to be about 1,000 units annually. To help you get a handle on the carrying and ordering costs, Kim has given you the list of last year's costs. He thought that these costs might be appropriate for the new product.

Cost Factor	Cost ($)	Cost Factor	Cost ($)
Taxes for the warehouse	2,000	Warehouse supplies	280
Receiving and incoming inspection	1,500	Research and development	2,750
New product development	2,500	Purchasing salaries & wages	30,000
Acct. Dept. costs to pay invoices	500	Warehouse salaries & wages	12,800
Inventory insurance	600	Pilferage of inventory	800
Product advertising	800	Purchase order supplies	500
Spoilage	750	Inventory obsolescence	300
Sending purchasing orders	800	Purchasing Dept. overhead	1,000

He also told you that these data were compiled for 10,000 inventory items that were carried or held during the year. You have also determined that 200 orders were placed last year. Your job as a new operations management graduate is to help Kim determine the economic order quantity for the new product.

•• 12.36 Cynthia Knott's oyster bar buys fresh Louisiana oysters for $5 per pound and sells them for $9 per pound. Any oysters not sold that day are sold to her cousin, who has a nearby grocery store, for $2 per pound. Cynthia believes that demand follows the normal distribution, with a mean of 100 pounds and a standard deviation of 15 pounds. How many pounds should she order each day? **Px**

•• 12.37 Henrique Correa's bakery prepares all its cakes between 4 A.M. and 6 A.M. so they will be fresh when customers arrive. Day-old cakes are virtually always sold, but at a 50% discount off the regular $10 price. The cost of baking a cake is $6, and demand is estimated to be normally distributed, with a mean of 25 and a standard deviation of 4. What is the optimal stocking level? **Px**

••• 12.38 University of Florida football programs are printed 1 week prior to each home game. Attendance averages 90,000 screaming and loyal Gators fans, of whom two-thirds usually buy the program, following a normal distribution, for $4 each. Unsold programs are sent to a recycling center that pays only 10 cents per program. The standard deviation is 5,000 programs, and the cost to print each program is $1.
a) What is the cost of underestimating demand for each program?
b) What is the overage cost per program?
c) How many programs should be ordered per game?
d) What is the stockout risk for this order size? **Px**

••••12.39 Emarpy Appliance is a company that produces all kinds of major appliances. Bud Banis, the president of Emarpy, is concerned about the production policy for the company's best-selling refrigerator. The annual demand for this has been about 8,000 units each year, and this demand has been constant throughout the year. The production capacity is 200 units per day. Each time production starts, it costs the company $120 to move materials into place, reset the assembly line, and clean the equipment. The holding cost of a refrigerator is $50 per year. The current production plan calls for

400 refrigerators to be produced in each production run. Assume there are 250 working days per year.
a) What is the daily demand of this product?
b) If the company were to continue to produce 400 units each time production starts, how many days would production continue?
c) Under the current policy, how many production runs per year would be required? What would the annual setup cost be?
d) If the current policy continues, how many refrigerators would be in inventory when production stops? What would the average inventory level be?
e) If the company produces 400 refrigerators at a time, what would the total annual setup cost and holding cost be?
f) If Bud Banis wants to minimize the total annual inventory cost, how many refrigerators should be produced in each production run? How much would this save the company in inventory costs compared to the current policy of producing 400 in each production run? **Px**

••••12.40 A gourmet coffee shop in downtown San Francisco is open 200 days a year and sells an average of 75 pounds of Kona coffee beans a day. (Demand can be assumed to be distributed normally with a standard deviation of 15 pounds per day). After ordering (fixed cost = $16 per order), beans are always shipped from Hawaii within exactly 4 days. Per-pound annual holding costs for the beans are $3.
a) What is the economic order quantity (EOQ) for Kona coffee beans?
b) What are the total annual holding costs of stock for Kona coffee beans?
c) What are the total annual ordering costs for Kona coffee beans?
d) Assume that management has specified that no more than a 1% risk during stockout is acceptable. What should the reorder point (ROP) be?
e) What is the safety stock needed to attain a 1% risk of stockout during lead time?
f) What is the annual holding cost of maintaining the level of safety stock needed to support a 1% risk?
g) If management specified that a 2% risk of stockout during lead time would be acceptable, would the safety stock holding costs decrease or increase?

▶ Refer to myomlab 🔘 for these additional homework
problems: 12.41–12.53

Case Studies

▶ Zhou Bicycle Company

Zhou Bicycle Company (ZBC), located in Seattle, is a wholesale distributor of bicycles and bicycle parts. Formed in 1981 by University of Washington Professor Yong-Pin Zhou, the firm's primary retail outlets are located within a 400-mile radius of the distribution center. These retail outlets receive the order from ZBC within 2 days after notifying the distribution center, provided that the stock is available. However, if an order is not fulfilled by the company, no backorder is placed; the retailers arrange to get their shipment from other distributors, and ZBC loses that amount of business.

The company distributes a wide variety of bicycles. The most popular model, and the major source of revenue to the company, is the AirWing. ZBC receives all the models from a single

manufacturer in China, and shipment takes as long as 4 weeks from the time an order is placed. With the cost of communication, paperwork, and customs clearance included, ZBC estimates that each time an order is placed, it incurs a cost of $65. The purchase price paid by ZBC, per bicycle, is roughly 60% of the suggested retail price for all the styles available, and the inventory carrying cost is 1% per month (12% per year) of the purchase price paid by ZBC. The retail price (paid by the customers) for the AirWing is $170 per bicycle.

ZBC is interested in making an inventory plan for 2010. The firm wants to maintain a 95% service level with its customers to minimize the losses on the lost orders. The data collected for the past 2 years are summarized in the preceding table. A forecast for

Demands for AirWing Model

Month	2008	2009	Forecast for 2010
January	6	7	8
February	12	14	15
March	24	27	31
April	46	53	59
May	75	86	97
June	47	54	60
July	30	34	39
August	18	21	24
September	13	15	16
October	12	13	15
November	22	25	28
December	38	42	47
Total	343	391	439

AirWing model sales in 2010 has been developed and will be used to make an inventory plan for ZBC.

Discussion Questions

1. Develop an inventory plan to help ZBC.
2. Discuss ROPs and total costs.
3. How can you address demand that is not at the level of the planning horizon?

Source: Professor Kala Chand Seal, Loyola Marymount University.

▶ Sturdivant Sound Systems

Sturdivant Sound Systems manufactures and sells sound systems for both home and auto. All parts of the sound systems, with the exception of DVD players, are produced in the Rochester, New York, plant. DVD players used in the assembly of Sturdivant systems are purchased from Morris Electronics of Concord, New Hampshire.

Sturdivant purchasing agent Mary Kim submits a purchase requisition for DVD players once every 4 weeks. The company's annual requirements total 5,000 units (20 per working day), and the cost per unit is $60. (Sturdivant does not purchase in greater quantities because Morris Electronics does not offer quantity discounts.) Because Morris promises delivery within 1 week following receipt of a purchase requisition, rarely is there a shortage of DVD players. (Total time between date of order and date of receipt is 5 days.)

Associated with the purchase of each shipment are procurement costs. These costs, which amount to $20 per order, include the costs of preparing the requisition, inspecting and storing the delivered goods, updating inventory records, and issuing a voucher and a check for payment. In addition to procurement costs, Sturdivant incurs inventory carrying costs that include insurance, storage, handling, taxes, and so forth. These costs equal $6 per unit per year.

Beginning in August of this year, Sturdivant management will embark on a companywide cost-control program in an attempt to improve its profits. One area to be closely scrutinized for possible cost savings is inventory procurement.

Discussion Questions

1. Compute the optimal order quantity of DVD players.
2. Determine the appropriate reorder point (in units).
3. Compute the cost savings that the company will realize if it implements the optimal inventory procurement decision.
4. Should procurement costs be considered a linear function of the number of orders?

Source: Reprinted by permission of Professor Jerry Kinard, Western Carolina University.

▶ Managing Inventory at Frito-Lay

Video Case

Frito-Lay has flourished since its origin—the 1931 purchase of a small San Antonio firm for $100 that included a recipe, 19 retail accounts, and a hand-operated potato ricer. The multi-billion-dollar company, headquartered in Dallas, now has 41 products—15 with sales of over $100 million per year and 7 at over $1 billion in sales. Production takes place in 36 product-focused plants in the U.S. and Canada, with 48,000 employees.

Inventory is a major investment and an expensive asset in most firms. Holding costs often exceed 25% of product value, but in Frito-Lay's prepared food industry, holding cost can be much higher because the raw materials are perishable. In the food industry, inventory spoils. So poor inventory management is not only expensive but can also yield an unsatisfactory product that in the extreme can also ruin market acceptance.

Major ingredients at Frito-Lay are corn meal, corn, potatoes, oil, and seasoning. Using potato chips to illustrate rapid inventory flow: potatoes are moved via truck from farm, to regional plants for processing, to warehouse, to the retail store. This happens in a matter of hours—not days or weeks. This keeps freshness high and holding costs low.

Frequent deliveries of main ingredients at the Florida plant, for example, take several forms:

- Potatoes are delivered in 10 truckloads per day, with 150,000 lbs consumed in one shift: the entire potato storage area will only hold 71/2 hours' worth of potatoes.
- Oil inventory arrives by rail car, which lasts only 41/2 days.
- Corn meal arrives from various farms in the Midwest, and inventory typically averages 4 days' production.
- Seasoning inventory averages 7 days.
- Packaging inventory averages 8 to 10 days.

Frito-Lay's product-focused facility is expensive. It represents a major capital investment that must achieve high utilization to be efficient. The capital cost must be spread over a substantial volume to drive down total cost of the snack foods produced. This demand for high utilization requires reliable equipment and tight schedules. Reliable machinery requires an inventory of critical components: this is known as MRO, or maintenance, repair, and operating supplies. MRO inventory of motors, switches, gears, bearings, and other critical specialized components can be costly but is necessary.

Frito-Lay's non-MRO inventory moves rapidly. Raw material quickly becomes work-in-process, moving through the system and out the door as a bag of chips in about 11/2 shifts. Packaged finished products move from production to the distribution chain in less than 1.4 days.

Discussion Questions*

1. How does the mix of Frito-Lay's inventory differ from those at a machine or cabinet shop (a process-focused facility)?
2. What are the major inventory items at Frito-Lay, and how rapidly do they move through the process?

3. What are the four types of inventory? Give an example of each at Frito-Lay.
4. How would you rank the dollar investment in each of the four types (from the most investment to the least investment)?
5. Why does inventory flow so quickly through a Frito-Lay plant?
6. Why does the company keep so many plants open?
7. Why doesn't Frito-Lay make all its 41 products at each of its plants?

*You may wish to view the video that accompanies this case before answering these questions.

Source: Professors Jay Heizer, Texas Lutheran University; Barry Render, Rollins College; and Bev Amer, Northern Arizona University.

▶ Inventory Control at Wheeled Coach

Video Case

Controlling inventory is one of Wheeled Coach's toughest problems. Operating according to a strategy of mass customization and responsiveness, management knows that success is dependent on tight inventory control. Anything else results in an inability to deliver promptly, chaos on the assembly line, and a huge inventory investment. Wheeled Coach finds that almost 50% of the $40,000 to $100,000 cost of every ambulance it manufactures is purchased materials. A large proportion of that 50% is in chassis (purchased from Ford), aluminum (from Reynolds Metal), and plywood used for flooring and cabinetry construction (from local suppliers). Wheeled Coach tracks these A inventory items quite carefully, maintaining tight security/control and ordering carefully so as to maximize quantity discounts while minimizing on-hand stock. Because of long lead times and scheduling needs at Reynolds, aluminum must actually be ordered as much as 8 months in advance.

In a crowded ambulance industry in which it is the only giant, its 45 competitors don't have the purchasing power to draw the same discounts as Wheeled Coach. But this competitive cost advantage cannot be taken lightly, according to President Bob Collins. "Cycle counting in our stockrooms is critical. No part can leave the locked stockrooms without appearing on a bill of materials."

Accurate bills of material (BOM) are a requirement if products are going to be built on time. Additionally, because of the custom nature of each vehicle, most orders are won only after a bidding process. Accurate BOMs are critical to cost estimation and the resulting bid. For these reasons, Collins was emphatic that Wheeled Coach maintain outstanding inventory control. The *Global Company Profile* featuring Wheeled Coach (which opens Chapter 14 in the text) provides further details about the ambulance inventory control and production process.

Discussion Questions*

1. Explain how Wheeled Coach implements ABC analysis.
2. If you were to take over as inventory control manager at Wheeled Coach, what additional policies and techniques would you initiate to ensure accurate inventory records?
3. How would you go about implementing these suggestions?

*You may wish to view the video that accompanies this case before answering these questions.

Active Model Exercises

ACTIVE MODEL 12.1 This explores the basics of a typical inventory decision and simulates the sensitivity of the model to changes in demand and costs. It uses the data from Examples 3, 4, and 5. It is illustrated at **www.myomlab.com** or **www.pearsonhighered.com/heizer**.

ACTIVE MODEL 12.2 This illustrates Example 8's production order quantity model. It is illustrated at **www.myomlab.com** or **www.pearsonhighered.com/heizer**.

Classroom Activity

▶ Inventory Application: He Shoots, He Scores

At a recent trade show, a Canadian company unveiled its radical new product for the sports equipment industry—a graphite hockey stick! The company, known as "*He Shoots, He Scores*," has enthusiastic plans for the stick. As owner of a medium-sized retail sporting goods store, you are aware of the various costs involved in ordering and holding inventory. Taking into account the respective costs, you are to develop an appropriate ordering policy for this brand-new item.

Since this is a new product, you have no historical data on which to base your forecast of demand. However, you have data on the number of sticks sold for other new, state-of-the-art sticks from prior years:

	2 Years Ago	Last Year		2 Years Ago	Last Year
Jul	20	24	**Jan**	34	68
Aug	35	44	**Feb**	41	62
Sep	59	49	**Mar**	38	33
Oct	79	100	**Apr**	19	26
Nov	42	51	**May**	27	26
Dec	83	81	**Jun**	25	21

As in any business, sales for any given month could be extremely volatile (or not). In this game, the demand for the next year is generated from a Normal distribution (which ranges from negative infinity to infinity). It is not necessary to know the parameters of the Normal distribution for this game, but they are given at the end of these instructions.

"*He Shoots, He Scores*" will allow you to purchase hockey sticks for $20. Market research results given at the recent trade show indicated that potential customers would pay up to $30 for the item. Thus, you plan to use $30 as your selling price. Note that the amount you sell in a given month is always the lowest of either monthly demand or (beginning inventory + quantity ordered).

Placing an order costs you $60 (note that the manufacturer allows at most one replenishment per month). Any unsatisfied demand (a stockout, or should we call it a "stick" out?) costs you $7 per unit short. Backorders are not allowed (since customers will most likely purchase the hockey stick from a competitor if you don't have enough on-hand). Inventory remaining at the end of a month costs you $1 per unit.

Your task is to plan replenishments (when to order, how much to order) on a month-by-month basis for the next 12 months. Assume that the first month in the planning horizon is July, and that there is no inventory on-hand. *After* you make your replenishment decision, the instructor will *announce the demand for that month*. Then, you may make the decision for next month. Use the table on page 12-22 to indicate your monthly replenishments, and to tabulate the results of your respective strategy. If a stockout occurs, write "0" for the ending inventory, and put a "0" for the beginning inventory of the subsequent month.

For example, assume that there were no units in beginning inventory, and that you ordered 15 sticks at the beginning of July. Assuming a demand of 23 sticks, you would face the following costs:

- revenue: $30 * $min(0 + 15,23) = \$30 * 15 = \$450$
- ordering cost: $\$60 + (\$20 * 15) = \$360$
- shortage cost: $\$7 * 8 = \$56$
- holding cost: $0 (since there is no ending inventory—i.e., we had a stockout)
- monthly profit $= \$450 - (\$360 + \$56) = \$34$

Parameters for Normal Distribution:

Normal $((D2 + D1 * 3) / 4,$ absvalue$(D1 - D2))$

where: D1 is demand last year
D2 is demand 2 years ago

Thus, demand for July is calculated from:

Normal $((20 + 24 * 3) / 4,$ absvalue$(24 - 20)$
Normal $(23,4)$

Note: This game has been developed for educational purposes. It may be used, disseminated, and modified for educational purposes, but it may not be sold. In all uses of the game, the original developers must be acknowledged (as has been done below).

© Keith Willoughby and Ken Klassen, 2003

He Shoots, He Scores Worksheet

		July	Aug.	Sept.	Oct.	Nov.	Dec.	Jan.	Feb.	March	April	May	June
1	Beg. Inventory	0											
2	Order Quantity												
3	Number Available $= (1) + (2)$												
4	Demand												
5	End. Inventory $= \max[(3) - (4), 0]$												
	Revenue:												
6	Sales $= \$30 \times \min[(3), (4)]$												
	Costs:												
7	Ordering If $(2) > 0, = \$60 + (\$20 \times 2)$ If $(2) = 0, = 0$												
8	Shortage $= -\$7 \times \min[0, (3) - (4)]$												
9	Holding $= \$1 \times (5)$												
10	**Total Costs** $= (7) + (8) + (9)$												
11	**Monthly Profit** $= (6) - (10)$												
12	**Annual Profit**												

Main Heading	Review Material	
THE IMPORTANCE OF INVENTORY (pp. 374–375)	Inventory is one of the most expensive assets of many companies. *The objective of inventory management is to strike a balance between inventory investment and customer service.* The two basic inventory issues are how much to order and when to order. ■ **Raw material inventory**—Materials that are usually purchased but have yet to enter the manufacturing process. ■ **Work-in-process (WIP) inventory**—Products or components that are no longer raw materials but have yet to become finished products. ■ **MRO**—Maintenance, repair, and operating materials. ■ **Finished-goods inventory**—An end item ready to be sold but still an asset on the company's books.	**VIDEO 12.1** Managing Inventory at Frito-Lay
MANAGING INVENTORY (pp. 375–379)	■ **ABC analysis**—A method for dividing on-hand inventory into three classifications based on annual dollar volume. ■ **Cycle counting**—A continuing reconciliation of inventory with inventory records. ■ **Shrinkage**—Retail inventory that is unaccounted for between receipt and sale. ■ **Pilferage**—A small amount of theft.	Problems: 12.1–12.4 Virtual Office Hours for Solved Problem: 12.1
INVENTORY MODELS (p. 380)	■ **Holding cost**—The cost to keep or carry inventory in stock. ■ **Ordering cost**—The cost of the ordering process. ■ **Setup cost**—The cost to prepare a machine or process for production. ■ **Setup time**—The time required to prepare a machine or process for production.	
INVENTORY MODELS FOR INDEPENDENT DEMAND (pp. 380–393)	■ **Economic order quantity (EOQ) model**—An inventory-control technique that minimizes the total of ordering and holding costs: $$Q^* = \sqrt{\frac{2DS}{H}} \qquad (12\text{-}1)$$ $$\text{Expected number of orders} = N = \frac{\text{Demand}}{\text{Order quantity}} = \frac{D}{Q^*} \qquad (12\text{-}2)$$ $$\text{Expected time between orders} = T = \frac{\text{Number of working days per year}}{N} \qquad (12\text{-}3)$$ $$\text{Total annual cost} = \text{Setup (order) cost} + \text{Holding cost} \qquad (12\text{-}4)$$ $$TC = \frac{D}{Q}S + \frac{Q}{2}H \qquad (12\text{-}5)$$ ■ **Robust**—Giving satisfactory answers even with substantial variation in the parameters. ■ **Lead time**—In purchasing systems, the time between placing an order and receiving it; in production systems, the wait, move, queue, setup, and run times for each component produced. ■ **Reorder point (ROP)**—The inventory level (point) at which action is taken to replenish the stocked item. *ROP for known demand:* $$\text{ROP} = (\text{Demand per day}) \times (\text{Lead time for a new order in days}) = d \times L \quad (12\text{-}6)$$ ■ **Safety stock**—Extra stock to allow for uneven demand; a buffer. ■ **Production order quantity model**—An economic order quantity technique applied to production orders: $$Q_p^* = \sqrt{\frac{2DS}{H[1 - (d/p)]}} \qquad (12\text{-}7)$$ $$Q_p^* = \sqrt{\frac{2DS}{H\left(1 - \dfrac{\text{Annual demand rate}}{\text{Annual production rate}}\right)}} \qquad (12\text{-}8)$$ ■ **Quantity discount**—A reduced price for items purchased in large quantities: $$TC - \frac{D}{Q}S + \frac{Q}{2}H + PD \qquad (12\text{-}9)$$ $$Q^* = \sqrt{\frac{2DS}{IP}} \qquad (12\text{-}10)$$	Problems: 12.5– 12.26, 12.35, 12.39 Virtual Office Hours for Solved Problems: 12.2–12.5 **ACTIVE MODELS 12.1, 12.2** **VIDEO 12.2** Inventory Control at Wheeled Coach Ambulance

Main Heading	Review Material	myomlab
PROBABILISTIC MODELS AND SAFETY STOCK (pp. 393–398)	■ **Probabilistic model**—A statistical model applicable when product demand or any other variable is not known but can be specified by means of a probability distribution. ■ **Service level**—The complement of the probability of a stockout. *ROP for unknown demand:* $$ROP = d \times L + ss \qquad (12\text{-}11)$$ Annual stockout costs = The sum of the units short for each demand level $\times$ The probability of that demand level $\times$ The stockout cost/unit $\qquad$ (12-12) $\times$ The number of orders per year *ROP for unknown demand and given service level:* $$ROP = \text{Expected demand during lead time} + Z\sigma_{dLT} \qquad (12\text{-}13)$$ $$\text{Safety stock} = Z\sigma_{dLT} \qquad (12\text{-}14)$$ *ROP for variable demand and constant lead time:* $$ROP = (\text{Average daily demand} \times \text{Lead time in days}) + Z\sigma_{dLT} \qquad (12\text{-}15)$$ *ROP for constant demand and variable lead time:* $$ROP = (\text{Daily demand} \times \text{Average lead time in days}) + Z(\text{Daily demand}) \times \sigma_{LT} \ (12\text{-}16)$$ *ROP for variable demand and variable lead time:* $$ROP = (\text{Average daily demand} \times \text{Average lead time}) + Z\sigma_{dLT} \qquad (12\text{-}17)$$ In each case, $\sigma_{dLT} = \sqrt{(\text{Average lead time} \times \sigma_d^2) + \bar{d}^2\sigma_{LT}^2}$ but under constant demand: $\sigma_d^2 = 0$, and while under constant lead time: $\sigma_{LT}^2 = 0$.	Problems: 12.27–12.34 Virtual Office Hours for Solved Problems: 12.6–12.9
SINGLE-PERIOD MODEL (pp. 398–399)	■ **Single-period inventory model**—A system for ordering items that have little or no value at the end of the sales period: $$\text{Service Level} = \frac{C_s}{C_s + C_o} \qquad (12\text{-}18)$$	Problems: 12.36–12.38
FIXED-PERIOD (P) SYSTEMS (pp. 399–400)	■ **Fixed-quantity (Q) system**—An ordering system with the same order amount each time. ■ **Perpetual inventory system**—A system that keeps track of each withdrawal or addition to inventory continuously, so records are always current. ■ **Fixed-period (P) system**—A system in which inventory orders are made at regular time intervals.	

Self Test

■ **Before taking the self-test,** refer to the learning objectives listed at the beginning of the chapter and the key terms listed at the end of the chapter.

LO1. ABC analysis divides on-hand inventory into three classes, based on:
  a) unit price.
  b) the number of units on hand.
  c) annual demand.
  d) annual dollar values.

LO2. Cycle counting:
  a) provides a measure of inventory turnover.
  b) assumes that all inventory records must be verified with the same frequency.
  c) is a process by which inventory records are periodically verified.
  d) all of the above.

LO3. The two most important inventory-based questions answered by the typical inventory model are:
  a) when to place an order and the cost of the order.
  b) when to place an order and how much of an item to order.
  c) how much of an item to order and the cost of the order.
  d) how much of an item to order and with whom the order should be placed.

LO4. Extra units in inventory to help reduce stockouts are called:
  a) reorder point.
  b) safety stock.
  c) just-in-time inventory.
  d) all of the above.

LO5. The difference(s) between the basic EOQ model and the production order quantity model is(are) that:
  a) the production order quantity model does not require the assumption of known, constant demand.
  b) the EOQ model does not require the assumption of negligible lead time.
  c) the production order quantity model does not require the assumption of instantaneous delivery.
  d) all of the above.

LO6. The EOQ model with quantity discounts attempts to determine:
  a) the lowest amount of inventory necessary to satisfy a certain service level.
  b) the lowest purchase price.
  c) whether to use a fixed-quantity or fixed-period order policy.
  d) how many units should be ordered.
  e) the shortest lead time.

LO7. The appropriate level of safety stock is typically determined by:
  a) minimizing an expected stockout cost.
  b) choosing the level of safety stock that assures a given service level.
  c) carrying sufficient safety stock so as to eliminate all stockouts.
  d) annual demand.

Answers: LO1. d; LO2. c; LO3. b; LO4. b; LO5. c; LO6. d; LO7. b.

13

Aggregate Planning

Chapter Outline

The Planning Process
The Nature of Aggregate Planning
Aggregate Planning Strategies
Methods for Aggregate Planning
Aggregate Planning in Services
Yield Management
Ethical Dilemma
Discussion Questions
Problems
Case Studies: Southwestern University:
   (G); Andrew-Carter, Inc.
Active Model Exercise
Rapid Review

Aggregate planning is concerned with determining the quantity and timing of production for the intermediate future, often from 3 to 18 months ahead. Operations managers try to determine the best way to meet forecasted demand by adjusting production rates, labor levels, inventory levels, overtime work, subcontracting rates, and other controllable variables. Usually, the objective of aggregate planning is to minimize cost over the planning period. However, other strategic issues may be more important than low cost. These strategies may be to smooth employment levels, to drive down inventory levels, or to meet a high level of service.

This chapter describes the aggregate planning decision, shows how the aggregate plan fits into the overall planning process, and describes several techniques that managers use when developing an aggregate plan.

BEFORE COMING TO CLASS, READ CHAPTER 13 IN YOUR TEXT AND ANSWER THESE QUESTIONS.

1. What do we mean by aggregate planning? _____

   _____

2. Identify 5 capacity options and 3 demand options for developing an

   aggregate plan. _____

   _____

3. What is the graphical method of aggregate planning? _____

   _____

4. How does the transportation method differ from the graphical method?

   _____

   _____

5. What is yield management, and in what industries is it popular? _____

   _____

   _____

THE PLANNING PROCESS (See Flexible Version pp. 410–411)

THE NATURE OF AGGREGATE PLANNING (See Flexible Version pp. 411–412)

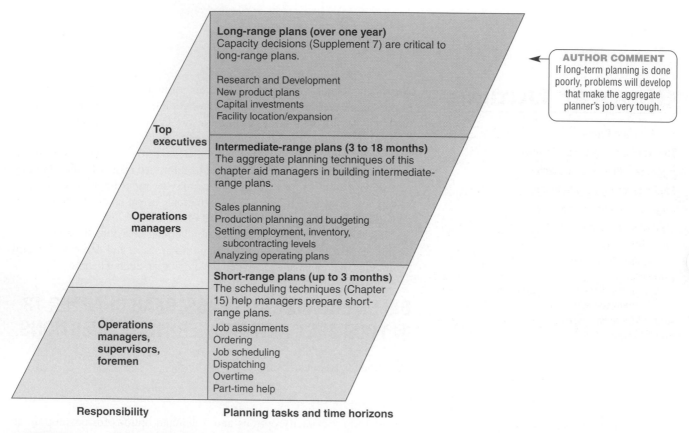

▲ FIGURE 13.1 Planning Tasks and Responsibilities

Disaggregation

Master Production Schedule

AGGREGATE PLANNING STRATEGIES (See Flexible Version pp. 412–415)

Capacity Options (See Flexible Version p. 413)

1. _____

2. _____

3. _____

4. _____

5. _____

Demand Options (See Flexible Version p. 414)

1. _____

2. _____

3. _____

Chase Strategy

Level Strategy

METHODS FOR AGGREGATE PLANNING (See Flexible Version pp. 415–422)

Graphical Methods (See Flexible Version pp. 415–420)

Five Steps

1. _____

2. _____

3. _____

4. _____

5. _____

PRACTICE PROBLEM 13.1 ■ Graphical Approach

Heyl Appliances produces industrial dishwashers. Jeff Heyl's per unit back order (shortage) cost is $100 per month and his inventory carrying cost is $30 per month per washer. The current workforce can produce 700 dishwashers per month at a cost of $700 each. The forecasted demand is as follows:

Month	Demand
January	500
February	600
March	700
April	700
May	800
June	900
July	800
	5,000

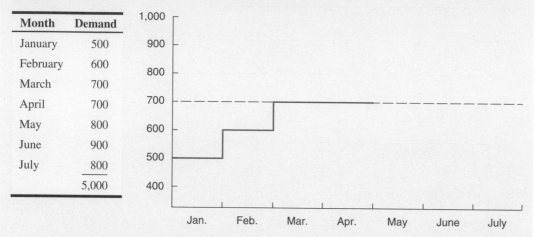

Using a pure strategy (one that holds production constant), complete the graph above and the partially completed aggregate production schedule below. You may want to evaluate other plans and the impact of changes in production levels.

Month	Beginning Inventory	Production	Production Cost	Demand	Ending Inventory	Shortage	Inventory Carrying Cost	Shortage Cost
January	0	700	$490,000	500	200	0	$6,000	$0
February	200	700	490,000	600	300	0	9,000	0
March	300	700	490,000	700	300	0	____	0
April	300	700	____	____	____	____	____	0
May	300	____	____	____	____	____	____	0
June	____	____	____	____	____	____	____	0
July	____	____	____	____	____	____	____	10,000
							$39,000	$10,000

Transportation Method of Linear Programming

(See Flexible Version p. 420)

PRACTICE PROBLEM 13.2 ■ Transportation Model Approach

Set up the following problem in transportation format, and solve for the minimum cost plan.

	Period		
	Feb.	**Mar.**	**Apr.**
Demand	55	70	75
Capacity			
Regular	50	50	50
Overtime	5	5	5
Subcontract	12	12	10
Beginning inventory	10		
Costs			
Regular time		$60 per unit	
Overtime		$80 per unit	
Subcontract		$90 per unit	
Inventory carrying cost		$1 per unit per month	
Back order cost		$3 per unit per month	

Table with a few numbers filled in:

		Demand for			Unused Capacity (dummy)	Total Capacity Available (supply)
		Feb.	**Mar.**	**Apr.**		
February	Beginning inventory	0	1	2	0	10
	Regular time	60	61	62	0	50
	Overtime	80	81	82	0	5
	Subcontract	90	91	92	0	12
March	Regular time				0	
	Overtime				0	
	Subcontract				0	
April	Regular time				0	
	Overtime				0	
	Subcontract				0	
	Demand	55	70	75	9	209

Additional Practice Problem Space

Other Models   (See Flexible Version p. 422)

AGGREGATE PLANNING IN SERVICES   (See Flexible Version pp. 422–425)

YIELD MANAGEMENT   (See Flexible Version pp. 425–428)

		Price	
		Tend to be fixed	**Tend to be variable**
Use	**Tend to be predictable**	Quadrant 1: Movies Stadiums/arenas Convention centers Hotel meeting space	Quadrant 2: Hotels Airlines Rental cars Cruise lines
	Tend to be uncertain	Quadrant 3: Restaurants Golf courses Internet service providers	Quadrant 4: Hospitals Continuing care

▲ FIGURE 13.7   Yield Management Matrix

Industries in quadrant 2 are traditionally associated with revenue management.

Source: Adapted from S. Kimes and K. McGuire, "Function Space Revenue Management," *Cornell Hotel and Restaurant Administration Quarterly* 42, no. 6 (December 2001): 33–46.

Ethical Dilemma

Airline passengers today stand in numerous lines, are crowded into small seats on mostly full airplanes, and often spend time on taxiways because of air-traffic problems or lack of open gates. But what gripes travelers almost as much as these annoyances is finding out that the person sitting next to them paid a much lower fare than they did for their seat. This concept of "yield management" or "revenue management" results in ticket pricing that can range from free to thousands of dollars on the same plane. Figure 13.8

illustrates what passengers recently paid for various seats on an 11:35 A.M. flight from Minneapolis to Anaheim, California, on an Airbus A320.

Make the case for, and then against, this pricing system. Does the general public seem to accept yield management? What would happen if you overheard the person in front of you in line getting a better room rate at a Hilton Hotel? How do customers manipulate the airline systems to get better fares?

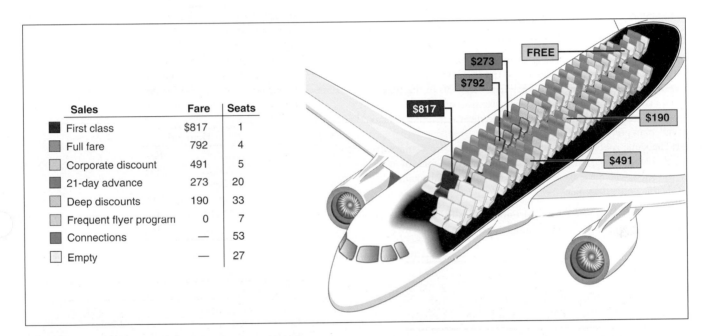

Sales	Fare	Seats
First class	$817	1
Full fare	792	4
Corporate discount	491	5
21-day advance	273	20
Deep discounts	190	33
Frequent flyer program	0	7
Connections	—	53
Empty	—	27

▲ **FIGURE 13.8** **Yield Management Seat Costs on a Typical Flight**

Discussion Questions

1. Define *aggregate planning*.
2. Explain what the term *aggregate* in "aggregate planning" means.
3. List the strategic objectives of aggregate planning. Which one of these is most often addressed by the quantitative techniques of aggregate planning? Which one of these is generally the most important?
4. Define *chase strategy*.
5. What is a pure strategy? Provide a few examples.
6. What is level scheduling? What is the basic philosophy underlying it?
7. Define *mixed strategy*. Why would a firm use a mixed strategy instead of a simple pure strategy?
8. What are the advantages and disadvantages of varying the size of the workforce to meet demand requirements each period?
9. Why are mathematical models not more widely used in aggregate planning?
10. How does aggregate planning in service differ from aggregate planning in manufacturing?13-7
11. What is the relationship between the aggregate plan and the master production schedule?
12. Why are graphical aggregate planning methods useful?
13. What are major limitations of using the transportation method for aggregate planning?
14. How does yield management impact an aggregate plan?

Problems*

• **13.1** Prepare a graph of the monthly forecasts and average forecasted demand for Industrial Air Corp., a manufacturer of a variety of large air conditioners for commercial applications.

Month	Production Days	Demand Forecast
January	22	1,000
February	18	1,100
March	22	1,200
April	21	1,300
May	22	1,350
June	21	1,350
July	21	1,300
August	22	1,200
September	21	1,100
October	22	1,100
November	20	1,050
December	20	900

•• **13.2** a) Develop another plan for the Mexican roofing manufacturer described in Examples 1 to 4 (pp. 416–419 in the Flexible Version) and Solved Problem 13.1 (pp. 429–430 in the Flexible Version). For this plan, plan 5, the firm wants to maintain a constant workforce of six, using subcontracting to meet remaining demand. Is this plan preferable?

b) The same roofing manufacturer in Examples 1 to 4 and Solved Problem 13.1 has yet a sixth plan. A constant workforce of seven is selected, with the remainder of demand filled by subcontracting.

c) Is this better than plans 1–5? **P✕**

••• **13.3** The president of Hill Enterprises, Terri Hill, projects the firm's aggregate demand requirements over the next 8 months as follows:

Jan.	1,400	May	2,200
Feb.	1,600	June	2,200
Mar.	1,800	July	1,800
Apr.	1,800	Aug.	1,400

Her operations manager is considering a new plan, which begins in January with 200 units on hand. Stockout cost of lost sales is $100 per unit. Inventory holding cost is $20 per unit per month. Ignore any idle-time costs. The plan is called plan A.

Plan A: Vary the workforce level to execute a "chase" strategy by producing the quantity demanded in the *prior* month. The December demand and rate of production are both 1,600 units per month. The cost of hiring additional workers is $5,000 per 100 units. The cost of laying off workers is $7,500 per 100 units. Evaluate this plan. **P✕**

•• **13.4** Using the information in Problem 13.3, develop plan B. Produce at a constant rate of 1,400 units per month, which will meet minimum demands. Then use subcontracting, with additional units at a premium price of $75 per unit. Evaluate this plan by computing the costs for January through August. **P✕**

•• **13.5** Hill is now considering plan C. Beginning inventory, stockout costs, and holding costs are provided in Problem 13.3:

a) Plan C: Keep a stable workforce by maintaining a constant production rate equal to the average requirements and allow varying inventory levels.

b) Plot the demand with a graph that also shows average requirements. Conduct your analysis for January through August. **P✕**

*Note: **P✕** means the problem may be solved with POM for Windows and/or Excel OM.

••• **13.6** Hill's operations manager (see Problems 13.3 through 13.5) is also considering two mixed strategies for January–August:

a) Plan D: Keep the current workforce stable at producing 1,600 units per month. Permit a maximum of 20% overtime at an additional cost of $50 per unit. A warehouse now constrains the maximum allowable inventory on hand to 400 units or less.

b) Plan E: Keep the current workforce, which is producing 1,600 units per month, and subcontract to meet the rest of the demand.

c) Evaluate plans D and E and make a recommendation. **P✕**

••• **13.7** Michael Carrigg, Inc., is a disk manufacturer in need of an aggregate plan for July through December. The company has gathered the following data:

Costs	
Holding cost	$8/disk/month
Subcontracting	$80/disk
Regular-time labor	$12/hour
Overtime labor	$18/hour for hours above 8 hours/worker/day
Hiring cost	$40/worker
Layoff cost	$80/worker

Demand*	
July	400
Aug.	500
Sept.	550
Oct.	700
Nov.	800
Dec.	700

*No costs are incurred for unmet demand.

Other Data	
Current workforce (June)	8 people
Labor-hours/disk	4 hours
Workdays/month	20 days
Beginning inventory	150 disks**
Ending inventory	0 disks

**Note that there is no holding cost for June.

What will each of the two following strategies cost?
a) Vary the workforce so that production meets demand. Carrigg had eight workers on board in June.
b) Vary overtime only and use a constant workforce of eight. **Px**

•• **13.8** You manage a consulting firm down the street from Michael Carrigg, Inc., and to get your foot in the door, you have told Mr. Carrigg (see Problem 13.7) that you can do a better job at aggregate planning than his current staff. He said, "Fine. You do that, and you have a 1-year contract." You now have to make good on your boast using the data in Problem 13.7. You decide to hire 5 workers in August and 5 more in October.

••• **13.9** Mary Rhodes, operations manager at Kansas Furniture, has received the following estimates of demand requirements:

July	Aug.	Sept.	Oct.	Nov.	Dec.
1,000	1,200	1,400	1,800	1,800	1,600

a) Assuming stockout costs for lost sales of $100 per unit, inventory carrying costs of $25 per unit per month, and zero beginning and ending inventory, evaluate these two plans on an *incremental* cost basis:
  • Plan A: Produce at a steady rate (equal to minimum requirements) of 1,000 units per month and subcontract additional units at a $60 per unit premium cost.
  • Plan B: Vary the workforce, which performs at a current production level of 1,300 units per month. The cost of hiring additional workers is $3,000 per 100 units produced. The cost of layoffs is $6,000 per 100 units cut back. **Px**
b) Which plan is best and why?

••• **13.10** Mary Rhodes (see Problem 13.9) is considering two more mixed strategies. Using the data in Problem 13.9, compare plans C and D with plans A and B and make a recommendation.
  • Plan C: Keep the current workforce steady at a level producing 1,300 units per month. Subcontract the remainder to meet demand. Assume that 300 units remaining from June are available in July.
  • Plan D: Keep the current workforce at a level capable of producing 1,300 units per month. Permit a maximum of 20% overtime at a premium of $40 per unit. Assume that warehouse limitations permit no more than a 180-unit carryover from month to month. This plan means that any time inventories reach 180, the plant is kept idle. Idle time per unit is $60. Any additional needs are subcontracted at a cost of $60 per incremental unit.

••• **13.11** Liz Perry Health and Beauty Products has developed a new shampoo and you need to develop its aggregate schedule. The cost accounting department has supplied you the cost relevant to the aggregate plan and the marketing department has provided a four-quarter forecast. All are shown as follows and in the next column:

Quarter	Forecast
1	1,400
2	1,200
3	1,500
4	1,300

Your job is to develop an aggregate plan for the next four quarters.
a) First, try a chase plan by hiring and layoffs (to meet the forecast) as necessary.
b) Then try a plan that holds employment steady.
c) Which is the more economical plan for Liz Perry Health and Beauty Products? **Px**

Costs	
Previous quarter's output	1,500 units
Beginning inventory	0 units
Stockout cost for backorders	$50 per unit
Inventory holding cost	$10 per unit for every unit held at the end of the quarter
Hiring workers	$40 per unit
Layoff workers	$80 per unit
Unit cost	$30 per unit
Overtime	$15 extra per unit
Subcontracting	Not available

••• **13.12** Missouri's Soda Pop, Inc., has a new fruit drink for which it has high hopes. Steve Allen, the production planner, has assembled the following cost data and demand forecast:

Quarter	Forecast
1	1,800
2	1,100
3	1,600
4	900

Costs/Other Data
Previous quarter's output = 1,300 cases
Beginning inventory = 0 cases
Stockout cost = $150 per case
Inventory holding cost = $40 per case at end of quarter
Hiring employees = $40 per case
Terminating employees = $80 per case
Subcontracting cost = $60 per case
Unit cost on regular time = $30 per case
Overtime cost = $15 extra per case
Capacity on regular time = 1,800 cases per quarter

Steve's job is to develop an aggregate plan. The three initial options he wants to evaluate are:
  • Plan A: a chase strategy that hires and fires personnel as necessary to meet the forecast.
  • Plan B: a level strategy.
  • Plan C: a level strategy that produces 1,200 cases per quarter and meets the forecasted demand with inventory and subcontracting.
a) Which strategy is the lowest-cost plan?
b) If you are Steve's boss, the VP for operations, which plan do you implement and why? **Px**

•• **13.13** Josie Gall's firm has developed the following supply, demand, cost, and inventory data. Allocate production capacity to meet demand at a minimum cost using the transportation method. What is the cost? Assume that the initial inventory has no holding cost in the first period and backorders are not permitted.

Supply Available

Period	Regular Time	Overtime	Subcontract	Demand Forecast
1	30	10	5	40
2	35	12	5	50
3	30	10	5	40

Initial inventory	20 units
Regular-time cost per unit	$100
Overtime cost per unit	$150
Subcontract cost per unit	$200
Carrying cost per unit per month	$ 4

PX

•• **13.14** Haifa Instruments, an Israeli producer of portable kidney dialysis units and other medical products, develops a 4-month aggregate plan. Demand and capacity (in units) are forecast as follows:

Capacity Source	Month 1	Month 2	Month 3	Month 4
Labor				
Regular time	235	255	290	300
Overtime	20	24	26	24
Subcontract	12	15	15	17
Demand	255	294	321	301

The cost of producing each dialysis unit is $985 on regular time, $1,310 on overtime, and $1,500 on a subcontract. Inventory carrying cost is $100 per unit per month. There is to be no beginning or ending inventory in stock and backorders are not permitted. Set up a production plan that minimizes cost using the transportation method. PX

•• **13.15** The production planning period for flat-screen monitors at Georgia's Fernandez Electronics, Inc., is 4 months. Cost data are as follows:

Regular-time cost per monitor	$ 70
Overtime cost per monitor	$110
Subcontract cost per monitor	$120
Carrying cost per monitor per month	$ 4

For each of the next 4 months, capacity and demand for flat-screen monitors are as follows:

	Period			
	Month 1	Month 2	Month 3[a]	Month 4
Demand	2,000	2,500	1,500	2,100
Capacity				
Regular time	1,500	1,600	750	1,600
Overtime	400	400	200	400
Subcontract	600	600	600	600

[a]Factory closes for 2 weeks of vacation.

Fernandez Electronics expects to enter the planning period with 500 monitors in stock. Back ordering is not permitted (meaning, for example, that monitors produced in the second month cannot be used in the first month to cover first month's demand). Develop a production plan that minimizes costs using the transportation method. PX

••• **13.16** A large Omaha feed mill, B. Swart Processing, prepares its 6-month aggregate plan by forecasting demand for 50-pound bags of cattle feed as follows: January, 1,000 bags; February, 1,200; March, 1,250; April, 1,450; May, 1,400; and June, 1,400. The feed mill plans to begin the new year with no inventory left over from the previous year and backorders are not permitted. It projects that capacity (during regular hours) for producing bags of feed will remain constant at 800 until the end of April, and then increase to 1,100 bags per month when a planned expansion is completed on May 1. Overtime capacity is set at 300 bags per month until the expansion, at which time it will increase to 400 bags per month.

A friendly competitor in Sioux City, Iowa, is also available as a backup source to meet demand—but can provide only 500 bags total during the 6-month period. Develop a 6-month production plan for the feed mill using the transportation method.

Cost data are as follows:

Regular-time cost per bag (until April 30)	$12.00
Regular-time cost per bag (after May 1)	$11.00
Overtime cost per bag (during entire period)	$16.00
Cost of outside purchase per bag	$18.50
Carrying cost per bag per month	$ 1.00

PX

•• **13.17** Lon Min has developed a specialized airtight vacuum bag to extend the freshness of seafood shipped to restaurants. He has put together the following demand cost data:

Quarter	Forecast (units)	Regular time	Over-time	Sub-contract
1	500	400	80	100
2	750	400	80	100
3	900	800	160	100
4	450	400	80	100

Initial inventory = 250 units
Regular time cost = $1.00/unit
Overtime cost = $1.50/unit
Subcontracting cost = $2.00/unit
Carrying cost = $0.50/unit/quarter
Back-order cost = $0.50/unit/quarter

Min decides that the initial inventory of 250 units will incur the 20¢/unit cost from each prior quarter (unlike the situation in most companies, where a 0 unit cost is assigned).
a) Find the optimal plan using the transportation method.
b) What is the cost of the plan?
c) Does any regular time capacity go unused? If so, how much in which periods?
d) What is the extent of backordering in units and dollars? PX

••• **13.18** José Martinez of El Paso has developed a polished stainless steel tortilla machine that makes it a "showpiece" for display in Mexican restaurants. He needs to develop a 5-month aggregate plan. His forecast of capacity and demand follows:

	Month				
	1	2	3	4	5
Demand	150	160	130	200	210
Capacity					
Regular	150	150	150	150	150
Overtime	20	20	10	10	10

Subcontracting: 100 units available over the 5-month period
Beginning inventory: 0 units
Ending inventory required: 20 units

Costs	
Regular-time cost per unit	$100
Overtime cost per unit	$125
Subcontract cost per unit	$135
Inventory holding cost per unit per month	$ 3

Assume that backorders are not permitted. Using the transportation method, what is the total cost of the optimal plan? **Px**

•••• **13.19** Chris Fisher, owner of an Ohio firm that manufactures display cabinets, develops an 8-month aggregate plan. Demand and capacity (in units) are forecast as follows:

Capacity Source (units)	Jan.	Feb.	Mar.	Apr.	May	June	July	Aug.
Regular time	235	255	290	300	300	290	300	290
Overtime	20	24	26	24	30	28	30	30
Subcontract	12	16	15	17	17	19	19	20
Demand	255	294	321	301	330	320	345	340

The cost of producing each unit is $1,000 on regular time, $1,300 on overtime, and $1,800 on a subcontract. Inventory carrying cost is $200 per unit per month. There is no beginning or ending inventory in stock, and no backorders are permitted from period to period.

a) Set up a production plan that minimizes cost by producing exactly what the demand is each month. Let the workforce vary by using regular time first, then overtime, and then subcontracting. This plan allows no backorders or inventory. What is this plan's cost?

b) Through better planning, regular-time production can be set at exactly the same amount, 275 units, per month. Does this alter the solution?

c) If overtime costs rise from $1,300 to $1,400, will your answer to part (a) change? What if overtime costs then fall to $1,200? **Px**

••• **13.20** Forrester and Cohen is a small accounting firm, managed by Joseph Cohen since the retirement in December of his partner Brad Forrester. Cohen and his 3 CPAs can together bill 640 hours per month. When Cohen or another accountant bills more than 160 hours per month, he or she gets an additional "overtime" pay of $62.50 for each of the extra hours: This is above and beyond the $5,000 salary each draws during the month. (Cohen draws the same base pay as his employees.) Cohen strongly discourages any CPA from working (billing) more than 240 hours in any given month. The demand for billable hours for the firm over the next 6 months is estimated below:

Month	Estimate of Billable Hours
Jan.	600
Feb.	500
Mar.	1,000
Apr.	1,200
May	650
June	590

Cohen has an agreement with Forrester, his former partner, to help out during the busy tax season, if needed, for an hourly fee of $125. Cohen will not even consider laying off one of his colleagues in the case of a slow economy. He could, however, hire another CPA at the same salary, as business dictates.

a) Develop an aggregate plan for the 6-month period.

b) Compute the cost of Cohen's plan of using overtime and Forrester.

c) Should the firm remain as is, with a total of 4 CPAs?

•• **13.21** Refer to the CPA firm in Problem 13.20. In planning for next year, Cohen estimates that billable hours will increase by 10% in each of the 6 months. He therefore proceeds to hire a fifth CPA. The same regular time, overtime, and outside consultant (i.e., Forrester) costs still apply.

a) Develop the new aggregate plan and compute its costs.

b) Comment on the staffing level with five accountants. Was it a good decision to hire the additional accountant?

•• **13.22** Southeastern Airlines's daily flight from Atlanta to Charlotte uses a Boeing 737, with all-coach seating for 120 people. In the past, the airline has priced every seat at $140 for the one-way flight. An average of 80 passengers are on each flight. The variable cost of a filled seat is $25. Katie Morgan, the new operations manager, has decided to try a yield revenue approach, with seats priced at $80 for early bookings and at $190 for bookings within 1 week of the flight. She estimates that the airline will sell 65 seats at the lower price and 35 at the higher price. Variable cost will not change. Which approach is preferable to Ms. Morgan?

▶ **Refer to** myomlab ○ **for these additional homework problems: 13.23–13.26**

Case Studies

▶ **Southwestern University: (G)***

With the rising demands of a successful football program, the campus police chief at Southwestern University, Greg Frazier wants to develop a 2-year plan that involves a request for additional resources.

The SWU department currently has 26 sworn officers. The size of the force has not changed over the past 15 years, but the following changes have prompted the chief to seek more resources:

• The size of the athletic program, especially football, has increased.

• The college has expanded geographically, with some new research facilities and laboratories now miles away from the main campus.

- Traffic and parking problems have increased.
- More portable, expensive computers with high theft potential are dispersed across the campus.
- Alcohol and drug problems have increased.
- The size of the surrounding community has doubled.
- The police need to spend more time on education and prevention programs.

The college is located in Stephenville, Texas, a small town about 30 miles southwest of the Dallas/Forth Worth metroplex. During the summer months, the student population is around 5,000. This number swells to 20,000 during fall and spring semesters. Thus demand for police and other services is significantly lower during the summer months. Demand for police services also varies by:

- Time of day (peak time is between 10 P.M. and 2 A.M.).
- Day of the week (weekends are the busiest).
- Weekend of the year (on football weekends, 50,000 extra people come to campus).
- Special events (check-in, checkout, commencement).

Football weekends are especially difficult to staff. Extra police services are typically needed from 8 A.M. to 5 P.M. on five football Saturdays. All 26 officers are called in to work double shifts. More than 40 law enforcement officers from surrounding locations are paid to come in on their own time, and a dozen state police lend a hand free of charge (when available). Twenty-five students and local residents are paid to work traffic and parking. During the last academic year (a 9-month period), overtime payments to campus police officers totaled over $120,000.

Other relevant data include the following:

- The average starting salary for a police officer is $28,000.
- Work-study and part-time students and local residents who help with traffic and parking are paid $9.00 an hour.
- Overtime is paid to police officers who work over 40 hours a week at the rate of $18.00 an hour. Extra officers who are hired part time from outside agencies also earn $18.00 an hour.
- There seems to be an unlimited supply of officers who will work for the college when needed for special events.
- With days off, vacations, and average sick leave considered, it takes five persons to cover one 24-hour, 7-day-a-week position.

Source: Adapted from C. Haksever, B. Render, and R. Russell, *Service Management and Operations*, 2nd ed. (Upper Saddle River, NJ: Prentice Hall, 2000), 308–309. Reprinted by permission of Prentice Hall, Inc.

The schedule of officers during fall and spring semesters is:

	Weekdays	Weekend
First shift (7 A.M.–3 P.M.)	5	4
Second shift (3 P.M.–11 P.M.)	5	6
Third shift (11 P.M.–7 A.M.)	6	8

Staffing for football weekends and special events is *in addition to* the preceding schedule. Summer staffing is, on average, half that shown.

Frazier thinks that his present staff is stretched to the limit. Fatigued officers are potential problems for the department and the community. In addition, neither time nor personnel has been set aside for crime prevention, safety, or health programs. Interactions of police officers with students, faculty, and staff are minimal and usually negative in nature. In light of these problems, the chief would like to request funding for four additional officers, two assigned to new programs and two to alleviate the overload on his current staff. He would also like to begin limiting overtime to 10 hours per week for each officer.

Discussion Questions

1. Which variations in demand for police services should be considered in an aggregate plan for resources? Which variations can be accomplished with short-term scheduling adjustments?
2. Evaluate the current staffing plan. What does it cost? Are 26 officers sufficient to handle the normal workload?
3. What would be the additional cost of the chief's proposal? How would you suggest that he justify his request?
4. How much does it currently cost the college to provide police services for football games? What would be the pros and cons of completely subcontracting this work to outside law enforcement agencies?
5. Propose other alternatives.

*This integrated case study runs throughout the text. Other issues facing Southwestern's football expansion include: (A) managing the stadium project (Chapter 3); (B) forecasting game attendance (Chapter 4); (C) quality of facilities (Chapter 6); (D) break-even analysis for food services (Supplement 7 Web site); (E) where to locate the new stadium (Chapter 8 Web site); and (F) inventory planning of football programs (Chapter 12 Web site).

▶ Andrew-Carter, Inc.

Andrew-Carter, Inc. (A-C), is a major Canadian producer and distributor of outdoor lighting fixtures. Its products are distributed throughout South and North America and have been in high demand for several years. The company operates three plants to manufacture fixtures and distribute them to five distribution centers (warehouses).

During the present global slowdown, A-C has seen a major drop in demand for its products, largely because the housing market has declined. Based on the forecast of interest rates, the head of operations feels that demand for housing and thus for A-C's products will remain depressed for the foreseeable future. A-C is considering closing one of its plants, as it is now operating with a forecast excess capacity of 34,000 units per week. The forecast weekly demands for the coming year are as follows:

Warehouse 1	9,000 units
Warehouse 2	13,000
Warehouse 3	11,000
Warehouse 4	15,000
Warehouse 5	8,000

Plant capacities, in units per week, are as follows:

Plant 1, regular time	27,000 units
Plant 1, on overtime	7,000
Plant 2, regular time	20,000
Plant 2, on overtime	5,000
Plant 3, regular time	25,000
Plant 3, on overtime	6,000

If A-C shuts down any plants, its weekly costs will change, because fixed costs will be lower for a nonoperating plant. Table 1 shows production costs at each plant, both variable at regular time and

▼ TABLE 1 Andrew-Carter, Inc., Variable Costs and Fixed Production Costs per Week

Plant	Variable Cost (per unit)	Fixed Cost per Week Operating	Fixed Cost per Week Not Operating
1, regular time	$2.80	$14,000	$6,000
1, overtime	3.52		
2, regular time	2.78	12,000	5,000
2, overtime	3.48		
3, regular time	2.72	15,000	7,500
3, overtime	3.42		

Source: Reprinted by permission of Professor Michael Ballot, University of the Pacific, Stockton, CA.

▼ TABLE 2 Andrew-Carter, Inc., Distribution Costs per Unit

From Plants	To Distribution Centers W1	W2	W3	W4	W5
1	$.50	$.44	$.49	$.46	$.56
2	.40	.52	.50	.56	.57
3	.56	.53	.51	.54	.35

overtime, and fixed when operating and shut down. Table 2 shows distribution costs from each plant to each distribution center.

Discussion Questions

1. Evaluate the various configurations of operating and closed plants that will meet weekly demand. Determine which configuration minimizes total costs.
2. Discuss the implications of closing a plant.

Active Model Exercise

ACTIVE MODEL 13.1 This example contains a 6-month aggregate planning problem, illustrated in Example 2 in the text, using a leveling strategy. You can adjust the base level of daily production during the month, the amount of daily overtime, and the amount of subcontracting to simulate the impact of different aggregate plans. It is illustrated at **www.myomlab.com** or **www.pearsonhighered.com/heizer.**

Main Heading	Review Material	PEARSON myomlab
THE PLANNING PROCESS (pp. 410–411)	■ **Aggregate planning** (or **aggregate scheduling**)—An approach to determine the quantity and timing of production for the intermediate future (usually 3 to 18 months ahead) Usually, *the objective of aggregate planning is to meet forecasted demand while minimizing cost over the planning period.* Four things are needed for aggregate planning: 1. A logical overall unit for measuring sales and output 2. A forecast of demand for a reasonable intermediate planning period in these aggregate terms 3. A method for determining the relevant costs 4. A model that combines forecasts and costs so that scheduling decisions can be made for the planning period ■ **Scheduling decisions**—Plans that match production to changes in demand.	
THE NATURE OF AGGREGATE PLANNING (pp. 411–412)	An aggregate plan looks at production *in the aggregate* (a family of products), not as a product-by-product breakdown. ■ **Disaggregation**—The process of breaking an aggregate plan into greater detail. ■ **Master production schedule**—A timetable that specifies what is to be made and when.	
AGGREGATE PLANNING STRATEGIES (pp. 412–415)	The basic aggregate planning capacity (production) options are: • *Changing inventory levels* • *Varying workforce size by hiring or layoffs* • *Varying production rates through overtime or idle time* • *Subcontracting* • *Using part-time workers* The basic aggregate planning demand options are: • *Influencing demand* • *Back ordering during high-demand periods* • *Counterseasonal product and service mixing* ■ **Chase strategy**—A planning strategy that sets production equal to forecasted demand. Many service organizations favor the chase strategy because the inventory option is difficult or impossible to adopt. ■ **Level scheduling**—Maintaining a constant output rate, production rate, or workforce level over the planning horizon. Level scheduling works well when demand is reasonably stable. ■ **Mixed strategy**—A planning strategy that uses two or more controllable variables to set a feasible production plan.	
METHODS FOR AGGREGATE PLANNING (pp. 415–422)	■ **Graphical techniques**—Aggregate planning techniques that work with a few variables at a time to allow planners to compare projected demand with existing capacity. Graphical techniques are trial-and-error approaches that do not guarantee an optimal production plan, but they require only limited computations. The five steps of the graphical method are: 1. Determine the demand in each period. 2. Determine capacity for regular time, overtime, and subcontracting each period. 3. Find labor costs, hiring and layoff costs, and inventory holding costs. 4. Consider company policy that may apply to the workers or to stock levels. 5. Develop alternative plans and examine their total costs. A *cumulative* graph displays visually how the forecast deviates from the average requirements. ■ **Transportation method of linear programming**—A way of solving for the optimal solution to an aggregate planning problem. The transportation method of linear programming is flexible in that it can specify regular and overtime production in each time period, the number of units to be subcontracted, extra shifts, and the inventory carryover from period to period. Transportation problems require that supply equals demand, so when it does not, a dummy column called "unused capacity" may be added. Costs of not using capacity are zero.	Problems: 13.2–13.19 Virtual Office Hours for Solved Problems: 13.1, 13.2 **ACTIVE MODEL 13.1**

Main Heading	Review Material	PEARSON myomlab

Demand requirements are shown in the bottom row of a transportation table. Total capacity available (supply) is shown in the far right column.

In general, to complete a transportation table, allocate as much production as you can to a cell with the smallest cost, without exceeding the unused capacity in that row or demand in that column. If there is still some demand left in that row, allocate as much as you can to the next-lowest-cost cell. You then repeat this process for periods 2 and 3 (and beyond, if necessary). When you are finished, the sum of all your entries in a row must equal total row capacity, and the sum of all entries in a column must equal the demand for that period.

The transportation method was originally formulated by E. H. Bowman in 1956. The transportation method does not work when nonlinear or negative factors are introduced.

- **Management coefficients model**—A formal planning model built around a manager's experience and performance.

AGGREGATE PLANNING IN SERVICES
(pp. 422–425)

Successful techniques for controlling the cost of labor in service firms include:
1. Accurate scheduling of labor-hours to ensure quick response to customer demand.
2. An on-call labor resource that can be added or deleted to meet unexpected demand.
3. Flexibility of individual worker skills that permits reallocation of available labor.
4. Flexibility in rate of output or hours of work to meet changing demand.

YIELD MANAGEMENT
(pp. 425–428)

- **Yield** (or **revenue**) **management**—Capacity decisions that determine the allocation of resources to maximize profit or yield.

Organizations that have *perishable inventory*, such as airlines, hotels, car rental agencies, and cruise lines, have the following shared characteristics that make yield management of interest:
1. Service or product can be sold in advance of consumption.
2. Demand fluctuates.
3. The resource (capacity) is relatively fixed.
4. Demand can be segmented.
5. Variable costs are low, and fixed costs are high.

To make yield management work, the company needs to manage three issues:
1. *Multiple pricing structures.*
2. *Forecasts of the use and duration of the use.*
3. *Changes in demand.*

Self Test

- **Before taking the self-test,** refer to the learning objectives listed at the beginning of the chapter and the key terms listed at the end of the chapter.

LO1. Aggregate planning is concerned with determining the quantity and timing of production in the:
   a) short term.
   b) intermediate term.
   c) long term.
   d) all of the above.

LO2. Aggregate planning deals with a number of constraints. These typically are:
   a) job assignments, job ordering, dispatching, and overtime help.
   b) part-time help, weekly scheduling, and SKU production scheduling.
   c) subcontracting, employment levels, inventory levels, and capacity.
   d) capital investment, expansion or contracting capacity, and R&D.
   e) facility location, production budgeting, overtime, and R&D.

LO3. Which of the following is not one of the graphical method steps?
   a) Determine the demand in each period.
   b) Determine capacity for regular time, overtime, and subcontracting each period.
   c) Find labor costs, hiring and layoff costs, and inventory holding costs.
   d) Construct the transportation table.
   e) Consider company policy that may apply to the workers or stock levels.
   f) Develop alternative plans and examine their total costs.

LO4. When might a dummy column be added to a transportation table?
   a) When supply does not equal demand
   b) When overtime is greater than regular time
   c) When subcontracting is greater than regular time
   d) When subcontracting is greater than regular time plus overtime
   e) When production needs to spill over into a new period

LO5. Yield management requires management to deal with:
   a) multiple pricing structures.
   b) changes in demand.
   c) forecasts of use.
   d) forecasts of duration of use.
   e) all of the above.

Answers: LO1. b; **LO2.** c; **LO3.** d; **LO4.** a; **LO5.** e.

14 Material Requirements Planning (MRP) and ERP

Chapter Outline

Dependent Demand

Dependent Inventory Model Requirements

MRP Structure

MRP Management

Lot-Sizing Techniques

Extensions of MRP

MRP in Services

Enterprise Resource Planning (ERP)

Ethical Dilemma
Discussion Questions
Problems
Case Studies: Hill's Automotive, Inc.;
    MRP at Wheeled Coach
Active Model Exercise
Rapid Review

The standard way to determine requirements for dependent demand is a material requirements planning (MRP) system. Dependent demand means that the demand for one item is related to the demand for another item. Once an item is scheduled, the demand for all of its components is known—they are *dependent* upon the scheduled item. For any item for which a schedule can be established, dependent techniques such as MRP are used.

MRP systems have evolved as a basis for enterprise resource planning (ERP) systems. ERP is an information system for identifying and planning for the enterprise-wide resources needed to purchase, make, ship, and account for customer orders.

BEFORE COMING TO CLASS, READ CHAPTER 14 IN YOUR TEXT AND ANSWER THESE QUESTIONS.

1. In a product structure tree, what is a parent and what is a child? _____

_____

_____

2. What is a gross requirements plan? _____

_____

3. What is a net requirements plan? _____

_____

4. What are four ways to determine lot sizes in an MRP system? _____

_____

_____

5. What is MRP II? _____

_____

6. What is a closed loop MRP? _____

_____

7. What is enterprise resource planning (ERP)? _____

_____

DEPENDENT DEMAND (See Flexible Version p. 436)

DEPENDENT INVENTORY MODEL REQUIREMENTS

(See Flexible Version pp. 436–441)

1. Master Production Schedule (MPS)
2. Bill-of-Material
3. Accurate Inventory Records
4. Purchase Orders Outstanding
5. Lead Time

MRP STRUCTURE (See Flexible Version pp. 441–445)

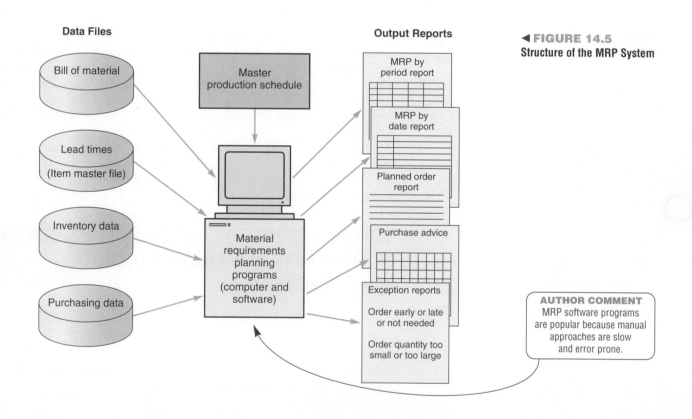

◀ FIGURE 14.5
Structure of the MRP System

AUTHOR COMMENT
MRP software programs are popular because manual approaches are slow and error prone.

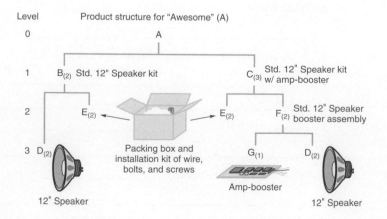

A Sample Product Structure Tree

PRACTICE PROBLEM 14.1 ■ Material Structure Tree

The Hunicut and Hallock Corporation makes two versions of the same file cabinet: the TOL (top-of-the-line) five-drawer file cabinet and the HQ (high-quality) five-drawer file cabinet.

The TOL and HQ use the same cabinet frame and the same locking mechanism. The drawer assemblies are different, although both use the same drawer frame assembly. The drawer assemblies for the TOL cabinet use sliding assemblies that require *four* bearings per side, whereas the HQ sliding assemblies require *only two* bearings per side. (These bearings are identical for both cabinet types.) Hunicut and Hallock needs to assemble 100 TOL and 300 HQ file cabinets in week 10. No current stock exists.

Develop a material structure tree for the TOL and the HQ file cabinets.

PRACTICE PROBLEM 14.2 ■ Gross Material Requirements Plan

Develop a gross material requirements plan for the TOL and HQ cabinets in the previous example.

Gross Requirements Plan

Week	1	2	3	4	5	6	7	8	9	10
TOL										
HQ										

PRACTICE PROBLEM 14.3 ■ Net Material Requirements Plan

Develop a net material requirements plan for the TOL and HQ file cabinets in the previous problems, assuming a current on-hand finished goods inventory of 100 TOL cabinets. The lead times are:

Painting and final assembly of both HQ and TOL require 2 weeks.
Both cabinet frames and lock assembly require 1 week for manufacturing.
Both drawer assemblies require 2 weeks for assembly.
Both sliding assemblies require 2 weeks for manufacturing.
Bearings require 2 weeks to arrive from supplier.

Answer Sheet for Practice Problem 14.3

		Week										Lead Time
		1	2	3	4	5	6	7	8	9	10	
TOL	Required date											weeks
	Order release date	None required; 100 in inventory										
HQ	Required date											weeks
	Order release date											
Cabinet frames and lock	Required date											week
	Order release date											
HQ drawer assembly	Required date											weeks
	Order release date											
Drawer frame	Required date											weeks
	Order release date											
HQ sliding assembly	Required date											weeks
	Order release date											
Bearings	Required date											weeks
	Order release date											

Scheduled receipts are:

	Quantity	In Week
Cabinet frames and lock		
HQ drawer assembly		
Drawer frame assembly		
HQ sliding assembly		
Bearings		

MRP MANAGEMENT (See Flexible Version pp. 446–447)

MRP Dynamics (See Flexible Version p. 446)

JIT (See Flexible Version pp. 446–447)

LOT-SIZING TECHNIQUES (See Flexible Version pp. 447–451)

1. Lot-for-Lot (See Flexible Version pp. 447–448)

PRACTICE PROBLEM 14.4 ■ Lot-for-Lot

If the TOL file cabinet has a gross material requirements plan as shown below and no inventory, and 2 weeks lead time is required for assembly, what are the order release dates and lot sizes when lot sizing is determined using lot-for-lot? Use a holding cost of $2 and a setup cost of $20, and assume no initial inventory.

Gross Material Requirements Plan

Week	1	2	3	4	5	6	7	8	9	10
TOL			50		100		50			100

2. Economic Order Quantity (See Flexible Version pp. 448–449)

PRACTICE PROBLEM 14.5 ■ EOQ

If the TOL file cabinet has a gross material requirements plan as shown below and no inventory, and 2 weeks of lead time is required for assembly, what are the order release dates and lot sizes when lot sizing is determined by EOQ (economic order quantity)? Use a holding cost of $2 and a setup cost of $20, and assume no initial inventory.

Gross Material Requirements Plan

Week	1	2	3	4	5	6	7	8	9	10
TOL			50		100		50			100

3. Part Period Balancing (See Flexible Version pp. 449–450)

PRACTICE PROBLEM 14.6 ■ Part Period Balancing

If the TOL file cabinet has a gross material requirements plan as shown below and no inventory, and 2 weeks of lead time is required for assembly, what are the order release dates and lot sizes when lot sizing is determined using PPB (part period balancing)? Use a holding cost of $2 and a setup cost of $20, and no initial inventory.

Gross Material Requirements Plan

Week	1	2	3	4	5	6	7	8	9	10
TOL			50		100		50			100

---

4. Wagner-Whiten (See Flexible Version p. 451)

EXTENSIONS OF MRP (See Flexible Version pp. 451–454)

1. MRP II

2. Closed Loop

3. Capacity Planning

MRP IN SERVICES (See Flexible Version pp. 454–455)

Restaurants

Hospitals

Hotels

Distribution Resource Planning (DRP) (See Flexible Version p. 454)

ENTERPRISE RESOURCE PLANNING (ERP)

(See Flexible Version pp. 455–458)

Advantages and Disadvantages of ERP

(See Flexible Version p. 458)

ERP in the Service Sector (See Flexible Version p. 458)

Efficient Consumer Response

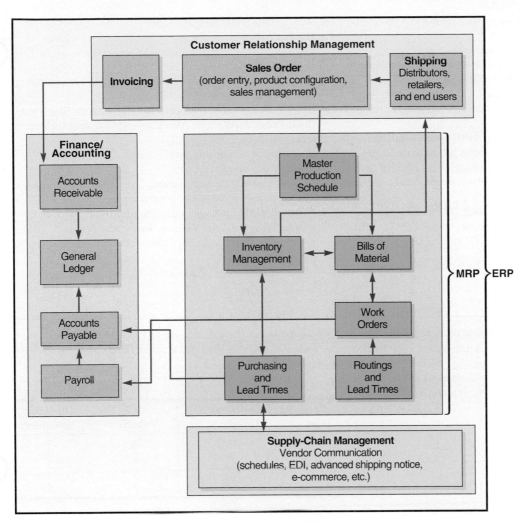

▲ **FIGURE 14.11**   **MRP and ERP Information Flows, Showing Customer Relationship Management (CRM), Supply Chain Management (SCM), and Finance/Accounting**

Other functions such as human resources are often also included in ERP systems.

Ethical Dilemma

For many months your prospective ERP customer has been analyzing the hundreds of assumptions built into the $900,000 ERP software you are selling. So far, you have knocked yourself out to try to make this sale. If the sale goes through, you will reach your yearly quota and get a nice bonus. On the other hand, loss of this sale may mean you start looking for other employment.

The accounting, human resource, supply chain, and marketing teams put together by the client have reviewed the specifications and finally recommended purchase of the software. However, as you

looked over their shoulders and helped them through the evaluation process, you began to realize that their purchasing procedures—with much of the purchasing being done at hundreds of regional stores—were not a good fit for the software. At the very least, the customizing will add $250,000 to the implementation and training cost. The team is not aware of the issue, and you know that the necessary $250,000 is not in the budget.

What do you do?

Discussion Questions

1. What is the difference between a *gross* requirements plan and a *net* requirements plan?
2. Once a material requirements plan (MRP) has been established, what other managerial applications might be found for the technique?
3. What are the similarities between MRP and DRP?

4. How does MRP II differ from MRP?
5. Which is the best lot-sizing policy for manufacturing organizations?
6. What impact does ignoring carrying cost in the allocation of stock in a DRP system have on lot sizes?

7. MRP is more than an inventory system; what additional capabilities does MRP possess?

8. What are the options for the production planner who has:
    a) scheduled more than capacity in a work center next week?
    b) a consistent lack of capacity in that work center?

9. Master schedules are expressed in three different ways depending on whether the process is continuous, a job shop, or repetitive. What are these three ways?

10. What functions of the firm affect an MRP system? How?

11. What is the rationale for (a) a phantom bill of material, (b) a planning bill of material, and (c) a pseudo bill of material?

12. Identify five specific requirements of an effective MRP system.

13. What are the typical benefits of ERP?

14. What are the distinctions between MRP, DRP, and ERP?

15. As an approach to inventory management, how does MRP differ from the approach taken in Chapter 12, dealing with economic order quantities (EOQ)?

16. What are the disadvantages of ERP?

17. Use the Web or other sources to:
    a) Find stories that highlight the advantages of an ERP system.
    b) Find stories that highlight the difficulties of purchasing, installing, or failure of an ERP system.

18. Use the Web or other sources to identify what an ERP vendor (SAP, PeopleSoft/Oracle, American Software, etc.) includes in these software modules:
    a) Customer relationship management.
    b) Supply-chain management.
    c) Product life cycle management.

19. The very structure of MRP systems suggests fixed lead times. However, many firms have moved toward JIT and kanban techniques. What are the techniques, issues, and impact of adding JIT inventory and purchasing techniques to an organization that has MRP?

Problems*

•   **14.1** You have developed the following simple product structure of items needed for your gift bag for a rush party for prospective pledges in your organization. You forecast 200 attendees. Assume that there is no inventory on hand of any of the items. Explode the bill of material. (Subscripts indicate the number of units required.)

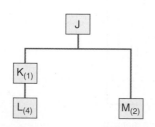

•• **14.2** You are expected to have the gift bags in Problem 14.1 ready at 5 P.M. However, you need to personalize the items (monogrammed pens, note pads, literature from the printer, etc.). The lead time is 1 hour to assemble 200 Js once the other items are prepared. The other items will take a while as well. Given the volunteers you have, the other time estimates are item K (2 hours), item L (1 hour), and item M (4 hours). Develop a time-phased assembly plan to prepare the gift bags.

•• **14.3** The demand for subassembly S is 100 units in week 7. Each unit of S requires 1 unit of T and 2 units of U. Each unit of T requires 1 unit of V, 2 units of W, and 1 unit of X. Finally, each unit of U requires 2 units of Y and 3 units of Z. One firm manufactures all items. It takes 2 weeks to make S, 1 week to make T, 2 weeks to make U, 2 weeks to make V, 3 weeks to make W, 1 week to make X, 2 weeks to make Y, and 1 week to make Z.
a) Construct a product structure. Identify all levels, parents, and components.
b) Prepare a time-phased product structure.

•• **14.4** Using the information in Problem 14.3, construct a gross material requirements plan. **Px**

•• **14.5** Using the information in Problem 14.3, construct a net material requirements plan using the following on-hand inventory. **Px**

Item	On-Hand Inventory	Item	On-Hand Inventory
S	20	W	30
T	20	X	25
U	40	Y	240
V	30	Z	40

•• **14.6** Refer again to Problems 14.3 and 14.4. In addition to 100 units of S, there is also a demand for 20 units of U, which is a component of S. The 20 units of U are needed for maintenance purposes. These units are needed in week 6. Modify the *gross material requirements plan* to reflect this change. **Px**

•• **14.7** Refer again to Problems 14.3 and 14.5. In addition to 100 units of S, there is also a demand for 20 units of U, which is a component of S. The 20 units of U are needed for maintenance purposes. These units are needed in week 6. Modify the *net material requirements plan* to reflect this change. **Px**

•• **14.8** As the production planner for Gerry Cook Products, Inc., you have been given a bill of material for a bracket that is made up of a base, two springs, and four clamps. The base is assembled from one clamp and two housings. Each clamp has one handle and one casting. Each housing has two bearings and one shaft. There is no inventory on hand.
a) Design a product structure noting the quantities for each item and show the low-level coding.
b) Determine the gross quantities needed of each item if you are to assemble 50 brackets.
c) Compute the net quantities needed if there are 25 of the base and 100 of the clamp in stock. **Px**

•• **14.9** Your boss at Gerry Cook Products, Inc., has just provided you with the schedule and lead times for the bracket in Problem 14.8. The unit is to be prepared in week 10. The lead times for the components are bracket (1 week), base (1 week), spring (1 week), clamp (1 week), housing (2 weeks), handle (1 week), casting (3 weeks), bearing (1 week), and shaft (1 week).

Lot Size	Lead Time (# of periods)	On Hand	Safety Stock	Allo- cated	Low- Level Code	Item ID		Period (week, day)							
								1	2	3	4	5	6	7	8
						Gross Requirements									
						Scheduled Receipts									
						Projected On Hand									
						Net Requirements									
						Planned Order Receipts									
						Planned Order Releases									
						Gross Requirements									
						Scheduled Receipts									
						Projected On Hand									
						Net Requirements									
						Planned Order Receipts									
						Planned Order Releases									
						Gross Requirements									
						Scheduled Receipts									
						Projected On Hand									
						Net Requirements									
						Planned Order Receipts									
						Planned Order Releases									
						Gross Requirements									
						Scheduled Receipts									
						Projected On Hand									
						Net Requirements									
						Planned Order Receipts									
						Planned Order Releases									
						Gross Requirements									
						Scheduled Receipts									
						Projected On Hand									
						Net Requirements									
						Planned Order Receipts									
						Planned Order Releases									

▲ **FIGURE 14.13** **MRP Form for Homework Problems in Chapter 14**
For several problems in this chapter, a copy of this form may be helpful.

a) Prepare the time-phased product structure for the bracket.
b) In what week do you need to start the castings? **Px**

•• **14.10**

a) Given the product structure and master production schedule (Figure 14.14 below), develop a gross requirements plan for all items.
b) Given the preceding product structure, master production schedule, and inventory status (Figure 14.14), develop a net materials requirements (planned order release) for all items. **Px**

••• **14.11** Given the following product structure, master production schedule, and inventory status (Figure 14.15 on the next page) and assuming the requirements for each BOM item is 1: (a) develop a gross requirements plan for Item C; (b) develop a net requirements plan for Item C. **Px**

•••• **14.12** Based on the data in Figure 14.15, complete a net material requirements schedule for:

a) All items (10 schedules in all), assuming the requirement for each BOM item is 1.

▼ **FIGURE 14.14** **Information for Problem 14.10**

Master Production Schedule for X1

PERIOD	7	8	9	10	11	12
Gross requirements		50		20		100

ITEM	LEAD TIME	ON HAND		ITEM	LEAD TIME	ON HAND
X1	1	50		C	1	0
B1	2	20		D	1	0
B2	2	20		E	3	10
A1	1	5				

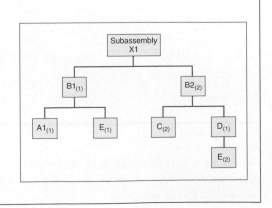

▶ **FIGURE 14.15**
Information for Problems 14.11 and 14.12

PERIOD	8	9	10	11	12
Gross requirements: A	100		50		150
Gross requirements: H		100		50	

ITEM	ON HAND	LEAD TIME	ITEM	ON HAND	LEAD TIME
A	0	1	F	75	2
B	100	2	G	75	1
C	50	2	H	0	1
D	50	1	J	100	2
E	75	2	K	100	2

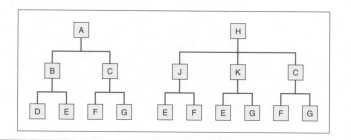

b) All 10 items, assuming the requirement for all items is 1, except B, C, and F, which require *2 each*. **Px**

••• **14.13** Electro Fans has just received an order for one thousand 20-inch fans due week 7. Each fan consists of a housing assembly, two grills, a fan assembly, and an electrical unit. The housing assembly consists of a frame, two supports, and a handle. The fan assembly consists of a hub and five blades. The electrical unit consists of a motor, a switch, and a knob. The following table gives lead times, on-hand inventory, and scheduled receipts.
a) Construct a product structure.
b) Construct a time-phased product structure.
c) Prepare a net material requirements plan. **Px**

Data Table for Problem 14.13

Component	Lead Time	On Hand Inventory	Lot Size*	Scheduled Receipt
20″ Fan	1	100	—	
Housing	1	100	—	
Frame	2	—	—	
Supports (2)	1	50	100	
Handle	1	400	500	
Grills (2)	2	200	500	
Fan Assembly	3	150	—	
Hub	1	—	—	
Blades (5)	2	—	100	
Electrical Unit	1	—	—	
Motor	1	—	—	
Switch	1	20	12	
Knob	1	—	25	200 knobs in week 2

*Lot-for-lot unless otherwise noted

••• **14.14** A part structure, lead time (weeks), and on-hand quantities for product A are shown in Figure 14.16. From the information shown, generate:

a) An indented bill of material for product A (see Figure 5.9 in Chapter 5 as an example of a BOM).
b) Net requirements for each part to produce 10 As in week 8 using lot-for-lot. **Px**

••• **14.15** You are product planner for product A (in Problem 14.14 and Figure 14.16). The field service manager, Al Trostel, has just called and told you that the requirements for B and F should each be increased by 10 units for his repair requirements in the field.
a) Prepare a list showing the quantity of each part required to produce the requirements for the service manager *and* the production request of 10 Bs and Fs.
b) Prepare a net requirement plan by date for the new requirements (for both production and field service), assuming that the field service manager wants his 10 units of B and F in week 6 and the 10 production units of A in week 8. **Px**

••• **14.16** You have just been notified via fax that the lead time for component G of product A (Problem 14.15 and Figure 14.16) has been increased to 4 weeks.
a) Which items have changed and why?
b) What are the implications for the production plan?
c) As production planner, what can you do? **Px**

Data Table for Problems 14.17 through 14.19*

Period	1	2	3	4	5	6	7	8	9	10	11	12
Gross requirements	30		40		30	70	20		10	80		50

*Holding cost = $2.50/unit/week; setup cost = $150; lead time = 1 week; beginning inventory = 40.

••• **14.17** Develop a lot-for-lot solution and calculate total relevant costs for the data in the preceding table. **Px**

••• **14.18** Develop an EOQ solution and calculate total relevant costs for the data in the preceding table. Stockout costs equal $10 per unit. **Px**

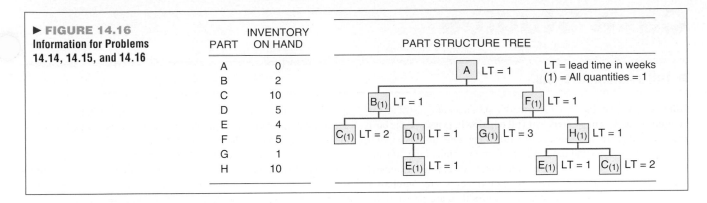

► FIGURE 14.16
Information for Problems 14.14, 14.15, and 14.16

PART	INVENTORY ON HAND
A	0
B	2
C	10
D	5
E	4
F	5
G	1
H	10

••• **14.19** Develop a PPB solution and calculate total relevant costs for the data in the table on page 14-10. P_X

••• **14.20** Using the gross requirements schedule in Examples 4, 5, and 6 in the text, prepare an alternative ordering system that always orders 100 units the week prior to a shortage (a fixed order quantity of 100) with the same costs as in the example (setup at $100 each, holding at $1 per unit per period). What is the cost of this ordering system? P_X

••• **14.21** Using the gross requirements schedule in Examples 4, 5, and 6 in the text, prepare an alternative ordering system that orders every 3 weeks for 3 weeks ahead (a periodic order quantity). Use the same costs as in the example (setup at $100 each, holding at $1 per unit per period). What is the cost of this ordering system? P_X

••• **14.22** Using the gross requirements schedule in Examples 4, 5, and 6 in the text, prepare an alternative ordering system of your own design that uses the same cost as in the example (setup at $100 each, holding at $1 per unit per period). Can you do better than the costs shown in the text? What is the cost of your ordering system? P_X

••• **14.23** Katharine Hepburn, Inc., has received the following orders:

Period	1	2	3	4	5	6	7	8	9	10
Order size	0	40	30	40	10	70	40	10	30	60

The entire fabrication for these units is scheduled on one machine. There are 2,250 usable minutes in a week, and each unit will take 65 minutes to complete. Develop a capacity plan, using lot splitting, for the 10-week time period.

••• **14.24** David Jurman, Ltd., has received the following orders:

Period	1	2	3	4	5	6	7	8	9	10
Order size	60	30	10	40	70	10	40	30	40	0

The entire fabrication for these units is scheduled on one machine. There are 2,250 usable minutes in a week, and each unit will take 65 minutes to complete. Develop a capacity plan, using lot splitting, for the 10-week time period.

•• **14.25** Heather Adams, production manager for a Colorado exercise equipment manufacturer, needs to schedule an order for 50 UltimaSteppers, which are to be shipped in week 8. Subscripts indicate quantity required for each parent. Assume lot-for-lot ordering. In the next column is information about the steppers:

Item	Lead time	On-Hand Inventory	Components
Stepper	2	20	$A_{(1)}, B_{(3)}, C_{(2)}$
A	1	10	$D_{(1)}, F_{(2)}$
B	2	30	$E_{(1)}, F_{(3)}$
C	3	10	$D_{(2)}, E_{(3)}$
D	1	15	
E	2	5	
F	2	20	

a) Develop a product structure for Heather.
b) Develop a time-phased structure.
c) Develop a net material requirements plan for F. P_X

•••• **14.26** You are scheduling production of your popular Rustic Coffee Table. The table requires a top, four legs, $\frac{1}{8}$ gallon of stain, $\frac{1}{16}$ gallon of glue, 2 short braces between the legs and 2 long braces between the legs, and a brass cap that goes on the bottom of each leg. You have 100 gallons of glue in inventory, but none of the other components. All items except the brass caps, stain, and glue are ordered on a lot-for-lot basis. The caps are purchased in quantities of 1,000, stain and glue by the gallon. Lead time is 1 day for each item. Schedule the order releases necessary to produce 640 coffee tables on days 5 and 6, and 128 on days 7 and 8. P_X

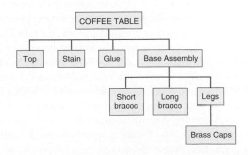

•••• **14.27** Using the data for the coffee table in Problem 14.26, build a labor schedule when the labor standard for each top is 2 labor hours; each leg including brass cap installation requires $\frac{1}{4}$ hour, as does each pair of braces. Base assembly requires 1 labor-hour, and final assembly requires 2 labor-hours. What is the total number of labor-hours required each day, and how many employees are needed each day at 8 hours per day?

► **Refer to** myomlab ⓞ **for these additional homework problems: 14.28–14.32**

Case Studies

▶ Hill's Automotive, Inc.

Hill's Automotive, Inc., is an aftermarket producer and distributor of automotive replacement parts. Art Hill has slowly expanded the business, which began as a supplier of hard-to-get auto air-conditioning units for classic cars and hot rods. The firm has limited manufacturing capability, but a state-of-the-art MRP system and extensive inventory and assembly facilities. Components are purchased, assembled, and repackaged. Among its products are private-label air-conditioning, carburetors, and ignition kits. The downturn in the economy, particularly the company's discretionary segment, has put downward pressure on volume and margins. Profits have fallen considerably. In addition, customer service levels have declined, with late deliveries now exceeding 25% of orders. And to make matters worse, customer returns have been rising at a rate of 3% per month.

Wally Hopp, vice president of sales, claims that most of the problem lies with the assembly department. He says that although the firm has accurate bills of materials, indicating what goes into each product, it is not producing the proper mix of the product. He also believes the firm has poor quality control and low productivity, and as a result its costs are too high.

Melanie Thompson, treasurer, believes that problems are due to investing in the wrong inventories. She thinks that marketing has too many options and products. Melanie also thinks that purchasing department buyers have been hedging their inventories and requirements with excess purchasing commitments.

The assembly manager, Kalinga Jagoda, says, "The symptom is that we have a lot of parts in inventory, but no place to assemble them in the production schedule. When we have the right part, it is not very good, but we use it anyway to meet the schedule."

Marshall Fisher, manager of purchasing, has taken the stance that purchasing has not let Hill's Automotive down. He has stuck by his old suppliers, used historical data to determine requirements, maintained what he views as excellent prices from suppliers, and evaluated new sources of supply with a view toward lowering cost. Where possible, Marshall reacted to the increased pressure for profitability by emphasizing low cost and early delivery.

Discussion Questions

1. Prepare a plan for Art Hill that gets the firm back on a course toward improved profitability. Be sure to identify the symptoms, the problems, and the specific changes you would implement.
2. Explain how MRP plays a role in this plan.

▶ MRP at Wheeled Coach
Video Case

Wheeled Coach, the world's largest manufacturer of ambulances, builds thousands of different and constantly changing configurations of its products. The custom nature of its business means lots of options and special designs—and a potential scheduling and inventory nightmare. Wheeled Coach addressed such problems, and succeeded in solving a lot of them, with an MRP system (described in the *Global Company Profile* that opens this chapter in the text). As with most MRP installations, however, solving one set of problems uncovers a new set.

One of the new issues that had to be addressed by plant manager Lynn Whalen was newly discovered excess inventory. Managers discovered a substantial amount of inventory that was not called for in any finished products. Excess inventory was evident because of the new level of inventory accuracy required by the MRP system. The other reason was a new series of inventory reports generated by the IBM MAPICS MRP system purchased by Wheeled Coach. One of those reports indicates where items are used and is known as the "Where Used" report. Interestingly, many inventory items were not called out on bills-of-material (BOMs) for any current products. In some cases, the reason some parts were in the stockroom remained a mystery.

The discovery of this excess inventory led to renewed efforts to ensure that the BOMs were accurate. With substantial work, BOM accuracy increased and the number of engineering change notices (ECNs) decreased. Similarly, purchase-order accuracy, with regard to both part numbers and quantities ordered, was improved. Additionally, receiving department and stockroom accuracy went up, all helping to maintain schedule, costs, and ultimately, shipping dates and quality.

Eventually, Lynn Whalen concluded that the residual amounts of excess inventory were the result, at least in part, of rapid changes in ambulance design and technology. Another source was customer changes made after specifications had been determined and materials ordered. This latter excess occurs because, even though Wheeled Coach's own throughput time is only 17 days, many of the items that it purchases require much longer lead times.

Discussion Questions*

1. Why is accurate inventory such an important issue at Wheeled Coach?
2. Why does Wheeled Coach have excess inventory, and what kind of a plan would you suggest for dealing with it?
3. Be specific in your suggestions for reducing inventory and how to implement them.

*You may wish to view the video that accompanies this case before answering the questions.

Active Model Exercise

ACTIVE MODEL 14.1 This example allows you to input an 8 period forecast, lead-time, inventory on hand, multiple of the lot size and minimum lot for up to 7 items. From this data, a Material Requirements Plan for scheduled order releases is generated. This Active Model permits a simulation of Examples 1-3 in the text. It is illustrated at **www.myomlab.com** or **www.pearsonhighered. com/heizer**.

Main Heading	Review Material	
DEPENDENT DEMAND (p. 436)	Demand for items is *dependent* when the relationship between the items can be determined. For any product, all components of that product are dependent demand items. ■ **Material requirements planning (MRP)**—A dependent demand technique that uses a bill-of-material, inventory, expected receipts, and a master production schedule to determine material requirements.	**VIDEO 14.1** MRP at Wheeled Coach Ambulances
DEPENDENT INVENTORY MODEL REQUIREMENTS (pp. 436–441)	Dependent inventory models require that the operations manager know the: (1) Master production schedule; (2) Specifications or bill of material; (3) Inventory availability; (4) Purchase orders outstanding; and (5) Lead times ■ **Master production schedule (MPS)**—A timetable that specifies what is to be made and when. The MPS is a statement of *what is to be produced*, not a forecast of demand. ■ **Bill of material (BOM)**—A listing of the components, their description, and the quantity of each required to make one unit of a product. Items above any level in a BOM are called *parents*; items below any level are called *components*, or *children*. The top level in a BOM is the 0 level. ■ **Modular bills**—Bills of material organized by major subassemblies or by product options. ■ **Planning bills (or kits)**—A material grouping created in order to assign an artificial parent to a bill of material; also called "pseudo" bills. ■ **Phantom bills of material**—Bills of material for components, usually subassemblies, that exist only temporarily; they are never inventoried. ■ **Low-level coding**—A number that identifies items at the lowest level at which they occur. ■ **Lead time**—In purchasing systems, the time between recognition of the need for an order and receiving it; in production systems, it is the order, wait, move, queue, setup, and run times for each component. When a bill of material is turned on its side and modified by adding lead times for each component, it is called a *time-phased product structure*.	Problems: 14.1, 14.3 Virtual Office Hours for Solved Problem: 14.1
MRP STRUCTURE (pp. 441–445)	■ **Gross material requirements plan**—A schedule that shows the total demand for an item (prior to subtraction of on-hand inventory and scheduled receipts) and (1) when it must be ordered from suppliers, or (2) when production must be started to meet its demand by a particular date. ■ **Net material requirements**—The result of adjusting gross requirements for inventory on hand and scheduled receipts. ■ **Planned order receipt**—The quantity planned to be received at a future date. ■ **Planned order release**—The scheduled date for an order to be released. Net requirements = Gross requirements + Allocations − (On hand + Scheduled receipts)	Problems: 14.2, 14.4–14.8 Virtual Office Hours for Solved Problem: 14.2 **ACTIVE MODEL 14.1**
MRP MANAGEMENT (pp. 446–447)	■ **System nervousness**—Frequent changes in an MRP system. ■ **Time fences**—A means for allowing a segment of the master schedule to be designated as "not to be rescheduled." ■ **Pegging**—In material requirements planning systems, tracing upward the bill of material from the component to the parent item. Four approaches for integrating MRP and JIT are (1) finite capacity scheduling, (2) small buckets, (3) balanced flow, and (4) supermarkets. ■ **Buckets**—Time units in a material requirements planning system. Finite capacity scheduling (FCS) considers department and machine capacity. FCS provides the precise scheduling needed for rapid material movement. ■ **Bucketless system**—Time-phased data are referenced using dated records rather than defined time periods, or buckets. ■ **Back flush**—A system to reduce inventory balances by deducting everything in the bill of material on completion of the unit. ■ **Supermarket**—An inventory area that holds common items that are replenished by a kanban system.	
LOT-SIZING TECHNIQUES (pp. 447–451)	■ **Lot-sizing decision**—The process of, or techniques used in, determining lot size. ■ **Lot-for-lot**—A lot-sizing technique that generates exactly what is required to meet the plan. ■ **Part period balancing (PPB)**—An inventory ordering technique that balances setup and holding costs by changing the lot size to reflect requirements of the next lot size in the future.	Problems: 14.17–14.22

Main Heading	Review Material
	■ **Economic part period (EPP)**—A period of time when the ratio of setup cost to holding cost is equal. ■ **Wagner-Whitin procedure**—A technique for lot-size computation that assumes a finite time horizon beyond which there are no additional net requirements to arrive at an ordering strategy. In general, the lot-for-lot approach should be used whenever low-cost deliveries can be achieved.
EXTENSIONS OF MRP (pp. 451–454)	■ **Material requirements planning II (MRP II)**—A system that allows, with MRP in place, inventory data to be augmented by other resource variables; in this case, MRP becomes *material resource planning*. ■ **Closed-loop MRP system**—A system that provides feedback to the capacity plan, master production schedule, and production plan so planning can be kept valid at all times. ■ **Load report**—A report for showing the resource requirements in a work center for all work currently assigned there as well as all planned and expected orders. Tactics for smoothing the load and minimizing the impact of changed lead time include: *Overlapping*, *Operations splitting*, and *Order* or *lot splitting*.
MRP IN SERVICES (pp. 454–455)	■ **Distribution resource planning (DRP)**—A time-phased stock-replenishment plan for all levels of a distribution network.
ENTERPRISE RESOURCE PLANNING (ERP) (pp. 455–458)	■ **Enterprise resource planning (ERP)**—An information system for identifying and planning the enterprise-wide resources needed to take, make, ship, and account for customer orders. In an ERP system, data are entered only once into a common, complete, and consistent database shared by all applications. ■ **Efficient consumer response (ECR)**—Supply-chain management systems in the grocery industry that tie sales to buying, to inventory, to logistics, and to production.

Self Test

■ **Before taking the self-test,** refer to the learning objectives listed at the beginning of the chapter and the key terms listed at the end of the chapter.

LO1. In a product structure diagram:
  a) parents are found only at the top level of the diagram.
  b) parents are found at every level in the diagram.
  c) children are found at every level of the diagram except the top level.
  d) all items in the diagrams are both parents and children.
  e) all of the above.

LO2. The difference between a gross material requirements plan (gross MRP) and a net material requirements plan (net MRP) is:
  a) the gross MRP may not be computerized, but the net MRP must be computerized.
  b) the gross MRP includes consideration of the inventory on hand, whereas the net MRP doesn't include the inventory consideration.
  c) the net MRP includes consideration of the inventory on hand, whereas the gross MRP doesn't include the inventory consideration.
  d) the gross MRP doesn't take taxes into account, whereas the net MRP includes the tax considerations.
  e) the net MRP is only an estimate, whereas the gross MRP is used for actual production scheduling.

LO3. Net requirements =
  a) Gross requirements + Allocations − On-hand inventory + Scheduled receipts.
  b) Gross requirements − Allocations − On-hand inventory − Scheduled receipts.

  c) Gross requirements − Allocations − On-hand inventory + Scheduled receipts.
  d) Gross requirements + Allocations − On-hand inventory − Scheduled receipts.

LO4. A lot-sizing procedure that assumes a finite time horizon beyond which there are no additional net requirements is:
  a) Wagner-Whitin algorithm.   b) part period balancing.
  c) economic order quantity.   d) all of the above.

LO5. MRP II stands for:
  a) material resource planning.
  b) management requirements planning.
  c) management resource planning.
  d) material revenue planning.
  e) material risk planning.

LO6. A(n) _____ MRP system provides information to the capacity plan, to the master production schedule, and ultimately to the production plan.
  a) dynamic   b) closed-loop
  c) continuous   d) retrospective
  e) introspective

LO7. Which system extends MRP II to tie in customers and suppliers?
  a) MRP III   b) JIT
  c) IRP   d) ERP
  e) Enhanced MRP II

Answers: **LO1.** c; **LO2.** c; **LO3.** d; **LO4.** a; **LO5.** a; **LO6.** b; **LO7.** d.

15 Short-Term Scheduling

Chapter Outline

The Importance of Short-Term Scheduling

Scheduling Issues

Scheduling Process-Focused Facilities

Loading Jobs

Sequencing Jobs

Finite Capacity Scheduling (FCS)

Scheduling Repetitive Facilities

Scheduling Services

Ethical Dilemma

Discussion Questions

Problems

Case Studies: Old Oregon Wood Store;
*   Scheduling at Hard Rock Cafe*

Active Model Exercise

Rapid Review

Scheduling involves the timing of operations to achieve the efficient movement of units through a system. This chapter addresses the issues of short-term scheduling in (1) process-focused, (2) repetitive, and (3) service environments. Process-focused facilities are production systems in which products are made to order; scheduling tasks in them is complex. There are several aspects and approaches to scheduling, loading, and sequencing of jobs, including Gantt charts, the assignment method of scheduling, priority rules, and Johnson's rule for sequencing.

Scheduling in service systems generally differs from scheduling in manufacturing systems. This leads to the use of appointment systems; first-come, first-served systems; and reservation systems, as well as to heuristics and linear programming approaches.

BEFORE COMING TO CLASS, READ CHAPTER 15 IN YOUR TEXT AND ANSWER THESE QUESTIONS.

1. How does a short-term schedule relate to a master schedule? _____

_____

2. How are Gantt charts used? _____

_____

3. What is the "assignment method"? _____

_____

4. Name five priority rules for sequencing. _____

_____

5. What is Johnson's rule? _____

_____

6. What is finite capacity scheduling? _____

_____

7. What is cyclical scheduling? _____

_____

THE IMPORTANCE OF SHORT-TERM SCHEDULING

(See Flexible Version p. 468)

SCHEDULING ISSUES (See Flexible Version pp. 468–471)

Capacity Planning
(Long term; years)
Changes in Facilities
Changes in Equipment
See Chapter 7 and Supplement 7

Capacity Plan for New Facilities
Adjust capacity to the demand suggested by strategic plan

Aggregate Planning
(Intermediate term; quarterly or monthly)
Facility utilization
Personnel changes
Subcontracting
See Chapter 13

Aggregate Production Plan for All Bikes
(Determine personnel or subcontracting necessary to match aggregate demand to existing facilities/capacity)

Month	1	2
Bike Production	800	850

Master Schedule
(Intermediate term; weekly)
Material requirements planning
Disaggregate the aggregate plan
See Chapters 13 and 14

Master Production Schedule for Bike Models
(Determine weekly capacity schedule)

	Month 1				Month 2			
Week	1	2	3	4	5	6	7	8
Model 22		200		200		200		200
Model 24	100		100		150		100	
Model 26	100		100		100		100	

Short-Term Scheduling
(Short term; days, hours, minutes)
Work center loading
Job sequencing/dispatching
See this chapter

Work Assigned to Specific Personnel and Work Centers
Make finite capacity schedule by matching specific tasks to specific people and machines

Assemble Model 22 in work center 6

▲ **FIGURE 15.1**   The Relationship between Capacity Planning, Aggregate Planning, Master Schedule, and Short-Term Scheduling for a Bike Co.

Forward and Backward Scheduling (See Flexible Version p. 470)

Scheduling Criteria (See Flexible Version pp. 470–471)

SCHEDULING PROCESS-FOCUSED FACILITIES

(See Flexible Version pp. 471–472)

LOADING JOBS   (See Flexible Version pp. 472–477)

Input–Output Control   (See Flexible Version pp. 472–473)

Gantt Charts   (See Flexible Version pp. 474–475)

Assignment Method   (See Flexible Version pp. 475–477)

Steps of the Assignment Method

1.
2.
3.
4.

PRACTICE PROBLEM 15.1 ■ Assignment Problem

Assume that Susan is a sorority pledge coordinator with four jobs and only three pledges. The table below gives the expected time for each pledge to do each job.

	Job 1	Job 2	Job 3	Job 4
Alice	4	9	3	8
Barbara	7	8	2	6
Jennifer	3	4	5	7

If Susan wishes to minimize the time taken, to whom should she assign which job?

Additional Practice Problem Space

SEQUENCING JOBS (See Flexible Version pp. 478–484)

Priority Rules for Dispatching Jobs (See Flexible Version pp. 478–480)

FCFS

SPT

EDD

LPT

PRACTICE PROBLEM 15.2 ■ Job Shop Sequencing

A custom furniture shop has the following five jobs to be done, and the managers are unsure how to sequence them through the shop.

Job	Days to Finish	Date Promised (in days from today)
A	2	5
B	8	8
C	6	12
D	4	10
E	1	4

Compare the effect of the scheduling methods (a) FCFS (first come, first served), (b) EDD (earliest due date), and (c) SPT (shortest processing time).

Additional Practice Problem Space

Critical Ratio   (See Flexible Version pp. 481–482)

$$CR = \frac{\text{Time remaining}}{\text{Workdays remaining}} = \frac{\text{Due date} - \text{Today's date}}{\text{Work (lead) time remaining}}$$

PRACTICE PROBLEM 15.3 ■ Critical Ratio Rule

A firm has the following six jobs waiting to be processed:

Job	Hours to Process	Time Due
#407	2	7
#281	8	16
#306	4	4
#429	10	17
#038	5	15
#998	12	18

Develop the appropriate sequencing for these jobs using the critical ratio criteria.

Additional Practice Problem Space

Scheduling N Jobs on Two Machines: Johnson's Rule (See Flexible Version pp. 482–483)

Four Steps

1.

2.

3.

4.

PRACTICE PROBLEM 15.4 ■ Johnson's Rule

Our furniture manufacturer has the following five jobs that must go through the two work centers, varnishing and painting.

	Hours Required	
Job	Varnishing (center 1)	Painting (center 2)
R	4	5
S	17	7
T	14	12
U	9	2
V	11	6

What is the appropriate sequence for these jobs?

Additional Practice Problem Space

Limitations of Rule-Based Dispatching Systems
(See Flexible Version pp. 483–484)

FINITE CAPACITY SCHEDULING (FCS) (See Flexible Version pp. 484–485)

SCHEDULING REPETITIVE FACILITIES (See Flexible Version pp. 485–486)

Level Material Use

SCHEDULING SERVICES (See Flexible Version pp. 486–489)

Cyclical Scheduling

Practice Problem Space

Ethical Dilemma

Scheduling people to work second and third shifts (evening and "graveyard") is a problem in almost every 24-hour company. The *OM in Action* box "Scheduling Workers Who Fall Asleep Is a Killer—Literally," on page 471 in the Flexible Version, describes potentially dangerous issues on the night shift at FedEx and a nuclear power plant. Perhaps even more significantly, ergonomic data indicate the body does not respond well to significant shifts in its natural circadian rhythm of sleep. There are also significant long-run health issues with frequent changes in work and sleep cycles.

Consider yourself the manager of a nonunion steel mill that must operate 24-hour days, and where the physical demands are such that 8-hour days are preferable to 10- or 12-hour days. Your empowered employees have decided that they want to work weekly rotating

shifts. That is, they want a repeating work cycle of 1 week, 7 A.M. to 3 P.M., followed by a second week from 3 P.M. to 11 P.M., and the third week from 11 P.M. to 7 A.M. You are sure this is not a good idea in terms of both productivity and the long-term health of the employees.

If you do not accept their decision, you undermine the work empowerment program, generate a morale issue, and perhaps, more significantly, generate a few more votes for a union. What is the ethical position and what do you do?

Discussion Questions

1. What is the overall objective of scheduling?
2. List the four criteria for determining the effectiveness of a *scheduling* decision. How do these criteria relate to the four criteria for *sequencing* decisions?
3. Describe what is meant by "loading" work centers. What are the two ways work centers can be loaded? What are two techniques used in loading?
4. Name five priority sequencing rules. Explain how each works to assign jobs.
5. What are the advantages and disadvantages of the shortest processing time (SPT) rule?
6. What is a due date?
7. Explain the terms *flow time* and *lateness*.
8. Which shop-floor scheduling rule would you prefer to apply if you were the leader of the only team of experts charged with defusing several time bombs scattered throughout your building? You can see the bombs; they are of different types. You can tell how long each one will take to defuse. Discuss.
9. When is Johnson's rule best applied in job-shop scheduling?
10. State the four effectiveness measures for dispatching rules.
11. What are the steps of the assignment method of linear programming?
12. What are the advantages of level material flow?
13. What is input–output control?

Problems*

•• **15.1** Ron Satterfield's excavation company uses both Gantt scheduling charts and Gantt load charts.
a) Today, which is the end of day 7, Ron is reviewing the Gantt chart depicting these schedules:
   • Job #151 was scheduled to begin on day 3 and to take 6 days. As of now, it is 1 day ahead of schedule.
   • Job #177 was scheduled to begin on day 1 and take 4 days. It is currently on time.
   • Job #179 was scheduled to start on day 7 and take 2 days. It actually got started on day 6 and is progressing according to plan.
   • Job #211 was scheduled to begin on day 5, but missing equipment delayed it until day 6. It is progressing as expected and should take 3 days.
   • Job #215 was scheduled to begin on day 4 and take 5 days. It got started on time but has since fallen behind 2 days.
Draw the Gantt scheduling chart for the activities above.
b) Ron now wants to use a Gantt load chart to see how much work is scheduled in each of his three work teams: Able, Baker, and Charlie. Five jobs constitute the current work load for these three work teams: Job #250, requiring 48 hours and #275 requiring 32 hours for Work Team Able; Jobs #210 and #280 requiring 16 and 24 hours, respectively, for Team Baker; and Job #225, requiring 40 hours, for Team Charlie.
Prepare the Gantt load chart for these activities.

•• **15.2** First Printing and Copy Center has 4 more jobs to be scheduled, in addition to those shown in Example 3 in the chapter. Production scheduling personnel are reviewing the Gantt chart at the end of day 4.
   • Job D was scheduled to begin early on day 2 and to end on the middle of day 9. As of now (the review point after day 4), it is 2 days ahead of schedule.
   • Job E should begin on day 1 and end on day 3. It was on time.
   • Job F was to begin on day 3, but maintenance forced a delay of 1½ days. The job should now take 5 full days. It is now on schedule.

*Note: **Px** means the problem may be solved with POM for Windows and/or Excel OM.

   • Job G is a day behind schedule. It started at the beginning of day 2 and should require 6 days to complete.
Develop a Gantt schedule chart for First Printing and Copy Center.

• **15.3** The Orange Top Cab Company has a taxi waiting at each of four cabstands in Evanston, Illinois. Four customers have called and requested service. The distances, in miles, from the waiting taxis to the customers are given in the following table. Find the optimal assignment of taxis to customers so as to minimize total driving distances to the customers.

		Customer		
Cab Site	**A**	**B**	**C**	**D**
Stand 1	7	3	4	8
Stand 2	5	4	6	5
Stand 3	6	7	9	6
Stand 4	8	6	7	4

Px

• **15.4** Molly Riggs's medical testing company wishes to assign a set of jobs to a set of machines. The following table provides the production data of each machine when performing the specific job:

		Machine		
Job	**A**	**B**	**C**	**D**
1	7	9	8	10
2	10	9	7	6
3	11	5	9	6
4	9	11	5	8

a) Determine the assignment of jobs to machines that will *maximize* total production.
b) What is the total production of your assignments? **Px**

• **15.5** The Johnny Ho Manufacturing Company in Columbus, Ohio, is putting out four new electronic components. Each of Ho's four plants has the capacity to add one more product to its current line of electronic parts. The unit-manufacturing costs for producing the different parts at the four plants are shown in the accompanying table. How should Ho assign the new products to the plants to minimize manufacturing costs?

Electronic Component	Plant			
	1	2	3	4
C53	$0.10	$0.12	$0.13	$0.11
C81	0.05	0.06	0.04	0.08
D5	0.32	0.40	0.31	0.30
D44	0.17	0.14	0.19	0.15

PX

• **15.6** Claire Consultants has been entrusted with the task of evaluating a business plan that has been divided into four sections—marketing, finance, operations and human resources. Chris, Steve, Juana, and Rebecca form the evaluation team. Each of them has expertise in a certain field and tends to finish that section faster. The estimated times taken by each team member for each section have been outlined in the table below. Further information states that each of these individuals is paid $60/hour.

a) Assign each member to a different section such that Claire Consultants's overall cost is minimized.

b) What is the total cost of these assignments?

Times Taken by Team Members for Different Sections (minutes)

	Marketing	Finance	Operations	HR
Chris	80	120	125	140
Steve	20	115	145	160
Juana	40	100	85	45
Rebecca	65	35	25	75

PX

•• **15.7** The Akron Police Department has five detective squads available for assignment to five open crime cases. The chief of detectives, Paul Kuzdrall, wishes to assign the squads so that the total time to conclude the cases is minimized. The average number of days, based on past performance, for each squad to complete each case is as follows:

Squad	Case				
	A	B	C	D	E
1	14	7	3	7	27
2	20	7	12	6	30
3	10	3	4	5	21
4	8	12	7	12	21
5	13	25	24	26	8

Each squad is composed of different types of specialists, and whereas one squad may be very effective in certain types of cases, it may be almost useless in others.

a) Solve the problem by using the assignment method.

b) Assign the squads to the above cases, but with the constraint that squad 5 cannot work on case E because of a conflict. **PX**

• **15.8** Tigers Sports Club has to select four separate co-ed doubles teams to participate in an inter-club table tennis tournament. The pre-selection results in the selection of a group of four men—Raul, Jack, Gray, and Ajay—and four women—Barbara, Dona, Stella, and Jackie. Now, the task ahead lies in pairing these men and women in the best fashion. The table below shows a matrix that has been designed for this purpose, indicating how each of the men complements the game of each of the women. A higher score indicates a higher degree of compatibility in the games of the two individuals concerned. Find the best pairs.

Game Compatibility Matrix

	Barbara	Dona	Stella	Jackie
Raul	30	20	10	40
Jack	70	10	60	70
Gray	40	20	50	40
Ajay	60	70	30	90

PX

••• **15.9** James Gross, chairman of the College of Oshkosh's business department, needs to assign professors to courses next semester. As a criterion for judging who should teach each course, Professor Gross reviews the past 2 years' teaching evaluations (which were filled out by students). Since each of the four professors taught each of the four courses at one time or another during the 2-year period, Gross is able to record a course rating for each instructor. These ratings are shown in the following table.

a) Find the assignment of professors to courses to maximize the overall teaching rating.

b) Assign the professors to the courses, with the exception that Professor Fisher cannot teach Statistics. **PX**

Professor	Course			
	Statistics	Management	Finance	Economics
W. W. Fisher	90	65	95	40
D. Golhar	70	60	80	75
Z. Hug	85	40	80	60
N. K. Rustagi	55	80	65	55

•• **15.10** The following jobs are waiting to be processed at the same machine center. Jobs are logged as they arrive:

Job	Due Date	Duration (days)
A	313	8
B	312	16
C	325	40
D	314	5
E	314	3

In what sequence would the jobs be ranked according to the following decision rules: (a) FCFS, (b) EDD, (c) SPT, and (d) LPT? All dates are specified as manufacturing planning calendar days. Assume that all jobs arrive on day 275. Which decision is best and why? **PX**

• **15.11** The following 5 overhaul jobs are waiting to be processed at Avianic's Engine Repair Inc. These jobs were logged as they arrived. All dates are specified as planning calendar days. Assume that all jobs arrived on day 180; today's date is 200.

Job	Due Date	Remaining Time (days)
103	214	10
205	223	7
309	217	11
412	219	5
517	217	15

Using the critical ratio scheduling rule, in what sequence would the jobs be processed? **Px**

•• **15.12** An Alabama lumberyard has four jobs on order, as shown in the following table. Today is day 205 on the yard's schedule.

Job	Due Date	Remaining Time (days)
A	212	6
B	209	3
C	208	3
D	210	8

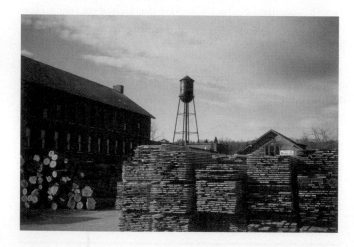

In what sequence would the jobs be ranked according to the following decision rules:
a) FCFS
b) SPT
c) LPT
d) EDD
e) Critical ratio

Which is best and why? Which has the minimum lateness? **Px**

•• **15.13** The following jobs are waiting to be processed at Rick Carlson's machine center. Carlson's machine center has a relatively long backlog and sets fresh schedules every 2 weeks, which do not disturb earlier schedules. Below are the jobs received during the previous 2 weeks. They are ready to be scheduled today, which is day 241 (day 241 is a work day). Job names refer to names of clients and contract numbers.

Job	Date Job Received	Production Days Needed	Date Job Due
BR-02	228	15	300
CX-01	225	25	270
DE-06	230	35	320
RG-05	235	40	360
SY-11	231	30	310

a) Complete the table below. (Show your supporting calculations.)
b) Which dispatching rule has the best score for flow time?
c) Which dispatching rule has the best score for utilization metric?
d) Which dispatching rule has the best score for lateness?
e) Which dispatching rule would you select? Support your decision.

Dispatching Rule	Job Sequence	Flow Time	Utilization Metric	Average Number of Jobs	Average Lateness
EDD					
SPT					
LPT					
FCFS					

Px

•• **15.14** The following jobs are waiting to be processed at Julie Morel's machine center:

Job	Date Order Received	Production Days Needed	Date Order Due
A	110	20	180
B	120	30	200
C	122	10	175
D	125	16	230
E	130	18	210

In what sequence would the jobs be ranked according to the following rules: (a) FCFS, (b) EDD, (c) SPT, and (d) LPT? All dates are according to shop calendar days. Today on the planning calendar is day 130, and none of the jobs have been started or scheduled. Which rule is best? **Px**

•• **15.15** Sunny Park Tailors has been asked to make three different types of wedding suits for separate customers. The table below highlights the time taken in hours for (1) cutting and sewing and (2) delivery of each of the suits. Which schedule finishes sooner: First-come, first-served (123) or a schedule using Johnson's rule?

Times Taken for Different Activities (hours)

Suit	Cut and Sew	Deliver
1	4	2
2	7	7
3	6	5

Px

•• **15.16** The following jobs are waiting to be processed at Jeremy LaMontagne's machine center. Today is day 250.

Job	Date Job Received	Production Days Needed	Date Job Due
1	215	30	260
2	220	20	290
3	225	40	300
4	240	50	320
5	250	20	340

Using the critical ratio scheduling rule, in what sequence would the jobs be processed? **Px**

•••• **15.17** The following set of seven jobs is to be processed through two work centers at George Heinrich's printing company. The sequence is first printing, then binding. Processing time at each of the work centers is shown in the following table:

Job	Printing (hours)	Binding (hours)
T	15	3
U	7	9
V	4	10
W	7	6
X	10	9
Y	4	5
Z	7	8

a) What is the optimal sequence for these jobs to be scheduled?
b) Chart these jobs through the two work centers.
c) What is the total length of time of this optimal solution?
d) What is the idle time in the binding shop, given the optimal solution?
e) How much would the binding machine's idle time be cut by splitting Job Z in half? **Px**

••• **15.18** Six jobs are to be processed through a two-step operation. The first operation involves sanding, and the second involves painting. Processing times are as follows:

Job	Operation 1 (hours)	Operation 2 (hours)
A	10	5
B	7	4
C	5	7
D	3	8
E	2	6
F	4	3

Determine a sequence that will minimize the total completion time for these jobs. Illustrate graphically. **Px**

•• **15.19** Jesse's Barber Shop at O'Hare Airport is open 7 days a week but has fluctuating demand. Jesse is interested in treating his barbers as well as he can with steady work and preferably 5 days of work with two consecutive days off. His analysis of his staffing needs resulted in the following plan. Schedule Jesse's staff with the minimum number of barbers.

	Day						
	Mon.	Tue.	Wed.	Thu.	Fri.	Sat.	Sun.
Barbers needed	6	5	5	5	6	4	3

•• **15.20** Given the following demand for waiters and waitresses at S. Ghosh Bar and Grill, determine the minimum wait staff needed with a policy of 2 consecutive days off.

	Day						
	Mon.	Tue.	Wed.	Thu.	Fri.	Sat.	Sun.
Wait staff needed	3	4	4	5	6	7	4

•• **15.21** Lifang Wu owns an automated machine shop that makes precision auto parts. He has just compiled an input–output report for the grinding work center. Complete this report and analyze the results.

Input–Output Report

Period	1	2	3	4	Total
Planned input	80	80	100	100	
Actual input	85	85	85	85	
Deviation					
Planned output	90	90	90	90	
Actual output	85	85	80	80	
Deviation					
Initial backlog: 30					

▶ **Refer to** myomlab◯ **for these additional homework problems: 15.22–15.27**

Case Studies

▶ Old Oregon Wood Store

In 2010, George Wright started the Old Oregon Wood Store to manufacture Old Oregon tables. Each table is carefully constructed by hand using the highest-quality oak. Old Oregon tables can support more than 500 pounds, and since the start of the Old Oregon Wood Store, not one table has been returned because of faulty workmanship or structural problems. In addition to being rugged, each table is beautifully finished using a urethane varnish that George developed over 20 years of working with wood-finishing materials.

The manufacturing process consists of four steps: preparation, assembly, finishing, and packaging. Each step is performed by one person. In addition to overseeing the entire operation, George does all of the finishing. Tom Surowski performs the preparation step, which involves cutting and forming the basic components of the tables. Leon Davis is in charge of the assembly, and Cathy Stark performs the packaging.

Although each person is responsible for only one step in the manufacturing process, everyone can perform any one of the steps. It is George's policy that occasionally everyone should complete several tables on his or her own without any help or assistance. A small competition is used to see who can complete an entire table in the least amount of time. George maintains average total and intermediate completion times. The data are shown in Figure 15.6.

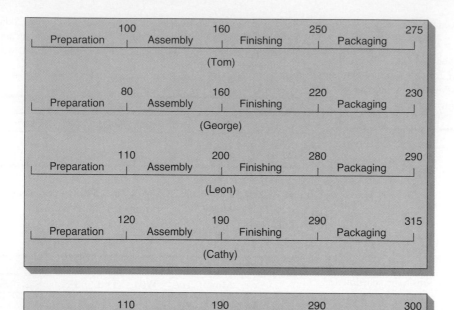

◄ FIGURE 15.6
Manufacturing Time in Minutes

◄ FIGURE 15.7
Randy's Completion Times in Minutes

It takes Cathy longer than the other employees to construct an Old Oregon table. In addition to being slower than the other employees, Cathy is also unhappy about her current responsibility of packaging, which leaves her idle most of the day. Her first preference is finishing, and her second preference is preparation.

In addition to quality, George is concerned with costs and efficiency. When one of the employees misses a day, it causes major scheduling problems. In some cases, George assigns another employee overtime to complete the necessary work. At other times, George simply waits until the employee returns to work to complete his or her step in the manufacturing process. Both solutions cause problems. Overtime is expensive, and waiting causes delays and sometimes stops the entire manufacturing process.

To overcome some of these problems, Randy Lane was hired. Randy's major duties are to perform miscellaneous jobs and to help out if one of the employees is absent. George has given Randy training in all phases of the manufacturing process, and he is pleased

with the speed at which Randy has been able to learn how to completely assemble Old Oregon tables. Randy's average total and intermediate completion times are given in Figure 15.7.

Discussion Questions

1. What is the fastest way to manufacture Old Oregon tables using the original crew? How many could be made per day?
2. Would production rates and quantities change significantly if George would allow Randy to perform one of the four functions and make one of the original crew the backup person?
3. What is the fastest time to manufacture a table with the original crew if Cathy is moved to either preparation or finishing?
4. Whoever performs the packaging function is severely underutilized. Can you find a better way of utilizing the four- or five-person crew than either giving each a single job or allowing each to manufacture an entire table? How many tables could be manufactured per day with this scheme?

▶ Scheduling at Hard Rock Cafe

Video Case

Whether it's scheduling nurses at Mayo Clinic, pilots at Southwest Airlines, classrooms at UCLA, or servers at a Hard Rock Cafe, it's clear that good scheduling is important. Proper schedules use an organization's assets (1) more effectively, by serving customers promptly, and (2) more efficiently, by lowering costs.

Hard Rock Cafe at Universal Studios, Orlando, is the world's largest restaurant, with 1,100 seats on two main levels. With typical turnover of employees in the restaurant industry at 80% to 100% per year, Hard Rock General Manager Ken Hoffman takes scheduling very seriously. Hoffman wants his 160 servers to be effective, but he also wants to treat them fairly. He has done so with scheduling software and flexibility that has increased productivity while contributing to turnover that is half the industry average. His goal is to find the fine balance that gives employees financially productive daily work shifts while setting the schedule tight enough so as to not overstaff between lunch and dinner.

The weekly schedule begins with a sales forecast. "First, we examine last year's sales at the cafe for the same day of the week," says Hoffman. "Then we adjust our forecast for this year based on a variety of closely watched factors. For example, we call the Orlando Convention Bureau every week to see what major groups will be in town. Then we send two researchers out to check on the occupancy of nearby hotels. We watch closely to see what concerts are scheduled at Hard Rock Live—the 3,000-seat concert stage next door. From the forecast, we calculate how many people we need to have on duty each day for the kitchen, the bar, as hosts, and for table service."

Once Hard Rock determines the number of staff needed, servers submit request forms, which are fed into the software's linear programming mathematical model. Individuals are given priority rankings from 1 to 9, based on their seniority and how important they are to fill each day's schedule. Schedules are then posted by day and by workstation. Trades are handled between employees, who understand the value of each specific shift and station.

Hard Rock employees like the system, as does the general manager, since sales per labor-hour are rising and turnover is dropping.

Discussion Questions*

1. Name and justify several factors that Hoffman could use in forecasting weekly sales.

2. What can be done to lower turnover in large restaurants?
3. Why is seniority important in scheduling servers?
4. How does the schedule impact productivity?

*You may wish to view the video that accompanies this case before answering the questions.

Active Model Exercise

ACTIVE MODEL 15.1 This exercise allows you to evaluate job shop sequencing/dispatching rules (FCFS, SPT, EDD, LPT, and CR) for Example 5 in the text. The computed metrics are: average completion time, utilization, average number of jobs in the system, and average lateness. It is illustrated at **www.myomlab.com** or **www.pearsonhighered.com/heizer**.

Main Heading	Review Material	
THE IMPORTANCE OF SHORT-TERM SCHEDULING (p. 468)	The strategic importance of scheduling is clear: • Effective scheduling means *faster movement* of goods and services through a facility. This means greater use of assets and hence greater capacity per dollar invested, which, in turn, *lowers cost*. • Added capacity, faster throughput, and the related flexibility mean better customer service through *faster delivery*. • Good scheduling contributes to realistic commitments, hence *dependable delivery*.	
SCHEDULING ISSUES (pp. 468–471)	*The objective of scheduling is to allocate and prioritize demand (generated by either forecasts or customer orders) to available facilities.* ▪ **Forward scheduling**—Begins the schedule as soon as the requirements are known. ▪ **Backward scheduling**—Begins with the due date by scheduling the final operation first and the other job steps in reverse order. The four scheduling criteria are (1) *minimize completion time*, (2) *maximize utilization*, (3) *minimize work-in-process (WIP) inventory*, and (4) *minimize customer waiting time*.	**VIDEO 15.1** Scheduling at Hard Rock
SCHEDULING PROCESS-FOCUSED FACILITIES (pp. 471–472)	A process-focused facility is a high-variety, low-volume system commonly found in manufacturing and services. It is also called an intermittent, or job shop, facility. Control files track the actual progress made against the plan for each work order.	
LOADING JOBS (pp. 472–477)	▪ **Loading**—The assigning of jobs to work or processing centers. ▪ **Input/output control**—Allows operations personnel to manage facility work flows by tracking work added to a work center and its work completed. ▪ **ConWIP cards**—Cards that control the amount of work in a work center, aiding input/output control. ConWIP is an acronym for *constant work-in-process*. A ConWIP card travels with a job (or batch) through the work center. When the job is finished, the card is released and returned to the initial workstation, authorizing the entry of a new batch into the work center. ▪ **Gantt charts**—Planning charts used to schedule resources and allocate time. The Gantt *load chart* shows the loading and idle times of several departments, machines, or facilities. It displays the relative workloads in the system so that the manager knows what adjustments are appropriate. The Gantt *schedule chart* is used to monitor jobs in progress (and is also used for project scheduling). It indicates which jobs are on schedule and which are ahead of or behind schedule. ▪ **Assignment method**—A special class of linear programming models that involves assigning tasks or jobs to resources. In assignment problems, only one job (or worker) is assigned to one machine (or project). The assignment method involves adding and subtracting appropriate numbers in the table to find the lowest *opportunity cost* for each assignment.	Problems: 15.1–15.9, 15.21 Virtual Office Hours for Solved Problems: 15.1
SEQUENCING JOBS (pp. 478–484)	▪ **Sequencing**—Determining the order in which jobs should be done at each work center. ▪ **Priority rules**—Rules used to determine the sequence of jobs in process-oriented facilities. ▪ **First-come, first-served (FCFS)**—Jobs are completed in the order in which they arrived. ▪ **Shortest processing time (SPT)**—Jobs with the shortest processing times are assigned first. ▪ **Earliest due date**—Earliest due date jobs are performed first. ▪ **Longest processing time (LPT)**—Jobs with the longest processing time are completed first: $$\text{Average completion time} = \frac{\text{Sum of total flow time}}{\text{Number of jobs}}$$ $$\text{Utilization metric} = \frac{\text{Total job work (processing) time}}{\text{Sum of total flow time}}$$	Problems: 15.10–15.18 Virtual Office Hours for Solved Problems: 15.2–15.5 **ACTIVE MODEL 15.1**

Main Heading	Review Material	myomlab

$$\text{Average number of jobs in the system} = \frac{\text{Sum of total flow time}}{\text{Total job work (processing) time}}$$

$$\text{Average job lateness} = \frac{\text{Total late days}}{\text{Number of jobs}}$$

SPT is the best technique for minimizing job flow and average number of jobs in the system.

FCFS performs about average on most criteria, and it appears fair to customers.

EDD minimizes maximum tardiness.

- **Critical ratio (CR)**—A sequencing rule that is an index number computed by dividing the time remaining until due date by the work time remaining:

$$CR = \frac{\text{Time remaining}}{\text{Workdays remaining}} = \frac{\text{Due date} - \text{Today's date}}{\text{Work (lead) time remaining}}$$

As opposed to the priority rules, the critical ratio is dynamic and easily updated. It tends to perform better than FCFS, SPT, EDD, or LPT on the average job-lateness criterion.

- **Johnson's rule**—An approach that minimizes processing time for sequencing a group of jobs through two work centers while minimizing total idle time in the work centers.

Rule-based scheduling systems have the following limitations: (1) Scheduling is dynamic, (2) rules do not look upstream or downstream, and (3) rules do not look beyond due dates.

FINITE CAPACITY SCHEDULING (FCS)
(pp. 484–485)

- **Finite capacity scheduling (FCS)**—Computerized short-term scheduling that overcomes the disadvantage of rule-based systems by providing the user with graphical interactive computing.

SCHEDULING REPETITIVE FACILITIES
(pp. 485–486)

- **Level material use**—The use of frequent, high-quality, small lot sizes that contribute to just-in-time production.

Advantages of level material use are (1) lower inventory levels, (2) faster product throughput, (3) improved component and product quality, (4) reduced floor-space requirements, (5) improved communication among employees, and (6) a smoother production process.

SCHEDULING SERVICES
(pp. 486–489)

Cyclical scheduling with inconsistent staffing needs is often the case in services. The objective focuses on developing a schedule with the minimum number of workers. In these cases, each employee is assigned to a shift and has time off.

Problems: 15.19–15.20

Self Test

- **Before taking the self-test,** refer to the learning objectives listed at the beginning of the chapter and the key terms listed at the end of the chapter.

LO1. Which of the following decisions covers the longest time period?
 a) Short-term scheduling
 b) Capacity planning
 c) Aggregate planning
 d) A master schedule

LO2. A visual aid used in loading and scheduling jobs is a:
 a) Gantt chart.
 b) planning file.
 c) bottleneck.
 d) load-schedule matrix.
 e) level material chart.

LO3. The assignment method involves adding and subtracting appropriate numbers in the table to find the lowest _____ for each assignment.
 a) profit
 b) number of steps
 c) number of allocations
 d) range per row
 e) opportunity cost

LO4. The most popular priority rules include:
 a) FCFS.
 b) EDD.
 c) SPT.
 d) all of the above.

LO5. The job that should be scheduled last when using Johnson's rule is the job with the:
 a) largest total processing time on both machines.
 b) smallest total processing time on both machines.
 c) longest activity time if it lies with the first machine.
 d) longest activity time if it lies with the second machine.
 e) shortest activity time if it lies with the second machine.

LO6. What is computerized short-term scheduling that overcomes the disadvantage of rule-based systems by providing the user with graphical interactive computing?
 a) LPT
 b) FCS
 c) CSS
 d) FCFS
 e) GIC

LO7. Cyclical scheduling is used to schedule:
 a) jobs.
 b) machines.
 c) shipments.
 d) employees.

Answers: **LO1.** b; **LO2.** a; **LO3.** e; **LO4.** d; **LO5.** e; **LO6.** b; **LO7.** d.

16 JIT and Lean Operations

Chapter Outline

Just-in-Time, the Toyota Production
    System, and Lean Operations

Just-in-Time (JIT)

JIT Layout

JIT Inventory

JIT Scheduling

JIT Quality

Toyota Production System (TPS)

Lean Operations

Lean Operations in Services

Ethical Dilemma
Discussion Questions
Problems
Case Studies: Mutual Insurance Company
    of Iowa; JIT after a Catastrophe; JIT at
    Arnold Palmer Hospital
Classroom Activity
Rapid Review

Just-in-time (JIT) and lean production are philosophies of continuous improvement. Lean production begins with a focus on customer desires, but both concepts focus on driving all waste out of the production process. Because waste is found in anything that does not add value, JIT and lean organizations are adding value more efficiently than other firms. Waste occurs when defects are produced within the production process or by outside suppliers. JIT and lean production attack wasted space because of a less-than-optimal layout; they attack wasted time because of poor scheduling; they attack waste in idle inventory; and they attack waste for poorly maintained machinery and equipment. The expectation is that committed, empowered employees work with committed management and suppliers to build systems that respond to customers with ever lower cost and higher quality.

BEFORE COMING TO CLASS, READ CHAPTER 16 IN YOUR TEXT AND ANSWER THESE QUESTIONS.

1. What are JIT, TPS, and lean operations? _____

_____

2. What are the seven wastes and the 5 Ss? _____

_____

3. What are the goals of JIT partnerships? _____

_____

4. Explain how to determine optimal setup time. _____

_____

5. What is a kanban? _____

_____

6. How do you compute the number of kanbans required? _____

_____

7. Explain the principles of TPS. _____

_____

JUST-IN-TIME, THE TOYOTA PRODUCTION SYSTEM, AND LEAN OPERATIONS (See Flexible Version pp. 498–500)

Eliminate Waste (See Flexible Version pp. 498–499)

7 Wastes

5 Ss

Remove Variability (See Flexible Version pp. 499–500)

Improve Throughput (See Flexible Version p. 500)

JUST-IN-TIME (JIT) (See Flexible Version pp. 500–503)

JIT Partnerships (See Flexible Version pp. 501–502)

Concerns of Suppliers (See Flexible Version pp. 502–503)

JIT LAYOUT   (See Flexible Version pp. 503–504)

◀ **TABLE 16.1**
Layout Tactics

Build work cells for families of products

Include a large number of operations in a small area

Minimize distance

Design little space for inventory

Improve employee communication

Use poka-yoke devices

Build flexible or movable equipment

Cross train workers to add flexibility

JIT INVENTORY   (See Flexible Version pp. 504–506)

◀ **TABLE 16.2**
JIT Inventory Tactics

Use a pull system to move inventory

Reduce lot size

Develop just-in-time delivery systems with suppliers

Deliver directly to point of use

Perform to schedule

Reduce setup time

Use group technology

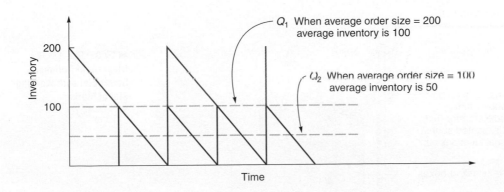

Q_1 When average order size = 200
average inventory is 100

Q_2 When average order size = 100
average inventory is 50

◀ **FIGURE 16.4**
Frequent Orders Reduce Average Inventory

A lower order size increases the number of orders and total ordering cost, but reduces average inventory and total holding cost.

Production Order Quantity Model

$$Q^* = \sqrt{\frac{2DS}{H[1 - (d/p)]}} \qquad \textbf{(16-1)}$$

where D = Annual demand
S = Setup cost
H = Holding cost
d = Daily demand
p = Daily production

Practice Problem Space

JIT SCHEDULING (See Flexible Version pp. 506–510)

◀ **TABLE 16.3**
JIT Scheduling Tactics

Communicate schedules to suppliers
Make level schedules
Freeze part of the schedule
Perform to schedule
Seek one-piece-make and one-piece-move
Eliminate waste
Produce in small lots
Use kanbans
Make each operation produce a perfect part

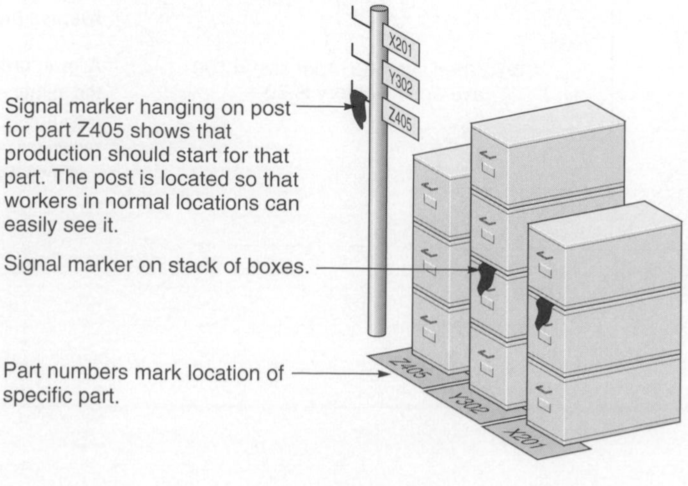

X201
Y302
Z405
Signal marker hanging on post for part Z405 shows that production should start for that part. The post is located so that workers in normal locations can easily see it.
Signal marker on stack of boxes.
Part numbers mark location of specific part.
Z405
Y302
X201

◀ **FIGURE 16.8**
Diagram of Outbound Stockpoint with Warning-Signal Marker

Level Schedules (See Flexible Version pp. 507–508)

Kanban (See Flexible Version pp. 508–510)

$$\text{Number of kanbans (containers)} = \frac{\text{Demand during lead time } + \text{ Safety stock}}{\text{Size of container}} \quad (16\text{-}3)$$

PRACTICE PROBLEM 16.1 ■ Number of Kanbans

Bryant Electronics produces short runs of battery-powered pocket lanterns. As the new materials manager, you have been asked to reduce inventory by introducing a kanban system. After several hours of analysis, you have developed the following data for connectors used in one work cell. How many kanbans do you need for this connector?

Daily demand: 1,500 units
Production lead time: 1 day
Safety stock: 1 day
Kanban size: 250 units

PRACTICE PROBLEM 16.2 ■ Size and Number of Kanbans

Perkins Lighting managers wish to employ a kanban in their new floor lamp production system. For the floor lamp base, they have provided the following information:

Daily demand: 300 units (with 300 business days per year)
Holding cost: $20 per unit per year
Order cost: $10 per order
Lead time: 2 days
Safety stock: 600 units

Assuming that the size of the kanban is the EOQ, find the size of the kanban and the number of kanbans required.

JIT QUALITY (See Flexible Version pp. 510–511)

Use statistical process control
Empower employees
Build fail-safe methods (poka-yoke, checklists, etc.)
Expose poor quality with small lot JIT
Provide immediate feedback

◀ **TABLE 16.4**
JIT Quality Tactics

TOYOTA PRODUCTION SYSTEM (TPS) (See Flexible Version pp. 511–512)

Continuous Improvement (See Flexible Version p. 511)

Respect for People (See Flexible Version p. 511)

Standard Work Practice (See Flexible Version pp. 511–512)

LEAN OPERATIONS (See Flexible Version pp. 512–513)

Building a Lean Organization (See Flexible Version pp. 512–513)

LEAN OPERATIONS IN SERVICES (See Flexible Version pp. 513–514)

Ethical Dilemma

In this lean operations world, in an effort to lower handling costs, speed delivery, and reduce inventory, retailers are forcing their suppliers to do more and more in the way of preparing their merchandise for their cross-docking warehouses, shipment to specific stores, and shelf presentation. Your company, a small manufacturer of aquarium decorations, is in a tough position. First, Mega-Mart wanted you to develop bar-code technology, then special packaging, then small individual shipments bar coded for each store (this way when the merchandise hits the warehouse it is cross-docked immediately to the correct truck and store and is ready for shelf placement). And now Mega-Mart wants you to develop RFID—immediately. Mega-Mart has made it clear that suppliers that cannot keep up with the technology will be dropped.

Earlier, when you didn't have the expertise for bar codes, you had to borrow money and hire an outside firm to do the development, purchase the technology, and train your shipping clerk. Then, meeting the special packaging requirement drove you into a loss for several months, resulting in a loss for last year. Now it appears that the RFID request is impossible. Your business, under the best of conditions, is marginally profitable, and the bank may not be willing to bail you out again. Over the years, Mega-Mart has slowly become your major customer and without them, you are probably out of business. What are the ethical issues and what do you do?

Discussion Questions

1. What is JIT?
2. What is a lean producer?
3. What is TPS?
4. What is level scheduling?
5. JIT attempts to remove delays, which do not add value. How then does JIT cope with weather and its impact on crop harvest and transportation times?
6. What are three ways in which JIT and quality are related?
7. How does TPS contribute to competitive advantage?
8. What are the characteristics of just-in-time partnerships with respect to suppliers?
9. Discuss how the Japanese word for *card* has application in the study of JIT.
10. Standardized, reusable containers have fairly obvious benefits for shipping. What is the purpose of these devices within the plant?
11. Does lean production work in the service sector? Provide an illustration.
12. Which lean techniques work in both the manufacturing *and* service sectors?

Problems*

• **16.1** Leblanc Electronics, Inc., in Nashville, produces short runs of custom airwave scanners for the defense industry. You have been asked by the owner, Larry Leblanc, to reduce inventory by introducing a kanban system. After several hours of analysis, you develop the following data for scanner connectors used in one work cell. How many kanbans do you need for this connector?

Daily demand	1,000 connectors
Lead time	2 days
Safety stock	$\frac{1}{2}$ day
Kanban size	500 connectors

• **16.2** Chip Gillikin's company wants to establish kanbans to feed a newly established work cell. The following data have been provided. How many kanbans are needed?

Daily demand	250 units
Production lead time	$\frac{1}{2}$ day
Safety stock	$\frac{1}{4}$ day
Kanban size	50 units

Note: **P✗** means the problem may be solved with POM for Windows and/or Excel OM.

•• **16.3** Chris Millikan Manufacturing, Inc., is moving to kanbans to support its telephone switching-board assembly lines. Determine the size of the kanban for subassemblies and the number of kanbans needed.

Setup cost = $30
Annual holding
        cost = $120 per subassembly
Daily production = 20 subassemblies
    Annual usage = 2,500 (50 weeks × 5 days each
                × daily usage of 10 subassemblies)
    Lead time = 16 days
    Safety stock = 4 days' production of subassemblies. **P✗**

•• **16.4** Maggie Moylan Motorcycle Corp. uses kanbans to support its transmission assembly line. Determine the size of the kanban for the mainshaft assembly and the number of kanbans needed.

Setup cost = $20
Annual holding cost
of mainshaft assembly = $250 per unit
    Daily production = 300 mainshafts
      Annual usage = 20,000 (= 50 weeks × 5 days each
                 × daily usage of 80 mainshafts)
    Lead time = 3 days
    Safety stock = $\frac{1}{2}$ day's production of mainshafts **P✗**

• 16.5 Discount-Mart, a major East Coast retailer, wants to determine the economic order quantity (see Chapter 12 for EOQ formulas) for its halogen lamps. It currently buys all halogen lamps from Specialty Lighting Manufacturers, in Atlanta. Annual demand is 2,000 lamps, ordering cost per order is $30, annual carrying cost per lamp is $12.
a) What is the EOQ?
b) What are the total annual costs of holding and ordering (managing) this inventory?
c) How many orders should Discount-Mart place with Specialty Lighting per year? **Px**

••• 16.6 Discount-Mart (see Problem 16.5), as part of its new JIT program, has signed a long-term contract with Specialty Lighting and will place orders electronically for its halogen lamps. Ordering costs will drop to $.50 per order, but Discount-Mart also reassessed its carrying costs and raised them to $20 per lamp.
a) What is the new economic order quantity?
b) How many orders will now be placed?
c) What is the total annual cost of managing the inventory with this policy? **Px**

•• 16.7 How do your answers to Problems 16.5 and 16.6 provide insight into a JIT purchasing strategy?

••• 16.8 Bill Penny has a repetitive manufacturing plant producing trailer hitches in Arlington, Texas. The plant has an average inventory turnover of only 12 times per year. He has therefore determined that he will reduce his component lot sizes. He has developed the following data for one component, the safety chain clip:

$$\text{Annual demand} = 31{,}200 \text{ units}$$
$$\text{Daily demand} = 120 \text{ units}$$
$$\text{Daily production (in 8 hours)} = 960 \text{ units}$$
$$\text{Desired lot size (1 hour of production)} = 120 \text{ units}$$
$$\text{Holding cost per unit per year} = \$12$$
$$\text{Setup labor cost per hour} = \$20$$

How many minutes of setup time should he have his plant manager aim for regarding this component?

••• 16.9 Given the following information about a product, at Phyllis Simon's firm, what is the appropriate setup time?

$$\text{Annual demand} = 39{,}000 \text{ units}$$
$$\text{Daily demand} = 150 \text{ units}$$
$$\text{Daily production} = 1{,}000 \text{ units}$$
$$\text{Desired lot size} = 150 \text{ units}$$
$$\text{Holding cost per unit per year} = \$10$$
$$\text{Setup labor cost per hour} = \$40$$

••• 16.10 Rick Wing has a repetitive manufacturing plant producing automobile steering wheels. Use the following data to prepare for a reduced lot size. The firm uses a work year of 305 days.

Annual demand for steering wheels	30,500
Daily demand	100
Daily production (8 hours)	800
Desired lot size (2 hours of production)	200
Holding cost per unit per year	$10

a) What is the setup cost, based on the desired lot size?
b) What is the setup time, based on $40 per hour setup labor?

▶ Refer to myomlab for these additional homework problems: 16.11–16.12

Case Studies

▶ Mutual Insurance Company of Iowa

Mutual Insurance Company of Iowa (MICI) has a major insurance office facility located in Des Moines, Iowa. The Des Moines office is responsible for processing all of MICI's insurance claims for the entire nation. The company's sales have experienced rapid growth during the last year, and as expected, record levels in claims followed. Over 2,500 forms for claims a day are now flowing into the office for processing. Unfortunately, fewer than 2,500 forms a day are flowing out. The total time to process a claim, from the time it arrives to the time a check is mailed, has increased from 10 days to 10 weeks. As a result, some customers are threatening legal action. Sally Cook, the manager of Claims Processing, is particularly

distressed, as she knows that a claim seldom requires more than 3 hours of actual work. Under the current administrative procedures, human resources limitations, and facility constraints, there appear to be no easy fixes for the problem. But clearly, something must be done, as the workload has overwhelmed the existing system.

MICI management wants aggressive, but economical, action taken to fix the problem. Ms. Cook has decided to try a JIT approach to claim processing. With support from her bosses, and as a temporary fix, Cook has brought in part-time personnel from MICI sales divisions across the country to help. They are to work down the claims backlog while a new JIT system is installed.

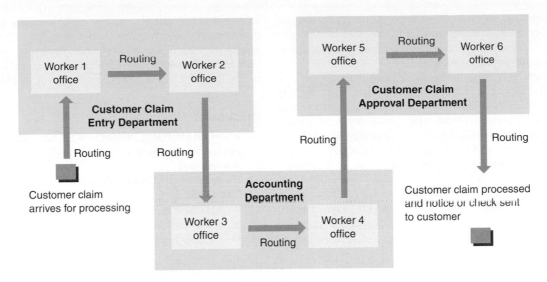

▲ **FIGURE 16.10** **Claims Processing Department Layout**

Meanwhile, Claims Processing managers and employees are to be trained in JIT principles. With JIT principles firmly in mind, managers will redesign jobs to move responsibilities for quality control activities to each employee, holding them responsible for quality work and any necessary corrections. Cook will also initiate worker-training programs that explain the entire claim processing flow, as well as provide comprehensive training on each step in the process. Data-entry skills will also be taught to both employees and managers in an effort to fix responsibility for data accuracy on the processor rather than on data entry clerks. Additionally, cross-training will be emphasized to enable workers within departments to process a variety of customer claim applications in their entirety.

Cook and her supervisors are also reexamining the insurance and claim forms currently in use. They want to see if standardization of forms will cut processing time, reduce data-entry time, and cut work-in-process.

They hope the changes will also save training time. Making changes in work methods and worker skills leads logically to a need for change in the layout of the Claims Processing Department. This potential change represents a major move from the departmental layout of the past, and will be a costly step. To help ensure the successful implementation of this phase of the changeover, Cook established a team made up of supervisors, employees, and an outside office layout consultant. She also had the team visit the Kawasaki motorcycle plant in Lincoln, Nebraska, to observe their use of work cells to aid JIT.

The team concluded that a change in the office facilities was necessary to successfully implement and integrate JIT concepts at MICI. The team believes it should revise the layout of the operation and work methods to bring them in line with "group technology cell" layouts. An example of the current departmental layout and claim processing flow pattern is presented in Figure 16.10. As can be seen in this figure, customer claims arrive for processing at the facility and flow through a series of offices and departments to eventually complete the claim process. Although the arrangement of the offices and workers in Figure 16.10 is typical, the entire facility actually operates 20 additional flows, each consisting of the same three departments. However, not all of the 20 flows are configured the same. The number of employees, for example, varies depending on the claim form requirements (larger claims have to be approved by more people). So while all forms must pass through the same three departments (Customer Claim Entry, Accounting, and Customer Claim Approval), the number of workers for each claim may vary from two to four. For this reason, the MICI facility currently maintains a staff of over 180 office workers just to process and route claims. All these people work for Ms. Cook.

Discussion Questions

1. Identify the attributes you would expect the Claims Processing Department at MICI to have once the new JIT system is in place.
2. What will the restructured cell layout for claim processing in Figure 16.10 look like? Draw it.
3. What assumptions are you making about personnel and equipment in the new group technology cell layout?
4. How will the new JIT oriented system benefit the MICI operation? Explain.

Source: Adapted from Marc J. Schniederjans, *Topics in Just-in-Time Management*, pp. 283–285. Reprinted by permission of Pearson Education, Inc., Upper Saddle River, NJ.

▶ JIT after a Catastrophe

You name the catastrophe, and JIT has been through it and survived. Toyota Motor Corporation has had its world-renowned JIT system tested by fire. The massive fire incinerated the main source of crucial brake valves that Toyota buys from the Aisin Seiki plant in Kariya, Japan, and uses in most of its cars. The impact was the loss of 70,000 cars not produced while Toyota got the supply chain repaired. Then an earthquake destroyed Toyota's transmission supplier, Riken, shutting down production in a dozen factories. Chrysler and many others had their JIT systems tested on September 11, 2001, when the terrorists attacks shut down their state-of-the-art air delivery systems. And on February 5, 2008, during the second shift at Caterpillar's high-pressure couplings plant in

Oxford, Mississippi, a tornado all but destroyed the facility. Despite these catastrophes, managers at these firms, like other executives all over the world, are still cutting costs by consolidating production, reducing inventory, and implementing JIT.

Consistent with JIT practice, these firms maintain minimal inventory of components and tight supply chains. There are very few components in these closely knit networks that constitute their respective supply chains. Without critical components, production comes to a rapid halt. And in Caterpillar's case, the Oxford plant is the only plant in the world that makes this unique coupling. The couplings link hydraulic hoses on *every* piece of machinery Caterpillar makes. Depending on a single source and holding little inventory is a risk, but it also keeps firms lean and costs low.

The morning after the tornado tore apart the Oxford plant, Greg Folley, who runs Caterpillar's parts division, toured the plant. Much of the roof, including 10-ton heating and air-conditioning units, had fallen onto three critical metal stamping machines. The first piece of equipment was up and running in 2 weeks; getting production back to normal would take 6 months. But the Oxford plant had been making over 1 million of the critical couplings each month; this left a huge hole in Caterpillar's supply line.

Discussion Questions

1. If you are Mr. Folley, looking over the devastation at the Oxford plant, what do you do to keep Caterpillar's worldwide production running?
2. Given the inherent risk in JIT and the trauma that the companies have experienced, why has JIT survived?
3. What do these experiences, and the continuing popularity of JIT, tell you about just-in-time?
4. What actions or changes in policy do you suggest for Caterpillar?

Sources: Case is based on material in: *The Wall Street Journal* (May 19, 2008): B1, B2; (July 20, 2007): B1; www.USAToday.com/money/world/2007-07-18-toyota-quake; and *Harvard Business Review* (September–October 1999): 97–106.

▶ JIT at Arnold Palmer Hospital

Video Case

Orlando's Arnold Palmer Hospital, founded in 1989, specializes in treatment of women and children and is renowned for its high-quality rankings (top 10% of 2000 benchmarked hospitals), its labor and delivery volume (more than 16,000 births per year, and growing), and its neonatal intensive care unit (one of the highest survival rates in the nation). But quality medical practices and high patient satisfaction require costly inventory—some $30 million per year and thousands of SKUs.* With pressure on medical care to manage and reduce costs, Arnold Palmer Hospital has turned toward controlling its inventory with just-in-time (JIT) techniques.

Within the hospital, for example, drugs are now distributed at nursing workstations via dispensing machines (almost like vending machines) that electronically track patient usage and post the related charge to each patient. The dispensing stations are refilled each night, based on patient demand and prescriptions written by doctors.

To address JIT issues externally, Arnold Palmer Hospital turned toward a major distribution partner, McKesson General Medical, which as a first-tier supplier provides the hospital with about one quarter of all its medical/surgical inventory. McKesson supplies sponges, basins, towels, mayo stand covers, syringes, and hundreds of other medical/surgical items. To ensure coordinated daily delivery of inventory purchased from McKesson, an account executive has been assigned to the hospital on a full-time basis, as well as two other individuals who address customer service and product issues. The result has been a drop in Central Supply average daily inventory from $400,000 to $114,000 since JIT.

JIT success has also been achieved in the area of *custom surgical packs*. Custom surgical packs are the sterile coverings, disposable plastic trays, gauze, and the like, specialized to each type of surgical procedure. Arnold Palmer Hospital uses 10 different custom packs for various surgical procedures. "Over 50,000 packs are used each year, for a total cost of about $1.5 million," says George DeLong, head of Supply-Chain Management.

The packs are not only delivered in a JIT manner but packed that way as well. That is, they are packed in the reverse order they are used so each item comes out of the pack in the sequence it is needed. The packs are bulky, expensive, and must remain sterile. Reducing the inventory and handling while maintaining an assured sterile supply for scheduled surgeries presents a challenge to hospitals.

Here is how the supply chain works: Custom packs are *assembled* by a packing company with *components supplied* primarily from manufacturers selected by the hospital, and *delivered* by McKesson from its local warehouse. Arnold Palmer Hospital works with its own surgical staff (through the Medical Economics Outcome Committee) to identify and standardize the custom packs to reduce the number of custom pack SKUs. With this integrated system, pack safety stock inventory has been cut to one day.

The procedure to drive the custom surgical pack JIT system begins with a "pull" from the doctors' daily surgical schedule. Then, Arnold Palmer Hospital initiates an electronic order to McKesson between 1:00 and 2:00 P.M. daily. At 4:00 A.M. the next day, McKesson delivers the packs. Hospital personnel arrive at 7:00 A.M. and stock the shelves for scheduled surgeries. McKesson then reorders from the packing company, which in turn "pulls" necessary inventory for the quantity of packs needed from the manufacturers.

Arnold Palmer Hospital's JIT system reduces inventory investment, expensive traditional ordering, and bulky storage, and supports quality with a sterile delivery.

Discussion Questions**

1. What do you recommend be done when an error is found in a pack as it is opened for an operation?
2. How might the procedure for custom surgical packs described here be improved?
3. When discussing JIT in services, the text notes that suppliers, layout, inventory, and scheduling are all used. Provide an example of each of these at Arnold Palmer Hospital.
4. When a doctor proposes a new surgical procedure, how do you recommend the SKU for a new custom pack be entered into the hospital's supply-chain system?

*SKU = stock keeping unit
**You may wish to view the video that accompanies this case before answering these questions.

Classroom Activity

▶ Simulating Push and Pull Assembly Lines

Your simulation activity is to create two identical assembly lines with three or more workstations each. A student at each workstation is assigned a task (making paper airplanes, assembly and stapling reports, putting Lego blocks together, etc.). Each station has a task that is substantially longer than the preceding one. Station 1 has unlimited raw material, while other stations start empty. One team is a "push" system and the other a "pull" system. Specifically, the "pull" has a green kanban card for Station 3 and a yellow card for Station 2. Only when Station 2 receives the green card should Station 2 begin production on a new unit. At that point, Station 2

should pass the yellow card to Station 1. When Station 2 completes the product, the yellow card is sent with the product to Station 2. Similarly, Station 1 should only begin work when the yellow card is received. And after completing a product, the yellow card is sent with the product to Station 2.

What observations can you make about work-in-process inventory and how would you address this issue? What do you observe about idle time and how would you address that issue?

Your instructor may want to introduce quality issues into the activity by having defective raw material enter the system.

Main Heading	Review Material	PEARSON myomlab
JUST-IN-TIME, THE TOYOTA PRODUCTION SYSTEM, AND LEAN OPERATIONS (pp. 498–500)	■ **Just-in-time (JIT)**—Continuous and forced problem solving via a focus on throughput and reduced inventory. ■ **Toyota Production System (TPS)**—Focus on continuous improvement, respect for people, and standard work practices. ■ **Lean operations**—Eliminates waste through a focus on exactly what the customer wants. *When implemented as a comprehensive manufacturing strategy, JIT, TPS, and lean systems sustain competitive advantage and result in increased overall returns.* ■ **Seven wastes**—Overproduction, queues, transportation, inventory, motion, overprocessing, and defective product. ■ **5Ss**—A lean production checklist: sort, simplify, shine, standardize, and sustain. U.S. managers often add two additional *S*s to the 5 original ones: *safety* and *support/maintenance*. ■ **Variability**—Any deviation from the optimum process that delivers perfect product on time, every time. Both JIT and inventory reduction are effective tools for identifying causes of variability. ■ **Throughput**—The time required to move orders through the production process, from receipt to delivery. ■ **Manufacturing cycle time**—The time between the arrival of raw materials and the shipping of finished products. ■ **Pull system**—A concept that results in material being produced only when requested and moved to where it is needed just as it is needed. Pull systems use signals to request production and delivery from supplying stations to stations that have production capacity available.	
JUST-IN-TIME (JIT) (pp. 500–503)	■ **JIT partnerships**—Partnerships of suppliers and purchasers that remove waste and drive down costs for mutual benefits. Some specific goals of **JIT** partnerships are: *removal of unnecessary activities*, *removal of in-plant inventory*; *removal of in-transit inventory*; and *obtain improved quality and reliability*. ■ **Consignment inventory**—An arrangement in which the supplier maintains title to the inventory until it is used. Concerns of suppliers in JIT partnerships include: (1) *diversification*; (2) *scheduling*; (3) *lead time*; (4) *quality*; and (5) *lot sizes*.	
JIT LAYOUT (pp. 503–504)	JIT layout tactics include building work cells for families of products, include a large number of operations in a small area, minimizing distance, designing little space for inventory, improving employee communication, using poka-yoke devices, building flexible or movable equipment, and cross-training workers to add flexibility.	
JIT INVENTORY (pp. 504–506)	■ **Just-in-time inventory**—The minimum inventory necessary to keep a perfect system running. The idea behind JIT is to eliminate inventory that hides variability in the production system. JIT inventory tactics include using a pull system to move inventory, reducing lot size, developing just-in-time delivery systems with suppliers, delivering directly to the point of use, performing to schedule, reducing setup time, and using group technology. $$Q^* = \sqrt{\frac{2DS}{H[1 - (d/p)]}} \qquad (16\text{-}1)$$ Using Equation (16-1), for a given desired lot size, Q, we can solve for the optimal setup cost, S: $$S = \frac{(Q^2)(H)(1 - d/p)}{2D} \qquad (16\text{-}2)$$	Problems: 16.8–16.10

Main Heading	Review Material	
JIT SCHEDULING (pp. 506–510)	JIT scheduling tactics include: communicate schedules to suppliers, make level schedules, freeze part of the schedule, perform to schedule, seek one-piece-make and one-piece-move, eliminate waste, produce in small lots, use kanbans, and make each operation produce a perfect part.	Problems: 16.1–16.6
	▪ **Level schedules**—Scheduling products so that each day's production meets the demand for that day.	
	▪ **Kanban**—The Japanese word for *card*, which has come to mean "signal"; a kanban system moves parts through production via a "pull" from a signal:	
	Number of Kanbans (containers) = $\dfrac{\text{Demand during lead time} + \text{Safety stock}}{\text{Size of container}}$ (16-3)	Virtual Office Hours for Solved Problem: 16.1
JIT QUALITY (pp. 510–511)	Whereas inventory *hides* bad quality, JIT immediately *exposes* it.	
	JIT quality tactics include using statistical process control, empowering employees, building fail-safe methods (poka-yoke, checklists, etc.), exposing poor quality with small lot JIT, and providing immediate feedback.	
TOYOTA PRODUCTION SYSTEM (pp. 511–512)	▪ **Kaizen**—A focus on continuous improvement. At Toyota, people are recruited, trained, and treated as knowledge workers. They are empowered. TPS employs aggressive cross-training and few job classifications.	
LEAN OPERATIONS (pp. 512–513)	Lean operations tend to share the following attributes: *use JIT techniques* to eliminate virtually all inventory; *build systems that help employees* produce a perfect part every time; *reduce space requirements* by minimizing travel distance; *develop partnerships with suppliers*, helping them to understand the needs of the ultimate customer; *educate suppliers* to accept responsibility for satisfying end customer needs; *eliminate all but value-added activities*; *develop employees* by constantly improving job design, training, employee commitment, teamwork, and empowerment; *make jobs challenging*, pushing responsibility to the lowest level possible; and *build worker flexibility* through cross-training and reducing job classifications.	
LEAN OPERATIONS IN SERVICES (pp. 513–514)	The features of lean operations apply to services just as they do in other sectors. Forecasts in services may be very elaborate, with seasonal, daily, hourly, or even shorter components.	**VIDEO 16.1** JIT at Arnold Palmer Hospital

Self Test

▪ **Before taking the self-test,** refer to the learning objectives listed at the beginning of the chapter and the key terms listed at the end of the chapter.

LO1. Continuous improvement and forced problem solving via a focus on throughput and reduced inventory is a reasonable definition of:
  a) lean operations.
  b) expedited management.
  c) the 5Ss of housekeeping.
  d) just-in-time.
  e) Toyota Production System.

LO2. The 5Ss for lean production are _____, _____, _____, _____, and _____.

LO3. Concerns of suppliers when moving to JIT include:
  a) small lots sometimes seeming economically prohibitive.
  b) realistic quality demands.
  c) changes without adequate lead time.
  d) erratic schedules.
  e) all of the above.

LO4. What is the formula for optimal setup time?
  a) $\sqrt{2DQ/[H(1 - d/p)]}$
  b) $\sqrt{Q^2 H(1 - d/p)/(2D)}$

  c) $QH(1 - d/p)/(2D)$
  d) $Q^2 H(1 - d/p)/(2D)$
  e) $H(1 - d/p)$

LO5. Kanban is the Japanese word for:
  a) car.   b) pull.
  c) card.   d) continuous improvement.
  e) level schedule.

LO6. The required number of kanbans equals:
  a) 1.   b) Demand during lead time/Q
  c) Size of container.   d) Demand during lead time.
  e) (Demand during lead time + safety stock)/Size of container.

LO7. TPS's standard work practices include:
  a) completely specified work.   b) "pull" systems.
  c) level scheduling.   d) kanbans.
  e) JIT techniques.

Answers: LO1. d; **LO2.** sort, simplify, shine, standardize, sustain; **LO3.** e; **LO4.** d; **LO5.** c; **LO6.** e; **LO7.** a.

17 Maintenance and Reliability

Chapter Outline

The Strategic Importance of Maintenance and Reliability

Reliability

Maintenance

Total Productive Maintenance

Techniques for Exchanging Maintenance

Ethical Dilemma
Discussion Questions
Problems
Case Study: Maintenance Drives Profits at Frito-Lay
Active Model Exercises
Rapid Review

High facility utilization, tight scheduling, low inventory, and consistent quality demand reliable systems. Variability in a system means inefficient use of plant, equipment, and human resources. Managers reduce variability and achieve effective and efficient operations by improving reliability and maintenance. Successful operations managers adopt a practice known as total productive maintenance (TPM). The objective of TPM is to maintain the capability of the system while controlling costs.

BEFORE COMING TO CLASS, READ CHAPTER 17 IN YOUR TEXT AND ANSWER THESE QUESTIONS.

1. What are two tactics for improving reliability? _____
   _____

2. How is system reliability determined? _____
   _____
   _____

3. Define *mean time between failures* (MTBF). _____
   _____

4. How do preventive and breakdown maintenance differ? _____
   _____
   _____

5. What are two tactics for improving maintenance? _____
   _____

6. What is the difference between preventive and breakdown maintenance costs? _____
   _____

7. What is autonomous maintenance? _____
   _____

THE STRATEGIC IMPORTANCE OF MAINTENANCE AND RELIABILITY (See Flexible Version pp. 520–521)

Reliability (See Flexible Version p. 520)

Improving Individual Components
Providing Redundancy

Maintenance (See Flexible Version pp. 520–521)

Implementing Preventive Maintenance
Increasing Repair Capability/Speed

RELIABILITY (See Flexible Version pp. 521–524)

$$R_s = R_1 \times R_2 \times R_3 \times \cdots \times R_n \qquad\qquad (17\text{-}1)$$

where R_1 = reliability of component 1
R_2 = reliability of component 2

and so on.

▶ **FIGURE 17.2**
Overall System Reliability as a Function of Number of Components and Component Reliability with Components in a Series

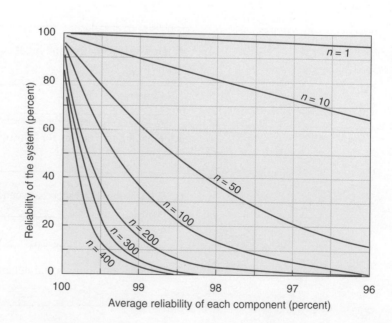

$$FR(\%) = \frac{\text{Number of failures}}{\text{Number of units tested}} \times 100\% \qquad (17\text{-}2)$$

$$FR(N) = \frac{\text{Number of failures}}{\text{Number of unit-hours of operation time}} \qquad (17\text{-}3)$$

$$MTBF = \frac{1}{FR(N)} \qquad (17\text{-}4)$$

PRACTICE PROBLEM 17.1 ■ Reliability

California Instruments, Inc., produces 3,000 computer chips per day. Three hundred are tested for a period of 500 operating hours each. During the test, six failed: two after 50 hours, two at 100 hours, one at 300 hours, and one at 400 hours.

Find FR(%) and FR(N).

PRACTICE PROBLEM 17.2 ■ Reliability

If 300 of the chips from Practice Problem 17.1 are used in building a mainframe computer, how many failures of the computer can be expected per month?

Additional Practice Problem Space

Redundancy (See Flexible Version pp. 523–524)

PRACTICE PROBLEM 17.3 ■ Reliability

Find the reliability of this system:

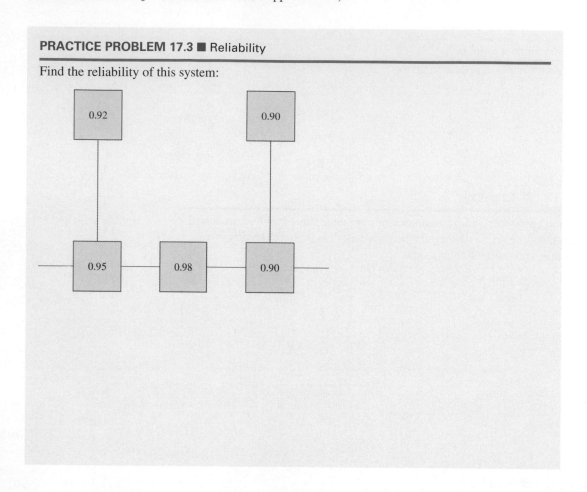

MAINTENANCE (See Flexible Version pp. 524–528)

Preventive Maintenance (See Flexible Version pp. 524–528)

Breakdown Maintenance (See Flexible Version pp. 525–528)

> **AUTHOR COMMENT**
> When all breakdown costs are considered, much more maintenance may be advantageous.

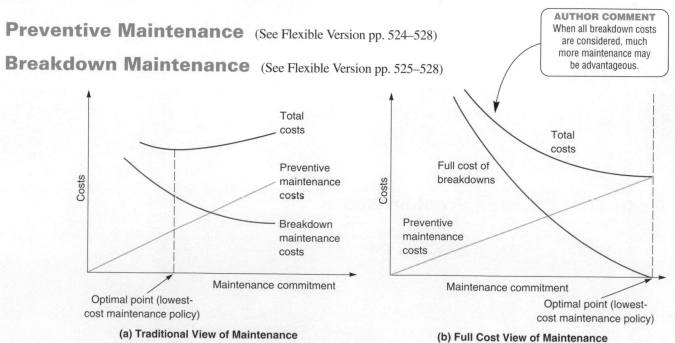

▲ **FIGURE 17.4** **Maintenance Costs**

PRACTICE PROBLEM 17.4 ■ Expected Breakdown Cost

Given the following probabilities, calculate the expected breakdown cost.

Number of Breakdowns	Daily Frequency
0	3
1	2
2	2
3	3

Assume a cost of $10 per breakdown.

Additional Practice Problem Space

TOTAL PRODUCTIVE MAINTENANCE (See Flexible Version pp. 528–529)

TECHNIQUES FOR ENHANCING MAINTENANCE

(See Flexible Version p. 529)

Ethical Dilemma

The Space Shuttle *Columbia* disintegrated over Texas on its 2003 return to Earth. The *Challenger* exploded shortly after launch in 1986. An *Apollo 1* spacecraft imploded in fire on the launch pad in 1967. In each case, the lives of all crew members were lost. The hugely complex shuttle may look a bit like an airplane, but it is very different. In reality, its overall statistical reliability is such that about 1 out of every 50 flights will have a major malfunction. In fact, there have been almost 130 shuttle flights to date.

NASA has cut safety inspections by more than 50% since 1989. Employees often face a cumbersome process for bringing safety issues to management. And the agency continues to face pressure to launch the shuttle on missions to the space station and elsewhere. Of course, as one aerospace manager has stated, "you can be perfectly safe and never get off the ground."

Given the huge reliability and maintenance issues NASA faces (e.g., seals cracking in cold weather, heat shielding tiles falling off), should astronauts be allowed to fly? (In earlier *Atlas* rockets, men were inserted not out of necessity but because test pilots and politicians thought they should be there.) What are the pros and cons of manned space exploration from an ethical perspective? Should the U.S. spend billions of dollars to return an astronaut to the moon?

Discussion Questions

1. What is the objective of maintenance and reliability?
2. How does one identify a candidate for preventive maintenance?
3. Explain the notion of "infant mortality" in the context of product reliability.
4. Why is simulation often an appropriate technique for maintenance problems?
5. What is the trade-off between operator-performed maintenance versus supplier-performed maintenance?
6. How can a manager evaluate the effectiveness of the maintenance function?
7. How does machine design contribute to either increasing or alleviating the maintenance problem?
8. What roles can information technology play in the maintenance function?
9. During an argument as to the merits of preventive maintenance at Windsor Printers, the company owner asked, "Why fix it before it breaks?" How would you, as the director of maintenance, respond?
10. Will preventive maintenance eliminate *all* breakdowns?

Problems*

• **17.1** The Beta II computer's electronic processing unit contains 50 components in series. The average reliability of each component is 99.0%. Using Figure 17.2, determine the overall reliability of the processing unit. **Px**

• **17.2** A testing process at Boeing Aircraft has 400 components in series. The average reliability of each component is 99.5%. Use Figure 17.2 to find the overall reliability of the whole testing process. **Px**

• **17.3** What are the *expected* number of yearly breakdowns for the power generator at Orlando Utilities that has exhibited the following data over the past 20 years? **Px**

Number of breakdowns	0	1	2	3	4	5	6
Number of years in which breakdown occurred	2	2	5	4	5	2	0

• **17.4** Each breakdown of a graphic plotter table at Airbus Industries costs $50. Find the expected daily breakdown cost, given the following data: **Px**

Number of breakdowns	0	1	2	3	4
Daily breakdown probability	.1	.2	.4	.2	.1

•• **17.5** A new aircraft control system is being designed that must be 98% reliable. This system consists of three components in series. If all three of the components are to have the same level of reliability, what level of reliability is required? **Px**

•• **17.6** Robert Klassan Manufacturing, a medical equipment manufacturer, subjected 100 heart pacemakers to 5,000 hours of testing. Halfway through the testing, 5 pacemakers failed. What was the failure rate in terms of the following:
a) Percentage of failures?
b) Number of failures per unit-hour?
c) Number of failures per unit-year?
d) If 1,100 people receive pacemaker implants, how many units can we expect to fail during the following year?

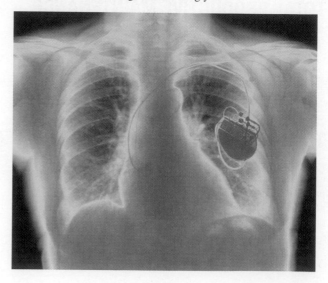

Note: **Px** means the problem may be solved with POM for Windows and/or Excel OM.

•• **17.7** A manufacturer of disk drives for notebook computers wants a MTBF of at least 50,000 hours. Recent test results for 10 units were one failure at 10,000 hrs, another at 25,000 hrs, and two more at 45,000 hrs. The remaining units were still running at 60,000 hours. Determine the following:
a) Percent of failures.
b) Number of failures per unit-hour
c) MTBF at this point in the testing

•• **17.8** What is the reliability of the following production process? $R_1 = 0.95$, $R_2 = 0.90$, $R_3 = 0.98$.

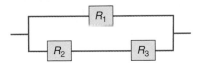

Px

•• **17.9** What is the reliability that bank loans will be processed accurately if each of the 5 clerks shown in the chart has the reliability shown?

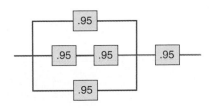

Px

•• **17.10** Merrill Kim Sharp has a system composed of three components in parallel. The components have the following reliabilities:

$$R_1 = 0.90, \quad R_2 = 0.95, \quad R_3 = 0.85$$

What is the reliability of the system? (*Hint:* See Example 3 in the text.) **Px**

• **17.11** A medical control system has three components in series with individual reliabilities (R_1, R_2, R_3) as shown:

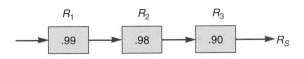

What is the reliability of the system? **Px**

•• **17.12** a) What is the reliability of the system shown?

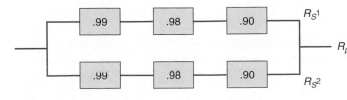

b) How much did reliability improve if the medical control system shown in Problem 17.11 changed to the redundant parallel system shown here? **Px**

••• **17.13** Assume that for cardiac bypass surgery, 85% of patients survive the surgery, 95% survive the recovery period after surgery, 80% are able to make the lifestyle changes needed to extend their survival to 1 year or more, and only 10% of those who do not make the lifestyle changes survive more than a year. What is the likelihood that a given patient will survive more than a year? **Px**

•• **17.14** Elizabeth Irwin's design team has proposed the following system with component reliabilities as indicated:

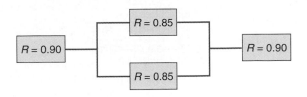

What is the reliability of the system? **Px**

•• **17.15** The maintenance department at Mechanical Dynamics has presented you with the following failure curve. What does it suggest?

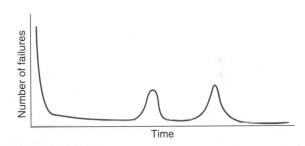

•• **17.16** Rick Wing, salesperson for Wave Soldering Systems, Inc. (WSSI), has provided you with a proposal for improving the temperature control on your present machine. The machine uses a hot-air knife to cleanly remove excess solder from printed circuit boards; this is a great concept, but the hot-air temperature control lacks reliability. According to Wing, engineers at WSSI have improved the reliability of the critical temperature controls. The new system still has the four sensitive integrated circuits controlling the temperature, but the new machine has a backup for each. The four integrated circuits have reliabilities of .90, .92, .94, and .96. The four backup circuits all have a reliability of .90.
a) What is the reliability of the new temperature controller?
b) If you pay a premium, Wing says he can improve all four of the backup units to .93. What is the reliability of this option? **Px**

••• **17.17** The fire department has a number of failures with its oxygen masks and is evaluating the possibility of outsourcing preventive maintenance to the manufacturer. Because of the risk associated with a failure, the cost of each failure is estimated at $2,000. The current maintenance policy (with station employees performing maintenance) has yielded the following history:

Number of breakdowns	0	1	2	3	4	5
Number of years in which breakdowns occurred	4	3	1	5	5	0

This manufacturer will guarantee repairs on any and all failures as part of a service contract. The cost of this service is $5,000 per year.
a) What is the expected number of breakdowns per year with station employees performing maintenance?
b) What is the cost of the current maintenance policy?
c) What is the more economical policy?

••• **17.18** As VP for operations at Brian Normoyle Engineering, you must decide which product design, A or B, has the higher reliability. B is designed with backup units for components R_3 and R_4. What is the reliability of each design?

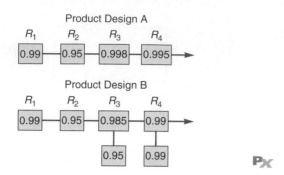

Product Design A

Product Design B

PX

•••• **17.19** A typical retail transaction consists of several smaller steps, which can be considered components subject to failure. A list of such components might include:

Component	Description	Definition of Failure
1	Find product in proper size, color, etc.	Can't find product
2	Enter cashier line	No lines open; lines too long; line experiencing difficulty
3	Scan product UPC for name, price, etc.	Won't scan; item not on file; scans incorrect name or price
4	Calculate purchase total	Wrong weight; wrong extension; wrong data entry; wrong tax
5	Make payment	Customer lacks cash; check not acceptable; credit card refused
6	Make change	Makes change incorrectly
7	Bag merchandise	Damages merchandise while bagging; bag splits
8	Conclude transaction and exit	No receipt; unfriendly, rude, or aloof clerk

Let the eight probabilities of success be .92, .94, .99, .99, .98, .97, .95, and .96. What is the reliability of the system, that is, the probability that there will be a satisfied customer? If you were the store manager, what do you think should be an acceptable value for this probability? Which components would be good candidates for backup, and which for redesign?

▶ **Refer to** myomlab🔵 **for these additional homework problems: 17.20–17.24**

Case Study

▶ **Maintenance Drives Profits at Frito-Lay**

Video Case Study 🎥

Frito-Lay, the multi-billion-dollar subsidiary of food and beverage giant PepsiCo, maintains 36 plants in the U.S. and Canada. These facilities produce dozens of snacks, including the well-known Lay's, Fritos, Cheetos, Doritos, Ruffles, and Tostitos brands, each of which sells over $1 billion per year.

Frito-Lay plants produce in the high-volume, low-variety process model common to the commercial baked goods, steel, glass, and beer industries. In this environment, preventive maintenance of equipment takes a major role by avoiding costly downtime. Tom Rao, vice president for Florida operations, estimates that each 1% of downtime has a negative annual profit

impact of $200,000. He is proud of the $1\frac{1}{2}$% unscheduled downtime his plant is able to reach—well below the 2% that is considered the "world-class" benchmark. This excellent performance is possible because the maintenance department takes an active role in setting the parameters for preventive maintenance. This is done with weekly input to the production schedule.

Maintenance policy impacts energy use as well. The Florida plant's technical manager, Jim Wentzel, states, "By reducing production interruptions, we create an opportunity to bring energy and utility use under control. Equipment maintenance and a solid production schedule are keys to utility efficiency. With every production interruption, there is substantial waste."

As a part of its total productive maintenance (TPM) program,* Frito-Lay empowers employees with what it calls the "Run Right" system. Run Right teaches employees to "identify and do." This means each shift is responsible for identifying problems and making the necessary corrections, when possible. This is accomplished through (1) a "power walk" at the beginning of the shift to ensure that equipment and process settings are performing to standard, (2) mid-shift and post-shift reviews of standards and performance, and (3) posting of any issues on a large whiteboard in the shift office. Items remain on the whiteboard until corrected, which is seldom more than a shift or two.

With good manpower scheduling and tight labor control to hold down variable costs, making time for training is challenging. But supervisors, including the plant manager, are available to fill in on the production line when that is necessary to free an employee for training.

The 30 maintenance personnel hired to cover 24/7 operations at the Florida plant all come with multi-craft skills (e.g., welding, electrical, plumbing). "Multi-craft maintenance personnel are harder to find and cost more," says Wentzel, "but they more than pay for themselves."

Discussion Questions**

1. What might be done to help take Frito-Lay to the next level of outstanding maintenance? Consider factors such as sophisticated software.
2. What are the advantages and disadvantages of giving more responsibility for machine maintenance to the operator?
3. Discuss the pros and cons of hiring multi-craft maintenance personnel.

*At Frito-Lay preventive maintenance, autonomous maintenance, and total productive maintenance are part of a Frito-Lay program known as total productive manufacturing.

**You may wish to view the video that accompanies this case before answering these questions.

Source: Professors Barry Render (Rollins College), Jay Heizer (Texas Lutheran University), and Beverly Amer (Northern Arizona University).

Active Model Exercises

ACTIVE MODEL 17.1, Series Reliability, allows you to substitute various reliabilities for a series of 3 components or workstations. The software computes the reliability of the series. It is illustrated at **www.myomlab.com** or **www. pearsonhighered.com/heizer**.

ACTIVE MODEL 17.2, Redundancy, allows a series of 3 components to each have up to 10 redundant (back-up) components of a given reliability. The software computes the reliability of the series with the selected number of redundant components. It is illustrated at **www.myomlab.com** or **www.pearsonhighered.com/heizer**.

Chapter 17 *Rapid Review*

Main Heading	Review Material	
THE STRATEGIC IMPORTANCE OF MAINTENANCE AND RELIABILITY (pp. 520–521)	Poor maintenance can be disruptive, inconvenient, wasteful, and expensive in dollars and even in lives. The interdependency of operator, machine, and mechanic is a hallmark of successful maintenance and reliability. Good maintenance and reliability management requires employee involvement and good procedures; it enhances a firm's performance and protects its investment. *The objective of maintenance and reliability is to maintain the capability of the system.* ■ **Maintenance**—All activities involved in keeping a system's equipment in working order. ■ **Reliability**—The probability that a machine part or product will function properly for a specified time under stated conditions. The two main tactics for improving reliability are: 1. Improving individual components 2. Providing redundancy The two main tactics for improving maintenance are: 1. Implementing or improving preventive maintenance 2. Increasing repair capabilities or speed	**VIDEO 17.1** Maintenance Drives Profits at Frito-Lay
RELIABILITY (pp. 521–524)	A system is composed of a series of individual interrelated components, each performing a specific job. If any *one* component fails to perform, the overall system can fail. As the number of components in a *series* increases, the reliability of the whole system declines very quickly: $$R_s = R_1 \times R_2 \times R_3 \times \ldots \times R_n \quad (17\text{-}1)$$ where R_1 = reliability of component 1, R_2 = reliability of component 2, and so on Equation (17-1) assumes that the reliability of an individual component does not depend on the reliability of other components. A .90 reliability means that the unit will perform as intended 90% of the time, and it will fail 10% of the time. The basic unit of measure for reliability is the *product failure rate* (FR). FR(N) is the number of failures during a period of time: $$FR(\%) = \frac{\text{Number of failures}}{\text{Number of units tested}} \times 100\% \quad (17\text{-}2)$$ $$FR(N) = \frac{\text{Number of failures}}{\text{Number of unit-hours of operation time}} \quad (17\text{-}3)$$ ■ **Mean time between failures (MTBF)**—The expected time between a repair and the next failure of a component, machine, process, or product. $$MTBF = \frac{1}{FR(N)} \quad (17\text{-}4)$$ ■ **Redundancy**—The use of components in parallel to raise reliability. The reliability of a component along with its backup equals: (Probability that 1st component works) + [(Prob. that backup works) × (Prob. that 1st fails)]	Problems: 17.1–17.2, 17.5–17.14, 17.16, 17.18, 17.19 Virtual Office Hours for Solved Problems: 17.1, 17.2 **ACTIVE MODEL 17.1**
MAINTENANCE (pp. 524–528)	■ **Preventive maintenance**—Involves routine inspections, servicing, and keeping facilities in good repair to prevent failure. ■ **Breakdown maintenance**—Remedial maintenance that occurs when equipment fails and must be repaired on an emergency or priority basis. ■ **Infant mortality**—The failure rate early in the life of a product or process. Consistent with job enrichment practices, machine operators must be held responsible for preventive maintenance of their own equipment and tools.	Problems: 17.3, 17.4, 17.15, 17.17

Main Heading	Review Material	PEARSON myomlab
	Reliability and maintenance are of such importance that most maintenance systems are now computerized. Costs of a breakdown that may get ignored include: • The cost of inventory maintained to compensate for downtime • Downtime, which can have a devastating effect on safety and morale and which adversely affects delivery schedules, destroying customer relations and future sales ■ **Autonomous maintenance**—Partners operators with maintenance personnel to observe, check, adjust, clean, and notify. Employees can predict failures, prevent breakdowns, and prolong equipment life. With autonomous maintenance, the manager is making a step toward both employee empowerment and maintaining system performance.	
TOTAL PRODUCTIVE MAINTENANCE (pp. 528–529)	■ **Total productive maintenance (TPM)**—Combines total quality management with a strategic view of maintenance from process and equipment design to preventive maintenance. Total productive maintenance includes: • Designing machines that are reliable, easy to operate, and easy to maintain • Emphasizing total cost of ownership when purchasing machines, so that service and maintenance are included in the cost • Developing preventive maintenance plans that utilize the best practices of operators, maintenance departments, and depot service • Training for autonomous maintenance so operators maintain their own machines and partner with maintenance personnel	
TECHNIQUES FOR ENHANCING MAINTENANCE (p. 529)	Three techniques that have proven beneficial to effective maintenance are simulation, expert systems, and sensors. Computer simulation is a good tool for evaluating the impact of various policies. Expert systems are computer programs that mimic human logic. Automatic sensors warn when production machinery is about to fail or is becoming damaged by heat, vibration, or fluid leaks.	

Self Test

■ **Before taking the self-test,** refer to the learning objectives listed at the beginning of the chapter and the key terms listed at the end of the chapter.

LO1. The two main tactics for improving reliability are _____ and _____.

LO2. The reliability of a system with *n* independent components equals:
   a) the sum of the individual reliabilities.
   b) the minimum reliability among all components.
   c) the maximum reliability among all components.
   d) the product of the individual reliabilities.
   e) the average of the individual reliabilities.

LO3. What is the formula for the mean time between failures?
   a) Number of failures ÷ Number of unit-hours of operation time
   b) Number of unit-hours of operation time ÷ Number of failures
   c) (Number of failures ÷ Number of units tested) × 100%
   d) (Number of units tested ÷ Number of failures) × 100%
   e) $1 \div FR(\%)$

LO4. The process that is intended to find potential failures and make changes or repairs is known as:
   a) breakdown maintenance.   b) failure maintenance.
   c) preventive maintenance.   d) all of the above.

LO5. The two main tactics for improving maintenance are _____ and _____.

LO6. The appropriate maintenance policy is developed by balancing preventive maintenance costs with breakdown maintenance costs. The problem is that:
   a) preventive maintenance costs are very difficult to identify.
   b) full breakdown costs are seldom considered.
   c) preventive maintenance should be performed, regardless of the cost.
   d) breakdown maintenance must be performed, regardless of the cost.

LO7. _____ maintenance partners operators with maintenance personnel to observe, check, adjust, clean, and notify.
   a) Partnering   b) Operator
   c) Breakdown   d) Six Sigma
   e) Autonomous

Answers: LO1. improving individual components, providing redundancy; **LO2.** d; **LO3.** b; **LO4.** c; **LO5.** implementing or improving preventive maintenance, increasing repair capabilities or speed; **LO6.** b; **LO7.** e.

Module Outline

The Decision Process in Operations

Fundamentals of Decision Making

Decision Tables

Types of Decision-Making Environments:
    Uncertainty, Risk, Certainty

Decision Trees

Discussion Questions
Problems
Case Study: Tom Tucker's Liver Transplant
Rapid Review

Every day operations managers make hundreds of decisions that alter the lives of customers, employees, and owners. These managers need to make those decisions in a logical, coherent way and with the right tools. Those tools include decision tables and decision trees, which we will discuss in this module. To understand these two tools we will also examine (1) states of nature and probabilities that provide the environment of decisions and (2) decision alternatives and decision criteria.

BEFORE COMING TO CLASS, READ MODULE A IN YOUR TEXT AND ANSWER THESE QUESTIONS.

1. What is the role of a decision tree? _____

_____

_____

2. What is a decision table? _____

_____

3. What are the three types of decision-making environments? _____

_____

_____

4. What is *expected monetary value* (EMV)? _____

_____

_____

5. What is expected value of perfect information (EVPI)? _____

_____

_____

6. How do you evaluate the nodes in a decision tree? _____

_____

_____

7. What is a decision tree with *sequential* decisions? _____

_____

_____

THE DECISION PROCESS IN OPERATIONS

(See Flexible Version pp. 532–533)

Six Steps (See Flexible Version pp. 532–533)

1. **Define the Problem**
2. **Develop Objectives**
3. **Develop a Model**
4. **Evaluate Alternative Solutions**
5. **Select the Best Alternative**
6. **Implement the Decision**

FUNDAMENTALS OF DECISION MAKING

(See Flexible Version pp. 533–534)

Alternatives (See Flexible Version p. 533)

States of Nature (See Flexible Version p. 533)

DECISION TABLES (See Flexible Version p. 534)

PRACTICE PROBLEM A.1 ■ EMV

The baseball souvenir concessionaire at Chicago's Wrigley Field has developed a table of the conditional values for various alternative stocking decisions of goods and states of nature (crowd attendance).

| | State of Nature (game attendance) | | |
Alternatives	45,000 crowd	30,000 crowd	15,000 crowd
Large inventory	$22,000	$12,000	−$2,000
Average inventory	15,000	12,000	6,000
Small inventory	9,000	6,000	5,000

The probabilities associated with the states of nature are 0.30 for a large crowd, 0.50 for a crowd of 30,000, and 0.20 for a smaller crowd. Find the alternative with the greatest EMV.

Additional Practice Problem Space

TYPES OF DECISION-MAKING ENVIRONMENTS:
UNCERTAINTY, RISK, CERTAINTY (See Flexible Version pp. 534–538)

Decision Making under Uncertainty (See Flexible Version p. 535)

1. Maximax
2. Maximin
3. Equally Likely

Decision Making under Risk (See Flexible Version p. 536)

Expected Monetary Value (EMV)

(See Flexible Version p. 536)

$$
\begin{aligned}
\text{EMV (Alternative } i) = \ & (\text{Payoff of 1st state of nature}) \\
& \times (\text{Probability of 1st state of nature}) \\
+ \ & (\text{Payoff of 2nd state of nature}) \\
& \times (\text{Probability of 2nd state of nature}) \\
+ \cdots + \ & (\text{Payoff of last state of nature}) \\
& \times (\text{Probability of last state of nature})
\end{aligned}
$$

Decision Making under Certainty (See Flexible Version p. 537)

Expected Value of Perfect Information (EVPI)

(See Flexible Version pp. 537–538)

EVPI = Expected Value with Perfect Information − Maximum EMV

$$
\begin{aligned}
\text{Expected value with perfect information} = \ & (\text{Best outcome or consequence for 1st state}) \\
& \times (\text{Probability of 1st state of nature}) \\
+ \ & (\text{Best outcome for 2nd state of nature}) \\
& \times (\text{Probability of 2nd state of nature}) \\
+ \cdots + \ & (\text{Best outcome for last state of nature}) \\
& \times (\text{Probability of last state of nature})
\end{aligned}
$$

PRACTICE PROBLEM A.2 ■ EVPI

For Practice Problem A.1, find the EVPI.

DECISION TREES (See Flexible Version pp. 538–543)

Five Steps (See Flexible Version p. 538)

1. **Define the Problem**
2. **Draw the Tree**
3. **Assign Probabilities**
4. **Estimate Payoffs**
5. **Compute EMVs by Working Right to Left**

PRACTICE PROBLEM A.3 ■ Decision Tree

Bascomb's Candy is considering the introduction of a new line of products. In order to produce the new line, the bakery is considering either a major or minor renovation of the current plant. The market for the new line of products could be either favorable or unfavorable. Bascomb's Candy has the option of not developing the new product line. Develop the appropriate decision tree.

PRACTICE PROBLEM A.4 ■ EMVs

With major renovation at Bascomb's Candy (see Practice Problem A.3), the payoff from a favorable market is $100,000 and from an unfavorable market it is −$90,000. With minor renovation, the payoff from a favorable market is $40,000 and from an unfavorable market it is −$20,000. Assuming that a favorable market and an unfavorable market are equally likely, solve the decision tree.

PRACTICE PROBLEM A.5 ■ EVPI

Jeff Heyl, the owner of Bascomb's Candy (Practice Problems A.3 and A.4), realizes that he should get more information before making his final decision. He decides to contract with a market research firm to conduct a market survey. How much should Jeff be willing to pay for accurate information (i.e., what is the expected value of perfect information [EVPI])?

Additional Practice Problem Space

Discussion Questions

1. Identify the six steps in the decision process.
2. Give an example of a good decision you made that resulted in a bad outcome. Also give an example of a bad decision you made that had a good outcome. Why was each decision good or bad?
3. What is the *equally likely* decision model?
4. Discuss the differences between decision making under certainty, under risk, and under uncertainty.
5. What is a decision tree?
6. Explain how decision trees might be used in several of the 10 OM decisions.

7. What is the expected value of perfect information?
8. What is the expected value *with* perfect information?
9. Identify the five steps in analyzing a problem using a decision tree.
10. Why are the maximax and maximin strategies considered to be optimistic and pessimistic, respectively?
11. The expected value criterion is considered to be the rational criterion on which to base a decision. Is this true? Is it rational to consider risk?
12. When are decision trees most useful?

Problems*

• **A.1** Given the following conditional value table, determine the appropriate decision under uncertainty using:
a) Maximax
b) Maximin
c) Equally likely **Px**

| | *States of Nature* | | |
Alternatives	Very Favorable Market	Average Market	Unfavorable Market
Build new plant	$350,000	$240,000	–$300,000
Subcontract	$180,000	$ 90,000	–$ 20,000
Overtime	$110,000	$ 60,000	–$ 10,000
Do nothing	$ 0	$ 0	$ 0

••• **A.2** Even though independent gasoline stations have been having a difficult time, Susan Helms has been thinking about starting her own independent gasoline station. Susan's problem is to decide how large her station should be. The annual returns will depend on both the size of her station and a number of marketing factors related to the oil industry and demand for gasoline. After a careful analysis, Susan developed the following table:

Size of First Station	Good Market ($)	Fair Market ($)	Poor Market ($)
Small	50,000	20,000	–10,000
Medium	80,000	30,000	–20,000
Large	100,000	30,000	–40,000
Very large	300,000	25,000	–160,000

For example, if Susan constructs a small station and the market is good, she will realize a profit of $50,000.
a) Develop a decision table for this decision, like the one illustrated in Table A.2 earlier.
b) What is the maximax decision?
c) What is the maximin decision?
d) What is the equally likely decision?
e) Develop a decision tree. Assume each outcome is equally likely, then find the highest EMV. **Px**

*Note: **Px** means the problem may be solved with POM for Windows and/or Excel OM.

• **A.3** Clay Whybark, a soft-drink vendor at Hard Rock Cafe's annual Rockfest, created a table of conditional values for the various alternatives (stocking decision) and states of nature (size of crowd):

| | *States of Nature (demand)* | | |
Alternatives	Big	Average	Small
Large stock	$22,000	$12,000	–$2,000
Average stock	$14,000	$10,000	$6,000
Small stock	$ 9,000	$ 8,000	$4,000

The probabilities associated with the states of nature are 0.3 for a big demand, 0.5 for an average demand, and 0.2 for a small demand.
a) Determine the alternative that provides Clay Whybark the greatest expected monetary value (EMV).
b) Compute the expected value of perfect information (EVPI). **Px**

•• **A.4** Raymond Jacobs owns a health and fitness center, the Muscle-Up, in Ashland. He is considering adding more floor space to meet increasing demand. He will either add no floor space (N), a moderate area of floor space (M), a large area of floor space (L), or an area of floor space that doubles the size of the facility (D). Demand will either stay fixed, increase slightly, or increase greatly. The following are the changes in Muscle-Up's annual profits under each combination of expansion level and demand change level:

| | *Expansion Level* | | | |
Demand Change	N	M	L	D
Fixed	$ 0	–$4,000	–$10,000	–$50,000
Slight Increase	$2,000	$8,000	$ 6,000	$ 4,000
Major Increase	$3,000	$9,000	$20,000	$40,000

Raymond is risk averse and wishes to use the maximin criterion.
a) What are his decision alternatives and what are the states of nature?
b) What should he do? **Px**

• **A.5** Howard Weiss, Inc., is considering building a sensitive new airport scanning device. His managers believe that there is a probability of 0.4 that the ATR Co. will come out with a competitive product. If Weiss adds an assembly line for the product and ATR Co. does not follow with a competitive product, Weiss's expected profit is $40,000; if Weiss adds an assembly line and ATR follows suit, Weiss still expects $10,000 profit. If Weiss adds a new plant addition and ATR does not produce a competitive product, Weiss expects a profit of $600,000; if ATR does compete for this market, Weiss expects a loss of $100,000.

a) Determine the EMV of each decision.
b) Compute the expected value of perfect information. PX

•• **A.6** Deborah Watson's factory is considering three approaches for meeting an expected increase in demand. These three approaches are increasing capacity, using overtime, and buying more equipment. Demand will increase either slightly (S), moderately (M), or greatly (G). The profits for each approach under each possible scenario are as follows:

	Demand Scenario		
Approach	**S**	**M**	**G**
Increasing Capacity	$700,000	$700,000	$ 700,000
Using Overtime	$500,000	$600,000	$1,000,000
Buying Equipment	$600,000	$800,000	$ 800,000

Since the goal is to maximize, and Deborah is risk-neutral, she decides to use the *equally likely* decision criterion to make the decision as to which approach to use. According to this criterion, which approach should be used? PX

• **A.7** The following payoff table provides profits based on various possible decision alternatives and various levels of demand at Amber Gardner's software firm:

	Demand	
	Low	**High**
Alternative 1	$10,000	$30,000
Alternative 2	$ 5,000	$40,000
Alternative 3	-$ 2,000	$50,000

The probability of low demand is 0.4, whereas the probability of high demand is 0.6.

a) What is the highest possible expected monetary value?
b) What is the expected value *with* perfect information (EVwPI)?
c) Calculate the expected value of perfect information for this situation. PX

• **A.8** Leah Johnson, director of Legal Services of Brookline, wants to increase capacity to provide free legal advice but must decide whether to do so by hiring another full-time lawyer or by using part-time lawyers. The table below shows the expected *costs* of the two options for three possible demand levels:

	States of Nature		
Alternatives	**Low Demand**	**Medium Demand**	**High Demand**
Hire full-time	$300	$500	$ 700
Hire part-time	$ 0	$350	$1,000
Probabilities	.2	.5	.3

a) Using expected value, what should Ms. Johnson do?
b) Draw an appropriate decision tree showing payoffs and probabilities. PX

•• **A.9** Chung Manufacturing is considering the introduction of a family of new products. Long-term demand for the product group is somewhat predictable, so the manufacturer must be concerned with the risk of choosing a process that is inappropriate. Chen Chung is VP of operations. He can choose among batch manufacturing or custom manufacturing, or he can invest in group technology. Chen won't be able to forecast demand accurately until after he makes the process choice. Demand will be classified into four compartments: poor, fair, good, and excellent. The table below indicates the payoffs (profits) associated with each process/demand combination, as well as the probabilities of each long-term demand level:

	Poor	**Fair**	**Good**	**Excellent**
Probability	.1	.4	.3	.2
Batch	–$ 200,000	$1,000,000	$1,200,000	$1,300,000
Custom	$ 100,000	$ 300,000	$ 700,000	$ 800,000
Group technology	–$1,000,000	–$ 500,000	$ 500,000	$2,000,000

a) Based on expected value, what choice offers the greatest gain?
b) What would Chen Chung be willing to pay for a forecast that would accurately determine the level of demand in the future? PX

•• **A.10** Consider the following decision table, which Dinesh Dave has developed for Appalacian Enterprises:

		States of Nature		
Decision	**Probability:**	**.40**	**.20**	**.40**
Alternatives		**Low**	**Medium**	**High**
A		$40	$100	$60
B		$85	$ 60	$70
C		$60	$ 70	$70
D		$65	$ 75	$70
E		$70	$ 65	$80

Which decision alternative maximizes the expected value of the payoff? PX

•• **A.11** The University of Dallas bookstore stocks textbooks in preparation for sales each semester. It normally relies on departmental forecasts and preregistration records to determine how many copies of a text are needed. Preregistration shows 90 operations management students enrolled, but bookstore manager Curtis Ketterman has second thoughts, based on his intuition and some historical evidence. Curtis believes that the distribution of sales may range from 70 to 90 units, according to the following probability model:

Demand	70	75	80	85	90
Probability	.15	.30	.30	.20	.05

This textbook costs the bookstore $82 and sells for $112. Any unsold copies can be returned to the publisher, less a restocking fee and shipping, for a net refund of $36.

a) Construct the table of conditional profits.
b) How many copies should the bookstore stock to achieve highest expected value? PX

•• **A.12** Palmer Cheese Company is a small manufacturer of several different cheese products. One product is a cheese spread sold to retail outlets. Susan Palmer must decide how many cases of cheese spread to manufacture each month. The probability that demand will be 6 cases is .1, for 7 cases it is .3, for 8 cases it is .5, and for 9 cases it is .1. The cost of every case is $45, and the price Susan gets for each case is $95. Unfortunately, any cases not sold by the end of the month are of no value as a result of spoilage. How many cases should Susan manufacture each month? **Px**

••• **A.13** Ronald Lau, chief engineer at South Dakota Electronics, has to decide whether to build a new state-of-the-art processing facility. If the new facility works, the company could realize a profit of $200,000. If it fails, South Dakota Electronics could lose $180,000. At this time, Lau estimates a 60% chance that the new process will fail.

The other option is to build a pilot plant and then decide whether to build a complete facility. The pilot plant would cost $10,000 to build. Lau estimates a 50-50 chance that the pilot plant will work. If the pilot plant works, there is a 90% probability that the complete plant, if it is built, will also work. If the pilot plant does not work, there is only a 20% chance that the complete project (if it is constructed) will work. Lau faces a dilemma. Should he build the plant? Should he build the pilot project and then make a decision? Help Lau by analyzing this problem. **Px**

•• **A.14** Karen Villagomez, president of Wright Industries, is considering whether to build a manufacturing plant in the Ozarks. Her decision is summarized in the following table:

Alternatives	Favorable Market	Unfavorable Market
Build large plant	$400,000	–$300,000
Build small plant	$ 80,000	–$ 10,000
Don't build	$ 0	$ 0
Market probabilities	0.4	0.6

a) Construct a decision tree.
b) Determine the best strategy using expected monetary value (EMV).
c) What is the expected value of perfect information (EVPI)? **Px**

•• **A.15** Deborah Kellogg buys Breathalyzer test sets for the Denver Police Department. The quality of the test sets from her two suppliers is indicated in the following table:

Percent Defective	Probability for Loomba Technology	Probability for Stewart-Douglas Enterprises
1	.70	.30
3	.20	.30
5	.10	.40

For example, the probability of getting a batch of tests that are 1% defective from Loomba Technology is .70. Because Kellogg orders 10,000 tests per order, this would mean that there is a .7 probability of getting 100 defective tests out of the 10,000 tests if Loomba Technology is used to fill the order. A defective Breathalyzer test set can be repaired for $0.50. Although the quality of the test sets of the second supplier, Stewart-Douglas Enterprises, is lower, it will sell an order of 10,000 test sets for $37 less than Loomba.

a) Develop a decision tree.
b) Which supplier should Kellogg use? **Px**

•• **A.16** Deborah Hollwager, a concessionaire for the Des Moines ballpark, has developed a table of conditional values for the various alternatives (stocking decision) and states of nature (size of crowd):

Alternatives	States of Nature (size of crowd)		
	Large	Average	Small
Large inventory	$20,000	$10,000	–$2,000
Average inventory	$15,000	$12,000	$6,000
Small inventory	$ 9,000	$ 6,000	$5,000

If the probabilities associated with the states of nature are 0.3 for a large crowd, 0.5 for an average crowd, and 0.2 for a small crowd, determine:
a) The alternative that provides the greatest expected monetary value (EMV).
b) The expected value of perfect information (EVPI). **Px**

• **A.17** Joseph Biggs owns his own sno-cone business and lives 30 miles from a California beach resort. The sale of sno-cones is highly dependent on his location and on the weather. At the resort, his profit will be $120 per day in fair weather, $10 per day in bad weather. At home, his profit will be $70 in fair weather and $55 in bad weather. Assume that on any particular day, the weather service suggests a 40% chance of foul weather.
a) Construct Joseph's decision tree.
b) What decision is recommended by the expected value criterion? **Px**

•• **A.18** Kenneth Boyer is considering opening a bicycle shop in north Chicago. Boyer enjoys biking, but this is to be a business endeavor from which he expects to make a living. He can open a small shop, a large shop, or no shop at all. Because there will be a 5-year lease on the building that Boyer is thinking about using, he wants to make sure he makes the correct decision. Boyer is also thinking about hiring his old marketing professor to conduct a marketing research study to see if there is a market for his services. The results of such a study could be either favorable or unfavorable. Develop a decision tree for Boyer. **Px**

•• **A.19** F. J. Brewerton Retailers, Inc., must decide whether to build a small or a large facility at a new location in south Texas. Demand at the location will either be low or high, with probabilities 0.4 and 0.6, respectively. If Brewerton builds a small facility and demand proves to be high, he then has the option of expanding the facility. If a small facility is built and demand proves to be high, and then the retailer expands the facility, the payoff is $270,000. If a small facility is built and demand proves to be high, but Brewerton then decides not to expand the facility, the payoff is $223,000.

If a small facility is built and demand proves to be low, then there is no option to expand and the payoff is $200,000. If a large facility is built and demand proves to be low, Brewerton then has the option of stimulating demand through local advertising. If he does not exercise this option, then the payoff is $40,000. If he does exercise the advertising option, then the response to advertising will either be modest or sizable, with probabilities of 0.3 and 0.7, respectively. If the response is modest, the payoff is $20,000. If it is sizable, the payoff is $220,000. Finally, if a large facility is built and demand proves to be high, then no advertising is needed and the payoff is $800,000.

a) What should Brewerton do to maximize his expected payoff?
b) What is the value of this expected payoff? **Px**

• • • **A.20**   Dick Holliday is not sure what he should do. He can build either a large video rental section or a small one in his drugstore. He can also gather additional information or simply do nothing. If he gathers additional information, the results could suggest either a favorable or an unfavorable market, but it would cost him $3,000 to gather the information. Holliday believes that there is a 50-50 chance that the information will be favorable. If the rental market is favorable, Holliday will earn $15,000 with a large section or $5,000 with a small. With an unfavorable video-rental market, however, Holliday could lose $20,000 with a large section or $10,000 with a small section. Without gathering additional information, Holliday estimates that the probability of a favorable rental market is .7. A favorable report from the study would increase the probability of a favorable rental market to .9. Furthermore, an unfavorable report from the additional information would decrease the probability of a favorable rental market to .4. Of course, Holliday could ignore these numbers and do nothing. What is your advice to Holliday? **Px**

• • • • **A.21**   Jeff Kaufmann's machine shop sells a variety of machines for job shops. A customer wants to purchase a model XPO2 drilling machine from Jeff's store. The model XPO2 sells for $180,000, but Jeff is out of XPO2s. The customer says he will wait for Jeff to get a model XPO2 in stock. Jeff knows that there is a wholesale market for XPO2s from which he can purchase an XPO2. Jeff can buy an XPO2 today for $150,000, or he can wait a day and buy an XPO2 (if one is available) tomorrow for $125,000. If at least one XPO2 is still available tomorrow, Jeff can wait until the day after tomorrow and buy an XPO2 (if one is still available) for $110,000.

There is a 0.40 probability that there will be no model XPO2s available tomorrow. If there are model XPO2s available tomorrow, there is a 0.70 probability that by the day after tomorrow, there will be no model XPO2s available in the wholesale market. Three days from now, it is certain that no model XPO2s will be available on the wholesale market. What is the maximum expected profit that Jeff can achieve? What should Jeff do? **Px**

• • • • **A.22**   The city of Segovia is contemplating building a second airport to relieve congestion at the main airport and is considering two potential sites, X and Y. Hard Rock Hotels would like to purchase land to build a hotel at the new airport. The value of land

has been rising in anticipation and is expected to skyrocket once the city decides between sites X and Y. Consequently, Hard Rock would like to purchase land now. Hard Rock will sell the land if the city chooses not to locate the airport nearby. Hard Rock has four choices: (1) buy land at X, (2) buy land at Y, (3) buy land at both X and Y, or (4) do nothing. Hard Rock has collected the following data (which are in millions of euros):

	Site X	Site Y
Current purchase price	27	15
Profits if airport and hotel built at this site	45	30
Sale price if airport not built at this site	9	6

Hard Rock determines there is a 45% chance the airport will be built at X (hence, a 55% chance it will be built at Y).

a) Set up the decision table.
b) What should Hard Rock decide to do to maximize total net profit? **Px**

• • • • **A.23**   Louisiana is busy designing new lottery scratch-off games. In the latest game, Bayou Boondoggle, the player is instructed to scratch off one spot: A, B, or C. A can reveal "Loser," "Win $1," or "Win $50." B can reveal "Loser" or "Take a Second Chance." C can reveal "Loser" or "Win $500." On the second chance, the player is instructed to scratch off D or E. D can reveal "Loser" or "Win $1." E can reveal "Loser" or "Win $10." The probabilities at A are .9, .09, and .01. The probabilities at B are .8 and .2. The probabilities at C are .999 and .001. The probabilities at D are .5 and .5. Finally, the probabilities at E are .95 and .05. Draw the decision tree that represents this scenario. Use proper symbols and label all branches clearly. Calculate the expected value of this game. **Px**

• • • • **A.24**   On the opening page of Module A and in Example A9, we follow the poker decision made by Paul Phillips against veteran T.J. Cloutier. Create a decision tree that corresponds with the decision made by Phillips. **Px**

► **Refer to** myomlab **for these additional homework problems: A.25–A.32**

Case Study

▶ Tom Tucker's Liver Transplant

Tom Tucker, a robust 50-year-old executive living in the northern suburbs of St. Paul, has been diagnosed by a University of Minnesota internist as having a decaying liver. Although he is otherwise healthy, Tucker's liver problem could prove fatal if left untreated.

Firm research data are not yet available to predict the likelihood of survival for a man of Tucker's age and condition without surgery. However, based on her own experience and recent medical journal articles, the internist tells him that if he elects to avoid surgical treatment of the liver problem, chances of survival will be approximately as follows: only a 60% chance of living 1 year, a 20% chance of surviving for 2 years, a 10% chance for 5 years, and a 10% chance of living to age 58. She places his

probability of survival beyond age 58 without a liver transplant to be extremely low.

The transplant operation, however, is a serious surgical procedure. Five percent of patients die during the operation or its recovery stage, with an additional 45% dying during the first year. Twenty percent survive for 5 years, 13% survive for 10 years, and 8%, 5%, and 4% survive, respectively, for 15, 20, and 25 years.

Discussion Questions

1. Do you think that Tucker should select the transplant operation?
2. What other factors might be considered?

Module A *Rapid* Review

Main Heading	Review Material	
THE DECISION PROCESS IN OPERATIONS (pp. 532–533)	To achieve the goals of their organizations, managers must understand how decisions are made and know which decision-making tools to use. Overcoming uncertainty is a manager's mission. Decision tables and decision trees are used in a wide number of OM situations.	
FUNDAMENTALS OF DECISION MAKING (pp. 533–534)	*Alternative*—A course of action or strategy that may be chosen by a decision maker. *State of nature*—An occurrence or a situation over which a decision maker has little or no control. Symbols used in a decision tree: 1. ☐—A decision node from which one of several alternatives may be selected. 2. ◯—A state-of-nature node out of which one state of nature will occur. When constructing a decision tree, we must be sure that all alternatives and states of nature are in their correct and logical places and that we include *all* possible alternatives and states of nature, usually including the "do nothing" option.	
DECISION TABLES (p. 534)	■ **Decision table**—A tabular means of analyzing decision alternatives and states of nature. A decision table is sometimes called a payoff table. For any alternative and a particular state of nature, there is a *consequence*, or an *outcome*, which is usually expressed as a monetary value; this is called the *conditional value*.	
TYPES OF DECISION-MAKING ENVIRONMENTS (pp. 534–538)	There are three decision-making environments: (1) decision making under uncertainty, (2) decision making under risk, and (3) decision making under certainty. When there is complete *uncertainty* about which state of nature in a decision environment may occur (i.e., when we cannot even assess probabilities for each possible outcome), we rely on three decision methods: (1) maximax, (2) maximin, and (3) equally likely. ■ **Maximax**—A criterion that finds an alternative that maximizes the maximum outcome. ■ **Maximin**—A criterion that finds an alternative that maximizes the minimum outcome. ■ **Equally likely**—A criterion that assigns equal probability to each state of nature. Maximax is also called an "optimistic" decision criterion, while maximin is also called a "pessimistic" decision criterion. Maximax and maximin present best case/worst case planning scenarios. Decision making under risk relies on probabilities. The states of nature must be mutually exclusive and collectively exhaustive, and their probabilities must sum to 1. ■ **Expected monetary value (EMV)**—The expected payout or value of a variable that has different possible states of nature, each with an associated probability. The EMV represents the expected value or *mean* return for each alternative *if we could repeat this decision (or similar types of decisions) a large number of times.* The EMV for an alternative is the sum of all possible payoffs from the alternative, each weighted by the probability of that payoff occurring: $$\text{EMV (Alternative } i) = (\text{Payoff of 1st state of nature})$$ $$\times (\text{Probability of 1st of state of nature})$$ $$+ (\text{Payoff of 2nd state of nature}) \times (\text{Probability of 2nd state of nature})$$ $$+ \ldots + (\text{Payoff of last state of nature}) \times (\text{Probability of last state of nature})$$ ■ **Expected value of perfect information (EVPI)**—The difference between the payoff under perfect information and the payoff under risk. ■ **Expected value with perfect information (EVwPI)**—The expected (average) return if perfect information is available. EVPI represents an upper bound on what you would be willing to spend on state-of nature information: $$\text{EVPI} = \text{EVwPI} - \text{Maximum EMV}$$ $$\text{EVwPI} = (\text{Best outcome for 1st state of nature}) \times (\text{Probability of 1st state of nature})$$ $$+ (\text{Best outcome for 2nd state of nature}) \times (\text{Probability of 2nd state of nature})$$ $$+ \cdots + (\text{Best outcome for last state of nature}) \times (\text{Probability of last state of nature})$$	Problems: A.1–A.12, A.14, A.16 Virtual Office Hours for Solved Problems: A.1, A.2

Main Heading	Review Material	

DECISION TREES
(pp. 538–543)

When there are two or more sequential decisions, and later decisions are based on the outcome of prior ones, the decision tree (as opposed to decision table) approach becomes appropriate.

- **Decision tree**—A graphical means of analyzing decision alternatives and states of nature.

Analyzing problems with *decision trees* involves five steps:

1. Define the problem.
2. Structure or draw the decision tree.
3. Assign probabilities to the states of nature.
4. Estimate payoffs for each possible combination of decision alternatives and states of nature.
5. Solve the problem by computing the expected monetary values (EMV) for each state-of-nature node. This is done by working *backward*—that is, by starting at the right of the tree and working back to decision nodes on the left:

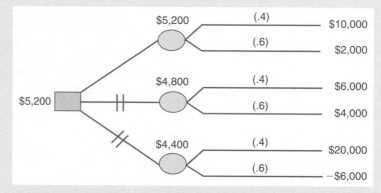

Decision trees force managers to examine all possible outcomes, including unfavorable ones. A manager is also forced to make decisions in a logical, sequential manner.

Short parallel lines on a decision tree mean "prune" that branch, as it is less favorable than another available option and may be dropped.

Problems: A.2, A.8, A.14, A.17, A.18, A.19, A.20, A.21, A.23, A.24

Virtual Office Hours for Solved Problem: A.3

Self Test

- **Before taking the self-test,** refer to the learning objectives listed at the beginning of the module and the key terms listed at the end of the module.

LO1. On a decision tree, at each state-of-nature node:
   a) the alternative with the greatest EMV is selected.
   b) an EMV is calculated.
   c) all probabilities are added together.
   d) the branch with the highest probability is selected.

LO2. In decision table terminology, a course of action or a strategy that may be chosen by a decision maker is called a(n):
   a) payoff.   b) alternative.
   c) state of nature.   d) all of the above.

LO3. If probabilities are available to the decision maker, then the decision-making environment is called:
   a) certainty.   b) uncertainty.
   c) risk.   d) none of the above.

LO4. What is the EMV for Alternative 1 in the following decision table?

	State of nature	
Alternative	*S1*	*S2*
A1	$15,000	$20,000
A2	$10,000	$30,000
Probability	0.30	0.70

   a) $15,000   b) $17,000
   c) $17,500   d) $18,500
   e) $20,000

LO5. The most that a person should pay for perfect information is:
   a) the EVPI.
   b) the maximum EMV minus the minimum EMV.
   c) the minimum EMV.
   d) the maximum EMV.

LO6. On a decision tree, once the tree has been drawn and the payoffs and probabilities have been placed on the tree, the analysis (computing EMVs and selecting the best alternative):
   a) is done by working backward (starting on the right and moving to the left).
   b) is done by working forward (starting on the left and moving to the right).
   c) is done by starting at the top of the tree and moving down.
   d) is done by starting at the bottom of the tree and moving up.

LO7. A decision tree is preferable to a decision table when:
   a) a number of sequential decisions are to be made.
   b) probabilities are available.
   c) the maximax criterion is used.
   d) the objective is to maximize regret.

Answers: LO1. b; LO2. b; LO3. c; LO4. d; LO5. a; LO6. a; LO7. a.

Module Outline

Why Use Linear Programming?

Requirements of a Linear Programming
    Problem

Formulating Linear Programming Problems

Graphical Solution to a Linear
    Programming Problem

Sensitivity Analysis

Solving Minimization Problems

Linear Programming Applications

The Simplex Method of LP

Discussion Questions
Problems
Case Study: Golding Landscaping
    and Plants, Inc.
Active Model Exercise
Rapid Review

Linear programming (LP) is a widely used mathematical tool that can help operations managers plan and make the decisions necessary to allocate resources. The technique requires the development of a mathematical objective function that defines the quantity to be maximized or minimized and the development of constraint equations that limit the degree to which resources are available.

LP problems with two variables can be solved graphically, while larger problems are solved with a technique known as the simplex method. Both types of problems can be solved by hand or by computer. Large LP problems are typically solved by computer.

BEFORE COMING TO CLASS, READ MODULE B IN YOUR TEXT AND ANSWER THESE QUESTIONS.

1. How do you formulate an LP problem? _____

   _____

2. What is an iso profit line and how is it used to solve an LP problem?

   _____

   _____

3. What is the *corner point method*? _____

   _____

4. What is sensitivity analysis and what are shadow prices? _____

   _____

   _____

5. How does a minimization problem differ from a maximization problem? _____

   _____

6. What is a product mix problem; a diet LP problem; a labor scheduling problem? _____

   _____

WHY USE LINEAR PROGRAMMING? (See Flexible Version pp. 548–549)

REQUIREMENTS OF A LINEAR PROGRAMMING PROBLEM

(See Flexible Version p. 549)

1. **Objective**

2. **Constraints**

3. **Alternatives**

4. **Linear**

FORMULATING LINEAR PROGRAMMING PROBLEMS

(See Flexible Version pp. 549–550)

GRAPHICAL SOLUTION TO A LINEAR PROGRAMMING PROBLEM (See Flexible Version pp. 550–555)

Decision Variables

Objective Function

Constraints

Feasible Region (See Flexible Version p. 551)

Iso-Profit Line Method (See Flexible Version pp. 551–553)

Corner-Point Method (See Flexible Version pp. 553–555)

PRACTICE PROBLEM B.1 ■ Maximization Problem

Chad's Pottery Barn has enough clay to make 24 small vases or 6 large vases. He has only enough of a special glazing compound to glaze 16 of the small vases or 8 of the large vases. Let X_1 = the number of small vases and X_2 = the number of large vases. The smaller vases sell for $3 each, and the larger vases would bring $9 each.

a. Formulate the problem.

b. Solve the problem graphically.

Additional Practice Problem Space

SENSITIVITY ANALYSIS (See Flexible Version pp. 555–557)

Changes in the Right-Hand-Side Values

(See Flexible Version pp. 556–557)

Shadow Price

Changes in the Objective Function Coefficient

(See Flexible Version p. 557)

Sample Excel Sensitivity Analysis Output (Using Text Example) (See Flexible Version p. 555)

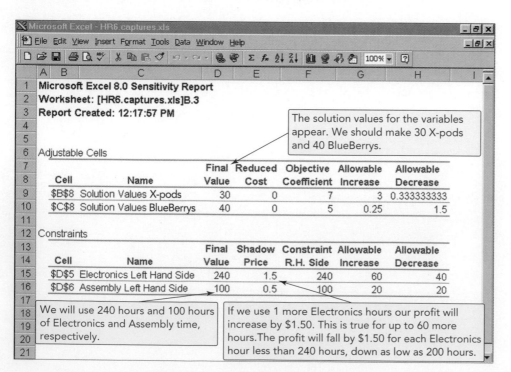

▲ **PROGRAM B.1** Sensitivity Analysis for Shader Electronics Using Excel's Solver

SOLVING MINIMIZATION PROBLEMS (See Flexible Version pp. 557–559)

PRACTICE PROBLEM B.2 ■ Minimization Problem

A fabric firm has received an order for cloth specified to contain at least 45 pounds of cotton and 25 pounds of silk. The cloth can be woven out of any suitable mix of two yarns, A and B. They contain the proportions of cotton and silk (by weight) as shown in the following table:

	Cotton	Silk
A	30%	50%
B	60%	10%

Material A costs $3 per pound, and B costs $2 per pound. What quantities (pounds) of A and B yarns should be used to minimize the cost of this order?

Additional Practice Problem Space

LINEAR PROGRAMMING APPLICATIONS (See Flexible Version pp. 559–562)

Production Mix

Diet Problem

Labor Scheduling

Practice Problem Space

THE SIMPLEX METHOD OF LP* (See Flexible Version p. 562)

*See Tutorial 3 on our website for extended discussion

Discussion Questions

1. List at least four applications of linear programming problems.
2. What is a "corner point"? Explain why solutions to linear programming problems focus on corner points.
3. Define the feasible region of a graphical LP problem. What is a feasible solution?
4. Each linear programming problem that has a feasible region has an infinite number of solutions. Explain.
5. Under what circumstances is the objective function more important than the constraints in a linear programming model?
6. Under what circumstances are the constraints more important than the objective function in a linear programming model?
7. Why is the diet problem, in practice, applicable for animals but not particularly for people?
8. How many feasible solutions are there in a linear program? Which ones do we need to examine to find the optimal solution?

9. Define shadow price (or dual value).
10. Explain how to use the iso-cost line in a graphical minimization problem.
11. Compare how the corner-point and iso-profit line methods work for solving graphical problems.
12. Where a constraint crosses the vertical or horizontal axis, the quantity is fairly obvious. How does one go about finding the quantity coordinates where two constraints cross, not at an axis?
13. Suppose a linear programming (maximation) problem has been solved and that the optimal value of the objective function is $300. Suppose an additional constraint is added to this problem. Explain how this might affect each of the following:
    a) The feasible region.
    b) The optimal value of the objective function.

Problems*

• **B.1** Solve the following linear programming problem graphically:

$$\text{Maximize profit} = 4X + 6Y$$
$$\text{Subject to:} \quad X + 2Y \le 8$$
$$5X + 4Y \le 20$$
$$X, Y \ge 0 \quad \text{P}_X$$

• **B.2** Solve the following linear programming problem graphically:

$$\text{Maximize profit} = X + 10Y$$
$$\text{Subject to:} \quad 4X + 3Y \le 36$$
$$2X + 4Y \le 40$$
$$Y \ge 3$$
$$X, Y \ge 0 \quad \text{P}_X$$

• **B.3** Solve the following linear program graphically:

$$\text{Minimize cost} = X_1 + X_2$$
$$8X_1 + 16X_2 \ge 64$$
$$X_1 \ge 0$$
$$X_2 \ge -2 \quad \text{P}_X$$

•• **B.4** Consider the following linear programming problem:

$$\text{Maximize profit} = 30X_1 + 10X_2$$
$$\text{Subject to:} \quad 3X_1 + X_2 \le 300$$
$$X_1 + X_2 \le 200$$
$$X_1 \le 100$$
$$X_2 \ge 50$$
$$X_1 - X_2 \le 0$$
$$X_1, X_2 \ge 0$$

a) Solve the problem graphically.
b) Is there more than one optimal solution? Explain. **P**$_X$

• **B.5** Solve the following LP problem graphically:

$$\text{Minimize cost} = 24X + 15Y$$
$$\text{Subject to:} \quad 7X + 11Y \ge 77$$
$$16X + 4Y \ge 80$$
$$X, Y \ge 0 \quad \text{P}_X$$

*Note: **P**$_X$ means the problem may be solved with POM for Windows and/or Excel OM.

•• **B.6** Ed Silver Dog Food Company wishes to introduce a new brand of dog biscuits composed of chicken- and liver-flavored biscuits that meet certain nutritional requirements. The liver-flavored biscuits contain 1 unit of nutrient A and 2 units of nutrient B; the chicken-flavored biscuits contain 1 unit of nutrient A and 4 units of nutrient B. According to federal requirements, there must be at least 40 units of nutrient A and 60 units of nutrient B in a package of the new mix. In addition, the company has decided that there can be no more than 15 liver-flavored biscuits in a package. If it costs 1¢ to make 1 liver-flavored biscuit and 2¢ to make 1 chicken-flavored, what is the optimal product mix for a package of the biscuits to minimize the firm's cost?
a) Formulate this as a linear programming problem.
b) Solve this problem graphically, giving the optimal values of all variables.
c) What is the total cost of a package of dog biscuits using the optimal mix? **P**$_X$

• **B.7** The Electrocomp Corporation manufactures two electrical products: air conditioners and large fans. The assembly process for each is similar in that both require a certain amount of wiring and drilling. Each air conditioner takes 3 hours of wiring and 2 hours of drilling. Each fan must go through 2 hours of wiring and 1 hour of drilling. During the next production period, 240 hours of wiring time are available and up to 140 hours of drilling time may be used. Each air conditioner sold yields a profit of $25. Each fan assembled may be sold for a $15 profit.

Formulate and solve this LP production-mix situation, and find the best combination of air conditioners and fans that yields the highest profit. **P**$_X$

• **B.8** The Lauren Shur Tub Company manufactures two lines of bathtubs, called model A and model B. Every tub requires blending a certain amount of steel and zinc; the company has available a total of 25,000 lb of steel and 6,000 lb of zinc. Each model A bathtub requires a mixture of 125 lb of steel and 20 lb of zinc, and each yields a profit of $90. Each model B tub requires 100 lb of steel and 30 lb of zinc and can be sold for a profit of $70.

Find by graphical linear programming the best production mix of bathtubs. **P**$_X$

•• **B.9** Spitzfire, Inc., manufactures specialty cars and trucks. It has just opened a new factory where the C1 car and the T1 truck can both be manufactured. To make either vehicle, processing in the assembly shop and in the paint shop are required. It takes 1/40 of a day and 1/60 of a day to paint a truck of type T1 and a car of type C1 in the paint shop, respectively. It takes 1/50 of a day to assemble either type of vehicle in the assembly shop.

A T1 truck and a C1 car yield profits of $300 and $220, respectively, per vehicle sold.

a) Define the objective function and constraint equations.
b) Graph the feasible region.
c) What is a maximum-profit daily production plan at the new factory?
d) How much profit will such a plan yield, assuming whatever is produced is sold? **Px**

•   **B.10** MSA Computer Corporation manufactures two models of minicomputers, the Alpha 4 and the Beta 5. The firm employs 5 technicians, working 160 hours each per month, on its assembly line. Management insists that full employment (that is, *all* 160 hours of time) be maintained for each worker during next month's operations. It requires 20 labor-hours to assemble each Alpha 4 computer and 25 labor-hours to assemble each Beta 5 model. MSA wants to see at least 10 Alpha 4s and at least 15 Beta 5s produced during the production period. Alpha 4s generate a $1,200 profit per unit, and Betas yield $1,800 each.

Determine the most profitable number of each model of minicomputer to produce during the coming month. **Px**

•   **B.11** The Sweet Smell Fertilizer Company markets bags of manure labeled "not less than 60 lb dry weight." The packaged manure is a combination of compost and sewage wastes. To provide good-quality fertilizer, each bag should contain at least 30 lb of compost but no more than 40 lb of sewage. Each pound of compost costs Sweet Smell 5¢ and each pound of sewage costs 4¢. Use a graphical LP method to determine the least-cost blend of compost and sewage in each bag. **Px**

•   **B.12** Consider Faud Shatara's following linear programming formulation:

$$\text{Minimize cost} = \$1X_1 + \$2X_2$$
$$\text{Subject to:} \quad X_1 + 3X_2 \geq 90$$
$$8X_1 + 2X_2 \geq 160$$
$$3X_1 + 2X_2 \geq 120$$
$$X_2 \leq 70$$

a) Graphically illustrate the feasible region to indicate to Faud which corner point produces the optimal solution.
b) What is the cost of this solution? **Px**

•   **B.13** The LP relationships that follow were formulated by Jeffrey Rummel at the Connecticut Chemical Company. Which ones are invalid for use in a linear programming problem, and why?

$$\text{Maximize} = 6X_1 + \tfrac{1}{2}X_1X_2 + 5X_3$$
$$\text{Subject to:} \quad 4X_1X_2 + 2X_3 \leq 70$$
$$7.9X_1 - 4X_2 \geq 15.6$$
$$3X_1 + 3X_2 + 3X_3 \geq 21$$
$$19X_2 - \tfrac{1}{3}X_3 = 17$$
$$-X_1 - X_2 + 4X_3 = 5$$
$$4X_1 + 2X_2 + 3\sqrt{X_3} \leq 80$$

••   **B.14** Kalyan Singhal Corp. makes three products, and it has three machines available as resources as given in the following LP problem:

$$\text{Maximize contribution} = 4X_1 + 4X_2 + 7X_3$$
$$\text{Subject to: } 1X_1 + 7X_2 + 4X_3 \leq 100 \text{ (hours on machine 1)}$$
$$2X_1 + 1X_2 + 7X_3 \leq 110 \text{ (hours on machine 2)}$$
$$8X_1 + 4X_2 + 1X_3 \leq 100 \text{ (hours on machine 3)}$$

a) Determine the optimal solution using LP software.
b) Is there unused time available on any of the machines with the optimal solution?
c) What would it be worth to the firm to make an additional hour of time available on the third machine?
d) How much would the firm's profit increase if an extra 10 hours of time were made available on the second machine at no extra cost? **Px**

••   **B.15** Consider the following LP problem developed at Jeff Spencer's San Antonio optical scanning firm:

$$\text{Maximize profit} = \$1X_1 + \$1X_2$$
$$\text{Subject to:} \quad 2X_1 + 1X_2 \leq 100$$
$$1X_1 + 2X_2 \leq 100$$

a) What is the optimal solution to this problem? Solve it graphically.
b) If a technical breakthrough occurred that raised the profit per unit of X_1 to $3, would this affect the optimal solution?
c) Instead of an increase in the profit coefficient X_1 to $3, suppose that profit was overestimated and should only have been $1.25. Does this change the optimal solution? **Px**

•••   **B.16** The Arden County, Maryland, superintendent of education is responsible for assigning students to the three high schools in his county. He recognizes the need to bus a certain number of students, because several sectors, A–E, of the county are beyond walking distance to a school. The superintendent partitions the county into five geographic sectors as he attempts to establish a plan that will minimize the total number of student miles traveled by bus. He also recognizes that if a student happens to live in a certain sector and is assigned to the high school in that sector, there is no need to bus him because he can walk to school. The three schools are located in sectors B, C, and E.

The accompanying table reflects the number of high-school-age students living in each sector and the distance in miles from each sector to each school:

	Distance to School			
Sector	School in Sector B	School in Sector C	School in Sector E	Number of Students
A	5	8	6	700
B	0	4	12	500
C	4	0	7	100
D	7	2	5	800
E	12	7	0	400
				2,500

Each high school has a capacity of 900 students.

a) Set up the objective function and constraints of this problem using linear programming so that the total number of student miles traveled by bus is minimized.

b) Solve the problem. **P✗**

•• **B.17** The National Credit Union has $250,000 available to invest in a 12-month commitment. The money can be placed in Treasury notes yielding an 8% return or in municipal bonds at an average rate of return of 9%. Credit union regulations require diversification to the extent that at least 50% of the investment be placed in Treasury notes. Because of defaults in such municipalities as Cleveland and New York, it is decided that no more than 40% of the investment be placed in bonds. How much should the National Credit Union invest in each security so as to maximize its return on investment? **P✗**

•• **B.18** Boston's famous Limoges Restaurant is open 24 hours a day. Servers report for duty at 3 A.M., 7 A.M., 11 A.M., 3 P.M., 7 P.M., or 11 P.M., and each works an 8-hour shift. The following table shows the minimum number of workers needed during the 6 periods into which the day is divided:

Period	Time	Number of Servers Required
1	3 A.M.–7 A.M.	3
2	7 A.M.–11 A.M.	12
3	11 A.M.–3 P.M.	16
4	3 P.M.–7 P.M.	9
5	7 P.M.–11 P.M.	11
6	11 P.M.–3 A.M.	4

Owner Michelle Limoges's scheduling problem is to determine how many servers should report for work at the start of each time period in order to minimize the total staff required for one day's operation. (*Hint:* Let X_i equal the number of servers beginning work in time period i, where $i = 1, 2, 3, 4, 5, 6$.) **P✗**

• **B.19** A craftsman named Chuck Synovec builds two kinds of birdhouses, one for wrens and a second for bluebirds. Each wren birdhouse takes 4 hours of labor and 4 units of lumber. Each bluebird house requires 2 hours of labor and 12 units of lumber. The craftsman has available 60 hours of labor and 120 units of lumber. Wren houses yield a profit of $6 each and bluebird houses yield a profit of $15 each.

a) Write out the objective and constraints.

b) Solve graphically. **P✗**

•• **B.20** Each coffee table produced by Robert West Designers nets the firm a profit of $9. Each bookcase yields a $12 profit. West's firm is small and its resources limited. During any given production period (of 1 week), 10 gallons of varnish and 12 lengths of high-quality redwood are available. Each coffee table requires approximately 1 gallon of varnish and 1 length of redwood. Each bookcase takes 1 gallon of varnish and 2 lengths of wood.

Formulate West's production-mix decision as a linear programming problem, and solve. How many tables and bookcases should be produced each week? What will the maximum profit be? **P✗**

•• **B.21** Par, Inc., produces a standard golf bag and a deluxe golf bag on a weekly basis. Each golf bag requires time for cutting and dyeing and time for sewing and finishing, as shown in the following table:

	Hours Required per Bag	
Product	Cutting and Dyeing	Sewing and Finishing
Standard Bag	1/2	1
Deluxe Bag	1	2/3

The profits per bag and weekly hours available for cutting and dyeing and for sewing and finishing are as follows:

Product	Profit per Unit ($)
Standard bag	10
Deluxe bag	8

Activity	Weekly Hours Available
Cutting and dyeing	300
Sewing and finishing	360

Par, Inc., will sell whatever quantities it produces of these two products.

a) Find the mix of standard and deluxe golf bags to produce per week that maximizes weekly profit from these activities.

b) What is the value of the profit? **P✗**

• **B.22** Solve the following linear programming problem graphically:

$$\text{Minimize cost} = 4X_1 + 5X_2$$
$$\text{Subject to:} \quad X_1 + 2X_2 \geq 80$$
$$3X_1 + X_2 \geq 75$$
$$X_1, X_2 \geq 0 \quad \textbf{P✗}$$

•• **B.23** Thompson Distributors packages and distributes industrial supplies. A standard shipment can be packaged in a class A container, a class K container, or a class T container. A single class A container yields a profit of $9; a class K container, a profit of $7; and a class T container, a profit of $15. Each shipment prepared requires a certain amount of packing material and a certain amount of time.

	Resources Needed per Standard Shipment	
Class of Container	Packing Material (pounds)	Packing Time (hours)
A	2	2
K	1	6
T	3	4

Total amount of resource available each week	130 pounds	240 hours

Jason Thompson, head of the firm, must decide the optimal number of each class of container to pack each week. He is bound by the previously mentioned resource restrictions but also decides that he must keep his 6 full-time packers employed all 240 hours (6 workers × 40 hours) each week.

Formulate and solve this problem using LP software. **P✗**

•• **B.24** How many corner points are there in the feasible region of the following problem?

$$\text{Minimize cost} = X - Y$$
$$\text{Subject to:} \quad X \leq 4$$
$$-X \leq 2$$
$$X + 2Y \leq 6$$
$$-X + 2Y \leq 8$$
$$Y \geq 0$$

(*Note:* X values can be negative in this problem.)

•• **B.25** The Denver advertising agency promoting the new Breem dishwashing detergent wants to get the best exposure possible for the product within the $100,000 advertising budget ceiling placed on it. To do so, the agency needs to decide how much of the budget to spend on each of its two most effective media: (1) television spots during the afternoon hours and (2) large ads in the city's Sunday newspaper. Each television spot costs $3,000; each Sunday newspaper ad costs $1,250. The expected exposure, based on industry ratings, is 35,000 viewers for each TV commercial and 20,000 readers for each newspaper advertisement. The agency director, Deborah Kellogg, knows from experience that it is important to use both media in order to reach the broadest spectrum of potential Breem customers. She decides that at least 5 but no more than 25 television spots should be ordered, and that at least 10 newspaper ads should be contracted. How many times should each of the two media be used to obtain maximum exposure while staying within the budget? Use the graphical method to solve. **Px**

••• **B.26** Libby Temple Manufacturing has three factories (1, 2, and 3) and three warehouses (A, B, and C). The following table shows the shipping costs between each factory and warehouse, the factory manufacturing capabilities (in thousands), and the warehouse capacities (in thousands). Management would like to keep the warehouses filled to capacity in order to generate demand.
a) Write the objective function and the constraint equations. Let $X_{1A} = 1{,}000$s of units shipped from factory 1 to warehouse A, and so on.
b) Solve by computer. **Px**

To From	Warehouse A	Warehouse B	Warehouse C	Production Capability
Factory 1	$ 6	$ 5	$ 3	6
Factory 2	$ 8	$10	$ 8	8
Factory 3	$11	$14	$18	10
Capacity	7	12	5	

•••• **B.27** A fertilizer manufacturer has to fulfill supply contracts to its two main customers (650 tons to Customer A and 800 tons to Customer B). It can meet this demand by shipping existing inventory from any of its three warehouses. Warehouse 1 (W1) has 400 tons of inventory on hand, Warehouse 2 (W2) has 500 tons, and Warehouse 3 (W3) has 600 tons. The company would like to arrange the shipping for the lowest cost possible, where the per-ton transit costs are as follows:

	W1	W2	W3
Customer A	$7.50	$6.25	$6.50
Customer B	6.75	7.00	8.00

a) Explain what each of the six decision variables (V) is. (*Hint:* Look at the Solver report below.)

V A1: _____

V A2: _____

V A3: _____

V B1: _____

V B2: _____

V B3: _____

b) Write out the objective function in terms of the variables (V A1, V A2, etc.) and the objective coefficients.
c) Aside from nonnegativity of the variables, what are the five constraints? In the below chart, write a short description for each constraint, and write out the formula (and circle the type of equality/inequality).

Description	Variables and Coefficients	What Type?	RHS
C1: _____	Formula: _____	(= > | = | = <) _____	
C2: _____	Formula: _____	(= > | = | = <) _____	
C3: _____	Formula: _____	(= > | = | = <) _____	
C4: _____	Formula: _____	(= > | = | = <) _____	
C5: _____	Formula: _____	(= > | = | = <) _____	

After you formulate and enter the linear program for Problem B.27 in Excel, the Solver gives you the following sensitivity report:

Adjustable Cells

Cell	Name	Final Value	Reduced Cost	Objective Coefficient	Allowable Increase	Allowable Decrease
B6	V A1	0	1.5	7.5	1E+30	1.5
C6	V A2	100	0	6.25	0.25	0.75
D6	V A3	550	0	6.5	0.75	0.25
E6	V B1	400	0	6.75	0.5	1E+30
F6	V B2	400	0	7	0.75	0.5
G6	V B3	0	0.75	8	1E+30	0.75

Constraints

Cell	Name	Final Value	Shadow Price	Constraint R.H. Side	Allowable Increase	Allowable Decrease
H7	C1	650	6.5	650	50	550
H8	C2	800	7.25	800	50	400
H9	C3	400	−0.5	400	400	50
H10	C4	500	−0.25	500	550	50
H11	C5	550	0	600	1E+30	50

d) How many of the constraints are binding?

e) How much slack/surplus is there with the nonbinding constraint(s)?

f) What is the range of optimality on variable V A3?

g) If we could ship 10 tons less to Customer A, how much money *might* we be able to save? If we could choose to short *either* Customer A or Customer B by 10 tons, which would we prefer to short? Why? **Px**

•••• **B.28** New Orleans's Mt. Sinai Hospital is a large, private, 600-bed facility complete with laboratories, operating rooms, and X-ray equipment. In seeking to increase revenues, Mt. Sinai's administration has decided to make a 90-bed addition on a portion of adjacent land currently used for staff parking. The administrators feel that the labs, operating rooms, and X-ray department are not being fully utilized at present and do not need to be expanded to handle additional patients. The addition of 90 beds, however, involves deciding how many beds should be allocated to the medical staff (for medical patients) and how many to the surgical staff (for surgical patients).

The hospital's accounting and medical records departments have provided the following pertinent information. The average hospital stay for a medical patient is 8 days, and the average medical patient generates $2,280 in revenues. The average surgical patient is in the hospital 5 days and generates $1,515 in revenues. The laboratory is capable of handling 15,000 tests per year more than it *was* handling. The average medical patient requires 3.1 lab tests, the average surgical patient 2.6 lab tests. Furthermore, the average medical patient uses 1 X-ray, the average surgical patient 2 X-rays. If the hospital were expanded by 90 beds, the X-ray department could handle up to 7,000 X-rays without significant additional cost. Finally, the administration estimates that up to 2,800 additional operations could be performed in existing operating-room facilities. Medical patients, of course, require no surgery, whereas each surgical patient generally has one surgery performed.

Formulate this problem so as to determine how many medical beds and how many surgical beds should be added to maximize revenues. Assume that the hospital is open 365 days per year. **Px**

•••• **B.29** Charles Watts Electronics manufactures the following six peripheral devices used in computers especially designed for jet fighter planes: internal modems, external modems, graphics circuit boards, jump drives, hard disk drives, and memory expansion boards. Each of these technical products requires time, in minutes, on three types of electronic testing equipment as shown in the following table:

	Internal Modem	External Modem	Circuit Board	Jump Drives	Hard Drives	Memory Boards
Test device 1	7	3	12	6	18	17
Test device 2	2	5	3	2	15	17
Test device 3	5	1	3	2	9	2

The first two test devices are available 120 hours per week. The third (device 3) requires more preventive maintenance and may be used only 100 hours each week. The market for all six computer components is vast, and Watts Electronics believes that it can sell as many units of each product as it can manufacture. The table below summarizes the revenues and material costs for each product.

Device	Revenue per Unit Sold ($)	Material Cost per Unit ($)
Internal modem	200	35
External modem	120	25
Graphics circuit board	180	40
Jump drive	130	45
Hard disk drive	430	170
Memory expansion board	260	60

In addition, variable labor costs are $15 per hour for test device 1, $12 per hour for test device 2, and $18 per hour for test device 3. Watts Electronics wants to maximize its profits.

a) Formulate this problem as an LP model.

b) Solve the problem by computer. What is the best product mix?

c) What is the value of an additional minute of time per week on test device 1? test device 2? test device 3? Should Watts Electronics add more test device time? If so, on which equipment? **Px**

•••• **B.30** You have just been hired as a planner for the municipal school system, and your first assignment is to redesign the subsidized lunch program. In particular, you are to formulate the least expensive lunch menu that will still meet all state and federal nutritional guidelines.

The guidelines are as follows: A meal must be between 500 and 800 calories. It must contain at least 200 calories of protein, at least 200 calories of carbohydrates, and no more than 400 calories of fat. It also needs to have at least 200 calories of a food classified as a fruit or vegetable.

At the bottom of this page is the list of the foods you can consider as possible menu items, with contract-determined prices and nutritional information. Note that all percentages sum to 100% per food—as all calories are protein, carbohydrate, or fat calories. For example, a serving of applesauce has 100 calories, all of which are carbohydrate, and it counts as a fruit/veg food. You are allowed to use fractional servings, such as 2.25 servings of turkey breast and a 0.33 portion of salad. Cost and nutritional attributes scale likewise: e.g., a 0.33 portion of salad costs $.30 and has 33 calories.

Formulate and solve as a linear problem. Print out your formulation in Excel showing the objective function coefficients and constraint matrix in standard form.

- Display, on a separate page, the full *Answer Report* as generated by Excel Solver.
- Highlight *and label as* Z the objective value for the optimal solution on the Answer Report.
- Highlight the nonzero decision variables for the optimal solution on the Answer Report.
- Display, on a separate page, the full *Sensitivity Report* as generated by Excel Solver. **Px**

▶ Refer to myomlab🔵 for these additional homework problems: **B.31–B.40**

Food	Cost/Serving	Calories/Serving	% Protein	% Carbs	% Fat	Fruit/Veg
Applesauce	$0.30	100	0%	100%	0%	Y
Canned corn	$0.40	150	20%	80%	0%	Y
Fried chicken	$0.90	250	55%	5%	40%	N
French fries	$0.20	400	5%	35%	60%	N
Mac and cheese	$0.50	430	20%	30%	50%	N
Turkey breast	$1.50	300	67%	0%	33%	N
Garden salad	$0.90	100	15%	40%	45%	Y

Case Study

▶ Golding Landscaping and Plants, Inc.

Kenneth and Patricia Golding spent a career as a husband-and-wife real estate investment partnership in Washington, DC. When they finally retired to a 25-acre farm in northern Virginia's Fairfax County, they became ardent amateur gardeners. Kenneth planted shrubs and fruit trees, and Patricia spent her hours potting all sizes of plants. When the volume of shrubs and plants reached the point that the Goldings began to think of their hobby in a serious vein, they built a greenhouse adjacent to their home and installed heating and watering systems.

By 2009, the Goldings realized their retirement from real estate had really only led to a second career—in the plant and shrub business—and they filed for a Virginia business license. Within a matter of months, they asked their attorney to file incorporation documents and formed the firm Golding Landscaping and Plants, Inc.

Early in the new business's existence, Kenneth Golding recognized the need for a high-quality commercial fertilizer that he could blend himself, both for sale and for his own nursery. His goal was to keep his costs to a minimum while producing a top-notch product that was especially suited to the northern Virginia climate.

Working with chemists at George Mason University, Golding blended "Golding-Grow." It consists of four chemical compounds, C-30, C-92, D-21, and E-11. The cost per pound for each compound is indicated in the following table:

Chemical Compound	Cost per Pound
C-30	$.12
C-92	.09
D-21	.11
E-11	.04

The specifications for Golding-Grow are established as:

a. Chemical E-11 must constitute at least 15% of the blend.
b. C-92 and C-30 must together constitute at least 45% of the blend.
c. D-21 and C-92 can together constitute no more than 30% of the blend.
d. Golding-Grow is packaged and sold in 50-lb bags.

Discussion Questions

1. Formulate an LP problem to determine what blend of the four chemicals will allow Golding to minimize the cost of a 50-lb bag of the fertilizer.
2. Solve to find the best solution.

Active Model Exercise

ACTIVE MODEL B.1 This exercise describes the Shader Electronics example maximization problem, which has two less-than-or-equal-to contraints. You can use the scrollbars to change any of the eight numbers in the example or to move the iso-profit line. It is illustrated at **www.myomlab.com** or **www.pearsonhighered.com/heizer**.

Module B *Rapid Review*

Main Heading	Review Material	
WHY USE LINEAR PROGRAMMING? (pp. 548–549)	■ **Linear programming (LP)**—A mathematical technique designed to help operations managers plan and make decisions relative to allocation of resources.	

REQUIREMENTS OF A LINEAR PROGRAMMING PROBLEM (p. 549)

■ **Objective function**—A mathematical expression in linear programming that maximizes or minimizes some quantity (often profit or cost, but any goal may be used).

■ **Constraints**—Restrictions that limit the degree to which a manager can pursue an objective.

All LP problems have four properties in common:
1. LP problems seek to *maximize* or *minimize* some quantity. We refer to this property as the *objective function* of an LP problem.
2. The presence of restrictions, or *constraints*, limits the degree to which we can pursue our objective. We want, therefore, to maximize or minimize a quantity (the objective function) subject to limited resources (the constraints).
3. There must be *alternative courses of action* to choose from.
4. The objective and constraints in linear programming problems must be expressed in terms of *linear equations* or inequalities.

FORMULATING LINEAR PROGRAMMING PROBLEMS (pp. 549–550)

One of the most common linear programming applications is the *product-mix problem*. Two or more products are usually produced using limited resources. For example, a company might like to determine how many units of each product it should produce to maximize overall profit, given its limited resources.

An important aspect of linear programming is that certain interactions will exist between variables. The more units of one product that a firm produces, the fewer it can make of other products.

Virtual Office Hours for Solved Problem: B.1

ACTIVE MODEL B.1

GRAPHICAL SOLUTION TO A LINEAR PROGRAMMING PROBLEM (pp. 550–555)

■ **Graphical solution approach**—A means of plotting a solution to a two-variable problem on a graph.
■ **Decision variables**—Choices available to a decision maker.

Constraints of the form $X \geq 0$ are called *nonnegativity constraints*.
■ **Feasible region**—The set of all feasible combinations of decision variables.

Any point inside the feasible region represents a *feasible solution*, while any point outside the feasible region represents an *infeasible solution*.

■ **Iso-profit line method**—An approach to identifying the optimum point in a graphic linear programming problem. The line that touches a particular point of the feasible region will pinpoint the optimal solution.
■ **Corner-point method**—Another method for solving graphical linear programming problems.

The mathematical theory behind linear programming states that an optimal solution to any problem will lie at a *corner point*, or an *extreme point*, of the feasible region. Hence, it is necessary to find only the values of the variables at each corner; the optimal solution will lie at one (or more) of them. This is the corner-point method.

Problems: B.1, B.2, B.4, B.15

Virtual Office Hours for Solved Problem: B.2

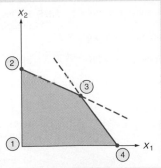

SENSITIVITY ANALYSIS (pp. 555–557)

■ **Parameter**—A numerical value that is given in a model.
■ **Sensitivity analysis**—An analysis that projects how much a solution may change if there are changes in the variables or input data.

Sensitivity analysis is also called *postoptimality analysis*.
There are two approaches to determining just how sensitive an optimal solution is to changes: (1) a trial-and-error approach and (2) the analytic postoptimality method.

Main Heading	Review Material	myomlab
	To use the analytic postoptimality method, after an LP problem has been solved, we determine a range of changes in problem parameters that will not affect the optimal solution or change the variables in the solution. LP software has this capability.	
	While using the information in a sensitivity report to answer what-if questions, we assume that we are considering a change to only a *single* input data value at a time. That is, the sensitivity information does not generally apply to simultaneous changes in several input data values.	
	▪ **Shadow price** (or **dual**)—The value of one additional unit of a scarce resource in LP.	
	The shadow price is valid as long as the right-hand side of the constraint stays in a range within which all current corner points continue to exist. The information to compute the upper and lower limits of this range is given by the entries labeled Allowable Increase and Allowable Decrease in the sensitivity report.	
SOLVING MINIMIZATION PROBLEMS (pp. 557–559)	▪ **Iso-cost**—An approach to solving a linear programming minimization problem graphically.	Virtual Office Hours for Solved Problem: B.3
	The iso-cost line approach to solving minimization problems is analogous to the iso-profit approach for maximization problems, but successive iso-cost lines are drawn *inward* instead of outward.	Problems: B.3, B.5, B.6, B.11, B.12, B.22, B.24
LINEAR PROGRAMMING APPLICATIONS (pp. 559–562)	The *diet problem*, known in agricultural applications as the *feed-mix problem*, involves specifying a food or feed ingredient combination that will satisfy stated nutritional requirements at a minimum cost level. *Labor scheduling problems* address staffing needs over a specific time period. They are especially useful when managers have some flexibility in assigning workers to jobs that require overlapping or interchangeable talents.	Problems: B.7–B.10, B.13, B.14, B.16–B.21, B.23, B.25–B.29
THE SIMPLEX METHOD OF LP (p. 562)	▪ **Simplex method**—An algorithm for solving linear programming problems of all sizes.	
	The simplex method is actually a set of instructions with which we examine corner points in a methodical fashion until we arrive at the best solution—highest profit or lowest cost. Computer programs (such as Excel OM and POM for Windows) and Excel's Solver add-in are available to solve linear programming problems via the simplex method.	

Self Test

▪ **Before taking the self-test,** refer to the learning objectives listed at the beginning of the module and the key terms listed at the end of the module.

LO1. Which of the following is *not* a valid LP constraint formulation?
a) $3X + 4Y \leq 12$
b) $2X \times 2Y \leq 12$
c) $3Y + 2Z = 18$
d) $100 \geq X + Y$
e) $2.5X + 1.5Z = 30.6$

LO2. Using a *graphical solution procedure* to solve a maximization problem requires that we:
a) move the iso-profit line up until it no longer intersects with any constraint equation.
b) move the iso-profit line down until it no longer intersects with any constraint equation.
c) apply the method of simultaneous equations to solve for the intersections of constraints.
d) find the value of the objective function at the origin.

LO3. Consider the following linear programming problem:

$$\text{Maximize} \quad 4X + 10Y$$
$$\text{Subject to:} \quad 3X + 4Y \leq 480$$
$$4X + 2Y \leq 360$$
$$X, Y \geq 0$$

The feasible corner points are (48,84), (0, 120), (0, 0), and (90,0). What is the maximum possible value for the objective function?
a) 1,032   b) 1,200   c) 360   d) 1,600   e) 840

LO4. A zero shadow price for a resource ordinarily means that:
a) the resource is scarce.
b) the resource constraint was redundant.
c) the resource has not been used up.
d) something is wrong with the problem formulation.
e) none of the above.

LO5. For these two constraints, which point is in the feasible region of this minimization problem?

$$14x + 6y \leq 42 \text{ and } x - y \leq 3$$

a) $x = -1, y = 1$
b) $x = 0, y = 4$
c) $x = 2, y = 1$
d) $x = 5, y = 1$
e) $x = 2, y = 0$

LO6. When applying LP to diet problems, the objective function is usually designed to:
a) maximize profits from blends of nutrients.
b) maximize ingredient blends.
c) minimize production losses.
d) maximize the number of products to be produced.
e) minimize the costs of nutrient blends.

Answers: LO1. b; **LO2.** a; **LO3.** b; **LO4.** c; **LO5.** d; **LO6.** e.

C

Transportation Models

Module Outline

Transportation Modeling

Developing an Initial Solution

The Stepping-Stone Method

Special Issues in Modeling

Discussion Questions
Problems
Case Study: Custom Vans, Inc.
Rapid Review

The transportation method finds the least cost means of shipping supplies from several *origins* to several *destinations*. Origin points (sources of supply) can be factories, warehouses, or any other points from which goods are shipped. Destinations are any points that receive goods.

Use of the transportation method requires (1) origin points with the supply for a given time period at each, (2) destination points with the demand for a given time period at each, and (3) the cost of shipping one unit from each origin point to each destination point.

These problems can be solved by hand and by computer.

BEFORE COMING TO CLASS, READ MODULE C IN YOUR TEXT AND ANSWER THESE QUESTIONS.

1. What is the difference between the northwest-corner and intuitive lowest-cost initial solution methods? _____

_____

_____

2. What is the stepping-stone method? _____

_____

_____

3. What happens when the quantity being supplied does not equal the quantity required? _____

_____

_____

4. What is meant by degeneracy in a transportation problem? _____

_____

_____

TRANSPORTATION MODELING (See Flexible Version pp. 568–569)

Origins

Destinations

You Need to Know

1. Origins and supply at each
2. Destinations and demand at each
3. Cost of shipping 1 unit from each origin to each destination

DEVELOPING AN INITIAL SOLUTION (See Flexible Version pp. 570–572)

The Northwest-Corner Rule (See Flexible Version pp. 570–571)

Steps

1. _____

2. _____

3. _____

The Intuitive Lowest-Cost Method

(See Flexible Version pp. 571–572)

Steps

1. _____

2. _____

3. _____

4. _____

THE STEPPING-STONE METHOD (See Flexible Version pp. 572–575)

Steps

1. _____

2. _____

3. _____

4. _____

5. _____

PRACTICE PROBLEM C.1 ■ Shipping Allocations

John Galt Shipping wishes to ship a product that is made at two different factories to three different warehouses. The company produces 18 units at Factory A and 22 units at Factory B. It needs 10 units in Warehouse 1, 20 units in Warehouse 2, and 10 units in Warehouse 3. Per-unit transportation costs are shown in the following table. How many units should be shipped from each factory to each warehouse?

	Warehouse 1	Warehouse 2	Warehouse 3
Plant A	$4	$2	$3
Plant B	$3	$2	$1

Additional Practice Problem Space

SPECIAL ISSUES IN MODELING (See Flexible Version pp. 575–577)

Demand Not Equal to Supply

Dummy Sources

Dummy Destinations

PRACTICE PROBLEM C.2 ■ Unbalanced Problem

Assume that in Practice Problem C.1 the demand at each warehouse is increased by 4 units. How many units now should be shipped from each factory to each warehouse?

Additional Practice Problem Space

Degeneracy (See Flexible Version pp. 576–577)

Rule about Shipping Routes

The number of occupied squares in any solution is equal to the number of rows in the table plus the number of columns minus 1. If not, degeneracy exists.

Discussion Questions

1. What are the three information needs of the transportation model?
2. What are the steps in the intuitive lowest-cost method?
3. Identify the three "steps" in the northwest-corner rule.
4. How do you know when an optimal solution has been reached?
5. Which starting technique generally gives a better initial solution, and why?
6. The more sources and destinations there are for a transportation problem, the smaller the percentage of all cells that will be used in the optimal solution. Explain.
7. All of the transportation examples appear to apply to long distances. Is it possible for the transportation model to apply on a much smaller scale, for example, within the departments of a store or the offices of a building? Discuss.

8. Develop a *northeast*-corner rule and explain how it would work. Set up an initial solution for the Arizona Plumbing problem analyzed in Example C1.
9. What is meant by an unbalanced transportation problem, and how would you balance it?
10. How many occupied cells must all solutions use?
11. Explain the significance of a negative improvement index in a transportation-minimizing problem.
12. How can the transportation method address production costs in addition to transportation costs?
13. Explain what is meant by the term *degeneracy* within the context of transportation modeling.

Problems*

•   **C.1**   Find an initial solution to the following transportation problem.

	To			
	Los		Panama	
From	**Angeles**	**Calgary**	**City**	**Supply**
Mexico City	$ 6	$18	$ 8	100
Detroit	$17	$13	$19	60
Ottawa	$20	$10	$24	40
Demand	50	80	70	

a) Use the northwest-corner method. What is its total cost?
b) Use the intuitive lowest-cost approach. What is its total cost?
c) Using the stepping-stone method, find the optimal solution. Compute the total cost. **Px**

•   **C.2**   Consider the transportation table below. Unit costs for each shipping route are in dollars. What is the total cost of the basic feasible solution that the intuitive least cost method would find for this problem? **Px**

Destination

Source	A	B	C	D	E	Supply
1	12	8	5	10	4	18
2	6	11	3	/	9	14
Demand	6	8	12	4	2	

•   **C.3**   a) Use the northwest-corner method to find an initial feasible solution to the following problem. What must you do before beginning the solution steps?

Note: **Px** means the problem may be solved with POM for Windows and/or Excel OM.

b) Use the intuitive lowest-cost approach to find an initial feasible solution. Is this approach better than the northwest-corner method?
c) Find the optimal solution using the stepping-stone method.

	To			
From	**A**	**B**	**C**	**Supply**
X	$10	$18	$12	100
Y	$17	$13	$ 9	50
Z	$20	$18	$14	75
Demand	50	80	70	**Px**

•   **C.4**   Consider the transportation table below. The solution displayed was obtained by performing some iterations of the transportation method on this problem. What is the total cost of the shipping plan that would be obtained by performing *one more iteration* of the stepping stone method on this problem?

Destination

Source	Denver	Yuma	Miami	Supply
Houston	$2 10	$8	$1	10
St. Louis	$4 10	$5 10	$6	20
Chicago	$6	$3 10	$2 20	30
Demand	20	20	20	

••   **C.5**   Tharp Air Conditioning manufactures room air conditioners at plants in Houston, Phoenix, and Memphis. These are sent to regional distributors in Dallas, Atlanta, and Denver. The shipping costs vary, and the company would like to find the least-cost way to meet the demands at each of the distribution centers. Dallas needs to receive 800 air conditioners per month, Atlanta needs 600, and Denver needs 200. Houston has 850 air conditioners available each month, Phoenix has 650, and Memphis has 300. The shipping cost per unit from Houston to Dallas is $8, to Atlanta $12, and to Denver $10. The cost per unit from Phoenix to Dallas is $10, to Atlanta $14, and to Denver $9. The cost per unit from Memphis to Dallas is $11, to Atlanta $8, and to Denver $12. How many units should owner Devorah Tharp ship from each plant to each regional distribution center? What is the total transportation cost? (Note that a "dummy" destination is needed to balance the problem.) **Px**

•• **C.6** The following table is the result of one or more iterations:
a) Complete the next iteration using the stepping-stone method.
b) Calculate the "total cost" incurred if your results were to be accepted as the final solution. **Px**

From \ To	1	2	3	Capacity
A	30 / 40	30	5 / 10	50
B	10	10 / 30	10	30
C	20	10 / 30	25 / 45	75
Demand	40	60	55	155

•• **C.7** The three blood banks in Franklin County are coordinated through a central office that facilitates blood delivery to four hospitals in the region. The cost to ship a standard container of blood from each

bank to each hospital is shown in the table below. Also given are the biweekly number of containers available at each bank and the biweekly number of containers of blood needed at each hospital. How many shipments should be made biweekly from each blood bank to each hospital so that total shipment costs are minimized?

From	Hosp. 1	Hosp. 2	Hosp. 3	Hosp. 4	Supply
Bank 1	$ 8	$ 9	$11	$16	50
Bank 2	$12	$ 7	$ 5	$ 8	80
Bank 3	$14	$10	$ 6	$ 7	120
Demand	90	70	40	50	250

Px

•• **C.8** In Solved Problem C.1 (pp. 579–580 in the *Flexible Version*), Williams Auto Top Carriers proposed opening a new plant in either New Orleans or Houston. Management found that the total system cost (of production plus distribution) would be $20,000 for the New Orleans site. What would be the total cost if Williams opened a plant in Houston? At which of the two proposed locations (New Orleans or Houston) should Williams open the new facility? **Px**

•• **C.9** For the following William Gehrlein Corp. data, find the starting solution and initial cost using the northwest-corner method. What must you do to balance this problem?

From	W	X	Y	Z	Supply
A	$132	$116	$250	$110	220
B	$220	$230	$180	$178	300
C	$152	$173	$196	$164	435
Demand	160	120	200	230	

Px

•• **C.10** The Tara Tripp Clothing Group owns factories in three towns (W, Y, and Z), which distribute to three Walsh retail dress shops in three other cities (A, B, and C). The following table summarizes factory availabilities, projected store demands, and unit shipping costs:

Walsh Clothing Group

From \ To	Dress Shop A	Dress Shop B	Dress Shop C	Factory availability
Factory W	$4	$3	$3	35
Factory Y	$6	$7	$6	50
Factory Z	$8	$2	$5	50
Store demand	30	65	40	135

a) Complete the analysis, determining the optimal solution for shipping at the Tripp Clothing Group.
b) How do you know if it is optimal or not? **Px**

•• **C.11** Consider the following transportation problem at Frank Timoney Enterprises in Clifton Park, NY.

From	Destination A	Destination B	Destination C	Supply
Source 1	$8	$9	$4	72
Source 2	$5	$6	$8	38
Source 3	$7	$9	$6	46
Source 4	$5	$3	$7	19
Demand	110	34	31	175

a) Find an initial solution using the northwest-corner rule. What special condition exists?
b) Explain how you will proceed to solve the problem.
c) What is the optimal solution? **Px**

•• C.12 Lawson Mill Works (LMW) ships pre-cut lumber to three building-supply houses from mills in Mountpelier, Nixon, and Oak Ridge. Determine the best shipment schedule for LMW from the data provided by James Lawson, the traffic manager at LMW. Use the northwest-corner starting procedure and the stepping-stone method. Refer to the following table. (*Note:* You may face a degenerate solution in one of your iterations.) **Px**

Lawson Mill Works

From \ To	Supply House 1	Supply House 2	Supply House 3	Mill capacity (in tons)
Mountpelier	$3	$3	$2	25
Nixon	$4	$2	$3	40
Oak Ridge	$3	$2	$3	30
Supply house demand (in tons)	30	30	35	95

••• C.13 Captain Cabell Corp. manufacturers fishing equipment. Currently, the company has a plant in Los Angeles and a plant in New Orleans. David Cabell, the firm's owner, is deciding where to build a new plant—Philadelphia or Seattle. Use the following table to find the total shipping costs for each potential site. Which should Cabell select?

| | Warehouse | | | |
Plant	Pittsburgh	St. Louis	Denver	Capacity
Los Angeles	$100	$75	$50	150
New Orleans	$ 80	$60	$90	225
Philadelphia	$ 40	$50	$90	350
Seattle	$110	$70	$30	350
Demand	200	100	400	

Px

•• C.14 Susan Helms Manufacturing Co. has hired you to evaluate its shipping costs. The following table shows present demand, capacity, and freight costs between each factory and each warehouse. Find the shipping pattern with the lowest cost. **Px**

Susan Helms Manufacturing Data

From \ To	Warehouse 1	Warehouse 2	Warehouse 3	Warehouse 4	Plant capacity
Factory 1	4	7	10	12	2,000
Factory 2	7	5	8	11	2,500
Factory 3	9	8	6	9	2,200
Warehouse demand	1,000	2,000	2,000	1,200	6,700 6,200

•• C.15 Drew Rosen Corp. is considering adding a fourth plant to its three existing facilities in Decatur, Minneapolis, and Carbondale. Both St. Louis and East St. Louis are being considered.

Evaluating only the transportation costs per unit as shown in the table, decide which site is best.

| | From Existing Plants | | | |
To	Decatur	Minneapolis	Carbondale	Demand
Blue Earth	$20	$17	$21	250
Ciro	$25	$27	$20	200
Des Moines	$22	$25	$22	350
Capacity	300	200	150	

| | From Proposed Plants | |
To	East St. Louis	St. Louis
Blue Earth	$29	$27
Ciro	$30	$28
Des Moines	$30	$31
Capacity	150	150

Px

•• C.16 Using the data from Problem C.15 and the unit production costs in the following table, show which locations yield the lowest cost.

Location	Production Costs ($)
Decatur	$50
Minneapolis	60
Carbondale	70
East St. Louis	40
St. Louis	50

Px

•••• C.17 Dalton Pharmaceuticals enjoys a dominant position in the southeast U.S. with over 800 discount retail outlets. These stores are served by twice-weekly deliveries from Dalton's 16 warehouses, which are in turn supplied daily by 7 factories that manufacture about 70% of all of the chain's products.

It is clear to Marilyn Helms, VP operations, that an additional warehouse is desperately needed to handle growth and backlogs. Three cities, Mobile, Tampa, and Huntsville, are under final consideration. The table on the next page illustrates the current and proposed factory/warehouse capacities/demands and shipping costs per average box of supplies.

a) Based on shipping costs only, which city should be selected for the new warehouse?

b) One study shows that Ocala's capacity can increase to 500 boxes per day. Would this affect your decision in part (a)?

c) Because of a new intrastate shipping agreement, rates for shipping from each factory in Florida to each warehouse in Florida drop by $1 per carton. How does this factor affect your answer to parts (a) and (b)? **Px**

▶ **Refer to** myomlab 🔵 **for these additional homework problems: C.18–C.22**

Table for Problem C.17

Factory	Warehouse								Capacity (cartons per day)
	Atlanta, GA	New Orleans, LA	Jackson, MS	Birmingham, AL	Montgomery, AL	Raleigh, NC	Asheville, NC	Columbia, SC	
Valdosta, GA	$3	$5	$4	$3	$4	$6	$8	$8	350
Ocala, FL	4	6	5	5	6	7	6	7	300
Augusta, GA	1	4	3	2	2	6	7	8	400
Stuart, FL	3	5	2	6	6	5	5	6	200
Biloxi, MS	4	1	4	3	3	8	9	10	600
Starkville, MS	3	3	1	2	2	6	5	6	400
Durham, NC	4	8	8	7	7	2	2	2	500
Requirements (cartons/day)	150	250	50	150	100	200	150	300	

Factory	Warehouse					Alternatives			Capacity (cartons (per day)
	Orlando, FL	Miami, FL	Jacksonville, FL	Wilmington, NC	Charlotte, NC	Mobile, AL	Tampa, FL	Huntsville, AL	
Valdosta, GA	$9	$10	$8	$8	$11	$4	$6	$3	350
Ocala, FL	2	3	2	6	7	5	2	5	300
Augusta, GA	7	9	6	8	9	3	5	2	400
Stuart, FL	2	2	3	5	5	6	3	5	200
Biloxi, MS	7	13	9	8	8	2	6	3	600
Starkville, MS	6	8	7	7	8	3	6	2	400
Durham, NC	6	8	5	1	2	8	7	8	500
Requirements (cartons/day)	250	300	300	100	150	300	300	300	

Case Study

▶ Custom Vans, Inc.

Custom Vans, Inc., specializes in converting standard vans into campers. Depending on the amount of work and customizing to be done, the customizing can cost less than $1,000 to more than $5,000. In less than 4 years, Tony Rizzo was able to expand his small operation in Gary, Indiana, to other major outlets in Chicago, Milwaukee, Minneapolis, and Detroit.

Innovation was the major factor in Tony's success in converting a small van shop into one of the largest and most profitable custom van operations in the Midwest. Tony seemed to have a special ability to design and develop unique features and devices that were always in high demand by van owners. An example was Shower-Rific, which was developed by Tony only 6 months after Custom Vans, Inc., was started. These small showers were completely self-contained, and they could be placed in almost any type of van and in a number of different locations within a van. Shower-Rific was made of fiberglass and contained towel racks, built-in soap and shampoo holders, and a unique plastic door. Each Shower-Rific took 2 gallons of fiberglass and 3 hours of labor to manufacture.

Most of the Shower-Rifics were manufactured in Gary in the same warehouse where Custom Vans, Inc., was founded. The manufacturing plant in Gary could produce 300 Shower-Rifics in a month, but this capacity never seemed to be enough. Custom Van shops in all locations were complaining about not getting enough Shower-Rifics, and because Minneapolis was farther away from Gary than the other locations, Tony was always inclined to ship Shower-Rifics to the other locations before Minneapolis. This infuriated the manager of Custom Vans at Minneapolis, and after many heated discussions, Tony decided to start another manufacturing plant for Shower-Rifics at Fort Wayne, Indiana. The manufacturing plant at Fort Wayne could produce 150 Shower-Rifics per month.

The manufacturing plant at Fort Wayne was still not able to meet current demand for Shower-Rifics, and Tony knew that the demand for his unique camper shower would grow rapidly in the next year. After consulting with his lawyer and banker, Tony concluded that he should open two new manufacturing plants as soon as possible. Each plant would have the same capacity as the Fort Wayne manufacturing plant. An initial investigation into possible manufacturing locations was made, and Tony decided that the two new plants should be located in Detroit, Michigan; Rockford, Illinois; or Madison, Wisconsin. Tony knew that selecting the best location for the two new manufacturing plants would be difficult. Transportation costs and demands for the various locations would be important considerations.

The Chicago shop was managed by Bill Burch. This shop was one of the first established by Tony, and it continued to outperform the other locations. The manufacturing plant at Gary was supplying 200 Shower-Rifics each month, although Bill knew that the demand for the showers in Chicago was 300 units. The transportation cost per unit from Gary was $10, and although the transportation cost from Fort Wayne was double that amount, Bill was always pleading with Tony to get an additional 50 units from the Fort Wayne manufacturer. The two additional manufacturing plants would certainly be able to supply Bill with the additional 100 showers he needed. The transportation costs would, of course, vary, depending on which two locations Tony picked. The transportation cost per shower would be $30 from Detroit, $5 from Rockford, and $10 from Madison.

Wilma Jackson, manager of the Custom Van shop in Milwaukee, was the most upset about not getting an adequate supply of showers. She had a demand for 100 units, and at the present time, she was only getting half of this demand from the Fort Wayne manufacturing plant. She could not understand why Tony didn't ship her all 100 units from Gary. The transportation cost per unit from Gary was only $20, while the transportation cost from Fort Wayne was $30. Wilma was hoping that Tony would select Madison for one of the manufacturing locations. She would be able to get all the showers needed, and the transportation cost per unit would only be $5. If not in Madison, a new plant in Rockford would be able to supply her total needs, but the transportation cost per unit would be twice as much as it would be from Madison. Because the transportation cost per unit from Detroit would be $40, Wilma speculated that even if Detroit became one of the new plants, she would not be getting any units from Detroit.

Custom Vans, Inc., of Minneapolis was managed by Tom Poanski. He was getting 100 showers from the Gary plant. Demand was 150 units. Tom faced the highest transportation costs of all locations. The transportation cost from Gary was $40 per unit. It would cost $10 more if showers were sent from the Fort Wayne location. Tom was hoping that Detroit would not be one of the new plants, as the transportation cost would be $60 per unit. Rockford and Madison would have a cost of $30 and $25, respectively, to ship one shower to Minneapolis.

The Detroit shop's position was similar to Milwaukee's—only getting half of the demand each month. The 100 units that Detroit did receive came directly from the Fort Wayne plant. The transportation cost was only $15 per unit from Fort Wayne, while it was $25 from Gary. Dick Lopez, manager of Custom Vans, Inc., of Detroit, placed the probability of having one of the new plants in Detroit fairly high. The factory would be located across town, and the transportation cost would be only $5 per unit. He could get 150 showers from the new plant in Detroit and the other 50 showers from Fort Wayne. Even if Detroit was not selected, the other two locations were not intolerable. Rockford had a transportation cost per unit of $35, and Madison had a transportation cost of $40.

Tony pondered the dilemma of locating the two new plants for several weeks before deciding to call a meeting of all the managers of the van shops. The decision was complicated, but the objective was clear—to minimize total costs. The meeting was held in Gary, and everyone was present except Wilma.

Tony: Thank you for coming. As you know, I have decided to open two new plants at Rockford, Madison, or Detroit. The two locations, of course, will change our shipping practices, and I sincerely hope that they will supply you with the Shower-Rifics that you have been wanting. I know you could have sold more units, and I want you to know that I am sorry for this situation.

Dick: Tony, I have given this situation a lot of consideration, and I feel strongly that at least one of the new plants should be located in Detroit. As you know, I am now only getting half of the showers that I need. My brother, Leon, is very interested in running the plant, and I know he would do a good job.

Tom: Dick, I am sure that Leon could do a good job, and I know how difficult it has been since the recent layoffs by the auto industry. Nevertheless, we should be considering total costs and not personalities. I believe that the new plants should be located in Madison and Rockford. I am farther away from the other plants than any other shop, and these locations would significantly reduce transportation costs.

Dick: That may be true, but there are other factors. Detroit has one of the largest suppliers of fiberglass, and I have checked prices. A new plant in Detroit would be able to purchase fiberglass for $2 per gallon less than any of the other existing or proposed plants.

Tom: At Madison, we have an excellent labor force. This is due primarily to the large number of students attending the University of Wisconsin. These students are hard workers, and they will work for $1 less per hour than the other locations that we are considering.

Bill: Calm down, you two. It is obvious that we will not be able to satisfy everyone in locating the new plants. Therefore, I would like to suggest that we vote on the two best locations.

Tony: I don't think that voting would be a good idea. Wilma was not able to attend, and we should be looking at all of these factors together in some type of logical fashion.

Discussion Question

Where would you locate the two new plants? Why?

Source: From *Quantitative Analysis for Management*, B. Render, R. M. Stair, and M. Hanna. 10th ed. Copyright © 2009. Reprinted by permission of Prentice Hall, Inc., Upper Saddle River, NJ.

Module C *Rapid* Review

Main Heading	Review Material

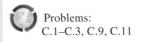

TRANSPORTATION MODELING
(pp. 568–569)

The transportation models described in this module prove useful when considering alternative facility locations *within the framework of an existing distribution system*. The choice of a new location depends on which will yield the minimum cost for the entire system.

- **Transportation modeling**—An iterative procedure for solving problems that involves minimizing the cost of shipping products from a series of sources to a series of destinations.

Origin points (or *sources*) can be factories, warehouses, car rental agencies, or any other points from which goods are shipped.

Destinations are any points that receive goods.

To use the transportation model, we need to know the following:

1. The origin points and the capacity or supply per period at each.
2. The destination points and the demand per period at each.
3. The cost of shipping one unit from each origin to each destination.

The transportation model is a type of linear programming model.

A **transportation matrix** summarizes all relevant data and keeps track of algorithm computations. Shipping costs from each origin to each destination are contained in the appropriate cross-referenced box.

To From	Destination 1	Destination 2	Destination 3	Capacity
Source A				
Source B				
Source C				
Demand				

DEVELOPING AN INITIAL SOLUTION
(pp. 570–572)

Two methods for establishing an initial feasible solution to the problem are the northwest-corner rule and the intuitive lowest-cost method.

- **Northwest-corner rule**—A procedure in the transportation model where one starts at the upper-left-hand cell of a table (the northwest corner) and systematically allocates units to shipping routes.

The northwest-corner rule requires that we:

1. Exhaust the supply (origin capacity) of each row before moving down to the next row.
2. Exhaust the demand requirements of each column before moving to the next column to the right.
3. Check to ensure that all supplies and demands are met.

The northwest-corner rule is easy to use and generates a feasible solution, but it totally ignores costs and therefore should be considered only as a starting position.

- **Intuitive method**—A cost-based approach to finding an initial solution to a transportation problem.

The intuitive method uses the following steps:

1. Identify the cell with the lowest cost. Break any ties for the lowest cost arbitrarily.
2. Allocate as many units as possible to that cell, without exceeding the supply or demand. Then cross out the row or column (or both) that is exhausted by this assignment.
3. Find the cell with the lowest cost from the remaining (not crossed out) cells.
4. Repeat steps 2 and 3 until all units have been allocated.

Problems:
C.1–C.3, C.9, C.11

THE STEPPING-STONE METHOD
(pp. 572–575)

- **Stepping-stone** method—An iterative technique for moving from an initial feasible solution to an optimal solution in the transportation method.

The stepping-stone method is used to evaluate the cost-effectiveness of shipping goods via transportation routes not currently in the solution. When applying it, we test each unused cell, or square, in the transportation table by asking: What would happen to total shipping costs if one unit of the product were tentatively shipped on an unused route? We conduct the test as follows:

1. Select any unused square to evaluate.
2. Beginning at this square, trace a closed path back to the original square via squares that are currently being used (only horizontal and vertical moves are

Problems: C.4, C.6–C.8, C.10, C.13, C.15, C.16, C.17

Virtual Office Hours for Solved Problem: C.1

Main Heading	Review Material	

permissible). You may, however, step over either an empty or an occupied square.

3. Beginning with a plus (+) sign at the unused square, place alternative minus signs and plus signs on each corner square of the closed path just traced.
4. Calculate an improvement index by first adding the unit-cost figures found in each square containing a plus sign and then subtracting the unit costs in each square containing a minus sign.
5. Repeat steps 1 through 4 until you have calculated an improvement index for all unused squares. If all indices computed are *greater than or equal to zero*, you have reached an optimal solution. If not, the current solution can be improved further to decrease total shipping costs.

Each negative index represents the amount by which total transportation costs could be decreased if one unit was shipped by the source–destination combination. The next step, then, is to choose that route (unused square) with the *largest* negative improvement index. We can then ship the maximum allowable number of units on that route and reduce the total cost accordingly. That maximum quantity is found by referring to the closed path of plus signs and minus signs drawn for the route and then selecting the *smallest number found in the squares containing minus sign*s. To obtain a new solution, we add this number to all squares on the closed path with plus signs and subtract it from all squares on the path to which we have assigned minus signs. From this new solution, a new test of unused squares needs to be conducted to see if the new solution is optimal or whether we can make further improvements.

SPECIAL ISSUES IN MODELING
(pp. 575–577)

- **Dummy sources**—Artificial shipping source points created when total demand is greater than total supply to effect a supply equal to the excess of demand over supply.
- **Dummy destinations**—Artificial destination points created when the total supply is greater than the total demand; they serve to equalize the total demand and supply.

Because units from dummy sources or to dummy destinations will not in fact be shipped, we assign cost coefficients of zero to each square on the dummy location. If you are solving a transportation problem by hand, be careful to decide first whether a dummy source (row) or a dummy destination (column) is needed. When applying the stepping-stone method, *the number of occupied squares in any solution (initial or later) must be equal to the number of rows in the table plus the number of columns minus 1*. Solutions that do not satisfy this rule are called *degenerate*.

- **Degeneracy**—An occurrence in transportation models in which too few squares or shipping routes are being used, so that tracing a closed path for each unused square becomes impossible.

To handle degenerate problems, we must artificially create an occupied cell: That is, we place a zero (representing a fake shipment) into one of the unused squares and *then treat that square as if it were occupied*. Remember that the chosen square must be in such a position as to allow all stepping-stone paths to be closed.

 Problem: C.5, C.9, C.11, C.12, C.14

Virtual Office Hours for Solved Problem: C.2

Self Test

- **Before taking the self-test,** refer to the learning objectives listed at the beginning of the module and the key terms listed at the end of the module.

LO1. With the transportation technique, the initial solution can be generated in any fashion one chooses. The only restriction(s) is that:
- a) the solution be optimal.
- b) one uses the northwest-corner method.
- c) the edge constraints for supply and demand be satisfied.
- d) the solution not be degenerate.
- e) all of the above.

LO2. The purpose of the stepping-stone method is to:
- a) develop the initial solution to a transportation problem.
- b) identify the relevant costs in a transportation problem.
- c) determine whether a given solution is feasible.
- d) assist one in moving from an initial feasible solution to the optimal solution.
- e) overcome the problem of degeneracy.

LO3. The purpose of a *dummy source* or a *dummy destination* in a transportation problem is to:
- a) provide a means of representing a dummy problem.
- b) obtain a balance between total supply and total demand.
- c) prevent the solution from becoming degenerate.
- d) make certain that the total cost does not exceed some specified figure.
- e) change a problem from maximization to minimization.

LO4. If a solution to a transportation problem is degenerate, then:
- a) it will be impossible to evaluate all empty cells without removing the degeneracy.
- b) a dummy row or column must be added.
- c) there will be more than one optimal solution.
- d) the problem has no feasible solution.
- e) increase the cost of each cell by 1.

Answers: LO1. c; **LO2.** d; **LO3.** b; **LO4.** a.

QUANTITATIVE MODULE

Waiting-Line Models

D-1

Module Outline

Queuing Theory

Characteristics of a Waiting-Line System

Queuing Costs

The Variety of Queuing Models

Other Queuing Approaches

Discussion Questions
Problems
Case Studies: New England Foundry;
    The Winter Park Hotel
Active Model Exercises
Rapid Review

Waiting lines, generally called queues, are a common occurrence in the life of an operations manager. Indeed, waiting lines are a common occurrence in the lives of most of us. Queues can be found at shipping and loading docks in factories and at service counters in post offices, banks, and your neighborhood supermarket. Therefore, operations managers need to understand them. Conveniently, many common queues can be analyzed with some straightforward equations.

This module will introduce and explain four common types of queuing models.

BEFORE COMING TO CLASS, READ MODULE D IN YOUR TEXT AND ANSWER THESE QUESTIONS.

1. What are the characteristics of arrivals, waiting lines, and service systems?

_____

_____

_____

2. In the basic queuing model (the M/M/1 model), arrivals are assumed to be what type of statistical distribution? _____

_____

_____

3. How do you conduct a cost analysis for a waiting line? _____

_____

_____

4. What is a multiple channel queuing model (the M/M/S model)? _____

_____

_____

5. What is a constant service time model? _____

_____

_____

6. What is a limited population model? _____

_____

_____

QUEUING THEORY (See Flexible Version p. 584)

CHARACTERISTICS OF A WAITING-LINE SYSTEM

(See Flexible Version pp. 585–588)

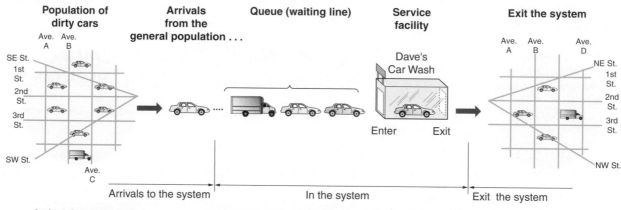

▲ **FIGURE D.1** **Three Parts of a Waiting Line, or Queuing System, at Dave's Car Wash**

Arrival Characteristics (See Flexible Version pp. 585–586)

1. **Size of Arrival Population**

2. **Pattern of Arrivals**

Poisson distribution often applies.

$$P(x) = \frac{e^{-\lambda}\lambda^x}{x!} \quad \text{for } x = 0, 1, 2, 3, 4, \ldots \qquad \text{(D-1)}$$

where $P(x)$ = probability of x arrivals
x = number of arrivals per unit of time
λ = average arrival rate
e = 2.7183 (which is the base of the natural logarithms)

3. **Behavior of Arrivals**

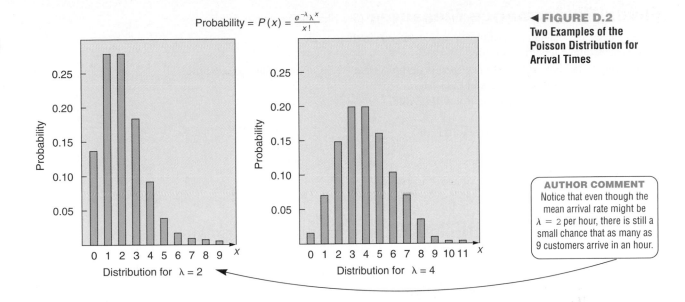

Probability = $P(x) = \dfrac{e^{-\lambda}\lambda^x}{x!}$

◀ **FIGURE D.2**
Two Examples of the Poisson Distribution for Arrival Times

Distribution for $\lambda = 2$

Distribution for $\lambda = 4$

> **AUTHOR COMMENT**
> Notice that even though the mean arrival rate might be $\lambda = 2$ per hour, there is still a small chance that as many as 9 customers arrive in an hour.

Waiting-Line Characteristics (See Flexible Version pp. 586–587)

Service Characteristics (See Flexible Version pp. 587–588)

Basic Designs of Queuing Systems

1. **Single Channel**
2. **Multiple Channel**
3. **Single Phase**
4. **Multiphase**

Service Time Distribution

Negative exponential probability distribution often applies.

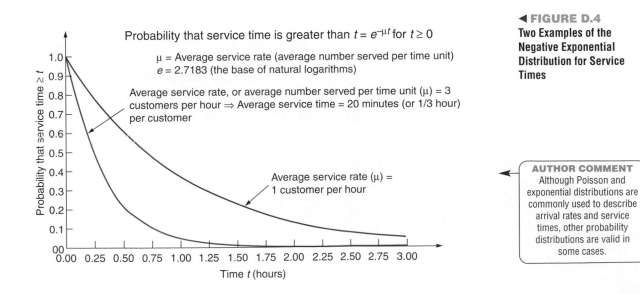

Probability that service time is greater than $t = e^{-\mu t}$ for $t \geq 0$

μ = Average service rate (average number served per time unit)
e = 2.7183 (the base of natural logarithms)

Average service rate, or average number served per time unit (μ) = 3 customers per hour $\Rightarrow$ Average service time = 20 minutes (or 1/3 hour) per customer

Average service rate (μ) = 1 customer per hour

Time t (hours)

◀ **FIGURE D.4**
Two Examples of the Negative Exponential Distribution for Service Times

> **AUTHOR COMMENT**
> Although Poisson and exponential distributions are commonly used to describe arrival rates and service times, other probability distributions are valid in some cases.

Seven Performance Measures (See Flexible Version p. 588)

1. Average time that each customer or object spends in the queue.
2. Average queue length.
3. Average time that each customer spends in the system (waiting time plus service time).
4. Average number of customers in the system.
5. Probability that the service facility will be idle.
6. Utilization factor for the system.
7. Probability of a specific number of customers in the system.

QUEUING COSTS (See Flexible Version pp. 589–590)

THE VARIETY OF QUEUING MODELS (See Flexible Version pp. 590–601)

▼ **TABLE D.2** Queuing Models Described in This Chapter

Model	Name (technical name in parentheses)	Example	Number of Channels	Number of Phases	Arrival Rate Pattern	Service Time Pattern	Population Size	Queue Discipline
A	Single-channel system (M/M/1)	Information counter at department store	Single	Single	Poisson	Exponential	Unlimited	FIFO
B	Multichannel (M/M/S)	Airline ticket counter	Multi-channel	Single	Poisson	Exponential	Unlimited	FIFO
C	Constant service (M/D/1)	Automated car wash	Single	Single	Poisson	Constant	Unlimited	FIFO
D	Limited population (finite population)	Shop with only a dozen machines that might break	Single	Single	Poisson	Exponential	Limited	FIFO

Model A: M/M/1 (See Flexible Version pp. 590–593)

Assumptions

1. _____
2. _____
3. _____
4. _____
5. _____
6. _____

λ = Mean number of arrivals per time period

μ = Mean number of people or items served per time period

L_s = Average number of units (customers) in the system (waiting and being served)

$$= \frac{\lambda}{\mu - \lambda}$$

W_s = Average time a unit spends in the system (waiting time plus service time)

$$= \frac{1}{\mu - \lambda}$$

L_q = Average number of units waiting in the queue

$$= \frac{\lambda^2}{\mu(\mu - \lambda)}$$

W_q = Average time a unit spends waiting in the queue

$$= \frac{\lambda}{\mu(\mu - \lambda)}$$

ρ = Utilization factor for the system

$$= \frac{\lambda}{\mu}$$

P_0 = Probability of 0 units in the system (that is, the service unit is idle)

$$= 1 - \frac{\lambda}{\mu}$$

$P_{n>k}$ = Probability of more than k units in the system, where n is the number of units in the system

$$= \left(\frac{\lambda}{\mu}\right)^{k+1}$$

PRACTICE PROBLEM D.1 ■ Basic Single-Channel Model

A new shopping mall is considering setting up an information desk manned by one employee.
Based on information obtained from similar information desks, it is believed that people will
arrive at the desk at a rate of 20 per hour. It takes an average of 2 minutes to answer a question.
It is assumed that the arrivals follow a Poisson distribution and answer times are exponentially
distributed.

a. Find the probability that the employee is idle.

b. Find the proportion of the time that the employee is busy.

c. Find the average number of people receiving and waiting to receive some information.

d. Find the average number of people waiting in line to get some information.

e. Find the average time a person seeking information spends in the system.

f. Find the expected time a person spends just waiting in line to have a question answered
(time in the queue).

PRACTICE PROBLEM D.2 ■ Costs in Practice Problem D.1

Assume that the information desk employee in Practice Problem D.1 earns $5 per hour. The cost of waiting time, in terms of customer unhappiness with the mall, is $12 per hour of time spent waiting in line. Find the total expected costs over an 8-hour day.

Additional Practice Problem Space

Model B: M/M/S (See Flexible Version pp. 593–597)

M = number of channels open

λ = average arrival rate

μ = average service rate at each channel

The probability that there are zero people or units in the system is:

$$P_0 = \frac{1}{\left[\displaystyle\sum_{n=0}^{M-1} \frac{1}{n!}\left(\frac{\lambda}{\mu}\right)^n\right] + \frac{1}{M!}\left(\frac{\lambda}{\mu}\right)^M \frac{M\mu}{M\mu - \lambda}} \quad \text{for } M\mu > \lambda$$

The average number of people or units in the system is:

$$L_s = \frac{\lambda\mu(\lambda/\mu)^M}{(M-1)!(M\mu - \lambda)^2} P_0 + \frac{\lambda}{\mu}$$

The average time a unit spends in the waiting line and being serviced (namely, in the system) is:

$$W_s = \frac{\mu(\lambda/\mu)^M}{(M-1)!(M\mu - \lambda)^2} P_0 + \frac{1}{\mu} = \frac{L_s}{\lambda}$$

The average number of people or units in line waiting for service is:

$$L_q = L_s - \frac{\lambda}{\mu}$$

The average time a person or unit spends in the queue waiting for service is:

$$W_q = W_s - \frac{1}{\mu} = \frac{L_q}{\lambda}$$

PRACTICE PROBLEM D.3 ■ Adding a Second Employee to Practice Problem D.1

The shopping mall has decided to investigate the use of two employees on the information desk.

a. Find the proportion of the time the employees will be idle.

b. Find the average number of people waiting in this system.

c. Find the expected time a person spends waiting in this system.

d. Assuming the same salary level and waiting costs as in Practice Problem D.2, find the total expected costs over an 8-hour day.

Additional Practice Problem Space

Use of Waiting Line Tables (See Table D.5 in Flexible Version p. 596)

Model C: M/D/1 (See Flexible Version pp. 597–598)

Average length of queue: $L_q = \dfrac{\lambda^2}{2\mu(\mu - \lambda)}$

Average waiting time in queue: $W_q = \dfrac{\lambda}{2\mu(\mu - \lambda)}$

Average number of customers in system: $L_s = L_q + \dfrac{\lambda}{\mu}$

Average time in system: $W_s = W_q + \dfrac{1}{\mu}$

◀ TABLE D.6
Queuing Formulas for Model C:
Constant Service, Also Called
M/D/1

PRACTICE PROBLEM D.4 ■ Constant Service Time Model

Three students arrive per minute at a coffee machine that dispenses exactly 4 cups per minute at a constant rate. Describe the system parameters.

Additional Practice Problem Space

Little's Law (See Flexible Version pp. 598–599)

$$L = \lambda W \qquad \text{(D-2)}$$

Model D: Limited Population (See Flexible Version pp. 599–601)

◀ **TABLE D.7**
Queuing Formulas and Notation for Model D: Limited Population Formulas

Service factor: $X = \dfrac{T}{T + U}$	Average number running: $J = NF(1 - X)$
Average number waiting: $L = N(1 - F)$	Average number being serviced: $H = FNX$
Average waiting time: $W = \dfrac{L(T + U)}{N - L} = \dfrac{T(1 - F)}{XF}$	Number in population: $N = J + L + H$

Notation

D = probability that a unit will have to wait in queue	N = number of potential customers
F = efficiency factor	T = average service time
H = average number of units being served	U = average time between unit service
J = average number running	requirements
L = average number of units waiting for service	W = average time a unit waits in line
M = number of service channels	X = service factor

PRACTICE PROBLEM D.5 ■ Limited Population Model

A repairperson at a local metal working shop services the shop's 5 drill presses. Service time averages 10 minutes and is exponentially distributed. Machines break down after an average of 70 minutes of operation (following a Poisson distribution). Describe the major system characteristics.

OTHER QUEUING APPROACHES (See Flexible Version p. 601)

Discussion Questions

1. Name the three parts of a typical queuing system.
2. When designing a waiting line system, what "qualitative" concerns need to be considered?
3. Name the three factors that govern the structure of "arrivals" in a queuing system.
4. State the seven common measures of queuing system performance.
5. State the assumptions of the "basic" single-channel queuing model (Model A, or M/M/1).
6. Is it good or bad to operate a supermarket bakery system on a strict first-come, first-served basis? Why?
7. Describe what is meant by the waiting-line terms *balk* and *renege*. Provide an example of each.
8. Which is larger, W_s or W_q? Explain.
9. Briefly describe three situations in which the first-in, first-out (FIFO) discipline rule is not applicable in queuing analysis.
10. Describe the behavior of a waiting line where $\lambda > \mu$. Use both analysis and intuition.
11. Discuss the likely outcome of a waiting line system where $\mu > \lambda$ but only by a tiny amount (e.g., $\mu = 4.1, \lambda = 4$).

12. Provide examples of four situations in which there is a limited, or finite, waiting line.
13. What are the components of the following queuing systems? Draw and explain the configuration of each.
    a) Barbershop.
    b) Car wash.
    c) Laundromat.
    d) Small grocery store.
14. Do doctors' offices generally have random arrival rates for patients? Are service times random? Under what circumstances might service times be constant?
15. What happens if two single-channel systems have the same mean arrival and service rates, but the service time is constant in one and exponential in the other?
16. What dollar value do you place on yourself per hour that you spend waiting in lines? What value do your classmates place on themselves? Why do the values differ?
17. Why is Little's Law a useful queuing concept?

Problems*

•   **D.1**   Customers arrive at Paul Harrold's Styling Shop at a rate of 3 per hour, distributed in a Poisson fashion. Paul can perform haircuts at a rate of 5 per hour, distributed exponentially.
a) Find the average number of customers waiting for haircuts.
b) Find the average number of customers in the shop.
c) Find the average time a customer waits until it is his or her turn.
d) Find the average time a customer spends in the shop.
e) Find the percentage of time that Paul is busy. **Px**

•   **D.2**   There is only one copying machine in the student lounge of the business school. Students arrive at the rate of $\lambda = 40$ per hour (according to a Poisson distribution). Copying takes an average of 40 seconds, or $\mu = 90$ per hour (according to an exponential distribution). Compute the following:
a) The percentage of time that the machine is used.
b) The average length of the queue.
c) The average number of students in the system.
d) The average time spent waiting in the queue.
e) The average time in the system. **Px**

•   **D.3**   Glen Schmidt owns and manages a chili-dog and soft-drink stand near the Georgeville campus. While Glen can service 30 customers per hour on the average (μ), he gets only 20 customers per hour (λ). Because Glen could wait on 50% more customers than actually visit his stand, it doesn't make sense to him that he should have any waiting lines.

Glen hires you to examine the situation and to determine some characteristics of his queue. After looking into the problem, you find it follows the six conditions for a single-channel waiting line (as seen in Model A). What are your findings? **Px**

•   **D.4**   Sam Certo, a Longwood vet, is running a rabies vaccination clinic for dogs at the local grade school. Sam can "shoot" a dog every 3 minutes. It is estimated that the dogs will arrive independently and randomly throughout the day at a rate of one dog every 6 minutes according to a Poisson distribution. Also assume that Sam's shooting times are exponentially distributed. Compute the following:
a) The probability that Sam is idle.
b) The proportion of the time that Sam is busy.
c) The average number of dogs being vaccinated and waiting to be vaccinated.
d) The average number of dogs waiting to be vaccinated.
e) The average time a dog waits before getting vaccinated.
f) The average amount of time a dog spends waiting in line and being vaccinated. **Px**

••   **D.5**   The pharmacist at Arnold Palmer Hospital, Saad Alwan, receives 12 requests for prescriptions each hour, Poisson distributed. It takes him a mean time of 4 minutes to fill each, following a negative exponential distribution. Use the waiting line table, Table D.5 and $W_q = L_q/\lambda$, to answer these questions.
a) What is the average number of prescriptions in the queue?
b) How long will the average prescription spend in the queue?
c) Alwan decides to hire a second pharmacist, Ajay Aggerwal, whom he went to school with and who operates at the same speed in filling prescriptions. How will the answers to parts (a) and (b) change? **Px**

•   **D.6**   Calls arrive at James Hamann's hotel switchboard at a rate of 2 per minute. The average time to handle each is 20 seconds.

There is only one switchboard operator at the current time. The Poisson and exponential distributions appear to be relevant in this situation.
a) What is the probability that the operator is busy?
b) What is the average time that a customer must wait before reaching the operator?
c) What is the average number of calls waiting to be answered? **Px**

••   **D.7**   Automobiles arrive at the drive-through window at the downtown Urbana, Illinois, post office at the rate of 4 every 10 minutes. The average service time is 2 minutes. The Poisson distribution is appropriate for the arrival rate and service times are exponentially distributed.
a) What is the average time a car is in the system?
b) What is the average number of cars in the system?
c) What is the average number of cars waiting to receive service?
d) What is the average time a car is in the queue?
e) What is the probability that there are no cars at the window?
f) What percentage of the time is the postal clerk busy?
g) What is the probability that there are exactly 2 cars in the system?
h) By how much would your answer to part (a) be reduced if a second drive-through window, with its own server, were added? **Px**

•   **D.8**   Missouri's Stephen Allen Electronics Corporation retains a service crew to repair machine breakdowns that occur on an average of $\lambda = 3$ per 8-hour workday (approximately Poisson in nature). The crew can service an average of $\mu = 8$ machines per workday, with a repair time distribution that resembles the exponential distribution.
a) What is the utilization rate of this service system?
b) What is the average downtime for a broken machine?
c) How many machines are waiting to be serviced at any given time?
d) What is the probability that more than one machine is in the system? the probability that more than two are broken and waiting to be repaired or being serviced? more than three? more than four? **Px**

••   **D.9**   Zimmerman's Bank is the only bank in the small town of St. Thomas. On a typical Friday, an average of 10 customers per hour arrive at the bank to transact business. There is one teller at the bank, and the average time required to transact business is 4 minutes. It is assumed that service times may be described by the exponential distribution. A single line would be used, and the customer at the front of the line would go to the first available bank teller. If a single teller is used, find:
a) The average time in the line.
b) The average number in the line.
c) The average time in the system.
d) The average number in the system.
e) The probability that the bank is empty.
f) Zimmerman is considering adding a second teller (who would work at the same rate as the first) to reduce the waiting time for customers. She assumes that this will cut the waiting time in half. If a second teller is added, find the new answers to parts (a) to (e). **Px**

••   **D.10**   Susan Slotnick manages a Cleveland, Ohio, movie theater complex called Cinema I, II, III, and IV. Each of the four auditoriums plays a different film; the schedule staggers starting times to avoid the large crowds that would occur if all four movies started at the same time. The theater has a single ticket booth and a cashier who can maintain an average service rate of 280 patrons per hour.

Service times are assumed to follow an exponential distribution. Arrivals on a normally active day are Poisson distributed and average 210 per hour.

To determine the efficiency of the current ticket operation, Susan wishes to examine several queue-operating characteristics.

a) Find the average number of moviegoers waiting in line to purchase a ticket.
b) What percentage of the time is the cashier busy?
c) What is the average time that a customer spends in the system?
d) What is the average time spent waiting in line to get to the ticket window?
e) What is the probability that there are more than two people in the system? more than three people? more than four? **Px**

•• **D.11** Bill Youngdahl has been collecting data at the TU student grill. He has found that, between 5:00 P.M. and 7:00 P.M., students arrive at the grill at a rate of 25 per hour (Poisson distributed) and service time takes an average of 2 minutes (exponential distribution). There is only 1 server, who can work on only 1 order at a time.

a) What is the average number of students in line?
b) What is the average time a student is in the grill area?
c) Suppose that a second server can be added to team up with the first (and, in effect, act as one faster server). This would reduce the average service time to 90 seconds. How would this affect the average time a student is in the grill area?
d) Suppose a second server is added and the 2 servers act independently, with *each* taking an average of 2 minutes. What would be the average time a student is in the system? **Px**

••• **D.12** The wheat harvesting season in the American Midwest is short, and farmers deliver their truckloads of wheat to a giant central storage bin within a 2-week span. Because of this, wheat-filled trucks waiting to unload and return to the fields have been known to back up for a block at the receiving bin. The central bin is owned cooperatively, and it is to every farmer's benefit to make the unloading/storage process as efficient as possible. The cost of grain deterioration caused by unloading delays and the cost of truck rental and idle driver time are significant concerns to the cooperative members. Although farmers have difficulty quantifying crop damage, it is easy to assign a waiting and unloading cost for truck and driver of $18 per hour. During the 2-week harvest season, the storage bin is open and operated 16 hours per day, 7 days per week, and can unload 35 trucks per hour according to an exponential distribution. Full trucks arrive all day long (during

the hours the bin is open) at a rate of about 30 per hour, following a Poisson pattern.

To help the cooperative get a handle on the problem of lost time while trucks are waiting in line or unloading at the bin, find the following:

a) The average number of trucks in the unloading system.
b) The average time per truck in the system.
c) The utilization rate for the bin area.
d) The probability that there are more than three trucks in the system at any given time.
e) The total daily cost to the farmers of having their trucks tied up in the unloading process.
f) As mentioned, the cooperative uses the storage bin heavily only 2 weeks per year. Farmers estimate that enlarging the bin would cut unloading costs by 50% next year. It will cost $9,000 to do so during the off-season. Would it be worth the expense to enlarge the storage area? **Px**

••• **D.13** Radovilsky's Department Store in Haywood, California, maintains a successful catalog sales department in which a clerk takes orders by telephone. If the clerk is occupied on one line, incoming phone calls to the catalog department are answered automatically by a recording machine and asked to wait. As soon as the clerk is free, the party who has waited the longest is transferred and serviced first. Calls come in at a rate of about 12 per hour. The clerk can take an order in an average of 4 minutes. Calls tend to follow a Poisson distribution, and service times tend to be exponential.

The cost of the clerk is $10 per hour, but because of lost goodwill and sales, Radovilsky's loses about $25 per hour of customer time spent waiting for the clerk to take an order.

a) What is the average time that catalog customers must wait before their calls are transferred to the order clerk?
b) What is the average number of customers waiting to place an order?
c) Radovilsky's is considering adding a second clerk to take calls. The store's cost would be the same $10 per hour. Should it hire another clerk? Explain your decision. **Px**

• **D.14** Karen Brown's Coffee Shop decides to install an automatic coffee vending machine outside one of its stores to reduce the number of people standing in line inside. Karen charges $3.50 per cup. However, it takes too long for people to make change. The service time is a constant 3 minutes, and the arrival rate is 15 per hour (Poisson distributed).

a) What is the average wait in line?
b) What is the average number of people in line?
c) Karen raises the price to $5 per cup and takes 60 seconds off the service time. However, because the coffee is now so expensive, the arrival rate drops to 10 per hour. Now what are the average wait time and the average number of people in the queue (waiting)? **Px**

••• **D.15** The typical subway station in Washington, DC, has six turnstiles, each of which can be controlled by the station manager to be used for either entrance or exit control—but never for both. The manager must decide at different times of the day how many turnstiles to use for entering passengers and how many to use for exiting passengers.

At the George Washington University (GWU) Station, passengers enter the station at a rate of about 84 per minute between the hours of 7 A.M. and 9 A.M. Passengers exiting trains at the stop reach the exit turnstile area at a rate of about 48 per minute during the same morning rush hours. Each turnstile can allow an average of 30 passengers per minute to enter or exit. Arrival and service times have been thought to follow Poisson and exponential distributions, respectively. Assume riders form a common queue at both entry and exit turnstile areas and proceed to the first empty turnstile.

The GWU station manager, Ernie Forman, does not want the average passenger at his station to have to wait in a turnstile line for more than 6 seconds, nor does he want more than 8 people in any queue at any average time.

a) How many turnstiles should be opened in each direction every morning?

b) Discuss the assumptions underlying the solution of this problem using queuing theory. **Px**

•• **D.16** Yvette Freeman's Car Wash takes a constant time of 4.5 minutes in its automated car wash cycle. Autos arrive following a Poisson distribution at the rate of 10 per hour. Yvette wants to know:

a) The average waiting time in line.

b) The average length of the line. **Px**

••• **D.17** Debra Bishop's cabinet-making shop, in Des Moines, has five tools that automate the drilling of holes for the installation of hinges. These machines need setting up for each order of cabinets. The orders appear to follow the Poisson distribution, averaging 3 per 8-hour day. There is a single technician for setting these machines. Her service times are exponential, averaging 2 hours each.

a) What is the service factor for this system?

b) What is the average number of machines available for drilling?

c) What impact on machines in service would there be if a second technician were available? **Px**

••• **D.18** Two technicians, working separately, monitor a group of 5 computers that run an automated manufacturing facility. It takes an average of 15 minutes (exponentially distributed) to adjust a computer that develops a problem. Computers run for an average of 85 minutes (Poisson distributed) without requiring adjustments. Determine the following:

a) The average number of computers waiting for adjustment.

b) The average number being adjusted.

c) The average number of computers not in working order. **Px**

••• **D.19** One mechanic services 5 drilling machines for a steel plate manufacturer. Machines break down on an average of once every 6 working days, and breakdowns tend to follow a Poisson distribution. The mechanic can handle an average of one repair job per day. Repairs follow an exponential distribution.

a) On the average, how many machines are waiting for service?

b) On the average, how many drills are in running order?

c) How much would waiting time be reduced if a second mechanic were hired? **Px**

••• **D.20** Richard Insinga, the administrator at an Onienta Hospital emergency room, faces the problem of providing treatment for patients who arrive at different rates during the day. There are four doctors available to treat patients when needed. If not needed, they can be assigned other responsibilities (such as doing lab tests, reports, X-ray diagnoses) or else rescheduled to work at other hours. It is important to provide quick and responsive treatment, and Richard feels that, on the average, patients should not have to sit in the waiting area for more than 5 minutes before being seen by a doctor. Patients are treated on a first-come, first-served basis and see the first available doctor after waiting in the queue. The arrival pattern for a typical day is as follows:

Time	Arrival Rate
9 A.M.–3 P.M.	6 patients/hour
3 P.M.–8 P.M.	4 patients/hour
8 P.M.–midnight	12 patients/hour

Arrivals follow a Poisson distribution, and treatment times, 12 minutes on the average, follow the exponential pattern.

a) How many doctors should be on duty during each period to maintain the level of patient care expected?

b) What condition would exist if only one doctor were on duty between 9 A.M. and 3 P.M.? **Px**

••• **D.21** The Pontchartrain Bridge is a 16-mile toll bridge that crosses Lake Pontchartrain in New Orleans. Currently, there are 7 toll booths, each staffed by an employee. Since Hurricane Katrina, the Port Authority has been considering replacing the employees with machines. Many factors must be considered because the employees are unionized. However, one of the Port Authority's concerns is the effect that replacing the employees with machines will have on the times that drivers spend in the system. Customers arrive to any one toll booth at a rate of 10 per minute. In the exact change lanes with employees, the service time is essentially constant at 5 seconds for each driver. With machines, the average service time would still be 5 seconds, but it would be exponential rather than constant, because it takes time for the coins to rattle around in the machine. Contrast the two systems for a single lane. **Px**

••• **D.22** The registration area has just opened at a large convention of building contractors in Las Vegas. There are 200 people arriving per hour (Poisson distributed), and the cost of their waiting time in the queue is valued at $100 per person per hour. The Las Vegas Convention Bureau provides servers to register guests at a fee of $15 per person per hour. It takes about one minute to register an attendee (exponentially distributed). A single waiting line, with multiple servers, is set up.

a) What is the minimum number of servers for this system?

b) What is the optimal number of servers for this system?

c) What is the cost for the system, per hour, at the optimum number of servers?

d) What is the server utilization rate with the minimum number of servers? **Px**

•• **D.23** Refer to Problem D.22. A new registration manager, Lisa Houts, is hired who initiates a program to entertain the people in line with a juggler whom she pays $15/hour. This reduces the waiting costs to $50 per hour.

a) What is the optimal number of servers?

b) What is the cost for the system, per hour, at the optimal service level? **Px**

•••• **D.24** The Chattanooga Furniture store gets an average of 50 customers per shift. Marilyn Helms, the manager, wants to calculate whether she should hire 1, 2, 3, or 4 salespeople. She has determined that average waiting times will be 7 minutes with one salesperson, 4 minutes with two salespeople, 3 minutes with three salespeople, and 2 minutes with four salespeople. She has estimated the cost per minute that customers wait at $1. The cost per salesperson per shift (including fringe benefits) is $70.

How many salespeople should be hired?

▶ **Refer to** myomlab ○ **for these additional homework problems: D.25–D.33**

Case Studies

▶ New England Foundry

For more than 75 years, New England Foundry, Inc. (NEFI), has manufactured wood stoves for home use. In recent years, with increasing energy prices, president George Mathison has seen sales triple. This dramatic increase has made it difficult for George to maintain quality in all his wood stoves and related products.

Unlike other companies manufacturing wood stoves, NEFI is in the business of making *only* stoves and stove-related products. Its major products are the Warmglo I, the Warmglo II, the Warmglo III, and the Warmglo IV. The Warmglo I is the smallest wood stove, with a heat output of 30,000 BTUs, and the Warmglo IV is the largest, with a heat output of 60,000 BTUs.

The Warmglo III outsold all other models by a wide margin. Its heat output and available accessories were ideal for the typical home. The Warmglo III also had a number of other outstanding features that made it one of the most attractive and heat-efficient stoves on the market. These features, along with the accessories, resulted in expanding sales and prompted George to build a new factory to manufacture the Warmglo III model. An overview diagram of the factory is shown in Figure D.6.

The new foundry used the latest equipment, including a new Disamatic that helped in manufacturing stove parts. Regardless of new equipment or procedures, casting operations have remained basically unchanged for hundreds of years. To begin with, a wooden pattern is made for every cast-iron piece in the stove. The wooden pattern is an exact duplicate of the cast-iron piece that is to be manufactured. All NEFI patterns are made by Precision Patterns, Inc. and are stored in the pattern shop and maintenance room. Next, a specially formulated sand is molded around the wooden pattern. There can be two or more sand molds for each pattern. The sand is mixed and the molds are made in the molding room. When the wooden pattern is removed, the resulting sand molds form a negative image of the desired casting. Next, molds are transported to the casting room, where molten iron is poured into them and allowed to cool. When the iron has solidified, molds are moved into the cleaning, grinding, and preparation room, where they are dumped into large vibrators that shake most of the sand from the casting. The rough castings are then subjected to both sandblasting to remove the rest of the sand and grinding to finish some of their surfaces. Castings are then painted with a special heat-resistant paint, assembled into workable stoves,

and inspected for manufacturing defects that may have gone undetected. Finally, finished stoves are moved to storage and shipping, where they are packaged and transported to the appropriate locations.

At present, the pattern shop and the maintenance department are located in the same room. One large counter is used by both maintenance personnel, who store tools and parts (which are mainly used by the casting department); and sand molders, who need various patterns for the molding operation. Pete Nawler and Bob Dillman, who work behind the counter, can service a total of 10 people per hour (about 5 per hour each). On the average, 4 people from casting and 3 from molding arrive at the counter each hour. People from molding and casting departments arrive randomly, and to be served, they form a single line.

Pete and Bob have always had a policy of first come, first served. Because of the location of the pattern shop and maintenance department, it takes an average of 3 minutes for an individual from the casting department to walk to the pattern and maintenance room, and it takes about 1 minute for an individual to walk from the molding department to the pattern and maintenance room.

After observing the operation of the pattern shop and maintenance room for several weeks, George decided to make some changes to the factory layout. An overview of these changes appears in Figure D.7.

Separating the maintenance shop from the pattern shop would have a number of advantages. It would take people from the casting department only 1 minute instead of 3 to get to the new maintenance room. The time from molding to the pattern shop would be unchanged. Using motion and time studies, George was also able to determine that improving the layout of the maintenance room would allow Bob to serve 6 people from the casting department per hour; improving the layout of the pattern department would allow Pete to serve 7 people from the molding shop per hour.

Discussion Questions

1. How much time would the new layout save?
2. If casting personnel were paid $9.50 per hour and molding personnel were paid $11.75 per hour, how much could be saved per hour with the new factory layout?
3. Should George have made the change in layout?

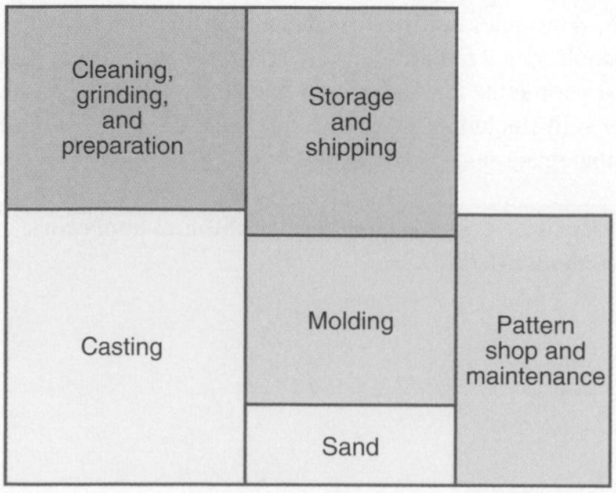

▲ FIGURE D.6 Overview of Factory

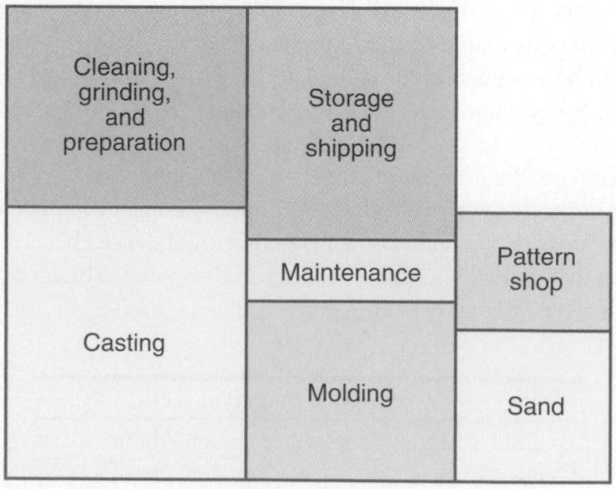

▲ FIGURE D.7 Overview of Factory after Changes

▶ The Winter Park Hotel

Donna Shader, manager of the Winter Park Hotel, is considering how to restructure the front desk to reach an optimum level of staff efficiency and guest service. At present, the hotel has five clerks on duty, each with a separate waiting line, during peak check-in time of 3:00 P.M. to 5:00 P.M. Observation of arrivals during this period shows that an average of 90 guests arrive each hour (although there is no upward limit on the number that could arrive at any given time). It takes an average of 3 minutes for the front-desk clerk to register each guest.

Ms. Shader is considering three plans for improving guest service by reducing the length of time that guests spend waiting in line. The first proposal would designate one employee as a quick-service clerk for guests registering under corporate accounts, a market segment that fills about 30% of all occupied rooms. Because corporate guests are preregistered, their registration takes just 2 minutes. With these guests separated from the rest of the clientele, the average time for registering a typical guest would climb to 3.4 minutes. Under this plan, noncorporate guests would choose any of the remaining four lines.

The second plan is to implement a single-line system. All guests could form a single waiting line to be served by whichever of five clerks became available. This option would require sufficient lobby space for what could be a substantial queue.

The use of an automatic teller machine (ATM) for check-ins is the basis of the third proposal. This ATM would provide about the same service rate as would a clerk. Because initial use of this technology might be minimal, Shader estimates that 20% of customers, primarily frequent guests, would be willing to use the machines. (This might be a conservative estimate if guests perceive direct benefits from using the ATM, as bank customers do. Citibank reports that some 95% of its Manhattan customers use its ATMs.) Ms. Shader would set up a single queue for customers who prefer human check-in clerks. This line would be served by the five clerks, although Shader is hopeful that the ATM will allow a reduction to four.

Discussion Questions

1. Determine the average amount of time that a guest spends checking in. How would this change under each of the stated options?
2. Which option do you recommend?

Active Model Exercises

ACTIVE MODELS D.1, D.2, D.3 These exercises allow you to simulate the behavior of the queues presented in Examples D1, D3, and D4, respectively, in the text. These are illustrated at **www.myomlab.com** or **www.pearsonhighered.com/heizer**.

Module D *Rapid* Review

Main Heading	Review Material
QUEUING THEORY (p. 584)	■ **Queuing theory**—A body of knowledge about waiting lines. ■ **Waiting line (queue)**—Items or people in a line awaiting service.

Main Heading	Review Material
CHARACTERISTICS OF A WAITING-LINE SYSTEM (pp. 585–588)	The three parts of a waiting-line, or queuing, system are: *Arrivals or inputs to the system; queue discipline, or the waiting line itself;* and *the service facility:* ■ **Unlimited, or infinite, population**—A queue in which a virtually unlimited number of people or items could request the services, or in which the number of customers or arrivals on hand at any given moment is a very small portion of potential arrivals. ■ **Limited, or finite, population**—A queue in which there are only a limited number of potential users of the service. ■ **Poisson distribution**—A discrete probability distribution that often describes the arrival rate in queuing theory:

$$P(x) = \frac{e^{-\lambda}\lambda^x}{x!} \quad \text{for } x = 0, 1, 2, 3, 4, \ldots \qquad \text{(D-1)}$$

A queue is *limited* when it cannot, either by law or because of physical restrictions, increase to an infinite length. A queue is *unlimited* when its size is unrestricted.

Queue discipline refers to the rule by which customers in the line are to receive service:

■ **First-in, first-out (FIFO) rule**—A queue discipline in which the first customers in line receive the first service.

■ **Single-channel queuing system**—A service system with one line and one server.

■ **Multiple-channel queuing system**—A service system with one waiting line but with more than one server (channel).

■ **Single-phase system**—A system in which the customer receives service from only one station and then exits the system.

■ **Multiphase system**—A system in which the customer receives services from several stations before exiting the system.

■ **Negative exponential probability distribution**—A continuous probability distribution often used to describe the service time in a queuing system.

Main Heading	Review Material
QUEUING COSTS (pp. 589–590)	Operations managers must recognize the trade-off that takes place between two costs: the cost of providing good service and the cost of customer or machine waiting time.

Cost

Minimum total → cost

Total expected cost

Cost of providing service

Cost of waiting time

Low level of service — Optimal service level — High level of service

Main Heading	Review Material	
THE VARIETY OF QUEUING MODELS (pp. 590–601)	*Model A: Single-Channel System (M/M/1):* *Queuing Formulas:*	Problems: D.1–D.24 Virtual Office Hours for Solved Problems: D.1–D.4 **ACTIVE MODELS D.1, D.2, D.3**

λ = mean number of arrivals per time period

μ = mean number of people or items served per time period

L_s = average number of units in the system = $\lambda/(\mu - \lambda)$

W_s = average time a unit spends in the system = $1/(\mu - \lambda)$

L_q = average number of units waiting in the queue = $\lambda^2/[\mu(\mu - \lambda)]$

Main Heading	Review Material	

W_q = average time a unit spends waiting in the queue = $\lambda/[\mu(\mu - \lambda)] = L_q/\lambda$

ρ = utilization factor for the system = λ/μ

P_0 = probability of 0 units in the system (i.e., the service unit is idle) = $1 - (\lambda/\mu)$

$P_{n>k}$ = probability of $> k$ units in the system = $(\lambda/\mu)^{k+1}$

Model B: *Multichannel System (M/M/S):*

$$P_0 = \frac{1}{\left[\sum_{n=0}^{M-1} \frac{1}{n!}\left(\frac{\lambda}{\mu}\right)^n\right] + \frac{1}{M!}\left(\frac{\lambda}{\mu}\right)^M \frac{M\mu}{M\mu - \lambda}} \quad \text{for } M\mu > \lambda$$

$$L_s = \frac{\lambda\mu(\lambda/\mu)^M}{(M-1)!(M\mu - \lambda)^2} P_0 + \frac{\lambda}{\mu}$$

$$W_s = L_s/\lambda \qquad L_q = L_s - (\lambda/\mu) \qquad W_q = L_q/\lambda$$

Model C: *Constant Service (M/D/1):*

$$L_q = \lambda^2/[2\mu(\mu - \lambda)] \qquad W_q = \lambda/[2\mu(\mu - \lambda)]$$

$$L_s = L_q + (\lambda/\mu) \qquad W_s = W_q + (1/\mu)$$

Little's Law
A useful relationship in queuing for any system in a steady state is called Little's Law:

$$L = \lambda W \quad \text{(which is the same as } W = L/\lambda) \tag{D-2}$$

$$L_q = \lambda W_q \quad \text{(which is the same as } W_q = L_q/\lambda) \tag{D-3}$$

Model D: *Limited Population*
With a limited population, there is a *dependent* relationship between the length of the queue and the arrival rate. As the *waiting* line becomes longer, the *arrival rate* drops.

OTHER QUEUING APPROACHES (p. 601)	Often, *variations* of the four basic queuing models are present in an analysis. Many models, some very complex, have been developed to deal with such variations.

Self Test

■ **Before taking the self-test,** refer to the learning objectives listed at the beginning of the module and the key terms listed at the end of the module.

LO1. Which of the following is *not* a key operating characteristic for a queuing system?
 a) Utilization rate
 b) Percent idle time
 c) Average time spent waiting in the system and in the queue
 d) Average number of customers in the system and in the queue
 e) Average number of customers who renege

LO2. Customers enter the waiting line at a cafeteria's only cash register on a first-come, first-served basis. The arrival rate follows a Poisson distribution, while service times follow an exponential distribution. If the average number of arrivals is 6 per minute and the average service rate of a single server is 10 per minute, what is the average number of customers in the system?
 a) 0.6 b) 0.9
 c) 1.5 d) 0.25
 e) 1.0

LO3. In performing a cost analysis of a queuing system, the waiting time cost is sometimes based on the time in the queue and sometimes based on the time in the system. The waiting cost should be based on time in the system for which of the following situations?
 a) Waiting in line to ride an amusement park ride
 b) Waiting to discuss a medical problem with a doctor
 c) Waiting for a picture and an autograph from a rock star
 d) Waiting for a computer to be fixed so it can be placed back in service

LO4. Which of the following is *not* an assumption in a multichannel queuing model?
 a) Arrivals come from an infinite, or very large, population.
 b) Arrivals are Poisson distributed.
 c) Arrivals are treated on a first-in, first-out basis and do not balk or renege.
 d) Service times follow the exponential distribution.
 e) Servers each perform at their own individual speeds.

LO5. If everything else remains the same, including the mean arrival rate and service rate, except that the service time becomes constant instead of exponential:
 a) the average queue length will be halved.
 b) the average waiting time will be doubled.
 c) the average queue length will increase.
 d) we cannot tell from the information provided.

LO6. A company has one computer technician who is responsible for repairs on the company's 20 computers. As a computer breaks, the technician is called to make the repair. If the repairperson is busy, the machine must wait to be repaired. This is an example of:
 a) a multichannel system. b) a finite population system.
 c) a constant service rate system. d) a multiphase system.
 e) all of the above.

Answers: LO1. e; LO2. c; LO3. d; LO4. e; LO5. a; LO6. b.

QUANTITATIVE MODULE
E Learning Curves

Module Outline

What Is a Learning Curve?

Learning Curves in Services and Manufacturing

Applying the Learning Curve

Strategic Implications of Learning Curves

Limitations of Learning Curves

Discussion Questions
Problems
Case Study: SMT's Negotiation with IBM
Active Model Exercise
Rapid Review

Most of us get better with practice. So do most processes. As firms and employees perform a task repeatedly, they learn how to perform those tasks more efficiently. We call this the learning curve.

The learning curve has application to (1) labor time, (2) purchased components, and (3) strategic decisions regarding costs and pricing.

The learning curve is based on a doubling of similar production units. That is, when production doubles, the decrease in time per unit determines the learning curve.

BEFORE COMING TO CLASS, READ MODULE E IN YOUR TEXT AND ANSWER THESE QUESTIONS.

1. What is the basic assumption of learning curves? _____

_____

_____

2. Explain the "doubling concept" of learning curves. _____

_____

_____

3. What three ways can learning curves be calculated? _____

_____

_____

4. How is the learning curve used for strategic decisions? _____

_____

_____

WHAT IS A LEARNING CURVE?   (See Flexible Version pp. 606–607)

LEARNING CURVES IN SERVICES AND MANUFACTURING

(See Flexible Version pp. 607–608)

Doubling Concept

$$T \times L^n = \text{Time required for the } n\text{th unit} \qquad \text{(E-1)}$$

where T = unit cost or unit time of the first unit
 L = learning curve rate
 n = number of times T is doubled

APPLYING THE LEARNING CURVE   (See Flexible Version pp. 608–611)

Arithmetic Approach   (See Flexible Version p. 608)

Logarithmic Approach   (See Flexible Version p. 609)

$$T_N = T_1(N^b) \qquad \text{(E-2)}$$

where T_N = time for the Nth unit
 T_1 = hours to produce the first unit
 b = (log of the learning rate)/(log 2) = slope of the learning curve

Learning-Curve Coefficient Approach

(See Flexible Version pp. 609–611)

$$T_N = T_1 C \qquad \text{(E-3)}$$

where T_N = number of labor-hours required to produce the Nth unit
 T_1 = number of labor-hours required to produce the first unit
 C = learning-curve coefficient found in Table E.3

▼ TABLE E.3   Learning-Curve Coefficients, Where Coefficient, $C = N^{(\text{log of learning rate/log 2})}$

Unit Number (N)	70%		75%		80%		85%		90%	
	Unit Time Co-efficient	Total Time Co-efficient	Unit Time Co-efficient	Total Time Co-efficient	Unit Time Co-efficient	Total Time Co-efficient	Unit Time Co-efficient	Total Time Co-efficient	Unit Time Co-efficient	Total Time Co-efficient
1	1.000	1.000	1.000	1.000	1.000	1.000	1.000	1.000	1.000	1.000
2	.700	1.700	.750	1.750	.800	1.800	.850	1.850	.900	1.900
3	.568	2.268	.634	2.384	.702	2.502	.773	2.623	.846	2.746
4	.490	2.758	.562	2.946	.640	3.142	.723	3.345	.810	3.556
5	.437	3.195	.513	3.459	.596	3.738	.686	4.031	.783	4.339
6	398	3 593	475	3 934	.562	4.299	.657	4.688	.762	5.101
7	.367	3.960	.446	4.380	.534	4.834	.634	5.322	.744	5.845
8	.343	4.303	.422	4.802	.512	5.346	.614	5.936	.729	6.574
9	.323	4.626	.402	5.204	.493	5.839	.597	6.533	.716	7.290
10	.306	4.932	.385	5.589	.477	6.315	.583	7.116	.705	7.994
11	.291	5.223	.370	5.958	.462	6.777	.570	7.686	.695	8.689
12	.278	5.501	.357	6.315	.449	7.227	.558	8.244	.685	9.374
13	.267	5.769	.345	6.660	.438	7.665	.548	8.792	.677	10.052
14	.257	6.026	.334	6.994	.428	8.092	.539	9.331	.670	10.721
15	.248	6.274	.325	7.319	.418	8.511	.530	9.861	.663	11.384
16	.240	6.514	.316	7.635	.410	8.920	.522	10.383	.656	12.040
17	.233	6.747	.309	7.944	.402	9.322	.515	10.898	.650	12.690
18	.226	6.973	.301	8.245	.394	9.716	.508	11.405	.644	13.334
19	.220	7.192	.295	8.540	.388	10.104	.501	11.907	.639	13.974
20	.214	7.407	.288	8.828	.381	10.485	.495	12.402	.634	14.608
25	.191	8.404	.263	10.191	.355	12.309	.470	14.801	.613	17.713
30	.174	9.305	.244	11.446	.335	14.020	.450	17.091	.596	20.727
35	.160	10.133	.229	12.618	.318	15.643	.434	19.294	.583	23.666
40	.150	10.902	.216	13.723	.305	17.193	.421	21.425	.571	26.543
45	.141	11.625	.206	14.773	.294	18.684	.410	23.500	.561	29.366
50	.134	12.307	.197	15.776	.284	20.122	.400	25.513	.552	32.142

PRACTICE PROBLEM E.1 ■ Learning Curve

The initial external tank for NASA's Space Shuttle took 400 hours of labor to produce. The learning rate is 80%. How long will the twentieth tank take?

Additional Practice Problem Space

PRACTICE PROBLEM E.2 ■ Learning Curve Costs

An operation has a 90% learning curve, and the first unit produced took 28 minutes. The labor cost is $20 per hour.

   a. How long will the second unit take?

   b. How much should the second unit cost?

PRACTICE PROBLEM E.3 ■ Cumulative Values

Using the data from Practice Problem E.1, how long will it take to produce all 20 tanks?

Additional Practice Problem Space

STRATEGIC IMPLICATIONS OF LEARNING CURVES

(See Flexible Version pp. 611–612)

LIMITATIONS OF LEARNING CURVES   (See Flexible Version p. 612)

Discussion Questions

1. What are some of the limitations of learning curves?
2. Identify three applications of the learning curve.
3. What are the approaches to solving learning-curve problems?
4. Refer to Example E2. What are the implications for Great Lakes, Inc., if the engineering department wants to change the engine in the third and subsequent tugboats that the firm purchases?

5. Why isn't the learning-curve concept as applicable in a high-volume assembly line as it is in most other human activities?
6. What are the elements that can disrupt the learning curve?
7. Explain the concept of the "doubling" effect in learning curves.
8. What techniques can a firm use to move to a steeper learning curve?

Problems*

• **E.1** Amand Heinl, an IRS auditor, took 45 minutes to process her first tax return. The IRS uses an 85% learning curve. How long will the:
a) 2nd return take?
b) 4th return take?
c) 8th return take? **Px**

• **E.2** Seton Hall Trucking Co. just hired Sally Kissel to verify daily invoices and accounts payable. She took 9 hours and 23 minutes to complete her task on the first day. Prior employees in this job have tended to follow a 90% learning curve. How long will the task take at the end of:
a) the 2nd day?
b) the 4th day?
c) the 8th day?
d) the 16th day? **Px**

• **E.3** If Professor Tacy Quinn takes 15 minutes to grade the first exam and follows an 80% learning curve, how long will it take her:
a) to grade the 25th exam?
b) to grade the first 10 exams? **Px**

• **E.4** If it took 563 minutes to complete a hospital's first cornea transplant, and the hospital uses a 90% learning rate, what is the cumulative time to complete:
a) the first 3 transplants?
b) the first 6 transplants?
c) the first 8 transplants?
d) the first 16 transplants? **Px**

•• **E.5** Beth Zion Hospital has received initial certification from the state of California to become a center for liver transplants. The hospital, however, must complete its first 18 transplants under great scrutiny and at no cost to the patients. The very first transplant, just completed, required 30 hours. On the basis of research at the hospital, Beth Zion estimates that it will have an 80% learning curve. Estimate the time it will take to complete:

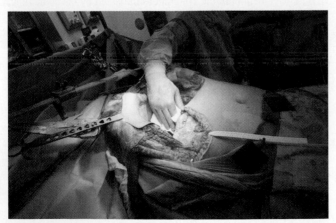

Note: **Px** means the problem may be solved with POM for Windows and/or Excel OM.

a) the 5th liver transplant.
b) all of the first 5 transplants.
c) the 18th transplant.
d) all 18 transplants. **Px**

•• **E.6** Refer to Problem E.5. Beth Zion Hospital has just been informed that only the first 10 transplants must be performed at the hospital's expense. The cost per hour of surgery is estimated to be $5,000. Again, the learning rate is 80% and the first surgery took 30 hours.
a) How long will the 10th surgery take?
b) How much will the 10th surgery cost?
c) How much will all 10 cost the hospital? **Px**

• **E.7** Manceville Air has just produced the first unit of a large industrial compressor that incorporated new technology in the control circuits and a new internal venting system. The first unit took 112 hours of labor to manufacture. The company knows from past experience that this labor content will decrease significantly as more units are produced. In reviewing past production data, it appears that the company has experienced a 90% learning curve when producing similar designs. The company is interested in estimating the total time to complete the next 7 units. Your job as the production cost estimator is to prepare the estimate. **Px**

• **E.8** John Howard, a student at the University of South Alabama, bought 6 bookcases for his dorm room. Each required unpacking of parts and assembly, which included some nailing and bolting. John completed the first bookcase in 5 hours and the second in 4 hours.
a) What is his learning rate?
b) Assuming the same rate continues, how long will the 3rd bookcase take?
c) The 4th, 5th, and 6th cases?
d) All 6 cases? **Px**

•• **E.9** Professor Mary Beth Marrs took 6 hours to prepare the first lecture in a new course. Traditionally, she has experienced a 90% learning factor. How much time should it take her to prepare the 15th lecture? **Px**

• **E.10** The first vending machine that Michael Vest, Inc., assembled took 80 labor-hours. Estimate how long the fourth machine will require for each of the following learning rates:
a) 95%
b) 87%
c) 72% **Px**

• **E.11** Kara-Smith Systems is installing networks for Advantage Insurance. The first installation took 46 labor-hours to complete. Estimate how long the 4th and the 8th installations will take for each of the following learning rates:
a) 92%
b) 84%
c) 77% **Px**

•••   **E.12** Baltimore Assessment Center screens and trains employees for a computer assembly firm in Towson, Maryland. The progress of all trainees is tracked and those not showing the proper progress are moved to less demanding programs. By the tenth repetition trainees must be able to complete the assembly task in 1 hour or less. Torri Olson-Alves has just spent 5 hours on the fourth unit and 4 hours completing her eighth unit, while another trainee, Julie Burgmeier, took 4 hours on the third and 3 hours on the sixth unit. Should you encourage either or both of the trainees to continue? Why? **PX**

••   **E.13** The better students at Baltimore Assessment Center (see Problem E.12) have an 80% learning curve and can do a task in 20 minutes after just six times. You would like to weed out the weak students sooner and decide to evaluate them after the third unit. How long should the third unit take? **PX**

••   **E.14** Wanda Fennell, the purchasing agent for Northeast Airlines, is interested in determining what she can expect to pay for airplane number 4 if the third plane took 20,000 hours to produce. What would Fennell expect to pay for plane number 5? number 6? Use an 85% learning curve and a $40-per-hour labor charge. **PX**

••   **E.15** Using the data from Problem E.14, how long will it take to complete the 12th plane? The 15th plane? How long will it take to complete planes 12 through 15 inclusive? At $40 per hour, what can Fennell, as purchasing agent, expect to pay for all 4 planes? **PX**

••   **E.16** Dynamic RAM Corp. produces semiconductors and has a learning curve of .7. The price per bit is 100 millicents when the volume is $.7 \times 10^{12}$ bits. What is the expected price at 1.4×10^{12} bits? What is the expected price at 89.6×10^{12} bits? **PX**

••   **E.17** Central Power owns 25 small power generating plants. It has contracted with Genco Services to overhaul the power turbines of each of the plants. The number of hours that Genco billed Central to complete the third turbine was 460. Central pays Genco $60 per hour for its services. As the maintenance manager for Central, you are trying to estimate the cost of overhauling the fourth turbine. How much would you expect to pay for the overhaul of number 5 and number 6? All the turbines are similar and an 80% learning curve is appropriate. **PX**

••   **E.18** It takes 28,718 hours to produce the eighth locomotive at a large French manufacturing firm. If the learning factor is 80%, how long does it take to produce the 10th locomotive? **PX**

••   **E.19** Eric Krassow's firm is about to bid on a new radar system. Although the product uses new technology, Krassow believes that a learning rate of 75% is appropriate. The first unit is expected to take 700 hours, and the contract is for 40 units.
a) What is the total amount of hours to build the 40 units?
b) What is the average time to build each of the 40 units?
c) Assume that a worker works 2,080 hours per year. How many workers should be assigned to this contract to complete it in a year? **PX**

•••   **E.20** As the estimator for Arup Mukherjee Enterprises, your job is to prepare an estimate for a potential customer service contract. The contract is for the service of diesel locomotive cylinder heads. The shop has done some of these in the past on a sporadic basis. The time required to service the first cylinder head in each job has been exactly 4 hours, and similar work has been accomplished at an 85% learning curve. The customer wants you to quote the total time in batches of 12 and 20.
a) Prepare the quote.
b) After preparing the quote, you find a labor ticket for this customer for five locomotive cylinder heads. From the notations on the labor ticket, you conclude that the fifth unit took 2.5 hours. What do you conclude about the learning curve and your quote? **PX**

••   **E.21** Sara Bredbenner and Blake DeYoung are teammates at a discount store; their new job is assembling swing sets for customers.

Assembly of a swing set has a learning rate of 90%. They forgot to time their effort on the first swing set, but spent 4 hours on the second set. They have 6 more sets to do. Determine approximately how much time will be (was) required for:
a) the 1st unit
b) the 8th unit
c) all 8 units **PX**

••   **E.22** Kelly-Lambing, Inc., a builder of government-contracted small ships, has a steady work force of 10 very skilled craftspeople. These workers can supply 2,500 labor-hours each per year. Kelly-Lambing is about to undertake a new contract, building a new style of boat. The first boat is expected to take 6,000 hours to complete. The firm thinks that 90% is the expected learning rate.
a) What is the firm's "capacity" to make these boats—that is, how many units can the firm make in 1 year?
b) If the operations manager can increase the learning rate to 85% instead of 90%, how many units can the firm make?

•••   **E.23** The service times for a new data entry clerk have been measured and sequentially recorded as shown below:

Report	Time (minutes)
1	66
2	56
3	53
4	48
5	47
6	45
7	44
8	41

a) What is the learning curve rate, based on this information?
b) Using an 85% learning curve rate and the above times, estimate the length of time the clerk will take to complete the 48th report. **PX**

••   **E.24** If the first unit of a production run takes 1 hour and the firm is on an 80% learning curve, how long will unit 100 take? (*Hint:* Apply the coefficient in Table E.3 twice.) **PX**

••••   **E.25** Using the accompanying log-log graph, answer the following questions:
a) What are the implications for management if it has forecast its cost on the optimum line?
b) What could be causing the fluctuations above the optimum line?
c) If management forecast the 10th unit on the optimum line, what was that forecast in hours?
d) If management built the 10th unit as indicated by the actual line, how many hours did it take?

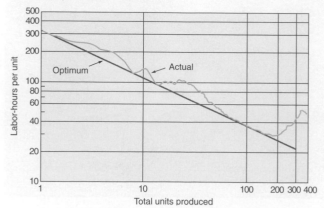

► **Refer to** myomlab○ **for these additional homework problems: E.26–E.32**

Case Study

▶ SMT's Negotiation with IBM

SMT and one other, much larger company were asked by IBM to bid on 80 more units of a particular computer product. The RFQ (request for quote) asked that the overall bid be broken down to show the hourly rate, the parts and materials component in the price, and any charges for subcontracted services. SMT quoted $1.62 million and supplied the cost breakdown as requested. The second company submitted only one total figure, $5 million, with no cost breakdown. The decision was made to negotiate with SMT.

The IBM negotiating team included two purchasing managers and two cost engineers. One cost engineer had developed manufacturing cost estimates for every component, working from engineering drawings and cost-data books that he had built up from previous experience and that contained time factors, both setup and run times, for a large variety of operations. He estimated materials costs by working both from data supplied by the IBM corporate purchasing staff and from purchasing journals. He visited SMT facilities to see the tooling available so that he would know what processes were being used. He assumed that there would be perfect conditions and trained operators, and he developed cost estimates for the 158th unit (previous orders were for 25, 15, and 38 units). He added 5% for scrap-and-flow loss; 2% for the use of temporary tools, jigs, and fixtures; 5% for quality control; and 9% for purchasing burden. Then, using an 85% learning curve, he backed up his costs to get an estimate for the first unit. He next checked the data on hours and materials for the 25, 15, and 38 units already made and found that his estimate for the first unit was within 4% of actual cost. His check, however, had indicated a 90% learning-curve effect on hours per unit.

In the negotiations, SMT was represented by one of the two owners of the business, two engineers, and one cost estimator. The sessions opened with a discussion of learning curves. The IBM cost estimator demonstrated that SMT had in fact been operating on a 90% learning curve. But, he argued, it should be possible to move to an 85% curve, given the longer runs, reduced setup time, and increased continuity of workers on the job that would be possible with an order for 80 units. The owner agreed with this analysis and was willing to reduce his price by 4%.

However, as each operation in the manufacturing process was discussed, it became clear that some IBM cost estimates were too low because certain crating and shipping expenses had been overlooked. These oversights were minor, however, and in the following discussions, the two parties arrived at a common understanding of specifications and reached agreements on the costs of each manufacturing operation.

At this point, SMT representatives expressed great concern about the possibility of inflation in material costs. The IBM negotiators volunteered to include a form of price escalation in the contract, as previously agreed among themselves. IBM representatives suggested that if overall material costs changed by more than 10%, the price could be adjusted accordingly. However, if one party took the initiative to have the price revised, the other could require an analysis of *all* parts and materials invoices in arriving at the new price.

Another concern of the SMT representatives was that a large amount of overtime and subcontracting would be required to meet IBM's specified delivery schedule. IBM negotiators thought that a relaxation in the delivery schedule might be possible if a price concession could be obtained. In response, the SMT team offered a 5% discount, and this was accepted. As a result of these negotiations, the SMT price was reduced almost 20% below its original bid price.

In a subsequent meeting called to negotiate the prices of certain pipes to be used in the system, it became apparent to an IBM cost estimator that SMT representatives had seriously underestimated their costs. He pointed out this apparent error because he could not understand why SMT had quoted such a low figure. He wanted to be sure that SMT was using the correct manufacturing process. In any case, if SMT estimators had made a mistake, it should be noted. It was IBM's policy to seek a fair price both for itself and for its suppliers. IBM procurement managers believed that if a vendor was losing money on a job, there would be a tendency to cut corners. In addition, the IBM negotiator felt that by pointing out the error, he generated some goodwill that would help in future sessions.

Discussion Questions

1. What are the advantages and disadvantages to IBM and SMT from this approach?
2. How does SMT's proposed learning rate compare with that of other industries?
3. What are the limitations of the learning curve in this case?

Source: Based on E. Raymond Corey, *Procurement Management: Strategy, Organization, and Decision Making* (New York: Van Nostrand Reinhold).

Active Model Exercise

ACTIVE MODEL E.1 This exercise allows you to simulate important elements in the learning curve model described in Examples E2 and E3 in the text. It is illustrated at **www.myomlab.com** or **www.pearsonhighered.com/heizer**.

Module E *Rapid Review*

Main Heading	Review Material	
WHAT IS A LEARNING CURVE? (pp. 606–607)	■ **Learning curves**—The premise that people and organizations get better at their tasks as the tasks are repeated; sometimes called experience curves.	

WHAT IS A LEARNING CURVE?
(pp. 606–607)

■ **Learning curves**—The premise that people and organizations get better at their tasks as the tasks are repeated; sometimes called experience curves.

Learning usually follows a negative exponential curve.

It takes less time to complete each additional unit a firm produces; however, the time *savings* in completing each subsequent unit *decreases*.

Learning curves were first applied to industry in a report by T. P. Wright of Curtis-Wright Corp. in 1936. Wright described how direct labor costs of making a particular airplane decreased with learning.

Learning curves have been applied not only to labor but also to a wide variety of other costs, including material and purchased components.

The power of the learning curve is so significant that it plays a major role in many strategic decisions related to employment levels, costs, capacity, and pricing.

The learning curve is based on a *doubling* of production: That is, when production doubles, the decrease in time per unit affects the rate of the learning curve.

$$T \times L^n = \text{Time required for the } n\text{th unit} \qquad \text{(E-1)}$$

where T = unit cost or time of the first unit
L = learning curve rate
n = number of times T is doubled

LEARNING CURVES IN SERVICES AND MANUFACTURING
(pp. 607–608)

Different organizations—indeed, different products—have different learning curves. The rate of learning varies, depending on the quality of management and the potential of the process and product. *Any change in process, product, or personnel disrupts the learning curve.* Therefore, caution should be exercised in assuming that a learning curve is continuing and permanent.

The steeper the slope of the learning curve, the faster the drop in costs.

By tradition, learning curves are defined in terms of the *complements* of their improvement rates (i.e., a 75% learning rate is better than an 85% learning rate).

Stable, standardized products and processes tend to have costs that decline more steeply than others.

Learning curves are useful for a variety of purposes, including:

1. *Internal:* Labor forecasting, scheduling, establishing costs and budgets.
2. *External:* Supply-chain negotiations.
3. *Strategic:* Evaluation of company and industry performance, including costs and pricing.

APPLYING THE LEARNING CURVE
(pp. 608–611)

If learning curve improvement is ignored, potential problems could arise, such as scheduling mismatches, leading to idle labor and productive facilities, refusal to accept new orders because capacity is assumed to be full, or missing an opportunity to negotiate with suppliers for lower purchase prices as a result of large orders.

Three ways to approach the mathematics of learning curves are (1) arithmetic analysis, (2) logarithmic analysis, and (3) learning-curve coefficients.

The arithmetic approach uses the production doubling Equation (E-1).

The logarithmic approach allows us to determine labor for *any* unit, T_N, by the formula:

$$T_N = T_1(N^b) \qquad \text{(E-2)}$$

where T_N = time for the Nth unit
T_1 = hours to produce the first unit
b = (log of the learning rate)/(log 2) = slope of the learning curve

The learning-curve coefficient approach makes use of Table E.3 and uses the formula:

$$T_N = T_1(C) \qquad \text{(E-3)}$$

where T_N = number of labor-hours required to produce the Nth unit
T_1 = number of labor-hours required to produce the first unit
C = learning-curve coefficient found in "Unit Time Coefficient" columns of Table E.3

 Problems: E.1–E.24

Virtual Office Hours for Solved Problems: E.1, E.2

ACTIVE MODEL: E.1

Main Heading	Review Material
	The learning-curve coefficient, C, depends on both the learning rate and the unit number of interest.
	Formula (E-3) can also use the "Total Time Coefficient" columns of Table E.3 to provide the total cumulative number of hours needed to complete the specified number of units.
	If the most recent or most reliable information available pertains to some unit other than the first, these data should be used to find a revised estimate for the first unit, and then the applicable formulas should be applied to that revised number.
STRATEGIC IMPLICATIONS OF LEARNING CURVES (pp. 611–612)	When a firm's strategy is to pursue a learning cost curve steeper than the industry average, it can do this by: 1. Following an aggressive pricing policy 2. Focusing on continuing cost reduction and productivity improvement 3. Building on shared experience 4. Keeping capacity growing ahead of demand Managers must understand competitors before embarking on a learning-curve strategy. For example, taking on a strong competitor in a price war may help only the consumer.
LIMITATIONS OF LEARNING CURVES (p. 612)	Before using learning curves, some cautions are in order: ■ Because learning curves differ from company to company, as well as industry to industry, estimates for each organization should be developed rather than applying someone else's. ■ Learning curves are often based on the time necessary to complete the early units; therefore, those times must be accurate. As current information becomes available, reevaluation is appropriate. ■ Any changes in personnel, design, or procedure can be expected to alter the learning curve, causing the curve to spike up for a short time, even if it is going to drop in the long run. ■ While workers and process may improve, the same learning curves do not always apply to indirect labor and material. ■ The culture of the workplace, as well as resource availability and changes in the process, may alter the learning curve. For instance, as a project nears its end, worker interest and effort may drop, curtailing progress down the curve.

Self Test

■ **Before taking the self-test,** refer to the learning objectives listed at the beginning of the module and the key terms listed at the end of the module.

LO1. A learning curve describes:
- a) the rate at which an organization acquires new data.
- b) the amount of production time per unit as the total number of units produced increases.
- c) the increase in production time per unit as the total number of units produced increases.
- d) the increase in number of units produced per unit time as the total number of units produced increases.

LO2. A surgical procedure with a 90% learning curve required 20 hours for the initial patient. The fourth patient should require approximately how many hours?
- a) 18
- b) 16.2
- c) 28
- d) 30
- e) 54.2

LO3. The first transmission took 50 hours to rebuild at Bob's Auto Repair, and the learning rate is 80%. How long will it take to rebuild the third unit? (Use at least three decimals in the exponent if you use the logarithmic approach.)
- a) under 30 hours
- b) about 32 hours
- c) about 35 hours
- d) about 60 hours
- e) about 45 hours

LO4. Which one of the following courses of action would *not* be taken by a firm wanting to pursue a learning curve steeper than the industry average?
- a) Following an aggressive pricing policy
- b) Focusing on continuing cost reduction
- c) Keeping capacity equal to demand to control costs
- d) Focusing on productivity improvement
- e) Building on shared experience

Answers: LO1. b; **LO2.** b; **LO3.** c; **LO4.** c.

F

Simulation

Module Outline

What is Simulation?

Advantages and Disadvantages of
    Simulation

Monte Carlo Simulation

Simulation of a Queuing Problem

Simulation and Inventory Analysis

Discussion Questions
Problems
Case Study: Alabama Airlines's Call Center
Classroom Activity
Rapid Review

Simulation is an attempt to duplicate the significant features of a real system by building a mathematical model. The model is then used to understand and evaluate the real-world system. The major advantage of mathematical simulation is that the real system need not be touched until an understanding and evaluation of the system has been accomplished.

Although simulation models can be developed manually, simulation by computer is a more realistic approach. The Monte Carlo technique uses random numbers to represent variables such as demand in inventory systems or arrivals and service times in a drive-through restaurant.

BEFORE COMING TO CLASS, READ MODULE F IN YOUR TEXT AND ANSWER THESE QUESTIONS.

1. What are the advantages and disadvantages of simulation? _____

_____

_____

2. What is meant by Monte Carlo simulation and what are its 5 steps? ____

_____

_____

_____

3. Why would one simulate a queuing problem? _____

_____

_____

4. What are the variables in an inventory simulation? _____

_____

_____

5. What are the tools available in Excel to help create a simulation? ____

_____

_____

WHAT IS SIMULATION?   (See Flexible Version pp. 616–617)

1. **Imitate Real-World Situation Mathematically**
2. **Study Its Properties**
3. **Take Action Based on Simulation**

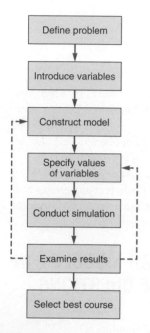

▲ **FIGURE F.1**
The Process of Simulation

ADVANTAGES AND DISADVANTAGES OF SIMULATION

(See Flexible Version p. 617)

MONTE CARLO SIMULATION (See Flexible Version pp. 618–621)

Five Steps

1. Setting up a probability distribution for important variables.

2. Building a cumulative probability distribution for each variable.

3. Establishing an interval of random numbers for each variable.

4. Generating random numbers.

5. Actually simulating a series of trials.

SIMULATION OF A QUEUING PROBLEM (See Flexible Version pp. 621–623)

PRACTICE PROBLEM F.1 ■ Queuing Simulation

The time between arrivals at a drive-through window of Kirby's Fast Food follows the distribution given in the following table. The service time distribution is also given in the table. Use the random numbers provided to simulate the activities of the first five arrivals. Assume that the window opens at 11:00 A.M. and that the first arrival after this is based on the first interarrival time.

Time between Arrivals	Probability	Service Time	Probability
1	0.2	1	0.3
2	0.3	2	0.5
3	0.3	3	0.2
4	0.2		

Random numbers for arrivals: 14, 74, 27, 03; Random numbers for service times: 88, 32, 36, 24

What time does the fourth customer leave the system?

SIMULATION AND INVENTORY ANALYSIS   (See Flexible Version pp. 623–626)

PRACTICE PROBLEM F.2 ■ Inventory Simulation

Average daily sales of a product are 8 units. The actual number of units each day is 7, 8, or 9, with probabilities 0.3, 0.4, and 0.3, respectively. The lead time for delivery of this product averages 4 days, although the time may be 3, 4, or 5 days with probabilities 0.2, 0.6, and 0.2, respectively. The company plans to place an order when the inventory level drops to 32 units (based on average demand and lead time). The beginning inventory is 32. The following random numbers have been generated:

Set 1: 60, 87, 46, 63, 50, 76, 11, 04, 97, 96, 65

Set 2: 52, 78, 13, 06, 99, 98, 80, 09, 67, 89, 45

Use Set 1 to generate lead times, and use Set 2 to simulate daily demand. Simulate two ordering periods, and determine how often the company runs out of stock before the shipment arrives.

Assume an order quantity of 32.

Additional Practice Problem Space

▼ TABLE F.4 Table of Random Numbers

52	06	50	88	53	30	10	47	99	37	66	91	35	32	00	84	57	07
37	63	28	02	74	35	24	03	29	60	74	85	90	73	59	55	17	60
82	57	68	28	05	94	03	11	27	79	90	87	92	41	09	25	36	77
69	02	36	49	71	99	32	10	75	21	95	90	94	38	97	71	72	49
98	94	90	36	06	78	23	67	89	85	29	21	25	73	69	34	85	76
96	52	62	87	49	56	59	23	78	71	72	90	57	01	98	57	31	95
33	69	27	21	11	60	95	89	68	48	17	89	34	09	93	50	44	51
50	33	50	95	13	44	34	62	64	39	55	29	30	64	49	44	30	16
88	32	18	50	62	57	34	56	62	31	15	40	90	34	51	95	26	14
90	30	36	24	69	82	51	74	30	35	36	85	01	55	92	64	09	85
50	48	61	18	85	23	08	54	17	12	80	69	24	84	92	16	49	59
27	88	21	62	69	64	48	31	12	73	02	68	00	16	16	46	13	85
45	14	46	32	13	49	66	62	74	41	86	98	92	98	84	54	33	40
81	02	01	78	82	74	97	37	45	31	94	99	42	49	27	64	89	42
66	83	14	74	27	76	03	33	11	97	59	81	72	00	64	61	13	52
74	05	81	82	93	09	96	33	52	78	13	06	28	30	94	23	37	39
30	34	87	01	74	11	46	82	59	94	25	34	32	23	17	01	58	73
59	55	72	33	62	13	74	68	22	44	42	09	32	46	71	79	45	89
67	09	80	98	99	25	77	50	03	32	36	63	65	75	94	19	95	88
60	77	46	63	71	69	44	22	03	85	14	48	69	13	30	50	33	24
60	08	19	29	36	72	30	27	50	64	85	72	75	29	87	05	75	01
80	45	86	99	02	34	87	08	86	84	49	76	24	08	01	86	29	11
53	84	49	63	26	65	72	84	85	63	26	02	75	26	92	62	40	67
69	84	12	94	51	36	17	02	15	29	16	52	56	43	26	22	08	62
37	77	13	10	02	18	31	19	32	85	31	94	81	43	31	58	33	51

Discussion Questions

1. State the seven steps, beginning with "Defining the Problem," that an operations manager should perform when using simulation to analyze a problem.
2. List the advantages of simulation.
3. List the disadvantages of simulation.
4. Explain the difference between *simulated* average demand and *expected* average demand.
5. What is the role of random numbers in a Monte Carlo simulation?
6. Why might the results of a simulation differ each time you make a run?
7. What is Monte Carlo simulation? What principles underlie its use, and what steps are followed in applying it?
8. List six ways that simulation can be used in business.
9. Why is simulation such a widely used technique?
10. What are the advantages of special-purpose simulation languages?
11. In the simulation of an order policy for drills at Simkin's hardware (Example F3, pp. 623–625 in the *Lecture Guide & Activities Manual*), would the results (of Table F.10) change significantly if a longer period were simulated? Why is the 10-day simulation valid or invalid?
12. Why is a computer necessary in conducting a real-world simulation?
13. Why might a manager be forced to use simulation instead of an analytical model in dealing with a problem of:
    a) inventory order policy?
    b) ships docking in a port to unload?
    c) bank-teller service windows?
    d) the U.S. economy?

Problems*

The problems that follow involve simulations that can be done by hand. However, to obtain accurate and meaningful results, long periods must be simulated. This task is usually handled by a computer. If you are able to program some of the problems in Excel or a computer language with which you are familiar, we suggest you try to do so. If not, the hand simulations will still help you understand the simulation process.

•   **F.1**   The daily demand for tuna sandwiches at a Roosevelt University cafeteria vending machine is either 8, 9, 10, or 11, with probabilities 0.4, 0.3, 0.2, or 0.1, respectively. Assume the following random numbers have been generated: 09, 55, 73, 67, 53, 59, 04, 23, 88, and 84. Using these numbers, generate daily sandwich sales for 10 days. **Px**

•   **F.2**   The number of machine breakdowns per day at Kristen Hodge's factory is either 0, 1, or 2, with probabilities 0.5, 0.3, or 0.2, respectively. The following random numbers have been generated: 13, 14, 02, 18, 31, 19, 32, 85, 31, and 94. Use these numbers to generate the number of breakdowns for 10 consecutive days. What proportion of these days had at least 1 breakdown? **Px**

•   **F.3**   The table below shows the partial results of a Monte Carlo simulation. Assume that the simulation began at 8:00 A.M. and there is only one server.

Customer Number	Arrival Time	Service Time
1	8:01	6
2	8:06	7
3	8:09	8
4	8:15	6
5	8:20	6

a) When does service begin for customer number 3?
b) When will customer number 5 leave?
c) What is the average waiting time in line?
d) What is the average time in the system?

•   **F.4**   Barbara Flynn sells papers at a newspaper stand for $.35. The papers cost her $.25, giving her a $.10 profit on each one she sells. From past experience Barbara knows that:
a) 20% of the time she sells 100 papers.
b) 20% of the time she sells 150 papers.
c) 30% of the time she sells 200 papers.
d) 30% of the time she sells 250 papers.

Assuming that Barbara believes the cost of a lost sale to be $.05 and any unsold papers cost her $.25, simulate her profit outlook over 5 days if she orders 200 papers for each of the 5 days. Use the following random numbers: 52, 06, 50, 88, and 53. **Px**

••   **F.5**   Children's Hospital is studying the number of emergency surgery kits that it uses on weekends. Over the last 40 weekends the number of kits used is as follows:

Number of Kits	Frequency
4	4
5	6
6	10
7	12
8	8

The following random numbers have been generated: 11, 52, 59, 22, 03, 03, 50, 86, 85, 15, 32, 47. Simulate 12 nights of emergency kit usage. What is the average number of kits used during these 12 nights? **Px**

•   **F.6**   Susan Sherer's grocery store has noted the following figures with regard to the number of people who arrive at the store's three checkout stands and the time it takes to check them out:

Arrivals/Minute	Frequency
0	.3
1	.5
2	.2

Service Time (minute)	Frequency
1	.1
2	.3
3	.4
4	.2

*Note: **Px** means the problem may be solved with POM for Windows and/or Excel OM or Excel. However, using software will generate random numbers that differ from those provided in the text.

Simulate the utilization of the three checkout stands over 5 minutes, using the following random numbers: 07, 60, 77, 49, 76, 95, 51, 16, and 14. Record the results at the end of the 5-minute period. Start at time = 0. **P**✗

• **F.7** A warehouse manager at Mary Beth Marrs Corp. needs to simulate the demand placed on a product that does not fit standard models. The concept being measured is "demand during lead time," where both lead time and daily demand are variable. The historical record for this product, along with the cumulative distribution, appear in the table. Random numbers have been generated to simulate the next 5 order cycles; they are 91, 45, 37, 65, and 51. What are the five demand values? What is their average? **P**✗

Demand During Lead Time	Probability	Cumulative Probability
100	.01	.01
120	.15	.16
140	.30	.46
160	.15	.61
180	.04	.65
200	.10	.75
220	.25	1.00

•• **F.8** The time between arrivals at the drive-through window of Barry Harmon's fast-food restaurant follows the distribution given in the table. The service-time distribution is also given. Use the random numbers provided to simulate the activity of the first 4 arrivals. Assume that the window opens at 11:00 A.M. and that the first arrival occurs afterward, based on the first interarrival time generated.

Time between Arrivals	Probability	Service Time	Probability
1	.2	1	.3
2	.3	2	.5
3	.3	3	.2
4	.2		

Random numbers for arrivals: 14, 74, 27, 03
Random numbers for service times: 88, 32, 36, 24
At what time does the fourth customer leave the system? **P**✗

• **F.9** Phantom Controls monitors and repairs control circuit boxes on elevators installed in multistory buildings in downtown Chicago. The company has the contract for 108 buildings. When a box malfunctions, Phantom installs a new one and rebuilds the failed unit in its repair facility in Gary, Indiana. The data for failed boxes over the last 2 years is shown in the following table:

Number of Failed Boxes per Month	Probability
0	.10
1	.14
2	.26
3	.20
4	.18
5	.12

Simulate 2 years (24 months) of operation for Phantom and determine the average number of failed boxes per month from the simulation. Was it common to have fewer than 7 failures over 3 months

of operation? (Start your simulation at the top of the 10th column of Table F.4 on page F-5, *RN* = 37, and go down in the table.) **P**✗

• **F.10** The number of cars arriving at Terry Haugen's Car Wash during the last 200 hours of operation is observed to be the following:

Number of Cars Arriving	Frequency
3 or fewer	0
4	20
5	30
6	50
7	60
8	40
9 or more	0
	200

a) Set up a probability and cumulative-probability distribution for the variable of car arrivals.
b) Establish random-number intervals for the variable.
c) Simulate 15 hours of car arrivals and compute the average number of arrivals per hour. Select the random numbers needed from column 1, Table F.4, beginning with the digits 52. **P**✗

•• **F.11** Leonard Presby's newsstand uses naive forecasting to order tomorrow's papers. The number of newspapers ordered corresponds to the previous day's demands. Today's demand for papers was 22. Presby buys the newspapers for $.20 and sells them for $.50. Whenever there is unsatisfied demand, Presby estimates the lost goodwill cost at $.10. Complete the accompanying table, and answer the questions that follow.

Demand	Probability
21	.25
22	.15
23	.10
24	.20
25	.30

Day	Papers Ordered	Random Number	Demand	Revenue	Cost	Goodwill Cost	Net Profit
1	22	37					
2		19					
3		52					
4		8					
5		22					
6		61					

a) What is the demand on day 3?
b) What is the total net profit at the end of the 6 days?
c) What is the lost goodwill on day 6?
d) What is the net profit on day 2?
e) How many papers has Presby ordered for day 5? **P**✗

•• **F.12** Simkin's Hardware simulated an inventory-ordering policy for Ace electric drills that involved an order quantity of 10 drills, with a reorder point of 5. This first attempt to develop a cost-effective ordering strategy was illustrated in Table F.10 of Example F3 (on p. 624 in the *Flexible Version*). The brief simulation resulted in a total daily inventory cost of $6.65 in Example F4.

Simkin would now like to compare this strategy to one in which he orders 12 drills, with a reorder point of 6. Conduct a

10-day simulation (using random numbers from the right hand column of Table F.4, starting with 07, and using a beginning inventory = 12). Discuss the cost implications. **Px**

•• **F.13** Every home football game for the last 8 years at Eastern State University has been sold out. The revenues from ticket sales are significant, but the sale of food, beverages, and souvenirs has contributed greatly to the overall profitability of the football program. One particular souvenir is the football program for each game. The number of programs sold at each game is described by the probability distribution given in the table:

Numbers of Programs Sold	Probability
2,300	0.15
2,400	0.22
2,500	0.24
2,600	0.21
2,700	0.18

Each program costs $.80 to produce and sells for $2.00. Any programs that are not sold are donated to a recycling center and do not produce any revenue.

a) Simulate the sales of programs at 10 football games. Use the last column in the random-number table (Table F.4 on p. F-5) and begin at the top of the column.

b) If the university decided to print 2,500 programs for each game, what would the average profits be for the 10 games that were simulated?

c) If the university decided to print 2,600 programs for each game, what would the average profits be for the 10 games that were simulated? **Px**

• **F.14** Refer to the data in Solved Problem F.1, on pages 628–629 in the *Flexible Version*, which deals with Higgins Plumbing and Heating. Higgins has now collected 100 weeks of data and finds the following distribution for sales:

Water Heater Sales per Week	Number of Weeks This Number Was Sold	Water Heater Sales per Week	Number of Weeks This Number Was Sold
3	2	8	12
4	9	9	12
5	10	10	10
6	15	11	5
7	25		100

a) Assuming that Higgins maintains a constant supply of 8 heaters, simulate the number of stockouts incurred over a 20-week period (using the seventh column of Table F.4).

b) Conduct this 20-week simulation two more times and compare your answers with those in part (a). Did they change significantly? Why or why not?

c) What is the new expected number of sales per week? **Px**

••• **F.15** Taboo Tattoo and Tanning has two tanning beds. One bed serves the company's regular members exclusively. The second bed serves strictly walk-in customers (those without appointments) on a first-come, first-served basis. Gary Clendenen, the store manager, has noticed on several occasions during the busy 5 hours of the day (2:00 P.M. until 7:00 P.M.) that potential walk-in customers will most often walk away from the store if they see one person

already waiting for the second bed. He wonders if capturing this lost demand would justify adding a third bed. Leasing and maintaining a tanning bed costs Taboo $600 per month. The price paid per customer varies according to the time in the bed, but Gary has calculated the average net income for every 10 minutes of tanning time to be $2. A study of the pattern of arrivals during the busy hours and the time spent tanning has revealed the following:

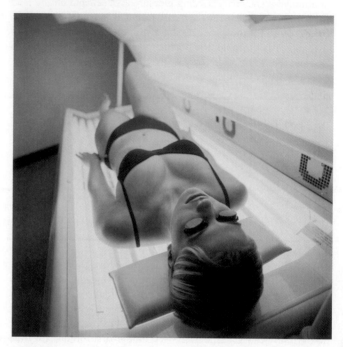

Time between Arrivals (minutes)	Probability	Time in Tanning Bed (minutes)	Probability
5	0.30	10	0.20
10	0.25	15	0.30
15	0.20	20	0.40
20	0.15	25	0.10
25	0.10		

a) Simulate 4 hours of operation (arrivals over 4 hours). Use the 14th column of Table F.4 (p. F-5) for arrival times and the 8th column for tanning times. Assume there is one person who has just entered the bed at 2:00 P.M. for a 20-minute tan. Indicate which customers balk at waiting for the bed to become available. How many customers were lost over the 4 hours?

b) If the store is open an average of 24 days a month, will capturing all lost sales justify adding a new tanning bed?

••• **F.16** Erin Davis owns and operates one of the largest Mercedes-Benz auto dealerships in Nebraska. In the past 36 months, her sales have ranged from a low of 6 new cars to a high of 12 new cars, as reflected in the following table:

Sales of New Cars/Month	Frequency
6	3
7	4
8	6
9	12
10	9
11	1
12	1
	36 months

Davis believes that sales will continue during the next 24 months at about the same historical rates, and that delivery times will also continue to follow the following pace (stated in probability form):

Delivery Time (months)	Probability
1	.44
2	.33
3	.16
4	.07
	1.00

Davis' current policy is to order 14 cars at a time (two full truckloads, with 7 autos on each truck), and to place a new order whenever the stock on hand reaches 12 autos.
a) What are the results of this policy when simulated over the next 2 years?
b) Davis establishes the following relevant costs: (1) carrying cost per Mercedes per month is $600; (2) cost of a lost sale averages $4,350; and (3) cost of placing an order is $570. What is the total inventory cost of this policy?

•• **F.17** Dumoor Appliance Center sells and services several brands of major appliances. Past sales for a particular model of refrigerator have resulted in the following probability distribution for demand:

Demand per week	0	1	2	3	4
Probability	0.20	0.40	0.20	0.15	0.05

The lead-time in weeks is described by the following distribution:

Lead time (weeks)	1	2	3
Probability	0.15	0.35	0.50

Based on cost considerations as well as storage space, the company has decided to order 10 of these each time an order is placed. The holding cost is $1 per week for each unit that is left in inventory at the end of the week. The stockout cost has been set at $40 per stockout. The company has decided to place an order whenever there are only two refrigerators left at the end of the week. Simulate 10 weeks of operation for Dumoor Appliance, assuming that there are currently 5 units in inventory. Determine what the weekly stockout cost and weekly holding cost would be for the problem. Use the random numbers in the first column of Table F.4 for demand and the second column for lead time.

•• **F.18** Repeat the simulation in Problem F.17, assuming that the reorder point is 4 units rather than 2. Compare the costs for these two situations. Again use the same random numbers as in Problem F.17.

••• **F.19** Johnny's Dynamo Dogs has a drive-through line. Customers arriving at this line during the busy hours (11:00 A.M. to 1:00 P.M.) either order items à la carte or on a value-meal basis. Currently 25% of meals are sold as value meals at an average contribution margin of $2.25. The à la carte meals earn $3.00 per meal but take longer to prepare and this slows the line. The following are the interarrival times that were recorded over the last 3 weeks of operation.

Interarrival Times for 500 Observations	
Time between Arrivals (minutes)	Number of Occurrences
1	100
2	150
3	125
4	100
5	25

In addition, the following service times for à la carte and value meals were recorded:

Customer Service Times for 500 Orders of Each Type			
Service Time (minutes)	À la carte	Service Time (minutes)	Value Meals
1	50	1	100
2	125	2	175
3	175	3	125
4	150	4	100

John Cottrell ("Johnny") has observed that because of street traffic the store loses all the potential customers who arrive when 4 cars are in the drive-through line (i.e., the line never exceeds four customers).
a) Simulate a 1-hour time period for the current mix of á la carte and value-meal orders. To start, assume two cars are in the line, each with 2-minute service times. Determine the number of meals served, the income from those meals, and the number of missed sales because customers go elsewhere.
b) Johnny is contemplating a reduction of $0.25 in the prices of value meals. He believes that this will increase the percentage of meals that are value meals from 25% to 40%. This will result in faster service times and fewer lost sales. Using simulation, determine if this change will be financially beneficial. Assume that the benefits will be available for 2 hours a day over a 20-day month.

••• **F.20** General Hospital in Richmond, Virginia, has an emergency room that is divided into six departments: (1) an initial exam station to treat minor problems or to make a diagnosis; (2) an X-ray department; (3) an operating room; (4) a cast-fitting room; (5) an observation room (for recovery and general observation before final diagnosis or release); and (6) an outprocessing department (where clerks check out patients and arrange for payment or insurance forms).

The probabilities that a patient will go from one department to another are presented in the following table:

From	To	Probability
Initial exam at emergency room entrance	X-ray department	.45
	Operating room	.15
	Observation room	.10
	Outprocessing clerk	.30
X-ray department	Operating room	.10
	Cast-fitting room	.25
	Observation room	.35
	Outprocessing clerk	.30
Operating room	Cast-fitting room	.25
	Observation room	.70
	Outprocessing clerk	.05
Cast-fitting room	Observation room	.55
	X-ray department	.05
	Outprocessing clerk	.40
Observation room	Operating room	.15
	X-ray department	.15
	Outprocessing clerk	.70

a) Simulate the trail followed by 10 emergency room patients. Proceed, one patient at a time, from each one's entry at the initial exam station until he or she leaves through outprocessing. You should be aware that a patient can enter the same department more than once.

b) Using your simulation data, determine the chances that a patient enters the X-ray department twice.

•••• **F.21** Management of First Syracuse Bank is concerned over a loss of customers at its main office. One proposed solution calls for adding one or more drive-through teller stations so that customers can get quick service without parking. President David Pentico thinks the bank should risk only the cost of installing one drive-through. He is informed by his staff that the cost (amortized over a 20-year period) of building a drive-through is $12,000 per year. It also costs $16,000 per year in wages and benefits to staff each new teller window.

The director of management analysis, Marilyn Hart, believes that the following two factors encourage the immediate construction of two drive-through stations. According to a recent article in *Banking Research* magazine, customers who wait in long lines for drive-through teller service will cost banks an average of $1 per minute in lost goodwill. Also, although adding a second drive-through will cost an additional $16,000 in staffing, amortized construction costs can be cut to a total of $20,000 per year if two drive-throughs are installed simultaneously, instead of one at a time. To complete her analysis, Hart collected 1 month's worth of arrival and service rates at a competing bank. These data follow:

Interarrival Times for 1,000 Observations

Time between Arrivals (minutes)	Number of Occurrences
1	200
2	250
3	300
4	150
5	100

Customer Service Time for 1,000 Customers

Service Time (minutes)	Number of Occurrences
1	100
2	150
3	350
4	150
5	150
6	100

a) Simulate a 1-hour time period, from 1:00 P.M. to 2:00 P.M., for a single-teller drive-through.

b) Simulate a 1-hour time period, from 1:00 P.M. to 2:00 P.M., for a two-teller system.

c) Conduct a cost analysis of the two options. Assume that the bank is open 7 hours per day and 200 days per year.

•••• **F.22** The Alfredo Fragrance Company produces only one product, a perfume called Hint of Elegance. Hint of Elegance consists of two secret ingredients blended into an exclusive fragrance that is marketed in Zurich. An economic expression referred to as the Cobb-Douglas function describes the production of Hint of Elegance, as follows:

$$X = \sqrt{(\text{Ingredient 1})(\text{Ingredient 2})}$$

where X is the amount of perfume produced.

The company operates at a level where ingredient 1 is set daily at 25 units and ingredient 2 at 36 units. Although the price Alfredo pays for ingredient 1 is fixed at $50 per unit, the cost of ingredient 2 and the selling price for the final perfume are both probabilistic. The sales price for Hint of Elegance follows this distribution:

Sales Price ($)	Probability
300	.2
350	.5
400	.3

The cost for ingredient 2 is as follows:

Ingredient 2 Cost ($)	Probability
35	.1
40	.6
45	.3

a) What is the profit equation for Alfredo Fragrance Company?

b) What is the expected profit to the firm?

c) Simulate the firm's profit for a period of 9 days, using these random numbers from Table F.4's top row: 52, 06, 50, 88, 53, 30, 10, 47, 99 for sales price, and 37, 66, 91, 35, 32, 00, 84, 57, 07 for ingredient 2 cost.

d) What is the expected daily profit as simulated in part (c)?

▶ Refer to myomlab◯ for these additional homework problems: F.23–F.29

Case Study

▶ Alabama Airlines's Call Center

Alabama Airlines opened its doors in December 2001 as a commuter service with its headquarters and hub located in Birmingham. The airline was started and managed by two former pilots, David Douglas and George Devenney. It acquired a fleet of 12 used prop-jet planes and the airport gates vacated by Delta Airlines's 2001 downsizing due to terrorist attacks.

With business growing quickly, Douglas turned his attention to Alabama Air's "800" reservations system. Between midnight and

▼ **TABLE 1**   **Incoming Call Distribution**

Time between Calls (minutes)	Probability
1	.11
2	.21
3	.22
4	.20
5	.16
6	.10

▼ **TABLE 3**   **Incoming Call Distribution**

Time between Calls (minutes)	Probability
1	.22
2	.25
3	.19
4	.15
5	.12
6	.07

6:00 A.M., only one telephone reservations agent had been on duty. The time between incoming calls during this period is distributed as shown in Table 1. Carefully observing and timing the agent, Douglas estimated that the time required to process passenger inquiries is distributed as shown in Table 2.

All customers calling Alabama Air go "on hold" and are served in the order of the calls received unless the reservations agent

▼ **TABLE 2**   **Service-Time Distribution**

Time to Process Customer Inquiries (minutes)	Probability
1	.20
2	.19
3	.18
4	.17
5	.13
6	.10
7	.03

is available for immediate service. Douglas is deciding whether a second agent should be on duty to cope with customer demand. To maintain customer satisfaction, Alabama Air wants a customer to be "on hold" for no more than 3 to 4 minutes; it also wants to maintain a "high" operator utilization.

Furthermore, the airline is planning a new TV advertising campaign. As a result, it expects an increase in "800" line phone inquiries. Based on similar campaigns in the past, the incoming call distribution from midnight to 6:00 A.M. is expected to be as shown in Table 3. (The same service-time distribution will apply.)

Discussion Questions

1. Given the original call distribution, what would you advise Alabama Air to do for the current reservation system? Create a simulation model to investigate the scenario. Describe the model carefully and justify the duration of the simulation, assumptions, and measures of performance.

2. What are your recommendations regarding operator utilization and customer satisfaction if the airline proceeds with the advertising campaign?

Source: Professor Zbigniew H. Przasnyski, Loyola Marymount University. Reprinted by permission.

Classroom Activity

▶ Let's Make a Deal

The old game show *Let's Make a Deal* had a contest with an optimal strategy that we can simulate in class. As described in "Which Door Has the Cadillac?" (*Decision Line*, Dec.–Jan., 1999, pp. 17–19), the game itself is relatively simple. A great prize is located behind one of three curtains, and the other two curtains hide some sort of joke prize. The player chooses the curtain that he or she thinks has the big prize. The master of ceremonies (MC) then opens one of the other two curtains (this one never has the big prize). The MC then gives the player the choice of *staying* with the original curtain or *switching*.

Conduct a simulation at least a hundred times (more if using software) and record each play with the columns: "1st Curtain," "Revealed Curtain," "Final Curtain," "Prize Curtain," and "Prize (Y/N)?" Generate a set of random integers between 1 and 3 inclusive (in Excel this is =*RANDBETWEEN(1,3)*) for the number of students that will be playing the game, and place the prize in the curtain indicated by your random draws.

Module F *Rapid* Review

Main Heading	**Review Material**

WHAT IS SIMULATION?
(pp. 616–617)

Most of the large companies in the world use simulation models.

- **Simulation**—The attempt to duplicate the features, appearance, and characteristics of a real system, usually via a computerized model.

The idea behind simulation is threefold:

1. To imitate a real-world situation mathematically
2. Then to study its properties and operating characteristics
3. Finally, to draw conclusions and make action decisions based on the results of the simulation

In this way, a real-life system need not be touched until the advantages and disadvantages of a major policy decision are first measured on the model.

To use simulation, an OM manager should:

1. Define the problem.
2. Introduce the important variables associated with the problem.
3. Construct a numerical model.
4. Set up possible courses of action for testing by specifying values of variables.
5. Run the experiment.
6. Consider the results (possibly modifying the model or changing data inputs).
7. Decide what course of action to take.

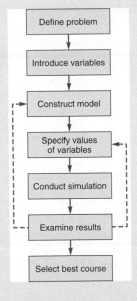

◄ **FIGURE F.1**
The Process of Simulation

ADVANTAGES AND DISADVANTAGES OF SIMULATION
(p. 617)

The main *advantages* of simulation are:

1. Simulation is relatively straightforward and flexible.
2. It can be used to analyze large and complex real-world situations that cannot be solved using conventional operations management models.
3. Real-world complications can be included that most OM models cannot permit. For example, simulation can use any probability distribution the user defines; it does not require standard distributions.
4. "Time compression" is possible. The effects of OM policies over many months or years can be obtained by computer simulation in a short time.
5. Simulation allows "what-if?" types of questions. Managers like to know in advance what options will be most attractive. With a computerized model, a manager can try out several policy decisions within a matter of minutes.
6. Simulations do not interfere with real-world systems. It may be too disruptive, for example, to experiment physically with new policies or ideas.
7. Simulation can study the interactive effects of individual components or variables in order to determine which ones are important.

The main *disadvantages* of simulation are:

1. Good simulation models can be very expensive; they may take many months to develop.
2. It is a trial-and-error approach that may produce different solutions in repeated runs. It does not generate optimal solutions to problems.

Main Heading	Review Material	
	3. Managers must generate all of the conditions and constraints for solutions that they want to examine. The simulation model does not produce answers without adequate, realistic input. 4. Each simulation model is unique. Its solutions and inferences are not usually transferable to other problems.	
MONTE CARLO SIMULATION (pp. 618–621)	■ **Monte Carlo method**—A simulation technique that selects random numbers assigned to a distribution. The Monte Carlo method breaks down into five simple steps: 1. Setting up a probability distribution for important variables 2. Building a cumulative probability distribution for each variable 3. Establishing an interval of random numbers for each variable 4. Generating random numbers 5. Actually simulating a series of trials One common way to establish a *probability distribution* for a given variable is to examine historical outcomes. We can find the probability, or relative frequency, for each possible outcome of a variable by dividing the frequency of observation by the total number of observations. ■ **Cumulative probability distribution**—The accumulation (summary) of probabilities of a distribution. ■ **Random-number intervals**—A set of numbers to represent each possible value or outcome in a computer simulation. ■ **Random number**—A series of digits that have been selected using a totally random process. Random numbers may be generated for simulation problems in two ways: (1) If the problem is large and the process under study involves many simulation trials, computer programs are available to generate the needed random numbers; or (2) if the simulation is being done by hand, the numbers may be selected from a table of random digits.	Problems: F.1–F.5 Virtual Office Hours for Solved Problems: F.1, F.2
SIMULATION OF A QUEUING PROBLEM (pp. 621–623)	An important use of simulation is in the analysis of waiting-line problems. The assumptions required for solving queuing problems are quite restrictive. For most realistic queuing situations, simulation may be the only approach available.	Problems: F.6, F.8, F.10
SIMULATION AND INVENTORY ANALYSIS (pp. 623–626)	The commonly used EOQ models are based on the assumption that both product demand and reorder lead time are known, constant values. In most real-world inventory situations, though, demand and lead time are variables, so accurate analysis becomes extremely difficult to handle by any means other than simulation.	Problem: F.7

Self Test

■ **Before taking the self-test,** refer to the learning objectives listed at the beginning of the module and the key terms listed at the end of the module.

LO1. Which of the following is *not* an advantage of simulation?
  a) Simulation is relatively straightforward and flexible.
  b) Good simulation models are usually inexpensive to develop.
  c) "Time compression" is possible.
  d) Simulation can study the interactive effects of individual variables.
  e) Simulations do not interfere with real-world systems.

LO2. The five steps required to implement the Monte Carlo simulation technique are ____, ____, ____, ____, and ____

LO3. Using simulation for a queuing problem:
  a) would be rare in a realistic situation.
  b) is an unreasonable alternative if the arrival rate is not Poisson distributed but can be plotted on a curve.
  c) would be appropriate if the service time was not exponential or constant.
  d) all of the above.

LO4. Two particularly good candidates to be probabilistic components in the simulation of an inventory problem are:
  a) order quantity and reorder point.
  b) setup cost and holding cost.
  c) daily demand and reorder lead time.
  d) order quantity and reorder lead time.
  e) reorder point and reorder lead time.

LO5. One important reason that spreadsheets are excellent tools for conducting simulations is that they can:
  a) generate random numbers.
  b) easily provide animation of the simulation.
  c) provide more security than manual simulations.
  d) prohibit "time compression" from corrupting the results.
  e) be programmed by anybody.

Answers: LO1. b; **LO2.** Set up a probability distribution for each of the important variables, build a cumulative probability distribution for each of the important variables, establish an interval of random numbers for each variable, generate sets of random numbers, actually simulate a set of trials; **LO3.** c; **LO4.** c; **LO5.** a.

Appendices

APPENDIX I
Normal Curve Areas

APPENDIX II
Solutions to Even-Numbered Problems

APPENDIX I NORMAL CURVE AREAS

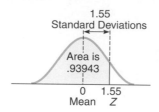

To find the area under the normal curve, you can apply either Table I.1 or Table I.2. In Table I.1, you must know how many standard deviations that point is to the right of the mean. Then, the area under the normal curve can be read directly from the normal table. For example, the total area under the normal curve for a point that is 1.55 standard deviations to the right of the mean is .93943.

TABLE I.1

Z	.00	.01	.02	.03	.04	.05	.06	.07	.08	.09
.0	.50000	.50399	.50798	.51197	.51595	.51994	.52392	.52790	.53188	.53586
.1	.53983	.54380	.54776	.55172	.55567	.55962	.56356	.56749	.57142	.57535
.2	.57926	.58317	.58706	.59095	.59483	.59871	.60257	.60642	.61026	.61409
.3	.61791	.62172	.62552	.62930	.63307	.63683	.64058	.64431	.64803	.65173
.4	.65542	.65910	.66276	.66640	.67003	.67364	.67724	.68082	.68439	.68793
.5	.69146	.69497	.69847	.70194	.70540	.70884	.71226	.71566	.71904	.72240
.6	.72575	.72907	.73237	.73565	.73891	.74215	.74537	.74857	.75175	.75490
.7	.75804	.76115	.76424	.76730	.77035	.77337	.77637	.77935	.78230	.78524
.8	.78814	.79103	.79389	.79673	.79955	.80234	.80511	.80785	.81057	.81327
.9	.81594	.81859	.82121	.82381	.82639	.82894	.83147	.83398	.83646	.83891
1.0	.84134	.84375	.84614	.84849	.85083	.85314	.85543	.85769	.85993	.86214
1.1	.86433	.86650	.86864	.87076	.87286	.87493	.87698	.87900	.88100	.88298
1.2	.88493	.88686	.88877	.89065	.89251	.89435	.89617	.89796	.89973	.90147
1.3	.90320	.90490	.90658	.90824	.90988	.91149	.91309	.91466	.91621	.91774
1.4	.91924	.92073	.92220	.92364	.92507	.92647	.92785	.92922	.93056	.93189
1.5	.93319	.93448	.93574	.93699	.93822	.93943	.94062	.94179	.94295	.94408
1.6	.94520	.94630	.94738	.94845	.94950	.95053	.95154	.95254	.95352	.95449
1.7	.95543	.95637	.95728	.95818	.95907	.95994	.96080	.96164	.96246	.96327
1.8	.96407	.96485	.96562	.96638	.96712	.96784	.96856	.96926	.96995	.97062
1.9	.97128	.97193	.97257	.97320	.97381	.97441	.97500	.97558	.97615	.97670
2.0	.97725	.97784	.97831	.97882	.97932	.97982	.98030	.98077	.98124	.98169
2.1	.98214	.98257	.98300	.98341	.98382	.98422	.98461	.98500	.98537	.98574
2.2	.98610	.98645	.98679	.98713	.98745	.98778	.98809	.98840	.98870	.98899
2.3	.98928	.98956	.98983	.99010	.99036	.99061	.99086	.99111	.99134	.99158
2.4	.99180	.99202	.99224	.99245	.99266	.99286	.99305	.99324	.99343	.99361
2.5	.99379	.99396	.99413	.99430	.99446	.99461	.99477	.99492	.99506	.99520
2.6	.99534	.99547	.99560	.99573	.99585	.99598	.99609	.99621	.99632	.99643
2.7	.99653	.99664	.99674	.99683	.99693	.99702	.99711	.99720	.99728	.99736
2.8	.99744	.99752	.99760	.99767	.99774	.99781	.99788	.99795	.99801	.99807
2.9	.99813	.99819	.99825	.99831	.99836	.99841	.99846	.99851	.99856	.99861
3.0	.99865	.99869	.99874	.99878	.99882	.99886	.99899	.99893	.99896	.99900
3.1	.99903	.99906	.99910	.99913	.99916	.99918	.99921	.99924	.99926	.99929
3.2	.99931	.99934	.99936	.99938	.99940	.99942	.99944	.99946	.99948	.99950
3.3	.99952	.99953	.99955	.99957	.99958	.99960	.99961	.99962	.99964	.99965
3.4	.99966	.99968	.99969	.99970	.99971	.99972	.99973	.99974	.99975	.99976
3.5	.99977	.99978	.99978	.99979	.99980	.99981	.99981	.99982	.99983	.99983
3.6	.99984	.99985	.99985	.99986	.99986	.99987	.99987	.99988	.99988	.99989
3.7	.99989	.99990	.99990	.99990	.99991	.99991	.99992	.99992	.99992	.99992
3.8	.99993	.99993	.99993	.99994	.99994	.99994	.99994	.99995	.99995	.99995
3.9	.99995	.99995	.99996	.99996	.99996	.99996	.99996	.99996	.99997	.99997

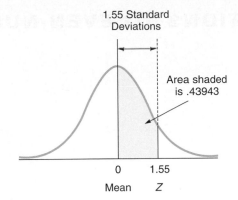

As an alternative to Table I.1, the numbers in Table I.2 represent the proportion of the total area away from the mean, μ, to one side. For example, the area between the mean and a point that is 1.55 standard deviations to its right is .43943.

					TABLE I.2					
Z	**.00**	**.01**	**.02**	**.03**	**.04**	**.05**	**.06**	**.07**	**.08**	**.09**
0.0	.00000	.00399	.00798	.01197	.01595	.01994	.02392	.02790	.03188	.03586
0.1	.03983	.04380	.04776	.05172	.05567	.05962	.06356	.06749	.07142	.07535
0.2	.07926	.08317	.08706	.09095	.09483	.09871	.10257	.10642	.11026	.11409
0.3	.11791	.12172	.12552	.12930	.13307	.13683	.14058	.14431	.14803	.15173
0.4	.15542	.15910	.16276	.16640	.17003	.17364	.17724	.18082	.18439	.18793
0.5	.19146	.19497	.19847	.20194	.20540	.20884	.21226	.21566	.21904	.22240
0.6	.22575	.22907	.23237	.23565	.23891	.24215	.24537	.24857	.25175	.25490
0.7	.25804	.26115	.26424	.26730	.27035	.27337	.27637	.27935	.28230	.28524
0.8	.28814	.29103	.29389	.29673	.29955	.30234	.30511	.30785	.31057	.31327
0.9	.31594	.31859	.32121	.32381	.32639	.32894	.33147	.33398	.33646	.33891
1.0	.34134	.34375	.34614	.34850	.35083	.35314	.35543	.35769	.35993	.36214
1.1	.36433	.36650	.36864	.37076	.37286	.37493	.37698	.37900	.38100	.38298
1.2	.38493	.38686	.38877	.39065	.39251	.39435	.39617	.39796	.39973	.40147
1.3	.40320	.40490	.40658	.40824	.40988	.41149	.41309	.41466	.41621	.41174
1.4	.41924	.42073	.42220	.42364	.42507	.42647	.42786	.42922	.43056	.43189
1.5	.43319	.43448	.43574	.43699	.43822	.43943	.44062	.44179	.44295	.44408
1.6	.44520	.44630	.44738	.44845	.44950	.45053	.45154	.45254	.45352	.45449
1.7	.45543	.45637	.45728	.45818	.45907	.45994	.46080	.46164	.46246	.46327
1.8	.46407	.46485	.46562	.46638	.46712	.46784	.46856	.46926	.46995	.47062
1.9	.47128	.47193	.47257	.47320	.47381	.47441	.47500	.47558	.47615	.47670
2.0	.47725	.47778	.47831	.47882	.47932	.47982	.48030	.48077	.48124	.48169
2.1	.48214	.48257	.48300	.48341	.48382	.48422	.48461	.48500	.48537	.48574
2.2	.48610	.48645	.48679	.48713	.48745	.48778	.48809	.48840	.48870	.48899
2.3	.48928	.48956	.48983	.49010	.49036	.49061	.49086	.49111	.49134	.49158
2.4	.49180	.49202	.49224	.49245	.49266	.49286	.49305	.49324	.49343	.49361
2.5	.49379	.49396	.49413	.49430	.49446	.49461	.49477	.49492	.49506	.49520
2.6	.49534	.49547	.49560	.49573	.49585	.49598	.49609	.49621	.49632	.49643
2.7	.49653	.49664	.49674	.49683	.49693	.49702	.49711	.49720	.49728	.49736
2.8	.49744	.49752	.49760	.49767	.49774	.49781	.49788	.49795	.49801	.49807
2.9	.49813	.49819	.49825	.49831	.49836	.49841	.49846	.49851	.49856	.49861
3.0	.49865	.49869	.49874	.49878	.49882	.49886	.49889	.49893	.49897	.49900
3.1	.49903	.49906	.49910	.49913	.49916	.49918	.49921	.49924	.49926	.49929

APPENDIX II SOLUTIONS TO EVEN-NUMBERED PROBLEMS

Chapter 1

1.2 (a) 2 valves/hr.
(b) 2.25 valves/hr.
(c) 12.5%

1.4 Varies by site and source.

1.6 Productivity of labor: 9.3%
Productivity of resin: 11.1%
Productivity of capital: −10.0%
Productivity of energy: 6.1%

1.8 (a) .0096 rugs/labor-dollar
(b) .00787 rugs/dollar

1.10 Productivity of capital dropped; labor and energy productivity increased.

1.12 (a) Before: 25 boxes/hr.
After: 27.08 boxes/hr.
(b) Increase: 8.3%
(c) 29.167 boxes/hr.

1.14 (a) .293 loaves/dollar
(b) .359 loaves/dollar
(c) Labor change: 0%; Investment change: 22.5%

1.16 (a) 220 hours per laborer; 66,000 labor hours
(b) 200 hours per laborer

Chapter 2

2.2 Cost leadership: Sodexho
Response: a catering firm
Differentiation: a fine-dining restaurant

2.4 The first few:
Arrow; Bidermann International, France
Braun; Procter & Gamble, U.S.
Lotus Autos; Proton, Malaysia
Firestone; Bridgestone, Japan
Godiva; Campbell Soup, U.S.

2.6 Some general thoughts to get you going:
(a) Energy costs change the cost structure of airlines.
(b) Environmental constraints force changes in process technology (paint manufacturing and application) and product design (autos).

2.8 Look at current ranking at **www.weforum.org**.

Chapter 3

3.2 Here are some detailed activities for the first two activities for Mefford's WBS:
1.11 Set initial goals for fundraising.
1.12 Set strategy, including identifying sources and solicitation.
1.13 Raise the funds.
1.21 Identify voters' concerns.
1.22 Analyze competitor's voting record.
1.23 Establish position on issues.

3.4

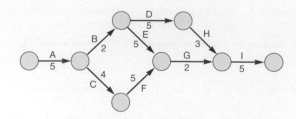

A–C–F–G–I is critical path; 21 days.
This is an AOA network.

3.6 (a)

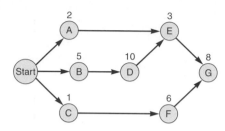

(b) B–D–E–G
(c) 26 days
(d)

Activity	Slack
A	13
B	0
C	11
D	0
E	0
F	11
G	0

3.8

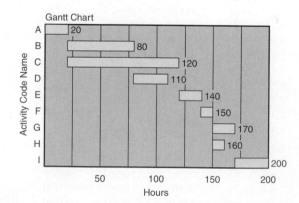

3.10

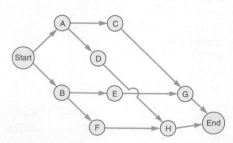

3.12 (a)

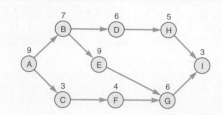

(b) A–B–E–G–I, is critical path.

(c) 34

3.14 (a) A, 5.83, 0.69   G, 2.17, 0.25
        B, 3.67, 0.11   H, 6.00, 1.00
        C, 2.00, 0.11   I, 11.00, 0.11
        D, 7.00, 0.11   J, 16.33, 1.00
        E, 4.00, 0.44   K, 7.33, 1.78
        F, 10.00, 1.78

(b) C.P. is C–D–E–F–H–K. Time = 36.33 days.

(c) Slacks are 7.17, 5.33, 0, 0, 0, 0, 2.83, 0, 2.83, 18, and 0, respectively, for A through K.

(d) $P = .946$

3.16 Crash C to 3 weeks at $200 total for one week. Now both paths are critical. Not worth it to crash further.

3.18 Critical path currently is C–E for 12 days. $1,100 to crash by 4 days. Watch for parallel critical paths as you crash.

3.20 (a) 16 (A–D–G)

(b) $12,300

(c) D; 1 wk. for $75

(d) 7 wk.; $1,600

3.22 (a) A–C–E–H–I–K–M–N; 50 days

(b) 82.1%

(c) 58 days

3.24 (a) .0228

(b) .3085

(c) .8413

(d) .97725

(e) 24 mo.

3.26 (a)

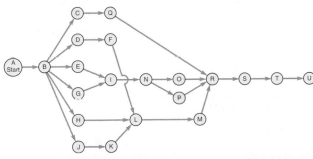

(b) Critical path is A–B–J–K–L–M–R–S–T–U for 18 days.

(c) i. No, transmissions and drivetrains are not on the critical path.

   ii. No, halving engine-building time will reduce the critical path by only 1 day.

   iii. No, it is not on the critical path.

(d) Reallocating workers not involved with critical-path activities to activities along the critical path will reduce the critical path length.

Chapter 4

4.2 (a) None obvious.

(b) 7, 7.67, 9, 10, 11, 11, 11.33, 11, 9

(c) 6.4, 7.8, 11, 9.6, 10.9, 12.2, 10.5, 10.6, 8.4

(d) The 3-yr. moving average.

4.4 (a) 41.6

(b) 42.3

(c) Banking industry's seasonality.

4.6 (b) Naive = 23; 3-mo. moving = 21.33; 6-mo. weighted = 20.6; trend = 20.67

(c) Trend projection.

4.8 (a) 91.3

(b) 89

(c) MAD = 2.7

(d) MSE = 13.35

(e) MAPE = 2.99%

4.10 (a) 4.67, 5.00, 6.33, 7.67, 8.33, 8.00, 9.33, 11.67, 13.7

(b) 4.50, 5.00, 7.25, 7.75, 8.00, 8.25, 10.00, 12.25, 14.0

(c) Forecasts are about the same.

4.12 72

4.14 Method 1: MAD = .125; MSE = .021
Method 2: MAD = .1275; MSE = .018

4.16 $y - 421 + 33.6x$. When $x = 6$, $y = 622.8$.

4.18 49

4.20 $\alpha = .1$, $\beta = .8$, August forecast = $71,303; MSE = 12.7 for $\beta = .8$ vs. MSE = 18.87 for $\beta = .2$ in Problem 4.19.

4.22 Confirm that you match the numbers in Table 4.1.

4.24 (a) Observations do not form a straight line but do cluster about one.

(b) $y = .676 + 1.03x$

(c) 10 drums

(d) $r^2 = .68$; $r = .825$

4.26 270, 390, 189, 351 for fall, winter, spring, and summer, respectively.

4.28 Index is 0.709, winter; 1.037, spring; 1.553, summer; 0.700, fall.

4.30 (a) 337

(b) 380

(c) 423

4.32 (a) $y = 50 + 18x$

(b) $410

4.34 (a) 28

(b) 43

(c) 58

4.36 (a) $452.50

(b) Request is higher than predicted, so seek additional documentation.

(c) Include other variables (such as a destination cost index) to try to increase r and r^2.

4.38 (a) $y = -.158 + .1308x$

(b) 2.719

(c) $r = .966$; $r^2 = .934$

4.40 131.2 → 72.7 patients; 90.6 → 50.6 patients

4.42 (a) They need more data and must be able to address seasonal *and* trend factors.

(b) Try to create your own naive model because seasonality is strong.

(c) Compute and graph your forecast.

4.44 Trend adjustment does not appear to give any significant improvement.

4.46 (a) $y = 1.03 + .0034x$, $r^2 = .479$

(b) For $x = 350$; $y = 2.22$

(c) For $x = 800$; $y = 3.75$

   (Some rounding may occur, depending on software.)

4.48 (a) Sales $(y) = -9.349 + .1121$ (contracts)

(b) $r = .8963$; $S_{xy} = 1.3408$

Chapter 5

5.2 House of quality for a lunch:

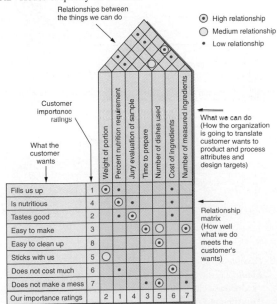

5.4 Individual answer. Build a house of quality similar to the one shown in Problem 5.2, entering the *wants* on the left and entering the *hows* at the top.

5.6 An assembly chart for the eyeglasses is shown below:

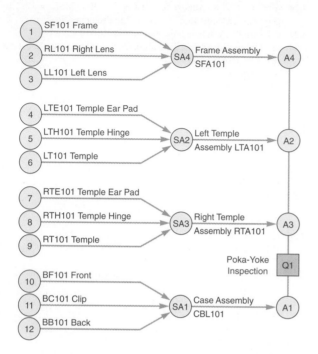

5.8 Assembly chart for a table lamp:

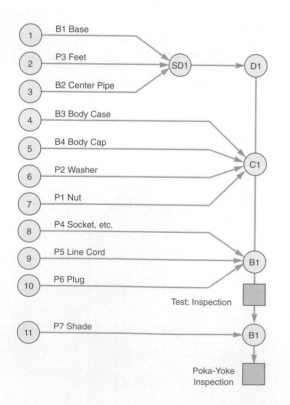

5.10 *Possible strategies:*

Kindle 2 (growth phase):
Increase capacity and improve balance of production system.
Attempt to make production facilities more efficient.

Netbook (introductory phase):
Increase R&D to better define required product characteristics.
Modify and improve production process.
Develop supplier and distribution systems.

Hand calculator (decline phase):
Concentrate on production and distribution cost reduction.

5.12 EMV of Proceed = $49,500,000
EMV of Do Value Analysis = $55,025,000
Therefore, do value analysis.

5.14

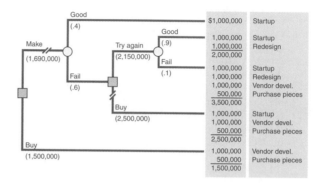

(a) The best decision would be to buy the semiconductors. This decision has an expected payoff of $1,500,000.
(b) Expected monetary value, minimum cost.
(c) The worst that can happen is that Ritz ends up buying the semiconductors and spending $3,500,000.
The best that can happen is that they make the semiconductors and spend only $1,000,000.

5.16 EMV (Design A) = $875,000
EMV (Design B) = $700,000

5.18 Use K1 with EMV = $27,500

Chapter 6

6.2 Individual answer, in the style of Figure 6.6(b).
6.4 Individual answer, in the style of Figure 6.6(f).
6.6 Partial flowchart for planning a party:

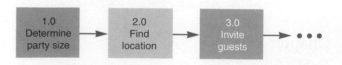

6.8 See figure on next page.
6.10 Individual answer, in the style of Figure 6.7 in the chapter.
6.12 Pareto chart, in the style of Example 1 with parking/drives most frequent, pool second, etc.
6.14 See figure on next page.
Materials: 4, 12, 14; Methods: 3, 7, 15, 16; Manpower: 1, 5, 6, 11; Machines: 2, 8, 9, 10, 13.
6.16 **(a)** A scatter diagram in the style of Figure 6.6(b) that shows a strong positive relationship between shipments and defects
(b) A scatter diagram in the style of Figure 6.6(b) that shows a mild relationship between shipments and turnover
(c) A Pareto chart in the style of Figure 6.6(d) that shows frequency of each type of defect
(d) A fishbone chart in the style of Figure 6.6(c) with the 4 *M*s showing possible causes of increasing defects in shipments

▼ *Figure for Problem 6.8.*

Fish-Bone Chart for Dissatisfied Airline Customer

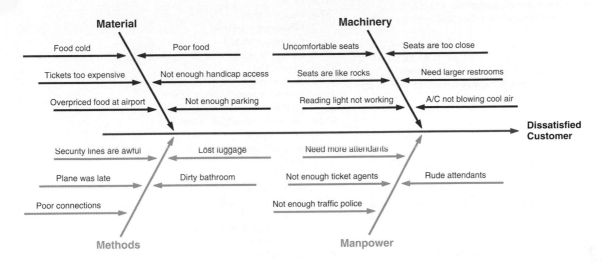

▼ *Figure for Problem 6.14*

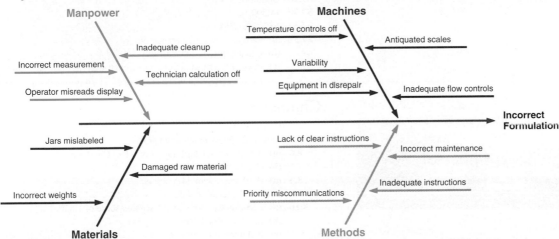

Chapter 6 Supplement

S6.2 (a) $UCL_{\bar{x}} = 52.31$
$LCL_{\bar{x}} = 47.69$
(b) $UCL_{\bar{x}} = 51.54$
$LCL_{\bar{x}} = 48.46$

S6.4 (a) $UCL_{\bar{x}} = 440$ calories
$LCL_{\bar{x}} = 400$ calories
(b) $UCL_{\bar{x}} = 435$ calories
$LCL_{\bar{x}} = 405$ calories

S6.6 $UCL_{\bar{x}} = 3.728$
$LCL_{\bar{x}} = 2.236$
$UCL_R = 2.336$
$LCL_R = 0.0$
The process is in control.

S6.8 (a) $UCL_{\bar{x}} = 16.08$
$LCL_{\bar{x}} = 15.92$
(b) $UCL_{\bar{x}} = 16.12$
$LCL_{\bar{x}} = 15.88$

S6.10 (a) 1.36, 0.61
(b) Using $\sigma_{\bar{x}}$, $UCL_{\bar{x}} = 11.83$, and $LCL_{\bar{x}} = 8.17$.
(c) Using A_2, $UCL_{\bar{x}} = 11.90$, and $LCL_{\bar{x}} = 8.10$.
(c) $UCL_R = 6.98$; $LCL_R = 0$
(d) Yes

S6.12 $UCL_R = 6.058$; $LCL_R = 0.442$
Averages are increasing.

S6.14

UCL	LCL
.062	0
.099	0
.132	0
.161	0
.190	.01

S6.16 $UCL_p = .0313$; $LCL_p = 0$
S6.18 (a) $UCL_p = 0.077$; $LCL_p = 0.003$
S6.20 (a) $UCL_p = .0581$
$LCL_p = 0$
(b) in control
(c) $UCL_p = .1154$
$LCL_p = 0$
S6.22 (a) c-chart
(b) $UCL_c = 13.35$
$LCL_c = 0$
(c) in control
(d) not in control

S6.24 (a) $UCL_c = 26.063$
$LCL_c = 3.137$
(b) No point out of control.
S6.26 $C_p = 1.0$. The process is barely capable.
S6.28 $C_{pk} = 1.125$. Process *is* centered and will produce within tolerance.
S6.30 $C_{pk} = .1667$
S6.32 AOQ = 2.2%
S6.34 (a) $UCL_{\bar{x}} = 61.131$, $LCL_{\bar{x}} = 38.421$, $UCL_R = 41.62$, $LCL_R = 0$
(b) Yes, the process is in control for both $\bar{x}$- and R-charts.
(c) They support West's claim. But variance from the mean needs to be reduced and controlled.

Chapter 7

7.2

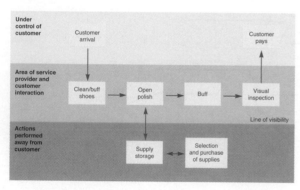

7.4

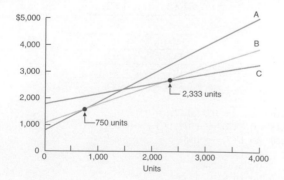

7.6 GPE is best below 100,000.
FMS is best between 100,000 and 300,000.
DM is best over 300,000.
7.8 Optimal process will change at 100,000 and 300,000.
7.10 (a)

(b) Plan c
(c) Plan b
7.12 Rent HP software since projected volume of 80 is above the crossover point of 75.
7.14 (a) Intermittent
(b) $200,000

Chapter 7 Supplement

S7.2 69.2%
S7.4 88.9%
S7.6 Design = 88,920
Fabrication = 160,680
Finishing = 65,520
S7.8 5.17 (or 6) bays
S7.10 15 min./unit
S7.12 (a) Process cycle time = 40 min.
(b) System process time = 12 min.
(c) Weekly capacity = 240 units
S7.14 (a) Work station C at 20 min./unit
(b) 3 units/hr.
S7.16 (a) 2,000 units
(b) $1,500
S7.18 (a) $150,000
(b) $160,000
S7.20 (a) $BEP_A = 1,667$;
$BEP_B = 2,353$
(b, c) Oven A slightly more profitable
(d) 13,333 pizzas
S7.22 (a) $18,750
(b) 375,000
S7.24 Yes, purchase new equipment and raise price. Profit = $2,500
S7.26 $BEP_\$ = \$7,584.83$ per mo.
Daily meals = 9
S7.28 Option B; $74,000
S7.30 $4,590
S7.32 NPV = $1,764
S7.34 (a) Purchase two large ovens.
(b) Equal quality, equal capacity.
(c) Payments are made at end of each time period. And future interest rates are known.

Chapter 8

8.2 China, $1.44
8.4 India is $.05 less than elsewhere.
8.6 (a) Atlanta = 53; Charlotte = 60; select Charlotte.
(b) Charlotte now = 66.
8.8 (a) Hyde Park, with 54.5 points.
(b) Present location = 51 points.
8.10 (a) Location C, with a total *weighted* score of 1,530.
(b) Location B = 1,360
(c) B can never be in first place.
8.12 (a) Great Britain, at 36;
(b) Great Britain is now 31; Holland is 30.
8.14 (a) Italy is highest.
(b) Spain always lowest.
8.16 (a) Site 1 up to 125, site 2 from 125 to 233, site 3 above 233
(b) Site 2
8.18 (a) Above 10,000 cars, site C is lowest cost
(b) Site A optimal from 0–10,000 cars.
(c) Site B is never optimal.
8.20 (a) (5.15, 7.31)
(b) (5.13, 7.67)
8.22 (a) (6.23, 6.08);   (b) safety, etc.
8.24 (a) Site C is best, with a score of 374
(b) For all positive values of w_7 such that $w_7 \leq 14$

Chapter 9

9.2 (a) $23,400
(b) $20,600
(c) $22,000
(d) Plan B
9.4 Benders to area 1; Materials to 2; Welders to 3; Drills to 4; Grinder to 5; and Lathes to 6; Trips × Distance = 13,000 ft.
9.6 Layout #1, distance = 600 with areas fixed
Layout #2, distance = 602 with areas fixed

9.8 Layout #4, distance = 609
Layout #5, distance = 478

9.10 (a) 1.68 minutes
(b) 4.76 ≈ 5
(c) cleaning

9.12 (b) Cycle time = 9.6 min.;
(e) Idle time/cycle = 15 min.
(f) 15 hours/day idle.
(g) 8 workstations with 76.6% efficiency is possible.

9.14 (a)

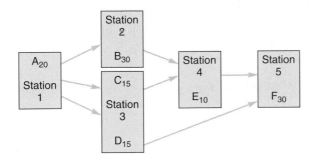

(b) cycle time = 30 sec./unit
(c) 4 stations = *theoretical* minimum, but 5 are needed
(d) Station 1–Task A; 2–B; 3–C, D; 4–E; 5–F
(e) Total idle = 30 sec.
(f) E = 80% with 5 stations; E = 66.6% with 6 stations

9.16 (a, b) Cycle time = 6.67 min./unit. Multiple solutions with 5 stations. Here is a sample: A, F, G to station 1; B, C to station 2; D, E to station 3; H to station 4; and I, J to station 5. (c) Actual efficiency with 5 stations = 83% (d) Idle time = 5 min./cycle.

9.18 (a) Minimum no. of workstations = 2.6 (or 3).
(b) Efficiency = 86.7%.
(c) Cycle time = 6.67 min./unit with 400 min./day; minimum no. of workstations = 1.95 (or 2).

9.20 Minimum (theoretical) = 4 stations. Efficiency = 93.3% with 5 stations and 6 min. cycle time. Several assignments with 5 are possible.

9.22 (a) Theoretical min. no. workstations = 5
(b) There are several possibilities. For example; Station 1–Task A; 2–C; 3–B and F; 4–D and G; 5–E, H, and I; 6–J. Or 1–A; 2–C; 3–B and F; 4–D and G; 5–E, H and I; 6–J.
(c) n = 6
(d) Efficiency = .7611

Chapter 10

10.2

Time	Operator	Time	Machine	Time
	Prepare Mill			
1	Load Mill	1	Idle	1
2		2		2
3	Idle	3	Mill Operating (Cutting Material)	3
4		4		4
5	Unload Mill	5	Idle	5
6		6		6

10.4 The first 10 steps of 10.4(a) are shown below. The remaining 10 steps are similar.

OPERATIONS CHART			SUMMARY						
PROCESS: CHANGE ERASER			SYMBOL		PRESENT		DIFF.		
ANALYST:					LH	RH	LH	RH	LH	RH
DATE:			○ OPERATIONS		1	8				
SHEET: 1 of 2			⇨ TRANSPORTS		3	8				
METHOD: (PRESENT) PROPOSED			□ INSPECTIONS		1					
REMARKS:			D DELAYS		15	4				
			▽ STORAGE							
			TOTALS		20	20				

LEFT HAND	DIST.	SYMBOL	SYMBOL	DIST.	RIGHT HAND
1 Reach for pencil		⇨	D		Idle
2 Grasp pencil		∩	∩		Idle
3 Move to work area		⇨	⇨		Move to pencil top
4 Hold pencil		D	○		Grasp pencil top
5 Hold pencil		D	○		Remove pencil top
6 Hold pencil		D	⇨		Set top aside
7 Hold pencil		D	⇨		Reach for old eraser
8 Hold pencil		D	○		Grasp old eraser
9 Hold pencil		D	○		Remove old eraser
10 Hold pencil		D	⇨		Set aside old eraser

10.6 Individual solution.

10.8

Process Chart		Summary	
Charted by *H. Molano*		○ Operation	*2*
		⇨ Transport	*3*
Date _____ Sheet *1* of *1*		□ Inspect	
		D Delay	*2*
Problem *Pit crew jack man*		▽ Store	
		Vert. Dist.	
		Hor. Dist.	
		Time (seconds)	*12.5*

Distance (feet)	Time (seconds)	Chart Symbols	Process Description
15	2.0	○⇨□D▽	*Move to right side of car*
	2.0	○⇨□D▽	*Raise car*
	1.0	○⇨□D▽	*Wait for tire exchange to finish*
10	1.8	○⇨□D▽	*Move to left side of car*
	2.0	○⇨□D▽	*Raise car*
	1.2	○⇨□D▽	*Wait for tire exchange to finish*
5	2.5	○⇨□D▽	*Move back over wall from left side*

10.10 The first portion of the activity chart is shown below.

ACTIVITY CHART

	OPERATOR #1		OPERATOR #2			
	TIME	%	TIME	%	OPERATIONS: Wash and Dry Dishes	
					EQUIPMENT: Sink, Drip Rack, Towels, Soap	
WORK	11.75	84	11.75	84	OPERATOR:	
IDLE	2.25	16	2.25	16	STUDY NO.: 1 ANALYST: HSM	

SUBJECT				DATE	
PRESENT (PROPOSED) DEPT. HOUSECLEANING				SHEET 1 CHART OF 1 BY Hank	
	TIME	Operator #1	TIME	Operator #2	TIME
		Fill sink w/dishes		Idle	
		Fill sink w/soap/ water		Idle	
		Wash dishes (2 min.)		Idle	
				Rinse (1 min.)	
		Fill sink w/dishes (1 min.)		Dry dishes (3 min.)	

10.12 The first portion of the process chart is shown below.

Present Method ☐	PROCESS CHART		
Proposed Method ☒			

SUBJECT CHARTED ___Printing and Copying Document___   DATE _____
CHART BY ___HSM___
CHART NO. ___1___
DEPARTMENT ___Clerical___   SHEET NO. _1_ OF _1_

DIST. IN FEET	TIME IN MINS.	CHART SYMBOLS	PROCESS DESCRIPTION
	0.25	●⇨☐D▽	Click on Print Command
50	0.25	O⇨☐D▽	Move to Printer
	0.50	O⇨☐▶▽	Wait for Printer
	0.10	O⇨▣D▽	Read Error Message
100	0.50	O⇨☐D▽	Move to Supply Room
	0.25	●⇨☐D▽	Locate Correct Paper

10.14 NT = 7.65 sec.; slower than normal
10.16 (a) 6.525 sec.
  (b) 6.2 sec.
  (c) 6.739 sec.
10.18 (a) 12.6 min.
  (b) 15 min.
10.20 (a) 12.0 sec.
  (b) 14.12 sec.
10.22 10.12 min.
10.24 (a) 3.24 min.
  (b) 4.208 min.
10.26 $n = 14.13$, or 15 observations
10.28 (a) 45.36, 13.75, 3.6, 15.09
  (b) 91.53 min.
  (c) 96 samples
10.30 (a) 47.6 min.
  (b) 75 samples
10.32 $n = 348$
10.34 73.8%
10.36 6.55 sec.
10.38 (a) 240 min.
  (b) 150 hr.
  (c) Clean 8 rooms; refresh 16 rooms; 38 housekeepers
  (d) 50 employees

Chapter 11

11.2 Donna Inc, 8.2; Kay Corp., 9.8
11.4 Individual responses. Issues might include: academics, location, financial support, size, facilities, etc.
11.6 (a) $3.13
  (b) $7.69
11.8 (a) Option a is most economical.
  (b) The customer requirements may demand a faster schedule.
11.10 (a) Go with faster subcontractor.
  (b) Internal production or testing may require a faster schedule.
11.12 (a) Weeks of supply = 3.85
  (b) % of assets in inventory = 11.63%
  (c) Turnover = 13.5
  (d) No, but note they are in different industries
11.14 (a) Last year = 10.4
  (b) This year = 9.67
  (c) Yes

Chapter 11 Supplement

S11.2 (a) Canada, 1.7
  (b) No change
S11.4 Mexico, 3.3
S11.6 Moscow Bell, 7.1

Chapter 12

12.2 (a) A items are G2 and F3; B items are A2, C7, and D1; all others are C.
12.4 108 items
12.6 (a) 600 units
  (b) 424.26 units
  (c) 848.53 units
12.8 (a) 80 units
  (b) 73 units
12.10 (a) 2,100 units
  (b) 4,200 units
  (c) 1,050 units
12.12 (a) 189.74 units
  (b) 94.87
  (c) 31.62
  (d) 7.91
  (e) $1,897.30
  (f) $601,897
12.14 (a) Order quantity variations have limited impact on total cost.
  (b) EOQ = 50
12.16 (a) 671 units
  (b) 18.63
  (c) 559 = max. inventory
  (d) 16.7%
  (e) $1,117.90
12.18 (a) 1,217 units
  (b) 1,095 = max. inventory
  (c) 8.22 production runs
  (e) $657.30
12.20 (a) EOQ = 200, total cost = $1,446,380
  (b) EOQ = 200, total cost = $1,445,880
12.22 (a) 16,971 units
  (b) $530.33
  (c) $530.33
  (d) $56,250
  (e) $57,310.66
12.24 (a) EOQ = 410
  (b) Vendor Allen has slightly lower cost.
  (c) Optimal order quantity = 1,000 @ total cost of $128,920
12.26 (a) EOQ (1) = 336; EOQ (2) = 335
  (b) Order 1,200 from Vendor 2.
  (c) At 1,200 lb., total cost = $161,275.
  (d) Storage space and perishability.
12.28 (a) Z = 1.88
  (b) Safety stock $= Z\sigma = 1.88(5) = 9.4$ drives
  (c) ROP = 59.4 drives
12.30 100 kilos of safety stock
12.32 (a) 2,291 towels
  (b) 291 towels
12.34 (a) ROP = 1,718 cigars
  (b) 1,868 cigars
  (c) A higher service level means a lower probability of stocking out.
12.36 103 pounds
12.38 (a) $3
  (b) $.90
  (c) 63,675 programs
  (d) 23.1%
12.40 (a) Q = 400 lb.
  (b) $600
  (c) $600
  (d) ROP = 369.99
  (e) 69.99
  (f) $209.97
  (g) Safety stock = 61.61

Chapter 13

13.2 (a) $109,120 = total cost
  (b) $106,640 = total cost
  (c) No, plan 2 is better at $105,152.

13.4 Cost = \$214,000 for plan B

13.6 (a) Plan D, \$122,000;
(b) plan E is \$129,000

13.8 Extra total cost = \$2,960.

13.10 (a) Plan C, \$92,000; (b) plan D, \$81,800, assuming initial inventory = 0

13.12 (a) Cost is \$314,000.
(b) Cost is \$329,000 (but an alternative approach yields \$259,500).
(c) Cost is \$222,000.
(d) Plan C.
(e) Plan C, with lowest cost and steady employment.

13.14 \$1,186,810

13.16 \$100,750

13.18 \$90,850

13.20 (a) Cost using O.T. and Forrester = \$195,625.
(b) A case could be made for either position.

13.22 Current model = \$9,200 in sales; proposed model yields \$9,350, which is only slightly better.

Chapter 14

14.2 The time-phased plan for the gift bags is:

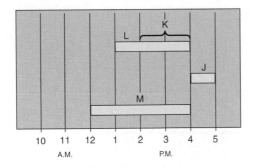

| | 10 | 11 | 12 | 1 | 2 | 3 | 4 | 5 |
| | A.M. | | | | | P.M. | | |

Someone should start on item M by noon.

14.4 Gross material requirements plan:

					Week					Lead Time
Item		1	2	3	4	5	6	7	8	(wk.)
S	Gross req.							100		
	Order release					100				2
T	Gross req.						100			
	Order release				100					1
U	Gross req.						200			
	Order release			200						2
V	Gross req.					100				
	Order release		100							2
W	Gross req.					200				
	Order release	200								3
X	Gross req.					100				
	Order release			100						1
Y	Gross req.				400					
	Order release	400								2
Z	Gross req.			600						
	Order release	600								1

14.6 Gross material requirements plan, modified to include the 20 units of U required for maintenance purposes:

					Week					Lead Time
Item		1	2	3	4	5	6	7	8	(wk.)
S	Gross req.							100		
	Order release					100				2
T	Gross req.							100		
	Order release					100				1
U	Gross req.							200	20	
	Order release				200	20				2
V	Gross req.							100		
	Order release		100							2
W	Gross req.							200		
	Order release	200								3
X	Gross req.							100		
	Order release				100					1
Y	Gross req.						400	40		
	Order release	400	40							2
Z	Gross req.						600	60		
	Order release		600	60						1

14.8 (a)

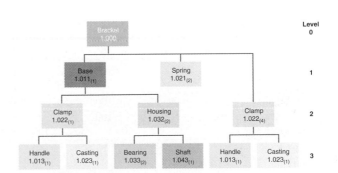

(b) For 50 brackets, the gross requirements are for 50 bases, 100 springs, 250 clamps, 250 handles, 250 castings, 100 housings, 200 bearings, and 100 shafts.

(c) For 50 brackets, net requirements are 25 bases, 100 springs, 125 clamps, 125 handles, 125 castings, 50 housings, 100 bearings, and 50 shafts.

14.10 (a) Gross material requirements plan for the first three items.

							Week							
Item		1	2	3	4	5	6	7	8	9	10	11	12
X1	Gross req.								50		20		100
	Order release							50		20		100	
B1	Gross req.								50		20		100
	Order release						50		20		100		
B2	Gross req.								100		40		200
	Order release							100		40		200	

(b) The net materials requirement plan for the first two items:

Level: 0 Item: X1	Parent: Lead Time:							Quantity: Lot Size: L4L			
Week No.	1	2	3	4	5	6	7	8	9	10	11	12
Gross Requirement								50		20		100
Scheduled Receipt												
On-hand Inventory								50		0		0
Net Requirement								0		20		100
Planned Order Receipt										20		100
Planned Order Release									20		100	

Level: 1 Item: B1	Parent: X1 Lead Time: 2							Quantity: 1X Lot Size: L4L			
Week No.	1	2	3	4	5	6	7	8	9	10	11	12
Gross Requirement									20		100	
Scheduled Receipt												
On-hand Inventory									20		0	
Net Requirement									0		100	
Planned Order Receipt											100	
Planned Order Release									100			

14.12 **(a)** Net material requirements schedule (only items A and H are shown):

	Week											
	1	2	3	4	5	6	7	8	9	10	11	12
A Gross Required								100		50		150
On Hand								0		0		0
Net Required								100		50		150
Order Receipt								100		50		150
Order Release							100		50		150	
H Gross Required								100		50		
On Hand								0		0		
Net Required								100		50		
Order Receipt								100		50		
Order Release							100		50			

(b) Net material requirements schedule (only items B and C are shown; schedule for items A and H remains the same as in part a.)

		Week											
	1	2	3	4	5	6	7	8	9	10	11	12	13
B Gross Requirements							200		100		300		
Scheduled Receipts													
Projected On Hand	100						100		0		0		
Net Requirements							100		100		300		
Planned Order Receipts							100		100		300		
Planned Order Releases					100		100		300				
C Gross Requirements							200	200	100	100	300		
Scheduled Receipts													
Projected On Hand	50						50		0		0		
Net Requirements							150	200	100	100	300		
Planned Order Receipts							150	200	100	100	300		
Planned Order Releases						150	200	100	100	300			

14.14 **(a)**

Level	Description			Qty
0	A			1
1		B		1
2			C	1
2			D	1
3				E	1
1		F		1
2			G	1
2			H	1
3				E	1
3				C	1

Note: with low-level coding "C" would be a level-3 code

(b) Solution for Items A, B, F (on next page):

14.14 (b)

Lot Size	Lead Time	On Hand	Safety Stock	Allo-cated	Low-Level Code	Item ID		1	2	3	4	5	6	7	8
Lot for Lot	1	0	—	—	0	A	Gross Requirement								10
							Scheduled Receipt								
							Projected On Hand								0
							Net Requirement								10
							Planned Receipt								10
							Planned Release							10	
Lot for Lot	1	2	—	—	1	B	Gross Requirement								10
							Scheduled Receipt								
							Projected On Hand	2	2	2	2	2	2	2	0
							Net Requirement								8
							Planned Receipt								8
							Planned Release							8	
Lot for Lot	1	5	—	—	1	F	Gross Requirement								10
							Scheduled Receipt								
							Projected On Hand	5	5	5	5	5	5	5	0
							Net Requirement								5
							Planned Receipt								5
							Planned Release							5	

14.16 (a) Only item G changes.

   (b) Component F and 4 units of A will be delayed one week.

   (c) Options include: delaying 4 units of A for 1 week; asking supplier of G to expedite production.

14.18 EOQ = 57; Total cost $ = $1,630

14.20 $650

14.22 $455

14.24 Selection for first 5 weeks:

Week	Units	Capacity Required (time)	Capacity Available (time)	Over/ (Under)	Production Scheduler's Action
1	60	3,900	2,250	1650	Lot split. Move 300 minutes (4.3 units) to week 2 and 1,350 minutes to week 3.
2	30	1,950	2,250	(300)	
3	10	650	2,250	(1,600)	
4	40	2,600	2,250	350	Lot split. Move 250 minutes to week 3. Operations split. Move 100 minutes to another machine, overtime, or subcontract.
5	70	4,550	2,250	2,300	Lot split. Move 1,600 minutes to week 6. Overlap operations to get product out door. Operations split. Move 700 minutes to another machine, overtime, or subcontract.

14.26 Here are the order releases for the table and the top:

Lot Size	Lead Time (# of periods)	On Hand	Safety Stock	Allo-catod	Low-Level Code	Item ID		1	2	3	4	5	6	7	8
Lot for Lot	1	—	—	—	0	Table	Gross Requirements					640	640	128	128
							Scheduled Receipts								
							Projected on Hand								
							Net Requirements					640	640	128	128
							Planned Order Receipts					640	640	128	128
							Planned Order Releases				640	640	128	128	
Lot for Lot	1	—	—	—	1	Top	Gross Requirements					640	640	128	128
							Scheduled Receipts								
							Projected on Hand								
							Net Requirements					640	640	128	128
							Planned Order Receipts					640	640	128	128
							Planned Order Releases				640	640	128	128	

Chapter 15

15.2

Job	Day 1	Day 2	Day 3	Day 4	Day 5	Day 6	Day 7	Day 8	Day 9
D									
E									
F									
G									

Now

15.4   (a) 1–D, 2–A, 3–C, 4–B
     (b) 40
15.6   Chris–Finance, Steve–Marketing, Juana–H.R., Rebecca–Operations, $210
15.8   Ajay–Jackie, Jack–Barbara, Gray–Stella, Raul–Dona, 230.
15.10 (a) A, B, C, D, E
     (b) B, A, D, E, C
     (c) E, D, A, B, C
     (d) C, B, A, D, E
     (e) SPT is best.
15.12 (a) A, B, C, D
     (b) B, C, A, D
     (c) D, A, C, B
     (d) C, B, D, A
     (e) D, C, A, B
     SPT is best on all measures.
15.14 (a) A, B, C, D, E
     (b) C, A, B, E, D
     (c) C, D, E, A, B
     (d) B, A, E, D, C
     EDD, then FCFS are best on lateness; SPT on other two measures.
15.16 1, 3, 4, 2, 5
15.18 E, D, C, A, B, F
15.20 7 employees needed; 6 have two consecutive days off. The 7th works only 3 days/week.

Chapter 16

16.2   3.75, or 4 kanbans
16.4   Size of kanban = 66; number of kanbans = 5.9, or 6
16.6   (a) EOQ = 10 lamps
     (b) 200 orders/yr.
     (c) $200
16.8   7.26 min.
16.10 (a) Setup cost = $5.74
     (b) Setup time = 8.61 min.

Chapter 17

17.2   From Figure 17.2, about 13% overall reliability.
17.4   Expected daily breakdowns = 2.0
     Expected cost = $100 daily
17.6   (a) 5.0%
     (b) .00001026 failures/unit-hr.
     (c) .08985
     (d) 98.83
17.8 $R_s = .9941$
17.10 $R_p = .99925$
17.12 (a) $R_p = .984$

(b) Increase by 11.1%.
17.14 $R = .7918$
17.16 (a) .972
     (b) .980
17.18 System B is slightly higher, at .9397.

Quantitative Module A

A.2   (a)

Size of First Station	Good Market ($)	Fair Market ($)	Poor Market ($)	EV Under Equally Likely
Small	50,000	20,000	−10,000	20,000
Medium	80,000	30,000	−20,000	30,000
Large	100,000	30,000	−40,000	30,000
Very large	300,000	25,000	−160,000	55,000

(b) Maximax: Build a very large station.
(c) Maximin: Build a small station.
(d) Equally likely: Build a very large station.
(e)

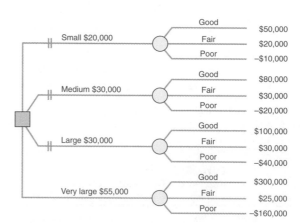

A.4   (a) Alternatives: N, M, L, D. States of nature: Fixed, Slight Increase, Major Increase
     (b) Use maximin criterion. No floor space (N).
A.6   Buying equipment at $733,333
A.8   (a) E(cost full-time) = $520
     (b) E(cost part-timers) = $475
A.10 Alternative B; 74
A.12 8 cases; EMV = $352.50
A.14 (a)

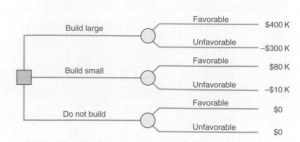

(b) Small plant with EMV = $26,000
(c) EVPI = $134,000

A.16 (a) Max EMV = $11,700
(b) EVPI = $13,200 − $11,700 = $1,500

A.18

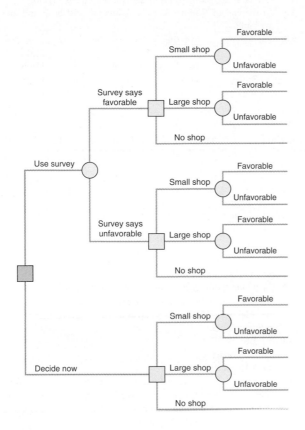

A.20 No information and build large; $4,500.
A.22 (b) EMV(Y) = 4.2, which is best

Quantitative Module B

B.2 Profit = $100 at $X = 0, Y = 10$
B.4 (b) Yes; $P = \$3{,}000$ at (75, 75) and (50, 150)
B.6 (a) Min $X_1 + 2X_2$
Subject to: $X_1 + X_2 \geq 40$
$2X_1 + 4X_2 \geq 60$
$x_1 \leq 15$
(b) Cost = $.65 at (15, 25)
(c) 65¢
B.8 $x_1 = 200, x_2 = 0$, profit = $18,000
B.10 10 Alpha 4s, 24 Beta 5s, profit = $55,200
B.12 (a) $x_1 = 25.71, x_2 = 21.43$
(b) Cost = $68.57
B.14 (a) $x_1 = 7.95, x_2 = 5.95, x_3 = 12.6, P = \$143.76$
(b) No unused time
(c) 26¢
(d) $7.86
B.16 (a) Let X_{ij} = number of students bused from sector i to school j.
Objective: minimize total travel miles =
$$5X_{AB} + 8X_{AC} + 6X_{AE}$$
$$+ \ 0X_{BB} + 4X_{BC} + 12X_{BE}$$
$$+ \ 4x_{CB} + 0X_{CC} + 7X_{CE}$$
$$+ \ 7X_{DB} + 2X_{DC} + 5x_{DE}$$
$$+ \ 12X_{EB} + 7X_{EC} + 0X_{EE}$$
Subject to:
$X_{AB} + X_{AC} + X_{AE} = 700$ (number of students in sector A)
$X_{BB} + X_{BC} + X_{BE} = 500$ (number students in sector B)
$X_{CB} + X_{CC} + X_{CE} = 100$ (number of students in sector C)
$X_{DB} + X_{DC} + X_{DE} = 800$ (number of students in sector D)
$X_{EB} + X_{EC} + X_{EE} = 400$ (number of students in sector E)

$X_{AB} + X_{BB} + X_{CB} + X_{DB} + X_{EB} \leq 900$ (school B capacity)
$X_{AC} + X_{BC} + X_{CC} + X_{DC} + X_{EC} \leq 900$ (school C capacity)
$X_{AE} + X_{BE} + X_{CE} + X_{DE} + X_{EE} \leq 900$ (school E capacity)

(b) Solution: $X_{AB} = 400$
$X_{AE} = 300$
$X_{BB} = 500$
$X_{CC} = 100$
$X_{DC} = 800$
$X_{EE} = 400$
Distance = 5,400 "student miles"

B.18 Hire 30 workers; three solutions are feasible; two of these are:
16 begin at 7 A.M.
9 begin at 3 P.M.
2 begin at 7 P.M.
3 begin at 11 P.M.
An alternate optimum is:
3 begin at 3 A.M.
9 begin at 7 A.M.
7 begin at 11 A.M.
2 begin at 3 P.M.
9 begin at 7 P.M.
0 begin at 11 P.M.

B.20 Max $P = 9x_1 + 12x_2$
Subject to:
$x_1 + x_2 \leq 10$
$x_1 + 2x_2 \leq 12$
$x_1 = 8, x_2 = 2$; profit = $96
B.22 $x_1 = 14, x_2 = 33$, cost = 221
B.24 5 corner points
B.26 (a) Minimize = $6X_{1A} + 5X_{1B} + 3X_{1C} + 8X_{2A} + 10X_{2B} +$
$8X_{2C} + 11X_{3A} + 14X_{3B} + 18X_{3C}$
Subject to:
$X_{1A} + X_{2A} + X_{3A} = 7$
$X_{1B} + X_{2B} + X_{3B} = 12$
$X_{1C} + X_{2C} + X_{3C} = 5$
$X_{1A} + X_{1B} + X_{1C} \leq 6$
$X_{2A} + X_{2B} + X_{2C} \leq 8$
$X_{3A} + X_{3B} + X_{3C} \leq 10$
(b) Minimum cost = $219,000
B.28 One approach results in 2,790 medical patients and 2,104 surgical patients, with a revenue of $9,551,659 per year (which can change slightly with rounding). This yields 61 integer medical beds and 29 integer surgical beds.
B.30 Apple sauce = 0, Canned corn = 1.33, Fried chicken = 0.46, French fries = 0, Mac & Cheese = 1.13, Turkey = 0, Garden salad = 0, Cost = $1.51.

Quantitative Module C

C.2 $208
C.4 $170
C.6 (a) A–1, 10; B–1, 30; C–2, 60; A–3, 40; C–3, 15
(b) $1,775
C.8 Houston, $19,500
C.10 Total cost − $505
C.12 Initial cost = $260
Final solution = $230
C.14 F1–W1, 1,000; F1–W4, 500; F2–W2, 2,000; F2–W3, 500; F3–W3, 1,500; F3–W4, 700; cost = $39,300
C.16 $60,900 with East St. Louis; $62,250 with St. Louis

Quantitative Module D

D.2 (a) 44%
(b) .36 people
(c) .8 people
(d) .53 min.
(e) 1.2 min.

D.4 (a) .5
  (b) .5
  (c) 1
  (d) .5
  (e) .05 hr.
  (f) .1 hr.
D.6 (a) .667
  (b) .667 min.
  (c) 1.33
D.8 (a) .375
  (b) 1.6 hr. (or .2 days)
  (c) .225
  (d) 0.141, 0.053, 0.020, 0.007
D.10 (a) 2.25
  (b) .75
  (c) .857 min. (.014 hr.)
  (d) .64 min. (.011 hr.)
  (e) 42%, 32%, 24%
D.12 (a) 6 trucks
  (b) 12 min.
  (c) .857
  (d) .54
  (e) $1,728/day
  (f) Yes, save $3,096 in the first year.
D.14 (a) .075 hrs (4.5 min.)
  (b) 1.125 people
  (c) .0083 hrs (0.5 min.), 0.083 people
D.16 (a) .113 hr. = 6.8 min.
  (b) 1.13 cars
D.18 (a) .05
  (b) .743
  (c) .793
D.20 (a) 3, 2, 4 MDs, respectively
  (b) Because $\lambda > \mu$, an indefinite queue buildup can occur.
D.22 (a) 4 servers
  (b) 6 servers
  (c) $109
  (d) 83.33%
D.24 2 salespeople ($340)

Quantitative Module E

E.2 (a) 507 min.
  (b) 456 min.
  (c) 410 min.
  (d) 369 min.
E.4 (a) 1,546 min.
  (b) 2,872 min.
  (c) 3,701 min.
  (d) 6,779 min.
E.6 (a) 14.31 hr.
  (b) $71,550
  (c) $947,250
E.8 (a) 80%
  (b) 3.51
  (c) 3.2, 2.98, 2.81
  (d) 21.5
E.10 (a) 72.2 hr.
  (b) 60.55 hr.
  (c) 41.47 hr.
E.12 Torri will take 3.67 hr. and Julie 2.43 hr. Neither trainee will reach 1 hr. by the 10th unit.
E.14 $748,240 for fourth, $709,960 for fifth, $679,960 for sixth
E.16 (a) 70 millicents/bit
  (b) 8.2 millicents/bit
E.18 26,755 hr.
E.20 (a) 32.98 hr., 49.61 hr.
  (b) Initial quote is high.
E.22 (a) Four boats can be completed.
  (b) Five boats can be completed.
E.24 .227 hr.

Quantitative Module F

F.2 0, 0, 0, 0, 0, 0, 0, 2, 0, 2
F.4 Profits = 20, −15, 20, 17.50, 20; average equals $12.50.
F.6 At the end of 5 min., two checkouts are still busy and one is available.
F.8

Arrivals	Arrival Time	Service Time	Departure Time
1	11:01	3	11:04
2	11:04	2	11:06
3	11:06	2	11:08
4	11:07	1	11:09

F.10 (a, b)

No. Cars	Prob.	Cum. Prob.	R.N. Interval
3 or fewer	0	0	—
4	.10	.10	01 through 10
5	.15	.25	11 through 25
6	.25	.50	26 through 50
7	.30	.80	51 through 80
8	.20	1.00	81 through 00
9 or more	0	—	—

  (c) Average no. arrivals/hr. = 105/15 = 7 cars
F.12 Each simulation will differ. Using random numbers from right-hand column of the random number table, reading top to bottom, in the order used, results in a $9.20 cost. This is greater than the $6.65 in Example F3.
F.14 (a) 5 times
  (b) 6.95 times; yes
  (c) 7.16 heaters
F.16 (a) Expected average demand is about 8.75, average lead time is 1.86, average end inventory = 6.50, average lost sales = 4.04. Values and costs will vary with different sets of random numbers.
  (b) $520,110, or $21,671 per month
F.18 Total stockout cost = $80; total holding cost = $40; so total cost = $120 with ROP = 4 vs. total cost = $223 with ROP = 2 in Problem F.17. Weekly costs are found by dividing by 10.
F.20 Here are the random-number intervals for the first two departments. Random number intervals correspond to probability of occurrence.

From	To	R.N. Interval
Initial exam	X-ray	01 through 45
	OR	46 through 60
	Observ.	61 through 70
	Out	71 through 00

From	To	R.N. Interval
X-ray	OR	01 through 10
	Cast	11 through 35
	Observ.	36 through 70
	Out	71 through 00

Each simulation could produce different results. Some will indeed show a person entering X-ray twice.
F.22 (a) Profit = 30 (sales price) − $1,250 − 36 (ingredient 2 cost)
  (b) Expected profit = $7,924/day
  (c) Expected profit from simulation = $7,770/day

Online Tutorial 1

T1.2 5.45; 4.06
T1.4 (a) .2743;
  (b) 0.5
T1.6 .1587; .2347; .1587
T1.8 (a) .0548;
  (b) .6554;
  (c) .6554;
  (d) .2119

Online Tutorial 2

T2.2 (selected values)

Fraction Defective	Mean of Poisson	$P(x \leq 1)$
.01	.05	.999
.05	.25	.974
.10	.50	.910
.30	1.50	.558
.60	3.00	.199
1.00	5.00	.040

T2.4 The plan meets neither the producer's nor the consumer's requirement.

Online Tutorial 3

T3.2 (a) $x_1 + 4x_2 + s_1 = 24$
$x_1 + 2x_2 + s_2 = 16$

(b) See the steps in the tutorial.

(c) Second tableau:

c_j	Mix	x_1	x_2	s_1	s_2	Qty.
9	x_2	.25	1	.25	0	6
0	s_2	.50	0	−.50	1	4
	z_j	2.25	9	2.25	0	54
	$c_j - z_j$	.75	0	−2.25	0	

(d) $x_1 = 8$, $x_2 = 4$, Profit $= \$60$

T3.4 Basis for 1st tableau:
$A_1 = 80$
$A_2 = 75$

Basis for 2nd tableau:
$A_1 = 55$
$X_1 = 25$

Basis for 3rd tableau:
$X_1 = 14$
$X_2 = 33$

Cost $= \$221$ at optimal solution

T3.6 (a) x_1
(b) A_1

Online Tutorial 4

T4.2 Cost $= \$980$; 1–A = 20; 1–B = 50; 2–C = 20; 2–Dummy = 30; 3–A = 20; 3–C = 40

T4.4 Total = 3,100 mi.; Morgantown–Coaltown = 35; Youngstown–Coal Valley = 30; Youngstown–Coaltown = 5; Youngstown–Coal Junction = 25; Pittsburgh–Coaltown = 5; Pittsburgh–Coalsburg = 20

T4.6 (a) Using VAM, cost = 635; A–Y = 35; A–Z = 20; B–W = 10; B–X = 20; B–Y = 15; C–W = 30.
(b) Using MODI, cost is also 635 (i.e., initial solution was optimal). An alternative optimal solution is A–X = 20; A–Y = 15; A–Z = 20; B–W = 10; B–Y = 35; C–W = 30.

Online Tutorial 5

T5.2 (a) $I_{13} = 12$
(b) $I_{35} = 7$
(c) $I_{51} = 4$

T5.4 (a) Tour: 1–2–4–5–7–6–8–3–1; 37.9 mi.
(b) Tour: 4–5–7–1–2–3–6–8–4; 39.1 mi.

T5.6 (a) Vehicle 1: Tour 1–2–4–3–5–1 = $134
(b) Vehicle 2: Tour 1–6–10–9–8–7–1 = $188

T5.8 The cost matrix is shown below:

	1	2	3	4	5	6	7	8
1	—	107.26	118.11	113.20	116.50	123.50	111.88	111.88
2		—	113.53	111.88	118.10	125.30	116.50	118.10
3			—	110.56	118.70	120.50	119.90	124.90
4				—	109.90	119.10	111.88	117.90
5					—	111.88	106.60	118.50
6						—	111.88	123.50
7							—	113.20
8								—

Photo Credits

CHAPTER 1: p. 1-8: Taras Vyshnya/Shutterstock.

CHAPTER 2: p. 2-4: © Michael Yamashita/CORBIS.

CHAPTER 3: p. 3-14: Markus Dlouhy/Peter Arnold, Inc.; p. 3-15 Paramount/Dreamworks/Picture Desk, Inc./Kobal Collection.

CHAPTER 4: p. 4-13: Getty Images – Photodisc-Royalty Free; p. 4-15: Condor 36/ Shutterstock; p. 4-19: Alan Copson/Photolibrary.com.

CHAPTER 5: p. 5-9: Nikolay Stefanvo Dimitrov/Shutterstock; p. 5-10: Maximillian Stock LTD/Phototake NYC.

CHAPTER 6: p. 6-10: Christophe Testi/Shutterstock

SUPPLEMENT 6: p. S6-13: Corbis RF.

CHAPTER 7: p. 7-6: © John Rodriguez/iStockphoto.com; p. 7-7: Eric Limon/Shutterstock.

SUPPLEMENT 7: p. S7-11: Corbis RF.

CHAPTER 8: p. 8-9: Andrea Catenaro Doherty/Shutterstock; p. 8-12: David Buffington/Getty Images, Inc.-Photodisc/Royalty Free.

CHAPTER 9: p. 9-8: David Young-Wolff/PhotoEdit, Inc.; p. 9-13: T. Matsumoto/CORBIS-NY; p. 9-15: Jonathan Bailey Associates.

CHAPTER 10: p. 10-13: Mark Winfrey/Shutterstock; p. 10-14: Lynn Goldsmith/CORBIS-NY; p. 10-15: www.comstock.com.

CHAPTER 11: p. 11-2 (top left): Bill Stormont/CORBIS-NY; p. 11-2 (top middle): Susan Van Etten/PhotoEdit Inc.; p. 11-2 (middle bottom): David de Lossy, Ghislain & Marie/Getty Images Inc. – Image Bank;

p. 11-2 (middle): Getty Images/Digial Vision; p. 11-2 (middle): Michael Newman/PhotoEdit Inc.; p. 11-2 (top right): Jose Manuel Riberio, REUTERS/CORBIS-NY; p. 11-2 (middle right): Peter Byron/PhotoEdit Inc.; p. 11-2 (bottom right): Richard Levine/Alamy.com; p. 11-7: Spencer Tirey/AP Wide World Photos; p. 11-8: Thomas Raupach/Peter Arnold, Inc.

CHAPTER 12: p. 12-13: Steve Dunwell/Getty Images Inc. – Image Bank.

CHAPTER 13: p. 13-8: Bobby Deal/Shutterstock; p. 13-11: Fernando Sanchez.

CHAPTER 15: p. 15-2 (top): Michael Newman/Photo Edit Inc.; p. 15-2 (bottom): Peter Endig/Landov Media; p. 15-7: Marcel Mooij/Shutterstock; p. 15-9: Dana Fisher/AP Wide World Photos; p. 15-10: Ann Prival/Omni-Photo Communications, Inc.

CHAPTER 16: p. 16-8: Green Gear Cycling, Inc.

CHAPTER 17: p. 17-6: PHT/Photo Researchers, Inc.

MODULE A: p. A-8: Jim Varney/Photo Researchers, Inc.; p. A-9: © MaxFK/Shutterstock.

MODULE B: p. B-8: Dennis MacDonald/PhotoEdit Inc.

MODULE C: p. C-6: Klaus Guldbrandsen/Science Photo Library/Photo Researchers, Inc.

MODULE D: p. D-12: Markus Matzel/Das Fotoarchiv./Peter Arnold, Inc.

MOUDLE E: p. E-5: Chris Anderson/Aurora Photos, Inc.

MODULE F: p. F-8: Getty Images-Stockbyte.